THE COVENANTERS

JAMES GRAHAM,
FIRST MARQUIS OF MONTROSE
1612-1650

THE
COVENANTERS

A HISTORY OF THE CHURCH IN SCOTLAND
FROM THE REFORMATION TO THE REVOLUTION

BY

James King Hewison

IN TWO VOLUMES

VOLUME II.

THE BANNER OF TRUTH TRUST

THE BANNER OF TRUTH TRUST

Head Office
3 Murrayfield Road
Edinburgh
EH12 6EL
UK

North America Office
PO Box 621
Carlisle
PA 17013
USA

banneroftruth.org

First published 1908
Revised and corrected edition 1913
This retypeset edition 2019

© The Banner of Truth Trust 2019

*

ISBN (Volume II.):
Print: 978 1 84871 924 8
Epub: 978 1 84871 925 5
Kindle: 978 1 84871 926 2

Two-volume set (print):
ISBN 978 1 84871 927 9

*

Typeset in 10.5/13.5 Adobe Garamond Pro
at The Banner of Truth Trust, Edinburgh

Printed in the USA by
Versa Press Inc.,
East Peoria, IL.

CONTENTS

ILLUSTRATIONS

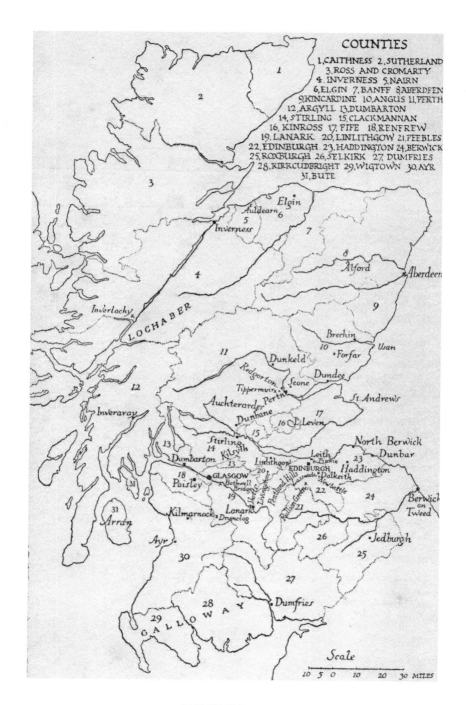

MAP OF SCOTLAND

CHAPTER EIGHTEEN

SCOTLAND'S THREE RULERS— CHURCH, CHARLES, AND CROMWELL

CHARLES arrived at Speymouth on the 23rd June 1650. Before he was permitted to place a foot on Scottish soil he was required to swear and subscribe both Covenants. He wished to subscribe with reservations, and struggled hard to be freed from the clause which bound him to give legal sanction to the Presbyterian system in both England and Ireland whenever he ascended the southern throne. His opposition gave rise to angry discussions on Sabbath morning before sermon. The Commissioners were inexorable. At length Charles appeared to surrender, and accepted the bitter terms. He vowed to be a Kirk-man. This compliance grieved John Livingstone, the preacher and exhorter that day, and he craved delay because he realised the King's hypocrisy in accepting the Covenants 'without any evidence of any reall change in his heart, and without forsaking former principles, counsells, and company.'[1] Livingstone was overruled and Charles was permitted to perjure himself, thus bringing guilt, according to Livingstone, on 'the Church and realm.' 'Our sin was more than his,' confessed Jaffray.[2] In Parliament, then sitting in Edinburgh, two of the Commissioners, 'Brodie and Libertone, made a full relation of all ther negotiation with his Maiestie; they producit the couenant, withe the Churche explanation, subscriued with the Kinge's hand, as also the Concessions subscriued by his Maiestie.'[3]

[1] 'Livingstone's Account,' *Select Biog.*, i. 183; *Rec. Com. Gen. Assem.* ii. 437.
[2] *Diary*, 55.
[3] 1st July 1650: Balfour, *Annals.*, iv. 67. For Breda propositions, cf. deed in *Clar.*

THE CONFESSION OF FAITH SUBSCRIBED AT FIRST BY THE KINGS.

Majesty and his household in the year of God 1580. Thereafter by persons of all rankes in the

Charles R.

Top: The Covenants signed by Charles II. at Speymouth
Bottom: Page of the Kirk-Session Record of Kirkinner, Wigtown (1711),
giving an Account of the Marrydom of Margaret Lauchlison—one of the Wigtown Martyrs

Official deputations of clergy and Parliament-men soon arrived to welcome Charles. The people, ignorant of the deceit practised upon them, were excited with joy at the news of the coming of their Prince. Edinburgh, in particular, was riotous with enthusiasm expressed by crackling bonfires, clanging bells, blaring trumpets, yelling dancers, and jovial kail-wives.[1] Contrary to the orders of Parliament, Charles had brought with him a retinue of Malignants, who were compelled to hive off and seek safety abroad. Only a select coterie, including Buckingham, Wentworth, Wilmot, Sir Edward Walker, Chiffinch, was allowed to remain. The following Scots were forbidden to accompany Charles until they had given satisfaction to Church and State: Hamilton, Lauderdale, Seaforth, Callendar, Forth, Dumfries, St. Clair, Napier, Sir Robert Dalziel, Thomas Dalyell of Binns, Lockhart, Charteris of Amisfield, Monro, and Cochrane. This rigour was long remembered and repaid with usury by these political convicts when the tables were turned in 1660.

Charles had entered into a tutelage which he little anticipated. His progress to Falkland Palace, of evil memory, by way of Aberdeen, Dunnottar, Kinnaird, St. Andrews, was officially appointed. In Aberdeen he passed under the uplifted arm of Montrose, but there is no record that the heartless opportunist felt any qualms at the gruesome sight. He reached Falkland on 5th July. One of his first acts was personally to instruct the Lyon-King as to a design for new colours for the Life

Marginal notes:
Rejoicings on the arrival of Charles II.

Progress of Charles.

State Pap. (June-September 1650), 55, 56, 57 (Bodleian Library). King Charles II. subscribed the Oath and Covenants more than once. First, on 26th March (O.S. 5th April) 1650 at Breda, he subscribed the original terms of the Oath. On 23rd June he subscribed both Covenants and the terms of the Declaration changed to include the words, 'Acts of Parliament, Bills or Ordinances, past or to be past.' The deed was signed 'aboard the *Skidam* of Amsterdam lying at anchor at the mouth of Spay, Sabboth, 23 Junii 1650,' according to John Livingstone (*Rec. Com. Gen. Assem.*, ii. 368, 370, 382, 392, 403, 438). The Covenants, with the Declaration, as signed by Charles—the deed which is preserved in the Bodleian Library (*Clarendon MSS.*, 40 f. 80)—shows the Oath amended on the margin and signeted by Charles, so that I conclude that it was signed after 20th May 1650, and in all likelihood on the 23rd June. It is endorsed by Archibald Johnston, Clerk-Register, and Andrew Ker, Clerk of the Assembly. It was read in Parliament on 1st July 1650 (*Act. Parl. Scot.*, VI. ii. 596), and Johnston was ordered to preserve it. Eleven days later it was also produced in the General Assembly. Cf. Appendix IV. vol. I..

[1] Nicoll, 16, 17.

4

Guards. The motto selected was significant: 'Covenant, For Religion, King and Kingdomes.' Charles was fast developing into a polished dissimulator.

Cromwell had already been recalled from Ireland, where he had constituted himself the well-paid minister of God's justice to avenge the massacres of the saints in 1641, and had completely subjugated that miserable isle.[1] The English Parliament, rightly interpreting all these sinister movements in the north to be a menace, determined to strike the first blow and to invade Scotland.[2] General Fairfax had conscientious scruples regarding this unconstitutional procedure, and declined the duty of leading the army. Cromwell, having consulted the Psalms, found the necessary authority to take command in the hope that the Lord would 'enable this poor worm and weak servant to do His will.'

Cromwell invades Scotland, 22nd July.

Cromwell crossed the Tweed on 22nd July with a force of 10,500 foot and 5500 horse. A naval squadron supported him along the coast.[3] In ordinary circumstances this was no formidable host for Scotland to oppose with the 20,000 regulars and levies who assembled on the Links of Leith under David Leslie, Cromwell's comrade at, and the hero of, Marston Moor. Cromwell's merciless massacres in Ireland had conferred on him a notoriety as fearful as the plague. It was Leslie's safest plan to avoid the terrible Ironsides. The Scots soon transformed into wastes those districts through which the invaders might pass, thus making local victualling impossible. None capable of bearing a weapon stayed to provoke a fight. The Covenanting host, however, wanted the strength and unity of former national armies. Before the campaign began, the purgation of the public services was carried out, on the demand of the Assembly's Commission, and afterwards of the Assembly, by the removal from the army 'of all men of a scandalous conversatione, and of a questionable integrity and affectione in the cause of God.'[4] This mistaken policy weakened the army of defence in

Leslie's Covenanted host.

---

[1] His salary was £45,000: *Cal. State Pap.* (Charles II.), i. 45.

[2] On 31st July 1650 the English Council ordered the demolition of the statues of James and Charles, and the publication of this inscription: Exit Tyrannus Regum ultimus anno primo restitutae libertatis Angliae ['The end of the final tyrannical king in the 1st year of the restoration of England's freedom], 1648': *ibid.*, ii. 261.

[3] Whitelocke, *Memoirs*, i. 450-71.

[4] Peterkin, 620. It is said 5000 men were cast out: *Cal. State Pap.*, ii. 324.

numbers, fighting power, and experience—many capable officers and privates being set aside. Probably Whitelocke was recording incredible gossip when he mentioned that some ministers in their prayers said, that 'if God did not deliver them from the Sectaries He would not be their God any longer.'[1]

Round the Capital Leslie made strenuous exertions to oppose Cromwell. A great entrenchment, strengthened with redoubts, was cut from the foot of the Canongate to the Port of Leith, and behind it encamped the Scots, from Broughton village to St. Leonard's Craigs.

Purging out Malignants. The Lammas floods befriended the Scots. The Covenanters have often been severely criticised for their intolerant suppression of the Malignant faction at this juncture. But extant records prove that Scotland was being threatened with a repetition of that moral decadence which a hundred years before sorely exercised Queen Mary and ruined the Church. The nobility, gentry, and clergy included many profligate members. The 'Old Man' was much in evidence. The advent of Charles II. alone was needed to popularise wickedness in Royalist society, and bring about that recrudescence of vice justly feared by the Covenanters. As yet the 'gracious' Lauderdale was not 'swollen with gluttony and brutalised with vice';[2] nor was young Rothes—'unhappily made for drunkenness,' as Burnet wrote—who afterwards was both and worse, indulging that sin they blamed his stricter father for:

> 'In the old cause your father led the van,
> But you bring up the rear with Lady Ann.'[3]

The gallant soldier Nathaniel Gordon had already been processed for adultery, and the similar scandals of Chancellor Loudoun and Ludovick Lindsay, Earl of Crawford, were coming into court.[4]

The wanton imitators of the Merry Monarch had many precursors and imitators, over whose unsavoury lives it might be better to draw a veil. It is to the national credit that there survived some honest and fearless men who were willing to tear the blister from the front of

---

[1] *Memoirs*, i. 465.
[2] Pref. *Lauderdale Papers*.
[3] Ballad, *Mitchel's Ghost*.
[4] Gordon, *Keith*, 150, 426; Lamont, *Diary*, 38, 130; Scot, *Staggering State*, 24.

virtue.[1] The Commission of Assembly, which was very representative, influential, and large, busied itself putting the stringent Acts against Engagers into operation in the autumn. In the visitation of lax Presbyteries they found and deposed many ministers and teachers guilty of vices incompatible with their offices, as well as doubtful characters whose chief fault seems to have been preference for the Royalist policy.[2] The growing lewdness of the Carolan age had even crept into manses and destroyed the usefulness of preachers, who incurred deposition for inefficiency, drunkenness, and immorality. With few exceptions the deposed Malignants were of no distinction. More notable were: Henry Guthry, minister of Stirling, who had been a member of the High Commission in 1634, was a noisy zealot in the Assembly, and survived to become Bishop of Dunkeld after the Restoration; Andrew Ramsay, the sturdy opponent of Laud's Liturgy, now senile and dotard, vented silly views regarding Presbytery and law; William Colvin, also an Edinburgh minister, was as loquacious a wire-puller in the Assembly as he was sly in concealing his Royalist leanings.[3] Scandalous facts like these grieved earnest men such as George Gillespie, who on 15th December 1648, on his death-bed, gave a testimony declaring the Malignant party to be 'the seed of the Serpent.'[4]

Lewdness in the Carolan age.

[1] Cf. *postea*, Chapter 21.

[2] *Rec. Com. Gen. Assem.*, ii. 125.

[3] Peterkin, 592.

[4] On 14th April 1650 the Earl of Buchan 'did stand up in his daske,' in Auchterhouse Church, confessed his sin of Engaging, held up his hand, swore to the Covenant, and subscribed it. In the same place fifteen years afterwards his widow, Marjory Ramsay, Countess of Buchan, confessed the sin of immorality with the parish minister, James Campbell, who also had to sit on the repentance pillar, December 1665 (*Kirk-Sess. Rec.*; Inglis, *Annals of Auchterhouse*, 108, 131, 132). 'At Bottarie, 15 Martii 1648, The Lady Altar, Jean Gordon,' was accused 'of ane barne in adulterie to Nathaniel Gordon, and also of ane uther bairne in fornication with Captain Mortimer.' 'May 21, 1651, Elspeth Crukshanks, Botarie, confessed adultery with Ludovick Lindsay, Earl of Crawfurd (*Pres. Rec. Strathbogie*; J. F. S. Gordon, *Keith*, 150, 426). Patrick Graham of Inchbrakie, *fidus Achates* of Montrose, an old man in 1678, knelt in the church of Auchterarder, confessing immorality, gave money to the poor and to Christian prisoners in Turkey, and on the bishop's recommendation was absolved (*Sess. Rec. of Auchterarder*, anno 1678). 'Patrick Lesley, Lord of Londors, was never married, but had aboue 67 basse children' (Balfour, *Annals*, 12th August 1649, iii. 423). '1651, Jun. ... The Commission of the kirk satt at Stirling, att which tyme Chancelour Campbell (Loudoun) was brought up

If purgation led to the disintegration of the Covenanted host in Scotland, as has been often asserted, Cromwell found it to be a method of selection of the fittest which rendered his Ironsides both stable and invincible.

On his northward march Cromwell, 'a God-intoxicated man,' composed and dispatched various Declarations, 'To all that are saints and Partakers of the Faith of God's Elect in Scotland,' and, 'To the People in Scotland,' repudiating the false accusations by Scottish enemies, that the Sectaries were brutal monsters, further asserting that in Charles II. there was no salvation possible, and assuring them that the English had come to fight for the substance of the Covenant.[1] Replies and counter-replies passed to and fro.[2] This correspondence called forth the oft-quoted letter of Cromwell, dated Musselburgh, 3rd August 1650, in which he accused the Scottish leaders of having 'a carnal confidence upon misunderstood and misapplied precepts, which may be called spiritual drunkenness.' This insobriety deluded them with the idea that their policy was established 'upon the Word of God.' He inquired, 'Is it therefore infallibly agreeable to the Word of God, all that *you* say? I beseech you, in the bowels of Christ, think it possible you may be mistaken. ... There may be a *Covenant* made with Death and Hell: I will not say yours was so.'[3]

Two days later the 'scornful men' of the Covenant answered the 'blasphemer'—such many styled Cromwell—with an emphatic disclaimer of Malignancy, which but made matters worse. Some influential members of the extreme section of the Covenanters—Colonels Ker, Strachan, and others—were not averse to contemplating an alliance with the Cromwellians in the event of the King not accepting their demands. But the unforeseen action of the unscrupulous Sovereign in consenting to promote the Covenants was a disappointment to Cromwell and to these concordant friends in the opposing camp.

---

before them and challenged for adulterie with ane Major Jhonston's wife, surnamed Lindsay. This Jhonston was he that went in shortlie before to Cromwell, and reveilled to him the purpose of a pairtie of our armie that went forth to beat up his quarters' (Lamont, *Diary*, 31).

[1] Aldis, *List*, 1407, *Declaration of the Army upon their March*, etc.

[2] Reply 1431; other Replies, 1410, 1411, 1417, 1428, 1429.

[3] Cromwell, Letter cxxxvi.

Cromwell came into contact with Leslie's insuperable barrier on 29th July, and the Scots had as little difficulty in rolling back his weary and wet troops to their fortified camp at Musselburgh as they in turn repulsed the assault on it two days later.[4] The King, on the invitation of the Earl of Eglinton, came from Stirling to Leith, where he was received with an enthusiasm which disconcerted the Government. They permitted him to watch the first conflict from the Castle, but were uneasy until he had left the lines. The extremists believed his presence would blight the holy army.[5] He was forced to retire to Dunfermline to prevent intrigues. Meantime the Committee of Purging was busy weeding out eighty officers and three thousand of the rank and file who were tainted with Malignancy and other offences distasteful to Covenanting purists—a handful of the elect being deemed more invincible than a legion of those lost by unpardonable sin.

Skirmishes before Edinburgh.

Cromwell, having retired to Dunbar to replenish his commissariat, returned to Musselburgh, whence he made a wide flank movement to the west, as he intended to assault Leslie to the rear of his own lines. He camped upon the Braid Hills and watched Leslie from Blackford Hill. Leslie would not be tempted to a general engagement. A strategist, and knowing the ground well, Leslie marched the Scots round to the slopes above Corstorphine, which now look down on green meadows, then marshy and impassable with water. Cromwell could not dislodge his wily opponent; the way to Queensferry and to the roadstead in the Forth was effectually barred; and there was no alternative to a retreat, more especially since disease was spreading in the English ranks. Cromwell made for Dunbar and arrived there on 1st September, closely chased by Leslie, who got between him and the Borders.

Cromwell retreats to Dunbar.

The Scottish army was miserably rent by factious parties, and military discipline had suffered severely in consequence of the loss of unity caused by the constant purging process and the growth of divisive views of the situation. Before John Livingstone took leave of his Sovereign he adjured him to divert the shock of the English invasion by making a personal declaration that, while maintaining his title to the English Crown, he would not prosecute it with the sword until

Dissensions among Covenanters

---

[4] Balfour, iv. 87; Douglas, *Cromwell's Scotch Campaigns*, 37-52.

[5] *Hist. MSS. Com. Rep.*, xi., App. vi. 132, No. 293 (*Hamilton MSS.*); Row, *Blair*, 235.

political confusions had vanished. Not relishing the proposal, Charles replied to his wise adviser, 'he hoped I would not wish him to sell his father's blood.'[1] This snub convinced the preacher that he was not 'called to meddle in any publick state matters.' The Covenanters were not unanimous in their idea of this demand. Cromwell knew this, and vainly hoped to win over the extremists to his side. He had formerly insisted on the passing of an Act of Classes, and subsequently tried to convince the Presbyterians that to trust another Malignant ruler was a fatal error. The leaders in the Church and Estates, especially in the former, were as determined to exact from Charles some safeguarding Declaration as he was obstinate in giving any satisfaction as to his intentions. Robert Douglas, like Livingstone, in a private interview with Charles, failed to convince him of the necessity for declaring his views. They were also resolved not to brook the well-timed taunt of Cromwell as to their inconsistency in professing the Covenants at the same time that they drew the sword in the Malignant cause.

The West Kirk resolution, 13th August 1650.

This is not to be wondered at. The demands of the Covenanters, who bitterly stigmatised the parents of King Charles as murderers and idolaters, were as humiliating and insulting as they could possibly be. Nevertheless Charles stooped to agree to them, merely stipulating that the harsh terms of the Declaration should be altered. The Protesters refused to do this after obtaining the King's signature.[2] He was further subdued by a resolution of the Church and of the Estates, subscribed at the West Kirk, Edinburgh, on the 13th August, for the purpose of satisfying the scruples of some officers, wherein it was declared that the Kirk and Kingdom would only fight for the settled Cause of the Covenant; disclaimed the sins of the Royal House; and would not own the King or his interest, unless he subordinated himself to God, prosecuted their holy aims in a holy manner, and repudiated the enemies of the Covenant.[3]

Robert Douglas, who had assented to this Act providing a private solace to the sensitive commanders of the Covenanters, was chagrined to learn that General Leslie had immediately forwarded the Resolution

---

[1] *Select Biog.*, i. 185.
[2] Wodrow, i. 47.
[3] Balfour, iv. 95.

to Cromwell, with the request that he should read it to his officers.[1] This was duly done. Cromwell sent back a masterly, scathing reply, wherein he disclaimed all intention to interfere with the religion of the Scots, and accused the Scots of inconsistency in condemning Malignancy, while they used the Covenant in order to impose a Malignant King upon England, who was actually then employing a Popish army to fight for him; nor could he see how any 'Godly Interest' could centre in such a man as Charles was, or make the English army enemies of the Presbyterians. Those Covenanters who agreed with Cromwell were in a minority and unable to coalesce with him. Doubtless their views were right, and they soon saw the error of trusting a ruler who never meant to keep his vows.[2]

Cromwell's disclaimer.

Cromwell was answered. Charles was terrified. He was afraid of being deserted by the army. He was practically a prisoner under the surveillance of Lord, captain of the Foot Guards, nor could he outwit, with lies and all, the astute Argyll—

> 'That Hylander whose conscience and whose eyes
> Play handy-dandy with deceit and lyes.'[3]

As an easy way out of his dilemma and present troubles Charles signed the Declaration at Dunfermline on 16th August. Its seven heads bore that Charles humbled himself for his father's opposition to the 'Worke of God' and to the Covenants, and for the idolatry, especially of his mother, in the royal household; acknowledged that he had no crooked design in signing the Covenant and would have no friends except Covenanters; annulled the Irish Treaty; would encourage trading by sea; would promote the Covenant in England and Ireland; would pass an act of oblivion for all except obstructors of the Reformation, traitors, and regicides; and would advise the well-affected English to help the Covenanters in preference to the Sectaries. Patrick Gillespie, minister in Glasgow, who placed the pen in the hand of Charles to subscribe the document, said to him 'that if he was not satisfied in his

Declaration at Dunfermline.

Deception by Charles.

---

[1] Wodrow, i. 48.

[2] Leslie's letter is printed in Cromwell, Letters (cxxxvi), ii. 171. Cromwell's reply is Letter cxxxvii. For Cromwell's letter written at Pentland Hills, of *Clar. State Pap.* (June-Sept., 1650), 171 (Bodleian Library).

[3] *Scot. Hist. Misc.*, ii. 287; *Hist. Man. Com. Rep.*, xi., App. vi. 132.

soul and conscience, beyond all hesitation, of the righteousness of the subscription, he was so far from over-driving him to ruin upon that, that as he obtested him, yea he charged him, in his Master's name and in the name of those who sent him, not to subscribe this declaration, no, not for the three kingdoms.' 'Mr. Gillespie,' replied the King, 'Mr. Gillespie, I am satisfied with the Declaration, and therefore will subscribe it.'[1] The unprincipled deceiver was but juggling with sacred things. With 'good and true natural inclinations to the Catholic faith,' Charles had already solicited Papal help, and at this very juncture, through the Dean of Tuam, he assured Ormond that he adhered to the Irish Peace: 'However I am forced by the necessity of my affairs to appear otherwise, yet that I am a true child of the Church of England, and still remain firm unto my first principles. Mr. King, I am a true Cavalier.'[2] He wrote to Nicholas from Perth on 3rd September: 'Nothing could have confirmed me more to the Church of England than being here seeing their hypocrisy.' How this discreditable artifice of a perfidious time-server could salve the consciences of the military champions of the Covenant it is hard to understand. Argyll, however, well aware of the hollowness of the King's professions, offered to him the consoling suggestion that his agreement was only a temporary expedient 'to please these madmen.'[3] Reaching the coast at Dunbar, Cromwell saw his 'poor, shattered, hungry, discouraged army' of 11,000 men in a trap. Leslie, almost simultaneously on Sabbath, 1st September, appeared with 23,000 men on the Dun, an eminence 600 feet high, one mile south from Dunbar, whose very name describes a military 'coign of vantage.' On the west it overlooks the course of the Broxburn, which had cut a deep and natural fosse 40 feet in depth and breadth, protecting the left declivity of the position. The front of the Dun is a steep, grassy slope with a gradient of 500 feet in half a mile facing the sea.

Cromwell in a trap at Dunbar.

The peninsula of Dunbar, on which the English had pitched their tents, extends 'about a mile from sea to sea'—from Belhaven Bay to Broxmouth House.[4] Eight miles further east Leslie had posted a force sufficient to guard a deep ravine called Peaths Dean, at Cockburnspath,

[1] A. Shields, *A Hind Let Loose*, 73.
[2] Gardiner, *Hist. of Commonwealth*, i. 268, 279.
[3] *Cal. State Pap.* (*Dom.*), ii. 325, 350.
[4] Cromwell, Letter cxl.

and thus doubly barred the Berwick Road into England. In the enemy's land Cromwell's only friend was the sea. 'Our condition was made very sad,' he wrote to Ireton, 'the Enemy greatly insulted and menaced us.' He might fortify the town and wait till relief came, or ship his foot and cut through with his sabres. But he had not transports enough to carry all his infantry. Leslie was sure he would attempt a massed cavalry charge. Indeed, 'the Scots boasted that they had Cromwell in a worse pound than the King had had Essex in Cornwall,'[1] and that his capture was inevitable.[2] Cromwell realised his peril, and, to inspire courage, openly lighted it. On Monday he wrote anxiously, marking on the letter 'Haste, Haste,' to Haselrig from the battlefield: 'We are upon an Engagement very difficult. The Enemy hath blocked up our way at the Pass of Copperspath, through which we cannot get without almost a miracle. He lieth so upon the Hills that we know not how to come that way without great difficulty; and our lying here daily consumeth our men, who fall sick beyond imagination.'[3] One can also gather from this letter that Cromwell intended to sit tight until Haselrig approached with reinforcements from Newcastle, which Cromwell had demanded and the Government had ordered.[4] In his account sent to the English Parliament Cromwell acknowledged that the Lord had 'reduced our Army into such straits that room was only left for Believing.'[5]

As the Scots faced the foe they proceeded with the ruinous purgation.[6] Their strength was further undermined by Royalist traitors, who kept Cromwell informed of Leslie's designs.[7] Leslie had the advantage

---

[1] Firth, *Cromwell*, 281.

[2] *Act. Parl. Scot.*, VI. ii. 808.

[3] Letter cxxxix.

[4] *Cal. State Pap.*, ii. 328.

[5] *Act. Parl. Scot.*, VI. ii. 808.

[6] That some incorrigible scamps were still left in the army is proved by the report of Haselrig on the Scots prisoners captured at Dunbar, whom he declared to be 'unruly, sluttish, and nasty'; 'they acted rather like beasts than men'; 'and some even murdered others for their money or clothes': Haselrig, *Letter*, 31st October 1650, quoted by Taylor, *Pictorial Hist. of Scot.*, ii. 978. One of Cromwell's spies was Mein, son to the staunch Anti-liturgists, John Mein and Barbara Hamilton—the 'Jenny Geddes' of tradition. The upright old Covenanter got his son apprehended. He was condemned to the gallows, but reprieved by Charles: Balfour, iv. 297, 299. 'Old Jhone Meane' and his wife died in 1654: Lamont, *Chron.*, 97.

[7] Balfour, iv. 97.

of what counsel the veteran Leven, who ran from Marston Moor, could give him before he fled again; and also the disadvantage of having to obey that advisory Council of War which ruined Baillie at Kilsyth. The fatal blunder at Kilsyth of moving to a less secure position in front of the foe was perpetrated again. For this tactical mistake the clergy have been wrongly blamed. The Protesters with reason repudiated the libel.[1] Cromwell himself testified that the clergy elected to fight, but the chief officers desired that he should escape, 'though it were by a golden bridge.'[2]

Leslie's position at Dunbar, 2nd September. On Monday, 'toward the evening,' when Cromwell was praying for deliverance out of his dilemma, the Scottish Horse were seen to descend from the Dun; the foot and guns followed, to extend east and to take up new positions, behind Little Pinkerton and nearer to the highway to Berwick. Cromwell marked this move to bar his road south. The fields in which the cavalry were picketed were yellow with the ripened corn. Leslie's object was to gain a better stand for threatening the unfinished embarkation, and for repelling the dash of the Ironsides. Besides, for days Leslie had been acting with the arrogance of a swaggerer, rather than the caution of a strategist.[3] If Leslie's scouts had not been inefficient and untrustworthy, he would not thus have acted on the mistaken belief that Cromwell had crippled his force by shipping those guns which next morning thundered out death over the Broxburn into his left wing. Tradition maintains that when Cromwell saw the unexpected turn of good fortune in that fatal descent, he exclaimed: 'The Lord hath delivered them into our hands.' That strategist instantly perceived that his opponent, Leslie, could no longer deploy his left wing for the ravine, nor yet could he re-form his right and centre on the hillside, should they be successfully assailed and thrown into disorder. Even with these unexpected advantages Cromwell had no justification for his assurance.

Carelessness of the Scots army. Had Leslie, in command of double the force of his antagonist, kept on guard, and his officers been worthy of the name, the surprise by Cromwell would have been ineffective. Cromwell's formations along the stream indicated a mere defence. During the evening he moved his

[1] M'Crie, *Sketches*, ii. 43 note.
[2] Letter cxlii.
[3] *Act. Parl. Scot.*, VI. II. 808; Cromwell, Letter cxlii.

divisions closer to the Broxburn, and was ready for crossing at daybreak. General Lambert, at the head of six regiments of horse, followed by three and a half regiments of foot, was ready to attack. The night was blustering, rainy, and cloudy. The Scots, shelterless, except those fortunate ones cowering behind the stooks of corn, spent a miserable night. Although they were ordered to stand to arms, sleep overpowered them. The cavalry off-saddled. Major-General Holborn in the dead of night relaxed the discipline, and permitted nearly all the musketeers to let their matches expire. Thus practically disarmed, the men lay down to rest. Some of the infantry officers slunk away to comfort and safety.[1]

Meantime the waning moon gave Cromwell light enough to carry out his crafty plan under the leadership of Generals Lambert, Fleetwood, and Monck. Before dawn the half-awakened Scots were attacked ere they well could form up for action. Soon the air was rent with trumpet calls, musket shots, cannonading, noise of clanging steel, and cries of 'The Lord of Hosts,' answered by 'The Covenant,' from the hillside. Pride's brigade of three regiments, supported by Cromwell's regiment of horse, during the darkness crossed the stream below Broxmouth House, and made a wide detour to reach the Scots cavalry on the right wing. The main body of the English, headed by Lambert's horse, crossed below Brant's Mill, and were supported by the great guns planted above it. A force of Scots, early astir to cross the ford on the Berwick road, met the English and for an hour gallantly contested the passage, at length being forced back.[2] Lambert headed for the Scottish cavalry, but his first onset was repulsed. The foot under Monck attacked the Scottish centre and were driven back. The check was temporary. Pride's brigade advanced to the attack, Monck's division rallied, and although one Scottish foot regiment, under Campbell of Lawers, gallantly withstood a flank attack from Lambert's infantry, until cavalry broke through their ranks, the Scottish centre gave way.

The left wing of the Scots, flanked by a small body of horse, was in too confined a position to act effectively, and was held in check by the English artillery. The right wing of the Scots was thus driven diagonally towards the left, the troopers, with all their colours flying,

The Battle of Dunbar, 3rd September 1650.

'Dunbar Drove.'

---

[1] Walker, *Hist. Disc.* 181.
[2] Douglas, *Cromwell's Campaigns*, 109 note.

riding pell-mell over their comrades. At this moment the red sun rose out of the German Ocean. Cromwell was heard to exclaim: 'Now let God arise, and His enemies shall be scattered'; then a little afterwards: 'I profess they run.' He recorded how the Scots were 'made as by the Lord of Hosts as stubble to their swords.'[1] It was a cowardly stampede. As many fugitives escaped unhurt as Cromwell had men to chase them. The Lord General sounded the rally, halted the victors, sang the hundred and seventeenth psalm, and unleashed the rested chargers again upon the bloody pursuit. It was the very shortest canticle which the avenger chose for praise, not wishing to defraud the thirsty sabres of their due. The singing veteran himself rode to the slaughter. Three thousand men fell and ten thousand men were taken, along with nearly two hundred standards and thirty guns.[2] The most notable among the mortally wounded was Winram, Lord Libbertoun, negotiator at Breda and Dunfermline. A few colonels died at their posts. The craven generals, Council of War, the entire cavalry, and the officers of the infantry fled and left the rank and file to their fate. Cromwell asserted that only twenty men and officers on his side were placed *hors de combat*. This indicates the absence of hand-to-hand combats, and of any serious defence by the Scots. An eye-witness declared that after the first onset 'wee lost none, they giving themselv's cheap to the execution.'[3] The craven Leslie laid the blame of the disaster on the chicken-hearted officers. He wrote to Argyll, 5th September: 'I tak God to witness wee might have as easily beaten them as wee did James Graham at Philiphaugh, if the officers had stayed by theire troops and regiments.'[4]

Cruel fate of Scots prisoners.

Cromwell released over five thousand wounded men, and marched nearly four thousand prisoners into England. These famished men, by hundreds, died of dysentery, contracted through the hardships of the campaign, and the eating of raw vegetables in a garden at Morpeth, where the prisoners were confined. In November only fourteen hundred of them survived. Cromwell gave the Countess of Winton a thousand

---

[1] Letter cxl.
[2] Alex. Jaffray, *Diary*, 163. Jaffray, Libbertoun, Gillespie, Waugh were taken prisoners.
[3] 'A Brief Relation,' Terry, *Leslie*, 478.
[4] *Ancram and Lothian Correspondence*, ii. 298.

'in a gallantry.'[1] The English Council of State ordered that the sound prisoners should be deported to the plantations of Virginia and New England, and to French military service, and some kept for English salt-works.[2] Few escaped from the scourge of disease to enter upon their servitude. Cromwell triumphantly wrote to Lenthall, the Speaker: 'It would do you good to see and hear our poor foot to go up and down making their boast of God for one of the most signal mercies God hath done for England and His people.'[3] Clarendon, on the other hand, noted the absence of lamentation in Royalist society: 'So the King was glad of it, as the greatest happiness that could befall him, in the loss of so strong a body of his enemies.' Charles was even credited with falling on his knees and thanking God for the victory. Rutherford and the Godly Party also indulged in a pious joy because God had testified to His wrath.

Cromwell gave God the glory for having appeared at Dunbar 'to the refreshment of His saints.' He speedily followed up his advantage and captured Edinburgh and Leith, the Castle of Edinburgh, however, holding out. Arriving at Edinburgh on Saturday, 7th September, Cromwell found that, while the military had converted St. Giles' Church into a store for munitions of war, the city ministers had sought safety in the Castle and deserted their pulpits. He invited them to return to their duty. They not only refused, but also sent to him an insolent reply, taunting him and the Sectaries with persecuting the English clergy. Even John Livingstone refused to meet Cromwell.[4] Cromwell took the trouble personally to answer their unfounded accusations.[5] He severely reprimanded them for not 'yielding to the mind of God in the great day of His power and visitation,' and pointed out their mistake in supposing that their present policy would work out the blessed Reformation. Never had the preachers received so well merited a castigation. Their craven conduct makes a poor contrast beside that of Zachary Boyd, who stayed to confront Cromwell in the Cathedral of Glasgow, a month later. That bold rhymer improved the occasion in flouting

Cromwell enters Edinburgh, 7th September.

---

[1] Walker, *Hist. Disc*, 181.
[2] *Cal. State Pap.*, ii. 334, 346.
[3] Letter cxl.
[4] *Select Biog.*, i. 186.
[5] Letters cxlvii., cxlviii.

the Sectaries to their faces. The irate Ironsides would have pistolled him on the spot had Cromwell not reserved the audacious railer for a worse revenge—a compulsory hearing of Old Noll's own interminable prayers.

If Cromwell could read the clerical mind he could also anticipate the next royal move. From the battlefield he wrote in a prophetic mood to Haselrig: 'Surely it's probable the Kirk has done their do. I believe their King will set up upon his own score now; wherein he will find many friends.'[1] Cromwell lost no time in seeking an encounter with Leslie, who had raked together his runaways at Stirling and occupied a position too strong for Cromwell to take. Leslie had more irritating opponents in his own camp. Colonels Strachan and Gilbert Ker, the victors of Carbisdale and other fights for the Covenant, the Gideons of the extreme party, the irreconcilable malcontents at the West Kirk meeting, with other anti-Malignants, publicly and rightly accused Leslie of losing the battle of Dunbar, and refused to serve under him, or Leven. It is painful to think that after Worcester fight Charles should have made a similar charge of cowardice and implied treachery against Leslie.[2] Leslie resigned his commission and, following the example of Baillie, resumed it on the entreaty of the Estates.

The Royalist party, including the King, resolved if possible to effect a conjunction of the diverse parties in the State and Church for the good of religion and the safety of the kingdom, and this proposal was discussed by the leaders of both Estates assembled in Stirling. Opinions differed as to the wisdom of acquiescing in this proposal, which afterwards was known as The Public Resolutions, and soon there were two opposing parties, laymen and clerics associated, for and against the proposal.

Harmony in the Scottish camp was now impossible. The opponents of the new policy of enlisting all and sundry into the Royalist ranks—Ker, Strachan, Chiesley, and others—were permitted to go into south-west Scotland and there to raise an independent command of untainted brethren in the valleys of Clyde, Ayr, and Nith. Sir Edward Walker is the authority for the story that Strachan wrote to Cromwell a

Marginal notes: Leslie's troubles. The Public Resolutions.

---

[1] Letter cxli.
[2] *Cal. State Pap.*, iii. xxi.; iv. 2.

letter, which was intercepted, assuring Cromwell that if he would quit Scotland, Strachan 'would so use the matter as that he should not fear any prejudice from this nation.'[1]

This Godly Party assured themselves that God would strengthen them to cope with the opponents of the Covenant without the aid of foreign arms.

While these dissensions tore the army, the Commission of the General Assembly also met in Stirling. The influence of James Guthrie, minister there, Patrick Gillespie, Johnston of Wariston, Samuel Rutherford, and other opponents of Malignancy was paramount. The fruit of their labours was *A Shorte Declaratione and Varninge* to all the congregations, which was issued on 12th September.[2] This document urged all parties to search for the iniquities which had provoked God to visit Scotland with His wrath, and summoned the King to mourn for the provocations of his guilty father and himself, as well as to consider if his hypocritical acceptance of the Covenant, in order to gain an earthly crown, was not another sin depriving him of a heavenly crown. The 'honest party' had not done. This summons prefaced another document, entitled 'Causes of a soleme public humiliatione vpone the defait of the Armey, to be keepit throughout all the Congregations of the Kirk of Scotland,' which, under thirteen heads, called on the kingdom to humble itself because of national sin, the provocation of the King's House, the home-coming of Malignants and the neglecting to expatriate them, the crooked ways of some negotiators sent to Breda, ingratitude to God, and the selfish policy of officials and officers in places of power and trust.[3] These edicts, however, were not well received in many places. Some ministers in Fife refused to publish the documents, and even went the length of demanding the restoration to public employment of such of their own parishioners as had satisfied the Church for the sin of the Engagement.

James Guthrie and the Protesters.

[1] *Hist. Disc,* 189.
[2] Balfour, iv. 98; Row, *Blair,* 246 note.
[3] Balfour, *Annals,* iv. 102. This document was the groundwork of Guthrie's famous *Causes of God's Wrath,* etc., published in 1653, the writing of which formed an item in his indictment. During these interminable dissensions David Calderwood, the historian of the Church, and a sufferer for Presbyterianism, died at Jedburgh in the seventy-fifth year of his age, 29th October 1650.

Sir John Chiesley of Kerswell, speaking of these would-be penitents, as he laid his hand significantly on his sword, said, 'I would rather join with Cromwell than with them.'[1] This was the voice of the 'honest party,' who preferred an alliance with the Sectaries to government by indifferent Discovenanters, whom Argyll, in his weak-kneed policy of moderation, was reintroducing into official life, at least such as were personally friendly to himself.

The King under surveillance.

During all this time Charles was treated with a courteous vigilance usually reserved for suspects, and for useful recreation he was expected to absorb, with the avidity of a proselyte, the Puritanical dogmatics he was treated to. In this enforced novitiate the carnal youth tried to look as grave as possible. Burnet testifies that Charles mortified his flesh, standing to hear prolix prayers and sitting to digest tedious sermons, no less than six on one occasion. Few princes would brook this pain for any crown. His guardians made him observe Sabbath within doors and week-days free from dancing and card-playing. They gave him no opportunity to write private letters. The sinless game of golf he might play with sentinels in sight. No doubt these national schoolmasters had good reason for stringency with one whose passions drove him into vice and crime.[2] There was another peril. He had won the hearts of the unthinking masses, who were scarce permitted to see the youth, and therefore invested him with many imaginary virtues. Marvel's description of him in after-years indicates his appearance:—

> 'Of a tall stature and a sable hue,
> Much like the son of Kish the lofty Jew,
> Ten years of need he suffered in exile,
> And kept his father's asses all the while.'

These months of penance made an ineffaceable impression on the young King's mind and confirmed him in his hatred of Presbyterianism. When, after the battle of Worcester, Charles appeared in France, Orleans told him that it was reported that he had gone back to Scotland. Charles replied, 'I had rather have been hanged.'[3]

---

[1] Cheisley or Chiesly: Walker, 187.
[2] Airy, *Charles II.*, 95.
[3] *Cal. State Pap.*, iv. 2.

The Commission of the Assembly urged the Committee of Estates to finish their half-done work of purging the King's House. The Lyon-King was commanded to discharge the offending courtiers who had been detected plotting for a Royalist rising. In vain had Charles pleaded for the retention of some of his favourites, but even the servile petition of Hamilton was rejected.[1] The King, smarting under these insults, and misled into the apprehension that the 'honest party'—the western army—under Strachan intended to seize and hand him over to Cromwell to be made an unwilling martyr, had completed a plan for escaping their toils. He arranged a secret meeting with his Royalist supporters in Fife. He cherished the fond dream that the raising of the royal banner and the mustering of the veterans of Montrose would create defection in the army of Leslie. However, too many were in the secret, which the Government learned from one of the plotters, probably Buckingham. The meeting was countermanded. Charles, nevertheless, on the afternoon of Friday, 4th October, accompanied by a few attendants, left Perth, as if on hunting bent in the south, crossed the Tay to Inchyra, and rode rapidly by Dudhope, Auchterhouse, and Cortachy to Clova, a distance of forty-two miles. He entered a wretched hovel and threw himself down to sleep on an old bolster laid on sedges and rushes.[2] A company of Highlanders—the army of his dreams—kept guard over the weary and terrified monarch, until Colonel Montgomery and his horse regiment surrounded the captive. They timed his return into Perth after the hour of public worship and treated him to a special private sermon,[3] so that in his sin he might not defraud his soul of the comforts of a Covenanter's sabbath.

'The Start,' 4th October 1650.

The Committee of Estates, realising the peril they had been saved from, met on 10th October, and for the first time gave the King a say in their councils. Next day he apologised for his credulity and his escapade, 'as he was a Christian man.' This ignominious incident is remembered under the name of 'The Start.'

The suppression of the armed Royalists in Angus and Athole was not so easily effected. Leslie mustered a force to crush them. With no little diplomacy the leaders of the rising forwarded to Leslie from Forfar

The Forfar Band, 26th October 1650.

[1] Balfour, iv. 110; *Cal. State Pap.*, ii. 321.
[2] Gardiner, *Hist. of Commonwealth*, i. 337.
[3] Balfour, iv. 113.

a copy of their Bond, in which they pleaded for national unity, and summoned all patriots to combine against the invaders. The terms of the Bond are as follows:—

> The Northerne band and Othe of Engagement, sent by Mideltone to L.-Generall Dauid Lesley, 26 of October, 1650.
>
> 'We wndersubscriuers, being tuoched with a deepe sence of the sade condition this our natiue kingdome of Scotland is in, by a prewailling armey of sectaries, quho hauing murthered our lait king, and ouerturned religione and gouuerniment in our nighboure kingdomes of England and Ireland, hath invaded this kingdome, and are in a way ... to reduce the quoll to a province. ...
>
> 'Therfor, and for satisfactione to all quho are satisfiable, wee doe promisse and sweare, that wee shall manteine the trew religione, as it is established in Scotland; the couenant, leauge and couenant; the Kings Maiesties persone, prerogatiue, gratnes, and authoritie; the preulidges of parliament and fredome of the subiects,
>
> So helpe ws God.
>
> Sic subscribitur,

Huntley.	Pat. Grhame.
Athole.	Sr Geo. Monro.
Seaforth.	Th. Mackenzie.
St. Clare.	Jo. Gordon.
Jo. Mideltone.	Wanderrosse.

> W. Horrie, etc'[1]

Middleton sent a covering letter explaining that the aim of the new Engagers was simply union and the avoiding of bloodshed among brother Scots.

The Commission of the Church, on the motion of James Guthrie, resolved on Middleton's summary excommunication.[2]

Collapse of Royalist rising.

Two days after the Bond was signed the King and the Committee of Estates published an 'Acte of Pardon and Indemnitie' to these rebels on condition that they laid down their arms. This alteration of the circumstances gave the King, Committee of Estates, and Commission a reason for requesting Guthrie to stay the excommunication, with which he was entrusted, but Guthrie was too much in earnest, and laid

[1] Balfour, iv. 129.
[2] Row, *Blair*, 244.

the ban on Middleton in Stirling Church. On 4th November Leslie received their submission at Strathbogie. The whole movement was a crafty device to unify the forces of the Crown on a field where the principle of patriotism was to be recognised as of first importance in the crisis. In taking action, men were to consider that patriotism took precedence of Covenanted religion. This was a demand the least likely to appeal to Strachan and his unbending Whiggamores. This party, which Carlyle styles 'the old Whiggamore Raid of 1648 under a new figure,' had already mustered over four thousand men in the western shires under Colonels Strachan and Gilbert Ker. They held a conference at Dumfries, when Wariston gave them assistance in framing a policy and pronouncement antagonistic to the new coalition.[1] Strachan had opened friendly correspondence with Cromwell, who, after sending to the Committee of Estates a firm letter stating that any blood further shed in defence of their Malignant King would lie on their heads, on 9th October marched to Glasgow, expecting a junction with the westland men.[2] On 17th October, the Dumfries manifesto was ready for presentation to the Estates by Patrick Gillespie and John Stirling. It had the following title: *The Humble Remonstrance of the Gentlemen, Commanders and Ministers, attending the Forces in the West.* This extraordinary document, prolix as all those viséed by Wariston are, attributed the Lord's wrath to—

Whiggamore conference at Dumfries.

The Remonstrance—a Western Covenant, 17th October 1650.

(1) The admission of Charles to the Covenant without proof of the reality of his professions.

(2) Provoking God by the hasty conclusion of the Treaty, after the 'unstraight dealling' of Charles stood disclosed, thus palliating his dissimulation.

(3) The King's action in conjunction with the apostate Montrose and other Malignants and Papists, in opposition to the work of God and the Covenant.

---

[1] 'The Remonstrant forces besieged and fired the house of Drumlanrig, wasting the lands and taking away the crops and plenishing of the tenantry, in October 1650. In 1661 the Earl of Queensberry pursued Wariston, Gilbert Ker, Stair, and other westland landlords with Captain John Gordon, 'wha burnt the gaits,' Patrick Gillespie, John Nevay, and other ministers. He was awarded £2000 sterling by Parliament: Ramage, *Drumlanrig and the Douglases*, 46-52; *Act. Parl. Scot.*, VI. ii. 637*b*; vii. 95.

[2] Letter cl; Balfour, iv. 161.

(4) The unjust design of some to invade England to obtain booty and to force a king upon an independent nation.

(5) Backsliding from the Covenant, neglecting to fill public offices with Covenanters, and tolerating Malignants.

(6) The sins of covetousness, extortion, self-seeking, and trust in the flesh instead of in God.[1]

'It closed,' wrote Baillie, 'with a solemn engagement on all their hearts (if God blessed their armies) to see all these things performed.'[2]

Views of the Remonstrants. The Remonstrants were careful to object to being classed with Sectaries and Levellers, and demanded the putting away of the sins of the King and people before they would join the royal army. This possibility of union, making these demands 'too low for his meridian,' was the factor constraining Strachan to resign the command of the Kirk regiment and to seek refuge with Cromwell. The fiery Patrick Gillespie afterwards crystallised in a few words the demands of his party, when in his 'pride of stomack' he declared, 'that a hypocrite ought not to reign over us; that we ought to treat with Cromwell and give him securitie not to trouble England with a king; and, who [soever] marred this treatie, the blood of the slaine in this quarrell should be on their head.'[3] There were extremer men than these, such as the two Cants of Aberdeen, who were so patriotic as to maintain that one crown was enough for any man.[4]

Committee of Estates condemn the Remonstrance. The Committee of Estates saw that the Remonstrance tended to undo their labours for unity, and after a fruitless conference with the Commission of Assembly on the subject, they, on 25th November, resolved to suppress it. Argyll, Balcarres, Lothian, and Lord Advocate Nicolson were loud in disapproval of it as a divisive, scandalous, and treasonable production, and of Hope, Guthrie, and Gillespie as contrivers of the national mischiefs. Burleigh, Wariston, and Sir James Hope as strongly defended it. However, the Remonstrance was voted to be scandalous, and Argyll and two others were commissioned to ask the Assembly to condemn it and its promoters, and to impeach Guthrie and Gillespie. The Commission of the Assembly on 28th November,

---

[1] Balfour, iv. 141; Peterkin, *Records*, 604; Row, *Blair*, 246.
[2] Letters, iii. 119.
[3] Baillie, *Letters*, iii. 124.
[4] Balfour, iv. 161.

with some diplomacy, admitted that the Remonstrance contained 'sad truths,' no doubt, 'apt to breid division in Kirk and Kingdom,' but, since they loved the 'godlie men' who framed it, they would defer criticism until these 'worthy gentlemen' had an opportunity, at another diet, to explain their intentions.[1] Guthrie, Patrick Gillespie, and others protested against this finding.

Perth was now the seat of the Government, and Parliament met there on 26th November 1650. The King, in his speech, acknowledged himself to be Sovereign of 'three Covenanted kingdoms,' and that God had 'moved me to enter a covenant with His people (a favour no other king can claime), and that He inclyned me to a resolutione, by His assistance, to live and dye with my people in defence of it. This is my resolutione, I professe it before God and you, and in testimony heirof, I desyre to renew it in your presence; and if it pleis God to lenthen my dayes, I houpe my actions shall demonstrat it.'[2] This blasphemous vow was of a piece with the vulgar outrage on religion about to be perpetrated in Scone, and with the dishonour of the political opportunists, who publicly enforced the Covenants and Act of Classes, while they welcomed the return to Parliament of men who hated these bonds. The Church was made the confessional for aspirants to place, and Parliament a meeting-house for pious dissemblers, from the hour when Argyll became bewitched with the promises of relief from his bankruptcy, of advancement to ducal honours, and of the marriage of Charles to his daughter, Ann—a king's barter for a subject's honesty.[3] Swashbucklers, such as James Turner, laughed at the credulity of the clergy.

Colonel Robert Montgomery was commissioned to crush the western army if it refused co-operation with the Nationalist party; but, while Parliament sat, he was able to report that General Lambert had routed the Covenanters at Hamilton on 1st December, and captured Ker, who was wounded. Ker was sent to an English prison, where he was consoled by sentimental letters from Samuel Rutherford. Strachan vainly made a final effort to rally the Whiggamores before he sought refuge at Cromwell's headquarters in Edinburgh. On 24th December

The King's vow.

Whiggamores crushed.

[1] Balfour iv. 174; Row, *Blair*, 248.
[2] Balfour, iv. 185; *Act. Parl. Scot.*, VI. ii. 608a.
[3] Gardiner, *Hist. of Commonwealth.*, i. 349.

the Castle of Edinburgh was delivered up, before Cromwell's heavy ordinance could pound it into submission, and soon the Lowlands, a few guerillas excepted, were in English hands.

Origin of the Resolutioners. The Estates agreed to the coronation of Charles, authorised that outward compliance with the Covenants should be the right of entrance to the Royalist ranks, and contemplated penal Acts against compliers with the Sectaries. Forgetting the old troubles over jurisdiction, they menacingly ordered Robert Douglas to convene the Commission of Assembly in Perth on 12th December, and to obtain a judgment on the main question then at issue, namely, whether it was lawful to reinstate those formerly purged out of the army by the Act of Classes. A quorum, chiefly of Fife ministers, assembled, and a majority, homologating the crafty proposition that it was a virtue to follow a Covenanted King, resolved to reply in the affirmative, that all persons except excommunicates, the forfeited, vicious, Discovenanters and professed enemies of God's cause, were eligible for defence of their country against the Sectaries. That was the first resolution. The Commission received a second query on 19th March as to the lawfulness of admitting to the Committee of Estates persons formerly debarred, but now after satisfaction admitted to the Covenant. On this point the second resolution was not intended to afford a full answer; at the same time, the Commission desired Parliament to admit to the Committee all save a few 'pryme actors against the state.'[1] Those who upheld those resolutions were henceforth styled Resolutioners, and those Remonstrants who protested against them were afterwards called Protesters.[2] The reply of the Commission gave great offence to the anti-Malignant party, and several of their leaders—Wariston, Chiesley, and others—dissociated themselves from assenters to the new policy, and with army officers left their appointments on the ground that there was a departure from principle. The Presbytery of Stirling made a strong protest, which Cromwell caused to be printed with the title: *A Remonstrance of the Presbytery of Stirling against the present conjunction with the*

[1] Balfour, iv. 197, 270.

[2] Six hundred ministers adhered to the resolutions, and, with the exception of forty, all conformed to Episcopacy in 1661: *Life of Blair*, 362 note. Other authorities reckon there were seven hundred and fifty Resolutioners: Thurloe, *State Pap.*, iv. 557-8; Baillie, *Letters*, iii. 299.

Malignant party.[1] The tendency of the extremists of the Covenanting party was towards an alliance with the English Sectaries, which caused the Commission, early in 1651, to issue an Act censuring those who complied with the Sectarian army. Some of the Protesters visited Cromwell in Glasgow and discussed the situation with him.

This acknowledgment by the ministers was all the politicians wanted. An Act summoning fresh levies, the penitents included, was passed on 23rd December. This was the signal for the King's supporters to rush to church to be shriven and made eligible to attend at the coronation on New Year's Day. On the other hand, all that could be done for the slaves taken at Dunbar was to read their petition before enlisting other dastards, who met a worse fate at Worcester. Before Parliament adjourned till 5th February, the Church, still anxious to secure a divine blessing on these dubious movements, ordained two preparatory services—Sabbath, 22nd December, being devoted to fasting and humiliation for the national sins, and the Thursday thereafter for the particular sins of the Stuart dynasty.[2] Charles was dutiful and gracious enough to fast and mourn with his subjects. After the penance was over he slyly said, 'I think I must repent too that ever I was born.' As remarkable a scene took place in Largo church, when the worldling, Lauderdale, compeared to own his sin, and heard Mr. James Makgill descant on Rehoboam from the text, 'And when he humbled himself the wrath of the Lord turned from him.' Thereafter Lauderdale lifted up his right hand and swore both Covenants.[3] General Middleton was even more docile, and donned the sackcloth uniform of a penitent excommunicate in Dundee church, on 12th January, in order to obtain his certificate. To keep the balance true, that very day in Perth, Strachan was excommunicated and 'delivered to the devil.'[4] Everything was in train for the restoration of the power of the Crown.

Church ordains fasting and humiliation.

Two miles north-west from Perth, overlooking the Tay, stood the ancient palace of Scone, and near by a new parish church, built out

---

[1] Row, *Blair*, 256.

[2] Cf. Patrick Gillespie's sermon, *Rulers' Sins the Causes of National Judgments, or a Sermon preached at the fast upon the 26th Day of December* 1650.

[3] Lamont, *Diary*, 25; *Minutes of Presbyteries of St. Andrews and Cupar*, 60, 61 (Abbotsford Club).

[4] Balfour, iv. 240.

of the old abbey. To that sacred 'Mount of Belief' the Kings of Alban came to sit on the *Lia Fail*, or Stone of Destiny, and be crowned. There Charles II. also came to take his 'tottering crown' and brook his realm, although the fabulous palladium now rested on foreign soil.

Coronation of Charles II. at Scone, 1st January 1651. Coronation day was 1st January 1651, but the brilliancy of that of 1633 could not be reproduced in the dead of winter, when many misfortunes had thrown a cloud over the land, and dissipated its seasonable joy.[1] The bishops were gone, the English glory shone in a hostile camp, and sour Scots faces looked from beneath clerical hats and iron bonnets. Into the upholstered church the Prince, the Honours, and the Estates of Scotland were ushered. The elevated throne was vacant. A chair afforded the Prince a seat before the pulpit, in which the then Moderator, Robert Douglas, a kinglike man, with royal blood in his veins according to whisperers about Queen Mary, and a manly Resolutioner, was standing. Charles could not forget him of the dark Dunfermline days. The ancient ceremonial he had to conduct was to be shorn of the anointing as savouring of superstition, and to be made more effective by sustained advices. After prayer, the celebrant expounded the coronation of Joash and the covenant of Jehoiada, and drew out every parallel to the case of his Prince. The sins of the Stuarts had made theirs a tottering crown, which now would fall if Charles put on crown and sin together. Unction was a popish device, with the 'limbs of Antichrist,' put to the door, and to be exchanged for the unction of Grace. The Covenant bound the King to the nation and to God, and must be renewed for the maintenance of Reformed Religion, the extirpation of false religion—Popery, Prelacy, profanity—and the unification of the people under the Crown, Parliament, and Church in the enjoyment of the national liberties. The people expected their King to remember his father's sins and turn good like Joash, to purge the Court, cleanse the Church, and reform the masses and himself. With the tormenting spirit of a risen Buchanan or Melville he trounced all round, and while disowning extremists, said a charitable word for the enlistment of penitent Malignants. The Covenant was the *sine qua non*. Although 'prayers are not much in request at Court,' said he, the King must pray and prevail. He must avoid the guilt of his meddlesome

---

[1] Baillie, *Letters*, iii. 127.

grandsire, who laid the foundation for the mischief done by his father. On this doctrine Douglas besought a blessing.

The representatives of the people in the General Assembly marched in and formed a bodyguard at the pulpit stairs. The two fateful Covenants, 1638 and 1643, written on one fair parchment, were produced and tediously read. The Moderator proceeded to pray that grace might be given to Charles to keep his vows. Charles knelt, held up his right hand, then swore this oath:—

'I, Charles, King of Great Britain, France and Ireland, do assert and declare, by my solemn Oath, in the Presence of Almighty God, the Searcher of Hearts, my Allowance and Approbation of the National Covenant, and of the Solemn League and Covenant, above written, and faithfully oblige myself to prosecute the Ends thereof in my Station and Calling; and that I for Myself and Successors shall consent and agree to all Acts of Parliament enjoining the National Covenant and Solemn League and Covenant, and fully establishing Presbyterial Government, the Directory for Worship, Confession of Faith, and Catechisms, in the Kingdom of Scotland, as they are approven by the General Assemblies of this Kirk, and Parliaments of this Kingdom; and that I shall give my royal assent to Acts or Ordinances of Parliament passed, or to be passed, enjoining the same in my other Dominions: And that I shall observe these in my own Practice and Family, and shall never make Opposition to any of these, or endeavour any change thereof.'[1]

King Charles's oath.

Charles then subscribed the Covenants—(National, and Solemn League)—to which the King's oath was subjoined. He ascended the platform, showing himself, and the Lyon-King demanded assent to his election. The audience responded, 'God save the King, Charles the Second.' He descended. The Moderator at the head of the clergy asked if he would take the Coronation Oath appointed by the first Parliament of James VI., and found him willing. He knelt again, lifted up his right hand, and swore the oath. After being robed in purple, the

The Coronation at Scone.

---

[1] The Covenant signed by Charles is preserved in the Bodleian Library: *Clarendon MSS.*, vol. 40f. 80 (*Cal. Clar. State Pap.*, 67, No. 347). Cf. Appendix. *Act. Parl. Scot.*, VI. ii. 161, 7 Feb. 1649; *Decl. Gen. Assem.*, 27 July 1649; Bute, *Scottish Coronations*, 192-3; Nicoll, 42-7.

Prince was asked to take the Sword of State in defence of the Faith, the Church, the Covenants, and Justice. Douglas prayed God to purge the Crown of the sins of Charles. Argyll placed it on his head. The nobles touched it and swore allegiance. The Earl of Crawford and Lindsay placed the sceptre in his hand, whereupon Argyll conducted him to the throne. For the first time in the national history had laymen ousted the Church from the office of proffering the symbols of sovereignty to the Monarch. Again Douglas interpreted the function, and warned Charles of the Stuart sins. A royal pardon was proclaimed. The King showed himself to the crowd, who shouted 'God save the King.'

On his return, the catalogue of the Scots Kings was recited. The Lords swore to be the King's liegemen according to the Covenants, then kissed the royal cheek. Standing, Charles received the benediction. Douglas had still his peroration to give, and, harping on the Covenants, adjured ruler and ruled that if they broke the Covenants, God would turn the King from his throne and the nobles from their possessions.

Charles, in order to evince his ingenuousness and sincerity, appealed to his lieges, 'that if in any time coming they did hear or see him breaking that Covenant, they would tell him of it, and put him in mind of his oath.'[1]

Charles, now a Covenanted King.

King James was once more flagellated, and then the climax was reached—'Sir, you are the only Covenanted King with God and His people in the world. ... Be strong and show yourself a man!' Prayer followed. The congregation sung the Twentieth Psalm, concluding—

> 'Deliver, Lord, and let the King
> Us hear, when we do call.'[2]

After the benediction was pronounced, the King, robed, sceptred, and crowned, escorted by the Court, re-entered the palace before returning to Perth. When night descended the hill-tops gleamed with bonfires. For an indecent outrage on religion and patriotism one could not readily find a match to that perpetrated at Scone by the libertine, Charles.

The secret policy of Charles.

Charles now had a good pretext for encouraging his secret aim to revenge his father's death, to oust and destroy the regicides, and to establish the autocracy cherished by the Stuart Kings. At the head of a

---

[1] Somers, *Tracts*, vi. 117; Row, *Blair*, 256.
[2] *Form of the Coronation*, Aldis, *List*, 1441-4.

Scottish army of Royalists, he might retrieve the fortunes of his house. In one ignorant of the complications of the times such enthusiasm was natural; and there was an unpardonable insult in the shrewd counsel of the Hope brothers, Craighall and Hopetoun, that Charles should 'treatt with Cromwell for one half of his cloake before he lost the quhole.'[1] He ostracised the Hopes and sought temporary comfort in the advice of Argyll, whose own influence was waning on account of his defection from the extremists of his own party. The increasing success of the new policy, whereby the King was surrounded by former opponents of the rigid system of the Covenanters, resulted in the depreciation of Argyll. Charles had already craved Hamilton to try to mitigate that 'rigidness,' and in the recall of Hamilton there was the plain signal to Argyll that his power was on the wane. Taking the hint, Argyll left the Court. Yet, because Charles conceived that the lever of Presbyterianism in Scotland and England could raise him to dominion, he tried to fulfil his Covenanted promises; and, to accomplish the end in view, offered to marry Argyll's daughter, Ann. He asked his mother to approve of this sacrifice to a hated faith. But the Queen-mother and Cardinal Mazarin abhorred the regicide tribe and their compatriots, and rejected the base artifice. No one could imagine Charles implementing his betrothal after he had utilised Argyll and his redshanks in the victorious campaign of his imagination. In due course the match was departed from.[2]

Charles II. and Lady Ann Campbell.

The raising of the northern levies went on apace, notwithstanding the vituperations of the Remonstrant clergy. For their offence of preaching against the resolutions 'as involving ane conjunctione with the malignant partie in the land,' which they considered contrary to the Word and Covenant, James Guthrie and David Bennet, ministers of Stirling, were cited before the Committee of Estates and ordered to remain in ward in Perth for a time. On 20th February, they in turn refused to acknowledge the jurisdiction of the Crown in such a purely ecclesiastical cause.[3]

Charles sat with the Parliament when it met in Perth on 13th March under the presidency of Lord Burleigh, who superseded Lord Loudoun. The latter too much favoured 'the Campbell faction' to be retained in

Parliament meets at Perth, 13th March 1651.

[1] Balfour, iv. 239.
[2] Gardiner, *Hist. of Commonwealth*, i. 201, 349, 352—citing authorities.
[3] Peterkin, *Records*, 639; Balfour, iv. 247-53, 263.

the chair at this crisis. The chief business was to elect Charles to be generalissimo of the army, to restore the known friends of the throne, and to propound a query to the Commission of the Church as to the advisability of reponing on the Committee of Estates those persons debarred under former acts of disability. While the Commission declined to give a full categorical answer to the query, as before stated (p. 26), they recommended the employment of all penitents, excepting a few notable persons. They further supported this recommendation by the issue from Perth, 20th March 1651, of an 'Exhortation and Warning,' in reality a patriotic manifesto, adjuring the people to rise under the King and defend their country. Even this was not a sufficient concession. The Commission of Assembly was next asked to agree to a repeal of the 'Act of Classes' and to promote a 'general unity.' The Commission, before agreeing to this recalcitrant measure, stipulated that Parliament should

Act securing Covenanters. first pass a statute 'for the security of religion, the worke of Reformation, and persons quho have beine steadfast in the Covenant and causse.' The King took an active part in the appointment of a War Committee, which provoked so much dissent from the Argyll party that the Chancellor and Lothian flouted the King with deserting his friends who set him on the throne. This desertion was more apparent after the return of the envoy with the ultimatum that Lady Ann Campbell was not to be Queen. The new national policy was not to be guided by Argyll, at least.

The Parliament met in Stirling in May, gave the Church the demanded security in an Act ratifying other relative Acts since 1649, and providing a bond whereby those excluded from Parliament should be readmitted on binding themselves not to carp at these Acts and their consequences.

Act of Classes repealed, 2nd June 1651. The Act of Classes, 1646, and the Act of 1649 were repealed on 2nd June. The King had proved a match for his astute opponents.[1]

Meantime Cromwell had failed to draw Leslie off his strong post on the hills south of Stirling, and had recourse to an unexpected movement. He established a camp under Lambert at North Queensferry, whence Lambert issued to attack and rout a force of Scots under Sir John Brown and Colonel Holborn at Inverkeithing, 20th July, where 2000 Scots fell, and Brown and 1500 men were captured. Cromwell crossed

---

[1] Balfour, iv. 301-7; *Act. Parl. Scot.*, VI. ii. 672-7; Act, 8th January 1646; Act, 23rd January 1649: *Act. Parl. Scot.*, VI. i. 503; VI. ii. 143.

the Forth and marched to Perth, thus getting between the northern army under Middleton and Leslie, and leaving the way into England open for the latter. The apparent peril of the situation was nullified by the arrangements made by Cromwell for the movement of his southern armies. Despair, not courage, constrained the War Committee to essay the rash enterprise to which Cromwell tempted them.[1] They counted on a Royalist rising in England and Wales. They were doomed to disappointment. The only man of influence who joined the invaders was the Earl of Derby with 300 retainers. Presbyterians and Episcopalians equally looked askance at the Scots. English Presbyterianism was in a moribund condition, and its leaders knew their own impotency. Military successes of Cromwell.

On 31st July, Charles and Leslie with 20,000 men left Stirling for Carlisle by way of Annandale and Eskdale. Argyll, Loudoun, and the party of conciliation stood aloof from this mad enterprise, and allowed Hamilton and the pretended penitents to march to disaster. Charles and his 16,000 wearied followers reached Worcester on 22nd August. Four days later he issued a manifesto declaring for the Covenant, and promising an Act of Oblivion for all except the regicides. Cromwell followed hard upon his heels, while the armies of Harrison, Fleetwood, and Lambert bore down upon Charles. Cromwell, taking the east coast road as far as Durham, crossed central England, passed through Stratford-on-Avon and entered Evesham, between Worcester and London, on 27th August. The Parliamentary forces were double those of the Scots. Charles and Scots army march into England.

Leslie drew up his army on the right or western bank of the Severn, in a corner where the Teme joins the Severn, and he destroyed the bridge over the Teme. It was the anniversary of the rout of Dunbar, 3rd September. Cromwell lay to the east across the river. He divided his force into three: one division lay across the road to London, another moved south and lay ready to cross the Severn, and the third crossed in the south and marched up to the Teme. The movement of these two divisions over two bridges of boats succeeded. The Scots were stubbornly driven from hedge to hedge into Worcester city. Charles watched the unequal fight from the cathedral tower. He saw the weakening of the division on the London road, and hurled troops Battle of Worcester, 3rd September 1651.

[1] Hamilton to Crofts, 8th August: Cary, *Memoirs*, ii. 305.

through the Sudbury gate, and himself gallantly charged against the enemy. At first the English gave way. Cromwell himself hurried back over the bridge of boats with reinforcements, and, gallantly leading his men, repelled the Scots and made them break. The Ironsides cut them to pieces. Capturing 'Fort Royal,' Cromwell turned its guns upon the fugitives fleeing through the streets. Charles was reluctant to fly. 'Shoot me dead,' said he, 'rather than let me live to see the sad consequences of this day.'[1] Into every avenue where the Scots ran they fell into cleverly prepared traps. Few escaped death or capture.[2] The peasantry helped the regulars to wipe out the invaders. The baggage and munitions of war were all taken. Of prisoners over six thousand were brought in, including Leslie, Rothes, Lauderdale, Kelly, Middleton, Montgomery, Thomas Dalyell (Binns), and many other officers, as well as nine ministers.[3] The Duke of Hamilton, before he died of his wounds, had four painful days given him in which to ponder over that essay on death and immortality which he wrote the night before the battle. The Earl of Derby, by recovering from his wounds, met a worse fate on the traitor's block at Bolton. The King escaped. For six weeks, there followed the romantic hunt and hair-breadth escapes in circumstances evincing devotion only equalled in that shown to 'Bonnie Prince Charlie.' His adherents scorned the reward offered for him. Yet he preferred his terrible privations to seeking security among the Scots. They afterwards had a feeble joke at his expense, saying their Achan hid himself in an *aik* (oak). At length, in the unsanitary plight of dirty vagrants, Charles, with his companion Wilmot, reached France on 16th October and cast himself, a starveling, on the charity of friends.[4] The Pope would not grant him a subsidy until he implemented in face of Holy Church his proposal to be converted to Romanism.[5]

Argyll, as soon as Charles took command of his army, with Hamilton as lieutenant-general and Leslie as major-general, realised that his Sovereign discounted the Campbells as a military factor.

Wanderings of King Charles.

---

[1] Airy, *Charles II.*, 161.

[2] Firth, *Oliver Cromwell*, 291.

[3] Lamont, 43.

[4] Cf. extant begging letters to John Knox, minister of Leith, 3rd and 4th August 1652, as to his 'straights and necesitys.' Sold by W. Brown, Bookseller, Edinburgh. His 'friend' Knox was deprived in 1662!

[5] Airy, 168.

While the Scots levies were being dragged reluctantly into the field, and cavaliers were counterfeiting repentance in order to obtain mercenary employment in the so-called army of patriots, the Assembly was endeavouring to silence the dissentients from the Royalist policy. It met in St. Andrews on 16th July, and Balcarres was Commissioner. Members had the unedifying experience of hearing Andrew Cant open the meeting with a condemnation of the recalcitrant policy, and Douglas, the Moderator, traverse Cant's opinions. Before the business was allowed to begin, Guthrie protested against certain members taking their seats, while Professor John Menzies, Aberdeen, proposed debarring the whole Commission for their defections. There was the usual wrangle, Douglas challenging this slander, and Blair offering mediation. Rutherford, and other twenty-one sympathisers, protested against the meeting as unconstitutional.[1] The Resolutioners voted Douglas into the chair. The temper of the diets was not improved by an impolitic request from the King that the opponents of the Resolutions should be censured, nor by a trenchant epistle from Wariston. Before they could settle to legislation, the news from Inverkeithing made them seek safety in Dundee. There, on 22nd July, Rutherford's cogent Protest declining the Assembly was read. Balcarres in vain demanded that the twenty-two absent Protesters should be reported for civil punishment for their reflections on the King, Parliament, and Church. The Assembly ordered Presbyteries to deal with them. It was ultimately agreed to cite Guthrie, Patrick Gillespie, James Simson, James Naismith, and John Menzies. They did not compear. The Assembly deposed Guthrie, Gillespie, and Simson, suspended Naismith, and referred Menzies to the Commission.[2]

Assembly at St. Andrews, Perth, and Dundee, in July 1651.

Deposition of Protestors.

After the meeting of the Assembly at St. Andrews, a work was published entitled *A Vindication of the Freedom and Lawfulness of the late Assembly*, etc.[3]

This was answered by *The Nullity of the Pretended Assembly at Saint Andrews and Dundee*.[4]

[1] Peterkin, *Records*, 631; Lamont, 40.

[2] Row, *Blair*, 278.

[3] *Vindication*, by James Wood: Review by Guthrie from notes of Wariston; cf. Baillie, *Letters*, iii. 213.

[4] 4to, pp. 312, 1652. *The Nullity*, p. 79, gives list of forty Remonstrants: Stranraer, Turnbull; Kirkcudbright, S. Row; Wigton, Richeson; Ayr, Wylie; Irvine, Mowet;

This ill-advised policy of the Moderates of conciliating a faithless King and worthless politicians while coercing their conscientious and wiser co-religionists—the Protesters—was for ever fatal to the unity of the Church of Scotland. That great schism, which the Covenant itself banned, and time never remedied, was not the only fruit of this Laodicean assembly.

The public Resolutions were a source of discord to both sections of the protesting party—those who, like James Guthrie, held them to be unscriptural, and those who maintained their incongruity with the former resolutions of the Church to be done with the Malignant party. But both sections, and many other Covenanters as well, held that Sin, personal, ministerial, official, regal, and national, was the root of all their domestic troubles and 'The Causes of God's Wrath' on a sinful land. They agreed that this opinion or fact should be publicly voiced, and promulgated in express terms. When they met to condescend on the form of the declaration, there was division of opinion and adjournment of debate. The Commission had, after Dunbar, published *Causes for Humiliation*, but the anti-Resolutionists did not consider them exhaustive, at a meeting held at Glasgow in September 1651, which was adjourned to meet at Edinburgh in October. Thither the Protesters came by urgent request,[1] The whole questions of the hour, religious

---

Dumbarton, Henry Semple; Paisley, A. Dunlop; Glasgow, P. Gillespie; Hamilton, Nasmith; Lanark, Sommerville; Auchterarder, Murray; Perth, Rollok; Dunkeld, Oliphant; Kirkcaldy, Moncrieff; Cupar, Macgill; St. Andrews, S. Rutherfurd; Forfar, Lindsay; Arbroath, Reynolds; Aberdeen, Cant; Kincardine, Cant; Dumfries, Henry Henderson; Penpont, Samuel Austine; Lochmaben, Thomas Henderson; Middlebie, David Lang; Jedburgh, John Livingston; Turriff, Mitchell; Garioch, Tellifer; Kelso, Summervail; Earlstoun, John Veitch; Chirnside, Ramsay; Edinburgh, Robert Trail; Linlithgow, Melvill; Biggar, Livingstone; Dalkeith, Sinclair; Stirling, James Guthrie; Deer, Keith; Elgin, Brodie; Inveraray, Gordon; Dundee, Oliphant.

[1] The ministers and elders who attended the 'Confessions' of the Ministers in 1651, which resulted in the production of *The Causes of God's Wrath*, were named in the Process against Wariston as follows:—

Thomas Ramsay	Alexander Moncrieff
Samuel Row	John Murray
Thomas Wyllie	Alexander Bartane
John Nevay	Hugh Kennedy
Hary Semple	John Sinclair
Patrick Gillespie	John Cleland
John Carstairs	Thomas Hog

and political, were discussed, but 'they only emitted some causes of a fast,' and declared the root sin to be the Restoration.[1] The ten 'General Heads of the Causes why the Lord contends with the land,' as agreed upon by the Commission, were accepted, and it was agreed that these should be amplified, after this meeting held in October, as stated in the work itself.

James Guthrie is usually credited with the clerical work of preparing the manifesto—Hugh Kennedy also being associated in it—which appeared with the title, *Causes of the Lords wrath against Scotland manifested in his sad late Dispensations. Whereunto is added a Paper, particularly holding forth the Sins of the Ministery.*[2] The manuscript, subscribed by Wariston, was given by him to John Ferrier, who carried it to Christopher Higgins the printer, who, in turn, executed the work as instructed by Colonel Fynick.[3]

The indictment of Guthrie bore that he was the compiler, but Guthrie in defence pleaded that he was only one of the compilers and enlargers of the 'Heads.'[4] The indictment of Wariston also accused him of being art and part in the compilation.[5] Setting apart the fact that King Charles was a pledged Covenanter, the pamphlet was the

James Nasmyth	William Wishart
Frances Aird	Robert Row, Elders,
Robert Lockhart	and laird of Hiltoune
William Jack	laird of Greinhead
William Somervell	laird Dolphinton
Alexander Livingston	Sir James Melvill
James Donaldson	Colonel Hacket
Samuel Rutherford	Lord Wariston
James Guthrie	Sir John Cheislie
Robert Traill	Archibald Porteous
John Stirling	Patrick Anderson
James Symson	George Gray
William Oliphant	Andrew Hay
George Nairn	Colonel Ker
Gilbert Hall	(Sir James Stewart?).
	Act. Parl. Scot., vii. App. 66.

[1] Row, *Blair*, 266, 270; *Suppl.*, 285, 286.
[2] 4to, n.p., 1653, pp. 98; Aldis, *List*, 1472.
[3] *Act. Parl. Scot.*, vii. App. 66.
[4] *Ibid.*, 35, 36-42.
[5] *Ibid.*, 10.

rankest treason possible. Otherwise it was both legal and justifiable. So widespread was the influence of this pamphlet that Parliament enjoined that Remonstrators and persons accessory to it should remove ten miles from the Capital.[1] It was burned by the common hangman.

The Assembly, as if ashamed of the West Kirk Declaration, authorised this interpretation of it: 'That the King's interest is not to be owned but in subordination to God, the Kirk being ever willing, as their duty is, to own and maintain in their station his Majesty's interest in that subordination, according to the Covenants.'[2]

[1] 1661, c. 11.
[2] Peterkin, *Records*, 636.

CHAPTER NINETEEN

THE RULE OF THE IRONSIDES

CROMWELL accepted his victory at Worcester as the divine sign of approval of a change of government.[1] The day after the battle he sent a dispatch to Lenthall, the Speaker, in which he restrained his great exultation, expressing the hope 'that the fatness of these continued mercies may not occasion pride and wantonness,' so that righteousness, justice, mercy, and truth might be the nation's 'thankful return to our gracious God.' ... 'The dimensions of this mercy are above my thoughts. It is for aught I know a crowning mercy.' That was prophetic; the sword of the Ironside returned to its scabbard. He had probably heard of the success of Monck in the north. While the hunt ran on in England, Monck and his subordinates were active. On 14th August the governor of Stirling Castle surrendered that hold, and left Monck free with seven thousand men to invest Dundee.

Dundee in 1651 was an exceedingly opulent, well-fortified city, whose roadstead was crowded with merchantmen, whose lock-fast places were filled with the valuables of the surrounding districts.[2] It was held for the Covenanters by an old campaigner with Gustavus Adolphus—Major-General Robert Lumsden of Mountquhanie—whom Cromwell had captured at Dunbar.

Acting-General Leven and the Committees of State and Church met in Alyth, on the Sidlaw Hills, in order to consider means for thwarting Monck and saving Dundee. Well informed of this intention, Colonel

Cromwell's 'crowning mercy.'

[1] Letters clxxxii, clxxxiii.
[2] *Scotland and Commonwealth*, ii. 66.

Alured captures Scots Council at Alyth.

Matthew Alured and eight hundred of Monck's Horse, after a bold night ride in the rain, surrounded the town early on Thursday 28th August, and captured the Council.[1] It is to be hoped that Monck spared the gallant defenders of Dundee the galling sight of the procession of these crestfallen patriots wending its way down to Broughty Ferry harbour to be shipped to English prisons—a goodly company, Leven, Crawford, Marischal, Ogilvy, Hepburn of Humbie, Fowlis of Colinton, Cockburn of Ormiston, Fotheringham of Powrie, Hamilton of Bargany, Archibald Sydserf, Colonel Andrew Mill, and the following clerics: the moderator Douglas, the clerk Andrew Ker, Mungo Law, John Smith, James Hamilton, John Rattray, minister of Alyth, George Pitilloch, junior, and the historical James Sharp, then minister at Crail. The people seemed to think 'the loons were weel away,' since they refused to pay a reek-tax to purchase the liberty of their ecclesiastical leaders. For grim Leven it was a sorrier ending than the *débâcle* at Dunbar. That argosy bore away the last hope of a crushed nation. On Monck's demand that the governor Lumsden should deliver up Dundee—a course recommended by the city ministers—a refusal was sent to that

Siege and fall of Dundee, 1st September 1651.

'collericke and merciless commander.'[2] Monck began to batter his way in, and succeeded on 1st September. According to Balfour, the 'drunken deboscht people' could not resist the English veterans, who entered the breaches shouting, 'God with us.' With no little humour in so grim a situation, each besieger displayed his shirt tail for a flying signal, distinguishing friend from foe in the gory pursuit. An indiscriminate carnage ensued. Age, sex, nor holy place was respected. The parish church was the last stand of Lumsden and his braves, who, it was said, were slaughtered after quarter was allowed. It is not to the credit of Monck that this brave man's head was fixed on a pike over the door of the old steeple, unless Lumsden had broken his parole.[3] The victors were unleashed for blood, lust, and loot. The sight of a puling infant sucking the breast of its dead mother staggered the butchers and stayed their hands.[4] After passion was surfeited in this red carnival, the soldiery gaily dressed themselves, being indistinguishable from officers,

[1] *Scot. and Common.*, ii. 9; Lamont, *Chron.*, 41.
[2] Balfour, iv. 315.
[3] Miller, *Fife Pictorial*, etc., ii. 313.
[4] Kidd, *Guide to Dundee*, 21.

and swaggered along loaded with fortunes. Prisoners were plentiful. A fleet of one hundred and ninety ships was captured in the anchorage. Monck has been accused of descending to personal barbarity when he threatened to 'scobe' the mouth of a minister who persisted in pleading for mercy.[1]

The other fortified towns be-north Tay soon capitulated, as did Huntly and his men on 21st November, and Balcarres on 3rd December. When Blackness was blown up, the Devil, according to report, was seen sitting on its walls.[2] Dunnottar, under Ogilvy, held out till 26th May 1652. Hunger alone compelled him to surrender that imperious rock washed by the German Ocean, and to treat with Colonel Morgan, its besieger. In Dunnottar were deposited the Honours of Scotland. By a well-conceived stratagem of Ogilvy and Mrs. Granger, wife of the minister of Kinneff, the ancient regalia were smuggled out, and hidden in Kinneff Church, before the English entered the fortress.[3]

Scotland, kingless, governmentless, beaten, lay at Cromwell's feet. A few garrisons terrorised it. In February 1652 Monck left the work of disarming and pacifying the Scots to his successor, Major-General Richard Deane. The aim of the conquerors was to unify the three kingdoms in a strong political confederation without regard to distinctive religious systems.[4]

Soon after the battle of Worcester, a bill was introduced into the English Parliament asserting the proprietorship of the Commonwealth in Scotland, and proposing the settlement of its government. A Council of twenty-one persons, of whom Cromwell was one, was appointed to govern the two conquered kingdoms. Early in 1652 eight Commissioners were elected to visit Scotland and inaugurate the Government. They were Generals Monck, Deane, and Lambert, Lord St. John, Sir Harry Vane the younger, Colonel Fenwick, Major Soloway, and

---

[1] *Scot. and Common.*, 12; Whitelocke, 490; Jervise, *Memorials*, 286; Maxwell, *Old Dundee*, 542; *Munic. Hist.*, 75; Gumble, *Monck*, 42; Gardiner, *Hist. of Common.*, ii. 67; Row, *Blair*, 281; Nicoll, 57; Balfour, iv. 315.

[2] Nicoll, 92.

[3] Scott, *Antiq.*, i. 1-49; Papers relative to the Regalia, Bann. Club, *The Honours of Scotland*, Scot. Hist. Soc. vol. xxvi.; Row, *Blair*, 332. For new details, cf. *Scot. Hist. Review*, iv. 15, 309, April 1907.

[4] Cf. *The Cromwellian Union*, C. S. Terry: Scot. Hist. Soc., 1902.

Alderman Tichborne.[1] Crushed and humiliated as Scotland was, she would not willingly assent to any incorporating union. Diverse parties in Church and State were unanimous in rejecting the English resolutions. In vain did the conciliatory Commission promulgate a manifesto, promising justice and protection, as well as enunciating a broad scheme of toleration, with liberty of worship to the peaceable and law-abiding. Laymen and clergy alike remonstrated that Protestantism was being menaced, Sectarianism intruded, spiritual independence abolished, the Covenants wiped out, evil encouraged, and the Constitution violated. The Commissioners prohibited the exercise of all judicatories not licensed by Parliament, and forbade the subscription of oaths and Covenants unless previously sanctioned. An Act abolishing the authority of Charles ii. was ceremonially proclaimed, 4th February, and the destruction at the Cross of Edinburgh of the Royal Arms with every mark of indignity showed the determination of the victors.[2]

'The Tender.'

Nine days later, the English Commissioners met at Dalkeith with representatives of the counties and burghs, and proffered to them the 'Tender,' or proposal of incorporation with England, after acceptance of which they were to be consulted as to practical details. Freedom of worship was guaranteed to the established and dissenting clergy. Some counties hailed the Tender with enthusiasm; trading centres were favourable to it; but the clergy, more truly interpreting the national feeling, would have none of it. James Guthrie and other stalwarts preached against it, and suffered for their patriotism in having troops quartered in their homes. Hatred of the Southron only slumbered, and frequently showed itself in armed risings. The Presbytery of Dunfermline went so far as to recommend the minister of Dalgetty not to marry an English soldier to a Scots girl on account of the unlawfulness of Cromwell's invasion.[3]

Appointment
of English
judges.

The Acts of the Executive, however, were approved of by the Council of State in England, who, on 6th April 1652, sent down four judges, Owen, Smith, Marsh, and Mosely, to administer justice. The Court of Session was thus superseded. To these four Englishmen three Scots were added—Sir John Hope of Craighall, William Lockhart of Lee,

[1] Heath, *Chronicle*, 304.
[2] Nicoll, 80-3.
[3] Ross, *Glimpses*, 220.

John Swinton of Swinton—Hope being appointed President. At a later date, the impecunious Johnston accepted one of these judgeships under the title of Wariston, or Judge Johnston.[1] The judges had full power to appoint subordinate magistrates, and, to their credit, it may be said that justice had never before been dispensed with so impartial a hand. The magistrates were as popular as they were effective. They undertook many duties now in the province of representative councils, such as Poor-law Boards, Road Boards, Trades Councils, Sanitary Authorities, and were a terror to evil-doers, and protectors of the well-doing.

Argyll was the last of the powerful lords to submit to Monck. After Worcester, Chancellor Loudoun and he had tried to galvanise into life a provisional government and to promote an arrangement with Monck. Monck replied that he could not negotiate without instructions from the English Parliament. Argyll, eager to vault into power again, lingered in his fastnesses and in vain endeavoured to parley with the Commissioners. That his diplomacy did not inspire much confidence in Monck is evidenced from the fact that after his submission, 26th April, Deane and an armed force penetrated the lordship of Argyle to establish garrisons, and to exact from Argyll an unequivocal submission. This he got in August, Lorne being nominated as the hostage for its exact fulfilment. Argyll, with his curious fear of contingencies, satisfied his conscience by declaring that he agreed to the civil part of Scotland being made into a Commonwealth with England—'My duty to religion according to my oath in the Covenant always reserved.' Argyll at his trial pleaded that he was not a free agent when he subscribed this submission.[2]

Submission of Argyll.

With the leading Resolutioners out of the way the Protesters held an Assembly in Edinburgh, Livingstone in the chair, and after disclaiming the Assemblies of their opponents, resolved to carry on the work of the Church.[3] The work of the Protesters was nugatory. Another Assembly, under the presidency of David Dickson, now Professor of Divinity in Edinburgh, met in the Capital on 21st July 1652. The Protesters compeared to lodge a protestation subscribed by sixty-three ministers and eighty laymen, who declared the Assembly to be 'unlawful, unfrie, and

Rival Assemblies in Edinburgh in 1652.

[1] Omond, 157 *et seq.*; *Act. Parl. Scot.*, VI. ii. 747.
[2] *State Trials*, v. 1427; Willcock, 280; Wodrow, i. 144.
[3] Lamont, 43; Row, *Blair*, 286.

unjust.' The Assembly threatened them with discipline.[1] They retaliated by making common cause with the Commonwealth. Others, persecuted for religion, also found a court of appeal in the alien Government. In 1652 the Presbytery of Aberdeen summoned Sir Alexander Irvine of Drum for alleged popery. He ignored their jurisdiction, and, on being excommunicated, appealed to Monck on the ground that Presbytery was not authorised by the Commonwealth. King Charles failed to allure Argyll from his new allegiance, but other Highland chieftains were more easily incited to take advantage of the conflict between England and Holland and to rise in arms while Monck was absent in England. Scotland was impoverished beyond description, and what with the confiscation of estates to English officers, and the general taxation for keeping up the army of occupation, no fewer than 35,000 arrestments for debt were made. With a beggared gentry it was not difficult to persuade Royalists such as Glencairn, Balcarres, Lorne, Kenmure, Glengarry, and others to take the field. Middleton was first selected to be leader of the enterprise, but sickness laid him aside. Glencairn received the royal commission and unfurled the standard at Killin on 27th July 1653.[2] Robert Lilburn, the Parliamentary commander, and the Commissioners considered Glencairn's military diversion to be a trivial outbreak, and reckoned that the influence of the Remonstrants would counterbalance the new rebellious movement. Still, the clergy could not be depended on. Judge Hope declared that few of them were honest, and that they twisted Scripture to the production of error.[3] The Church still hankered after a Covenanted King, and the ministers prayed for Charles till the custom was declared illegal. Two of their number, Waugh and Knox, were long in prison for breaking this law.[4] Others evaded the statute by circumlocutions, as the Jacobites, a century afterwards, evaded similar orders. Patrick Gillespie was one of the few who openly prayed for Cromwell, and he had his reward in being appointed Principal of Glasgow University, to the chagrin of Baillie and others.

Meantime great events had happened in England. On 20th April 1653, Cromwell and the officers had, in a high-handed manner, dissolved the

[margin note:] Highlanders rise under Glencairn, 1653.

[1] Lamont, 55.
[2] *Scot. and Common.*, 186.
[3] Nicoll, 124.
[4] Baillie, iii. 253.

Long Parliament (truncated after Pride's purge of Royalist members in 1648), and convened in its place the short-lived Barebones Parliament. The Cromwellian party in this Parliament immediately dissolved it in order to invest Cromwell with supreme authority as Lord Protector. A subsequent instrument of government modified the autocratic nature of this appointment, and provided for the establishing of a Parliament and Council of State. One result of this reformation was the promulgation of a scheme of religious toleration, to all but Papists, which provided for the establishment of Puritanism, with any of its many forms of ecclesiastical government, and for the permission of Episcopal worship when performed in private. The unbending Royalists so harassed the Government that ten major-generals were appointed to keep order in the provinces. Neither the first nor the second Protectorate Parliament was an unqualified success, and both were dissolved, the one in January 1655, the other in February 1658.

Cromwell appointed Lord Protector.

The contending clerics indicted their Assemblies to meet in Edinburgh on 20th July 1653. In St. Giles' Church only a thin partition separated Resolutioners from Protesters. Lilburn associated these conventions with the Highland rising and asked an injunction from Cromwell to suppress them. That astute diplomatist did not reply, and Lilburn determined to act on his own authority.[1] In the Resolutioners' Assembly Dickson appositely expounded the differences of Peter and Paul, and further exhorted the Church to unity and peace. He was followed by his successor in the chair, Douglas, who dilated upon schism. This preparatory service ended at four o'clock. The prayer of Dickson constituting the Assembly was nearly finished when the clatter of hoofs and the tramp of infantry were heard, and Lieutenant-Colonel Cotterel, some officers, and a guard of musketeers with lighted matches appeared in church. A loud voice with English accent broke the silence. It came from Cotterel, who stood up on a bench and said: 'Gentlemen, I am commanded to ask you by what authority you sit here: if you have none from the Parliament, Commander-in-chief, or Judges, you are to go with me.' The Moderator, having cleared out non-members, replied: 'We sit here by the authority of Jesus Christ and by the law of this land, whereby we are authorised to keep General Assemblies from year to

Edinburgh Assembly dissolved by Colonel Cotterel, 20th July 1653.

[1] Colville, *Byeways—Scotland under the Roundheads*, 236.

45

year, according to the several Acts of Parliament, and every Assembly meets by appointment of the former.' Cotterel bade them begone, 'or else he would make them rise on other terms.' Dickson craved time to constitute the meeting and to appoint the next Assembly. Cotterel was peremptory and summoned the musketeers. The Moderator's final prayer and protest was interrupted rudely by one of the officers. They stood waiting with their helmets on. Out between the lines of soldiers the ministers were led, and were conducted through the west gate over Bruntsfield Links, and drawn up near the spot where the trunk of Montrose lay buried. On this spot, set apart for the bodies of criminals, the roll was taken.[1] Baillie, who was there, describes the scene: 'When he had led us a myle without the towne, he then declared what further he had in commission. That we should not dare to meet any more above three in number; and that against eight o'clock tomorrow, we should depart the towne, under pain of being guiltie of breaking the public peace. And the day following, by sound of trumpet, we were commanded off towne under paine of present imprisonment. Thus our General Assembly, the glory and strength of our Church upon earth, is, by your souldarie, crushed and trod under feet, without the least provocatione from us, at this time, either in word or deed.'[2] What made the situation more vexing was that the Protesters sat on a while unmolested; but their meeting was also dissolved. And to their credit they drew up a protestation against the unjustifiable suppression of the Assembly.[3] Of nine hundred parish ministers, seven hundred and fifty were computed to be Resolutioners, and this majority had now no supreme judicatory. This collapse, without a blow struck, and with few regrets expressed in favour of the Church, showed how very wearied the people were with the conflicts and intrigues in connection with religion. Times had changed since the interference of a foreign prelate had roused the nation as one man.

The Remonstrants made use of their friendship with the English Sectaries by appointing to vacant charges sympathisers with both interests. In some cases the parishioners resented this intrusion. At

Protest of
Protestors.

---

[1] 'An Account of the late violence,' etc., *King's Pamphlets*, E. 708 (23); Lamont, 69; *Scot. and Common.*, 163.

[2] Letters, iii. 225.

[3] *Scot. and Common.*, 163; Row, *Blair*, 308.

Douglas, the Protesters ordained Francis Kidd on a hillside, the Aggressive-
ness of the
Protestors. celebrants being protected from the furious people by English troopers. At Bothkennar, John Galbraith was deposed, but remained in charge. The two opposing Presbyteries of Stirling prepared to settle another pastor. The parishioners nominated another Galbraith, while Guthrie's Presbytery chose a preacher named Blair. When the latter judicatory came to settle Blair, the parishioners defended the church with missiles until the sheriff appeared and protected the celebrants.[1] Nevertheless the Remonstrants at heart were not favourable to the intruded Republican Government;[2] the Protesters were openly antagonistic to it. At the communion dispensed by Rutherford and Alexander Moncrieff, at Scoonie, in June 1652, all persons who had taken the Tender, as well as Englishmen, were debarred from the table.[3] While a blight fell on the Moderate party the Protesters became more enthusiastic and tireless in ranging over the land, resuscitating the almost forgotten sacraments, rebuking sin, and re-inspiring evangelical fervour. By their zeal this remnant held itself together as the nucleus of the Church whose rehabilitation at the Revolution Settlement preserved Presbyterianism for Scotland.[4]

Although at this time Cromwell in England was in a maze of Cromwell's
policy. religious difficulties he shrewdly saw that 'the root of the matter' was in the Protesting party, and, at the suggestion of Lilburn, sent for its leaders to deliberate on the deadlock and 'a way to satisfye the godly in Scotland.'[5] Patrick Gillespie, John Livingstone, and James Menzies went, but Douglas, Blair, and Guthrie refused the invitation.[6] The result of this visit of the triumvirate was the arrangement of subsidies to the Universities of Glasgow and Aberdeen, and the framing of an ordinance for the government of the Church.

This ordinance, 8th August 1654, practically established a 'Commission of Triers' for Scotland, in the instruction of the Council of State to the Commissioners for visiting Universities to see that godly

---

[1] Baillie, iii. 247, 258.
[2] Broghill to Cromwell, 26th February 1655; *Act. Parl. Scot.*, VI. ii. 899, 900.
[3] Lamont, 51.
[4] Burnet, *Hist.*, i. 113; Lee, *Hist.*, ii. 376.
[5] Johnston to Guthrie, 29th March 1654; Baillie, iii. 567.
[6] *Ibid.*, iii. 243, 253.

presentees, who were capable preachers, as certified by four or more ministers and elders in each of five districts, were settled in livings. All parties spurned this method of extinguishing presbyterial power and privilege.

Monck returned to Scotland to restore peace by the sword. George Monck, first Duke of Albemarle (1608-70), was a Devonshire man, in the prime of life, of knightly lineage, a daring soldier for Crown and Parliament. His loyalty to Charles got him two years of imprisonment in the Tower. He became a Covenanter and a devoted adherent of the Parliamentary party. His success in the Irish wars was repeated at Dunbar. Cromwell trusted him. His manliness and moderation made him a suitable administrator. His sympathies were with the Moderates in the Church.[1] On 4th May 1654, Monck with pomp announced at the Cross of Edinburgh the establishment of the Protectorate and the assumption of Scotland as an integral part of the Commonwealth. Throne, Parliament Courts, and other authorities were abolished, and new representative forms of government were to be set up. He heralded a new era of free trade, proportionate taxation, and national prosperity. Malcontents from civil rule alone would suffer punishment. Persons in authority would be responsible for rebels issuing from their estates, or presbyteries, or families. A reward of £200 was offered for Middleton, Seaforth, Kenmure, and Dalyell.[2] This conciliatory policy did not appeal to the highest instincts, but it was popular and effective in view of the impoverished condition of the country, where bankrupt landlords became rebels out of sheer necessity. Argyll was arrested in London for debt. Despite his father's wishes Lorne joined the rebels, now in arms under Middleton. Monck hunted them from Inverlochy by Kintail to Inverness, and down to Blair-Athole. He left his mark on the charred homesteads of the Camerons, Macdonalds, Mackenzies, and other clans, and in retaliation Middleton devastated the lands of the Campbells and their allies.

Still King Charles could not be prevailed upon to land and lead his supporters, giving as his reason that they were not agreed among themselves. He asked the Assembly's Commission to pray for him and

[1] Baillie, iii., 567, 685.
[2] Thurloe, ii. 261.

send chaplains to the forces.[1] The peace made with Holland made these prayers belated.

On 19th July Colonel Morgan and the Parliamentary troops came into touch with Middleton at Dalnaspidal and dispersed the Royalists among the hills, capturing many, who were sent to the plantations and to foreign military service. A skirmish at Aberfoyle and an attack upon Campbeltown by Kenmure were unimportant incidents in this rising. Before the end of summer Glencairn and Kenmure submitted; Middleton fled to the Continent early in 1655. The Scots were forbidden the use of arms. Argyll loyally supported Monck in the suppression of the insurgents, and the informative letters he then sent to Monck were produced at the trial of Argyll, to the dishonour of Monck.

Dispersion of Royalist forces.

In 1655 Gillespie and his party received a Commission from Cromwell for settling the troubled affairs of the Church on the lines set forth in the Ordinance of 1654. In this Commission, Cromwell expressed his approval of a national establishment of religion. It was evidently intended to put the Church under the charge of the Protesters, but had a different result in splitting up that party over the question of the lawfulness of the Commission, Wariston and Guthrie rejecting it for its Erastian character.[2] In 1655 a Council of Eight, under the presidency of Lord Broghill (Roger Boyle, younger son of the first Earl of Cork, created Earl of Orrery after the Restoration, died 1679), was constituted in Edinburgh, and one of its good offices was the persuasion of the Resolutioners to accept the substance of the Ordinance and to live quietly under the Government. Lord Broghill informed Cromwell that he set himself to win the body of the ministry to accept his rule, but found the Wariston and Guthrie Protesting party to be like the Fifth Monarchy and All-hallows-men, impossible to conciliate. Douglas, Dickson, Wood, Hutchison, Smith, and 'Mr. Sharpe of Fife' were more reasonable and well disposed. This party was willing to coerce their intractable brethren and pray for the English Government. Of Douglas he wrote: 'I may truly say, he is the leadingest man in all the Church of Scotland.' His record of Sharp is noteworthy: 'Mr. Sharpe is a man I have made good use of in all this business, and one who, I thinke, is devoted

Cromwell's attempt to settle religion

---

[1] *Scot. and Common.*, 28, 29, 32, 198.
[2] Nicoll, 163-6.

to your service.'[1] These men were to gain over Patrick Gillespie, John Livingstone, and the Moderates to their party of conciliation. Deposed pastors who had suffered for Malignancy and the Engagement, such as Ramsay, Henry Guthry, Colville, and others, were now welcomed back to the ministry. The Protesters had only one panacea for the troubles— a fresh thorough purgation all round. Cromwell had marked the failure of Presbyterianism to establish itself on English soil.

Unpopularity of Presbyterianism in England.

In June 1646, the English Parliament established Presbyterianism, but parishes were slow to appoint elderships, and ministers were tardy in assembling in 'Classes,' as the ministerial courts were called. Questions as to discipline and excommunication made the system unpopular. On 29th August 1648, a final ordinance was passed, authorising 'triers' to test the fitness of the officials of the Church, so that elderships, classical precincts, or presbyteries, and provincial and national assemblies should be legally constituted. The toleration extended to the sects rendered the scheme inoperative.[2] The Westminster Assembly debated the matter thoroughly, and declared that uniformity and toleration were incompatible, and that no platform could peacefully accommodate Presbyterians and Sectaries. The sword of the New Model at Naseby put a different complexion on this conflict of theologians, and gave the Independents a new status. The sword gave a title to the sects which Parliament had to legalise in an indulgence for tender consciences. The Scottish Covenanters opposed toleration as tending to schism and atheism. In the meantime, King Charles agreed with the Scots in order to gain influence.

The second Civil War ended in the establishment of the principle of toleration. This was formulated in the 'Agreement of the People' presented by the officers to Parliament in January 1649, but a long struggle ensued before Parliament legislated on the subject. Cromwell's own aim was to unify Protestantism throughout Christendom under the aegis of the Commonwealth, and he tried to make his dream substantial by promoting a secular policy which was unpopular abroad.

Cromwell supports toleration.

His idea of toleration may be gathered from his declaration to the Irish: 'As for the people, what thoughts in the matter of religion they have

---

[1] Broghill to Cromwell, 26th February 1655; *Act. Parl. Scot.*, VI. ii. 900.
[2] Shaw, ii. 1-33.

in their own breasts, I cannot reach; but shall think it my duty if they walk honestly and peaceably, not to cause them in the least to suffer for the same.'[1]

Cromwell's first Parliament took into consideration a pronouncement on toleration embodied in the 'Instrument of Government,' of December 1653, and failing to define the limits of liberty of conscience, appointed a committee to nominate a council of theologians, who were to specify the fundamentals of religion. They duly reported their finding. But it was not till 1657 that the second Cromwellian Parliament resolved that the Scriptures should be the rule of faith, and believers in the Trinity and in the Scriptures should suffer no disability, unless they were Popish, prelatic, profligate, and blaspheming persons. Cromwell accepted these resolutions; so did the revived Rump Parliament in May 1659. The next Parliament, however, reverted to the Confession of Faith, and enacted that the Solemn League and Covenant should be read annually and hung up in every parish church.[2]

The Commonwealth did not by statute supersede Presbytery and establish Independency. The Classes simply disappeared through innate constitutional weakness. The easy, tolerant, good-natured Englishman did not take kindly to the disciplinary office of elder. The average layman then had not the education to make him a critic, nor the coercive spirit to justify his judgments on men. The majority liked the old, easy-going, non-compulsive way they had been accustomed to. There was also an active opposition to the Presbyterians from the Independents, who considered that they had as good a title to worship in the parish churches as the unwelcome Presbyters. The inability of the latter to enforce discipline tended to laxity, so that the people were in many places not catechised, and had no opportunity, for long periods, of partaking of the Lord's Supper. This scandal in the State Church gave rise in 1653 to Voluntary Associations, who undertook to dispense the sacraments and to revive decadent piety. With no middle ground between Presbytery and Independency, and hating the thrall of Puritanism, the English people yearned for a truce between Church and State. The last General Assembly in England was held in May 1659.[3]

Presbyterianism failed through inherent weakness of system.

[1] Morley, *Cromwell*, 296.
[2] Baillie, iii. 405; *Com. Jour.*, vii. 662, 862, 1st March 1660.
[3] Shaw, ii. 161; Heath, 439.

THE COVENANTERS

At this crisis the most active promoter of a union between parties was Robert Blair, who with Durham, minister of Glasgow, and some brethren in Fife, regretted the censures passed on the Protesters.[1] It was impossible to heal the rupture of the parties, who waged a pamphlet war against each other. The Resolutioners deemed it expedient that Cromwell should have authoritative information regarding Church affairs, but were unable to select a suitable delegate to present their case. At this point James Sharp, minister of Crail in Fife, was talked of in this relation. His neighbours, Wood of St. Andrews and Carmichael of Markinch, suggested his appointment; but Blair, with remarkable insight, was unfavourable both to the delegate and his mission to an Erastian ruler. Sharp was now (1656) in his forty-third year. He was born in Banff Castle, on 4th May 1613, his father, William, being factor to the Earl of Findlater, and his mother being a kinswoman of the Earl of Rothes. His reputed connection with some bagpiper is a jest or myth, like that regarding Montrose, who in his youth was said to have swallowed the devil in a toad. Sharp graduated at King's College, Aberdeen, where he imbibed the tenets of the famous Doctors, and repudiated the Covenant in 1638. He went to Oxford, and, it is said, would have taken orders in the English Church had not his health given way. His contemporaries accused him of carnal frailties during his college days, and even of the murder of Al his own illegitimate child; but there is no evidence to sustain the horrid charges.[2] He returned to Scotland and became a professor of philosophy in St. Andrews. A sympathiser with the Malignant faction, he found a patron in the Earl of Crawford, who appointed him to the Church of Crail, where he began his ministry on 27th January 1649. His portrait conveys the impression of a man of no great mental vigour or manly character, but rather of a cunning busybody. Burnet declared that 'he had a very small proportion of learning and was but an indifferent preacher.'[3] He was ambitious. His idols were power, pelf, and persons of position. His first cross was laid

Advent of James Sharp, 1613-1679.

---

[1] Row, *Blair*, 303.

[2] *Miscell. Scot.*, ii. ('Life of Sharp');, Pref. v., Sharp accused of immorality with his sister-in-law; p. 19, with Isobel Lindsay; p. 22, strangles baby. Cf. also pp. 94, 97, 101. *Eccl. Records* (St. Andrews and Cupar, 1641-98), Edin. Abbots. Club, p. 89: 'Isbell Lyndsay spouse to John Wilson in St. Andrews,' banished for reviling Sharp.

[3] *Hist.*, i. 114.

on him when the General Assembly refused to sanction his transfer from Crail to Edinburgh—that Mecca of ambitious committeemen and vain babblers of the Church.[1] He managed to keep in touch with the Resolutioners and with the Executive Government. He was sent a prisoner from Alyth to London, but through the influence of Wariston he was soon liberated, and returned, 10th April 1652, to take the Tender, and to become a friend of Monck and the English judges.[2] His friend. Lord Broghill, considered Sharp to be a suitable minister to accompany him to London in August 1656. He was then instructed by Dickson, Douglas, and Wood as to what he should represent to Cromwell regarding the National Church.[3] So early as this, Baillie describes Sharp as 'our professed friend.' Cromwell was pleased with the manner in which Sharp conducted his business, but Argyll advised him to stay his judgment until he heard his opponents. The adroitness of Sharp drew from Cromwell the remark: 'That gentleman after the Scotch way ought to be called Sharp of that Ilk.'[4] The credulous Resolutioners hailed him as 'the great instrument of God,' sent to cross the designs of the Protesters and Remonstrants, especially of Wariston, who was a member of the Upper House in the Second Protectorate Parliament, 1656-8.[5] They lived to change their judgment upon 'that very worthie, pious, wise, and diligent young man,' and to call their 'dear James' a Judas.

Sharp sent as envoy to Cromwell, August 1656.

To nullify his specious pleading and to promote their own formulated demands for the appointment of committees to plant the Church and settle its quarrels, especially by the renewal of the Act of Classes, the Protesters also sent up a spokesman to Cromwell. This was James Simson, minister at Airth, already mixed up in a vile scandal and deposed by the Assembly.[6] He was joined by powerful advocates in Guthrie and Gillespie, and three elders, Wariston, Inglestoun, and Greenhead, who brought with them an incisive indictment of their ecclesiastical persecutors. At the same time the partisans Cant, Rutherford, and Trail,

Envoys of the Protestors.

---

[1] Peterkin, *Records*, 589.

[2] *Cal. State Pap.*, 1651-2, p. 213; A. Hay, *Diary*, 42.

[3] Baillie, iii. 324, 330, 352, 568; Row, *Blair*, 328.

[4] *True and Impartial Account*, 34.

[5] Baillie, iii. 352; Row, *Blair*, 336.

[6] Baillie, iii. 353, 573.

wrote to Cromwell explaining the perplexing situation. Cromwell summoned the parties to a debate, and with a cynical shrewdness appointed a council of twelve to listen to the wrangle, in which Sharp had an opportunity of denying plain facts. In the spirit of Felix, Cromwell said he would hear them at a more convenient season, and bade them go home and live in peace. That they would not do. The Protesters so far prevailed as to get the Act of Classes renewed, while Sharp had compensation in being led to understand that this statute would remain a dead letter. The Resolutioners in 1658, in a Declaration, accused the Protesters of subverting the ecclesiastical government, and drew forth a pungent reply from the pen of James Guthrie, it is said, entitled *Protesters no Subverters, and Presbytery no Papacy*. A fresh war of pamphlets began. Rutherford wrote *A Survey of the Survey of that Summe of Church Discipline, penned by Mr. Thomas Hooker*.[1] The preface accused the Resolutioners of being worse persecutors than the bishops, and of being soul-murdering ministers who encouraged the vicious and ignorant.[2] In August, Sharp wrote to his correspondent in London, Patrick Drummond, declaring that 'no peace can be had with these men [Remonstrants] but upon their own termes, how destructive soever to truth and order.'[3] Shortly afterwards we find Sharp urging the prosecution of his opponents.

One unexpected result of the conference was the confirmation of the allegiance of Wariston to the Protector. Wariston had seen his country flourishing under the Ironsides, and realised that Cromwell was a friend to religion and education. For his patriotism he had lost office, and now with his large family was poverty-stricken. He reaccepted his former post of Lord Clerk Register, and together with Cassillis and Sir William Lockhart, was elevated to Cromwell's House of Peers, wherein he continued to sit during the regime of Richard Cromwell. He also took a share in the new administration which succeeded Richard's rule, until he was dispossessed of his office in 1659.

On 3rd September 1658, his day of fate, Oliver Cromwell, weary of the interminable strife of political and religious parties, found rest, and died expressing his confidence in these words: 'I am a conqueror

A war of pamphlets.

Wariston becomes a Cromwellian.

Death of Cromwell, 3rd September 1658.

---

[1] London, 1658.
[2] Baillie, iii. 362, 375.
[3] *Add. MSS.*, 23113, f. 66.

and more than a conqueror through Christ that strengtheneth me,' and praying earnestly for the people for whom he had fought. He was unquestionably the greatest Briton of his age. His Celtic blood determined his ideas in a religious mould. The secret of his power lay in his conviction that he was a humble instrument predestined to act for his country's welfare, under the guidance of the Divine hand. It moved him to become the representative and defender of Protestantism in Europe, in opposition to its Catholic rulers. In this action he was ably supported by the poet Milton. He strove to confer unity and peace on the British Empire, and if he followed the patterns of the Old Testament rather than the more gentle teachings of the New, he always at least sought a warrant for his actions in *The Souldiers Pocket Bible*, which every Ironside carried in his holster.[1]

If Cromwell achieved nothing more than the laying the foundations of that religious liberty which was re-established at the Revolution in 1688, he deserves to be held in esteem by all lovers of true religious and political freedom, such as Britain enjoys today. His character and place in British politics are well described by the late Principal Tulloch: 'Cromwell then was no hypocrite and no mere enthusiast. He was simply the greatest Englishman of his time: the most powerful, if not the most perfect expression of its religious spirit, and the master-genius of its military and political necessities.'[2]

On the accession of Richard Cromwell, a Parliament purged of Royalists assembled in January 1659, and was in May forced to resign along with Richard.[3] The military faction invited the Rump to assume session in May, but finding it too severe on their order, turned it out of power again. The attempt of the military to govern was a fiasco, and, finding affairs lapsing into chaos, they restored the Rump to Westminster on 26th December 1659. During summer, Sharp had been making himself so officious in London, that the Government ordered him to cease meddling in public affairs, to return to Scotland,

[margin note:] Accession of Richard Cromwell.

---

[1] '*The Souldiers Pocket Bible containing the most (if not all) those places contained in holy Scripture which doe show the qualifications of his inner man that is a fit souldier to fight the Lord's Battels both before the fight, in the fight, and after the fight*, etc. London, 1643.'

[2] *English Puritanism and its Leaders*, 160.

[3] Baker, *Chron.*, 636 *et seq.*

and 'to keep within the compass of his own calling.'[1] Sharp was not to be suppressed. The influence of Wariston, opponent of the toleration proposed to be granted to all kinds of schismatics, and soon to be advanced to be President of the Committee of Safety, was to be short-lived.

General Monck was taking a lively interest in all the perplexing moves in England. The exiled King had been in communication with Monck, but had failed to break down the gallant soldier's allegiance to the Cromwells. Monck, however, after the death of Oliver Cromwell, and the usurpation of the officers in barring out the Rump, felt himself called upon to interpose and redeem the country from anarchy.[2] The sequel seems to indicate that he had a secret aim which it was not opportune to divulge to any one. He was the most reserved man living. He convened his officers in the historic church of Greyfriars in Edinburgh and announced his opposition to the English military party, and called for those willing to join him to 'make the military power subservient to the civil.' All offered him their swords. He next secured the Cromwellian citadels and a loyal army. He issued declarations, which Sharp helped him to frame, wherein he announced that he stood for popular liberties and the freedom of Parliament.

On New Year's Day 1660, Monck crossed the Borders, and marched with six thousand men on London, which he reached on 3rd February. He boldly walked between files of soldiers into Westminster, and saw the Presbyterian members reseated who had been excluded by Pride. Thus obtaining the desired majority, Monck arranged for an early dissolution and for an appeal to the country for the election of a free Parliament. On the rising of the Long Parliament on 16th March, the first stage in the restoration of monarchy began.[3] The Presbyterian party made the best use of the time at their disposal to have the still unauthorised Confession of Faith legalised. A committee was appointed to consider it, and two days later it was agreed to, with the exception of chapters thirty and thirty-one, being finally placed in the Statute Book on 5th

Monck opposes militarism.

Monck at Westminster.

Confession of Faith legalised, 1660.

---

[1] 29th June 1659: *Add. MSS.*, 23113, f. 69. '1659, Feb. 7. Mr. James Sharpe, Mr. of Craill, tooke journey from Edinborughe to London sent by the ministrie for the public resolutions to withstand the actings of the protesters': Lamont, *Chron.*, 141.

[2] Baker, *Chron.*, 651, 663; Heath, *Chron.*, 430 *et seq.*; Row, *Blair*, 339.

[3] Heath, 439; Baker, 677.

March 1660.[1] This was the more readily agreed to since the Parliament men considered the Confession to be a simple corollary to the Solemn League and Covenant. The Solemn League and Covenant was also ordered to be reprinted, read annually in all churches, and hung up in Parliament House. This was the expiring effort, at this crisis, of ill-fated Presbytery in England. The Restoration of the King soon rendered these enactments inoperative. By agreeing to a dissolution the Covenanters threw away the only chance they had of reviving their unpopular cause in monarchical England. The elections went for the Crown and King.

Monck, by his urbanity, had so ingratiated himself with the Moderate party in the Church of Scotland, that their good wishes and prayers followed him across the Borders. A few days after his departure, David Dickson and Robert Douglas requested Monck to permit James Sharp to accompany him and keep him informed of ecclesiastical affairs. But Monck, who assured his correspondents that the welfare of the Church was the object of his solicitude, had already invited Sharp to London on a mission which was to be mentioned to none but Douglas.[2] Thus encouraged, the Resolutioners met in Edinburgh on 6th February, and drafted instructions to their envoy, who was to advocate:—

[margin note: Monck and Sharp take Council.]

(1) That the Church was to be guaranteed in her freedoms, privileges, and legal judicatories.

(2) That lax toleration productive of sin and error should be remedied.

(3) That the malversation of vacant stipends should cease.

(4) That ministers should enter into enjoyment of their stipends and benefices by the Church's Act of Admission.

This memorandum was subscribed by Dickson, Douglas, Wood, Smith, Hutchison, and the Clerk of Assembly, Andrew Ker.[3] The Resolutioners also put themselves into touch with the Presbyterian leaders in England.

Monck welcomed 'Mr. Sharp' … 'his good friend,' on 13th February. Edward Calamy and other nonconformists also welcomed him to London. Monck soon gave the Scots ministers to understand that 'it

---

[1] *Com. Jour.*, vii. 855, 862; Whitelocke, iv. 401.

[2] Wodrow, i. 4 *et seq.*; Row, *Blair*, 344; *Correspondence of Mr. James Sharp with Mr. Robert Douglas, David Dickson, etc., in the year* 1660, in Glasgow University Library. Press mark, BE. 8, d. 18.

[3] Wodrow, i. 5.

shall be his care that the Gospel ordinances and privileges of God's people may be established both here and there.' This equivocal language gave rise to a vision of Presbytery, restored, imperialised, glorified, by their new Joshua—'called of God in a strait.' But when Monck, probably at the suggestion of Sharp, although Sharp disclaimed the idea, reinstated the secluded members of Parliament in order to outvote the Rump, he plainly declared for 'Presbyterian government not rigid,' a differentiation which somewhat blurred the vision of Douglas and the other restorers of Presbytery then allied to Monck. These enthusiasts failed to comprehend wherein the rigid nature of Presbyterianism should make it unpopular and undesirable, and wrote Sharp to this effect. Sharp and Monck understood each other. Reading between the lines, and with the light thrown from subsequent events, one cannot fail to perceive that Sharp was early cognisant of the hatching of a policy which would take his co-presbyters by surprise. What other could it be than the entire discarding of their 'rigid' religious system? However, it is difficult to determine the exact date on which Sharp abandoned the idea, if he ever cherished it, that a King pledged to the Covenant was the only panacea for the national distemper. His constant asseverations that he was a genuine Presbyter, and that Lauderdale was no Episcopalian, ill harmonise with the agility he soon afterwards displayed in leaping into prelatic place and power. In his long correspondence with Douglas, Sharp gave a partial and prejudiced account of current affairs in the Capital, always contriving to leave out, as if unknown or unimportant, those facts which were indicators of the hidden movements of the friends of Episcopacy and the exiled King. His written memoranda are equivocal and difficult to interpret.

Sharp reported that it was hinted that if the Parliament rose without securing religion, then 'the King would come in without terms,' that moderate Episcopalians were coming to the front, and the populace was demanding the return of the King. In these circumstances Sharp thought that some of the Scots prisoners, who had been released on the advent of Monck, such as Crawford and Lauderdale, should be retained in London as representatives of Scotland. Monck had not yet shown his hand. Sharp endeavoured to work Douglas into a state of nervousness by informing him that the authorities reckoned the Resolutioners also to be republican and disloyal, and that Douglas's republished sermon, delivered at the Scone coronation, was being received with disfavour. Douglas and his associates wished to send special delegates to Monck and the Parliament to confer on the crisis. Sharp then desired to be recalled, but, in a subsequent letter, 5th April, he reported that Monck was averse to Commissioners being sent—Lauderdale and the emancipated Scots, in Monck's opinion, being able enough advocates of the Cause. He further mentioned Monck's distrust of the Remonstrants, and his promise, 'if we be quiet, our business would be done to our mind'; and, what staggered Douglas and his friends, Monck's avowal that none but Sharp would gain his confidence. To further hoodwink these simple believers, Sharp narrated how a trusty party of Presbyterian clergy, with Lauderdale and himself, met and came to an agreement as to the Restoration of the King on Covenant lines.[1] As a correspondent, Sharp seemed to be quite transparent and honest, as Mr. Andrew Lang would have us believe.[2] But Sharp never told the half of what he knew, and the other half he couched in oracular terms. After mentioning how Monck would not let him depart, how the King knew every move and Scotland's affection, how the King was on the eve of returning, to the joy of Presbyterians, and how the very Episcopalians were humbly seeking an accommodation from the Presbyterians, Sharp thus sums up the matter (7th April): 'The Lord having opened a fair door of hope, we may look for a settlement upon the grounds of the Covenant, and thereby a foundation laid for security against the prelatic and fanatic assaults; but I am dubious if this shall be the result of the agitations now on foot.' The sly diplomatist did not inform his masters what he expected and was working for. He adjured them to make no approach to the King till the King came, warned them against Middleton's design, and blamed Murray's mission to the King. To throw them off the true scent he confessed by the way: 'I smell that moderate episcopacy is the fairest accommodation, which moderate men who wish well to religion expect … we (the Scots) shall be left to the King, which is best for us.'[3] The Resolutioners realising the peril, the more that they now knew how tired of rigid Presbytery the youth of Scotland were, let Sharp understand that Episcopacy was the prelude to prelatic tyranny, and that if

Sharp's negotiations and craft.

---

[1] Wodrow, i. 18.
[2] *Hist. Scot.*, iii. 284.
[3] Wodrow, i. 20.

the King would not accept their conditions, they undeterred would maintain their Covenanted rights.

Triumph of
Hyde's
diplomacy.

All this time Charles and Chancellor Hyde were exerting themselves, by communicating with sympathisers in England, to create a public feeling in favour of the Restoration, and in this they succeeded so well that, before the Convention Parliament met on 25th April, the King had formulated his terms of settlement. On 4th April he signed the Declaration of Breda, wherein he offered a general pardon to all except to those whom Parliament might exempt, promised to allow Parliament to settle possible disputes over confiscated estates, and, in a word, invited Parliament to specify the terms of his return to the Throne. On receipt of this document on May-day, Parliament resolved that, 'according to the ancient and fundamental laws of the kingdom, the government is, and ought to be, by Kings, Lords, and Commons.' As far as England was concerned the Puritan Revolution was at an end. The faithful Hyde at length had triumphed.

Sharp's share
in the Resto-
ration.

Sharp had no little share in bringing about this consummation. Both Monck and Douglas, and, according to Blair, the ministers in London also, requested him to go and interview the King in exile. Before Douglas had an opportunity to send Sharp fresh instructions on that point, Sharp had assumed the function of a legate and crossed the Channel to negotiate for the Church, and in its name. Sharp must have been sure of his ground before he took such an unwarrantable liberty. Since the release of the Scots nobles Charles had been in communication with them, writing to Lauderdale 'as entirely my owne,' as his royal father had done twenty-one years before, congratulating him on his release from prison, and also trusting him to raise a Royalist party. Sharp was in their secrets. That rake, Rothes, owned him as 'our caynd, honist, Sherp Frend' who among other ministers was 'not to be compared uithe.'[1] Lauderdale, therefore, entrusted his reply to his Sovereign to Sharp, therein informing the King that 'God hath made him [Sharp] as happy ane instrument in your Service all along as any I know of his country. ... Nor need I say anything by so knowing a bearer, who is employed by him [Monck] who under God hath done this worke to give you a full account of those great transactions which

---

[1] Airy, *Laud. Pap.*, i. 10.

layd the foundacion of this happiness we are now I hope so neir.'[1] In fine, Sharp was a secret envoy for Monck. The Earl of Glencairn went even further, according to Burnet, and recommended Sharp to Hyde 'as the only person capable to manage the design of setting up Episcopacy in Scotland.'[2]

Monck was too wary to trust himself to a proved knave like Sharp, and employed his own cousin, Sir John Grenville, to convey his message to the King, verbatim, after Monck had repeated it several times in the hearing of Grenville. His advice was embodied in the Declaration of Breda. While on his way to Breda, Sharp wrote to his friend Wood, cryptic, equivocal, and lugubrious letters confessing how he was passing through distractions and a toilsome life.[3] He longed to be home. He had five interviews with the King, and, according to Douglas, he utilised these to prove that 'he was a great enemy to the Presbyterian interest.'[4] On that very day on which Sharp had his first interview with Charles, 8th May, Douglas and the brethren in Edinburgh penned a petition to the King, in which they rejoiced at his proposed restoration, and urging him not to repent of taking the Covenant and its pledge to maintain the Church. Douglas insisted on Sharp telling the King that Scotland was pledged to the Establishment, and that only 'naughty men' desired toleration. A few days after this, in a hyper-excited state of joy, they wrote to Charles 'as the man of God's right hand,' congratulating him on his recent profession of adherence to the Reformed Faith and on his moderation. In a letter from Brussels, 10th April, Charles professed this adherence, and vindicated himself from the charge of leading a vicious life.[5] This letter, transmitted by Rothes, was burked by Sharp, who treacherously had effected his purpose before his orders reached him. In his account of his mission, Sharp stated with verbosity and vagueness that 'he found his Majesty resolved to restore the kingdom to its former civil liberties, and to preserve the settled government of our church'; and that the King refrained from prosecuting uniformity, as it 'would be a most disgustful employment and successless,' since he knew

Marginal notes: Monck, a cautious plotter. / Resolutioners congratulate the King.

---

[1] *Additional MSS.*, 23113, fol. 100; *Laud. Pap.*, i. 24.
[2] *Hist.* i. 165; Wodrow, i. 28.
[3] *Add. MSS.* 23113, fol. 103.
[4] Wodrow, i. 28.
[5] *Wodrow MSS.*, xxxii. 5.

that 'there was no English party for uniformity.'[1] Charles, he wrote, was much improved by his afflictions. To these precisians this counted for sanctity. If his spiritual condition needed an illustration, it was afforded by Mr. Case, one of the deputation of ministers from London who also visited Charles. He declared that he was taken where he might, by eavesdropping, hear the royal saint at his devotions. He heard him groaning and saying: 'Lord, since thou art pleased to restore me to the throne of my ancestors, grant me a heart constant in the exercise and protection of thy true Protestant religion.' This trick of a scarcely disguised Papist was worse than the travesty of religion witnessed at Scone.

[1] Wodrow, i. 30.

CHAPTER TWENTY

THE RESTORATION

CHARLES, exalted from beggary to kingship, left Holland amid demonstrations of joy, and landed at Dover on 25th May 1660. There the jubilant ministers proffered him a clasped Bible; victorious Monck as appropriately offered him his sword. His progress towards and entry into London resembled a Roman triumph. Indeed, Evelyn declared it was like the return of the Jews from Babylon. He entered the Capital on 29th May—his thirtieth birthday. That night, when the jubilation and racket had ceased, and the godly were in prayer bearing up their Covenanted Monarch at the Throne of Grace, he first made an oblation of thanks to God in the presence-chamber before seeking carnal repose within the arms of the beautiful adulteress, Barbara Villiers.[1] He thus early inaugurated England's worst era of lust and falsehoods.

On realising the Restoration of the King, the people became frantic with joy, and soon their hilarity degenerated into ribaldry amid scenes of drunkenness and immorality.[2]

In Edinburgh a day of thanksgiving—19th June—was appointed, and Restoration Day was observed with sermons, noises hallowed and unhallowed, feasting, and strong drink. A farce in fireworks was presented on the Castle Hill, and redoubtable Cromwell was depicted being pursued by the Devil till both were blown up, to the merriment of the crowds.[3]

Popular joy at the Restoration.

---

[1] Kirkton, 61. She bore six children to Charles: Burnet, i. 168 and note (Airy's edit.).

[2] Burnet, i. 166; Clarendon, *Cont.*, 36-8.

[3] Nicoll, 294.

Later, on Coronation Day, the otherwise staid magistrates of Edinburgh converted the area round the Cross into a bacchanalian paradise, in which Bacchus, Silenus, and other bibulous divinities and wanton goddesses held court and revel, and the magistrates acted like coryphées in this fantastic vineyard. The mad orgy was prolonged until the citizens became 'not only drunk but frantic,' and worse.[1]

As vultures swoop on a carcase, the needy Scots nobility and hungry unemployed soldiers of fortune made for London to welcome Charles, and to present petitions asking for the removal of the English garrison, the restoration of forfeited estates, the resuscitation of privileges, and patronage in view of other attainders.[2]

At Crawford's levée Charles gave them a pleasant reception. Fortune now smiled on the Engagers, since the other extreme parties in the State—Montrosians and Argyllians—were defunct. Sharp, too, remained in London negotiating, as he would make his colleagues believe. Burton, I think, rightly interpreted the intentions of the new authorities when he wrote: 'While all these things were written, Sharp was Archbishop of St. Andrews and virtually Primate of Scotland. It was believed, indeed [he should have added "soon afterwards"], that the bargain was struck at

Sharp plays the Resolutioners false, June 1660.

once when he arrived at Breda.'[3] On 2nd June, the Primate-elect wrote to Douglas that in London he found 'the presbyterian cause wholly given up and lost,' while the leaders of that party were willing to accept a modified Episcopacy after Ussher's model, with an amended liturgy and curtailed ceremonies.[4] 'The cassock men swarm here,' he averred. He continued discouraging the sending up of more delegates, Douglas excepted—he had hopes of Douglas apostatising—on the ground that it would 'give suspicion of driving a disobliging design.' He disclaimed any personal manoeuvre. Douglas and his friends, instead of falling into the net, became fixed in their resolutions, and more emphatically

---

[1] *Edinburgh's Joy for His Majesties Coronation in England*, 1661; Kirkton, 65; Crookshanks, 81.

[2] Kirkton, 66; *Laud. Pap.*, i. 32-3.

[3] *Hist.*, vii. 134.

[4] Hallam, *Const. Hist.*, ii. 319: 'This consisted, first, in the appointment of a suffragan bishop for each rural deanery, holding a monthly Synod of the presbyters within his district; and, secondly, in an annual diocesan Synod of suffragans and representatives of the presbyters, under the presidency of the bishop, and deciding upon all matters before them by a plurality of suffrages.'

advised him to oppose the defections, prelacy, and the liturgy. It is not likely that Sharp repeated these instructions. When Douglas was bent on coming south, Sharp as firmly and plausibly discountenanced the proposed advocacy, declaring that the King was against it, since he was pledged to Presbytery already, and their advent would prejudice the cause. By these concoctions he kept them in their fool's paradise. His tactics were clever but dishonourable. In the middle of June he writes: 'Discerning men see that the gale is like to blow for the prelatic party, and those who are sober will yield to a liturgy and moderate episcopacy which they phrase to be *effectual presbytery*.' This was a specious fly well cast. This equation of 'effectual presbytery' explains the frequent boast of Sharp after he came to be suspected, that he 'had done more for the interest of presbyterian government than any minister who can accuse me.'[1] The peculiarity of Sharp's letters is that, while prolix, they do not contain, except in his paraphrase, the substantial communications which he must have been receiving from others. On 19th June, when the Scottish deputation was imminent, he wrote that the King was about to grant all their demands—their wildest dream—and with the royal letter he would come home. It was a mean trick to hold back the deputies. While trying to make his brethren discard the chimera of uniformity, be it said to his credit, he declared, 'If we knew how little our interests are regarded by the most part here, we would not much concern ourselves in theirs.' It was probably on this principle that Sharp, while narrating the various moves for the restoration of prelacy and moderate Episcopacy, and even the fact that the Royalists attributed the King's misfortunes to his acquiescence in Presbytery, omitted to mention that the Commissioners from Ireland thought it expedient to drop, in their negotiations, all mention of the Covenant and prelacy.[2]

Monck, created Duke of Albemarle in July, was no politician, yet he had the shrewdness to advise his Sovereign to select both Cavaliers and Presbyterians for his new Privy Council. In Chancellor Hyde the King possessed a Grand Vizier adept in statecraft and capable of anticipating and executing unswervingly the royal will. Hyde had the gift

The office of Hyde.

[1] Sharp to Drummond, 13th December 1660: *Laud. Pap.*, i. 47.
[2] Reid, *Hist. of Pres. Church in Ireland*, ii. 334-6.

of selecting trustworthy subordinates to carry out the meanest policy. In this uncompromising Episcopalian and Monarchist, Charles had an effective agent in executing the terms of the Declaration of Breda, so that soon the short-lived Convention Parliament set an example to successive legislatures of the way to dishonour the regicides, alive or dead, in their enactments and even in their persons.

Considering his past career, Argyll would have appeared hypocritical had he been an early visitant to Court. Yet, anxious to stand well with his Sovereign, Argyll, much against the advice of Douglas and other friends, sought the King's presence in the hope that in a personal interview Charles would accept his explanations for his apparent discourtesy and his disloyalty under the Cromwellian régime. There are discrepant accounts of the origin of the visit. According to some he went of his own accord; to others that Charles invited him; to still others that Lorne, being well received, was used as a decoy to the trap, **The arrest of Argyll.** having informed his father that there was no danger.[1] Sharp warned Douglas that the King would receive Argyll badly. Lauderdale, now Secretary of State, was not averse to the extinction of his new rival, if he had not already determined on vengeance for his old enemy. Consequently, when Argyll appeared in the presence-chamber the King had him promptly arrested there in circumstances which betokened a public affront. From the Tower he was conveyed by ship, along with Judge Swinton, down to Scotland to be tried for treason. He arrived at Leith on 20th December and was thrown into Edinburgh Castle. A similar warrant was sent to Major-General Morgan to seize Sir James Stewart, Provost of Edinburgh, Sir John Chiesley of Carsewell, and Lord Wariston. Wariston escaped to the Continent for a time. This was a foretaste of the arbitrary government which the country was to experience for twenty-eight years.

The King reconstitutes the Government in Scotland. The first care of Charles was to have a government reconstituted for Scotland.[2] The following appointments were made: Middleton, Commissioner to Parliament and Generalissimo; Glencairn, Chancellor;

---

[1] Fraser, *Red Book of Grandtully*, ii. 151; *Argyll Papers*, 17; Mackenzie, *Memoirs*, 13; Willcock, *The Great Marquess*, 302 note; Burnet, i. 193.

[2] Mackenzie's *History* is valuable here. According to a letter of Mackenzie to Lauderdale of date 1678, the first part of the book was revised by Lauderdale: *Wodrow MSS.*, xxxii. 212 Advocates' Library.

Lauderdale, Secretary; Rothes, President of Council; Crawford, Treasurer; Sir William Fleming, then Primrose, Clerk-Register. Lauderdale chose Sharp's brother, William, to be his secretary—a fateful appointment. This Council was meant to be a domestic one, associated with Hyde and other English statesmen close to the person of the King. The Committee of Estates, nominated in 1651, which Monck swept away from Alyth, was indicted to meet in Edinburgh on 23rd August, and to form a provisional government till Parliament should assemble. This Committee had limitless powers.[1]

While all former attempts at effecting a reconciliation between the Resolutioners and Remonstrants and Protesters had failed, the sinister reports and intrigues of Sharp helping to widen the gulf between them, the Protesters, after a final effort to induce the Resolutioners to join them in presenting an address of welcome to the King, resolved to make it on their own account. On the requisition of five ministers, James Guthrie, Trail, and others, they met at Edinburgh in the house of Robert Simpson, on the same day (23rd August) on which the Committee of Estates assembled. The Privy Council declared the meeting to be an unwarrantable and illegal convocation tending to sedition and the rekindling of civil war, and three times ordered them to disperse. On their refusal, soldiers were dispatched to seize them and their papers and lodge them in the Castle. They apprehended James Guthrie of Stirling; Robert Trail, Edinburgh; John Stirling, Edinburgh; Alexander Moncrieff, Scone; George Nairn, Burntisland; Gilbert Hall, Kirkliston; John Murray, Methven; John Scott, Oxnam; John Semple, Carsphairn; Gilbert Ramsay, Mordington, ministers; and Kirko of Sandywell, Dunscore, an elder. They were committed to close prison in Edinburgh Castle. Robert Row, Abercorn, William Wishart, Kinneil, left the meeting before the soldiers arrived, and Andrew Hay of Craignethan escaped capture.[2]

Protesters met to petition King are arrested, 23rd August 1660.

A Supplication, seized at their capture, testifies that their intentions were harmless and praiseworthy. Loyally they congratulated Charles on his restoration, totally banned the regicides and their acts, including toleration, warned him of popery, prelacy, and prayer-books, prayed

---

[1] *Privy Council Register: Acta* 1661-7, MSS. in Register House. Edinburgh.

[2] Lamont, 158; Row, *Blair*, 357; Nicoll, 298; Mackenzie, 16; *Act. Privy Council*, 23rd August 1660.

him to preserve the Scottish Church, craved him to own and make all others own the Covenant and the Westminster Standards. They concluded by praying that his piety would make him 'a king with all the virtues of all the godly kings of Israel.' The innocents did not know Charles, nor his abettors.[1] Glencairn and his fellows read treason into the document at once. The prisoners maintained that the printing of their Supplication would convince the public that their aims were laudable, and they petitioned to be relieved, promising to fall away from their Remonstrance of 1650. From his cell, Stirling wrote to his kirk-session: 'Yet this is my comfort that whatever the world say or believe, the cause I suffer for is the Lord's, and no less than the avowing of his marriage contract in a sworn covenant betwixt the three kingdoms.'[2] To prevent other contemplated assemblies the Committee of Estates issued another illegal proclamation, 24th August, prohibiting under highest pains all meetings, conventicles, and seditious papers unauthorised by the Crown. Victims were next singled out for punishment. During September, John Graham, Provost of Glasgow, John Spreul, town clerk there, Patrick Gillespie, Principal of Glasgow University, John Jaffray, Provost of Aberdeen, and William Wishart, minister of Kinneil, were thrown into jail. Gillespie and Guthrie were carried off to Stirling Castle into safest custody.

At this very juncture Sharp returned from his mission. Although we find him in December informing his clerical correspondent in London, Patrick Drummond, that he had pleaded for Guthrie and his fellows in misfortune, this boast is not in harmony with the implacable hatred he evinced towards the Remonstrants in his letters to Lauderdale, wherein he urged Lauderdale to take extreme measures against the 'hairbrain' rebels. He rendered Guthrie's petition inept by asserting that Guthrie not only justified the murder of the King, but proclaimed that Scotland's revulsion from the deed was a sin. A little later he practically recommended to Lauderdale the extinction of these 'leading impostors, Guthiree, Gillespy, Rutherford, which will daunt the rest of the hotheads who in time may be beat into sound minds and sober practises.'[3] Sharp knew this was palatable counsel to his patron

Severities of Privy Council.

Return of Sharp.

[1] Wodrow, i. 68-71.
[2] 11th September 1660: Wodrow, i. 73 note.
[3] *Laud. Pap.*, i. 41, 57, 59, App. lxx.

and master, to his peer in treachery and deceit. For years Lauderdale had disdained to look upon the extreme Covenanters as worthy to be reckoned Scotsmen.[1]

Lauderdale's regard for Presbyterianism, and the Covenants which he subscribed, was now merely the memory of the obsolete faith of his callow youth. Through dark days he had clung to his early love, but on the advent of regal splendour and pleasure, that affection sickened and died in a heart which had grown corrupt. He actually told Burnet that he had recommended Presbytery to the King, who replied, 'Let that go, for it was not a religion for a gentleman.'[2] Lauderdale would be a loyal gentleman; and, after that rebuff, Presbytery to him was a mere temporary political expedient to be cast out whenever it suited the King. Since no solitary fiat could in a trice obliterate the Free Scottish Constitution—Church and State—Charles needed complotters in his nefarious design. The vision of an archiepiscopal throne glamoured the Judas of the Covenant, and a greed for pelf, power, and the pleasures which these can procure entangled the vulgar Lauderdale. Charles had got both rogues in the hollow of his hand. *The volte face of Lauderdale.*

In the royal closet the trio completed a plan, the first detail of which was a letter to be borne to the King's Scottish lieges by Sharp. This royal missive, dated 'At Whitehall, the 10th of August 1660,' signed 'Lauderdale,' was addressed to Robert Douglas and to the Presbytery of Edinburgh. The crafty document began by assuring the Presbyters that Sharp had loyally executed his mission, and fully explained the ecclesiastical situation. It animadverted on some disloyal brethren, of course hinting at the Protesters and extremists generally, without considering that Sharp too had, as already narrated, supported Cromwell and taken the Tender. No mention was made of the Covenant. With studied craft the royal intentions regarding the Church were expressed thus: 'We do also resolve to protect and preserve the government of the Church of Scotland, as it is settled by law, without violation,' as well as the ministry living peaceably, 'as becomes men of their calling.' The joyful receivers did not perceive the quirk which Sir George Mackenzie afterwards pointed out: 'When Episcopacy was restored and this letter objected *The plan of the treacherous trio.*

[1] *Add. MSS.*, 23114, fol. 84.
[2] *Hist.*, i. 195.

by the Presbyterians, it was answered, that before the restoration of Episcopacy all the acts whereby Episcopacy was abrogated or presbyterial government asserted, were annulled by the Act Rescissory; so that Episcopacy being the only church government then established by law, his Majesty was by that letter obliged to own it.[1] The letter further owned the legislation of the Assembly (of St. Andrews and Dundee) in 1651, promised another Assembly, adjured the Church courts to attend to ecclesiastical business only (then, as if pointing directly to the Protesters and anti-Prelatists), while stamping out conventicles—the seedplots of disaffection—and invited the Church to pray God to give the King 'fresh and constant supplies of His grace.'[2] If the Devil ever appeared as an angel of light to the unsophisticated, he did so then in Charles. The jubilant Presbyters enshrined the letter in a silver casket. On 3rd September copies of it were transmitted to other Presbyteries. The rude, mercenary Middleton, who knew the intention of Charles to establish Episcopacy, flouted Sharp for this trick, and could never get over its meanness.[3] To Primrose 'he spake often of it with great indignation, since it seemed below the dignity of a king thus to equivocate with his people, and to deceive them.'[4] Sharp, however, somewhat mollified Middleton by declaring that the letter was only a temporary expedient, and that the King could be relieved of his promise whenever the existing establishment was abolished. It was, and was intended to be, a base incitement to clerical persecutors.

Churchmen grateful and jubilant.

These Presbyterians prepared a gracious address to their ruler, subscribed by thirty-two ministers, in which they confessed how much their spirits had been revived by his royal intentions, and they transmitted it along with a grateful letter to Lauderdale, whom they still reckoned to be as dutiful a son of 'our Mother Church' as he was that day he stood a penitent in Largo Church.[5] The Synod of Lothian also blessed the King for his favours. While the dominant party in the Church was considering what steps might be taken with their own recalcitrant brethren, the Committee of Estates was forging new fetters for both

[1] *Memoirs*, 16.
[2] Wodrow, i. 80-4.
[3] *Laud. Pap.*, ii. App. lxxviii: Sharp to Middleton, 21st May 1661.
[4] Burnet, i. 198.
[5] Wodrow, i. 83.

discredited parties. On 19th September a proclamation was published calling in all copies of Rutherford's *Lex Rex* and Guthrie's *Causes of God's Wrath*, as works poisonous and treasonable, with certification that refusers would be held to be enemies of the King, and punishable according to the Committee's discretion. The executive government wished no aftermath of horrid reminiscences. The tombs of Henderson in the Greyfriars' Churchyard, and of George Gillespie in Kirkcaldy, had their inscriptions erased.[1] In another proclamation a wider net was spread to catch all injudicious critics of the authorities, and to silence glib pulpiteers, satirical rhymers, scurrilous rakers of unpalatable tales, sympathisers with the Remonstrance, listeners who failed to report libellers, and orators outside the lawful courts of Church and State.[2] The mesh was small enough to catch the least that had an idea of his own. Every hearer was a catchpole to entrap his pastor. Dates were immaterial. A hair was made a tether of. Words once feeble enough appeared treasonable in an official 'hue and cry.' An unconstitutional inquisition was thus sprung upon the exhausted country. A reign of terror began. Great men tried to protect the little. Eglinton writes to Lauderdale craving pardon for one Ralston, probably a vassal, 'for he is a very pretty man.'[3] Every suspect, when disowning the Remonstrance, had to produce a substantial cautioner. The sermons of John Dickson, Rutherglen, James Naismith, Hamilton, and James Simpson, Airth, brought these honest men to jail. This Act of Silencing struck equally at Remonstrants, Protesters, and Resolutioners—meddlers in the affairs of State. Colonels Barclay and Ker preferred flight and ostracism to the tender mercies of the inquisitors. Wariston, for whom a reward of five thousand merks was offered, sought a refuge on the Continent. Not to be foiled in his scheme, Lauderdale sent down another proclamation,

Inquisition instituted by Privy Council inspired by Lauderdale.

---

[1] Mackenzie, 17. Nicoll, 373-9, records the defacement at a later date: 'For ... Mr. Alexander Hendirsone, minister at Edinburgh, a learned and pious man, depairttit this lyff upon the 18 day of August 1646. Efter quhais death thair wes ane monument or sepulcher erectit with ane pyramite abone the sepulcher, to his honor and commendation, bot withall, a relatioun to the League and Couenant, ingrauen in great letters hewin out of stone; quhilkis letters wer all hewit doun and blottit out by ordour of the Estaites of Parliament now sitting in Edinburgh in Junii 1662.' The Cromwellian citadels were also speedily demolished.

[2] 20th September 1660: 'A Proclamation against all seditious railers,' etc.

[3] *Add. MSS.*, 23111, fol. 66: October 1660.

12th October, referring to a Parliament to be convened in order to assert the royal prerogative, and to be constituted as the final judge of the conduct of the lieges. The sting was at the end: no subject was to 'presume to go out of the country, without licence of the Committee of the Estates, under pain of being esteemed and pursued as a contemner of our authority.' In the autumn the bench was packed with Royalists. The King's prerogative was the substitute for the Covenant, and the new touchstone to effect everything. Corrupt officials began to scent fines and forfeitures, while poverty produced many parasites content with the leavings of these persecuting extortioners. To this fact can be traced clearly the motives for the inhuman prosecution of the Covenanters. Many landed gentry were summoned before the Committee of Estates, and were forced to sign bonds for their good behaviour.

The tortuous course which Sharp continued to pursue in order to rehabilitate the Scots Church on a basis of usefulness and influence, according to his own conception of the function of the Church, is now easily explained by means of the *Lauderdale Papers*.[1] Sharp's letters prove that he had the gift of hiding his ideas and intentions in copious language which seemed to reveal them. He could express a superfine distinction which an ordinary mind would not have noticed. They also prove that Sharp, dissimulator, liar, and traitor, well styled by Patrick Walker 'a compound of wickedness,' was not without a politic aim. I entirely homologate Mr. Dodds in this conclusion of his estimate of Sharp: 'For well-concocted, cold-blooded, systematic dissimulation, he stands almost without a match in history.'[2] Nevertheless, what in March 1661 he confessed to his correspondent, Patrick Drummond, seems to have been a conception of long standing, that Presbytery had a foundation in Scripture, but that Scottish Presbytery was not *ex jure divino*.[3] He could not conscientiously affirm with his co-prelate Leighton, that forms of government and ceremonies were merely

Reason for the persecution.

Sharp partly an enigma.

Views of Sharp.

---

[1] These papers in twenty-six volumes are preserved in the British Museum. I have consulted the originals. They consist of letters, reports, petitions, and memoranda which Lauderdale received while he was Secretary. A selection of them have been ably edited by Mr. Osmund Airy for the Camden Society, 1884. A large transcript of Sharp's letters is preserved in Edinburgh University Library. In Glasgow University copies of a few letters exist: press mark BE. 8, d. 18.

[2] *The Fifty Years' Struggle*, 99.

[3] *Laud. Pap.*, i. 88.

human, happy expedients, and that the hierarchy might, with advantage to Church and State, retire altogether.[1] Nor could he quite brook the purely Erastian conception that the King was head of the Church, which was merely a bureau of the State. Ten years after he had ascended the Episcopal throne he protested to Lauderdale that he had never been 'in the habitude of parting by my own consent with the rights of the episcopal order which have been ever acknowledged by the Christian Church.'[2] He convinced himself that he had the part of a patriotic reformer to play in 'restoring the King's interest to its lustre in Scotland by removing the Church's encroachments *in civilibus*,[3] and restoring what the Crown had evacuated *in ecclesiasticis*.[4] He could well say, 'I am a Scot and a Presbyter,' if he believed in the primitive equation of bishop and presbyter, as scholars do now.[5] He claimed spiritual independence for the Church, and the right of the Church, in Assembly met, to make and alter her own polity. He disclaimed any personal intention of transforming Presbytery into Diocesan Episcopacy, but asserted the right of the Church to arrange the conditions of the inter-relationship of regal authority and ecclesiastical jurisdiction. He desired a reference to a General Assembly.[6] The sequel compels one to imagine that this professed gospeller after the primitive model, all the same, had his tongue in his cheek while he was writing: 'Whatever lot I may meet with I scorne to prostitute my conscience and honesty to base unbecoming allurements,' such as a crozier, mitre, and throne![7] With Charles, Lauderdale, and Royalists generally, he abhorred extreme Presbyterians, Protesters, and suchlike, whom he designated impostors venting 'antimagistratical and pernitious principles and devoid of reason and understanding.' Douglas never suspected that his envoy had prelatical leanings, and the moderate Covenanters entrusted to Sharp the realisation of their most hallowed hopes. His error lay in concealing his predilections; his crime, in cunningly executing his predetermination. His fall was not

Sharp's sin, ambition.

[1] Leighton to Lauderdale, 9th Nov. 1673: *Laud. Pap.*, ii. 238.
[2] *Ibid.*, ii. 215.
[3] [Latin: in civil matters.]
[4] [Latin: in church matters.]
[5] *Add. MSS.*, 23114, fol. 94; *Laud. Pap.*, i. 50.
[6] *Laud. Pap.*, i. 48.
[7] *Ibid.*, i. 50.

gradual, but was the quick result of his predetermination. We must admit that he had an ambition to serve and save the Church. Of quick wit and of open eyes and ears, Sharp could not fail to observe the low morale of King, courtiers, and country. The aristocracy made no secret of hating the disciplinary Church and rigid ministry, while legislators made religion subservient to private interests. He was convinced that Parliament-men aimed at humiliating the clergy to beggary, slavery, and contempt, against which, having no representation in the Government, they had no redress. As it was, pastoral livings were sublimated away and jurisdiction was ineffective. There was another danger which he must have noted—five thousand Papists had swarmed into Scotland on the downfall of the Commonwealth and the return of Charles.[1] But there is no evidence to show that Sharp might also have abjured Protestantism and become a Papist. Unconscious of his own weakness and inability to stem the rising tide, Sharp may have become one of those obstructionists out of whom Lauderdale said he would drive the conceit. Without the genius of Mazarin to outmanoeuvre the King's secular advisers, Sharp condescended to deception, and simply incited his fellow-conspirators, who were still more clever at dissembling, to use him as one knave to foil others. When the supreme crisis came

Sharp's alternatives.

in 1660, Sharp had one out of three choices to make: to throw in his lot with the Church in her ultramontane, bureaucratic, or Erastian form. The Church might be (1) rehabilitated in prestige and spiritual independence under Presbytery and its parties, divisive and internecine; or (2) reconstituted as a department of State under the control of Parliament, in which the pastors had no seats (for the seculars in the Estates did not care for clerical colleagues); or (3) re-established as a fief of the Crown and subject to the Sovereign's will alone. When the choice was between the rule of the many, of the select few, and of one. Sharp thought that the jurisdiction of the King was the safest—safest too for himself. His choice he afterwards, with other bishops, gratefully called the 'settlement of this Church upon its ancient basis.'[2]

Earl of Middleton, 1619-1674.

On Hogmanay night 1660, a night of national carnival, John, first Earl of Middleton,[3] with Doctor James Sharp, his chaplain, took up

---

[1] *Laud. Pap.*, i. 170.

[2] Bishops to King, 12th September 1662: *Hist. MSS. Com. Rep.*, IX. ii. 446.

[3] Son of John Middleton, proprietor of Caldhame, Marykirk, killed by the soldiers

residence in Holyrood House. On the morrow this counterfeit of a noble, a mercenary hungry for forfeitures, was to represent the King on the throne of Scotland in its Parliament. The Capital was thronged with the needy—with bankrupt landlords, deprived ministers, restored exiles, weeping widows, all swearing they had suffered for the Crown and clamouring for compensation, which many got out of the estates of their ecclesiastical opponents. The Estates in all splendour rode up the Canongate with the ancient Honours, now restored from their romantic place of burial. Again Douglas was the preacher, and his inaugural sermon, based on the text (2 Chron. xix. 6), 'Take heed what ye do; for ye judge not for man, but for the Lord, who is with you in the Judgment,' must have sounded as a jest in the ears of that unprincipled convention. There the bankrupt legislators sat in purple and fine linen, in fur and feather, all anxious till their petitions for ratification of their lands and honours should be granted by the Crown. 'Never any parliament was so obsequious to all that was proposed to them,' wrote Mackenzie,[1] for, 'tamed into a slavish subjection by the usurpers, they were ashamed to allow less power to their own king.' Baillie corroborated this fact, stating 'The parliament's pulse was quickly felt: for when Cassilis moved that the election of president should be by vote of parliament, the Commissioner obtained that the Chancellor should preside by virtue of his office, as before it wont to be.'[2] Glencairn, a reliable courtier, accordingly took the chair. Subscription of the Covenant, exacted by former Parliaments, was not demanded.[3]

First Restoration Parliament, 1st January 1661.

Middleton's instructions under fourteen heads were explicit—to assert the ancient royal prerogative and the King's right to call Parliaments, to disown the Covenanting legislation of 1643-9 and relative statutes, to pass an Act of Oblivion, to encourage trade, to annul confiscations, to give precedence to the officers of the Crown, and to give sepulture to the remains of Montrose.[4] Middleton was also to discover privately the popular view of Episcopacy.[5]

Middleton's instructions.

---

of Montrose in 1645 as he sat in his chair: Fraser, *Laurencekirk*, 55; Jervise, *Mem. Ang.*, ii. 154.

[1] *Hist.* 19.
[2] *Letters*, iii. 463.
[3] *Act. Pal. Scot.*, vii. 7.
[4] *Laud. Pap.*, i. 39: signed at Whitehall, 29th Nov. 1660.
[5] Burnet, i. 199.

THE COVENANTERS

The exhumation of Montrose.

On 7th January 1661, Middleton, Parliament, magistrates, citizens, military, and the clan Graham, wended their way to the gallows-foot on Boroughmuir, now Morningside, a suburb of Edinburgh. There lay the hashed trunk of Montrose, without head, heart, or limbs, beside the bones of his comrade, Sir William Hay of Dalgety.[1] In a casket, with canopy and black pall over it, the remains were borne away by peers and barons, amid military music and popular huzzas, Kenmure leading the jubilant cavalcade. They halted at the Tolbooth till Graham of Gorthie, kinsman of Montrose, had climbed the lofty gable and removed from the rusty pike a grinning skull, alleged to be that of the hero.[2] Amid the plaudits of the onlookers he lovingly kissed the head, then descended to have it circled with a coronet and laid beside the trunk to be borne away to Holyrood Abbey. Four days the two heroes lay in state. A

The burial of Montrose.

rainstorm ceased awhile, on the 11th May, to permit the sun to burst through and glorify the most extraordinary burial ever witnessed in the Capital of Scotland. In splendour it vied with the coronation of Charles I. As an exhibition of tragic irony this demonstration has no parallel. It was virtually the public penance of King Charles II., who was there in proxy in the person of Middleton, to honour the bones he gave to the gallows-birds. Middleton, whose unoffending father fell to the swords of the raiders of Montrose, who himself had given Montrose's home to the flames and shot his domestics at a post—a Malignant, Cromwellian, and whitewashed Covenanter by turn—was paid to mourn and drink that day, and to safely house in Holy Church the fragments of a comrade he fought with, an antagonist he pursued. Nobles who had sent Montrose to his doom—Tweeddale, Roxburgh, Forrester—joined Cavaliers, who bled with him, in making his burial memorable. With 'wedding countenances,' we are told, they in a magnificent cortège, with honours, arms, colours, and relics, accompanied the remains through files of soldiery, over the very spot where the hangman hashed his body,

---

[1] Cf. Register House, Hist. Dept., Q. 299, for Hay.

[2] Cf. *antea*, vol. I. 454. Sir Edward Walker made the following interesting note regarding Cromwell's actions in Edinburgh: 'For now having settled the minds of the People at Edenborough, blockt up the Castle, released all the prisoners there, and (as I hear) caused the Head of the Marquess of Montrose to be taken down and buried, upon Saturday the 15th of September, he marched thence to Leithgow, having got a Recruit of 600 men out of England': *Hist. Disc.*, 187.

up to the renovated 'eastmost' Church of St. Giles. In the Montrose aisle they deposited Montrose in a splendid tomb. Charles, no doubt, imagined that he had thus appeased the *manes* of his faithful servant whom he had forsaken. The Covenanting clergy did not countenance the significant, prophetic pageant. According to a quaint narrative, the ministers like howlets kept out of sight, the superstitious giving this reason, 'lest the bones of both should bleed.'[1]

The fearful Argyll in his prison in the Castle could hear the salvoes of artillery and the shouts of the merry crowds that day, and probably the lively music and the hilarity of the gentry who danced out that funeral night. His jailer, obliging or vindictive, could easily point out to the prisoner the pike which gallant Gorthie had left vacant for another skull—it was to be that of Argyll himself—for mobs to hiss at and Castle gunners to make a target of. Gorthie would not enjoy this revenge. He died that night, after his act of devotion, and the Covenanters said it was a judgment.

From January till 12th July the eager Parliament-men, under their taskmaster, Middleton, worked at their tale of bricks,—nearly four hundred enactments, many of them having the stamp of Lauderdale upon them.

The first statute, entitled 'Act constituting the Chancellor President in all time coming; and for taking the oath of Parliament,' at the very outset, made Charles master of the situation.[2] The kernel of the 'Oath of Allegiance,' which was to have such momentous issues, was: 'I acknowledge my said Soverane only supream Governor of this Kingdome over all persons and in all causes ... renunce and forsake all foreign Power ... and shall never decline his Majesties Power and Jurisdiction, as I shall answer to God.' This oath and acknowledgment of the King's prerogative was required of all public officials[3] and burgh magistrates.[4] Cassillis himself was proceeded against for ignoring this statute, and debarred from holding any office of trust.[5] Here in a

Statutes of 1661.

---

[1] Wilson, *Mem. of Edin.*, 100; Nicoll, 330; Baillie, iii. 466; Napier, *Memoirs*, ii. 819-37. For relics of Montrose, cf. *Proc. Soc. Antiq. Scot.*, xxxi. 65.

[2] *Act. Parl. Scot.*, vii. 7, Act 1.

[3] *Ibid.*, Act 62, p, 44.

[4] *Ibid.*, Act 255, p. 236.

[5] *Ibid.*, vii. 163.

moment was a *coup d'état* which patriots, Parliament-men, and pastors did not expect, and could not remedy till the Revolution. Realising its import and far-reaching intention, they then demanded the insertion of the word 'civil' before 'supream authority,' but Melville, Cassillis, and another member from Ayrshire failed to get this qualification inserted. Middleton and Glencairn assured the timorous that no ecclesiastical jurisdiction was aimed at. The westland men, inflexibly loyal to the Presbyterian cause, feared the destruction of their freedom gained in 1592, and their protest now was the expiring voice of political liberty.[1]

King Charles, Pope of Scotland.

In this way, Charles II. became Pope of Scotland—a Hildebrand, with no vestige of religion, however. He was monarch of all he surveyed. His Parliament, in several statutes, declared the King's prerogative to select the officers of state, to call and dissolve Parliaments and all meetings, to nullify all future convocations, leagues, and bands made without royal sanction, to make peace or war, to annul the convention which resulted in the League with England in 1643,[2] to rule arbitrarily, irresponsibly. The second Act turned Wariston out of office and declared him fugitive and traitor.[3] Another Act (10) granted two thousand merks to the brave Mrs. Christian Fletcher or Granger of Kinneff Manse, for saving the Honours of Scotland at Dunnottar Castle. These enactments were followed on 25th January by one of supreme importance,[4] entitled 'Act concerneing the League and Covenant and dischargeing the renewing thereof without his Majesties warrant and approbation.'[5] It declares that document and the Acts relative to it not obligatory on the kingdom or lieges, who are henceforth forbidden to interpose by arms or in any seditious way in religious or secular affairs in the three kingdoms, or to renew any Covenant or Oath without royal warrant. This was a sore blow to enthusiasts with visions of a universal Presbyterian brotherhood. Worse was to follow. Indeed, it was not easily seen where the Government was tending to. It was not enough to ban Anabaptists, Quakers, mass-priests, to banish the Remonstrators out of the city, to approve of the Engagement of 1648, and rescind

Statute repudiating the Covenant, 25th January 1661.

[1] Baillie, iii. 463; Wodrow, i. 93.
[2] *Act. Parl. Scot.*, vii. 16, Act 18.
[3] *Ibid.*, vii. 7.
[4] *Ibid.*, vii. 18, Act 22.
[5] Cf. Test or Declaration that Covenants are seditious, August 1663: *Ibid.*, 462.

the Parliament's work in 1649, and other judicial proceedings during the usurpation.[1] One result of this Act was the restoration of Church patronage to loyal subjects, who might appoint Royalists to vacant charges.[2] Sir Archibald Primrose, half in jest, proposed to consummate this nefarious work by passing an Act rescinding all the legislation of the period 1640-8, on the ground that it was unconstitutional. Middleton and his friends considered this over their cups. 'When they had drunk higher, they resolved to venture on it.'[3] A rough draft extracted from Primrose, when he was sick or maudlin, sufficed the Committee of Articles, and it became law, 28th March.[4] The obfuscated Commissioner saw no inconsistency in expunging records at whose making Charles had been present, or which he had afterwards ratified—under restraint, Middleton alleged—so long as he secured more power for the new ruler. This calamitous legislation razing the foundations of the Church, and obliterating the indemnities agreed to by the Crown, as Burnet truly wrote, was 'only fit to be concluded after a drunken bout.'[5] The unscrupulous legal advisers of Middleton—Primrose, Mackenzie of Tarbet, Urquhart, and Fletcher, knaves all—knew what they were driving at. That same day on which this Act Rescissory passed, another bill entitled 'Act concerning religion and Church Government' became law.[6] It was the King's latest thank-offering to God for his preservation and restitution! It was also his first papal rescript. In it he resolved to maintain the national Reformed Protestant religion, 'in its purity of doctrine and worship as it was established in this kingdome dureing the reigne of his royall father and grandfather of blessed memory,' to give protection to ministers who stuck to their calling, to settle and secure Church government in a frame most in accordance with God's Word, monarchy, and national peace, and 'in the meantime to allow the present administration by sessions, presbyteries, and Synods.' The grateful bacchanalian legislators reciprocated this condescension in an

Rescissory statute annulling legislation in period 1640-1648.

Act concerning religion, 28th March 1661.

[1] *Act. Parl. Scot.*, vii. 30, Act 46.

[2] Act 291, *Act. Parl. Scot.*, vii, 272.

[3] Burnet, i. 215.

[4] *Act. Parl. Scot.*, vii. 86, Act 126: 'Act rescinding and annulling the pretendit Parliaments in the yeers 1640, 1641,' etc.

[5] *Hist.*, i. 216.

[6] *Act. Parl. Scot.*, vii. 87, Act 127.

Act creating the Royalists' Sabbath, according to the Gospel of the *Book of Sports.* In Mosaic terms, Act 210 ordains Restoration Day (29th May), to be for ever set apart as an holy day unto the Lord, and that in all the churches of the kingdom it be imployed in publict prayers, preaching, thanksgiving, and praises to God, for so transcendent mercies.' When public worship ended, then they might have 'lawfull divertissments.' Were men ever so mad since the sycophants of Tyre and Sidon shouted to the glittering Herod, 'It is the voice of a god, and not of a man'? These lawfull divertissments had one meaning to honest, holy men like Rutherford and Guthrie, another to bibulous Middleton junketing on the first anniversary with Principal Leighton in the University hall, and still another to the royal head of the Church in his convocation of painted harlots, where he practised what he taught: 'All appetites are free, and that God will never damn a man for allowing himself a little pleasure.'[1] The Parliament was next engaged on the indictments of Argyll, Wariston, Guthrie, and others, in simplifying poinding (Act 218), in denouncing excommunicates (Act 238), in penalising actors in marriages performed by pastors not authorised by the established Church (Act 246), in passing Acts on the Sabbath, on swearing, and drinking, in providing a grant for the King of £40,000, partly out of ale and beer, and in commissioning judges to execute witches—mostly women—who scared the Earl of Haddington's tenantry off his lands.[2] By a proclamation, strangers and sympathisers with Guthrie's *Causes of Gods Wrath* were ostracised from the Capital.

This legislation terrorised the country. A few presbyteries and synods, bolder than the rest, prepared prolix overtures and declarations in order to oppose the measures, but, as in the case of Fife, Lothian, and Dumfries, they were menaced and dispersed. The Presbyterians generally still had confidence in Lauderdale and Sharp, the hollow reeds that were about to break and pierce those who leaned on them. But the disillusionment was not long delayed. The more faithful of the ministers warned their flocks of the impending danger.

These enactments left no room for dubiety in the public mind who the Pontifex Maximus of Scotland was; and Charles soon was

---

[1] Baillie, iii. 469 note, quoting *The Work Goes Bonnely On* (Edin., 1661); Burnet, *Foxcroft Supp.*, 50.

[2] *Act. Parl. Scot.*, vii. App. 31.

accompanied to the altar by many assistants carrying the sacrificial knives and sharing in the oblations which he seized and offered. To Whom he offered cannot be postulated.

Argyll was destined to be the first victim of the reign of terror, having been devoted to this end by the King himself, as being representative of what was worst in a Parliament too free of the Crown, and the basest of a nation accused of selling their Sovereign to regicides![1] Middleton, in a maudlin moment, divulged this malice aforethought of his master. James Guthrie would afford a similar satisfaction on behalf of the Covenanters and their 'rigid' Church and system. Lieutenant William Govan, in place of a more suitable victim, would atone for the disloyal army of the Remonstrants. These three lay tied to the horns of the altar. On the last day of January, Parliament, in the exercise of its judicial prerogative, sent a herald to summon Argyll to compear on a charge of treason. The procedure which followed can hardly be designated a trial. To Argyll's junior counsel—the bloody Sir George Mackenzie of the persecuting days—we are indebted for a concise account of what happened.[2] Argyll petitioned Parliament to grant him counsel, preferably John Nisbet, afterwards Lord Advocate; but Nisbet, probably forecasting the foregone conclusion, refused, so Parliament nominated six advocates, including Sinclair, Dean of Faculty, Robert Burnet, Junior, and Mackenzie, to undertake the defence. Mackenzie was then a vivacious pleader, twenty-five years old, budding into fame as Scotland's first novelist, and, in his idle hours, a moraliser on toleration and stoicism. The prosecutor was Lord Advocate Fletcher, a base, bribable, and truculent fellow, of whom his biographer asserts, 'At a time when bad men were common he was one of the worst.'[3] The indictment was a list of nearly all the offences on the statute-book— treason, arson, rebellion, murder, accession to the murder of the King. It was in reality a prejudiced narrative of Scots affairs for a generation.

Argyll's doom.

Argyll summoned to trial.

Indictment and defences

[1] *Act. Parl. Scot.* vii. App.; *Naphtali*, 193; *Argyll Papers, Hist. MSS. Com. Rep.*, vi. 617; *Hist. MSS. Com. Rep.*, v. 203; Baillie, *Letters*, iii. 466; Burnet, *Hist.*, i. 220; Row, *Blair*, 384-5; Mackenzie, *Works*, i. 80-4; Mackenzie, *Memoirs*, 34; Kirkton, *Hist.*, 98; Lamont, *Chron.*, 171; Law, *Mem.*, 10; Nicoll, *Diary*, 321, 334; Omond, *Lord Advocates*, i. 201; Wodrow, *Hist.*, i. 130; *Wodrow MSS.* (Advocates' Library), xxvii. 44-54; xxxii. 11-17; Willcock, *The Great Marquess*, 308, 378.

[2] *Memoirs*, 34.

[3] Omond, i. 199.

In a dignified speech to his peers and judges the accused showed how unlike him such crimes were, claimed protection under the indemnity of 1651, and pleaded that like others, he was compelled to submit to Cromwell, and, against his inclination, to appear to be disloyal. From the first the simplest elements of justice were ignored and obstacles thrown in the way of the defence. His demand for trial by justiciars, impartial and expert, for time to lodge answers and bring witnesses, and the request of his counsel to have freedom of pleading, were refused. With a thirst for blood, worthy of Shylock, Fletcher, himself a repentant complier, so far lost all sense of decency that he called Argyll 'an impudent villain,' regarding him as a doomed man. During the early stages of the case efforts were made in London, especially by his son Lorne, who had married a niece of the Countess of Lauderdale, to render the trial null. Afraid of their success, the Royalists on 29th April dispatched Glencairn, Rothes, and the useful Doctor Sharp, up to Court, ostensibly to report progress, but with a sinister purpose. They succeeded in confirming the animus of Monck, Hyde, and Lauderdale against the panel. In the debates, in which Burnet and Mackenzie shone, the honest attempts of Sir John Gilmour, President of the Court of Session, to excise the unjustifiable part of the libel, stood Argyll in good stead. The daring thrusts of Mackenzie went home, when he accused his hearers of being old compliers too, and demanded if it were not unjust 'that he [Argyll] should suffer for acts of frailty, when the ringleaders and malitious plotters pass unnoticed.' Gilmour justified this impeachment, and roused Middleton to retort: 'We are all of us, or most, guilty, and the King may pitch on any he pleases to make examples.' Gilmour's opinion made the House pause and favour Argyll, when a fatal incident occurred at the last moment. Argyll was at the bar. Debate and probation were closed. A rude knock was heard, and up to the throne passed one Campbell, servant of Macnaughton, and handed a packet to the Commissioner.[1] Campbell arrived from London, and the packet he bore contained six letters or more, three of which Argyll had written to Lilburn in 1653, three to Monck in 1654, while Cromwell

Sir John Gilmour's opinion.

Monck's six incriminating letters.

[1] Alexander Macnaughton of that Ilk was knighted by Charles II. In 1653, Argyll discharged a lieutenant of the same name, who vowed, 'if he were but able to command one man he should be revenged on them [i.e. English] and not leave them one reeking house in Kintyre': Willcock, Letter iii., 383.

was master of Scotland. Middleton had them read at once, and they proved so far incriminating, by showing that Argyll had honestly kept the letter of the Tender and oath, promising to keep, and make others, even his son Lorne, keep the peace. The plea of compulsory submission to the usurper—'the contagion of these times,' as Argyll phrased it on the scaffold—was no longer acceptable. The Argyllians, crestfallen, left the Court, which adjourned to meet on the morrow, 24th May. Then the charges were voted proven, young Montrose alone magnanimously refusing to vote. The next question was 'hang or head.' It was concluded to decapitate Argyll and to fix his head on the very spike which bore that of Montrose so long. In the absence of the President, Crawford pronounced with tears the doom of traitor's-death and forfeiture, which Argyll on his knees received with calmness and dignity, thereafter protesting his lifelong fidelity and affection to the King. There was no bitterness in his plaint, 'I had the honour to set the crown upon the King's head, and now he hastens me to a better crown than his own.' He wrote to the King asseverating his fidelity. He was hurried away to the felon's cell. Three days were given him to prepare for eternity. In vain he pleaded for more. Middleton, ignoring the King's command that no verdicts were to be executed without his approbation, was in hot haste, and had the bloody deed over, a day before the royal warrant was subscribed. Middleton and Glencairn were gaping for the broad acres of Argyll and could not wait.[1]

Argyll sentenced to die.

The champion of Presbyterianism and Parliamentary freedom never showed to more advantage than in the dungeon and on the scaffold. The Tolbooth—the well-known Heart of Midlothian—with its Iron House, was then a scene of levées, and frequently a loose place, where criminals unseen might even exchange clothes with their visitors. Timorous to the last, Argyll, rather than hazard an old and easy trick, cast off the dress which his faithful wife had persuaded him for a little to put on for a disguise. One of the brutal customs of that epoch was to deal frankly with departing friends. But the moribund often met death with equal familiarity. The bluff Mackenzie, on a final visit to his client, told him that the people believed he was a coward, and

Argyll in prison.

---

[1] Burnet, 223; Wodrow, *Anal.*, ii. 52, 103; *Hist. MSS. Com. Rep.*, v. 203.

expected he would die timorously.[1] To this Argyll replied 'he would not die as a Roman braving death, but he would die as a Christian without being affrighted.'[2] In prison, Argyll had acquired that ecstasy of faith which makes the martyr defiant and serene. He held discourse with the ministers, Douglas, Hutchison, Dickson; and he settled his earthly affairs with precision. But gentle Leighton, busy with a Latin eulogy of Middleton, did not trouble to cross the Cowgate to bid farewell to Argyll and Guthrie.

How different David Dickson! He was Argyll's bedfellow on the night before his execution.[3] Yet Professor Reid writes: 'Contrasted with him [Leighton], these unbending Presbyters are apt to appear in an unlovely light.' After the deed, Middleton met Crawford and asked him if he did not believe that his [Argyll's] soul was in hell. 'Not at all,' exclaimed Crawford, 'Argyll was naturally a very great coward and was always afraid of dying; so since he had heard he had died with great resolution, he was persuaded that was from some supernatural assistance; he was sure it was not his natural temper.'[4]

On Monday 27th May, as Argyll was leaving for execution, he called forth Guthrie for a parting embrace, during which Guthrie happily said: 'My Lord, God hath been with you. He is with you, and God will be with you; and such is my respect for your Lordship, that if I were not under sentence of death myself, I could cheerfully die for your Lordship.' He walked down to the scaffold at the Cross on High Street. Standing beside The Maiden, his heart, according to Cunningham, his physician, beating no stroke the more, he bade a chaste farewell to the crowd.[5] He blessed God and pardoned men; gloried in his share of the Reformation; declared the Covenant to be heaven-inspired and binding, even on the unborn; asserted his unwavering devotion to the reigning House, and his repugnance at the death of Charles; and rebuked the sins of the day. He turned to gaze upon the glittering blade, while he spoke of sufferers for sin in these terms: 'Mine is but temporal, theirs shall be eternal; when I shall be singing, they shall be howling.'

Argyll on the scaffold, 27th May 1661.

[1] *Memoirs*, 47.
[2] Kirkton, 103.
[3] Lee Lecture (1899), 11.
[4] Burnet, i. 226.
[5] Mackenzie preserves it, *Memoirs*, 41.

His final audible prayer was for the King, Government, and Council. He knelt, laying his neck on the block, and the loaded blade sheared off his head. Friends bore his body to the Magdalen Chapel in the Cowgate, to await transportation, first to Lothian's vault at Newbattle, thence to the mausoleum at Kilmun; the hangman fixed the head on the Tolbooth top.[1]

There are three remarkable facts connected with the death of Argyll which are worthy of mention: the original record of his trial has disappeared, and only references to the trial appear in the statute-book; none of the Campbell clan drew a dirk to save their chief; no westland Whig nor Bauld Buccleuch dared to break the prison of their leader. This latter fact may be explained on the supposition that Argyll had never created enthusiasm among the Covenanters, as his rival Montrose fascinated his following, and that the Covenanters always attributed the timidity, caution, and diplomacy of Argyll to a lack of righteous earnestness in the good cause. His noble ending put a different complexion upon his intentions and operations. It can hardly be gainsaid that his death was a gross offence against all the best traditions of the Judicial Courts of Scotland, and an unpardonable exhibition of the subservience of freemen to an arbitrary will for the sake of, it is almost certain, unrighteous gains. One well able to judge asserted: 'The crowning iniquity, however, was the mode in which a conviction was obtained. … The conviction of Argyll was a gross miscarriage of justice.'[2]

Difficulty in appraising the aim and character of Argyll.

The suppression by the Privy Council in November of the last speech of Argyll, circulating in print along with that of Guthrie, indicates that the Covenanters were now realising the loss of their mainstay—long feared by English statesmen—who, they now believed, had, with all his observable defects of character, battled in vain for a noble cause, which seemed to have found a grave with him.[3]

If that Monday was a red-letter day in the hagiology of the Covenanters, the Saturday following, 1st June, was even more notable, since on it Guthrie, 'the secretary and champion of his party,' was to

The death of Guthrie.

---

[1] In the chapel the table on which the body lay is still shown. The vault still exists. The Maiden is preserved in the Museum of the Society of Antiquaries in Edinburgh. The head was taken down on 8th June 1664.

[2] Omond, i. 174.

[3] Aldis, *List*, 1689; *Speech upon the Scaffold*, etc, (1661), fol.

die. Between these two bloody events came the first anniversary of the Restoration, and on it a banquet given to the Royal Commissioner, in the College Great Hall, Edinburgh, in honour of these happy times now come. Principal Leighton, who had sworn and also broken the Covenant, eulogised Middleton in Latin, and broke glasses with him— the then noble inaugurator of 'a mad time,' from which he was soon to be a despised outcast himself.[1]

Leighton toasts Middleton.

Dr. Sharp, in February, settled in St. Andrews as Professor of Divinity, was aware of the doom that had been arranged for Guthrie; and a week before Guthrie was called to the Bar of Parliament, Sharp wrote to Drummond to this effect: 'Poor Mr. James Guthrie is to appear upon Tuesday nixt, and though less criminous than others, is lyke to be the only sacrifice of our coat.'[2] Sharp wrote to Lauderdale in favour of this friend he accused as a traitor, but after Guthrie made his manly and exculpatory defence, the patronage of Sharp ceased, and Sharp deserted him, he confessed, because of his 'pertinatiousnes.' On 20th February, Guthrie was brought to the bar to receive his dittay. On 10th April, he heard the full indictment for treason under five heads read out.[3] He was accused under statutes of James vi. of (1) treasonable utterances against the Crown and Government, and especially of writing and promulgating the Remonstrance; (2) writing and publishing a seditious book entitled *The Causes of God's Wrath*; (3) calumniating the King and Government, intermeddling in civil affairs, and trying to subvert the Church and State; (4) unlawfully convening the lieges as if the King was menacing Protestantism; (5) ignoring the jurisdiction of the King when he was summoned to Perth in 1651. No mention was made of the excommunication of Middleton by Guthrie nor of the Commissioner's animus on that account. Guthrie made a noble defence worthy of an ingenuous patriot. The replies of the accused were simple and direct, asserting that he had no share in composing the Remonstrance; never uttered, nor intended uttering, disloyal expressions; acted according to a conscience directed by the Bible, the standards of the Church, the Covenants, and the laws of the land—all legal instruments; ever 'keeping himself within the bounds of what was competent to a minister of the

Indictment of James Guthrie.

Guthrie's defence.

[1] Nicoll, 335.
[2] *Laud. Pap.*, i. 74, 14th Feb. 1661.
[3] *Act. Parl. Scot.*, vii. App. 34.

Gospel.' He avowed a consistent loyalty, and gave two striking illustrations of it in proving that he opposed Cromwell as a usurper, and had preached against the Tender, for which he was ejected from his pulpit and had soldiers quartered upon him for six months.[1] His speech on the 11th April was the brilliant effort of a man imbued with genuine piety, a pure conscience, and a deep sense of responsibility for his ministerial duty to men.[2] Behind that dreamy, mystical face, there lurked a fire that kindled in him, as he spoke, a fervour similar to what filled the seers of old, and he concluded a high-toned apology, which has few like it in the martyrologies, with these words no less brave than prophetic: 'I know for certain that the Lord hath commanded me to speak all those things, and that if you put me to death, you shall bring innocent blood on yourself, and upon the inhabitants of this city. My Lord, my conscience I cannot submit, but this old crazy body and mortal flesh I do submit [he was but forty-nine] to do with it whatsoever you will, whether by death, or banishment, or imprisonment, or anything else; only I beseech you to ponder well what profit there is in my blood: it is not the extinguishing me or many others, that will extinguish the Covenant and work of Reformation since the year 1638. My blood, bondage, or banishment will contribute more for the propagation of those things, than my life or liberty could do, though I should live many years.' This vision he expanded as he stood on the ladder top—his Pisgah height of glory. Its fulfilment was exact. Here was all the enthusiasm of Andrew Melville revived in the cause of spiritual and political freedom, and voiced in the fearless spirit of John Knox. Four days later they found the charges proved, but his eloquence had staggered his judges, and they withheld sentence, doubtless delaying to see if highland pride or westland faith would dare anything for Argyll.

On the day after Argyll's execution, the day before the wild revelry in which Middleton and Leighton engaged, Guthrie was brought once more to the bar to learn his ignominious fate and barbarous doom—as a traitor to be hanged, his possessions forfeited, his coat-of-arms torn and dishonoured, his head fixed on the Nether Bow, and his children, a little boy and a girl, Willie and Sophia, and their posterity made

Doom of Guthrie.

---

[1] *Act. Parl. Scot.*, vii. App. 37.
[2] Wodrow, i. 171.

beggars for ever.[1] It fired the blood of Guthrie, who began to harangue his judges, adjuring heaven 'that his innocent blood might not be charged on the throne, and hoping that his head would preach more on the Port than ever in the pulpit.' He was interrupted and violently dragged away to his cell.[2] The Earl of Tweeddale, who was of a humane temperament and moderate views, horrified at such an unprecedented punishment for a pastor, voted against the sentence, so that he became a suspect and soon found himself lingering in prison and under surveillance for eight months.[3]

The case of Govan.

At the same time an old decree of forfeiture obtained in 1651 against Lieutenant William Govan for his desertion to the Cromwellian ranks was revived, and the panel also sent to the same fate, the verdict being varied to the small extent that his head was to adorn the West Bow.

Govan was a small land-holder, married, had been a subaltern of Remonstrating Strachan in the west, had followed him to the north and proudly brought back to Parliament the standard of Montrose; but gossip had it that he too played an ignobler part on the scaffold of King Charles, as headsman or guardsman, and actually brought first news of his execution into Edinburgh.[4]

Guthrie in prison.

The weary weeks of waiting in the Tolbooth Guthrie spent conversing with his wife, children, and friends, among whom was the staunch Covenanter, William Guthrie of Fenwick, his cousin; composing his last speech; and in communion with the Most High. Taking his little Willie on his knee, he counselled him thus: 'Willie, they will tell you and cast up to you that your father was hanged; but think not shame of it, for it is upon a good cause.' His last speech, couched in chaste and charitable terms, is a striking testimony to his invincible faith. He declared that he died willingly; he might have escaped the enemy by staining his innocency, but would not; he might have eluded his warders, but would not act dishonourably even to jailers; he had been asked to comply, but 'durst not redeem my life with the loss of my integrity,' he wrote; 'I judge it better to suffer than to sin'; he had always been loyal and commended loyalty, which springs from piety; he could

---

[1] *Act. Parl. Scot.*, vii. App. 74.
[2] Row, *Blair*, 386.
[3] *Laud. Pap.* i. 99; Burnet, i. 228-31.
[4] *Act. Parl. Scot.*, vii. 75; Mackenzie, *Memoirs*, 51.

not accuse himself of being unfaithful to his ministry; he had been a man of contention and sorrow only for Christ's sake; he was a Protester against Malignancy; and events made the righteousness of the Protest now manifest to many consciences (that sentence must have given a sore heart to Robert Douglas); he blessed and forgave all. As Argyll had uttered a final doleful note, so did he in repeating the causes of God's wrath—profanity, the broken Covenants, national ingratitude for past blessings, and the corruptions of many carnal ministers. Animadverting upon modern Babylon, with its prelacy, liturgy, and ceremonies, he penned the malison: 'Whosoever else be he that buildeth this Jericho again let him take heed of the curse of Hiel, the Bethelite, and of that flying roll threatened, Zechariah v.' This utterance is usually, without much authority, appended to the speech of Henderson at the close of the Glasgow Assembly. Guthrie further testified to his personal faith, to his adherence to Presbytery and the Church of Scotland, to the Covenants, and to the crucified Christ. Of the Covenants he affirmed: 'These sacred, solemn, public oaths of God, I believe can be loosed nor dispensed with, by no person, or party or power on earth, but are still binding … and will be for ever hereafter.' With such a faith, 'he would not exchange this scaffold with the palace or mitre of the greatest prelate in Britain.' He was ready, like Simeon, to depart, for his eyes had seen salvation.[1] Tolbooth life had aggravated the lameness of the prisoner, formerly known as 'Sickerfoot.' *Guthrie's testimony.*

On the fatal afternoon, he, staff in a loosely roped hand, tottered down the High Street, side by side with martial Govan, into the ring of glittering pikes and blades around the scaffold, on which the blood of Argyll was barely dry. Having ascended a few rungs of the ladder, Guthrie spoke for an hour. Bishop Burnet saw him suffer, and declared that he gave his testimony 'with the composedness of a man that was delivering a sermon.'[2] He mounted still higher when he exclaimed: 'Art Thou not from everlasting, O Lord my God. I shall not die, but live.' Before the hangman turned the ladder, Guthrie lifted the napkin from his pensive face and uttered the prophetic cry, long the watchword of the persecuted, 'The Covenants, the Covenants shall yet be Scotland's *The Martyrdom of Guthrie, 1st June 1661.*

[1] Wodrow, i. 192.
[2] *Hist.*, i. 228.

reviving.' According to Sir George Mackenzie, Guthrie was executed simply for declining the jurisdiction of the King and Council at Stirling, *i.e. laesa majestas,*[1] just as Andrew Crichton had suffered in 1610.[2]

The execution of Govan.

While thus one 'hothead' had cooled, another 'hairbrain' was waiting his turn. These are Sharp's designations for the men no gibbet could 'daunt.' As the martyr dangled in the air Govan looked up, and being reminded of Christ's cross, exclaimed: 'It is sweet, it is sweet; otherwise how durst I look upon the corpse of him who hangs there, and smile upon these sticks and that gibbet as the gates of heaven.'[3] This Puritan soldier was in his prime, thirty-eight years old, and having found Christ twenty-four years before, was now able to re-echo Guthrie and confess, 'Sin and suffering have been presented to me, and I have chosen the suffering part.' When the halter was adjusted the bold campaigner fired his parting shot: 'The Commissioner and I went out to the fields together for one cause; I have now the cord about my neck, and he is promoted to be his Majesty's Commissioner; yet for a thousand worlds I would not change lots with him,—praise and glory be to Christ for ever.'

Devotion of Guthrie's admirers.

The hackster kept the heads, but handed the bodies of the executed to friends in waiting. As Guthrie's corpse lay in the Old Kirk aisle, where ladies dressed it, enthusiasts came to dip handkerchiefs in the blood and prayed for vengeance; while a young man, afterwards the famous surgeon, George Stirling, sprinkled the body with a perfume that sweetly pervaded the sacred building. There is a gruesome story told of the blood oozing down from the pike till it dropped on the royal coach of Middleton, as he drove through the Netherbow Port on his way to or from Holyrood. Nothing could erase the martyr's blood. The skull remained there till after the disastrous fight at Bothwell Brig, when it was ordered that the heads and hands of the two ministers, Kid and King, captured after the fight, were to be fixed beside it, 14th August 1679.[4] Shortly after this date the head was taken down by a student, Alexander Hamilton (1662-1738), afterwards minister at Ecclesmachen and Airth and also of the charge in Stirling held by Guthrie.[5]

---

[1] [Latin: treason.]

[2] *Laws and Customs,* etc., 25.

[3] Wodrow, i, 195.

[4] Fountainhall, *Observes,* i. 228.

[5] Scott, *Fasti,* iv. 675. The forfeiture of Guthrie was rescinded on 22nd July 1696.

Thus passed Guthrie, who is generally looked upon as the proto-martyr of the Covenant,[1] a man of high, consistent character, deep spirituality, and lovable nature, unbending where he deemed that God had revealed His judgment, yet confessedly human and humble as a follower of Jesus Christ.

The fate of other suspects and prisoners must now be considered. On 19th September 1660 the Committee of Estates proclaimed Rutherford's *Lex Rex* and Guthrie's *Causes of God's Wrath* to be infamous, seditious works, poisoning the springs of loyalty; and they ordered all copies to be handed to the authorities to save their possessors from the charge of treason, and in order to be burned at the public crosses by the hangmen, as was done in Edinburgh and St. Andrews. Rutherford was cited to compear before the Committee, but being certified to be sick and unable to travel, was punished by a sentence of deposition from his licence, professorship, stipend, and personal freedom, and also summoned to the bar of Parliament. Now that Guthrie was in the noose, and Gillespie quaking on the repentance stool, Parliament, not to be balked of the prey foredoomed by Sharp, sent a herald to hale the dying professor to Edinburgh. He found the old enthusiast bedfast. There was still as much of the piping voice left as to answer: 'Tell them that sent you that I have got summons already before a Superior Judge and Judicatory, and I behove to answer to my first summons, and ere your day come, I will be where few kings and great folks come.' This was the last bolt that Uriel hurled before returning to

The summons of Samuel Rutherford.

> 'God's presence, nearest to His throne.'

The defiant message worse incensed the prosecutors, who would have ejected the dying man out of college, had not a taunt from Burleigh restrained them: 'Ye have voted that honest man out of the college, but ye cannot vote him out of heaven.' They retorted: 'He would never win [get] there; hell was o'er good for him.' To this Burleigh made rejoinder: 'I wish I were as sure of heaven as he is, and I would reckon myself happy to get a grip of his sleeve, to hale me in, when Mr. Rutherford enters the gates.'[2]

---

[1] Some students consider Argyll a sufferer for his politics more than for his faith.

[2] Walker, *Six Saints*, i. 359; ii. 197; Wodrow, i. 205; Gilmour, *Rutherford*, 225; Smellie, *Men of Covenant*, 49; Row, *Blair*, 366.

Death of
Rutherford,
29th March
1661.

As Rutherford's end drew near, he seems to have become exalted in the ecstasy of his spirit into Paradise itself, where he beheld the same wonders that the apostle had no words to describe on earth—the veil, the glory, the Bread of Life, the angelic choir. 'Glory shines in Immanuel's Land,' he exclaimed shortly before 'he gave up the ghost, and the renowned eagle took its flight unto the mountains of spices,' on 29th March 1661. He was buried next day.[1] In his death Rutherford offered the best illustration of his own book on *The Trial and Triumph of Faith*, 1645. Twelve days before he passed, he emitted his manifesto: *A Testimony to the Covenanted Work of the Reformation in Britain and Ireland from 1638 to 1649.*

The character and place of Rutherford are difficult to define, he being almost a combination of two antagonistic personalities. One can readily imagine him perched high on some supreme judicatory, piping with his shrill voice, from underneath a full-bottomed wig, a dry judgment from his own text-book of law upon an uninteresting subject of dispute, and never conceive that the same cold, judicial eye, when lifted from leafy Anwoth into the heaven of his own imagination, could see, so as to describe, the glories of the fair country he longed sorrowless and sinless to dwell in for ever, freed from law and only guided by love. A legalist and yet a lover of all; a philosopher and yet a prose-poet; a narrow-minded patriot and yet a citizen warring for heaven; a man of 'passions wild and strong,' wrestling with himself in a mystic's dream, was Samuel Rutherford.

Escape of
Patrick
Gillespie.

It looked ominous for Gillespie, the third of the 'antimagistratical' enemies of the Crown, as the jaundiced imagination of Sharp conceived of him. On 6th March he appeared at the bar of Parliament and received his dittay. He had powerful friends in the legislature, and, being of a more elastic temperament in face of peril than were his fellow-prisoners, he was induced to put an acceptable construction upon his attitude to the Remonstrance and to the 'Causes,' and to prepare a petition or recantation which Parliament recommended to the King in his mercy. The result was that on 6th July Gillespie was liberated, but his liberty was curtailed, and he was confined within a certain rural

---

[1] Lamont, *Chron.*, 167.

circle.[1] Surprised at this clemency, the King exclaimed: 'Well, if I had known that you would have spared Mr. Gillespie, I would have spared Mr. Guthrie.'[2]

On 7th June, Robert M'Quair or MacWard, collegiate minister of the Outer High Church of Glasgow, was also found guilty of sedition. His simple offence was, that in February 1661 he, in order to be free of guilt, protested against all Acts passed or to be passed against the Covenants and the Covenanted work of Reformation in Scotland.[3] He modified his expressions till they simply bore that he testified against such legislation. The recantation was insufficient. On 12th July, Parliament gave him six months in which to pack up and seek a refuge on the Continent. He became Scots pastor in Rotterdam and his manse was for long the rendezvous of the exiled, the headquarters whence issued many communications, and sometimes pistols, to the persecuted at home. He died in December 1681.[4] *(Banishment of Robert MacWard.)*

Alexander Moncrieff, minister of Scoonie, a staunch Protester, a temporary chaplain to Charles II., and during the Commonwealth a consistent opponent of the Usurpers, was brought before Parliament, and being found intractable was declared incapable of holding any place of trust and evicted from his parish.[5] His popularity as a Conventicler led to his being persecuted from place to place. He escaped confinement, but had letters of intercommuning passed against him in 1675. He survived till 1688.[6] *(Alexander Moncrieff evicted.)*

Confinement in prison for ten months broke the health of Robert Trail, who, after compearing before Parliament and making a manly answer to his libel, was permitted liberty to live in the city, from which in December 1662 he was banished out of the kingdom on pain of death.[7] For even corresponding with him, his wife, Jean Annan, was sent to prison in June 1665. *(Robert Trail banished.)*

---

[1] *Act. Parl. Scot.*, vii. App. 18, 66, 75, 81.

[2] Wodrow, i. 180.

[3] *Ibid.*, i. 207.

[4] Steven, *Scot. Church in Rotterdam*, 336.

[5] *Act. Parl. Scot.*, vii. 367a;. He was grandfather of Alex. Moncrieff of Abernethy, the Seceder.

[6] Row, *Blair*, 248, 358, 418, 561.

[7] *Ibid.*, 364, 416, 430. He sailed for Holland in March 1663, and returned to Edinburgh, where he died in 1678.

James Kirko, laird of Sundaywell, Dunscore, after lying four months in jail was discharged, soon to find himself on Middleton's list of fines for £360, then plundered for years into beggary by Sir James Turner and other soldiers, who had free quarters on his estate. He became a wanderer, and with Maxwell of Monreith went to Ireland, after Rullion Green. Probably it was he who returned to get the martyr's crown, being shot on the White Sands of Dumfries in 1685.[1]

The case of Sir John Chiesley of Kerswell, a staunch Covenanter, knighted by Charles I., Secretary to the Commissioners in 1646, and to Parliament, who had suffered for his fidelity to the King, was discreditable to the Government. He was charged with invading Drumlanrig in 1650 and with treason, fined £2400 and committed to one prison after another for ten years, till the King ordered his release in 1670.[2]

The process against Wariston, who had evaded arrest and escaped to Holland, was followed up on 1st February by a summons for him to compear like his associates and answer to the charge of treason. In his case they were careful to take depositions from witnesses and to prove the indictment framed. It specified in detail his treasonable acts, compassing the subversion of the Government, aiding and abetting the rebels against, and murderers of, the late King, associating with the usurpers, rising in arms against Charles II., tyrannising over the lieges, murdering some, notably Montrose, endeavouring to destroy the King's majesty after deserting him, and many other felonious acts punishable with death. On 15th May, Parliament found the fugitive guilty, and recorded a 'Decreit of Forfaltour' against him, stripping him of everything, and ordaining him to suffer the doom of traitors at the Cross of Edinburgh. A subsequent judgment honoured his head with a place on the Netherbow Port beside that of Guthrie.[3]

The Government, satisfied that they had made a good beginning of the reign of law and order, concluded it best meantime to stay the headsman's hand, and they left Judge Swinton, twice forfeited of life, lands, and estate, languishing in the Tolbooth, banished Simson of

In the margin:

James Kirko, martyr.

Sir John Chiesley.

Judgment on Wariston.

---

[1] *Memoirs of Veitch and Bryson*, 49, 50, 400, 403. His house and its inscription, 'J. K. and S. W. [S. Welsh] 1651,' remain. For his epitaph, cf. Thomson, *Martyr Graves*, 472, 474.

[2] *Act. Parl. Scot.*, vii, App. 17; *ibid.*, 96, 423*a*; Row, *Blair*, 531.

[3] *Act. Parl. Scot.*, vii. App. 7-11, 66, 69, 95.

Airth, held a few suspects in jail, while allowing others out on bail, such as John Livingstone, and Nevay—the grim councillor at Dunaverty— whose hour had not yet come.[1]

At this time a melancholy sight might have given Middleton pause in his wild career, had he seen it. It was none other than one of his predecessors in viceregal office—the Earl of Traquair—standing on the streets of the Capital soliciting alms from passers-by. Fraser, in his *Diary*, thus records the fact: 'I saw him (anno 1661) begging in the streetes of Edinburgh. He was in an antick garb, wore a broad old hat, short clock, and pannien breeches; and I contributed in my quarters in the Canongate at that time, which amounted to a noble which we gave him, and his hat off, the Master of Lovat, Culbocky, Glenmoriston, and myselfe; which piece of money he received from my hand as humbly and thankfully as the poorest supplicant. It is said that at a time he had not to pay for cobling his bootes, and died as we hear (1668) in a poor coblers house; so that of him we may say with the poet, who describes him well—

> 'Fortunae speculum, Tracuerus scandit in altum;
> Ut casu graviore ruat, regisque favore
> Tollitur; hincque cadit.'[2]

After these tragedies were over, Tweeddale, with a light heart, enter-tained the Commissioner to a sumptuous banquet, and the only return which the Commissioner thought that this friendliness deserved was an accusation conveyed in his report to the King, to the effect that Tweeddale endeavoured to frustrate the work in Parliament which Middleton had been sent to see accomplished. Such were the 'gentlemen' for whom Charles II. declared that Episcopacy was most suitable![3]

The Earl of Traquair, a beggar.

---

[1] Row, *Blair*, 388. Simson died in Holland. Sharp declared to Primrose, Lord Register, that he begged the lives of Guthrie and Gillespie, 'which his Majesty denied'; but that he was successful in his request for a mitigation of the charge against Simson: Wodrow, i, 197 note.

[2] [Latin: 'A mirror of fortune, Traquair ascends on high,
  so that his fall is all the sharper. It was a king's favour
  that lifted him up, and was also responsible for his downfall.']
Chron. of the Frasers (Wardlaw MS.), 476 (Scot. Hist. Soc, edit, 1905).

[3] The Lauderdale-Tweeddale Correspondence, in the possession of the Marquis of Tweeddale, was not available for consultation, having temporarily gone amissing. The volume has been restored to Yester House.

John, first Earl of Traquair

John, sixth Earl of Rothes

Sir George McKenzie of Rosehaugh

Archibald, Marquis of Argyll

General Thomas Dalyell

Archbishop Laud

Bishop Leighton

ROYALIST AND COVENANTING LEADERS

CHAPTER TWENTY-ONE

CONDITION OF THE COUNTRY IN THE SEVENTEENTH CENTURY— THE COVENANTERS: THE GENTLEMEN OF THE RESTORATION

THE bitterest indictment ever penned against the Presbyterian system as it existed in the middle of the seventeenth century will be found in Buckle's *History of Civilisation in England.* He expressed his conclusion thus: 'I will not be deterred from letting this age see the real character of a system which aimed at destroying all human happiness, exciting slavish and abject fear, and turning this glorious world into one vast theatre of woe.' In another passage he wrote: 'Whatever was natural was wrong. The clergy deprived the people of their holidays, their amusements, their shows, their games, and their sports: they repressed every appearance of joy; they forbade all merriment; they stopped all festivities; they choked up every avenue by which pleasure could enter; and they spread over the country an universal gloom.' Of their sermons he declared: 'There is in these productions a hardness of heart, an austerity of temper, a want of sympathy with human nature, such as have rarely been exhibited in any age, and I rejoice to think, have never been exhibited in any other Protestant country.' The Scots preachers 'sought to destroy not only human pleasures but also human affections. ... A Christian had no business with love or sympathy.'[1] No more jaundiced critic ever essayed

Buckle's libel of the Covenanters.

---

[1] *Hist. of Civil.*, iii. 255, 269, 275, 276.

the measurement of the Scottish intellect or showed himself so incompetent to gauge it. Aliens, ill-informed and inclined to bias, should have a care when they emerge from their own cave to find themselves in light that confuses the untried eye. The following facts will serve as a corrective of Buckle's erroneous views of Scottish civilisation, at least in the Covenanting age.[1]

The student, keeping in view the fact that the Covenanters had high ideals and noble aims, namely, to make every individual recognise his own responsibility for the temporal and eternal welfare of himself and his neighbours, in accordance with the law of love in Jesus Christ, has a key to unlock all the mysteries of the distracted age of the Covenants. If he turns to the Life of Andrew Donaldson, minister of Dalgety, he will find these ideals and aims largely realised in one man, who may be accepted as the type of the true Presbyterian, and also made practical in that Fifeshire parish where the minister laboured to elevate peer and peasant alike, to educate all the children, to feed, clothe, and protect the poor, to assist the indigent at home and the unfortunate abroad, to act the soldier in the hour of peril, and to repress vice. It can be demonstrated that the Covenanters practised what they preached; purity of life, truthfulness, and honesty; and further, that nearly every one of those repressive measures inspired by the Church for the curbing of vice and mitigating disease, drunkenness, profanity, Sabbath-breaking, have been, or are being, in our own day, re-enacted by intelligent governments, so that, for the good of the many, the suspect, the unsavoury, and the undesirable, whether alien or not, are being constantly policed. The most enlightened republics to-day ask from emigrants the same certificate of respectability and ability to work which kirk-sessions two centuries and a half ago demanded from incomers.[2] Nor is it to be forgotten that these sessions were virtually magisterial courts with one educated cleric presiding over many laymen judging petty offences—surely as good a system of local government and magistracy as our present rural and burghal system, whereby many an ill-informed justice of the peace disposes of trivial cases to the best of his judgment.

Donaldson, pastor of Dalgety.

[1] Dean Stanley, in *Lectures on the History of the Church of Scotland*, 97, pointed out the incorrectness of Buckle's 'frightful picture.'

[2] Cf. a very striking instance of policing, *Glasgow Herald*, 21st August 1905.

The Scots pre-Restoration clergy were not the 'plebeian class' nor the illiterates that Macaulay made out their English brethren 'on the whole' in 1685 to be, the generality of whom were considered unusually lucky if each of them had 'ten or twelve dog-eared volumes among the pots and pans on his shelves.'[1]

The Scots clergy, abhorring celibacy, cultivated domestic and social happiness, and were noted for hospitality, toleration, and humanity, which they enjoined on others. Few histories can produce so many illustrations of parental and filial affection as are found in the biographies of the persecuted—the pathetic stories of Guthrie and his Willie, the Johnstons, Humes, Baillies, Blackadders, Campbells, and of scores of other families being well known to readers generally. So far from burking human joys and banning amusements, the clergy encouraged every elevating custom, and only set themselves against those scenes of riot where vicious men purveyed incitements to wickedness for the debased and lascivious, at 'penny bridals,' paying 'dredgies' or wakes, and prolonged baptismal functions and funerals. The absurd extravagance at these debaucheries had to be restrained by Act of Parliament in 1681.[2] No rigidness of the most fanatical legislators in Covenanting days ever exceeded that of the Episcopal *parlementaires* of 1681, who forbade even a bride from putting off her 'braws'—her wedding garments—on her marriage day.[3] The Covenanters by two hundred years anticipated the decorum now normally exhibited on those solemn occasions. Indeed, according to Kirkton, 'Nobody complained more of our Church government than our taverners, whose ordinary lamentation was, their trade was broke, people were become so sober.'[4]

Virtues of the Covenanters.

Many instances of the Lowland hatred of the Celtic bagpipes (declared to be the favourite musical instrument of Satan) imply no more than that the more musical Saxons could not bear the sound of an instrument which brought to their remembrance ruthless foes who, it is said, also played the pipes during the Irish massacres in 1641. In 1641 Lord Lothian had a piper in every company when his regiment lay at Newcastle, and at the same time there was not a sober fiddler in the

Music and mirth.

---

[1] *Hist.*, chap. iii.
[2] 1681, c. 80, viii. 350.
[3] *Act. Parl. Scot.*, viii. 350.
[4] Kirkton, 65.

Scots army there.[1] The Scots loved the harp, the harpsichord, the viol, and the flute, and still more the sweet voices which sang those martial ballads and love lyrics which still charm the dainty ear.

Simon, the Master of Lovat, 'had a wonderful fancy for musick, variety of which he had still by him, the harp, virginels, base and trible viol in consort. ... Mr. John Houstoun, the Minister of Wardlaw (a Covenanter and member of 1638 Assembly), and his sone Mr. Thomas, were great musitians, vocal and instrumentall, who frequently attended.'[2] Simon died in 1640.

In 1642, the year before the Solemn League and Covenant was made, the new Master, Hugh Fraser, married Anna, daughter of Lord Leven, in Holyrood House. They came to Bunchrew, and the diarist wrote:

'It is an extravagant rant to speake of the glory and expense of this sumptuous wedding feast,' where, we are informed, the 'merry, jovial, facetious society'—the Earl of Sutherland, a notable Covenanter, and his friends—had 'liquors of all sorts, meat, mirth, musick, and good management of all things,' besides indulging in Highland games and sport.[3] Twenty years later similar festivities took place in Darnaway Castle at the wedding of Sir Hugh Calder. 'The kingdom could not afford better wines than was drunk, and musick of all sorts; Edam Smith, master of the musicians in Murray, for virginall, violins, harp, and organ, was Calder's domestic. ... We spent that day in a charming converse of sport, gamming, and singing.'[4] Nor must it be forgotten that the time-hallowed sports and games connected with Hogmanay, Candlemas, Beltane, Halloween, have all survived till our own day. There is a passage in the *Life of John Livingstone* where he mentions the famous Principal of Glasgow University, Robert Boyd: 'Sometimes he would call me and some other three or four, and lay down books before us, and have us sing setts of music, wherein he took great delight.'[5] The manse of Logie often resounded with the music of Hume the poet's 'jolie lute,' and he lent his instruments to his brother poet, the Earl of

---

[1] K. Sharpe, *Witchcraft*, 136.
[2] Fraser, *Polichronicon*, 265.
[3] *Ibid.*, 278.
[4] *Ibid.*, 453.
[5] Wodrow, *Select Biog.*, i. 134.

Stirling.[1] William Veitch left the following anecdote regarding Henry Erskine, father of Ralph and Ebenezer, who was ejected from Cornhill in 1662: 'One evening he, his wife and children went to bed with a light supper, which made the children cry in the morning when they awaked for meat. But there being none in the house he bade them be still, and he would play them a spring upon the citren [guitar]. He played and wept. ... Before he had done playing, a charitable lady sent him a horse-load of provisions.'[2]

John Erskine of Carnock, the Covenanter, recorded in his diary that his father sent him to learn dancing, and that he also enjoyed a game at byas-bowls and went 'gunning' and 'tod-hunting.'[3] The more strait-laced, like Patrick Walker, who had escaped the gallows and plantations, would not 'crook a hough to fyke and fling at pipers' and fidlers' springs.' He gives a satisfactory reason thus: 'I bless the Lord that ordered my lot so in my dancing days, that made the fear of the bloody rope and bullets to my neck and head, the pain of boots, thumbikens and irons, cold and hunger, wetness and weariness, to stop the lightness of my head and the wantonness of my feet.'[4] Argyll, with his family and household, in January 1667, celebrated a marriage, drinking, dancing, 'as merrie as you could wish us.'[5] *Scottish sports.*

William Guthrie of Fenwick was both a fowler and a fisher, and his primitive curling-stone is still preserved.[6] Leven and King Charles played golf at the Scottish camp. In the Covenanting period not a single Act against games appears on the Statute Book.

The men of the Covenant were imbued with a deep-seated love for every good thing, but as they had to fight for essentials they had no more opportunities than other soldiers in a protracted campaign to become occupied with arts, crafts, or ephemeral entertainments that did not make for the moral welfare of the people. They loved their kind. Old Scots churchyards contain many tombs with epitaphs illustrative of this domestic felicity. No better instance can be found than on the grave of *Humanitarianism of the Covenanting ministry.*

[1] Fergusson, *Alexander Hume*, 95, 97.
[2] M'Crie, *Veitch*, 204.
[3] Erskine, *Journal*, Introd. xxv.; xxxviii. 5.
[4] Walker, *Six Saints*, i. 240.
[5] Argyll, *Letters*, 44.
[6] *Select Biog.*, ii. 39.

Lillias Sanderson, whose husband's manse at Keir, Dumfriesshire, was wrecked by Colonel Nathaniel Gordon.[1] Livingstone narrates how he got a 'marriage affection' for his bride after prayer. 'But thereafter,' he honestly confesses, 'I had a great difficulty to moderate it.' The character which the northern Covenanters gave their Boanerges, Andrew Cant, whom they reckoned to be the 'greatest man of his age,' was that he was 'ardent and loving.'[2]

The epitaph of Patrick Purdie, minister of Newlands, a stalwart Covenanter (1634-61), declared that he

> 'to his dying day did never tire
> To feed and lodge a Lazarus at his fire;
> A man ingenuous far beyond the fashion,
> Wholly composed of pity and compassion.'

Many ministers left money for the poor; others, like Alexander Henderson, for education, and many subscribed handsomely for the library in Glasgow University. Ker, minister of Lyne, gave nearly all he had to the poor, also catechising the vagrants whom he relieved. Walter Pringle of Greenknowe in his *Memoirs* testifies to the humanity of Guthrie the martyr: 'At Stirling I advised with my dear friend, Mr. James Guthrie, anent mine own and my brother's children (to whom that faithful man had ever a most tender respect) concernements.'[3] Pringle's own narration of his anxiety for his wife and unborn babe, for whom he prayed under a plum-tree in the garden, does not lack pathos. The persecutions to which these men were subjected did not turn the milk of human kindness into gall and wormwood. Some retained their mother-wit till death, even on the scaffold. William Guthrie, minister of Fenwick, was 'cheerful and facetious, yet tempered with gravity as

Wit of
William
Guthrie.

---

[1] HERE LYIS INTERRED BENETH THIS BRITLE STONE
'A LILIE ONCE SO RARE AS FEW OR NONE
WITHIN THE PRECINCTS OF FAIR FLORA'S TREASURE
COULD PARALEL FOR GRACE OR VIRTUE'S MEASURE
WHO BEING MUCH WEARIED BY THIS WORLD'S TOYLE
GOD HATH TRANSPLANTEFD TO A BETTER SOYLE.'

[2] 'Vir suo seculo ... ardens et amans ... Boanerges et Barnabas, Magnes et Adamas'; April 30, 1663, aged seventy-nine. Tombstone in St. Nicholas, Aberdeen: Menteith, *Theater*.

[3] *Select Biog.*, i. 432.

becometh a minister of Christ.' He was wont to indulge in 'singular sallies of wit and innocent mirth.'[1] No one who ever read Guthrie's sermon on Sympathy would ever class him among the 'hard-hearted.'[2] So deep was the love of the persecuted for each other that there is scarce an instance of any one, even when writhing in the torture-chamber in Edinburgh, betraying a fellow-wanderer.

It must be conceded that many of the literary fragments left by these popular preachers are blemished with gross absurdities and strange vulgarities of expression, but it has to be borne in mind that many of these works were unauthorised reports written out from memory, while others are the fabrications of enemies. Many are posthumous, and should be appraised with some consideration. There remain sufficient Session and Presbytery Records to show the net results of the doctrines taught by the 'hard-hearted.' Side by side with passages proving hard dealings with evil-doers, are others displaying humanitarianism of the highest kind—indeed, of a higher kind than any of which we have any knowledge in connection with modern religious institutions. Knox's generous consideration of the evicted priests has already been referred to. What finer spirit of tolerance could be shown than that of John Livingstone of Ancrum, who after receiving sentence of expatriation said: 'Well, though it be not permitted me that I should breathe in my native air, yet I trust what part of the world soever I go to, I shall not cease to pray for a blessing to these lands, and to his Majesty, and the Government, and the inferior magistrates thereof, but especially to the land of my nativitie.'[3] He died at Rotterdam, 9th August 1672. The poor, helpless, broken, the victims of Irish kerns or Turkish pirates, aspiring youths, bankrupt merchants, harassed natives of Orkney and Shetland, stranded foreigners, lepers, and insane folk, were special wards of the Church.[4] The modern Church has fallen from its high estate. A nobler fellowship than ours bound the Covenanted Church together. Yet to have expected men and women to fling and sing, to play and be gay, to carry out the Gospel of the *Book of Sports* on Sabbaths, and, in fine, to exhibit the wantonness that made the reigns of the last

Kindness of Covenanting times.

---

[1] *Select Biog.*, ii. 65.
[2] *Ibid.*, ii. 66.
[3] 'Ane Accompt,' etc., *Select Biog.*, i. 219 (11th December 1662).
[4] Stevenson, *The Presbytrie Booke of Kirkcaldy*, 36, *et passim*.

Fears of the Covenanters.

Stuart kings unbearable, all the while the Covenanters had just grounds for fearing the recrudescence of popery, were repressed for refusing the political nostrums of James I., were lamenting the thousands whom the policy of Charles I. sent into bankruptcy, bloody graves, and burning plantations, were stunned with horror at the idea that Jesus Christ was removed from His throne in the Church in order to permit a ribald ruler, no better than an atheist, to quit his divan of painted harlots and salacious courtiers and to take upon himself the governance of the Church, suggests a way of thinking which Scotsmen have always contemned. The greatest intellect of the age, Milton, declared Popery and idolatry to be insufferable—the former being usurped political authority, and the latter impiety; and it is not to be wondered at that northern views of toleration coincided with this conclusion.

The commonest intellect in the north was able to appraise the King's 'religion of a gentleman,' as well as Hallam, who pertinently corroborated the Covenanters thus: 'It was a religion of the boots and the thumbscrew, which a good man must be very cold-blooded indeed if he did not hate and reject it from the hands that offered it.'[1]

Spiritual condition of Scotland.

I am not inclined to discredit and discard, as so many writers have done, the remarkable account of the spiritual condition of Scotland, or at least of some districts of it, in the Covenanting period, furnished by Kirkton the historian.[2] His narrative bears: 'In the interval betwixt the two kings [1649-1651 or 1661], religion advanced the greatest step it hade made for many years; now the ministry was notably purified, the magistracy altered, and the people strangely refined. ... Scotland hath been even by emulous foreigners called Philadelphia; and now she seemed to be in her flower ... as the bands of the Scottish Church were strong, so her beauty was bright ... no scandalous person could live ... most part were really godly, or at least counterfeited themselves Jews ... this seems to me to have been Scotland's high noon. The only complaint of prophane people was, that the government was so strict they hade not liberty enough to sin.'

He further makes the important averment that the hurt to religion through the contentions of the Resolutioners and Protesters was

[1] *Const. Hist.*, iii. 334.

[2] *Hist.*, 48-64. Kirkton was a graduate of Edinburgh in 1647, settled first in Lanark, then in Mertoun.

'inconsiderable in regard of the great successe the Word preached hade in sanctifying the people of the nation.'[1] … 'At the king's return every paroche hade a minister, every village hade a school, every family almost had a Bible, yea, in most of the country, all the children of age could read the Scriptures, and were furnished of Bibles, either by the parents or by the ministers. … Every minister was obliged to preach thrice a week, to lecture and catechise once, beside other private duties. … Indeed, in many places the Spirit seemed to be poured out with the Word, both by the multitude of sincere converts, and also by the common work of Reformation upon many who never came the length of a communion: there were no fewer than sixty aged people, men and women, who went to school, that even then they might be able to read the Scriptures with their own eyes. I have lived many years in a parish where I never heard ane oath, and you might have ridden many miles before you hade heard any.'[2] Every family, too, had family worship. An almost identical account of this golden age is given in the *Life of Alexander Reid, a Scottish Covenanter, written by himself.*[3] He says he was born in Kirkliston in 1646, 'that flourishing time of the Gospel,' and had a splendid education in the Scriptures and the principles laid down in the Westminster Standards. In New Mills, during the ministry of James Greig (1597-1635), 'in one winter forty persons all above forty years of age learned to read, that they might profit by reading the Scriptures.'[4] In the parish of Dalgety, in Fife, we find a district which fully justified the encomium of Kirkton, and there is evidence that it was not unique. In Dalgety from 1644 till 1662, when he was ejected, laboured Andrew Donaldson, M.A., a Protester and noble sufferer for the Covenant.[5] The parish was fully equipped. Nobility, gentry, and humble parishioners formed a Kirk-session, fifteen in number. A reader was still in office. Six deacons cared for the poor. During the ministry of Donaldson the church was repaired, and a school and schoolhouse were erected for the first time. A committee of the Session regularly visited the school, in which poor and rich were taught together—the poor

Kirkton's testimony corroborated.

Donaldson's grand work.

---

[1] *Hist.*, 54.
[2] *Ibid.*, 64.
[3] Manchester, 1822. He was the father of Rev. George Reid of Ochiltree.
[4] Scott, *Fasti*, iii. 183.
[5] Ross, *Glimpses of Pastoral Work*, q.v.

being provided with fees and food. It was enacted that little herd-boys be not neglected, but sent to church and to the catechising every second or third Sabbath, so as to 'be bred up in the knowledge of the grounds of religion'— all being kept at school till they were able to read the Bible. The General Assembly of 1642 had appointed 'The Three R's' as the minimum of rural education, namely, Reading, Writing, and Religion. 'Poor bodie' got Bibles free; no fewer than eleven Bibles, costing £2 Scots each, being given away in one month in 1654. In 1645 the minister himself went to the war. Under such a pastor—and he was only one among many such—the whole tone of the parish was raised. Humanitarianism was the rule. Hence we find the poor cared for, a 'lame soldier' provided for, a collection taken for a man whose horses were suffocated, the pestilence fought, and the uncharitable publicly rebuked for their 'hardness of heart.'[1] Elders visited all the congregation once a month to deepen the Christian life. Could the English critic have produced any individual or parochial parallels to such love of the brethren?

It is an identical picture which the two authors of *Naphtali*—both competent to write authoritatively—give of the state of Scotland before the Restoration. James Stewart (afterwards Lord Advocate), with his experience of the Lothians, in the Preface declaring: 'The land that was sometimes *Holiness unto the Lord* is become *the borders of wickedness* and an Aceldama.' Stirling, minister in Paisley, an Ayrshire man, evidently conversant with affairs in the south-west, testifies, 'before the end of the year 1638, the work of God was revived with more Glory and Splendour than ever formerly it had attained.'[2] The Restoration was the terminal of this phenomenal movement for the edification of the people, if the testimonies of John Livingstone and the Marquis of Argyll are trustworthy. Livingstone acknowledged that 'some two or three years after the English had in a manner subdued the land, there began some reviving of the work of God in the land in several parts.'[3] Yet Brodie, in his *Diary* in 1655, laments the awful sins 'abounding in everie congregation, drunkenness, adulterie,' etc.[4] Argyll on the scaffold declared: 'I

[1] January 14, 1653, Ross, *Glimpses*.
[2] *Naphtali*, 46, 50.
[3] *Life*, 186.
[4] *Diary*, 128.

The three R's in 1642.

Pictures from *Naphtali*.

hear assuredly that whoring, swearing, and drinking were never more common and never more countenanced than now.'

This was too true, as the sequel will show.

It cannot be denied, however, that, in spite of the earnest efforts of the clergy to outroot superstitions, survivals of old pagan faith and custom were looked upon as obligatory and potent as the Gospel. Recording his experience in the Highlands in 1652, Clark informed the Speaker of the House of Commons: 'The people [are] very simple and ignorant in the things of God, and some of them live even as bruitish as heathen ... heard our preaching with great attentions and groanings.'[1] A visitor to Scotland in 1659 wrote a terrible description of the immorality and dirt he discovered there, and his indictment was not minimised by another writer in 1679.[2] The latter writer refers to the show of religion in the country, where 'if you crack a nut there is a grace for that,' while there is 'nor decency nor order in their divine or contumelious service.'[3] He also mentions the barbarity of the Scots in cutting collops out of living bestial.[4] The people generally believed that spirits, good and evil, roamed everywhere, persons murdered haunting the scene of their dispatch. For this reason, according to Fountainhall, five men were executed and hung in chains at Magus Moor to 'expiate and appease the Archbishop's [Sharp] ghost who was there murdered.'[5] Ghosts of the dying or dead appeared to their friends, as Balbegno did to Middleton, and Claverhouse to Balcarres.[6] Fairies danced round the 'wirrikow'; little men in green inhabited the knolls, and virile spirits lurked in wells and streams.[7] Malcolm Cameron—Calum Mor Nan Seilag—in Kilmodan was wont to disperse these spirits by constant expectorations.[8] The spittle spell was

Survivals of paganism.

Belief in spirits.

[1] *Scot. and Common.*, 363.
[2] *A Perfect Description*, etc., by J. S. (Lond., 1659), 22 pp.; *A Modern Account*, etc., 1679, pp. 18. However, I do not find these indictments borne out by a reference to the manuscript judicial records of the time when compared with those of earlier and later periods.
[3] *A Modern Account*, etc., 7, 8.
[4] *Ibid.*, 13.
[5] *Decisions*, i. 62 (Nov. 10, 1679).
[6] Kirkton, 67 note; Sharpe, *Witchcraft*, 170.
[7] Cf. Allt an Spiorad in Kilmodan; the Wishing Well at St. Blane's, Bute.
[8] MacInnes, *The Kyles of Bute*, 7.

in widespread use.[1] The Beltane fire was lit with awe, and each glowing hearth was watched with vestal care on New Year morn, lest an expired fire should presage some calamity. The Devil was a real personage, able to transfigure and transform himself into the shapes of animals, persons, and things.[2] He held hilarious court with wizards, witches, warlocks, crones ('cailleaich'), till jovial Burns drove him for ever from Kirk Alloway. Into the satanic service the deluded sold themselves in a weird ceremonial in order to purchase the vaunted power to bless and curse their fellow-creatures. Even saintly Leighton sent to doom

Witchcraft. these covenanters with the Devil.[3] The punishment of witchcraft—a legacy from the Papists—was as much insisted upon by the educated laity and gentry as by the ministers, and the craze decreased during the ascendency of the Covenant. The soldiers of Cromwell (1650) would not permit the torture of the suspected witches, who were probed by professional 'prickers,' hung up by their thumbs tied behind their backs, whipped, had lighted candles put to their soles, into their mouths, and upon their heads, before being burned to ashes, drowned, or relegated to the dungeon to die of their wounds.[4] With the advent of Episcopacy there was an increase of witchcraft, according to the urgent petition

Auspices and portents. of the Earl of Haddington to the Government in 1660.[5] Auspices were read from birds, and portents from unusual sights in earth and sky. Some 'uncanny' persons were credited with power of second-sight, prophecy, casting 'the evil eye,' and glamoury. The hapless Montrose believed in astrology; Rothes was said to have been bewitched by Lady Ann Gordon; and Primate Sharp, it was reported, met his death while carrying in a box an unavailing talisman beside his own familiar—a humble bee. The godly, on the other hand, exhibited their intimacy with the Most High by showing 'motions' of the Spirit which agitated them into a Pythonic ecstasy. Few of the later Covenanters doubted the

---

[1] *Presby. Booke of Kirkcaldy*, Sept. 10, 1640: Margaret Lindsay accused of 'spitting on a bairne's face of the fallen sickness.'

[2] Stevenson, 'A Rare Comforting Cordial,' etc., in *Select Biog.* (Wodrow Soc., ii. 445); Fergusson, *Scottish Social Sketches*, etc., 88-105.

[3] *Presby. Rec. of Dalkeith*, quoted by Butler, *Leighton*, 223, 233.

[4] *Scot. and Common.*, 368.

[5] *Act. Parl. Scot.*, vii., App. 31. The printed Records of the Justiciary Court substantiate the petition (cf. vol. i. pref. xxi-xxvii, 2-8, 11, 13, 19, 20, 22, 24, 34, 121; vol. ii. 11, 17, 56, 57, 58, 75, 104, 269 (Scot. Hist. Soc).

prophecies of the famous Peden. But it is noteworthy that superstition of an offensive character lingered longest where Roman Catholicism and Episcopal Royalism continued to resist the more enlightening influences of the faith, as expounded by the rigid Covenanters, whose imaginations were of the most ecstatic, spiritual nature.

During the period prior to 1638, the public worship of the Church consisted of prayer, reading of Scripture, psalmody, and preaching. Public and private catechising was not neglected. There was a daily service in church for the reading of prayers and of Scripture. In the larger centres there were two services each Sabbath, and on that day, generally speaking, the first bell rang at seven in the morning, the second at eight, and the third at nine. The congregation assembled at eight to hear the reader in the 'latron' (reader's desk) read the common prayers from *The Book of Common Order*, lead the singing of the psalms, with the 'conclusion'—'Glorie to the Father,' etc., and read the portions of Scripture selected, as well as the Decalogue and the Creed. It is not known to what extent, or for what length of time, Carswell's translation of *The Book of Common Order* (*Foirm na nvrrnvidheadh*, 1567) was used in the Highlands.[1] Besides the reader, there was in many churches a precentor or 'uptaker of the psalm.' The minister entered the pulpit at nine o'clock after the reader concluded. The action in the service was as follows:—

Public worship.

A. {
    (1) Prayer—confession of sin—read to people kneeling and uncovered.
    (2) The Psalm, with one of thirty-two of the printed Doxologies in conclusion.
}

B. {
    (3) Minister's private prayer in pulpit, where he knelt.
    (4) Sermon to people (with hats on their heads).
    (5) Minister's prayer for the whole estate of Christ's Church, either read, or extemporised, concluding with the Lord's Prayer and the Creed.
    (6) Psalm with Doxology.
    (7) Benediction.
}

The service lasted about an hour according to the hour-glass.[2] The same

---

[1] A copy of this rare work was sold a few years ago for over £500.
[2] 'It is ordenit that quhen he [David Philp, A.M., 1617-32] teitches, that he turne

procedure was observed at an afternoon service, special prayers being introduced as occasion required. Children of twelve were admitted to the Sacrament of the Lord's Supper. In 1613 the people, fasting, took the Sacrament.[1] Welsh's *Catechism* was then in use in churches.

The spread of Brownism and the influence of the nonconformist ministers expelled by the prelates of Ireland led to the introduction of innovations, and the gradual discarding of the 'three nocent ceremonies—Paternoster, Gloria Patri, and kneeling in the pulpit.' Sitting at the Communion of the Lord's Supper was also reintroduced. The authorisation of the *Westminster Directory*, which was in the hands of Presbyteries in July 1645, led to 'novations,' which Montrose in his defence declared to be violations of the National Covenant for which he had taken up arms.[2] One early result of the Westminster Assembly was the dropping of the daily service, of private prayer on entering church, of the printed prayers, of the regular reading of the chapters, and of the Doxology. The uplifting of the collection was made an integral part of the service. In course of time the Lord's Prayer, being considered formal, was also omitted. The exposition of a chapter, or part of it, developed into the lecture before sermon. On Sabbaths, the minister thus came to have two lectures and two sermons, which tended to make worship in unventilated buildings wearisome afflictions of the flesh. On a week day another sermon was preached—in some parishes two days were set apart for preaching—while on another, catechising took place.[3] Another innovation in 1650 was the discarding of the old Scottish Psalm Book, in order to introduce the revised edition of the 'New Paraphrase,' by Francis Rouse; and this poor production, rendered more obnoxious by the puerile custom of the precentor reading out each line before he sang it, resulted in the deterioration of congregational singing. Organs were

Results of Westminster Assembly.

Introduction of the 'New Paraphrase.'

---

the glass, quhen he goes to the pulpit, that the prayer, psalme, and preitchings be all endit within the hour, under the pain of vis., viiid.': *Kirk-Sess. Rec. Elgin*, 14th October 1621; *Fasti*, v. 151. For the innovation of interposing the singing of a Psalm between the reading and exposition of the chapter, a minister was presbyterially censured: *Presby. Booke of Kirkcaldy*, 304.

[1] Row, *Blair*, 6.

[2] Napier, *Memoirs*, i. App. L.

[3] John Makgill, in Cupar, in 1654 had services on Sabbath, Tuesday, and Friday, catechised two days in town, one in country, besides doing other duties: Scott, *Fasti*, iv. 461.

no longer approved of. What was worse, the confusion and bitterness gendered in the land during the internecine wars, and the deposition of so many pastors, resulted in the discontinuance of the Lord's Supper for years in some parishes; while the spiritual tone of the masses was not improved by the example of the Cromwellian soldiery, who frequently converted the churches into stables and barracks, although others, of the type of Nehemiah Solsgrace, on occasion doffed their weapons of war in the pulpit before beginning their holy harangues. According to a contemporary, a fit of preaching came on Cromwell twice a day like a fit of ague. All these innovations tended to exalt the human element in the service at the expense of the divine—the topical conceptions of the preacher taking the place of the two chapters ordered to be read each Sabbath, of the inspiring psalms, of the essence of the faith concentrated in the Creed. The national idiom changed. Men went to hear a preacher—not to worship. The temple had lost its character.

Innovations in church services.

Presbytery had taken root in Scotland, and all the efforts of the hierarchy and of the Carolan government could not dislodge it. Hence Sir George Mackenzie in his *Vindication of the Government of Charles Second*[1] averred, 'The Reader will be astonished when we inform him that the way of Worship in our Church differed nothing from what the Presbyterians themselves practised (except only, that we used the Doxologie, the Lords Prayer, and in Baptism the Creed, all which they rejected). We had no Ceremonies, Surplice, Altars, Cross in Baptisms, nor the meanest of those things which would be allowed in England by the Dissenters, in way of Accomodation.' Burnet, when minister at Saltoun, East Lothian, was wont to use the Liturgy, as did Principal Monro in Edinburgh University, and some curates in Ayrshire.[2]

Quakerism spread under the tolerant regime of Cromwell, but 'dishaunting of ordinances, professing quakaristrie, and resetting

---

[1] London, 1691, p. 9.

[2] Crichton, *Mem. of Blackader*, 104, 2nd edit., note, citing authorities: Burnet; Foxcroft, *Suppl.*, 471; *Presby. Inquisition*, 27 (Lond., 1691); Cramond, letter, *Scotsman*, 29th August 1890; Hewison, letter, *Scotsman*, 24th May 1907; Sage, *Case of the Present Afflicted Clergy* (Lond., 1690), Pref.; Grub, iii. 217. Burnet, however, qualified his statement of the practice thus: 'I was the only man that I heard of in Scotland that used the forms of the common praier, not reading, but repeating them': Foxcroft, *Suppl.*, 471.

persons of that sect' became a serious ecclesiastical offence visited by penalties.[1]

At this point it is opportune for the reader to consider a brief account of the chief personages and classes whom he will see in full perspective upon the tragic stage during the 'Reign of Terror,' now to be described. A mere outline of the lives, principles, and practices of these unrestrained profligates in high places ought to be sufficient to create the impression that the chronic state of rebellion in Scotland was not to be wondered at, was more than justifiable, was indeed imperative, and that the untamable preachers and men of the moss hags—all defects duly appraised—were on the whole patterns of forbearance, toleration, and humanity, without equals in similar circumstances.[2]

According to Hallam, 'The Court of James I. was incomparably the most disgraceful scene of profligacy which this country has ever witnessed; equal to that of Charles II. in the laxity of female virtue, and without any sort of parallel in some other respects.'[3]

Charles II.

With disgust all right-minded Scots thought of their ruler, Charles II., sitting on his far-off throne, odious, vicious, repulsive-looking with his snuff-plugged nose. The story of his vulgar amours was a commonplace. No Lely could refine that face, no Clarendon that hideous character. Charles was absolutely devoid of friendship, morality, and religion. He idolised the flesh and became a victim to the most debased passions. He justified and patronised the worst forms of carnality. His pessimism led him to believe that no one did good except for self-interest. A secularist, he shook off Presbyterianism as a viper, utilised Episcopacy as the readiest political tool, and finally put on Popery as a comfortable shroud to die in.[4]

James II.

His royal brother, James, afterwards King, was a Bohemian not a whit better than the King, only less audacious in his amours, since he paid more painfully for them, and a trifle more honest, inasmuch as he sooner owned Popery, which was the prevailing interest at Court.[5] From the standpoint of the Puritans, whom he hated, he is not inaccurately

[1] Nicoll, 250; *Record of Exercise of Alford*, 66 and Index, 407 note.
[2] Cf. pp. 6, 7 and notes.
[3] *Cont. Hist.*, i. 332.
[4] Burnet, *Hist.*, ii. 466-74; Foxcroft, *Suppl.*, 48-50, 142.
[5] Foxcroft, 50-2, 78.

described on the gravestone of James Harkness, in Dalgarno, one of the persecuted, as 'that Beist the Duke of York.' All readers know of the painted seraglios which these Defenders of the Faith set up in the national palaces, and of the vicious cabals which met at midnight in 'Mistress Palmer's Lodging.' Macaulay's picture of that Court, as lewd as Nero's, suffices.[1] The rhyming satirist, who chronicled the slaughter of the London beadle by 'The Three Dukes,' the royal bastards, declared the impotence of justice thus:—

> 'Yet shall Whitehall, the innocent, the good,
> See these men dance all daubed with lace and blood.'[2]

Scotland has enough to answer for. In Parliamentary circles there were the royal Commissioner, Middleton, risen from a pike to a peerage, and his associates, all beggars on horseback, living in a bacchanalian paradise, plundering on all hands, and never so deliriously drunk as to become incapable of conducting an administration which aggrandised themselves and plunged the nation into penury. Greater power lay in the hands of Lauderdale, Secretary of State, an uncouth learned savage, about to develop into a bare-faced adulterer, toper, and inquisitor. Contemporaries left an uninviting portrait of this great but disagreeable statesman, with his red head, fiery face, spectacled nose, gross cheeks, thick sensual lips, and blubbering tongue, speaking vulgar English in a most offensive manner, with his hand always rifling the King's snuffbox, and his cup filled with a disgusting liquor by the tricky courtiers, who wished to illustrate his incomparable obsequiousness to the King.[3] We shall see him and his shameless consort, 'the Bess of old Noll,' together with his brother Maitland of Hatton, hectoring and plundering Scotland. Yet Lauderdale it was that Sharp and his co-prelates said they were delighted to serve as the saviour of their Church. The Duke of Hamilton accused Hatton of 'Injustice and brutalety palpable to all persons.'[4]

In John, sixth Earl of Rothes, Lauderdale had an accomplice who rivalled Silenus at the cask and Faunus in the indecent gratification of

Lauderdale.

Rothes.

[1] *Review of Hallam's Const. Hist.*
[2] *Poems on Affairs of State*, i. 147.
[3] Ailesbury, *Memoirs*, i. 14.
[4] *Hist. MSS. Com. Rep.*, xi. App. vi. 151.

every base appetite, until this notorious adulterer was 'either always sick or drunk.'[1] His oaths were malefic indeed, if they were as foully mouthed as they were badly spelled in his extant unique letters. The editor of the *Lauderdale Papers* concluded that 'with Rothes extortion appears to have been the only object, and brutality the only method.'[2] The Earl of Loudoun, whose early piety and promise charmed Samuel Rutherford, fell into adultery.[3] The Duke of Richmond (Lennox) was immoral and profane.[4] The story of Southesk is too abominable to repeat.[5] The Earl and Countess of Menteith accused each other of adultery and bigamy before the High Courts.[6] The story ran that the Earl of Eglinton, condemned to the stool of repentance, with a delightful assurance which would have charmed the Ayrshire bard, declined to sit anywhere else afterwards, because he thought it the best seat and himself the best man in the church.[7] It is not recorded what Abercromby, Balvaird, Durie, the third Duke of Hamilton, and others of their class thought of their prominence in the same place. Ross,[8] Lindores, Kinnear, General James Wemyss, General Dalyell, Captain Bruce, and many others of the nobility and gentry were guilty of sins of the flesh.[9] Christian Hamilton was beheaded at the Cross of Edinburgh in November 1679 for killing with a sword James, Lord Forester, who in drink criminally assaulted her.[10] Robertson of Athole was 'an incestuous and excommunicate person,' and escheated by Parliament.[11] The aristocracy was not totally vicious. The Earls of Kincardine and Tweeddale were positively good; Crawford was indiscreet; Lorne was on his good behaviour, although he could recommend torture for the

---

[1] Burnet, i. 73, 186, 187; ii. 310. 'The Earle of Rothes is put in the castle on a most shameful occasion,' adultery with Lady Howard: Baillie, *Letters*, iii. 367, an. 1658.

[2] Airy, *Laud. Pap.*, i. Pref. xii.

[3] Burnet, i. 72; Lamont, 38.

[4] Row, *Blair*, 420.

[5] Burnet, i. 406.

[6] *Book of Adjournal*, 4th August 1684.

[7] Burnet, i. 273 note.

[8] 'My Lord Ross, a good young youth, as was supposed, fallen in adulterie with his child's nurse': Baillie, *Letters*, iii. 366, an. 1658.

[9] Baillie, iii. 366; Lamont, 10, 13, 18, 84; *Binns Papers*; *Presby. of St. Andrews Minute Book*.

[10] Fountainhall, *Hist. Notices*, i. 231, 232.

[11] Balfour, *Annals*, iv. 207. Lord Kinnoul died of 'glengore' in 1650: Lamont, 17.

Whigs. Ancram was a man 'of small fortune, and of no principles either as to religion or virtue,' according to Burnet.[1] The heirs to Eglinton, Murray, and Kenmure were wanton lads. The young Earl of Leven died in 1664, after a carouse with the Earl of Dundee. The whole of society was infected with loose principles, from University chairs to cot houses.[2]

The gentry were bankrupt in estate as well as in morals, and the persecution of the thrifty mercantile and agricultural classes became the only lucrative business to which they could turn to retrieve their fortunes. The story is sickening, and it throws a strange sidelight on the national struggle to read how the nobles, Annandale, Airlie, Atholl, Drumlanrig and others were 'dependent on fines to save their fortunes.'[3] The creditors of Annandale stayed his bankruptcy by giving him time to exact fines from the rebels. It was easy getting men to farm the wages of sin. The Duke of Hamilton became chief publican in due course. Queensberry flourished and built Drumlanrig Castle when he was in office. The vultures nested in the Halls of Justice, and the Lord Advocate did not blush to fleece the timorous.[4] When ruining the Dissenters was the order of the day, exactors like bankrupt Carmichael of Easter Thurston, who just escaped the squinting eyes of Burly at Magus Moor, got the fines of the peasantry, so long as the Commissioners took one-half of the plunder of landed estates, while the other half went to the Crown.[5] Parasitism became infectious. Hunger for land, greed of money, the coveting of movables tainted all from duke to dragoon. Argyll plundered Huntly's estate; Middleton expected Argyll's; Lauderdale and his brother Hatton became rich by everything they touched; Aberdeen and Queensberry waited for the ill-gotten gains the coiner Hatton had to disgorge; Sharp got Inchaffray, but handed it over to the victors of Rullion Green; Dalyell legally obtained Caldwell, but illegally seized the marriage portion of its lady as well; Glencairn got Dinmurchie; Perth got Melville's lands; Drummond, Claverhouse, and Nithsdale respectively got Kersland, French, and Whyteside, from which zealous Covenanters had been evicted. Lesser officials grabbed

Bankrupt gentry.

---

[1] *Hist.*, ii. 29.
[2] Baillie, iii. 248, 284; Lamont, 35, 69.
[3] Rothes to Lauderdale in 1666: *Laud. Pap.*, i. 237, 257.
[4] Omond, i. 172.
[5] *Privy Council Warrant*, 11th March 1679; *Wodrow MSS.*, xliii. 26.

what they could manage to remove unmolested.[1] The Treasury was in
the hands of villains, according to Moray.[2]

The biographer of the Lord Advocates does not present a flattering
picture of the politicians and lawyers of the Restoration period. He
depicts cruel, avaricious ruffians.[3] They are continually drunk, both at
the Council-table and at home. When the ghastly shrunken head of
Montrose was taken down for burial, the Lord Advocate gave a feast
in honour of the event, and one of the guests drank himself to death.
The Council-chamber reeked like a charnel-house. The air was tainted
with the smell of blood. The judges in a circuit town drank the Devil's
health, at midnight, at the town's cross. Further, he describes the Lord
Clerk-Register as 'Sir Archibald Primrose, astute, wary, and unscrupulous'; and the Lord Advocate as 'Fletcher, the "Inquisitor-general"
whose cruelty could be averted only by a bribe.'[4] Ermine and silk were
soiled with mud and blood. Fletcher fell a victim to his own rapacity
and unscrupulousness, and was forced to resign, 14th September 1664.
His successor, Sir John Nisbet, Lord Dirleton, was no more immaculate
as Lord Advocate and Judge, and being accused of collusion and fraud
was also compelled to resign in 1677. Omond sums up his character
thus: 'At a time when bad men were common, he was one of the worst;
and it does not appear that, in the course of his public career, he ever
did one deed which lightens the darkness of his servile and mercenary
life.'[5] Dirleton was succeeded by George Mackenzie, who deservedly
earned the nickname 'The Bluidy Mackenzie,' upon whom so many
left their martyr blood.

These legislators did not lack for executors and executioners to carry
out their designs and dooms. The noblest of birth in the land lent them
service. Foreign trade in war was dull, and many blood-stained hands
idle at home were ready to draw blades for pay. To get a regiment (and
the chance to hold up the pay), a troop, a commission of any sort,
a collectorship of fines or of imposts, made the lucky one a soldier
of fortune in a true sense. We mark Thomas Dalyell of Binns, fresh

---

[1] For later grants, cf. *postea*; *Act. Parl. Scot.*, viii. 582.
[2] *Laud. Pap.*, ii. 68.
[3] Omond, i. 170.
[4] *Ibid.*, 177.
[5] *Ibid.*, 186, 198.

from the Polish wars, dubbed 'the Muscovy Beast' because he was so 'The
boorish, brutal, and overbearing. 'Dalyell is a rough man,' wrote Burnet Muscovy
to Sheldon, 'but of incomparable loyalty and integrity, a faithful friend Beast.'
to all that serve the King or Church.'[1] In his wild youth a brawler on
the streets of Linlithgow; he brawls on for years for blood and booty,
inventing war scares to frighten the Government. He also drinks
'hoolie and fairly,' and, in his cups and out, howls for blood, for liberty
to roast, hang, exterminate the Covenanters.[2] Hackston of Rathillet,
in an extant letter, records an instance of Dalyell's brutality at Lanark,
where he even threatened to roast Hackston, then suffering from his
untended wounds got at Ayrsmoss.[3] Dalyell, who was never married,
and left his property to his illegitimate children, was banned by Cargill
in the Torwood Excommunication 'for his lewd and impious life, led in
adultery and uncleanness from his youth, with a contempt of marriage.'[4]
On the field Dalyell and Drummond acted like bandits.[5] Sir William
Drummond, Dalyell's comrade on foreign fields, exhibited a rapacity
which brought him under suspicion and into prison as a fomenter of
rebellion.[6] Two prime hacksters, before the gory days of Claverhouse
and Lag, were Sir William Ballantine and Sir James Turner. The Sir James
memory of the atrocities committed by these licensed bandits has never Turner.
died out. A Galloway minister at the time informed Sir Robert Moray
that 'Turner was a saint to Balantine.'[7] For beggaring the westlands by
their unparalleled extortions and cruelties both saint and sinner were
dismissed by the Government. Burnet's true portrait of the mercenary
Turner, punctilious only in obeying his orders, and happy in his cups, is
not pleasing, and explains the hatred of the peasantry, who nicknamed
Turner 'Bloody Bite-the-Sheep.'[8]

---

[1] Aug. 9, 1667: *Laud. Pap.*, ii. xlvi. App.

[2] *Linlithgow Burgh Records*, July 1639; *Laud. Pap.*, *q.v.*

[3] Wodrow, *Hist.*, iii. 219 note.

[4] *Cloud of Witnesses*, 510, Thomson's edit.; *Binns Family Papers*.

[5] *Laud. Pap.*, ii. 65.

[6] Row, *Blair*, 552.

[7] *Laud. Pap.*, ii. 83.

[8] Burnet, i, 378, 440. Moray writing to Lauderdale corroborates Burnet; cf. *Laud. Pap.*, ii. 65, 82, 83. Defoe, *Memoirs*, 208: 'This butcher, for such he was rather than a soldier.'

John Graham
of Claver-
house.

Of the same militant and accipitrine order was John Graham of Claverhouse, a greedy rather than a needy soldier, anxious to be famous like his idol and kinsman, James, Marquis of Montrose, and also to found a family. With this itch for land and honours on him, Graham chaffered for the title of Menteith, sighed for its fair heiress, Eleanor Graham, swore a dragoon's oath as to his pure love, lied to Queensberry, to whom he often clamoured for 'movabilles,' and never lost the main chance to promote himself, although his track was stained with blood.[1] Queensberry accused him of upholding the fines and made him disgorge; he retaliated by accusing Queensberry's brother of defrauding the soldiery.[2] The dexterity which Claverhouse displayed in keeping himself out of the clutches of jealous opponents led contemporaries to conclude that he was a noble specimen of the swashbucklers of his day; so Burnet sums up his character thus—'a proud and passionate man, though in all other respects a man of virtue and probity.'[3]

To say that Claverhouse was better than his comrades is faint praise indeed, when we mark his associates in butchery with which, as soldiers, they had less to do than Dalyell and Claverhouse, who were most active

Carnal
Carolan
cavaliers.

members of the Privy Council. For example, Captain Andrew Bruce of Earlshall, whose only epitaph is found on martyrs' tombs, was a vile specimen of the Carolan cavalier. The Kirk-session of Leuchars charged him with stealing the endowments left by Alexander Henderson to the parish school; and the Presbytery of St. Andrews pressed a worse indictment—stealing the virtue of one of his own household.[4] With some satisfaction the chronicler of Coltness recorded that Irvine of Bonshaw, the captor of Cargill, 'in a drucken quarrel at Lanrick was stabbed to death on a dunghill by one of his own gange; a proper exit for such a blood-hound.'[5] 'Black Pate' Graham of Inchbrakie, kinsman of Claverhouse, already referred to, 'satisfied' the Church for sins of the flesh.'[6] The cruelties of Grierson of Lag, and the oppressions of other persecutors, stand on record. Defoe gives an instance of a humane

[1] *Book of Menteith*, ii. 197; *Hist. MSS. Com. Rep.*, xv. viii. 266, 267, 276.
[2] Terry, *John Graham of Claverhouse*, 182, 188.
[3] Foxcoft, *Suppl.*, 305.
[4] *Leuchars Kirk-sess. Rec.*, vol. i.; *St. And. Pres. Rec.*, iv. 151.
[5] *Coltness Collections*, 76.
[6] *Ibid.*, p. 5 note.

officer protesting against the brutal conduct of his fellows.[1] Claver-house, in his peculiar frenzy, desired his countrymen to think well of him as a sacrificial 'cleanser'—the chief of a new Order of Religious, a just Caiaphas clad in iron jack and 'scull'—at the national altar slaying Whigs to stay the plague of Whiggery from destroying other innocents. With such rude and lewd mercenaries at the head of regiments and troops of soldiers paid sixpence a day—when their officers did not defraud them of their pay—there was little likelihood of any other state of matters than that described by contemporary chroniclers and clerks of court—namely, abuse of the people, uniformed aristocrats stealing from poor packmen on the roads, justices fleecing the defenceless, and high officials tampering with the coinage. There was ample justification for Stewart declaring that 'worse than bears or tigers were let loose upon innocent families.'[2]

The Church was in a worse condition than the State. Sheldon was Primate in England, Sharp in Scotland. Their accomplishments can be cited in a word. Sheldon gave his Church the Act of Uniformity, Sharp gave his—'the boots.' According to Burnet, Sheldon 'seemed to have no great sense of religion nor of the true concerns of the Church, of which he spoke commonly rather as of a matter of policy than of conscience.'[3]

Sharp appears in his true colours, verily the 'base, clattering claw-back' of his contemporaries; to the Church, 'a knave *pur sang*, to his friends, a spy; to his foes, a persecutor; to his peers, a caitiff, whom they used but despised: in fine, one of the meanest Scots that ever wore a holy robe.[4]

A policy compromising, soothing, compassionate, did not seem to appeal to the better instincts left in Sharp. We have no mention of him remonstrating with the flagitious men of the age, as outspoken Wariston and Guthrie did with Charles II., and as even the latter and Richard Baxter did with tippling Lauderdale. We hear no voice lifted up against the recurrent tragedies of his time; no piteous appeal for the victims of the rope and axe, for the broken in boots and the tortured by thumbscrews; no effort to redeem the men, mothers, and babes who, often forgotten altogether, lay starved and rotting in noisome

The rôle of Claverhouse.

Archbishop Sheldon.

Archbishop Sharp.

Character of Sharp.

---

[1] *Memoirs*, 281.
[2] *Coltness Collections*, 76.
[3] Foxcroft, *Suppl.*, 67.
[4] Airy, *Laud. Pap.*, Introd. x.

tolbooths; and no mercy for the gifted pastors who were held in unholy and unwholesome ward.

Like Laud, he had as little sympathy with the sacrifices of the lawgivers as with the victims of the lawless. The weight of his hand and the strength of his will was in every blow with which the hangman drove the wedges home in the torture vaults of the Parliament House. If Sharp did not keep the pardons back, for which he was blamed,[1] he pressed forward no petitions for mercy. An infinite charity could not veneer the character of Sharp with a semblance of humanity.

Others of the prelates were exceedingly carnal. Archbishop Alexander Burnet was not secretive enough with his illicit loves to please his clerical namesake.[2]

Paterson, Bishop of Galloway, signalised his episcopate among the wild Whigs by inventing or re-introducing the thumbscrews.[3] 'This Paterson was one of the most notorious liars in his time, and vicious, base, and loose liver.'[4] Paterson was 'The Bishop Band-strings' whose obscenity is lashed by George Ridpath.[5] He was dismissed from the Privy Council in 1684 for obtaining a pension on false pretences and keeping churches vacant, so that, as patron, he might draw the stipends for his own pocket.[6]

Bishop Fairfull, a teller of 'merry tales' which disgusted Leighton, was 'scarce free of scandal.'[7] Even the nervous Leighton approved of exterminating rebel Whigs.

The Episcopal incumbents who dispossessed the Presbyterian pastors were, generally speaking,

'Hireling wolves whose gospel is their maw.'

This terrible indictment is endorsed by friends and foes alike. Bishop Gilbert Burnet designated the Episcopal clergy 'a disgrace to orders,' and 'dregs and refuse.' The Earl of Tweeddale, in his correspondence with Lauderdale in 1670, corroborated what the authors of *Naphtali*

[1] Row, *Blair*, 504.
[2] Burnet, i. 371: 'He kept his mistresses very avowedly.'
[3] Mackail to Adams, 16th November 1678; *Cal. State Pap.*, Charles II., 408.
[4] Row, *Blair*, 542.
[5] *An Answer to the Scotch Presbyterian Eloquence*, 87.
[6] *Hist. Observes*, 133.
[7] Burnet, i. 238; Foxcroft, *Suppl.*, 16.

and *A Hind Let Loose* called them—'scatterers and devourers, not pastors of the flock.'[1] Even the bibulous Turner confessed his shame at serving such 'debauched and worthless' creatures, a squeamishness which, incredible to tell, also overcame the bloodthirsty Dalyell.[2]

Gilbert Burnet's verdicts and generalisations were founded on sufficient data and personal experience of the men and times. Early in 1666, then the young minister of Saltoun, he issued *A Memorial of Diverse Grievances and Abuses in this Church*, copies of which he sent to some of the bishops.[3] He animadverted severely on the evils of the time, the corruptions of the clergy, and the vices of the gentry and the masses. He accused the prelates of being non-resident, seldom preaching, becoming politicians, acting with intolerance and pride, and sacrilegiously peculating Church property. He blamed many of the regular and indulged clergy for Simoniacal practices, entering the Church for gain, for being haughty, worldly-minded frequenters of taverns, who worried the people with 'long preachments' of 'mean stuff,' neglected the Communion, made dull, disorderly prayers, and gave out a few lines of psalms to 'slow, long tunes.' He timed the downfall of the masses to the advent of the bishops: 'At your coming in there hath been a deluge of wickedness, that hath almost quite overflowen the land; scoffing at religion, swearing, drunkenness, and uncleanness can not but meet you where ever yow are.' For this plain speaking the young minister barely escaped deposition on the motion of Sharp himself.[4]

On the other hand, the outed ministers and evicted rebels no doubt retained a large portion of the old Adam while on their wet and weary wanderings ever facing death; and their freedom from the spirit and practice of revenge would have testified to a special accession of supernatural power. We shall find one exasperated 'Stickit Minister,' James Mitchell, drawing a bad shot at Archbishop Sharp; another pietist, Skene, justifying the poisoning of the balls of his blunderbuss; the hunters of merciless Carmichael murderously grounding the very

Burnet's Memorial.

Character of the persecuted clergy.

---

[1] *Laud. Pap.*, ii. 207.

[2] Burnet, i. 426.

[3] *Misc. Scot. Hist.*, ii. 340-58.

[4] Burnet, *Hist.*, i. 387-9; *Suppl.*, 472; Clarke and Foxcroft, *A Life of Gilbert Burnet*, 62-8 (Cambridge, 1907).

Primate on Magus Moor; and a few cases of the shedding of the blood of soldiers, curates, and informers, in open fray, midnight raids, and tavern brawls; but these indefensible acts, even were all reckoned to be blots on the fair escutcheon of the Covenant, are out of all ratio to the bloodshed and excesses laid to the account of the ruthless suppressors of the Covenanters. Bearing in mind the rudeness of the age, the illegal acts of the King and his subordinates, and the provocation received, one is astonished that retaliation was not oftener resorted to, that offences were so infrequent, and that the persecuted exhibited so much Christian restraint. There is scarcely a parallel to it. Rulers who demand good subjects must afford good examples. Charles ii., Buckingham, and Lauderdale would have corrupted a 'Pagan suckled in a creed outworn.' Their infamous associates appear more like the flowers of *The Newgate Calendar* than the responsible governors of a civilised state and supporters of a Christian Church. The modern detractor of the Covenanters and eulogiser of their oppressors, who calls such men his 'cheerful friends,' keeps strange company among the dead.[1] We shall see these votaries of Vice sitting at the fountainhead of every purifying stream that flowed through Scottish life, save one, and pouring in their vile poison, which could not fail to make a nauseous taste in the mouths of what poor clergy and citizens were left in the miserable land. The stream of influence that welled out of the Covenant they were not allowed to vitiate. The struggle was not for a form of Church government merely, for the maintenance of the nostrums of illiterate fanatics, or for the justification of obstinate demagogues. The fight was for freedom, morality, virtue, and religion. No candid student can evade the fact that agitators like Guthrie, Cargill, Cameron, and Renwick, and fighters like Hamilton, Balfour, Hackston, Paton and others, in order to save their country, families, and innocents, from corrupters, seducers, and destroyers, resisted unto blood that Government, which they considered to be an agency of Satan. These purists of the Covenant, at least, do not figure in the records of scandal. Yet because the incorruptible ministers manfully denounced those Royalist scapegraces, and maintained a high standard of morality and religion, they have been frequently discredited by those who are ignorant of the vicious

Corrupt rulers.

Aims of the Covenanting agitators.

[1] Lang, *Hist. of Scot.*, iii. 305.

environments in which they contended. In these dark strata were being generated the disturbing movements which enflamed a once peaceable community. The Presbyterian ministers, by their honest ministries, pure lives, and creditable writings, form a contrast to other leaders of this epoch, and these attainments rightly gained for them the esteem in which the populace generally held them. According to Burnet, although they were 'a sour and supercilious people, their faults were not so conspicuous.' Our researches prove that their antagonists very seldom 'streaked honey in their mouths.' An impartial account of the lives of the persecutors will always form a sufficiently black framework wherein to set the picture of many saintly lives offered for Christ's Kingdom, Crown, and Covenants.[1]

---

[1] For an account of the literary men living between 1625 and 1690, and of their works, see Appendix 1., in this volume.

JOHN GRAHAM OF CLAVERHOUSE,
VISCOUNT DUNDEE

CHAPTER TWENTY-TWO

RECONSTRUCTION OF THE CHURCH

T HE plot was now laid for the final assault on Scottish liberties and for the realisation of the dream of the Stuart kings of Britain. The times were auspicious. The populace was tired of a rigid religion which conferred no temporal benefits; the gentry, bankrupt, servile, and growing habituated to English manners and customs, hung around the Commissioner's throne clamouring for ratifications of all sorts, knowing that to oppose the Crown was to frustrate their own designs; while the clergy were divided into two main classes—true-blue Presbyterians who saw a jailer haunting every church, and a party who were of the opinion of Robert Leighton, that the external apparatus of the faith was of little importance so long as the faith itself was professed, some even approving of the principle by which Gavin Young, minister of Ruthwell, held his charge happily through all the changes between 1617 and 1671, and thus expressed by him: 'Wha wad quarrel wi' their brose for a mote in them?'

Various parties in Scotland in 1661.

Shortly after the Parliament of 1661 began its reconstructive work, the leaders of the Church in Edinburgh pointed out to Middleton that some of the new Rescissory Acts abrogated statutes legalising the Covenants and Westminster Standards, and also other Acts enumerating indictable offences, and they overtured Parliament to renew these indispensable laws.[1] The Presbytery of Edinburgh sent a Committee to Middleton to appeal to him to constrain the legislature to delay considering a statute so revolutionary as the Rescissory Act was.

---

[1] Wodrow, i. 110.

Middleton politely cajoled the deputation until he got time to have the statute passed. Professor David Dickson, also sent to remonstrate, was cavalierly received and told by the Commissioner that he was not afraid of papers by ministers, a remark which drew from Dickson the biting retort—'he well knew his Grace was no coward since the Bridge of Don.' Impolitic then was this rejoinder, which raked up memories of the time when Middleton fought for the Covenant. Middleton was not to be moved. The ministers next addressed Lauderdale, whose love to Mother-Church they praised, hoping through his intervention with the King to have the incoming tide turned back by means of a General Assembly, which they desired to be convened for the settlement of peace. Lauderdale, too, was a broken reed. No longer an advocate for Covenants, he now viewed Presbyterianism as a temporary expedient. Besides, this statesman had a correspondent in Sharp, who disavowed the resolutions of Douglas, Dickson, and Wood, and pressed a conjunction of Lauderdale and Middleton 'for good to poor Scotland,' while he himself in hypocrisy prayed: 'Let me bear the punishment maybe intended for Mr. Guthrie, who hath made the frame of our religion heer to be nothing else but a contexture of treason and sedition.'[1] The King was personally indifferent, except to the democratic aspect of the Church question.

In April the Synod of Glasgow and Ayr met and considered the situation. William Guthrie, minister of Fenwick, failed to persuade all his brethren to transmit a suitable address to the Crown which he had prepared; dissent on the ground of inexpediency and inopportuneness being expressed by James Hamilton, Cambusnethan; Robert Wallace, Barnweill; and James Ramsay, Linlithgow (representative from Lothian), afterwards the Bishops of Galloway, the Isles, and Dunblane respectively. A milder declaration, emphasising adherence to Presbyterianism, was unanimously agreed to, even by the Episcopal dissentients. They adjourned this meeting, and on assembling again found themselves proclaimed as an illegal convocation.

The Synod of Fife also met to prepare a petition craving the Commissioner to have an Act passed establishing the Scots Church, Reformed and Presbyterian, and to draw up a pastoral admonition suitable in

---

[1] Sharp to Lauderdale, 25th April 1661: *Laing MSS.*, 784.

the crisis. They had passed from the first business to the second when Rothes rose, and, in the King's name, ordered them to desist and disperse. Taken by surprise, the Synod broke up without a protest.

In a similar manner the Earls of Queensberry and Hartfell, in sweet revenge for their unforgotten imprisonment, dissolved the Synod of Dumfries, which agreed to an Act deposing compliers. The Earl of Galloway dispersed the Synod of Galloway, which had prepared a prolix, wild, Whig manifesto in favour of Covenants and uniformity, the moderator duly protesting against this intrusion of Galloway. The Earl of Callendar and Sir Archibald Stirling of Carden broke up the Synod of Lothian and Tweeddale. This Synod purged itself of several members of the party of Protesters,[1] but Callendar's request that the Synod should re-introduce the old customs of Scripture reading, reciting the Lord's Prayer, singing 'Glore to the Father,' and saying the Creed in baptism, was refused.[2]

Synod of Dumfries dissolved.

In the Synod of Ross, Thomas Hog, minister at Kiltearn, and James Fraser of Ling, elder, were challenged to disown the Protestation, and, on their refusal, Hog was deposed and Fraser was suspended from the eldership.

The Synod of Aberdeen exhibited the powerful influence exercised on the ministry of the north by the Aberdeen doctors. This Synod acquiesced in the recent statutes, and asked the legislature to petition the King to settle the affairs of the Church according to his own conception of the warrant of Scripture, the example of the early Church, and his own sense of the fitness of things. Never had monarchy such champions of its divine prerogative as these ecclesiastics by the Bridge of Don, who now showed that they had recovered from that 'rigidity' resulting from the coercive and well-paid efforts of Andrew Cant and his associates.[3] Burnet, who was present at this meeting, records that he heard one of its members say 'that no man could decently oppose those words, since by that he would insinuate that he thought presbytery was not conform to these'—the Word of God and the practice of the primitive Church.

Erastianism of Aberdeen Synod.

---

[1] Livingstone of Biggar, Greig of Skirling, Porteous of Covington, Donaldson of Dolphinton, also Hall of Kirkliston. At the same time Weir of Linlithgow and Creighton of Bathgate were deprived.

[2] Grub, iii. 180.

[3] Cant was awarded £2000 for his labours in the north.

Thus even Presbyterians were craftily drawn into supporting a motion for this address to the Commissioner.[1]

New Church legislation.

One result of the meeting of the Scots councillors in London was the instruction given to Lauderdale and Sharp to draft and dispatch to Middleton a proclamation on Church affairs, which was duly issued on 10th June.[2] According to Sharp, it was Hyde's 'present expedient' until the time was ripe for that final rescript of which Middleton was expectant.[3] It was a cunningly devised document calling attention to the recent statute of 28th March, in which it was resolved to maintain the Church as it was established by James, and Charles I., and continuing the same 'in the meantime' until the King had secured it in 'a frame as shall be agreeable to the Word of God most suitable to monarchical government, and most complying with the public peace and quiet of the kingdom.'

Sharp's progress in defection.

This letter to Middleton is worth quoting to show the progress Sharp had made in his defection since he wrote to his friend Drummond denying the truth of the whispers concerning his treachery. On 19th March he wrote: 'No person heer or with you can say without injuring of me that Ever I spoke or cooperated for introducing a change.' Two days later he declares: 'But if a change come, I make no question it will be grievous and bring on suffering upon many honest men, in which I would be very loath to have any hand.' Rather than witness the confusion he would change his country and breathe a freer air, he declared.[4] In the interval between the opening of Parliament and his journey to London, early in May, Sharp had been chagrined to see the Church ignored in the making of Acts bearing on her welfare, but it can hardly be doubted that this solicitude for the enslaved Scots Church does not wholly account for the terms of the letter which follows:—

Letter of Sharp to Middleton, May 1661.

'He [Clarendon] spoke to me of the method to be usit for bringing about our church settlement, and bid me give my opinion of a present expedient, which, when I had offered, he was plesit to approve, so did the bishops of London and Worcester; and after consultation with our Lords, it was agreed that Lauderdale and I should draw a proclamation

---

[1] Burnet, i. 218; Grub, iii. 182.
[2] Aldis, *List*, 1713; Wodrow, i. 151.
[3] Sharp to Middleton, 21st May: *Laud. Pap.*, ii. App. lxxviii.
[4] *Ibid.*, i. 89.

from the king to be sent to your grace, with which I trust you will be satisfied … that the perfecting of the work may be upon your hand from whom it had its beginning, and under whose countenance and protection it must thrive and take rooting. … The proclamation will suffice to the disposing of minds to acquiescence to the king's pleasure … but now I trust all opposing designs are dashed, and a foundation laid for a superstructure, which will render your name precious to the succeeding generations.'[1]

The opinion that Sharp hoped to get an Assembly called to settle on a *modus vivendi* is not borne out by this letter or by the proclamation, which made no mention or promise of such a convocation. Nor is Sharp's statement to Drummond (21st March)—'I declare to you I have not acted directly or indirectly for a change among us, nor have I touched upon Church Government in sermons and conferences at our Court or elsewhere'—credible in face of the narrative relating the contempt of Middleton for the trick played on the Presbytery of Edinburgh, and of his own statement in May, that he had often been conversing with Middleton on the subject.

The first session of the Parliament of 1661 came to an end on 12th July.[2] On Middleton's return to Court to report progress, the government of the land was left to the Privy Council. According to Burnet, 'it was a mad, roaring time, full of extravagance; and no wonder it was so, when the men of affairs were almost perpetually drunk.'[3] The Scottish delegates were still in London.[4] Middleton gave to the King an account of his commission at a meeting of the Scots Council in London, at which Clarendon was present.[5] Middleton said, that since the Church of Scotland was now without a government it behoved the King to settle one. Glencairn and Rothes declared that 'six for one in Scotland longed for Episcopacy'—an assertion which drew a direct denial from the testy Earl of Crawford, who retorted that Presbytery had the ascendency. Lauderdale, who as yet had not openly discarded his early choice, feeling his way, suggested the middle and prudent

Middleton's report to the King.

---

[1] London, 21st May 1661: *Laud. Pap.*, ii. App. C. lxxviii.

[2] 1st January to 12th July: *Act. Parl. Scot.*, vii. 3-367.

[3] *Hist.*, i. 220.

[4] Row, *Blair*, 390.

[5] Mackenzie, *Memoirs*, 52.

course of taking counsel with the ecclesiastical courts before settling the matter. Hamilton and Sir Robert Moray supported this proposal, the former asserting that the King's promise to the Presbyters of Edinburgh to continue the faith established had prevented the rise of opposition to the Rescissory Acts. Middleton demurred to this proposal on the ground that the verdict would not be impartial, since the less influential clergy and elders 'durst not quarrel the resolution of their Rabbis, who would not adhere to the oath.' Clarendon finished the debate with the taunt—'God preserve me from living in a country where the church is independent from the state and may subsist by their own Acts: for there all churchmen may be kings.'[1]

Charles resolves to restore Episcopacy.

Thereupon the King of his own motion resolved to establish Episcopacy and to impose his uniformity upon the kingdoms this time. Accordingly Lauderdale was instructed to write to the Privy Council (14th August) intimating the King's desire for a better harmony between the churches and 'our firm resolution to interpose our royal authority for restoring of that church to its right government by bishops,' and commanding them to inhibit synodical meetings, and to mark those persons evilly disposed to the Crown and Government. Yet not a year had passed since Lauderdale had written to Douglas regarding 'our Mother Kirk,' that 'it is no small comfort to me, in serving my master, to find that his Majesty is so fixt in his intention not to alter anything in the government of that church,' and that he had drawn a proclamation convening an Assembly (23rd October 1660).

To Edinburgh Glencairn, Rothes, and Sharp brought the fatal letter whose terms referred to the former communication of 10th August 1660, to the recent Act investing the Crown with power to settle ecclesiastical affairs, and to the King's resolution to restore the Church to the position it held before the troubles began, and as it now stood settled by law. The Privy Council met on 5th September, and after refusing to accept the suggestion of Tweeddale and Kincardine that the King should be asked to refer the matter first to the Synods, resolved to

Royal decree proclaimed, 6th September 1661.

comply with the royal commands. Accordingly the regal fiat was, by command of the Privy Council, proclaimed at the Cross of Edinburgh with the usual heraldic ceremony, in presence of the city magistrates,

[1] Mackenzie, *Memoirs*, 55, 56.

on 6th September, and it was ordered to be read at every burgh cross. The proclamation announced the abolition of Presbytery, because of 'the unsuitableness thereof to his Majesty's monarchical estate,' restored right government by bishops, enjoined compliance, forbade clerical courts, banned all objectors, and ordained all magistrates to commit all nonconformists to prison. This edict, announcing that the Acts since 1638 had been rescinded, became the interpreter of the deceptive letter of August which promised the maintenance of a church 'as it now stands settled by law.' Now the law on the Statute Book in existence prior to 1638 legalised Episcopacy, and it was thus revived.[1] Strong efforts were made to seduce the leading Resolutioners from their allegiance to Presbytery, and promises of preferment were held out to and refused by Douglas, Baillie, Wood, Dickson, Ferguson, and others.[2]

In a moment the Church had been degraded to the low estate into which it had been thrust in the days of King James, when the obsequious Spottiswood hailed new-born Prelacy as the happy creation of his Majesty. The royal whim was now 'the Church's one foundation.'[3] *Degradation of Church.*

The first exercise of the powers of the Privy Council was seen in the interdicting Presbyteries meeting to ordain pastors without Episcopal collation, and the citing the Presbytery of Peebles for ignoring this injunction. At this juncture, a letter came to the Privy Council from Lauderdale (7th September) enjoining the Council to immure Tweeddale in Edinburgh Castle for treasonable speeches uttered at Guthrie's trial. This was done. After three weeks' imprisonment Tweeddale was released, having given satisfactory explanations of his conduct, on finding caution for 100,000 merks, and remaining under surveillance. He was finally relieved in the following May. *Tweeddale in prison.*

Consequent on instructions received from the King through Lauderdale, the Privy Council, 9th January 1662, issued a proclamation

---

[1] Nicoll, 342; Mackenzie, *Memoirs*, 56-60; Wodrow, i. 230 *et seq.*; Grub, iii. 184; Row, *Blair*, 392.

[2] Wodrow, i. 215.

[3] The councillors who surrendered the national liberties were Glencairn, Rothes, Montrose, Morton, Hume, Eglinton, Moray, Linlithgow, Roxburgh, Haddington, Southesk, Wemyss, Callendar, Sinclair, Duffus, President Gilmour, Primrose, Ley, Blackball, Niddrie, Alexander Bruce, Sir George Kinnaird, and Sir Robert Moray.

interdicting all clerical courts meeting until they were authorised by the bishops, who were about to be appointed, deacons alone being permitted to distribute the parochial alms in the interval.

Protest of Robert Baillie.

In clerical circles the new policy had leaked out as early as April, and when Sharp was busy protesting his ingenuousness and innocence to Patrick Drummond, Robert Baillie wrote adjuring Lauderdale to be no party to foisting Episcopacy on Scotland, and to persuading the King 'to tak ministers heids,' as he would have 'to answer to God for that grit sin and opening a door, which in hast will no be closit, for persecution of the best persons and most loyal subjects that ar in the thrie dominions.'[1] He closed the letter with these sad words: 'If yow or Mr. Sharp, whom we trusted as our own soules, have swerved towards Chancellor Hyde's principles, as now we see many doe, you have much to answer for.'

This answer the men of Fife soon demanded from Sharp on his appearance. He wrote from Crail Manse, on 6th September, that he now stood for the maintenance of royal authority. About the same time,

Blair accuses Sharp of treachery.

the Presbytery of St. Andrews sent a deputation, consisting of Robert Blair, and David Forret, minister of Kilconquhar, to interview Sharp, to recount the then current report that he had already received a patent appointing him Archbishop, to call upon him to repent for his treachery and wicked ways, to depict the disasters which befell previous occupants of the primatial throne, and to demand his refusal of the crozier. Blair was eloquent: Sharp was taciturn. Persuasive Blair, who had been able under the shadow of the scaffold to woo and win to Jesus Christ the gay gallant, Nathaniel Gordon, entirely failed with Sharp. Their meeting was futile, Sharp having determined 'to ride the ford where his predecessor drouned.' Blair left Forret with Sharp, when the latter became atrabilious and vowed the vengeance he afterwards took.[2] Throwing away the cloak, Sharp became bolder in public, essaying to cry the Covenants down, and to seduce his friends from their allegiance to the Presbyterian faith and forms, thus setting a snare for his opponent Blair.

Ejectment of Blair.

The latter soon found himself in the noose so deftly set, being cited to appear before the Council in October and November. His sentence

---

[1] 18th April 1661; *Laud. Pap.*, i. 95; Baillie, *Letters*, iii. 458-60.

[2] Row, *Blair*, 392.

was, that he confine himself to his own chamber in Edinburgh, and live unattended save by members of his own family. Under this restraint Blair's health soon failed, and he had further to humiliate himself by asking liberty from the Council to retire to Inveresk, where with recuperated vigour he got leisure to write his projected *Commentary on the Book of Proverbs.*[1]

The parish church of St. Andrews was declared vacant, and soon Sharp and Honeyman reigned there in Blair's stead. Petty persecutions still awaited the estimable sufferer for conscience' sake in his places of retirement in Kirkcaldy and Aberdour. When in the latter place he was nearing his death in 1666, and in all likelihood lay watching the little boats struggling in the offing,

'Half oure, half oure to Aberdour
Full fifty fathoms deep,'

he pointedly yet sympathetically expressed what so many sufferers for Christ, Crown, and Covenant were yet to experience: 'O Sharp! Sharp! there is no rowing with thee; Lord, open thine eyes, and give thee repentance and mercy, if it be Thy will. ... I would not exchange my condition, though I be now lying on my bed of languishing and dying, with thine, O Sharp, for thy mitre and all thy riches and revenues, nay, though all that's betwixt thee and me were red gold to the boot.'[2]

The King and his advisers had the vacant sees to fill with suitable dignitaries, and to reconstitute the cathedral chapters. Sharp took credit to himself for keeping worse men out than those let into office.[3] All the nominees were staunch Resolutioners. None of the Jacobite bishops were alive with the exception of Thomas Sydserf, formerly Bishop of Galloway, the prosecutor of Samuel Rutherford, and now almost a nonagenarian. The Church may have expected his elevation to the primatial throne, and the promotion of clergy who had remained faithful to their Episcopal vows. The advisers of the Crown thought otherwise. Sydserf had not the appearance, qualifications, nor character to recommend him for the highest dignity. The unenviable notoriety

Blair's death, 1666.

The new bishops: Sydserf.

---

[1] Row, *Blair*, 402.

[2] *Ibid.* 493: he died at Couston, Aberdour, on 27th August 1666, aged seventy-two.

[3] Sharp to Brodie, 9th August 1661: Brodie, *Diary*, 201.

given to him by Drummond of Hawthornden, who pilloried 'Galloway Tam, that squint-eyed, stridling asse,' and 'Roman snakie viper,' as well as the injurious verdict of the Glasgow Assembly, had damaged his popularity at home, which he did not retrieve during his exile in England, where he alienated the southern bishops by conferring orders in an unconstitutional manner. The Crown, however, assigned to the aged man the well-paid and easily managed diocese of Orkney, which he enjoyed till his death on Michaelmas Day 1663.[1]

It was a foregone conclusion that the archiepiscopal dignity of St. Andrews should go to the active pastor and politician of Crail, Dr. James Sharp. In the interval between the proclamation of the restoration of Episcopacy and the public announcement of the selected bishops, Sharp paid a visit to Robert Douglas to discuss the situation. Sharp then disclosed, as he said, the King's desire to elevate Douglas to the primacy, whereupon Douglas emphatically and testily replied that he would have nothing to do with it. The persistent Sharp could not have forgotten what Douglas had written to him: 'We must leave that business to the Lord, who will root out that stinking weed in His own time whatever pains men take to plant it and make it grow.'[2] Argument was useless, and Sharp rose to leave the house. As he was passing out Douglas called him back and said: 'James, I see you will engadge; I perceive that you are clear, you will be bishop of St. Andrews: and take it, and the curse of God with it.'[3]

Douglas refuses to apostatise.

On 14th November, a patent was issued nominating Sharp to the Metropolitan See of Scotland, and granting him all the rights, privileges, and immunities pertaining to the office when held by its last occupant, Spottiswood.[4] The terms of the patent indicate what a creature of the Crown the Primate was, thus exalted *ex authoritate regali, et potestate regia, certa scientia, proprioque motu.*[5] He had no 'call.'

Sharp appointed Primate, 14th November 1661.

Andrew Fairfull was chosen for Glasgow. Master of Arts of St. Andrews, he had been chaplain to Rothes (who owed him gratitude

Fairfull, Archbishop of Glasgow.

[1] Grub, *Hist.*, iii. 188, 214, 215.

[2] Wodrow, i. 38: 14th June 1660.

[3] *Ibid.*, i. 228; Douglas's *Brief Narration*; Kirkton, 135.

[4] Grub, iii. 189.

[5] [Latin: 'by royal authority and through royal power, assured knowledge and his own initiative.']

for irregularly restoring him from the stool of repentance to the pew), and minister of Leslie, North Leith, and Duns. Burnet and Kirkton's descriptions are not flattering: a wag, insinuating, crafty, lecherous, a veritable Dr. Hornbook—better at drugs than divinity. In his coarse way he answered an objector to the Covenant: 'There were some very good medecines that could not be chewed, but these were to be swallowed down in a pill or bolus: and since it was plain that a man could not live in Scotland unless he sware it, therefore it must be swallowed down without any further examination.'[1] Death ended his gay life on 2nd November 1663.

The see of Galloway was allotted to James Hamilton, minister of Cambusnethan, second son of Sir John Hamilton of Broomhill. He was a graduate of Glasgow. He was deposed for contumacy in 1639, and on being reponed became ostensibly so rigid a Covenanter that he compelled communicants to renew the Covenant before partaking at the Communion table, and excommunicated those who did not comply.[2] The Government in 1661 made him a substantial grant of £100 sterling in recognition of his sufferings and his loyalty.[3] He survived till 1674. *[margin: Hamilton, Bishop of Galloway.]*

The most notable appointment was that of Robert Leighton, Principal of the University of Edinburgh, of which he was also a student and graduate, now sixty years of age.[4] He was selected for Dunblane— *[margin: Leighton, Bishop of Dunblane.]*

'A grey old minster on the height,

.   .   .   .   .   .

A quaint old gabled place,
With church stamped on its face.'

Leighton was a miserable invertebrate, whom ill-health, largely due to his habits, kept shivering on the boundary line between what he styled 'this weary, weary, wretched life' and death—a mere reed piping with every wind over the bog he could not purify. He meandered through life as in a dream, fated to dwell in Scotland, but anxious to

[1] Burnet, i. 238; 'All the Merse talked of his amours': Kirkton, 135.
[2] Burnet, i. 238; *Fasti*, iii. 275; *Naphtali*, 135.
[3] *Act. Parl. Scot.*, vii. 234a.
[4] Butler, *Life and Letters* (Lond., 1903), *passim*; Aikman, *Works* (with Life) *of Leighton* (Edin., 1842).

pass through England into Heaven, and very envious that the young preacher, Andrew Gray, 'has got the start of us and not for long.' Jet black hair made the ghastliness of his cadaverous features more conspicuous, and added the charm of mysterious godliness to a personality naturally repellent to vulgar Cavaliers. The expression of his desire to die as he did in an inn drew from the more human Dean Swift the bitter comment—'canting puppy.'[1] Yet his dream was not that of Laud, who longed to be reconciled to Rome, but rather that Rome, with its filial, still unreformed Churches—the Scots among the number—should be reconciled to its former, better self—the model Church of primitive times.

Leighton a hypochondriac and mystic.

According to Burnet, who knew him well, Leighton never laughed, seldom smiled, and rarely said an idle word.[2] Leighton's description of himself in 'his diseased, defiled cottage,' with feeble voice, 'great defluxion,' and his 'pressingest desire' to rest in the grave, is the murmur of a hypochondriac, or, as he styled it, 'ye peevish humour of a melancholy monk.' Such a passionless mummy, 'whose bones were marrowless, whose blood was cold,' is not the personage portrayed in a painting of the Principal preserved by the University of Edinburgh, which rather suggests a Christian colonel as hard-mouthed as any contemporary Cavalier. Leighton had an immoral brother, Sir Elisha, a man in high places, who, with some diplomacy, had the name and fame of Robert brought under the notice of the King, who nominated him for promotion.

That such a dreamer should have accepted a diocese as a gift from the carnal Charles makes another mystery to be unfolded. With a celestial air he confessed that he took office not of choice but 'as a mortification, and that greater than a cell and haircloth.'[3] Brodie, no mean judge of men, records in his *Diary*: 'I heard Mr. Leighton inclined to be a Bishop, and did observe his loos principles befor, anent surplic, ceremonie and Papists.'[4] As became the son of that cultured doctor who had almost rotted to death, *sans* ears and nose, in an English dungeon for promulgating *Sion's Plea against the Prelacie*, Robert Leighton, in his student

Leighton a satirist of the bishops.

---

[1] Irving, *Lives of Scots Writers*, ii. 145 note.
[2] Burnet, i. 239 *et seq.*
[3] Butler, 338.
[4] 30th Sept. 1661: *Diary*, 216.

days, satirised 'the decaying kirk' and its bishops in verses which
'Deplore the mischiefes of this uncouth change.'

After he went to the Continent to complete his studies—and he was a
finished scholar—his association with the followers of Jansen and St.
Cyran resulted in his holding lofty spiritual and mystical views, devotion to which Leighton realised within himself, while he failed in the
hard arena of Scots ecclesiastical life to make others illustrate it. He
found uncongenial employment in the parish and church of Newbattle,
where, after taking the Covenant of 1581, he also subscribed the Solemn League and Covenant in 1643, and made others sign it, too, up
till 1650.[1] He did not feel comfortable among querulous kirkmen and
unbending Covenanters, whose devoteeism he deemed inconsequential.

Leighton signs the Covenant in which he did not believe.

Harmless as a dove, yet wise as a serpent, he 'judged it uselesse and
impertinent to tell them so.'[2] In 1661 this triple-bound Covenanter
confessed to Brodie that this 1643 Covenant was a mistake: 'The Covenant was rashli enterd in, and is now to be repented for.'[3] What was
worse, he confessed he had always believed that. During his term
of office as Principal of the University of Edinburgh (1653-62)—a
function relieving him of much of the irksomeness he felt in pulpit
and parochial duty—he continued preaching to the professors and
students in what Baillie designated 'the new guyse,' which he further
explains to be discoursing 'on some common head, in a high, romancing,
unscriptural style, tickling the ear for the present, and moving the
affection in some, bot leaving … little or nought to the memorie and
understanding.'[4]

[1] The Newbattle copy of the Covenant subscribed by Leighton is preserved in the
National Museum of Antiquities, Edinburgh, catalogued MSS. OA19.

[2] Leighton to Lothian, 23rd Dec. 1661: *Ancram Corres.*, 455.

[3] Brodie, *Diary*, 221. Robert Blair, a contemporary most likely to be well
informed, accused Leighton as much as Sharp of betraying the liberties of the
Church (Wodrow, i. 228). When that redoubtable champion of the Covenant, Sir
James Stewart of Coltness, reminded Leighton that he used to recommend the
National Covenant to his flock in Newbattle before the dispensation of the Sacra-
ments, Leighton justified his change on the ground that 'man is a mutable changing
essence both in body and in mind and frequently is misinformed,' backing up this
view with the text: 'When I was a child, I spake as a child,' etc. Stewart also accused
Leighton of nullifying his ordination vows. The incisive lawyer apparently reckoned
Leighton to be a Pharisee (*Coltness Collections*, 68, 69).

[4] Baillie, *Letters*, iii. 258.

Leighton a
theoretical
Christian.

If Dr. Flint's estimate of him be accurate—'a purer, humbler, holier spirit never tabernacled in Scottish clay,' it is another mystery that his sympathy found no voice in a protest at those meetings of Presbytery at which his brethren consigned to the doom of the Privy Council two wretched women who 'confessed to having maid a covenant with the devil'; nor when the petition of the Provincial Assembly of Lothian (8th November 1649) to obtain Parliamentary 'commissiounes for tryall and burning of witches' gratis was transmitted.[1] I have searched in vain for instances of the personal efforts of this saintly minister to mitigate the brutalities and crimes perpetrated in the name of law and justice upon hapless Protesters and other Covenanters; and, apart from purely academic and forensic attempts to bring about a millennial harmony, I have failed to find in him any phenomenal illustrations of compassion.[2] Indeed, before retiring from the Archbishopric of Glasgow, Leighton, while approving of Lauderdale pressing the Separatists to give reasons for their rebellious opposition, did not remonstrate against the policy whereby 'those coercions and civill restraints that for a time were intermitted are now found needful to be renewed.'[3]

Difficulties as
to consecra-
tion of Scots
bishops.

The four divines were commanded to London to receive regular consecration; and as only Fairfull and Hamilton had been regularly ordained in the Episcopal period, Sharp and Leighton, set apart by Presbyters only, were compelled, in the first place, privately to obtain orders of deacon and priest before they could seek the higher dignity.[4] Sharp at first demurred; with the pertinacity of a Scot argued the validity of imposition of hands by Presbyters, and quoted precedents for exemption from a second ceremony. Leighton, on the other hand, with a nobler indifference than Lauderdale displayed, who was prepared to take 'cartloads of oaths,' was ready to observe any rites which did not weaken the substance of the faith, so long as he was speedily furnished for his mission of reconciliation.[5]

At length, with difficulties surmounted, the quartette appeared in Westminster Abbey, on the 15th December 1661, and were consecrated by

---

[1] *St. Giles' Lectures*, 204 (Edin.); *Rec.*, 223, 233, quoted by Butler.

[2] Row, *Blair*, 410, 518.

[3] Leighton to Lauderdale, 16th June 1674: *Laud. Pap.*, iii. 50.

[4] Mr. Andrew Lang rashly asserts that the four were 'rushed through deacons' and priests' orders to the discontent of Sharp': *Hist. Scot.*, iii. 300.

[5] Row, *Blair*, 399; Wodrow, *Anal.*, i. 133; Burnet, i. 247; Kirkton, 137.

the Bishops of London, Worcester, Llandaff, and Carlisle with a stately ceremonial. A banquet was made for them and for the Scots aristocracy at Court in the house of Sir Abraham Williams, but the joviality of the party made the hypersensitive Leighton feel the incongruity of merriment and the sad travail he felt coming on the bishops of souls. Sharp had no such forebodings. Just a year previously Sharp wrote to Lauderdale in these terms: 'Whatever lot I may meet with, I scorn to prostitute my conscience and honesty to base unbecoming allurements.'[1] The Scots bishops lingered amid the allurements of Court till spring, before going north to bestow the apostolical afflatus upon their less favoured brethren. Leighton, eager to inaugurate a peaceable scheme for composing the unhappy differences in the land, lost no time in introducing his *irenicon* to the other bishops, only to discover that Sharp, with the craft of a diplomatist, had nothing to suggest nor do meantime, and the jocund Fairfull, light of heart, skipped away into lighter veins of thought.[2] The homeward journey of the four bishops in Sharp's brand-new coach afforded the dreamer another mortification.[3] But at Morpeth he dropped the penance and the society of the bishops, when he learned that a triumph was planned for their entry into Edinburgh. He preceded his colleagues and arrived in the Capital early in April. While some supporters went as far as the Borders, the Chancellor, Privy Council, and magistrates marched out of the city to greet and bring them back. Burnet witnessed their advent, heard the roaring, obsequious crowds, but was not impressed with the humility of the triumvirate forming the idols in that tawdry show, which was intended for an ovation, on the historic High Street of Edinburgh.[4]

One of the first acts of the bishops was the rehabilitation of the hierarchy to its completeness. The see of Edinburgh was assigned to Dr. George Wishart, a staunch sufferer for Monarchy and Episcopacy. He was the son of Sir John Wishart of Logie, in Angus, a graduate of Edinburgh, appointed by King James to Monifieth in 1624, and translated to the second charge of St. Andrews in 1626. Adhering to Episcopacy, he fled to England in 1637, and, two years later, was deposed for deserting his flock, and for heresy, immorality, and harsh discipline.

[1] 13th December 1660: *Laud. Pap.*, i. 50.
[2] Burnet, i. 248, 249.
[3] *Ibid.*, 251.
[4] *Ibid.* 252.

Wodrow accuses him of profane swearing on the streets of Edinburgh, of being 'a known drunkard,' and of writing immodest Sapphics, a 'scandal to all the world.'[1] He became a lecturer in Newcastle, where he was captured by the Scots in 1644, and sent down to the Tolbooth of Edinburgh for seven months. He joined Montrose, accompanied him as his chaplain, and went to the Continent, where he found leisure to write the history of that hero's campaigns.[2] He visited England in 1660 in the capacity of chaplain to Elizabeth of Bohemia.[3] It is recorded to his credit that, remembering the horrors of the Tolbooth, he daily sent some provisions to the prisoners taken at Rullion Green in 1666—a rare instance of practical millenarianism.

Mitchell, Bishop of Aberdeen.

For Aberdeen was selected Dr. David Mitchell, formerly in the Old Church of St. Giles, Edinburgh, from which he was removed in 1638 for declining the jurisdiction of the General Assembly and for alleged Arminianism. He went into exile in Holland, and returned to England at the Restoration to become a prebendary in Westminster. He had his doctor's degree from Oxford. Death deprived him of office in January 1663.

Consecration of other bishops, 1662.

On Wednesday, 7th May, the Bishops-designate of Moray,[4] Brechin, Dunkeld, Ross, Caithness, and the Isles were consecrated in Holyrood Abbey Church by the two Archbishops and Bishop Hamilton, in the presence of the Royal Commissioner, Middleton, the Estates, and the Town Council. The preacher, Dr. James Gordon, of Drumblade, in his sermon had the honesty to remind the bishops of the frailties of their predecessors, and to counsel them to sobriety, humility, and attention to their spiritual functions. Next day nine out of the fourteen prelates took their seats in Parliament. The consecration of the Bishops of Edinburgh and Aberdeen was postponed till 3rd June and took place at

---

[1] *Hist.*, i. 236.

[2] De Rebus auspiciis Serenissimi et Potentissimi Caroli sub imperio Jacobi Montisrosarum Marchionis supremi Scotiae,' Gubernatoris anno 1644 ... Interprete A. S. Agricola Sophocardia, *i.e.* George Wishart. The Government gave him a grant for his loyalty and sufferings.

[3] He died at Lammas, 1671, aged seventy-two.

[4] Murdoch M'Kenzie, minister of Elgin, 1645, was so zealous a Covenanter that in 1659 he searched the town to deprive the people of their Christmas goose: Scott, *Fasti*, v. 151. He became Bishop of Orkney in 1677.

St. Andrews, while that of the Bishop of Argyle took place in Glasgow that summer, Fairfull being the celebrant.[1]

None of the new bishops and none of the clergy who conformed to the new order were again ordained priests and deacons, as might have been expected at the hands of the Westminster neophytes.

The following table gives the names of the bishops and their emoluments:—

James Sharp, D.D., Archbishop of St. Andrews,	£ 1544	6	1	List of
Andrew Fairfull, A.M., Archbishop of Glasgow	1294	5	7	bishops and their salaries.
George Wishart, D.D., Bishop of Edinburgh,	93	6	10	
Murdoch Mackenzie, A.M., Bishop of Moray,	198	8	1	
David Strachan, A.M., Bishop of Brechin,	76	6	11	
David Mitchell, D.D., Bishop of Aberdeen,	288	10	11	
George Haliburton, A.M., Bishop of Dunkeld,	152	8	8	
Robert Leighton, D.D., Bishop of Dunblane,	43	19	1[2]	
Patrick Forbes, A.M., Bishop of Caithness,	547	4	10	
John Paterson, A.M., Bishop of Ross,	452	0	7	
Thomas Sydserf, D.D., Bishop of Orkney,	1366	2	8	
James Hamilton, A.M., Bishop of Galloway,	1366	2	8	
Robert Wallace, A.M., Bishop of Isles,[3]	140	0	0	
David Fletcher, A.M., Bishop of Argyle,	(The stipend of Melrose.)			

The hierarchy was now equipped for its mission, which turned out to be a militant one, Leighton confessing it was 'fighting against God,' and multitudes of his countrymen resisting the bishops as their natural enemies. From the very beginning Leighton appears to have felt no confidence in the wisdom, pleasure in the society, nor satisfaction in the work of his colleagues, and 'quickly lost all heart and hope.' His letters entirely bear out the impression left by the conversations of the dispirited visionary upon the mind of Burnet, who thus recorded what he had heard: 'He who had the greatest hand in it [*i.e.* Sharp

[1] Row, *Blair*, 406; Nicoll, 365; *Act. Parl. Scot.*, vii. 368.

[2] To this sum are to be added revenues from Crossraguel, Monymusk, and the Chapel Royal.

[3] Bishop Wallace is buried in Rothesay churchyard. His tomb was lately renovated. He was cousin-german of the Earl of Glencairn, and was noted for his big stomach. His epitaph indicates that he was a man of vigour and intellect.

and the restoration of the bishops] proceeded with so much dissimulation, and the rest of the order were so mean ['carnal' in the original MS.] and so selfish, and the Earl of Middleton, with the other secular men that conducted it, were so openly impious and vicious, that it did cast a reproach on everything relating to religion, to see it managed by such instruments.'[1] There is one noticeable illustration of the evil of this change of Government. In 1660 the Synod of Argyle resolved on translating the Scriptures into Gaelic, and appointed a large committee of Gaelic-speaking ministers to execute the work.[2] Two years later the majority of them were deprived by Act of Parliament and of Privy Council. His epitaph in Rothesay gives Bishop Wallace the credit of restoring the preached evangel to the diocese of Sodor. There was a gloomy outlook and a miserable future for distressed Scotland in 1662, and none the less because Sharp, on preaching his first sermon after his consecration at St. Andrews, on 20th April 1662, chose for his text 1 Cor. ii. 2: 'For I determined not to know anything among you, save Jesus Christ, and Him crucified.' To the master Christian of Scotland a crozier was no 'unbecoming allurement' now, and his sermon glorified the crozier, not the Cross.

Middleton again presided as Commissioner in the second session of Parliament, which sat from 8th May till 9th September. Its first statute enacted that, 'It is fit the parliament be returned to its antient constitution, and that the clergie have their place and vote in parliament as formerlie.' On this being agreed to, six commissioners were sent to conduct from Sharp's lodgings, near the Netherbow, where they were assembled, in Episcopal vestments, the two Archbishops and the Bishops of Galloway, Dunkeld, Moray, Ross, Brechin, Caithness, and the Isles, who came in and took the oath of allegiance and the oath of Parliament.[3] After the ceremony the completed Estates, in pomp, marched down to Holyrood to feast. Leighton kept away, being anxious to stand well with the opponents of these clerical members of the civil

[1] Burnet, i. 249. Hallam accepted this estimate and declared 'the new prelates were odious as apostates, and soon gained a still more indelible title to popular hatred as persecutors': *Const. Hist.*, iii. 337, 328, 329.

[2] *Synod Record*, 30th May, 2nd November 1660. Dugald Campbell, minister of Knapdale, was appointed Editor.

[3] *Act. Parl. Scot.*, vii. 370, 371.

Government. The Estates soon proceeded to sound the death-knell of Covenanted Presbyterianism, and to proclaim the autocracy of the King.

The third Act, entitled 'Act for the Restitution and Re-establishment of the Antient Government of the Church by Archbishops and Bishops,' was based on the dictum—'Forasmuch as the ordering and disposall of the external government and Policie of the Church doth properlie belong unto his maiesty and an inherent right of the Crown by virtue of his Royal Prerogative and Supremacie in Causes ecclesiastical.'[1] This new statute revived all relative Acts, annulled the Charter of Presbytery (Act 1, 1592), restored to the bishops the jurisdiction of commissariats (Act 6, 1609), and made bishops the superiors of lands held by persons off the Crown since 1638. Act 7, 'Concerning Benefices,' declared all parishes to be vacant whose ministers had been appointed since 1649, unless they applied for and got presentations from the former patrons, as well as collation from the bishops, before 20th September.[2] Thus the sinister Act of Patronage was revived and a test of Episcopacy provided at the outset. The test of loyalty came next. Act 8[3] ordained that any person who refused to celebrate the King's anniversary should *ipso facto* lose his appointment and should not enjoy any benefice.

Re-establishment of Episcopacy.

Tests of loyalty.

Act 12[4]—'Act for preservation of his Maiesties person and government'—was so drawn as to embrace every kind of treason conceivable, and declared all the official doings throughout the Covenanting epoch (1638-60) to be illegal, all bonds made or to be made, including the National Covenant and the Solemn League and Covenant, to be unlawful, the General Assembly of Glasgow to have been treasonable, inhibiting all persons in rebellion by word, writing, or deed against regal and ecclesiastical authority, and declaring all offenders against these provisions to be incapable of civil employment. This statute was supplemented by another Act, whereby 'persons in public trust' were to make a declaration acknowledging the Covenants to be unlawful and not obligatory.[5] This last enactment was meant

Acts declaring Covenanting to be treason 24th June 1662.

[1] 27th May, Act 3: *Act. Parl. Scot.*, vii. 372-4.
[2] *Ibid*, 376: 11th June.
[3] *Ibid.*, 376.
[4] *Ibid.*, 377: 24th June.
[5] Act 54: *Act. Parl. Scot.*, vii. 405. (The deed of Renunciation signed by Glencairn,

for a trap to ensnare Lauderdale and Crawford-Lindsay, and to lead to their displacement from power and place; but 'Lauderdale laughed at this contrivance, and told them he would sign a cartful of such oaths before he would lose his place.'[1] Crawford was not so pliant, and ultimately was turned out of office. Act 13[2] made it imperative that all principals, professors, and teachers in colleges should own allegiance to the bishop, that all ministers attend diocesan meetings, and that all private chaplains, tutors, and public teachers should be licensed by the ordinary, so that conventicles should not interfere with public worship and alienate parishioners from the legal pastors. In order that disloyalty should be totally stamped out, exemptions were made in the Act of Oblivion,[3] and Argyll, Wariston, Swinton, Guthrie, Govan, Home, Dundas, some Campbells, and regicides, were reserved for justice. By Act 73, rebels and their families were stripped of everything making existence possible, and by it even supplicants for mercy to the rebels made themselves liable to prosecution for disloyalty. In contrast with this drastic procedure the Reverend Father in God, Sharp, was ratified in his possession of the priory and abbacy of St. Andrews—a fatal gift.[4] As if to display the royal magnanimity, Act 80[5] authorised an indemnity, pardon, and oblivion to many rebels, with special exceptions of about eight hundred persons supposed to be able to pay heavy fines, ranging from £200, up to £18,000 (Scots)—that of Sir William Scot of Harden. Some for no offence, others then dead, minors, and mere names of persons unknown were placed on this list.[6] In the list are seen the names of Loudoun, Lothian, Borthwick, Balmerino, Balfour, Cowpar, Ruthven, nobles, knights, lairds, and of the Kirkos of Sundaywell and Bogrie, Neilson of Corsock, Maclellans, Gordon of Earlstoun, and other westland Whigs, who were to figure yet at Rullion

Act of Oblivion.

Rothes, Argyll, Lauderdale, many other nobles and gentlemen, Protestant and Catholic, about two hundred in all, is extant in the Register House, Hist. Dep., Q. 247.)

[1] Mackenzie, *Memoirs*, 64.
[2] *Act. Parl. Scot.*, vii. 379.
[3] Act 71: *ibid.*, 415.
[4] Act 88: *ibid.*, 432.
[5] *Ibid.*, 420.
[6] *Naphtali*, 100.

Green, Drumclog, and Bothwell Brig.[1] The total amount of the fines amounted to £1,917,353, 6s. 8d. Scots. Never before had the Church in Scotland suffered in one season the triple calamity of being oppressed with patronage, prelacy, and Parliamentary control.

Middleton, not content with executing this unpopular policy, cunningly planned the downfall of his powerful rivals, Lauderdale, Crawford-Lindsay, and Sir Robert Moray, so that he might the more easily enjoy the forfeitures and fines, which he reckoned on for his self-aggrandisement. He all but succeeded. He asked Parliament on the one hand to believe that the King wished, and he made the King on the other hand to understand that Parliament desired, that there should be an exception in the Act of Indemnity of twelve persons who were considered incapable of holding places of public trust—the names of the proscribed to be found out from the votes of members of Parliament voting secretly by billets. The Estates were led into passing the Billeting Act on 9th September 1662.[2] Lauderdale and his henchman, Sir Robert Moray, were among the proscribed.[3] The influence of Lauderdale at Court had been on the wane during the winter through the intrigues of Middleton and others; but when Middleton returned in February[4] to give to the King and Council an account of his Commissionership, Lauderdale was prepared to expose the mean trick of his enemy, his dishonourable attack upon the liberties of Parliament, as well as the affront put on his Majesty by the proposed insult to servants chosen by himself. He accused Middleton of overstepping his function, disregarding the King's behests, usurping the royal power by touching statutes with the sceptre without the King's authority, and other fraudulent offences. Middleton's defence was unavailing. He was hoist with his own petard by a cleverer tactician. His subsequent interference with a proclamation regarding the fines, which he still intended to

[1] 1662, Act 80: 'Act containing some Exceptions from the Act of Indemnitie': *Act. Parl. Scot.*, vii. 420. Loudoun was mulcted in £12,000: *ibid.*, vii. 425*b*.

[2] 1662, c. 30: 'Act rescinding two Acts passed in the second session of the Parliament, the one for Excepting of persons from public trusts, and the other for voting the same by billets': *ibid.*, vii. 471, 450. 'Act appoynting the maner of voteing by Billets': *ibid.*, vii. 472.

[3] *Laud. Pap.*, i. 106-34; Mackenzie, *Memoirs*, 49; Burnet, i. 258 *et seq.*; *Add. MSS.*, Brit. Mus., 23246 (*Middleton Pap.*, 1662-4).

[4] He left Edinburgh on 30th December, according to Nicoll.

peculate, led to the recall of his commission on 10th March, and to the appointment of his rival to the Captaincy of Edinburgh Castle. 'And thus the fines,' wrote Mackenzie, 'which were imposed by Middleton to enrich his friends, proved his ruin.'[1] Exactly one year afterwards Lauderdale had the gratification of getting the two over-reaching measures erased from the Statute Book.[2]

Degradation of Solemn League and Covenant, 29th May 1662, at Linlithgow.

On the turn of the tide in political affairs, the Royalists lost no opportunity of bringing into contempt what the Covenanters looked upon as the palladium of the country—the Solemn League and Covenant. On 29th May, Restoration Day was observed everywhere as 'a holiday to the Lord.' At the Cross of Edinburgh the common hangman tore the Covenants to pieces. Linlithgow that day held high carnival, under the guidance of the Earl of Linlithgow, the minister James Ramsay,[3] and Bailie Robert Miln. A great festal baldachin was erected beside the Cross. It was surmounted by an effigy of the Devil, from whose mouth issued a scroll with the words on it, 'Stand to the Cause.' On one side appeared the effigy of an old hag carrying the Covenant, and holding up an inscription: 'A glorious Reformation.' The King's health was honoured; fire was set to the erection, and after every possible indignity shown to the Covenants and the relative Acts of Parliament and Assembly, these documents were torn and reduced to ashes in the flames amid the plaudits of a hilarious crowd. The burgh fountain ran with wine, sweetmeats were distributed, and the revellers finished with a carouse in the Palace.[4]

Parliament rose on 9th September. Middleton and the Privy Council met next day, and ratified a resolution of the bishops to meet with their clergy in the various dioceses in October. All persons holding ecclesiastical appointments were enjoined to meet with their respective

[1] *Memoirs*, 113.

[2] The discarded Middleton ventured to approach and kneel before the King at Bath, only to find his master pass him by as an unknown cur: *Laud. Pap.*, i. 189. He became governor of Tangier, and died there in 1673 after a drinking-bout: *Art. Dict. Nat. Biog.*, for authorities.

[3] Afterwards Dean of Hamilton, combatant at Rullion Green, and Bishop of Dunblane,—a sworn Covenanter!

[4] *Diurnal, Wodrow MSS.*, xxxii. 34. *A Dismal Account of the Burning*, etc. (Stevenson's reprint, 1832); Chambers, *Dom. Annals*, ii. 292; Fergusson, *Ecclesia Antiqua*, 192 (Edin., 1905).

ordinaries on a day notified, refusers to be held to be contemners of authority and liable to censure, while those convening religious meetings were to be certified as seditious. Trouble was anticipated in the west and south, only conformity in the north. The ministers in many Synods were tardy in declaring their allegiance to their new overseers. In the diocese of Glasgow only a moiety appeared to welcome the Archbishop, and not one of those popularly elected since 1649 acknowledged his jurisdiction.

Middleton, accompanied by Glencairn, Hamilton, Montrose, Middleton and Morton, Eglinton, Linlithgow, Callendar, Newburgh, and Sinclair, Privy Councillors bearing names familiar to all signatories of the Covenants, imagining that their influential presence might stimulate the moribund interest of the westland Whigs in the new frame of religion, resolved on a semi-royal progress through Clydesdale, Nithsdale, Galloway, and Ayrshire, by way of Glasgow, Hamilton, Paisley, Dumfries, Wigtown, Ayr, and Dumbarton. With the tinsel and noise of a triumph they displayed the unmistakable symbols of the new regime—maces, swords, and drums. Middleton and riot went together. These exponents of the new Evangel held their love-feasts at night, like the early Christians, but it was Satan whose health they pledged at the cross of Ayr.[1] According to Burnet this surcharge of gaiety rendered Middleton fuddled and obfuscated.

Middleton and the Court visit the west country in October 1662.

When this Court arrived in Glasgow, Archbishop Fairfull had a woeful tale to narrate of the obstinacy of younger ministers, who had neither come to welcome Episcopacy and himself, nor taken the necessary steps for remaining in their charges. When asked to suggest a remedy, he proposed that a peremptory order be issued enjoining all pastors to submit to authority forthwith or quit their manses and remove into other Presbyteries. He acted on the supposition that the clergy having flexible consciences would rather comply than suffer, and that no more than ten pastors would be obstinate. The maudlin legislators, fired with this inspiration, met in the Fore College Hall on 1st October, and heedless of the consequences, authorised an edict of eviction to this effect: ministers who have not obeyed the recent Acts shall forthwith cease the exercise of the ministry; their pulpits shall

Edict of eviction.

[1] Wodrow, i. 282; Kirkton, 152.

be declared vacant; parishioners are relieved from payment to them of stipend, and from acknowledgment of their ministry, on pain of being convicted as conventiclers; non-compliers shall remove beyond the bounds of the Presbytery before 1st November; neglecters of the anniversary thanksgiving shall be mulcted in one year's stipend, and be liable to the full penalty fixed by the Act.[1] All signed the ordinance. The Duke of Hamilton informed Burnet that 'they were all so drunk that day, that they were not capable of considering anything that was laid before them, and would hear of nothing but the executing of the law, without any relenting or delay.'[2]

The ministers were now in even a worse case than the civil servants of the Crown, who had in their declaration to repudiate the Covenanted Work of Reformation, because the stipends in grain were not yet converted into money, and the nonconforming ministers had to leave their homes in winter. They had a recent noble precedent in the action of two thousand English clergy, who on St. Bartholomew's Day preferred eviction to conformity. So great indeed was the number of the pastors of Scotland who refused compliance, that the majority of the Council on becoming sober grew alarmed at their own headstrong mistake. Middleton raged and cursed at having been befooled, and endeavoured to get the Archbishops to contrive, 'for the good of the people,' some way of undoing the evil effects of the order. Fairfull was in no hurry to retract. Sharp professed to be shocked at the proclamation, 'nor did he imagine that so rash a thing could have been done till he saw it in print.'[3] His method was to break his opponents one by one. The Council, at their first meeting on 23rd December, authorised another proclamation by which the rigour of their former order was mitigated, and ministers were indulged until 1st February to obtain legalised presentation and collation, but were ordered to stay in their own parishes; while wanderers from their own parish churches were ordered to be fined in twenty shillings Scots, and extra-parochial gatherings at Communions or 'Holy Fairs' were proclaimed as 'a special engine to debauch people from their duty.' This respite was a convenience to a very few waverers. The debauchery of the Commissioner, Council, and legislators had

[1] Wodrow, i. 282.
[2] *Hist.*, i. 269.
[3] Burnet, i. 269.

given the earnest preachers too good a theme for proving the manifest evil accompaniments of prelatic government, and the aroused hearers in turn, trusting to that lead, encouraged their pastors to throw off the yoke of a coercive government and to become conventiclers.

While Leighton's peers on the Episcopal bench were preparing to set in order their 'precincts'—thus Presbyteries were sometimes designated—he had summoned the clergy of Dunblane to meet on 15th September 1662. Few absented themselves. They began the business with sermon, prayer, and reading; and he said he would preside, unless 'brethren of the exercise' wished to choose their own moderator. He was pawky, and left nothing to chance or to clerical ingenuity. He read aloud a document, which was a miniature Book of Discipline and Ordinal combined, in which he enjoined judicial government of church members, family worship, decorous public worship—the Lord's Prayer, Doxology, and Creed being restored—extra services, the use of the Catechism, popular sermons, and piety on the part of the clergy. The ministers accepted the proposals.[1] Leighton's humility in offering to sit at the foot of the table while the brethren dined was thought by some to be 'but straking cream in their mouths at first.'[2] In other dioceses the functions of Presbyteries and kirk-sessions were little interfered with. _{Leighton's diocesan work, September 1662.}

Leighton's diocesan work, September 1662.

In St. Andrews, the archbishop was neither so tactful nor so successful, and many of the wilful pastors of Fife refused to compear and own Sharp's exaltation. The names of the defaulters were sent to the Privy Council. Sharp introduced innovations, and nominated a constant moderator for each Presbytery.[3] Bishop Wishart and fifty-eight of the brethren met and constituted the Synod of Edinburgh, in the presence of the Lord Advocate, city magistrates, and persons of influence. He chose 'Moderation' for his text.[4] Among other innovations he arranged for public prayers, morning and evening daily, and for the preparation of the Synod business by a committee.

Innovations of the prelates.

In King's College Chapel, Aberdeen, Bishop Mitchell was met by nearly all the clergy of his diocese, the absentees sending valid excuses.

Changes in Aberdeen.

[1] Wilson, *Register*, 1-4.

[2] Row, *Blair*, 427.

[3] *Ibid.*, 425.

[4] Nicoll, 381.

With 'these light men about Aberdeen, who have been ever for all changes,' as Baillie informed Lauderdale, the reforming ordinary could use a firmer hand.[1] He restored the reader and the Psalm Book with the Form of Prayers, and improved the service by enjoining the reader to observe a form of service in which the Paternoster, Decalogue, Doxology, and Creed were recited, and lessons from the Psalter and the Testaments were read. The Synod also agreed to appoint morning and evening prayers in the larger congregations in the diocese. The Directory was forbidden. Private baptism and communion were permitted in certain circumstances. The bishop required that the resolutions of the Presbyteries in reference to discipline should be ratified by himself; that canonical obedience of the clergy to himself be given; and prayers for the King and bishops by name be made.[2] John Menzies, minister of Greyfriars, and Professor of Divinity in Marischal College, and George Meldrum, minister of the second charge in Aberdeen, were among the few who at first refused canonical obedience, but the deposition of the one and the suspension of the other ultimately brought them into ostensible conformity, until the test of 1681 discovered them again in a recalcitrant mood. Mitchell did not long enjoy his Episcopal elevation, dying in February 1663.

During all this turmoil, the foremost ranks of the Covenanters were being decimated by death or defection. Chancellor Loudoun was gathered to his fathers, and the hand that once so boldly subscribed the Covenant, but afterwards gave itself to vicious acts, was laid in the aisle of Loudoun Church in March 1662. This summer also saw Principal Robert Baillie declining to his grave, and confessing, 'I tell you, my heart is broken with grief.'[3] Officially he had welcomed his Grace of Glasgow and the Privy Council, appropriately offering them 'sack and ale.' Conscience permitted no other courtesy to the hierarchy. Every reed Baillie had leant upon had broken and pierced his trustful heart. Even the 'dear James' Sharp, whom he applauded as 'the most wise, honest, diligent, and successful agent of the nation in the late dangers of our church,' and whom he had pleaded with to help his 'old friends out of beggarie and dyvorie [bankruptcy],' had already brought

Robert Baillie dies of a broken heart, August 1662.

---

[1] Baillie to Lauderdale: *Laud. Pap.*, iii. 477.

[2] Grub, iii. 205, for authorities.

[3] Baillie to Lauderdale, 18th April 1661.

ruin on these starving scholars, and had worse to offer—'a fearfull persecution ... of the old Canterburian stamp.'[1] The pain of recording the gossip, that 'Mr. Sharp had bought a fair, new coach at London, at the sides whereof two lakqueys in purple does run,' was nothing to the confession that the same 'dear James,' 'piece by piece, in so cunning a way has trepanned us.' Baillie's last letters afford sad reading. Lauderdale, to whom he once wrote: 'My Lord, ye are the nobleman of the world I esteem most and love best,' had not deigned to answer his last epistle. The zest of life was gone. There are tears as he writes: 'I care for no vanities; ... God be merciful to our brethren who hes no help of man, nor any refuge but in God alone.' Death was welcome 'in these very hard tymes,' and came in the end of August 1662. His relict and children reared no monument to mark his grave. No portrait of him exists. His many works are his best memorial.[2] The pen-portrait of Carlyle is characteristically appreciative: 'this headlong, warm-hearted, blundering, babbling, "sagacious jolterhead" of a Baillie! For there is real worth in him, spite of its strange guise; something of the Boswell; rays of clear genial insight, sunny illumination, which alternate curiously with such babblement, oily vehemence, confused hallucination, and sheer floundering platitude! An incongruous, heterogeneous man; so many inconsistencies, all united in a certain prime-element of most turbid, but genuine and fertile radical warmth.'[3]

Carlyle's portrait of Baillie.

'*Scotia sub Cruce*'—'Scotland under the Cross,' was the suggestive title which Robert Wodrow, the historian, selected for his manuscript,[4] which he published with the title, *The History of the Sufferings of the Church of Scotland from the Restoration to the Revolution*.[5] A persistent persecution of the Covenanters for twenty-eight years began, as soon as the Privy Council obtained legal authority and means to exercise a spirit which showed itself to be most vindictive, because it was fed on

Scotia sub Cruce.

---

[1] *Letters*, iii. 473, 474.

[2] *Ladensium Autokatacrisis* ... 1640; *A Parallel ... of Liturgie with the Masse Book* ... 1641; *An Antidote against Arminianisme* ... 1641; *The Unlawfullnes ... of Prelacie* ... 1641; *A Dissuasive from the Errors of the Time* ... 1645; *An Hist. Vindication of the Government of the Church* ... 1646, 1647; *Letters and Journals*, 1775; 1842; *Sermons*; and other works.

[3] Carlyle, *Misc.*, vi., 'Baillie the Covenanter.'

[4] *Wodrow MSS.*, xli., xlvii., xlviii. (4to).

[5] Edinburgh, 2 vols., fol., 1721-2; edit. by Rev. Dr. R. Burns, 4 vols., Glasgow, 1835.

the memories of the hardships borne by the loyal followers of Charles. The need of the gentry, not their love of the Carolan policy, accounts for the excesses into which they fell in expunging nonconformity, in order to enrich themselves and their minions with the possessions of their opponents. The hierarchy became a cabal of procurers and panders, not always cloaked in holy vestments. Where the carcase was, there were the vultures also. The air was full of visions of forfeitures, fairs for favourites, imposts for squanderers, offices for idlers, and benefices for the disciples of Simon Magus.

Expulsion of parish ministers.

On the 7th August, Parliament passed a special Act discharging from the ministry in Edinburgh three ministers, Hamilton, Smyth, and Hutcheson; and the Privy Council followed this Act up by ordering them and all other nonconformists out of town, unless they accepted the Government's terms before October. Only Robert Lawrie, thereafter designated 'The Nest Egg,' remained in office, wherein he qualified for the deanery of Edinburgh and the see of Brechin.[1] 'They choosed rather to suffer than to sin,' said their compatriot, Robert Douglas, who with his family was expelled by a macer from the court. He had been invited to a conference with the Chancellor and Bishop Wishart, who hoped to convert him into compliance; but he refused on the ground that 'they were setting up men who would tread them upon, as they had done in former times.' The prophecy was soon verified. The Act made it impossible for professors and teachers to remain in office without the approbation of their ordinaries. In October, David Dickson, now an octogenarian, was removed from his professorship of divinity and charge in Edinburgh, where he had distinguished himself as the champion of the public Resolutions, a hymnologist, and a cultured commentator.[2]

Eviction of Donald Cargill.

By the eviction of Donald Cargill from the parish of Barony, Glasgow, the Government created a source of disturbance for long years to come. This young minister, eldest son of Laurence Cargill of Bonnytoun of Rattray, Perthshire, Notary Public, and of Marjory Blair, was a student of St. Salvator's College in 1645, licentiate of St. Andrews Presbytery in 1653, and was called to, and ordained in, the Barony in

---

[1] *Act. Parl. Scot.*, vi. 391: Act 37, 7th August 1662.

[2] *Commentary on Matthew; Hebrews; Psalms; Epistles; Therapeutica Sacra; A Treatise of the Promises*, are among his works: Wodrow, *Select Biog.*, ii. 5-15.

1655 in succession to Zachary Boyd. He was so ardent a Presbyterian that on Restoration Day he prophetically declared that the return of the King was 'the wofulest sight that ever the poor Church of Scotland saw. Wo, wo, wo to him; his name shall stink while the world stands, for treachery, tyranny, and leachery.'[1] Heroic, fiery, affectionate, clever, eloquent, of swift foot and tough constitution, Cargill was the leader best fitted to become the ubiquitous apostle of religious rebellion. His happy essays at judgment brought him the credit of having second sight. His marvellous escapes gave him, like Peden, the character of one who could assume the coat of darkness.[2] This was not the type of man to seek Episcopal benediction. For this and other alleged irregularities the Council, when in Glasgow, ordered him to transport himself and his household be-north of Tay before the first of November.

The young Earl of Argyll was next selected for sacrifice. Middleton, who had an eye on his vast domain, had Argyll apprehended, sent down to Scotland, and tried for treasonable expressions. On 26th August the usual doom of traitors was passed, and he might have gone to the heading-block had not Lauderdale, his surety, and the godfather of his children, obtained from the King a remission of his sentence in June 1663.[3] For this salvation he became the tool of Lauderdale, and, as a Privy Councillor, forgot his own peril when he saw Cargill and other martyrs in the talons of their captors. *(margin: Doom of Argyll averted.)*

Two notable ministers to whom the Glasgow Act applied, were John Blackadder of Troqueer and his neighbour, John Welsh of Irongray. Troqueer church overlooks Dumfries across the Nith. Irongray, four miles from that town, is charmingly situated in a pastoral scene hallowed with many memories of the Covenant. Of the twenty-one members of the Presbytery of Dumfries, only two conformed. Blackadder occupied his pulpit till the last Sabbath of October, and on that occasion enlarged on the sin of intruding hireling curates on Christ's flock, and of compliance with the order of eviction. The auditors were in tears. An alarm was raised that the horse-guards were approaching to seize him. He retired, but returned to advise his friends to disperse *(margin: Eviction of John Blackadder.)*

[1] Patrick Walker, Life, in Dr. D. Hay Fleming's *Six Saints of the Covenant* (Lond., 1901), ii. 8.
[2] *Ibid.*, ii. 1-62, and notes.
[3] *Act. Parl. Scot.*, vii. 380, 381, 387; Mackenzie, *Memoirs*, 70; Nicoll, 393.

quietly. Leaving his wife and young family in the manse, he sought shelter in the house of William Fergusson of Caitloch, in Glencairn, a staunch Covenanter. Next Sabbath morning, thinking to catch Blackadder, Turner and the guardsmen revisited the manse. The scene left an ineffaceable impression on one of the minister's sons—the guards in the yard cursing and blaspheming: the children hidden in a loft: this boy peering through a chink to view the roaring scene, 'a murdering ruffian' below detects the tiny face, draws, thrusts, and, just by 'scarce an inch,' misses the chink and glittering eye. The manse was emptied, the little ones packed in cadgers' creels, and as the evicted family made for Glencairn, one of the children cried through the Brigen', 'I'm banish't, I'm banish't; Byte-the-Sheep has banish't me.'[1] Blackadder, in his flight, appears to have witnessed the eviction of Welsh. This John Welsh was the son of Josias Welsh, minister in Templepatrick, grandson of John Welsh of Ayr, and great-grandson of John Knox. He was by heredity a Reformer, and of the stuff saints and martyrs are made of. In his sermons he had not minced words, and styled the Estates 'a drunken parliament.' Such freedom of expression was not to be tolerated. The Stewart-depute, Maxwell of Munches, a Papist, was ordered to bring his parish minister into Edinburgh. With some discretion he permitted Welsh to fulfil his duties at a communion at Holywood, an adjoining parish, on a Sacrament Monday. The crowds of dalesmen and women who accompanied him home would have defended him if necessary, had he not wished to go peaceably with his guards. An extraordinary scene occurred on the green banks of the Cluden, where he was to take horse. The other ministers gathered round him, knelt and prayed. The excited people groaned and cried. They held him there. He had to dash across the ford, only to be chased by the crowd of wailing men and women, who followed the cavalcade a long way. After compearing before the Committee of Parliament, he was put under surveillance, and was ultimately dismissed in June 1663.[2]

These are not solitary instances of the tyranny in vogue. In order to strike terror into western dissenters, a number of the prominent pastors were selected for examination before Parliament re-assembled.

Expulsion of John Welsh.

Parliament summons ministers, May 1662.

[1] Blackadder, *Memoirs*, 85-7, 91.
[2] *Ibid.*, 89 note.

At the end of May 1662, while Parliament was in session, the Commissioner and Lords of Articles had summoned John Carstairs, St. Mungo's Collegiate Church, Glasgow, James Naismith, Hamilton, Matthew Mowat, and James Rowat, of the first and second charges, Kilmarnock, Alexander Blair, Galston, James Veitch, Mauchline, and William Adair, Ayr, to sign the oath of allegiance, which they were willing to do with the explanation that the King's authority did not extend to things spiritual. Otherwise their loyalty was unimpeachable, and to prove it, all, except Adair, subscribed a paper to that effect. They compeared before Parliament, which considered their scruples to be treasonable, and relegated all but Adair to the foul cells, where they lay till 16th September, when they were discharged under another sentence of deposition and eviction of themselves and families from their respective parishes.[1] Carstairs, a man of herculean strength, who could exhort as many as fourteen tables at one communion, left the prison wrecked in health. The suave bishop, Leighton, was sent to try and conciliate the prisoners, only to be taunted with his own apostasy and defections by these honester sufferers for conscience' sake.

(margin: Ministers in prison.)

Thomas Wylie, a protégé of Loudoun, and formerly minister at Mauchline, where he stood against the King and Middleton in the Mauchline Moor fray, now that he was translated to disaffected Kirkcudbright, was a marked man to be tested in a personal compearance at Edinburgh. Wylie for a time kept out of the way, and refused to seek collation and to take the oath. Ultimately he succumbed to the pressure of the authorities, and removed with his family from the parish, not without leaving on record a list of the lamentable evils entailed on the Church.[2]

(margin: Thomas Wylie.)

The Act encouraging spies soon served its intended purpose, and among the first reported on was Hugh M'Kail, then chaplain to Sir James Stuart of Kirkfield, at one time Provost of Edinburgh, and father of James, a dangerous opponent of the Government.[3] The usual seditious speeches and acts were attributed to M'Kail.

(margin: Hugh M'Kail.)

The youth had preached an offensive political sermon, possibly too true, and Sir James and his son Walter had been hearers that day.

[1] Wodrow, *Hist.*, i. 294-6.
[2] *Ibid.* 300-3.
[3] Afterwards joint-author of *Naphtali*, and Lord Advocate.

John Brown
of Wamphray,
1610?-1679.

Walter, too, had made a fiery remark or two in a smithy. All three were summoned. Sir James cleared himself; M'Kail fled abroad; Walter compeared, and the Council, thinking his explanation weak, sent him to the Tolbooth.[1] Lying in the same noisome prison was John Brown, minister of Wamphray, in the presbytery of Lochmaben, a graduate of Edinburgh, an ardent Covenanter and an erudite theologian. In his native Galloway he had won the heart of Samuel Rutherford on account of his faithful discipleship, or of similarity of uncompromising views, so that Rutherford said of him: 'I never could get my love off that man. I think Christ has something to do with him.' The manly spirit in him could not help expressing itself in contempt of his weak-kneed co-presbyters who acknowledged diocesan Episcopacy, and he publicly styled them knaves and villains. Five weeks' incarceration in November and December brought him to death's door. After petitioning for liberty, and agreeing to leave the country and not to return without a licence under pain of death, he was released. At first he was too poor to buy a passage. Across the seas, the inspiration of kindred spirits, rebels and the ostracised, kept his powerful and untiring pen writing in English and Latin those able and damaging works, which forced King Charles in 1676 to demand from the States of Holland the expulsion of Brown, Robert MacWard, and Colonel James Wallace.[2] It was an irreparable loss to theological learning and to Scotland when a cruel fate forced this gifted scholar to become a mere polemic, devoting his talents to the petty measuring out of the 'mint, anise, and cummin' for the ordinary sacrifice, while the 'weightier matters of the law' were left without an interpreter. His extant works prove the vast capabilities of this accomplished Calvinist.[3]

Ministers
summonded.

Citations were directed to the following ministers, as well as to local magistrates, ordering them to ensure the compearance of the accused in the Capital on 9th December: John Livingstone, Ancrum; Samuel Austin, Penpont; John Nevay, Newmills; John Carstairs, St. Mungo,

[1] Wodrow, *Hist.*, i. 304: 11th November.
[2] *Ibid.*, i. 305.
[3] Scott, *Fasti*, ii. 663; Walker, *Scot. Theol.*, 24, 48, 107, 144; M'Crie, *Veitch*, 362, etc. Brown died in exile in 1679. His chief works are: *An Apologetical Relation*, ... 1665; *The Banders Disbanded*; *Libri Duo*, ... 1670; *Apology ... for Persecuted Ministers*, ... 1677; *Christ the Way*, ... 1677; *Quakerisme*, ... 1678; *The History of the Indulgence*, ... 1678; and several others.

Glasgow; Matthew Mowat, Kilmarnock; Robert Trail, Edinburgh; James Naismith, Hamilton; Andrew Cant, senior, and Andrew Cant, junior, Aberdeen; John Menzies, Aberdeen; George Meldrum, Aberdeen; Alexander Gordon, Inveraray; John Cameron, Kilfinan; James Gardiner. Saddle. Among others who were summoned for examination were: Gilbert Rule; John Drysdale; Alexander Dunlop, Paisley; James Warner, Balmaclellan. Livingstone, Trail, and Gardiner were duly examined on the 11th December by the Council. Livingstone recorded the procedure observed. Questioned regarding his scruples to keep Restoration Day, and to take the Oath of Allegiance, he declared that he had no clearness that God approved of anniversary holy days, and that he did acknowledge the King to be the supreme civil governor. This implied that Presbytery had co-ordinate jurisdiction in spiritual affairs—a recrudescence of the odious dogmas of the Knox-Buchanan school. The judges were satisfied, and sentenced Livingstone to banishment, and to lie in prison till his ship sailed to Rotterdam, unless he signed an assent to the sentence. His crave for permission to return and say farewell to his wife and family was refused. With that noble spirit so seldom credited to the Covenanters, Livingstone replied to his doomsters: 'Well, although it be not permitted me that I should breathe in my native air, yet I trust, what part of the world so ever I go to, I shall not cease to pray for a blessing to these lands, to his Majesty, and the government, and the inferior magistrates thereof, but especially to the land of my nativitie.' Filled with the same Christian spirit, he wrote to his flock admonishing them 'to love and help one another, have a care to breed your children to know the Lord, and to keep themselves unspotted from the pollutions of ane evill world. ... Let ane care be had of the poor and sick.' In a later letter he adjured the flock not to molest the intruded curate: 'As for the poor wretch that is thrust in upon you, do not hate him, do not injure him, rather pray for him, and use means if it be possible, that he may recover: but do not countenance or join with him: ye may easily be sensible that he is not a messenger from the Lord for your spiritual good.' Livingstone left his fatherland grieving that he had not lifted up a louder voice in defence of the faith and in opposition to defections. Livingstone died in Rotterdam on 9th August 1672, aged sixty-nine.[1]

John Livingstone, 1603-1672.

[1] Wodrow, *Hist.*, i. 310-2; *Select Biog.*, 'Life,' i. 190-241.

Trail and Nevay, not to be bent, subscribed the order for banishment, 'and not to return, under the pain of death'; but Menzies and Meldrum showed a faint heart and signed the Oath of Allegiance. Cameron found shelter as chaplain to Locheil in the ruined castle of Inverlochy. Austin appears to have retired to quiet Penpont, where he rests. Gordon for a time was left unmolested. Dunlop, father of Principal Dunlop, as became a Protester refused the Oath and was confined to Culross. He died in Bo'ness in his forty-seventh year, the defeat at Pentland having hastened his end. In Rotterdam the exiles formed that remarkable coterie of 'fiery instruments' which kept Scotland lively for many years by their writings and intrigues.

Similar evictions were carried out in several counties, but the purgation was greatest in the Synods of Glasgow and Ayr, Dumfries, Galloway, Lothian and Tweeddale, and Merse and Teviotdale. Various calculations have been made regarding the number of parish ministers deprived through the introduction of Episcopacy, Wodrow reckoning 'near four hundred'; Burnet, 350; Brown, 'the third part of the ministry,' i.e. 320; Mr. W. L. Mathieson, 271 from 1660 to 1666.[1] The Rev. Robert Logan's table, compiled from Scott's *Fasti*, makes out 952 charges, of which 72 were vacant. The ministers of 329 were deprived, and 551 adhered.[2] Probably not more than 200 manses were emptied up till the end of 1662, in the Synods undernoted:—

Synod of		Synod of	
Glasgow and Ayr	63	Aberdeen	6
Dumfries,	30	Ross,	3
Galloway,	23	Angus and Mearns,	1
Lothian and Tweeddale,	23	Orkney,	1
Merse and Teviotdale,	19	Glenelg,	0
Fife,	10	Moray,	0
Argyle,	12	Sutherland,	0
Perth and Stirling,	11	Zetland,	0
			203

[1] *Politics and Religion*, ii. 193 note.
[2] *The United Free Church* App., 213 (Edin., 1906).

Many of the more timid and peaceable clergy remained in their offices without conforming in strict legality, being overlooked for a time through the influence of friends at Court—a notable instance being William Guthrie of Fenwick. The Privy Council, learning that few ministers in Dumfries and Galloway had conformed, issued warrants ordering thirteen ministers in the Presbytery of Kirkcudbright, six in Stranraer, six in Wigtown, and two in Dumfries to cease their work, give up the ministry, remove themselves and their households beyond the bounds of their respective Presbyteries, before the 20th day of March, and to compear before the Council for their acts of disobedience.[1] A similar warrant was sent to fourteen ministers in the Synods of Fife, Perth, and Stirling, among whom was the estimable and typical Covenanter, Andrew Donaldson, pastor at Dalgety. Donaldson's friend and patron, the Earl of Dunfermline, who got his summons cancelled by the King, was not able to keep Donaldson in his parish after Sharp astutely got an Act passed preventing restored ministers returning to their former charges. Donaldson was suspended by the Synod, but continued preaching. The Synod proceeded to depose him in October 1664. He still officiated, his flock remaining staunch to him in spite of heavy finings. He had to seek safety wandering about—a homeless conventicler, put to the horn in July 1674, intercommuned two years later, taken and immured in Linlithgow prison for a year, indulged, and living on after the Restoration. He had the satisfaction of being reinstated in his church and manse. He died after 1693.[2]

Andrew Donaldson.

On the failure of the patrons to nominate successors to these honourable pastors, the Church had difficulty in filling the vacancies; and now it cannot be denied that the ordinaries promoted ignorant, worthless, contemptible creatures, well nicknamed 'The King's Curates.' Contemporary authorities of various parties are unanimous on this point. Burnet is not too bitter when he records: 'They were the worst preachers I ever heard: they were ignorant to a reproach: and many of them were openly vicious. They were a disgrace to orders, and the sacred functions: and were indeed the dregs and refuse of the northern

'The King's Curates.'

[1] Wodrow, *Hist.* i. 362.
[2] *Ibid.*, i. 409; ii. 325, 343; iii. 152; Ross, *Glimpses*, 222-35; App., 239.

parts.'[1] Kirkton corroborates Burnet, declaring that they were 'a sort of young lads unstudied and unbred, who hade all the properties of Jeroboams priests ... and so profane and void of conscience themselves that they believed there were none in any other. ... A gentleman in the north cursed the Presbyterian ministers, because, said he, since they left their churches, wee cannot get a lad to keep our cows, they turn all ministers.'[2] Tweeddale described them to Lauderdale as 'insufficient, scandalous, impudent fellows.'[3] It is satisfactory now to know that the almost incredible statements uttered by Stewart, Stirling, Brown, Wellwood, Shields, and commonly supposed to be gendered in Covenanting hatred and spite, were substantiated by Sir Robert Moray, Lauderdale's depute, who, after personal inquiry and observation, concluded that it was impossible to support such ignorant and scandalous men, 'unless the greatest part of them could be turned out.'[4]

Sir Robert Moray's testimony.

Riots at churches.

The evicted clergy harangued the people on the sin of intrusion. Apart from this, it is not natural to expect that the Scottish temper would have tamely submitted to these cruel and unwarrantable acts of tyranny, and the substitution of lewd clodpates for their loved and learned leaders. In Irongray, men and women convened to prevent the serving of the edict regarding Welsh; and William Arnot of Littlepark, drawing his sword as he placed his back to the church door, cried out boldly: 'Let me see who will place a minister here this day.' Another ebullition occurred when Bernard Saunderson came from the neighbouring parish of Keir, accompanied by his co-presbyters and an armed bodyguard, to fill Welsh's pulpit. A crowd of women, generalled by Margaret Smith, occupied the walled-in churchyard, a natural coign of vantage, and, after a hot skirmish of stones easily got from the Cluden, made the prelatic intruders beat a hasty retreat.[5]

Origin of the Galloway Rising.

A similar riot occurred on the attempt to settle John Jaffray of Monquhitter in Kirkcudbright, early in 1663. The Council took the matter up in May, and appointed a committee consisting of

---

[1] *Hist.*, i. 275.

[2] *Hist.*, 160-1.

[3] *Laud. Pap.*, ii. 207.

[4] Dodds, *Fifty Years*, 124; cf. *Naphtali*, 119, 135, 301, 302; Brown, *Apol. Narr.*, 270; Wellwood, *Sermon on* 1 *Peter* iv. 18; Burnet, i. 379, 441; *Laud. Pap.*, ii. 20.

[5] Wodrow, i. 365-7; Blackadder, *Memoirs*, 102 note; Kirkton, 162.

Linlithgow, Galloway, Annandale, Drumlanrig, and Wauchope of Niddrie (Montrose and Eglinton were afterwards added), to proceed to the district, to bring the offenders to justice, and to inquire if all the officials had obeyed the recent statutes. One hundred horse and two hundred foot of the Guards were told off to accompany the Commission and to exact for themselves free quarters and generous pay for officers and men. This order inaugurated the policy of repression by arms which resulted in the Galloway Rising. The Commission first sat at Kirkcudbright on 25th May, and examined Lord Kirkcudbright (who was a Protester and old friend of Wariston), John Carsan of Senwick, and John Euart (the latter two having formerly acted as provosts of the burgh), and also thirty-three widows and servants. They decerned that the three magistrates, being privy to the revolt, and five women rioters should be apprehended and removed to Edinburgh for trial, while other fourteen women should be put in the local bridewell till they found caution for their compearance before the Council. Some men went to prison for their wives. The Commission examined the Irongray delinquents at Dumfries on 30th May, and remitted Arnot to Edinburgh for trial, sending George Rome of Beoch to prison till he found caution to appear when called on. As a penalty for undiscovered culprits, they quartered soldiery on the parish, and exacted a bond of one hundred pounds from the heritors. The trial in August resulted in Carsan and Arnot being respectively fined eight thousand and five thousand merks—Arnot being forced to stand two Sabbaths in the public place of repentance in Irongray Church. Euart was finally sentenced to banishment. The five women from Kirkcudbright, Agnes Maxwell, Marion Brown, Jean Rennie, Christian M'Cavers, and Janet Biglaw, were ordered home to stand for two market-days at the Cross of Kirkcudbright, with a placard on each face announcing the crime, and the magistrates were empowered to scourge and banish the criminals if they tried to evade this doom. After sixteen weeks' imprisonment, and on finding caution, the male vicarious sufferers were released.[1]

It was while this Commission was visiting Galloway that the incident occurred which brought so much distress upon William Gordon, laird

The Earlston Gordons.

[1] Wodrow, i. 364-8.

of Earlston in Dalry, to be afterwards referred to.[1] The family of Gordon was strong in the Glenkens, and the Earlston Gordons had favoured Lollardy and other reform movements. They had also an influential local connection by marriage. John M'Michan, minister of Dalry, was evicted, and the bishop presented George Henry to the vacant charge. The Commissioners enjoined Earlston to take steps to have the presentee settled. Earlston replied, on 22nd May, declining the order, refusing to intrude, claiming the right of patronage, and stating that he too had nominated a pastor. They replied citing him to the Council to answer for contempt.[2] Before leaving Kirkcudbright the Commission appointed a bench of loyal magistrates under heavy caution, and left a party of the Guards to aid them in keeping order.

It was soon manifest that the would-be religious King and Council were not to brook bucolic pietists interfering with their sacred prerogatives and mission, or thwarting their infallible purposes.

Peden the Prophet, 1626-1686.

A remarkable and unique personage came into prominence at this critical time. Alexander Peden (1626-86), Pethein, or Peathine, was a native of Auchincloich, in the parish of Mauchline (now Sorn). Like his ancestry he was a bonnet-laird. He studied in Glasgow, and before entering the ministry became a teacher and precentor in Tarbolton and Fenwick. He was appointed minister of the Moorkirk of Glenluce in 1660. He did not conform and was deprived in 1662. Nevertheless, according to the charge preferred against him by the Privy Council on 24th February 1663, he continued in his office, 'labouring to keep the hearts of the people from the present government in Church and State.' At length, compelled to desist, he finished his parochial ministry with a dramatic climax. His sorrowful flock came to church to hear his farewell discourses. From morn till night he continued preaching, the hearers the while sobbing incessantly, all the more that he prophesied that they would never see his face in that pulpit again, for he was to become a homeless vagrant for his Master's cause. Then he lifted the sacred book to bear it away, and closed the pulpit door. 'He knocked hard upon it three times with his Bible, saying three times over, "I arrest thee in my Master's name, and never none enter thee, but such as come

---

[1] The Castle of Earlston still stands. It bears the inscription '1651;, W. G. M. H.'
[2] Wodrow, i. 369.

in at the door, as I did."' This malison rested on the pulpit long after Peden's death, his first successor being William Kyle, in 1693.[1]

The migrations through the south-west of Scotland of so many reputable, influential, and dogged opponents of the new repressive policy made the Lowlands lively, and created the necessity for the installation of a government agent as unique and as notorious as the elusive Peden. It was in September 1663 that the despot, Sir James Turner, was sent to the south to quell the disturbances. The vexation consequent on the operation of the obnoxious statutes was not confined to embittered Presbyterians. The less scrupulous opponents of Episcopacy showed antipathy in an offensive way. Church doors were locked in the incumbent's face: the tongues of bells were removed to make the hour of worship uncertain: the intruded pastors were terrified by rough-tongued men or stone-throwing termagants who adjured them to stay away and ruin no more souls: an ingenious herd-lad emptied a box full of pismires into a curate's boots, so as to torment him during service; and even more vulgar and vicious pranks were played upon the unhappy presentees.[2] On the other hand, the decorous multitudes of worshippers who gathered to hear the evicted clergy soon became armed convocations of the lieges.

The Lowlanders incensed.

---

[1] Wodrow, *Hist.*, ii. 4; iii. 73-5; iv. 396; *Analecta*, ii. 85, 86; Walker, *Some Remarkable Passages*, etc., in Fleming, *Six Saints*, i. 1-177; ii. 129.

[2] Kirkton, 161.

Barscob House, Balmaclellan

Irongray Church

The Clachan, Dalry

Sir James Turner

Dumfries

St. Bride's Church, Douglas

The battlefield at Rullion Green

THE PENTLAND RISING—FROM DALRY TO RULLION GREEN

CHAPTER TWENTY-THREE

THE RULE OF ROTHES AND
THE RISING OF RULLION GREEN

I N June 1663, Holyrood House once more resounded with revelry The mission of Lauderdale June 1663. when the new Commissioner, Rothes, and the Secretary of State, Lauderdale, took up residence there. Lauderdale had returned to displace Middleton, to undo the Billeting business, to make vengeance overtake Wariston, for whom formerly he had owned 'great friendship,' to guide Parliament in framing repressive measures for dissenters, to take the conceit out of the Church dignitaries, and generally to advance his own interests by proving to the King how clever and indispensable he was. His first step in debasing Middleton was the promotion of the bibulous Rothes to be Commissioner; and his second was his personal compearance in Parliament to get the crafty Acts of his rival expunged from the Statute Book.

John Leslie, seventh Earl and first Duke of Rothes, a coarse, illit- The Dukes of Rothes, 1630-1681. erate boor, salacious in talk and indecent in behaviour, was the best fitted to give effect to the atrocities conceived in the cunning brain of Archbishop Sharp. His greed of gain made him a tool most amenable to a persecutor. His carnal characteristics distinguished him as the type of man the King loved. He roguishly excused his own uncleanness of life by asserting that 'the King's Commissioner ought to represent his person.'[1] When Rothes arrived to preside, on 18th June, in the third Session of Parliament, 1663. session of Charles's first Parliament, 167 members met, including 2 archbishops, 8 bishops, 1 duke, 1 marquis, 35 earls, 4 viscounts,

[1] Burnet, i. 374-5.

26 lords, 48 county members, and 42 representatives of burghs. Rothes intimated the King's desire for the restoration of the Lords of Articles— the preparatory committee on business—a step which, by the aid of the bishops' votes, threw the legislative initiative and power into the hands of the King and his advisers.[1]

Johnston,
Lord
Wariston.

While the Estates were in session, a distinguished Covenanter lay in the Tolbooth— a political victim tied to the horns of the altar. This was none other than Lord Wariston. Long a fugitive abroad under sentence of death, Wariston was tracked by English spies to Rouen, where he was apprehended, and, on a writ of extradition, brought to London. While in Holland, according to Brown of Wamphray, an authority likely to know, Wariston had been cupped with evil intent by Dr. Bates, a royal physician, and left a wreck, weak, despondent, deprived of memory.[2] Middleton, who, with Dumfries and Secretary Bennet, examined him in London, found him to be the most timorous man he had ever seen, and suspected him of shamming.[3] He was sent to Edinburgh by sea and escorted to the Tolbooth with the usual indignity shown to traitors. On 8th July he was brought to the bar of Parliament to hear the doom pronounced in 1661, sending him to death by rope and axe at the Market Cross.[4] During this judicial interlude, according to Mackenzie, he was 'running up and down upon his knees begging mercy.'[5] Lauderdale also informed Moray of this wretched exhibition: 'I have often heard of a man feared out of his wits, but never saw it before; yet what he said was good sense enough, but he roared and cried and expressed more fear than ever I saw.'[6] His judges asked him if he had any reason to crave a delay of his execution. In a voice broken with sobs he replied that 'his memory was lost, that he remembered neither matter of law, nor matter of fact, nor a word of the bible'; and he begged a postponement so that ministers and physicians might prepare him for his end.[7] The more humane of the Parliament-men would have delayed his execution,

[1] *Act. Parl. Scot.*, vii. 449.
[2] Epistle, *Apol. Rel.*, 9.
[3] Middleton to Primrose, 3rd February 1663: *Wodrow MSS.*; Kirkton, 170 note.
[4] *Act. Parl. Scot.*, vii. 69, App. 95.
[5] *Memoirs*, 135.
[6] *Laud. Pap.*, i. 152, 155.
[7] *Ibid.*

but Lauderdale was anxious to have the bloody deed accomplished. Fourteen days' grace were allowed. On the 22nd July he was brought to 'ane gallous of extraordiner heicht ... set up at the Mercat Croce of Edinburgh.' On the scaffold he recovered his composure and read his 'Last Speech and Testimony,' which is a chaste confession of his sins, regret for compliance with Cromwell, an assertion of his innocence of the death of Charles, and an expression of his dying regard for the Royal House and for his own family. He publicly pleaded the merits of the Redeemer, and while crying out 'O pray, pray, praise, praise!' was turned over by the executioner. His head was fixed beside that of James Guthrie, and remained on the Netherbow for years, till it was removed at the instance of Sir William Drummond of Cromlix, his son-in-law, and Dalyell's lieutenant at Rullion Green.[1] The King was pleased to hear the news of Wariston's death.[2] Lauderdale, in response to the appeal of Archbishop Burnet, wrote apparently in Wariston's favour, but at the same time he advised his under-secretary, Moray, to be shy of the business and leave the matter alone. The heartless creature indicated his anxiety to receive his Bible in Hebrew without points, and his scent-bottles, rather than a pardon for his old friend.[3]

Execution of Wariston.

Thus passed from the very spot where he had often been the herald of constitutional freedom this eminent Scot, who, despite the defects of his impetuous nature and Border blood, was one of the most sincere and devout upholders of the Reformed faith in its Covenanted form. A pious lawyer—a rare phenomenon in his day—a conscientious politician—an equally rare subject (he had doubts about complying with the Sectaries), and a pure-minded man, Wariston possessed so many other-worldly characteristics that his son-in-law, Jerviswood, best described him as 'a man with God.' On the way to his own execution, Jerviswood looked over to Wariston's Close and exclaimed to Wariston's daughter, Helen: 'Many a sweet day and night with God had your now glorified father in that chamber.'

Character of Wariston.

While Wariston was lying in his blood, another bright luminary in the Church, James Wood, Professor of Divinity, and Principal of the

James Wood testimony.

---

[1] Nicoll, 394-6; *Naphtali*, 209; Omond, *Lord Advocates*, i. 182-5; Aldis, *List*, No. 1774, *Last Discourse of ... Wariston*; Wodrow, i. 355-62.

[2] *Laud. Pap.*, i. 153.

[3] *Ibid.*

Old College of St. Andrews, was summoned to the Council to be taken to task for retaining an office which he got from Cromwell. Wood was an able man, a staunch Resolutioner, a negotiator at Breda, the bosom friend and promoter of Sharp. Now his presence near the palace of the Archbishop was offensive; and the champion of Nonconformity, even although enfeebled in health, had to be removed. Not content with this, Sharp, after paying a visit to the sick man, promulgated the false report that Wood had confessed his defection, and intimated his willingness to live and die under the new discipline. This slander so hurt the dying Presbyter's feelings that he subscribed, before credible witnesses, a testimony asserting his 'wonted zeal for Presbyterial government,' and 'taking God, men, and angels to be witnesses, that I would count it my glory to seal this word of my testimony with my blood.' He died on 15th March 1664.[1] Sharp declared this document to be a testimony fraudulently obtained from a facile, moribund man, and caused the witnesses to it, and other recusant visitors of Wood, to be prosecuted as contemptuous, peace-breaking conventiclers. The Commission took up the case on 15th April, sent William Tullidaff, minister of Wemyss, to the Tolbooth for being a witness, ordered the deposition or suspension of Wood's visitors for conventicling in St. Andrews, and dispatched the seditious declaration to the hangman's fires. Another witness, John Carstairs, Wood's brother-in-law, wrote an account of the incident to Chancellor Glencairn, narrating the circumstances as above.[2] The affair afforded the Archbishop a lever for removing from the ministry several influential opponents of his policy. The Archbishop of Glasgow was equally assiduous in displacing the recusants, and there was good reason for the lament of the author of *Naphtali*, that the shepherds were smitten and the flocks scattered, the teachers removed, and the vineyard and sanctuary laid desolate, so that in whole provinces no preaching was heard, and the Sabbath was only known in sorrowful remembrance.[3] Hitherto the retributive statutes only applied to ministers ordained since 1649: that too was soon remedied, and the older Covenanters were netted as well.

Archbishop Sharp's vindictiveness.

[1] *Add. MSS.* 23251, fol. 9; Row, *Blair*, 465-7; Wodrow, i. 391, 404-6.
[2] M'Crie, *Veitch*, App. 491.
[3] *Naphtali*, III.

Naturally Lauderdale was anxious, until Parliament passed the 'Act rescinding the Acts of September 9, 1662, regarding Trusts and Billeting.'[1] He wrote to Moray: 'No dogg leads so buse a life. I am perfectly dazed.'[2] No wonder! He had to carouse with Rothes, examine Wariston, inquire into Middleton's peculation of £30,000 of army pay, and the fraud of Middleton's vicereine, who imagined that the furniture in Holyrood was her own, to mention the penalties for dissenters, and to explain the pretence of associating Papists with these unfortunates. There was a spice of blasphemy in his thought when he wrote to the King, the day after Saint Billeting's day, thus: 'By yesterday's Act you will see that Billeting is dead, buried, and descended.' Middleton, branded as a liar and peculator, degraded from position, despised by the nobility as an upstart, and 'de-courted,' as Nicoll happily phrased the dismissal, was relegated to the governorship of Tangier, where he died of a fall when drunk, in 1674.[3] Lauderdale had triumphed. Sharp's day-dream of a conjunction of these two rivals 'for good to poor Scotland' was dissipated. Still, in Rothes—Silenus enthroned on his cask—this 'Father in God' had a potentate who suited his purpose as well as Middleton.

Lauderdale's exacting duties.

Fate of Middleton.

The Government, influenced by English repressive legislation, on 10th July, passed an 'Act against separation and disobedience to ecclesiastical authority.'[4] It was popularly known as 'The Bishops' Drag-net.' It ordered ministers appointed before 1649 to obtain collation before 20th September; absentees and nonconformists to be suspended and deposed for persisting in disobedience; the Privy Council to remove delinquents and punish preachers not collated; parishioners to attend their own parish churches—withdrawers ('whether upon account of Popery or other disaffection') being liable to heavy fines as seditious persons; and, worst of all, enjoined the ministers to admonish delinquents, and send the names of the withdrawers to the Privy Council, who got power to inflict 'corporal punishment as they shall think fit.' These facts are worthy of attention: every parish had a Government informer; the Council could punish dissenters as they pleased. The latter fact explains the subsequent procedure of the truculent Councillors.

'The Bishops' Drag-net.'

---

[1] *Act. Parl. Scot.*, vii. 450, 471, Act 30; Mackenzie, *Memoirs*, 118, etc.

[2] *Laud. Pap.*, i. 148-71.

[3] Burnet, *Hist.*, i. 364 note.

[4] *Act. Parl. Scot.*, vii. 455, Act 9.

The Earl of Kincardine was one of the minority who recoiled from the new inquisition, which was an imitation of the cruel policy and deeds approved of by Primates Whitgift and Bancroft when dealing with English dissenters.[1]

Lauderdale, in writing to Moray, explained the meaning of this Statute thus: 'Penalties [are] calculated for our western dissenters (thogh the word papist be put in of course to beare them company), and it is hoped the penalties will be stronger arguments to move them to outward conformitie than any divines could use.' Charles, too, was pleased with the Act, caring nothing what cloak of religion men put on, so long as they were orderly citizens. Parliament further enacted that all persons holding offices of trust should take the Oath of Allegiance.[2] A Militia Act was also passed.[3] Thereafter, Lauderdale, vowing vengeance,

yielded to a clamour in certain circles for a National Synod as a panacea for the country's distemper and countenanced the Act for constituting it.[4] Never was a more Erastian Assembly contemplated. It made the clergy into puppets manipulated by the King, or his kinglets. The hierarchy, with its long tail of paid functionaries—the lay-elder was abolished—were to convene when and where the King ordered them to meet, under the Archbishop of St. Andrews, in presence of himself or deputy, to discuss subjects prescribed by the King, and to frame Acts only obligatory when confirmed by the King. By this deft touch of Lauderdale, the Church was converted into a college of pious scribes, and the Monarch into an infallible Pope. To complete the farce, the Synod never met.

In December 1660, Sharp boasted to Drummond: 'I have done more for the interest of Presbyterian Government in Scotland than any minister who can accuse me.' In November 1663, Sharp adjured Lauderdale: 'Your Lordship can never doubt but that my service and obsequiousness to his Majesty and to your Lordship will draw in a line.'[5] Sharp might reconcile these statements by his belief that extinction was the best interest of the Church he had betrayed. It was

---

[1] Hallam, *Const. Hist.*, i. 199, 213, 394.
[2] *Act. Parl. Scot.*, vii. 17, 463.
[3] *Ibid.*, 42, 480.
[4] *Ibid.*, 22, 465, August 21; Wodrow, i. 353.
[5] *Laud. Pap.*, i. 47, 89; *Laing MSS.*, 784.

not inappropriate that, on the last day on which the Estates met, a grant of the precious metals in the Ochils should be given to astute Lauderdale,[1] who returned to London satisfied that he had restored the 'good old form of government'—he should have added 'called Despotism.'

The two archbishops were advanced to the Privy Council, and the clerical brains were at work that day, 13th August 1663, when the famous 'Twenty Mile Act' was passed, 'by which the turbulent and disaffected ministers' got other twenty days wherein to conform, or remove with their whole households twenty miles from their churches, six miles outside a cathedral city, and three miles outside a royal burgh.'[2]

'Twenty Mile Act,' 13th August 1663.

Under this Act withdrawers from Synods were to be proceeded against. The bishops were busy pressing the constant moderators to deal with their refractory brethren; and the Privy Council had plenty to do giving effect to their latest proclamation, that the religious meetings of 'the outed ministers' were seditious convocations.[3] Repression made conventicling more popular; and Prelacy grew more distasteful to crowds, who listened to many vagrant Presbyterian pastors evicted from Ireland at the Restoration. Episcopacy, not having been legally suppressed there, was more easily re-established by the displacement of these nonconformists, who crossed the channel into Galloway. The Scots Council decreed that these 'wasps should have no countenance,' and, if found without passports, that they should be sent to prison. Turner and the Guards were set on to ferret them out. The churches became emptier. Discontent was on the increase.

The exactions from the nine hundred persons mentioned in the Act of Indemnity, 1662, had been made with such cruel exorbitancy that the victims were beggared and their best instincts violated. There was a short surcease of the extortion. Then a military party arrived in a district, and its commander demanded not only the unpaid fine, but three shillings a day for every trooper to be quartered till the fine was paid. There was no remeid of law. Seizure of goods was authorised.[4] There could be no error,

Exactions by Government officials.

---

[1] *Act. Parl. Scot.*, vii. 524.

[2] *Privy Counc. Rec.*: Twenty-eight Councillors present, including Rothes; Row, *Blair*, 447; Aldis, *List*, 1747.

[3] Proclaimed, 13th August; Aldis, *List*, 1759.

[4] *Act. Parl. Scot.*, vii. 203.

because the fine was *debitum fundi*,[1] whoever the occupier might be. No excuses were valid. None were too poor to pay. The exactors were thus licensed brigands, who beat, tortured and imprisoned, to gain their ends. The method for levying the sum of twenty shillings for withdrawing from public worship was simple. After sermon the incumbent called the congregational roll, and, marking the absentees, sent their names to the fining officer. He rode to quarters and waited for the fine. Or the troop rode up to church, called the congregation out, and seizing the visitors from other districts fined them, stripped them of their clothing, or detained them for further fleecing. They also drove the absentees to church, abusing the invalids on the march thither.[2] Insult was heaped on injury when the maltreated were coerced into signing a certificate, 'that the Captain had used them civilly and discreetly.' Corruption reigned everywhere. Moray is explicit on this point. From peer to pedee there was a vile lust for fines and loot, as will be proved. On the day Parliament rose, Sharp wrote to Sheldon pleading that Dumfries, who stuck to the peculating Middleton to the last, might get a share of the fines.[3]

People goaded to desperation.

The Advocate Mackenzie's excuse for the enormities—that no just government could be responsible for the extravagances of the soldiery—was mere trifling with the subject.[4] Guilty and innocent alike were goaded to desperation when the slightest show of disapproval led to sympathisers being registered as rebels. Yet despair lasted for years before defensive arms were resorted to by the persecuted.

Disturbances in Galloway.

Lieutenant Rattray and the foot guards in Kirkcudbright did not quell the Gallovidians, especially those of Anwoth, where the defiant spirit of Rutherford still lingered. From his pulpit John Mein, a true-blue Covenanter, had been ousted, and a young expectant, Alexander Robertson, son of the minister of Urr, in September boldly took his place, in spite of the guards. He it was who shortly afterwards encouraged the Balmaclellan rioters, marched with them to Dumfries and on to the Pentlands, for which he ultimately suffered.[5] Sir James Turner was sent by the Council to reinforce Rattray and to

---

[1] [Latin: 'a debt on the land'.]

[2] *Naphtali*, 130-4, App., 287; Kirkton, 200, 201; *Hind Let Loose*, 184.

[3] *Laud. Pap.*, ii. 20, App. i.

[4] *Vindication*, 10.

[5] Wodrow, ii. 21, 49, 50; *Just. Rec.*, i. 186.

put the disturbance down.[1] In Turner, who, as a soldier, knew Galloway well, the Government had a veteran agent, punctilious, remorseless, thorough. He was a product of an age which utilised men who emasculated themselves of the higher virtues, to become butchers of each other under a semi-chivalrous code of warfare, for pay, loot, and fame.[2] Romance was bred in him near the ruined castles of Borthwick and Dalkeith, where his father, a parish minister, read books and made poor rhymes.[3] By graduating at Glasgow in 1631, Turner redeemed himself from the illiterate condition which distinguished the other 'Dugald Dalgettys' in the pay of the Crown. In the evening of his life he employed his pen writing *Pallas Armata*, and other productions in prose and verse. Penniless, he sought advancement in Continental wars, and became a typical mercenary selling his sword for any cause. In his *Memoirs* he confessed: 'I had swallowed without chewing in Germanie a very dangerous maxime which militarie men then too much followed, which was that so we serve our master honestlie it is no matter what master we serve.' Loyal to this immoral maxim, he fought for foreigner, Covenanter, Engager, Montrose, Solemn Leaguers, for and against the King, for and against Presbytery and Prelacy. The King knighted him in 1662. Astonishingly, he never bled, save when he was drunk—a vulgar sin which 'brought me many inconveniences,' he wrote.[4] It only needed a licence to convert this bibulous brawler into a merciless brigand where there was a house to harry, or a fatted calf to kill. Yet with an incredible assurance, in an essay entitled 'A Christian under the Covenant,' Mr. Andrew Lang asserts that Turner was 'infinitely more of a Christian than the Saints of the Covenant.'[5] He, of course, in his special pleading, omits the fact that the Privy Council dismissed Turner upon receipt of an incriminating report on his cruelties.[6] Moray reported similarly. Defoe was nearest the truth when he asserted: 'It is impossible to give the details of the cruelties and inhuman usage the poor people suffered

---

[1] Turner, *Memoirs*, 139 (Bann. Club ed.).

[2] Cf. Scott, *A Legend of Montrose*, chap. ii.

[3] Professor Lee made the curious mistake of describing Turner as 'an Englishman': *Lectures on the History of the Church of Scotland*, ii. 331.

[4] *Memoirs*, 43.

[5] *Blackwood's Magazine*, clxxiv., 41-3, July 1903.

[6] *Memoirs*, 207, 209; *Privy Counc. Rec.* (20th February 1668)—*Decreta*, 36; *Laud. Pap.*, ii. 83, 100.

from this butcher, for such he was rather than a soldier.'[1] Turner, on the contrary, asseverated that Rothes and Sharp chid him for his leniency.[2]

Changes in the hierarchy, 1663.

In this unhappy period the hierarchy suffered several changes and losses. Sydserf, Bishop of Orkney, died on 29th September, 'little more than a year after his translation,' which made Burnet cynically record: 'He had died in more esteem if he had died a year before it.'[3] He was succeeded by Andrew Honyman, Archdeacon of St. Andrews, once a zealot for Presbytery, now the loyal understudy of Sharp. On 2nd November, Fairfull, Archbishop of Glasgow, also died in Edinburgh, and his see was given to Alexander Burnet of Aberdeen, who, in turn, was succeeded by Patrick Scougal, minister at Salton. The ceremonials of consecration and of installation were held in St. Andrews on 11th April 1664.'[4]

Status of the Church.

Again the Church was fully equipped with diocesan overseers. The system of government was unique. The bishops were virtually officers of the Crown: Kirk-Sessions, authorised by the bishop, might meet: the Exercise or Presbytery met with the bishop as moderator, or under the presidency of a 'constant moderator' nominated by the bishop: the diocesan Synod met and was presided over by the bishop: the national Synod was a Parliamentary chimera only.

Sharp miserable.

Sharp was miserable. He realised that the country was not at his back. His early friends flouted him as the Judas who had betrayed their Church. The aristocracy despised him as an upstart. The masses arrived at the same conclusion as James Mitchell, that he was the instigator of the national woes. Some needy hirelings and unbending Royalists gave him countenance. Sharp even confessed that 'the gangrene of separation from the Church' was spreading and making the position of the prelates precarious. This idea became fixed, got on his nerves, so that he began insinuating that the Privy Council was in league with recusants hatching some sinister plot. He entered himself heir to Laud's fatal policy of repression, which also recoiled on his own head when he tried the dragooning of other wills. At this juncture the King was willing to tolerate dissent for sake of shielding Popery; Lauderdale was indifferent

---

[1] *Hist.*, 208.
[2] Burnet, i. 379.
[3] *Hist.*, i. 237; Nicoll, 400.
[4] Nicoll, 403, 408; Row, *Blair*, 467.

as to what form of faith held the field; but Sharp felt an inward call to display a superior wisdom in the curative results of his policy.[1] He would establish the Court of High Commission, a weapon which other tyrants had found as impotent on the people as fatal to themselves; and for this purpose he betook himself to London, to advance his cherished policy, and to blame Chancellor Glencairn and others for their pusillanimity. His arrival was chronicled at home by the receipt of recriminating letters ordering rigorous treatment of the disaffected. The Oath of Allegiance was the touchstone. Many prominent citizens— Dalrymple of Stair, Dundas of Arniston, Mackenzie of Tarbet, and others—refused to disclaim the old Covenants.[2] Others gave up offices of trust. Charles was gracious to Sharp, who had an inquisitional ally in the Primate, Sheldon. Lauderdale, Moray, Argyll, Tweeddale, and Kincardine favoured conciliatory measures, but Lauderdale meantime acquiesced in Sharp's demands, 'persuaded he would ruin all: but, he said, he was resolved to give him line, for he had not credit enough to stop him.'[3] Lauderdale had for a second time to humiliate the treacherous Sharp and bring him to his knees in tears before the King, who henceforth was to recognise his servant as a knave, poltroon, and liar, to be used but not trusted.[4]

Court of High Commission, 1664.

Sharp humbled.

Early in the year 1664, Sharp returned to Edinburgh carrying a portfolio full of warrants, patents of bishoprics, and patronages. He was an exalted personage, Primate and Metropolitan of all Scotland, with the highest precedence in the land, and styled 'His Grace.' Douglas's prophecy had complete fulfilment: 'Pick a bishop to the bones, and he'll soon gather flesh and blood again.'[5]

Sharp exalted.

Sharp produced a warrant, dated 16th January 1664, for constituting a 'Commission for executing the laws in Church affairs,' which was another name for a Star Chamber, superseding the Privy Council. It was nicknamed *The Crail Court.* The tribunal was to last till November. Its members were specified—Sharp (President), Chancellor, Treasurer, Archbishop of Glasgow, Hamilton, Montrose, Argyll, Atholl, Eglinton,

The new Commission.

---

[1] Mathieson, *Politics*, ii. 210; Dodds, 125; Wodrow, i. 384; Burnet, i. 369 note.

[2] Wodrow, i. 345, 395; Row, *Blair*, 469.

[3] Burnet, i. 370, 378.

[4] *Ibid.*, i. 360; *Scottish Review*, iv. 6, 14; v. 76.

[5] Row, *Blair*, 462.

Linlithgow, Hume, Galloway, Annandale, Tweeddale, Leven, Moray, seven bishops, six lords, four law-lords, four gentlemen, five provosts of burghs, the Dean of Guild of Edinburgh for the provost, and Sir James Turner; any five, including a bishop, to be a quorum.[1] Every ecclesiastical offence was to come under their survey, and they had power to fine or imprison at will, and to have their orders implicitly executed by all officers of the Crown, without requiring indictments, defences, or evidence led. Their net had the smallest mesh. With Sharp at the head and Turner at the tail of this 'illegal monster,' as the author of *Naphtali* designated the Commission, the country was in peril of being cruelly devoured. It was no wonder that ostracised Brown wrote from Holland those telling chapters demonstrating the unlawfulness of hearing such heralds of the Gospel, and of obeying such a Commission.[2] The minutes of this Court have not yet been found. The well-informed contemporary author of *Naphtali* has recorded a few instances of the barbarities perpetrated, 'whereof there is no corner in the whole country, nor parish almost in the west, which cannot give evidence.'[3] *Ex ungue disce leonem.*[4]

Barbarities of the Commission.

The case of Ancrum was a typical one and the minister affected was likely to obtain the best protection of the authorities. James Scott was presented, at the end of 1665, to the pastorate of Livingstone— exiled for his faith. The antecedents of the unwelcome presentee, who got no call, were too well known.[5] He was a Borderer, a graduate of Edinburgh, a former Presbyter of Jedburgh, having been ordained in Kirktown, forty-nine years before, whence in 1619 he was translated to quiet Tongland in Galloway. There he contracted unholy habits. He became a *bon vivant*. He kept few of the laws. He left his pulpit empty for weeks; he helped himself to the church funds; he 'tabled' or enjoyed cards, draughts, dice; he was friendly to excommunicated Papists; he declined the superior Church courts; and he opposed the Covenant. The Assembly deposed him in 1639. Across the Border he became Episcopal minister of Ford in 1660, and had the ban of excommunication removed from him by the Bishop of Galloway in 1664. He was

James Scott of Ancrum.

[1] Wodrow, i. 384-6.
[2] *Apol. Narr.*, 270, 316.
[3] *Naphtali*, 130.
[4] [Latin: 'From the mark of its claw discover the lion.']
[5] Scott, *Fasti*, ii. 484, 503, 723; Peterkin, *Records*, 261.

an object of special solicitude to the first Restoration Parliament, which voted him a grant of one hundred pounds, increased to one hundred and fifty pounds, out of the diocese of Glasgow, or Galloway, because he was 'an extraordinary sufferer these twenty-four yeers byegone.'[1]

This was also a case for a conscientious congregation. Scott arrived in Ancrum to preach and be placed: his hearers, men and women, came to object—they confessed to be 'pressed in conscience' to declare to him their dissatisfaction with his entry. The women had a local pattern for being more valiant, in their own 'maiden Lylliard,' resting close by, whose epitaph declares:— *The rabbling of Scott.*

'Upon the English louns she laid mony thumps,
And, when her legs were cutted off, she fought upon her stumps.'

A young married woman, Turnbull, desirous of pressing home her rural views, seized Scott, the presentee, by his cloak. The ungallant Scott drew and used his pastoral staff. There were the usual Border cries. Her two brothers joined in the fray and took revenge. The local bench fined and imprisoned the rioters. That was not enough for the Council or the Commission. Four culprits were brought before the Commission to be sentenced 'as contemners of the Ordinances, to be scourged through the town, stigmatised with the letter T[raitor] at the Cross of Edinburgh, and thereafter imprisoned, and with the first ship to be carried to the Barbadoes Islands.' The Turnbull brothers of Ashieburn, married men, were afterwards sentenced to banishment in Barbadoes, and their sister to be scourged through the town of Jedburgh.[2] As the burghal hangman flogged the well-padded heroine, who was led through the streets by her brother, he turned his hateful duty into a popular, laughable pantomime. Mr. Grub, when animadverting on Wodrow and his acceptors for crediting Kirkton's version of what Mr. Grub designated a 'probably untrue story,' had not consulted the very credible contemporary book, *Naphtali*, the author of which points out, as if worthy of note, that the Commission had acted *ultra vires*[3] in ordering the stigma and transportation.[4] *Banishment of the offenders.*

[1] 23rd September 1663: *Act. Parl. Scot.*, vii. 81*a*, 484.
[2] *Naphtali*, 128; Row, *Blair*, 484; Kirkton, 209; Wodrow, i. 393.
[3] [Latin: outwith its powers.]
[4] Grub, *Hist.*, iii. 221 note; *Naphtali*, 125.

Another case which created a stir at the time was that of Alexander Smith, a graduate of Edinburgh, evicted minister of Colvend, who, after residing quietly at Leith, was charged with conventicling. At his examination he addressed Sharp as 'Sir,' instead of 'Your Grace.' Rothes demanded if Smith knew who the president was, when Smith intrepidly confessed that he recognised 'Mr. James Sharp, sometime fellow-minister with himself.' This reply was deemed treasonable, and Rothes ordered the hangman to put the minister in irons in 'The Thieves' Hole'—a filthy place—beside a furious, unfettered maniac, the intention being obvious. When his judges learned that the prisoner was visited and sustained by charitable friends they removed him into the Iron House, and ultimately ostracised him to Shetland. He was brought back to Edinburgh and was thereafter sent to North Ronaldshay, whence he returned to die on the Castlehill in 1673. Kirkton records: 'I heard him say he was in one island four years, where he had neither food nor fire to keep in a miserable life, his food being only barley, his feuel sea-tangle.'[1]

For somewhat similar offences a man named Black was scourged through Edinburgh.[2] The laird of Aikenhead, near Cathcart, James Hamilton, and his tenantry, became embroiled with a greedy local curate, who sought revenge by calling in the bishop as referee. The latter employed Sir James Turner. When the Commission heard Hamilton's defences, they mulcted him in a quarter's rent, and on his refusal to promise attendance on the new curate's services, they exacted another quarter, and handed him over to the tender mercies of Archbishop Burnet, who soon had him back before the Commission. No persuasion would induce him to take the oath of allegiance, unless the obnoxious clause regarding the supremacy was deleted. Rothes said he deserved hanging. They fined him £300 and banished him to Inverness. His estate was sequestrated to pay these fines; and even after his sentence was remitted, he was again incarcerated in the Tolbooth of Edinburgh, where he lay for months until another fine was paid, when he was liberated.[3]

---

[1] Nicoll, 441; Scott, *Fasti*, ii. 577; Kirkton, 209; *Naphtali*, 129.
[2] *Ibid.*, 129.
[3] Wodrow, i. 391-2.

John Porterfield, laird of Duchall, Kilmalcolm, absented himself from the services of his calumniating curate, and in consequence was invited by the Commission to take the oath, which in its amended form he was willing to do, had that been admissible. A fine of £500, to pay which the estate was sequestrated, and an injunction to reside in Elgin, were the beginning of a lifetime of persecution of this staunch non-juror.[1] For having like scruples about the oath, Walter Pringle of Greenknowes was fined £100 and sent to Elgin.[2]

The Court made a progress to the west to investigate similar cases, and to strengthen the hands of Burnet and his clergy. Among the ministers ordained before 1649 was William Guthrie in Fenwick, proprietor of Pitforthie, cousin of Guthrie the martyr, and a favourite student of Rutherford. An unbending Covenanter, he marched against Montrose, opposed the Engagement, was in the scuffle at Mauchline Moor, joined the Protesters, became a 'trier' under Cromwell—in a word, had done everything to make himself a marked man. He had found time to write a small book entitled *The Christian's Great Interest*, which had a great circulation at home and abroad. The patronage of the Earl of Eglinton, and his son-in-law, the Chancellor, Glencairn, saved him from the ejection which his brother John, in Tarbolton, now an outlaw, had suffered. Burnet insisted on displacing Guthrie, and in July 1664 sent Forbes, incumbent at Cadder, to announce his suspension. Notwithstanding, he was permitted to remain in Fenwick till October 1665, when he went north to Brechin, and on the tenth of that month died there, at the premature age of forty-five. Guthrie was one of the best specimens of the old Scots clergy, gentle of birth, scholarly, genial and witty, intensely evangelical, and yet not so straitlaced as to despise a sportsman's shot, cast of a fly, or an end at curling. According to Dr. John Owen he was 'one of the greatest divines that ever wrote.'[3]

The day after Guthrie's demise Burnet had the satisfaction of deposing Robert Maxwell, minister at Monkton, another persistent absentee from his Synod.[4]

[1] Wodrow, i. 392; ii. 226; iv. 137; *Naphtali*, 123.

[2] Wodrow, i. 394, 422.

[3] For Guthrie's Life, cf. Wodrow, i. 406; Row, *Blair*, 318 note, 430; *Select Biog.*, i. 335; ii. 33-80; *Analecta*, i. 47, 169; iii. 69; *Fasti*, iii. 168; Carslaw, *Life*, 1-118; Aldis, *List*, 1659.

[4] Wodrow, i. 411.

In 1660 vengeance had overtaken John Spreul, town-clerk of Glasgow, who, after a term in the Tolbooth of Edinburgh, found himself not able to break the Covenant, and exiled himself to escape a worse doom. He returned to skulk about by night. He was caught, offered the oath, which he refused, and was ordered out of the kingdom on pain of death. This sentence was remitted seven years later, when, as a frail old man,[1] he again ventured home to seek repose, and found it only in the jail.

The laity suffered crudest tribulation after the royal warrant of 17th September 1664 was issued, calling up all the fines payable by the eight hundred rebels according to the Act, 9th September 1662, and fixing the places of receipt. Stringent statutes and proclamations against clerical and lay conventiclers were repeated *ad nauseam*, so that an honest man dare hardly sneeze in public.

Meantime, on 30th May 1664, Chancellor Glencairn died of fever. The story ran that he was distressed over the persecutions which he had encouraged, lamented that he had raised a devil (Sharp) he could not lay again, and cried, when it was too late, for Douglas and other Presbyterian clergy to give him a soul-comforting viaticum.[2] Two months later the King gave his loyal servant a state funeral in St. Giles, and left his family to defray the charges.[3] In vain Sharp angled for the vacant Chancellorship, which, after a vacancy of three years, was given to Rothes.

Foreign politics as well as domestic troubles caused uneasiness and anxiety in the King and his advisers. By the English Uniformity Act the nonconformist clergy had been ejected from their pulpits without being forbidden to hold conventicles. In May 1664, a strict Conventicle Act discharged private religious conventions. Discontent grew and became dangerous. Malcontents sought safety over the seas, keeping in touch with their friends by correspondence, or by secret agents, who flitted about fomenting discord. For daring to write wifely letters to

her husband, Mrs. Robert Trail was put in prison.[4] Before hostilities broke out between England and the Dutch Republic in 1664, some exiled incendiaries promoted an insurrection in Britain, in which they

[1] Wodrow, i. 75, 413; ii. 196.
[2] Row, *Blair*, 469; Nicoll, 428.
[3] Wodrow, i. 417 note.
[4] *Ibid.*, 423.

expected subsidy and aid from Holland and France. It came to nought. Colonel Gibby Ker, who escaped seizure as an accomplice of Colonel Blood, gave the States glowing accounts of what the westland Whigs would do. Anticipating the peril, the Scots Estates, presided over by Sharp, voted the King a handsome subsidy, although the country was confessedly bankrupt.[1] The combination of Holland and France emboldened the Scots malcontents still more, till the English fleet crippled the Dutch. The States-General passed a secret resolution to assist the Scots with arms and money as soon as the 'friends of religion' possessed themselves of suitable towns and forts.[2] Spies had wormed out these designs, and the terrified Council kept alert. Sharp advocated the mobilisation of military, ostensibly to meet the Dutch, but in reality to quell the Covenanters. Directed by Lauderdale, Rothes, fortified by many new commissions, the choicest of which was Chief Collector of the Fines, managed Scotland. He was too much a man of the world to be an implacable persecutor, and tradition asserted that when his conventicling wife invited some rebel ministers to Leslie House, where the Chancellor saw them, he said, 'My Lady, I would advise you to keep your chickens in about, else I may pick up some of them.'[3] He was a drag on the truculent bishops. When muddled, he had visions of the invading 'Butterboxes'; when sober, he declared, 'The ffayns [fines] torments me.'[4]

Chancellor Rothes.

In their alarm the Scots Privy Council dispatched Archbishop Burnet (who, in writing to Arlington, mentioned the assembling of armed fanatics, and recommended the employment of the fines in moulding a militia) to London to expose the danger, and obtain a warrant for apprehending some westland gentlemen most likely to lead the Whigs if occasion served.[5] Orders came for the incarceration of these influential suspects in the very fortresses which the insurgents hoped to seize. Among their number were Major-General Robert Montgomery, brother of the Earl of Eglinton, Cunningham of Cunninghamhead, Maxwell of Nether Pollok, Campbell of Cessnock, Mure of Rowallan, Stewart of Coltness, Holborn of Menstrie, Sir George Munro, Colonel

Alarm of Privy Council.

[1] *Act. Parl. Scot.*, vii. 530; *Laud. Pap.*, i. 202, 206, 220.
[2] Dodds, *Fifty Years*, 132-7; M'Crie, *Veitch*, 378.
[3] M'Crie, *Veitch*, 295.
[4] *Laud. Pap.*, i. 206-20.
[5] 10th February 1666: *Rec. Off. State Papers*, cxxxvii. 239.

Robert Halket, Chiesley of Kerswell, Dunlop of that Ilk, and others.[1]
Sir Patrick Hume and other gentlemen were also imprisoned at this

Measures for
suppressing
the Whigs.

time. The activity and brutality with which the officers of the law and the soldiery executed the proclamation of 3rd October, exacting the fines of the non-jurors, made the law-abiding peasants sullen, their bolder brethren roused and revolutionary. Itinerant hosts of armed worshippers now assembled wherever John Osburn, preacher in Keir—'the Mountain Beadle'—convened the faithful to hear, or partake of the ordinances dispensed by Welsh, Semple, Blackadder, Arnot, Douglas, Peden, Reid, Wilkie, and Crookshanks. These fleet-footed heralds, following Peden's example, rode about in hodden-grey clothes, armed, and sometimes in masks. Rothes informed Lauderdale of their gatherings for worship and sacraments in the wilds, and that he

Turner
employed in
the west.

had sent troops to 'have a hit at them.'[2] That hard hitter was Sir James Turner, who, with one hundred and forty horse and foot guards, was let loose in the south-west for two months in the autumn of 1665.[3] Turks never behaved worse. He in vain locked Osburn in the Thieves' Hole in Dumfries, without food, 'keeping the key the space of three days himself,' in order to force him to confess the hiding-place of Welsh and Semple.[4]

'A gentleman in Galloway' gave the authors of *Naphtali* 'Some Instances of the Sufferings of Galloway and Nithsdale,' which for barbarity have few parallels in our annals. The soldiers exceeded the fines scheduled, took quarters where they pleased, rioted on the best, travelled with hounds and took the nearest sheep, and sometimes threw the children's broth for dog's-meat, raided cattle, ejected widows, beat complainers, violated women, mocked and cursed during family

Turner's
device.

worship, and desolated many a happy home.[5] To add insult to injury, the oppressed were compelled to subscribe a certificate 'that Sir James had used them civilly and discreetly,' which excluded them from all

---

[1] Wodrow, i. 425; Dodds, 139; *Laud. Pap.*, i. 206; ii. App. A. xxxi.; Burnet, i. 377.
[2] Reply to Lauderdale, 24th November 1665: *Laud. Pap.*, i. 233.
[3] *Memoirs*, 140.
[4] *Wodrow MSS.*, xl. T. 54; M'Crie, *Veitch*, 51 note.
[5] *Naphtali*, 136, 287; Wodrow, ii. 9 note; cf. Barmagechan's sufferings, Wodrow, iv. 334-6.

hope of redress.[1] When these and worse offences were afterwards charged against Turner and Ballantine by the Crown, Turner pleaded that he never exceeded his orders, and had actually shown leniency.[2] This infamous business of fining was a diabolical method of enriching the beggared Royalist gentry at the expense of the thrifty middle classes, as is proved by the correspondence of Rothes. The mustering of forces to oppose the Dutch, in reality a cunning suggestion of Sharp for procuring available exterminators of the Whigs, so alarmed Rothes, that he informed Lauderdale that the embodiment of the militia would ruin Annandale, Atholl, and Airlie, who were dependent on the fines to save their fortunes—the creditors of Annandale having staved off his bankruptcy to allow him time to scoop in fines, else he 'will immediately perish in his ffortune yeay at this verie next tearme.'[3] In these circumstances is it to be marvelled at that a vulgar curate in Galloway vowed in his pulpit: 'God nor I be hanged over this pulpit, but I shall gar [force] you all come in from the highest to the lowest.'[4]

Sharp reported that the Scots in 1665 were 'aloft and discomposed,' unwilling to comply with the Government measures, deluded, turbulent, and 'gadding after those who are disorderly.'[5] His coadjutor, Burnet, feared a conspiracy between the Ulster Presbyterians and the westland Whigs, a year before Rothes complained of their actual co-operation in Dumfries in March 1666.[6] The 7th December 1665 was a fateful day in the Privy Council. An Act of Eviction was then passed, by which the last of the ministerial recusants and their households were forced to leave the manses for homes in other parishes to save themselves from jail, while another Act declared all conventicles to be 'seminaries of separation and rebellion,' and frequenters of them to be traitors to be apprehended by 'all our public ministers.'[7] Another proclamation demanded the compearance of the eleven leading field-preachers: Welsh of Irongray, Semple (Kirkpatrick-Durham), Black-

Unrest in the Westlands

---

[1] *Reg. of Synod of Galloway*, 52-3.

[2] *Memoirs*, 192.

[3] *Laud. Pap.*, i. 237-8: Charles gave Atholl a precept of £6000 on the fines; *Chron. of Atholl*, 155: Countess of Atholl to Countess of Lauderdale, 20th February 1666.

[4] Wodrow, ii. 9 note.

[5] *Laing MSS.*, 784.

[6] *Laud. Pap.*, i. 235; ii. xviii.

[7] Wodrow, i. 428, 430 note.

adder (Troqueer), Archibald (Dunscore), Arnot (Tongland), John Douglas (Crailing?), Peden (Glenluce), William Reid (Rattray), Wilkie (Twynholm), John Crookshanks, (Rogerton), and John Osburn (Keir).[1] In April 1666 the Synod of Galloway drew Sir James Turner's attention to some of these preachers.[2] The order was ignored.

Early in the year 1666 the Council was staggered by the dissemination of a little epoch-making book entitled '*An Apologeticall Relation of the particular sufferings of the faithfull ministers and professours of the Church of Scotland since 1660, etc. etc.*, By a well-wisher to the good old cause.' It was printed abroad in 1665 (12mo, 424 pp.). Its author, John Brown of Wamphray, had timeously returned a Roland for an Oliver out of his place of exile. This treatise in twenty-three sections deals trenchantly with every aspect of the dispute, and powerfully maintains the righteousness of the principles and actions of the Covenanters, even to justifying their resistance to their unconstitutional governors. Acknowledging its dangerous import the Council at once proclaimed it seditious, ordered the hangman to burn it at the Cross, and attached a fine of £2000 Scots to any possessor of it. When Sharp forwarded it to Lauderdale he unclerically styled it 'a damned book,' which had fired the west and had turned the country's quarrel into a defiance of the Crown.[3] Mrs. James Guthrie and Sophia, the widow and daughter of the martyr, had a copy—probably a present from the author, who vindicates the martyr in it. Because they refused to state what they knew about the work they were banished to a close prison in Zetland.[4]

In March Turner was again sent south with one hundred and twenty foot-guards.[5] From his headquarters in Dumfries he gladly sent out his booted apostles to begin business 'at the old rate,' as Burnet grimly recorded the fact. Irritation succeeded irritation. The 'Commission for Discipline,' passed on 7th December, was now operating, so that influential persons who refused to help the curates in their so-called discipline and informing were liable to be fined and outlawed. Still worse, a 'Proclamation for procuring obedience to ecclesiastical

---

[1] Proclaimed 25th January 1666: *ibid.* ii. 4

[2] *Register*, 48.

[3] *Laing MSS.*, 784, 9th February 1666.

[4] Wodrow, ii. 7; *Reg. Sec. Conc.*, 8th February 1666.

[5] *Memoirs*, 142.

authority, October 11, 1666,' made proprietors liable for the orderliness of all residents on their lands, with power to evict the nonconformists, also magistrates liable for citizens in burghs, and heads of houses for their servants—the escheits as a reward falling to the proprietors, whom failing, to the informers.[1] Repressive measures, conceived by Sharp, Burnet, and the Privy Council, and now so specialised that there was no hole for a church mouse to escape by, made the stalwart men of the Glenkens ripe for a rising had they dared, being aware that two veterans, Dalyell and Drummond, with terrible reputations from Russian wars, now commanded the army. In October 1666 the Bishop and Synod of Galloway remonstrated with Turner for his illegalities in Kelton and Girthon of which the heritors complained.[2]

The atrocities of Turner's ruffians were more than Gallovidian blood could longer stand. It was reported that the leaders of the insurgents incited them by stating that Dalyell was coming to hang every man at his own door and that one hundred had been hanged in Glasgow.[3] They rose in arms.[4] It fell out thus: John Maclellan, laird of Barscob,[5] in Balmaclellan parish, with three other fugitives for conscience' sake, forsook their hiding in the rainy hills to seek food in the quaint clachan of St. John's, Dalry, on Tuesday morning, 13th November 1666. On their way they met some peasants, driven by Corporal George Deanes

Cause of the rising in the Glenkens, 1666.

[1] Wodrow, ii. 15 note; cf. *Act. Parl. Scot.*, vii. 455, 456; *Laud. Pap.*, ii. lxxiv.

[2] *Register of Synod*, 68.

[3] *State Papers* (Charles II.), 76, 110.

[4] I have compiled this account of the rising from the following works: *Naphtali*, 137; Turner, *Memoirs*, 146; Nicoll, 451; Kirkton, 229; Burnet, i. 418; Blackadder, *Memoirs*, 121; *Laud. Pap.*, i. 245, 248, 251; M'Crie, *Wallace's Narrative*, 355; *ibid.*, *Sempil MS.*, 380; *Hind Let Loose*, 108; Row, *Blair*, 501; *Life of A. Reid*, 17; Wodrow, ii. 17; *Wodrow MSS., Declaration of Whigs*, xxxii., 59; *ibid., True Relation of the Sufferings in Nithsdale and Galloway*, 60, 61, 62; *Mein's Letters*, Record Office (Charles II.), 76, 110; 102, 268; 156 275; 106, 107, 295; Dodds, *Fifty Years*, 144; *Narr. of Battle* (1856); Law, 16; *Chron. of Frasers*, 463; Fleming, *Six Saints*, var. loc.; *Scots Worthies*, art. M'Kail, Paton, etc.; *Just. Rec.*, i. 159-86 (Scot. Hist. Soc.); *Ayrshire Ballads*—'The Battle,' etc.—40; Omond, *Lord Advocates*, i. 189; J. K. Hewison (*Scotsman*, 14th September 1901), 'Fresh Light on Rullion Green'; Terry, *The Pentland Rising*, (1905); *The Register of the Synod*, (Kirkcudbright, 1856); Stark, *Book of Kirkpatrick-Durham*, 78; Thomson, *Martyr Graves*, 1-18; R. L. Stevenson, *The Pentland Rising: a Page of History*, 1666; *Reg. Sec. Conc.*

[5] Barscob House still stands. On the door lintel are the initials and arms of William Maclellan and M. Gordon, his wife; on a window the date 1648.

and three soldiers of Sir Alexander Thomson's company of the guards—
the fine-raising garrison of Dalry—proceeding to thresh the corn of a
poor old farmer named Grier, in order to obtain the fine for absence
from church, which Grier had not paid before fleeing from his home.
The wanderers were angry, but passed by, meantime saying nothing.
They had reached the clachan alehouse and sat down to breakfast when
the village resounded with the cry that Grier had been seized, bound
'hand and foot like a beast, ready to be carried along,' and that his
captors 'were threatening to strip him naked and set him on a hot
gridiron because he could not pay.' Barscob's party ran and caught the
fiends red-handed.[1]

Rescue by Barscob.

'Why do you use the honest man so?' cried Barscob. 'How dare you
bind the old man?' asked others. 'How dare you challenge?' replied
the King's men. Swords were drawn. Barscob, for lack of ball, rammed
his tobacco pipe into his pistol, fired, and grounded Deanes beside his
victim. The comrades of Deanes, after a spirited defence, surrendered.
The news soon reached Balmaclellan, where a conventicle, probably
conducted by Alexander Robertson, was in progress.[2] At this very time
the evicted minister, Thomas Verner, Robertson, and other preachers
were engaging the attention of Turner, by request of the Synod.[3] The
conventiclers, fearing punishment for implication in the affair at Dalry,
boldly captured the local garrison of sixteen men, killing one in the
ruffle, on Wednesday. Thus one rash emergent led to another. These
united parties, forecasting trouble, concluded that their only safety lay
in now capturing Turner himself, and holding him as hostage till their
grievances were redressed.[4] With Turner in custody they could approach
the King and Council with a chance of being listened to. To march to
the Capital and in person present their petition was an after-resolve.

Muster of conventicles.

Turner's 'inconveniences' made it possible. Fleet feet ran through
friendliest of parishes, and a muster of well-wishers was summoned
to the historic church of Irongray, four miles west of Dumfries, before

[1] M'Crie, *Sempil MS.*, Notices of Wallace in *Veitch*, 382.

[2] *Just. Rec.*, i. 186.

[3] Vernor or Warner, April 1666: *Register*, 48.

[4] Brit. Mus., *Add. MSS.*, 23245, fol. 6, *Declaration of Pentland Rebels*; *ibid.*, fol. 7,
Council to Charles II. Turner was appointed Lieutenant-Colonel on 28th July 1666:
Reg. Sec. Conc., Acta, 52.

sundown.[1] That night dauntless Deanes rode in to Turner and, showing his wounds, swore he had been shot for refusing to subscribe the Covenant.[2] The jovial colonel sent for his men and retired to bed indisposed. The increasing band of insurgents, fifty-four riders in cloaks on Galloway nags led by Barscob, and one hundred and fifty pedestrians led by John Neilson of Corsock and probationer Robertson, were impeded by torrential rain and the fallen night, and did not reach the rendezvous till after break of day on Thursday. Here a mysterious person called 'Mr.' or 'Captain' Andrew Gray, whose antecedents remained a puzzle to Turner, appeared and, producing a commission, installed himself as commander. He rode on 'a little beast' at the head of Barscob's troop over Devorgilla's Bridge into Dumfries, where a small party beset Bailie Finnie's house and called on Turner to surrender. No warrior bold replied. At the window appeared a vision of 'night cap, night gown, drawers, and socks,' and a voice was heard crying for quarter. Neilson, who was 'a meek and generous gentleman,' promised it, and the fierce dragoon descended between two rows of drawn blades and primed pistols—a ludicrous picture of peace. Gray was about to shoot him there, when Neilson, interposing, gallantly said: 'You shall as soon kill me, for I have given him quarters.' It was about nine o'clock. Gray ransacked Turner's chest and secured his papers and over six thousand merks. He mounted the colonel's charger, and had Sir James in his flannels placed on the little, discarded, barebacked Galloway, which was led by a halter to the Cross, where the Covenanters, as was their wont, pledged a health to the King, swore allegiance to the Covenant, and reviled the bishops. Then they marched to Nith Sands, opposite the green slope where Blackadder's church stood, in order to hold a council of war. Meantime arms were searched for, and in a scuffle another soldier was killed. They permitted Turner to dress before taking him with them. The cavalcade, now better armed, resumed its fateful march up Cluden and Cairn to Glencairn Kirk, where a halt was made. All night they marched over the moorland to Dalry, some thirty-two

Capture of Turner in Dumfries.

---

[1] The local landlords were interrelated by blood and marriage. In the Glenkens the strong clan of the Gordons, one of whom married Barscob, were supporters of the Covenant. Neilson of Corsock married Mary Maclellan. Corsock is in Kirkpatrick-Durham parish, Kirkcudbrightshire.

[2] Turner, *Memoirs*, 148.

miles in all, that day (16th). On an alarm they marched through part of the next night to the safer wilds of Carsphairn. They had no plans and no leader, for Gray mysteriously disappeared at this place. They used Turner well. Robertson and other messengers were dispatched to Ayrshire and Edinburgh to solicit succour and encouragement from sympathisers.

Irvine rides to Edinburgh with news. Meantime Stephen Irvine, a Dumfries bailie, rode to the Capital with the news.[1] Rothes was on his way to London. Sharp, as interim president of the Council, had the acceptable opportunity to gratify his vindictive spirit, which is manifested in the communication from the Council to Rothes recommending, as a first precaution, the apprehension of all landlords still refusing to disown the Covenant. The new commander-in-chief, Lieutenant-General Dalyell, was ordered to march to the west, with the regulars and probably some Midlothian Fencibles, in all two thousand five hundred foot and six troops of horse.[2] A proclamation on the 21st declared the rising to be rebellion, and all who refused to lay down arms 'incorrigible and desperate traitors incapable of mercy and pardon.'[3] The Fencibles were mustering in selected counties.

March of the regulars and insurgents in November 1666. The regulars under Dalyell and Drummond began their march from all quarters on Sabbath, 18th November, and reached Glasgow on the 20th, Kilmarnock 22nd, Mauchline 24th, Strathaven 25th, Lanark, afternoon of 26th, Calder 27th, Currie and Rullion Green 28th.[4] The insurgents were moving advisedly through districts well known to be hallowed by memories of struggles for faith and freedom, bivouacking in the parish churches by night, and inviting recruits by day, as they passed through Dalmellington (18), Tarbolton (19), Ayr (20), Coylton (21), Ochiltree (22), Cumnock (23), Muirkirk and Douglas (24), Lesmahagow and Lanark (Sunday, 25), Bathgate and Newbridge (26-27), Colinton (27-28), Rullion Green (Wednesday, 28).

The march of the Covenanters was not without curious episodes. The host was a moving conventicle sounding with prayer and sermon. At Dalmellington, Welsh of Irongray came into camp, and social Turner,

---

[1] *Reg. Sec. Conc., Acta*, 602.

[2] *State Papers* (Charles II.), 116, 248.

[3] Wodrow, ii. 20; *Reg. Sec. Conc., Acta*, 628.

[4] Drummond to Rothes, 29th November 1666: *Scot. Hist. Rev.*, iii. 12, 451; iv. 13, 114.

anxious to hear this famous divine's inordinate grace, pledged a tankard of ale to the field-preacher, to enjoy whose intemperate eloquence many flocked in. Welsh went home to beat up recruits. John Ross, a Mauchline man, and John Shields, Mearns, were sent to scout, and being captured near Kilmarnock, were afterwards tried and hanged.[1]
At the Bridge of Doon, James Wallace, proprietor of Auchans—of the stout stock that gave Scotland its greatest hero, an old campaigner in the Civil Wars, who had fought for Crown and Covenant, and been taken at Kilsyth and Dunbar, a former lieutenant-colonel of the foot-guards—joined the expedition and was appointed commander. This Christian soldier, like Havelock of our day, was a man of piety and purity, whose patriotism and love of justice impelled him to the side of the persecuted, so that he formed a striking contrast to the mercenary swashbucklers he opposed. To the admiration of Turner, he drilled his seven hundred men splendidly.

Commander James Wallace.

Fearing an attack from Dalyell, the Covenanters turned into the wild country round Cumnock, and in a tempest of rain plunged over disastrous Ayrsmoss on to the Moor Kirk of Kyle, wherein they lay all night drenched, and without food or fire. No wonder Turner recorded: 'I never sawe lustier fellows then these foote were, or better marchers.'[2] Daunted and dashed, some more craven, counselled by the Irish preacher Andrew M'Cormick and the probationer Robertson, wished to give up the enterprise. Even sapient, prophetic Peden disappeared through the mist. Intrepid Wallace defied the storm, pushed into Douglasdale, and gave his men shelter in St. Bride's among the tombs of the warrior Douglases. A council of war was held, with the usual religious exercises. Their resolve to proceed was fixed. Their aim was defence of the Faith. They had the honour and chivalry to reject a motion that Turner now should be pistolled. When the force arrived in Lanark they were a thousand strong, one-half being mounted, with four or five experienced officers only to lead them.

Turner's opinion of his captors.

When daylight broke on Monday the 26th, they assembled to renew the Solemn League and Covenant. John Guthrie, evicted minister of Tarbolton, standing on the stairs of Lanark Tolbooth, preached to the

Covenant renewed at Lanark.

[1] 'Their heads are buried in the Laigh Churchyard, Kilmarnock; cf. Thomson, *Martyr Graves*, 287-9.
[2] *Memoirs*, 164.

infantry; at the Townhead, Gabriel Semple addressed the horsemen. The Covenant was recited and all joyfully swore it with uplifted hands. At this time a preliminary manifesto, explaining the origin and aim of the insurrection, was framed, to the effect that they were assembled to maintain a bond of self-defence, to uphold the trust in the Covenant, to protest against the apostasy of the times, and to resist cruel usage.[1]

At Lanark a suspected intriguer, William Laurie of Blackwood, factor to the Earl of Douglas, came to express the desire of the Duke of Hamilton for a peaceable settlement; and again at Newbridge he arrived on his fruitless errand. To Colinton he brought a proposal from Dalyell that the rebels should accept the terms of the Government, to which they replied that they were simply going to the Council to petition for redress. Dalyell honourably sent this communication to the Council, who being dissatisfied, responded that all the Government could accede to was their submission, with the liberty to petition for mercy. The persecuted knew exactly what this meant to 'Sharp of that Ilk,' but it seems certain that the terms of this reply never reached the petitioners, who considered that there was a 'cessation' sinfully broken by the commencement of hostilities.[2]

March to Edinburgh.

Dalyell entered Lanark the day Wallace left it. Wallace's route was north to Bathgate, 'through pitiful broken moores,' so closely pressed by Drummond's horse that he was forced to march on through a sleet storm in the darkest of nights (26th-27th), rather than halt and be chilled to death in the shelterless waste. When they arrived at Newbridge they were a bewildered, wretched rabble—still unconquerable. Rather than fall out of the ranks they tied themselves together, and but few deserted. At length the frowning citadel of Edinburgh came in view, and the sheltering church of Colinton, four miles from the Capital. They had been advised to expect allies in Midlothian who never showed face. The miserable bivouack in Colinton Churchyard, newly mantled with frosted snow, was disturbed early in the morning of the 28th by sounds of musketry. It was an affair of outposts, and the Edinburgh Fencibles drew the first Covenanting blood. Wallace lifted his eyes to the hills for aid and safety. The Pentlands looked pure and glorious: they proved

[1] *Wodrow MSS.*, xxxii. 59; *Hist.*, ii. 25; *Declaration of the Western Party why they Lifted Arms*; *Add. MSS.*, Brit. Mus., 23245, fol. 6.
[2] *Naphtali*, 140.

cold, pitiless, cruel. Up and away trudging to their doom, the insurgents, still encouraged by thirty-two ministers, followed Wallace over ground where formerly Cromwell and Leslie manoeuvred, swinging round the hillfoots by way of Dreghorn Castle, Fulford (Woodhouselee), and Flotterstone (Ingliston) Bridge to Rullion Green—an ancient mart.[1]

Rullion Green was well known to southern herds and drovers. Never had 'such beasts'—that is the bitter taunt of Maitland of Hatton, one of their slayers—entered that tryst—soon to be a shambles. They looked like hunted sheep that had escaped the shearing, ragged in pelt and dirty in cloot—veritable 'rullions,' as Ayrshire folk style unkempt characters to this day. As fast as foot could carry him, Dalyell was on the way from Currie, down the old drove road between Capelaw and Bellshill, past Kirktown and St. Catherine's Chapel—now submerged in the Compensation Pond. The last stand at Rullion Green.

Wallace's trained eye chose the last stand on the south-east base of Turnhouse Hill, on a slope called Rullion Green, Rullim Green, Yorling's Green, Gallowhill. A broad, verdant glacis stretches up to a small plateau, carpeted with wire grass and bilberry bushes. It lies to the south-west of the monument to his fallen comrades.[2] A deep natural ditch bounds the slope on the north-west, intersecting the old drove road. Overhead was Turnhouse Hill, 1500 feet high. To the south rose Lawhead, a lovely green boss in summer. To the west and south the ground stretches in solid waves, as if frozen in their rolling, to the base of Carnethy Hill. Between Lawhead and Turnhouse the Covenanters stood. The trysting-place had on the north a declivity of three hundred feet in half a mile till it reached the red-breasted braes of the Castlelaw Hill, beneath which the Glencorse Burn 'drums and pours in cunning wimples in that glen.'[3]

Wallace made three dispositions. Barscob and his Galloway troop he stationed on his right, near Lawhead. Major Joseph Learmont, laird of Newholm, was in command of the horse on the left wing. Wallace directed the foot in the centre. A pioneer party of Drummond's cavalry, under Ogilvy, made a gallant onset upon Learmont, only emptying a Disposition of the Whig forces.

[1] 'House of Muir' market is mentioned in *Act. Parl. Scot.* (1581), iii. 238.

[2] 'This stone was formerly placed more to the north-east, and was lifted to this position by a late proprietor.

[3] R. L. Stevenson to Crockett.

few saddles before retreating. The armed pastors joined in the fray, and two of them, Crookshanks and M'Cormick, bit the dust. Drummond, perceiving that he could not dislodge Wallace without infantry reinforcements, drew off his cavalry and waited on Castlelaw Hill till the tardy Dalyell appeared. It was near sunset before Dalyell had his army marshalled in regulation order—himself, Atholl, and Airlie at the head of a body of cavalry on the left wing, Drummond with the Life Guards, Commissioner's troop, and other horse on the right wing, and the infantry under Linlithgow in the centre, and kept as the reserve.

General Dalyell's position.

The Covenanters watched Dalyell coolly riding about examining their position—a figure too 'kenspeckle' to be mistaken or forgotten, grim and grizzly of aspect, with his long beard unshorn since the fall of Charles's head, the very 'Muscovite Beast' of their imagination. The Royalists, on the other hand, saw against the dusky sky-line the figures of ecstatic preachers—Welsh and Semple throwing their arms into the air like the seers of old, and heard them crying 'The Great God of Jacob,' 'The Great God of Jacob,' 'See the Lord of Hosts fighting for us!' and other Judaic slogans meant to fan the courage of their doomed brethren.[1] The hillsides re-echoed the melodies of the 71st and 78th Psalms. It was not till after an exercise of prayer and praise that the Covenanters resolved to fight should they be attacked; still they expected some peaceful answer from the Council, and they disclaimed all desire to shed blood. For them it was an unequal fight. They had only sixty muskets, forty pair of pistols, and twenty pounds of loose powder.[2] It must have been

Condition of the insurgents.

with great contempt that Dalyell, supported by three thousand well-armed and disciplined troops, saw the nine hundred irregulars, under Wallace and Learmont, stand before him. Their sorry condition is best described in a contemporary manuscript:—

> 'It was a Januar or December,
> Or else the end of cauld November,
> When I did see the outlaw Whigs
> Lye scattered up and down the rigs.
> Some had hoggers,[3] some straw boots;

---

[1] Rothes to Lauderdale: *Laud. Pap.*, i. 267.
[2] *Ibid.*, ii. 63.
[3] Knitted leggings.

Some uncovered legs and coots;
Some had halbards; some had durks;
Some had crooked swords like Turks;
Some had slings, and some had flails
Knit with eel and oxen tails;
Some had spears and some had pikes;
Some had spades which delvyt dykes;
Some had guns with rusty ratches;
Some had firey peats for matches;
Some had bows but wanted arrows;
Some had pistols without marrows;
Some the coulter of a plough;
Some had syths men and horse to hough;
And some with a Lochaber axe
Resolved to give Dalyell his paiks.'

Turner, who was still under guard near the Lawhill, made a compact The fight on Rullion Green. with the guardsmen to save his life, and that in the event of the Covenanters losing the day he would give them quarter and plead for their release. When victory crowned the royal arms, Turner marched down with the guard to his comrades. But the Privy Council ignored his promise of quarter. On the rally of the trumpets and the roll of the drums a squadron of cavalry from Drummond's extreme right advanced uphill and poured a volley into Learmont's men. The fire was returned with spirit. A sword-fight ensued in which Captain John Paton of Meadowhead and Captain Arnot showed prowess, turning the enemy 'after they stuck in each other's birse for ane quarter of ane hour.' 'They mixed like chessmen in a bag,' was Drummond's graphic description of the struggle.[1] Wallace's pike-and-scythe-men rushed down the steep and drove first the foot and then the dragoons into flight. Drummond shot out his Commissioner's troop to rally the fugitives, but the headlong assault of the ugly scythes tied to long poles repelled these supports. In this melee the Duke of Hamilton just escaped death or capture by the timely interference of his neighbour, Dean, afterwards Bishop, Ramsay; while Learmont, in the opposite interest, escaped death just by the skin

---

[1] Drummond to Rothes, 'Pentland, November 1666.' This graphic letter from the battlefield, preserved in the *Carte MSS.*, LXXII. § iii., is printed in the *Scot. Hist. Rev.*, iii. No. 12, 451.

of his teeth. The Covenanters pursued too far. With the King's guard Drummond caught the struggling mass on the flank and hurled them into confusion. Wallace opposed this movement by sending supports which weakened his right command. That was Dalyell's opportunity. His centre and left were unimpaired. He rode his three regiments of horse right among the half-armed mob of pedestrians forming Wallace's main battle. Barscob, with his eighty little gallant Galloways, might vainly try to break such a shock before it reached the swaying mass; nor was Paton's notched blade of any avail. Fierce Dalyell and his fresh irresistible horse swept through the crowd as over a field of grass, and the white snow was reddened with blood. Till this charge Linlithgow's infantry were looking on and blowing their matches, affording light for Turner and stragglers to return. They followed Dalyell and consummated his victory. The blaring trumpets, rolling drums, and blazing firearms created an irretrievable stampede.

Dalyell's victorious charge.

Little knots of men fought it out. Among the last to leave was Paton—altogether, in the language of that day, 'a pretty man,' burly, keen-eyed, hero-like, a veteran of the German wars, a campaigner at Kilsyth, Philiphaugh, and Worcester. Dalyell, his old comrade, would fain have captured him. Pistols they emptied on each other. As the story still is told at westland firesides—when the smoke cleared, bold Paton saw his 'pistol ball to hop down upon Dalyell's boots,' and smelled the devil. He carried the antidote in his pocket. Superstitiously believing his antagonist to be lead-proof, he charged his second pistol with silver and presented it. But the necromantic Dalyell wilily stepped aside and let his servant get the fatal bullet. Troopers were urged to seize Paton. As one trooper fell at his feet with a cloven skull, Paton cried to his baffled pursuers, 'Take my compliments to your master, and tell him I cannot come to sup tonight.' Many others, light of foot, escaped down the gullies and over the hills, but others, discovered by the rising moon, fell to the relentless blades that followed them for miles. A miserable ballad has it thus:—

Captain Paton's heroism.

> 'The cleverest men stood in the van.
> The Whigs they took their heels and ran;
> But such a raking ne'er was seen
> As the raking o' the Rullion Green.'

The fighting horsemen had a better fate meantime, for we may infer from the lists of country gentlemen penalised for their participation in the fight that the better mounted and unwounded men escaped in the darkness.

The moon gave the soldiers light while they stripped the bodies of the slain.[1] Victors and vanquished lay on the field all night. Mein, in his account of the fight, declares: 'The army say they never saw men fight more gallantly than the rebels nor endure more; the general was forced to use stratagem to defeat them.'[2] What is not credible—he boasts: 'Not one of the King's men was killed and only a few wounded.'[3] Charles Maitland of Hatton, who fought with Dalyell, mentions that one hundred Covenanters fell on the field, and three hundred in flight.[4] Both averments are open to question, even although the Council had the Justices forewarned to intercept all fugitives. Rothes acknowledged the capture of one hundred and twenty prisoners. The peasantry of the Lothians were blamed for murdering some of the fugitives.[5] The Royalist gentry made diligent search for insurgents. Annandale and Drumlanrig, who were desperate for fines, forfeitures, and remunerative military employment, brought in the most prisoners.[6]

Losses by the fight.

Sharp was delighted with the victory of Dalyell, and wrote at once to the King assuring him that only nightfall prevented the extermination of his enemies, and to Lauderdale, praying: 'God make us thankful and give us hearts to improve this so seasonable a mercy for the furtherance of his Majesty's service in the Kingdom.' Shortly afterwards he resigned a grant of Inchaffray Abbey in favour of the hero of the hour.[7] The victory was celebrated by the firing of the guns of the Castle. While the half-naked prisoners filed into Haddock's Hole and other prisons—eighty wounded were confined in Heriot's Wark—the Council sat down to frame a letter craving the King's

Sharp's delight after the victory.

[1] Next day the godly women of Edinburgh went out and buried them in shrouds. Wallace, *Narrative*, in M'Crie, *Veitch*, 428.
[2] Mein to Williamson, 30th November: *State Papers* (Charles II.), 106, 301.
[3] *Ibid.*, 295.
[4] *Laud. Pap.*, i. 251. *Naphtali*, 144, gives forty westland men slain and '130 and upward' captured; four or five soldiers slain.
[5] Wallace, *Narrative*, 425.
[6] *Laud. Pap.*, i. 257.
[7] *Ibid.*, 259.

authority to proclaim their policy of extirpation.[1] Some fugitives fled to Kintyre, which Rothes described as a 'nest of Cneaffs'—worthless persons. Argyll now had no doubt as to what course to follow. He wrote to Lauderdale: 'The outed ministers that medled in the late rebellion I think deserve torture,' while those who refused submission 'should be put wher ther needs no troops to suppress them.' Truly times had changed quickly, when the heir of the proto-martyr should be among the first advocates of racks, boots, halters, and hangmen's knives for Covenanters, whom he styled 'fighting phanaticks.' He vowed that if they abused his tenderness, 'they shall need no other to cute their throats.'[2] After this, is it surprising that 'The Muscovite Beast' and other mercenaries, with a like keen scent for blood and loot, should plead the gospel of extermination, praying as Dalyell did to Lauderdale, 'heist us moir armes and bandeliers,' since there was no other remedy 'vithout the inhabetens be remouet or destroiet'?[3] Such sons of the saints and martyrs goaded on the persecutors, while the very prelates sharpened the swords of these executioners of the faithful and law-abiding adherents of a Covenant which the bishops and many clergy subscribed—and broke.

Dalyell clamours for the extermination of the Whigs.

Rothes rushed down from London angry at his removal from its scenes of pleasure. The Council, concluding that the rising was preconcerted, probably by Loudoun and other suspects, resolved to discover its origin by torture. The day after the battle they asked sanction for Sharp's policy of extirpation, and issued a proclamation making it treason to harbour fifty-seven leaders of the insurgents, including Colonel Wallace, Captain Maxwell, younger of Monreith, Maclellan of Barscob, Welsh of Scar, Welsh of Cornley, Kirko of Sundaywell, Mure of Caldwell,[4] Ker of Kersland, many clergy, and others who were not concerned in the affair. Rothes made a progress to pacify 'those parts where the frenzy first took its rise.' The King appointed a Justiciary

---

[1] Wodrow, ii. 35, 36; *Passages in the Lives of Helen Alexander*, etc., 4; *Reg. Sec. Conc., Acta*, 628.

[2] Argyll to Lauderdale, 28th January 1667: *Letters*, 41, 47, 56.

[3] Dalyell to Lauderdale, 6th December 1666: *Laud. Pap.*, i. 255.

[4] Dalyell got his estate, 11th July 1670, for his 'great losses … much hardship and sufferings by long imprisonment, banishment, and otherwise for his constant loyalty to his Majesty': Wodrow, ii. 75 note; *Reg. Sec. Conc., Acta*, 628.

Commission, composed of nobles, barons, and officers—Hamilton, Montrose, Argyll, Dalyell, etc.—to itinerate and try rebels.[1]

The Council thought they had secured two prisoners, M'Kail and Neilson of Corsock, who could divulge everything. M'Kail had been leading a fugitive life since he fled after preaching the too true sermon, in which he said 'that the Church and People of God had been persecuted both by a Pharaoh upon the Throne, a Haman in the State, and a Judas in the Church.' This bonny lad of twenty-five years— *Hugh M'Kail's fate.*

> 'For he had beauty which might well endear,
> No blemish in his body did appear'—

was now a fainting consumptive unable to keep step with the Galloway herds, whom he left at Cramond. He fell into the hands of the scouts of Dalyell on the Braids. M'Kail would tell nothing. They showed him the suggestive boots, and asked him to ponder them, and to become ingenuous to prevent their use. Meantime they experimented on Neilson, whose excruciating yells might 'have moved a heart of stone.'[2] M'Kail's simple story was that Turner caused the rising. Into the marrow-squirting boots his limbs must go; and strike never so lightly as Dunmore, the bribable hangman, might, his eleven blows on the emaciated spindle-shank afforded the devil's own entertainment to the patrons of bishops. Inflammatory fever held the victim in his dungeon on his trial day. All Rothes could report was, that the precipitancy of the insurgents had spoiled the designs of others, who 'were not to have sturd yet for several months.'[3] *Torture of Neilson and M'Kail.*

Lest the wounded might die, batches of them were brought to trial in the Justiciary Court in Edinburgh—the first on the 5th December—Nisbet[4] being prosecutor, and Lockhart and Mackenzie being the counsel in defence. The indictment bore that the prisoners were guilty of treason, rebellion—*laesa majestas*,[5] having taken Turner, *Trial of the Prisoners.*

[1] Wodrow, i. 51 note.

[2] Kirkton, 252; *Naphtali*, 163, 268; *A True Relation*, etc.

[3] Rothes to Lauderdale, 20th December 1666: *Laud. Pap.*, i. 265.

[4] It was to Lord Advocate Nisbet that Sir Archibald Primrose said: 'Thou old rotten devill, what art thou doing? thou wilt never rest till thou turn the fury of this people from the bishop upon thy self and gett thy self stabbed some day': Kirkton, 284; Wodrow, ii. 39.

[5] [Latin: treason.]

plundered houses, renewed the Covenant, and slain the King's soldiers. Their plea, that they had received quarter, was met by Nisbet's reply that there was no just war. Others pleaded that had they known of the proclamation they would have laid down their arms. All acknowledged participation in the rebellion. 'The Assize all in one voice by the mouth of Sir Alexander Urquhart of Cromarty their chancellor fand all and every one of the pannels guilty ... ffolows the Sentence. My Lord Justice Clerk and Justice Deputes decerns and adjudges the saids Captain Andrew Arnot, Major John M'Culloch, Gavin Hamilton in Maudslie in Carlouk Parish, John Gordon of Knockbreck, Cristall Strang, tenant in Kilbride, Robert Gordon, brother to John Gordon of Knockbreck, John Parker, walker in Kirkbride Parishin, John Ross in Mauchline, James Hamilton, tenant in Kithemoor, and John Shiells in Titwood, as being found guilty by an Assize, of the treasonable crimes forsaid, to be taken ffriday the 7th December instant betwixt 2 and 4 hours afternoon to the Mercate Cross of Edinbrugh and there to be hanged upon a Gibbett till they be dead, and after they are dead, their heads and right arms to be cutt off and disposed upon as the Lords of his Majesties Privy Council shall think fitt, and all their lands, heretages, goods and gear to be forfault and escheat to his Majesties use for the treasonable crimes forsaids which was pronounced for Doom.'[1]

Execution of ten insurgents, 7th December 1666. The ten were simultaneously hanged on a huge cross-tree, and thereafter mutilated: the ten right hands being sent for fixture on Lanark Tolbooth; the heads of the Gordons and M'Culloch to Kirkcudbright; the heads of the Hamiltons, Parker, and Strang to Hamilton; those of Ross and Shiells to Kilmarnock; and that of Arnot to the Watergate.[2] They died gallantly, wrote a correspondent of the time, 'adhering to the Covenant, declaring they never intended in the least any rebellion, and all of them prayed most fervently for His Majesty's interest and against his enemies ... [and that] their blood lay only at the prelates' door.'[3]

---

[1] Book of Adjournal; Just. Rec., i. 159-85. Their 'Joint Testimony' is in Naphtali, 215.

[2] Naphtali, 162; Martyr Graves, 244, 287. To the general reader an excellent guide to the places famous in Covenanting story is A. B. Todd's The Homes, Haunts, and Battlefields of the Covenanters (Edin., 1886, 1888), 2 vols.; also Rev. J. H. Thomson, The Martyr Graves of Scotland, 1903. For the 'Testimonies' of Arnot and Shiells, cf. Naphtali, 224, 226.

[3] Mein to Sir Joseph Williamson, Under-Secretary of State, 6th December 1666: State Papers (Charles II.), 106, 107, 325; Dodds, in his Fifty Years, quotes many of these important letters.

The brothers Gordon died locked in each other's arms. Their Joint Testimony corroborates that of others describing the atrocities in Galloway.[1] A few instances may suffice: M'Culloch of Barholm paid 1500 merks as Middleton's exaction, had thirty soldiers at eight-pence a day quartered on him, paid Turner a hundred pounds, had his estate forfeited, had his eldest son thrown into prison for a year after his father's execution, while his wife's portion was forfeited and given to Queensberry in 1681 and afterwards repurchased. Knockbreck, in Borgue, paid dearly for the laird's religion—the fines, crops seized, plenishing twice sold, the house thrice turned into a garrison and cleaned out by Highlanders, all except the trenchers and spoons—useless to these rogues—which were left for Grierson of Lag, together with some bestial they had not devoured, and two sons, right 'gallant Gordons,' hanged.

John Neilson, a godly man, sheltered the evicted Welsh of Irongray and Semple of Kirkpatrick-Durham, and turned Corsock mansion into a church for them.[2] For nonconformity he was sent to Kirkcudbright jail, had Corsock turned into a cavalry barracks, was mulcted in about two thousand pounds Scots, and made a bankrupt wanderer. His wife and family were evicted by soldiers, who destroyed his plenishing and sold his stock. His tenantry fared no better. Yet this noble fellow stood between Gray's pistol and its just mark, for which, be it remembered to Turner's credit, he tried to requite Neilson by pleading for his life after Pentland. Wodrow records that he failed to save Neilson on account of the representations of Dalgleish, a curate. Neilson's devoted wife, 'the eminently godly Mary Maclellan,' was brutally used; in her absence her house was sacked, her household, five children and a baby, turned adrift, the tenantry rooked by Ballantine, and one of them, with a wife and infant, put in prison for speaking to the laird; and, last hardship of all, 'Bonnie Dundee' came and 'eated up the Whigues,' as he confessed. So what with John, the heir, forfeited and in exile, and Thomas, his brother, in jail for non-churchgoing, no one could have hailed the Restoration more gladly than the godly wife who rests in the churchyard of Kirkpatrick-Durham since 1697.[3]

---

[1] *Naphtali*, 215, etc.

[2] Wodrow, ii. 49-53.

[3] Stark, *Book of Kirkpatrick-Durham*, 84; for Neilson's 'Testimony,' cf. *Naphtali*, 234-7.

Doom of
Neilson,
Robertson
and others,
14th Decem-
ber 1666.

On the 7th December, Mein again informed Williamson: 'On Tuesday next there is as many of the same kind of lay elders to fill the stage, and so along, till the remnant of the damned old cause be ferreted out of their Conventicles of retreat.' He referred to Neilson, Alexander Robertson, the preacher,[1] George Crauford in Cumnock, John Lindsay in Edinburgh, John Gordon in Irongray, tried on the 12th December, and sentenced to death, dismemberment, and forfeiture two days later.[2] M'Kail's case was adjourned till he could compear, on the 18th December, with Thomas Lennox, Humphry Colquhoun, Mungo Kaip in Evandale,

Executions
on 22nd
December.

Ralph Shiells, collier in Ayr, William Peddan, merchant there, John Wodrow or Wardrop, merchant in Glasgow, Robert M'Millan, merchant in Glasgow, John Wilson in Kilmaurs. They too were sentenced to the death of traitors on the 22nd December. They did not conceal the manly stand they had taken. M'Millan, Peddan, Lennox, and Lindsay were reprieved. The rest joyfully accepted their fate.[3] To their credit many gentlemen chose to be fined rather than sit on the assize. While these horrors went on, bands of little children paraded the streets carrying toy pikes and batons, and beating drums.[4]

The Testimonies emitted by all these sufferers are very affecting and afford illustrations of piety, purity, and patriotism which are in striking contrast with the vices of their judges. They rejoiced in becoming

Testimonies
of the
Pentland
martyrs.

witnesses and martyrs for Christ, Reformation, 'in the power and sweetness thereof,' and the Covenants. There is no trace of bitterness in their farewells in which they forgave their persecutors. All these champions of the Covenant had the assurance of Neilson: 'If I had many Worlds, I would lay them all down, as now I do my life for Christ and His Cause.'[5] None would purchase his life by abjuring the Covenants.

M'Kail's
Testimony.

'The Last Speech and Testimony of Mr. Hew M'Kaile,' etc., is a dying message worthy of the first martyrs, a bold manifesto full of the spirit

---

[1] This Alexander Robertson is supposed to have been the son of Alexander Robertson, minister of Urr, who died in 1639. The 'Testimonies' of Robertson, Crauford, Wodrow, Shiells, and Wilson appear in *Naphtali*, 228, 237, 247, 254, 259.

[2] *Just. Rec.*, i. 185-7.

[3] *Ibid.*, 187: Wodrow, ii. 52.

[4] Mein to Williamson: *State Papers*, 106, 348.

[5] *Naphtali*, 236.

of Luther and Knox.[1] His faith was exultant. He blessed God because He had 'keeped my soul free from all amazement and fear of death.' His final interview with his father was touching. 'I called thee a good olive tree of fair fruits, and now a storm hath destroyed the tree, and his fruits and branches; I have sinned: thou poor sheep, what hast thou done?' said the old father in tears. The penitent youth replied, 'Through coming short of keeping the Fifth Commandment'; and 'God's controversy with him was for overvaluing his children, especially himself.' This belief in the intimate care of God made Hew happy even to facetiousness. Though suffering, he exclaimed: 'Oh, the fear of my neck makes me forget my leg!' The night before the execution, he cheered his fellow-prisoners by saying merrily: 'Eat to the full, and cherish your bodies, that we may all be a fat Christmas Pie to the Prelates.'[2] His cousin. Dr. Matthew M'Kail, brought the influence of the Douglases to bear on Sharp and Burnet, but these callous Fathers in God did not interpose. A manuscript, probably written by the Doctor, records that 'there came a letter from the King discharging the execution of moe: but the Bishop of St. Andrews kept it up till Mr. Hew was executed: and then no moe were pannelled for that business.' Gilbert Burnet asserts that Archbishop Burnet brought and then withheld the letter. Row also chronicles this atrocity.[3]

As the fair youth, crippled and broken, dragged his way down High Street to the gallows, crowds viewed the scene in tears. He was now ecstatic. Scanning that bewildering sea of solemn faces he gladly said: 'So is there a greater and more solemn preparation in heaven to carry my soul to Christ's bosom.' He boldly read his memorable Testimony, which is a singularly beautiful confession of fidelity and devotion.[4] He next confirmed his resolution by singing the 31st Psalm:—

Scene at M'Kail's execution, 22nd December 1666.

'In Thee, O Lord, I put my trust,
  Shamed let me never be.'

As he mounted the ladder he cried out: 'I care no more to go up this ladder, and over it, than if I were going home to my father's house,' and as he touched every rung, he said: 'Every step is a degree nearer

[1] *Naphtali*, 239.
[2] *Ibid.*, 'A True Relation,' etc., 278.
[3] M'Crie, *Veitch*, 35 note; Row, *Blair*, 506; Burnet, i. 425; Defoe, 217.
[4] *Naphtali*, 239.

heaven.' Coolly turning round, he sat on a spar in order to address the onlookers, assuring them that their judges were to be exonerated, and their blood laid at the prelates' door. He was ready to embrace the rope for the Cause of God and of the Covenants—once the glory of the land. Opening his pocket Bible he read encouragement from the last chapter. With the napkin over his eyes he fancied he saw angels coming to bear his soul away, and, in a marvellous voice, referred to by Burnet, he burst into a tender rhapsody of 'Farewells' to his kindred, and 'Welcomings' to God, 'sweet Jesus Christ,' death, eternal life, and glory. The crowd wailed. Scotland had 'tint a byous lad'—an extraordinary youth.

Dr. Matthew M'Kail's devotion.

The compassionate Matthew, who slept with Hew in prison the night before, now stood beneath the beam, watching for the critical moment, to hang on to the dangling legs and give his cousin easy death. He had already arranged with the hangman, Dunmore, for Hew's black hair-cloth coat, which he wore for mourning as long as it held together, and for his unmutilated body, which was first borne into the Magdalene Chapel in a coffin; then being dressed, a usage forbidden to felons, it was accompanied by many and laid in Greyfriars' Churchyard, 'near the east dyke, a little above the stair, at the entry.'[5]

Gallant ending of Colquhoun, 22nd December.

Equally bold was Colquhoun, who, asking for a fellow victim's Bible, laid it on his wounded arm and read out with rapture the Scriptural grounds for his fearless faith and felicity.[6] 'I die not a fool,' he testified; 'it is better for me to suffer the worst of deaths, then to preserve my life by breaking the Oaths of God.'[7] Rothes might describe these heroes as 'damd incorrigeable phanaticks,' and 'damd fules' cursed with 'unparalleled obdurdness,' whom he would extinguish,—'not that I am wearie of causing hang such rebellious traitors.'[8] The bravery of pious peasantry, as inspirational as their eloquence was pentecostal, is best explained by the confession of M'Kail, that they had 'got a clear ray of the Majesty of the Lord.'

The Justices in Glasgow.

The Justiciary Commission, consisting of Linlithgow, Wigtown, Montgomery (eighth Eglinton), and Mungo Murray, held a court

[5] Wodrow, ii., 8; *Naphtali*, 283; M'Crie, *Veitch*, 35 note. Visible mourning—dress coffins, etc., being tokens of sympathy—was prohibited afterwards.

[6] Wodrow, ii. 58.

[7] 'Testimony' in *Naphtali*, 257.

[8] *Laud. Pap.*, i. 254.

in Glasgow on 17th December, and sent to the gallows, two days afterwards, Robert Buntein in Fenwick, John Hart in West Quarter, Glassford, Robert Scott in Shavock, Dalserf, and Matthew Paton, shoemaker, New Milns. When the condemned men attempted to address the spectators from the scaffold, the soldiers silenced them with drums. That was an old trick of Turner—and Rothes and Turner spent a merry Yule together in Glasgow.[1]

Similar tragedies occurred at Ayr, where a court presided over by Kellie, Drummond, Crichton, sheriff of Nithsdale, and Hatton (afterwards Lauderdale), on the 24th December, sentenced John Grier in Four Merkland, John Graham in Midtoun of Old Crachan,[2] James Smith in Old Crachan, Alexander MacCulloch in Carsphairn, James MacMillan in Marduchat, George MacCartney in Blairkennie, John Short in Dalry, James Blackwood in Fenwick, William Welsh in Kirkpatrick, John M'Coull in Carsphairn, Cornelius Anderson, tailor in Ayr, and James Muirhead in Irongray, to be forfeited and hanged, and their heads and right hands exposed at Ayr, on the 27th December, excepting two, Grier and Welsh, who were to die, be lopped, and be exhibited at Dumfries Market Cross on 2nd January.[3] The Ayr hangman ran away, and his neighbour in Irvine refused to act. In their dilemma the authorities with terrors, bribe of life, and intoxicants, induced the defective Cornelius to hang his brethren, two of whom were removed to Irvine and died joyfully there.[4]

The case of this Irvine hangman, William Sutherland, is unique. Sutherland tells his own soul's story.[5] He was a Strathnaver Highlander, illiterate, yet anxious to learn, who left cattle-herding and came to Paisley,

Marginal notes:
Judicial tragedies in Ayr.

Sutherland, the Christian hangman.

[1] *Just. Rec.*, i. 188; Row, *Blair*, 506; Tombstone, Glasgow Cathedral: *Martyr Graves*, 138.
[2] Clachan(?) of Dalry, Kirkcudbrightshire; *Book of Adjournal*, 24th December.
[3] *Just. Rec.*, i. 189; *Laud. Pap.*, i. 266. The tombstone in Ayr churchyard has MacMillan for MacCulloch: *Martyr Graves*, 310; similarly Patrick Walker, *Six Saints*, i. 319. In a very inaccurate doggerel epitaph on the back of the Ayr tombstone, 'Pontius M'Adam' is made the judge, and thumbkins are mentioned out of time. Two fine table stones in Dumfries churchyard keep green the memory of *William* (sic) Grierson and William Welsh, 'whose head once fixd up on the Bridge port stood': *Martyr Graves*, 471, 472.
[4] Cornelius perished a wretched outcast in Ireland: Wodrow, ii. 53-4; *Six Saints*, i. 318.
[5] Wodrow, ii. 54 note; *Naphtali*, 162.

where he eked out life by sweeping chimneys and hanging an odd witch. Paisley then slighted their obliging 'Dougal Cratur,' who, discovering that a more liberal spirit prevailed in Irvine, went thither and offered to hang all and sundry so long as the survivors kindly aided him in learning to read the Bible. In that Lollard atmosphere the rude Celt learned to love the Scriptures, to hate bishops, and to contract a moral sensibility which made him sometimes scruple at his killing work—a virtue which Turner and Claverhouse never knew. Fearing to be needed in Ayr, he contemplated flight, but first went to church to hear a sermon. His Bible opened at the text, 'Ye have not yet resisted unto blood, striving against sin,' and he interpreted the oracle in favour of the Covenanters. When the Provost called him out of church to go to Ayr, the hangman refused and was clapped in jail, whence a guard removed him to that 'auld toun.' Before setting out he sought strength in a 'mutchkin of ale.' In the Tolbooth of Ayr, White, a curate, plied him with Jewish precedents for killings, which Sutherland nullified by gospel texts—their dispute affording sport to the guardsmen. White, beaten, gave in, and believed the devil to be in the hangman. The judges next took him in hand, and found him obdurate in his refusal to execute. Dalyell, Drummond, and others tried the Muscovite method, threatening him with the boots, to which the waggish prisoner invited them to add the spurs too, with boiling lead, hanging, shooting, a barrel full of spikes, but it was to no purpose; Sutherland would neither be coerced nor persuaded to butcher his fellow-Christians, and was liberated.[1]

Trial of
fugitives.

It was not till the 15th August that the trial of the Pentland fugitives began under Atholl, when fifty-six rebels were called and did not compear.[2] In their absence the trial proceeded, and after an assize was sworn, Sir William Ballantine being one of them, and Turner and Lawrie of Blackwood gave evidence, all the accused were condemned as traitors to forfeiture and death, and were sentenced and denounced accordingly.

Sharp an in-
cubus on the
politicians.

Sharp had long been riding for a fall. He crushed the little war without feeling appeased. His communication to the Government

[1] Hatton, in a letter to Sharp, 6th May 1675, refers to Sutherland, the hangman, concerning whom Ross spoke to the Privy Council: *Miscell. Scot. Hist. Soc.*, 288 (Edin., 1893).

[2] For process and names, cf. *Just. Rec.*, i. 230; Wodrow, ii. 66.

saying Scotland was orderly required some explanation, after the King read another letter to a courtier wherein the Primate said, 'All was wrong; no man was faithful to the King, they were all sold.'[1] Tweeddale and the Treasurer-Depute, Bellenden, kept Lauderdale informed of the pitiless violence of the party for annihilation, and of the hatred borne towards Sharp and his abettors, the clergy being looked on as wolves. Lauderdale now appears with feline cunning sporting with his victim, Sharp. Since 1665 Bellenden had been warning Lauderdale of Sharp's hidden malignity, and now that victory had made the Primate insufferable, the terrified Bellenden, in bad French, implored the Secretary to rid Scotland of its miserable incubus.[2] Politic Lauderdale bided his time.

The unpreparedness of the Government to oppose a local rising, or Dutch landing-parties, necessitated a meeting of the Estates, on 9th January, to vote ample supplies to the King.[3] By the King's instructions, Hamilton, instead of Sharp, was made president, and to emphasise this rebuff, Rothes had the royal mandate to enjoin the Primate to confine himself to his own diocese. It gave Rothes pleasure to inform Lauderdale that Sharp was 'strangely cast down, yeay, lower than the dust.'[4] An abject melancholy brought the proud priest to death's door. He was not able to carry that 'sanctified cross' which, ten years before, he adjured Lauderdale in the Tower to bear for 'conscience, country, and Christ's church in it,' thereby testifying to 'that established [*then Presbyterian*] doctrine and discipline purchased at no small cost.' Sharp was fully paying up in shame, tears, and blood for his treachery. Gossip ran that he was to be deposed. Lauderdale, however, knew how to make him obedient to whip, and still had a use for the Primate who might keep the clergy 'from flying out to impertinencies.'[5]

Two proclamations (25th March) calling up the personal weapons and horses of non-jurors and non-churchgoers, opened new doors to

Meeting of Parliament, 1667.

Licence to spoil.

[1] Kirkton, 255.

[2] *Add. MSS.* 23123, fol. 212; 23125, fol. 167, 175: 'Pour l'amour de Dieu livré nous de cet maheureus et mal intentioné person … car le fardau d'un prester et trop pisant pour mais epoles'; *Laud. Pap.*, i. 240, 259.

[3] *Act. Parl. Scot.*, vii. 540.

[4] *Laud. Pap.*, i. 269, 270, 285.

[5] *Add. MSS.* 23127, fol. 191.

the spoilers. Another proclamation (13th June) rendered heritors and parishioners liable for fines and compensation exigible for assaults on, or affronts to, the well-affected clergy. This was a new licence to rob. These orders were no dead letters in face of the King's threat that the leniency of judges would not be brooked. Papists, however, were overlooked.[1]

Atrocities of Dalyell and Drummond.

After the battle of Rullion Green, the troops under Dalyell and Drummond marched to Ayrshire. *Naphtali* chronicles the atrocities which followed.[2] Dalyell, having tasted blood, 'acted the Muscovite too grossly,' and thus expressed his one idea regarding the 'mad phanaticks,'—'ther was noe mor to be doune bot tak them out and hang them.'[3] Archbishop Burnet also informed Sheldon that, if Dalyell's policy of extermination had been followed, 'I am confident this kingdome had by this tyme (9th August 1667) been in a very happy and quiet condition.'[4] After the fight, Dalyell's red hand wrote to Lauderdale: 'This Much I dar saye that fanatik parte vil never be redemit bot vit Much moir atemps then this And I beseik your Loirdship not to expek anay good from anay favors tham fr I am Confedent thay vil all Join vit the Couenant or anay hououer to overturn Episkopase.'[5] This illiterate demon set his uniformed bandits a cruel example. When ordinary tortures did not make ingenuous confessors, Dalyell threatened to kill, spit, roast, or burn alive his prisoners. Other victims, stripped half-naked, were crammed into filthy jails wherein they could only stand up.

The shooting of David Finlay.

He caused David Finlay in New Mills to be taken and examined as to his business in Lanark, on that day on which the rebels visited it; and because he could not name these strangers, he ordered a party to shoot him at the gallows-foot. The simple man, thinking that the goat-like monster was jesting, prevailed on the lieutenant to return and ask Dalyell for a respite till morning. Dalyell, in a rage, threatened the officer, declaring that 'he would teach him to obey his orders precisely.' The lieutenant accordingly ordered the soldiers to shoot and strip this unoffending man.

[1] Wodrow, ii. 83, 84, 86, 87.
[2] *Naphtali*, 169-75.
[3] *Laud. Pap.*, ii. 11.
[4] *Ibid.*, ii., App., Letter xxxii.
[5] *Add. MSS.* 28747, fol. 8.

The revolting story reached Sir Robert Moray, who informed Lauderdale that *Naphtali* 'tells exactly the whole story as I have heard it related.'[1] In all likelihood another murder is referred to by Burnet in this connection, thus, 'for he was then drunk, when he ordered one to be hanged, because he would not tell where his father was, for whom he was in search.'[2] Wodrow instances the brutality of Mungo Murray, who hanged to a tree, tied by the thumbs, two peasants who gave shelter to two insurgents. They would have perished had not two merciful soldiers cut them down.[3] Fines came in; churches began to fill with nervous hearers, as a result of Dalyell's practical gospel. Sir Robert Moray corroborates *Naphtali*.

In Nithsdale and Galloway, Turner and Ballantine[4] with their redcoats devoured the country with the pitilessness of locusts. The almost incredible indictment in *Naphtali*—stabbing, stripping, burglary, rape, torture by match, imprisoning, spoiling the innocent— is fully corroborated now.[5] Villainies of the soldiery.

Wodrow gives a concrete example of the villainy of Ballantine, who suggested immorality to the wife of the landlord of an alehouse in Balmaghie in his very presence. For resisting the assault, Ballantine struck the host dead. A Royalist gentleman interposed and seized Ballantine, who called in his men, and had the gentleman thrown down to lie all night roped like a beast, till, on Sabbath morning, friends arrived and became surety for the sufferer. After a debauch the soldiers fell on plundering the house, and, in sheer devilry, ran off the drink they could not consume.[6]

If Government agents could thus be procured publicly to commit atrocities, more like the acts of heathen than of Scots, what share of the reported crimes of the day is to be apportioned to the unbridled scum of the population, who professed no morality? The Books of Adjournal testify how rife certain kinds of crime were.[7] Up till now, in defence or retaliation, the Covenanters had not resented their treatment much

---

[1] *Laud. Pap.*, ii. 88, 10th December 1667; *Naphtali*, 170, 171; Wodrow, ii. 63.
[2] *Hist.*, i. 426.
[3] Wodrow, ii. 64.
[4] Or Bannatyne.
[5] Page 174; *Laud. Pap.*, ii. 25, 26, 62, 82, 83.
[6] Wodrow, ii. 65.
[7] *Just. Rec.*, i. 2 *passim*; also the unpublished *Minutes*.

further than in entering the manses of Borgue, Glencairn, Dunscore, Irongray, Closeburn, and other places, probably more to terrify informers than to wreak vengeance—loot being out of the question.

The insurgents not criminals.

The accusation is contemporary that the soldiers masqueraded as Whigs in order to plunder; and there is no proof that the insurgents were criminals.[1] Dalyell, with blood in his nostrils, was continually scenting incipient rebellion and writing to London creating a scare. Incidents were exaggerated.[2] Even Drummond and Burnet were sent to court to 'blow that coal,' and Dalyell also clamoured to go to secure forfeitures.

Lauderdale's investigations.

Now that Charles II. was promoting toleration in England, and Clarendon, its opponent, was in consequence to be 'decourted,' Lauderdale, influenced by the peace-loving antagonists of the military ring, had no better policy than the dispatch, in June 1667, of his trusty under-secretary, Sir Robert Moray, to discover the true trend of affairs in the north, and to see 'how the bowles roll.'

Moray, now getting old, was one of the most reputable men of his age. By family a Perthshire gentleman, a veteran colonel of the continental wars, a staunch friend of the two Charleses, a former Senator of Justice and Privy Councillor, a distinguished naturalist, physicist, astronomer, and mathematician, a wise diplomatist, who preferred study to politics, and a spring on his violin to the clangour of camps, Moray was a man whose kindliness of nature ever made him an advocate for clemency and moderation.[3]

Sir Robert Moray's report, 9th July 1667.

This 'cunning and dexterous man,' as Clarendon so aptly designated Moray, at once discovered the source of the troubles. The cabal of booted apostles aimed at being permanent governors battening on legal loot. Official life was rotten, and smelled of liquor and dirt. 'Now let me tell you,' he reported, 'that all any body can tell you of the corrupt state of things and persons here can as little make you imagine it as it is, as one who never saw the ruins of London can comprehend it by any

---

[1] *Wodrow*, ii. 18.

[2] Tweeddale reports that some rebels had sorely beat 'if not kild one old man, Black, minister of Closeburn.' He was aged forty-nine, and lived till 1684: *Laud. Pap.*, ii. 19. Black refused the Test in 1681, but, after petitioning the Council, and taking it, was reponed in 1682.

[3] *Scot. Rev.*, v. 22.

description any body can make of it.'[1] He enlarged on his experiences to this effect—the rumour regarding 'mad phanaticks' about to rebel were false 'starrlight stories'; officers were defrauding their men of their pay; Hamilton, Dalyell, and others were so mean, on the one hand, as to compound with rebels for a few merks 'and one for a stick,' while, on the other, they illegally exacted £1700 from Loudoun's tenantry; Ballantine was a notorious spoiler, and Steel, minister of Kells, had informed him that Turner, who beggared his parish so that the parishioners were unable to pay his stipend, 'was a saint to Balantine,'[2] the treasury was a den of robbers; his country sorely needed an autocrat to suppress its greedy oppressors.[3]

Thus the official reporter outrivalled the description of the miseries of Scotland, then recently published in an anonymous work entitled '*Naphtali, or the Wrestlings of the Church of Scotland for the Kingdom of Christ, etc.* … 1667.' Moray also referred to this book as 'all that a toung set on fire by hell can say of things and persons hereaway.'[4] Moray noted the veering round to Lauderdale of the battered weathercock, Sharp, who was now hinting that Rothes and Dalyell had arranged the rebellion, discarding these bloodstained buttresses of the Church, praying for reconciliation with the Secretary, wishing the abolition of the militia, standing for 'lenity and gentleness at present.' Moray naively advised his chief 'to make use of a knave as well as another,' for 'certainly you are not to learn to know him—Sharp.' How the two diplomatists must have chuckled when they saw bishops and clergy following that 'tinkling cymbal' of a bellwether, as Moray wrote: 'What a silly company of people they are, and how useful one of them is to manage the rest!'[5] Lauderdale brought Sharp to his reward and became reconciled, saying he wished 'fair play in time to come,' as he stood strong for crown and crozier.[6] Sharp swallowed the bait. It was in the drama, concocted by Moray and staged by Lauderdale, that the Sovereign should again

The Covenanters' testimony corroborated.

---

[1] *Laud. Pap.*, ii. 20, 9th July 1667.

[2] This was in keeping with a complaint of the papist Herries to Tweeddale: *Laud. Pap.*, ii. 24.

[3] Moray's Letters, *Laud. Pap.*, ii. 13, 14, 20, 34, 39, 62, 65, 68, 70.

[4] Cf. *postea*, 210-11 and note 1: *Laud. Pap.*, ii. 88.

[5] Moray to Lauderdale, 20th September: *Ibid.*, ii. 71, 86, 87.

[6] *Ibid.*, ii. 40, 41.

honour the Primate. The King sent a commendatory letter to Sharp, which made him so mad with joy that he replied to Lauderdale that he was 'wholly his'; and that 'His Majesties hand with the diamond seal was to me as a resurrection from the dead.'[7] Into that polluted hand the stronger Sheldon once refused to put the communion cup.[8] But the cowed whelp licks the hand that feeds and whips it.

Conciliation
advocated by
Moray.

The conciliatory policy inspired by Moray was soon announced, and with a change of managers, the reduction of Rothes to the Chancellorship, the disbanding of all but a few regulars—peace with Holland having been made—it was intended to return the sword to its scabbard. Dalyell found his list of forfeitures useless, and Burnet felt as if 'the Gospell was banished out of his diocey that day.'[9]

Moray's proposal that all who took a bond of peace—a few undesirables excepted—should receive pardon and indemnity, was approved by Charles, and opposed by the blood-and-booty cabal, because it killed their paying trade. The proclamation of this act of grace breathed a kindly spirit towards those obliging themselves not to rise in arms without authority, and producing a cautioner before New Year's Day. The three classes excepted were: (1) forty lay and sixteen clerical insurgents—Wallace, MacLellan, and other westlandmen; (2) the forfeited already scheduled; and (3) molesters of the settled incumbents.[10]

Moray's bond
of peace.

To render the Act effective, heritors were enjoined to summon all on their lands to subscribe the bond, and to dispossess them should they refuse. The hair-splitting Scots, with tender consciences, read more into this surety of lawburrows than Moray intended, as if it bound them to the past and future policy of the Crown. Others—Campbell, Dunlop, Montgomery, etc.—welcomed it and got release from prison. Of those aimed at by the Act two hundred and eighteen came to terms, and three hundred, mostly 'mean persons,' remained obdurate. Many were sceptical of the royal clemency and refused to surrender, and others took advantage of it by demanding an inquiry into the grievances at the bottom of the Rising. There was no little irony in the circumstance

[7] Sharp to Lauderdale, 18th January 1668: *Add. MSS.* 23128, fol. 273.
[8] Burnet, i. 313 note.
[9] *Laud. Pap.*, ii. 68; Kirkton, 269.
[10] *Reg. Sec. Conc., Acta*, 726-34, 9th October 1667; Wodrow, ii. 92, 93, 94.

that on the first anniversary of Rullion Green, the Council appointed a Committee to report on the excesses of the troops under Turner in Galloway, and on the same day Clarendon was preparing to flee into exile. The country rang with the terrible charges of *Naphtali*, which Sharp said he expected to 'debauch the people to a Munster tragedy'; but neither the frequent banning and burning of the book, nor the answer by Bishop Honyman, diminished the sensation it produced. Mackenzie attributed the murderous intentions of James Mitchell to the principles set forth in *Naphtali*.[1]

The effect of *Naphtali*.

The Privy Council met on 20th February to receive the report on the Turner scandals, and, as was to be expected from undeniable facts, and from the foregone conclusion that some scapegoats should be turned adrift with the crimes of greater offenders on their heads, the Committee detailed under twenty-one heads the offences complained of, and concluded that 'every one of the foregoing articles is made out by information upon oath.'[2] Turner's defence was that he had only lifted £30,000 Scots, and had always mitigated the severity authorised. The Council sent the report to the King, who ordered Turner to be discharged from the service. Dreading the fate of becoming 'ane absolute beggar,' this pitiless oppressor of the innocent wrote a whining letter to Lauderdale, imploring him to intercede with the King to save him from the 'ruine of a poor gentleman.'[3] It is to the credit of his cruel abettor, Archbishop Burnet, that the prelate wrote to Secretary Williamson pleading for this 'very honest gentleman,' and minimising his offences on the ground: 'I have heard him recommended for the same acts for which he is now condemned: and soldiers think they do not offend when they obey their superior officers' orders.'[4] The Council afterwards took a more lenient view of Turner's practices.[5] A similar investigation into the ledgers of, and into the ruffianism alleged against, Ballantine also justified the authorities in sending that gory-handed Gentleman

The Council and the military scandals.

Turner discharged.

Ballantine banished, 1668.

---

[1] *Memoirs*, 326; Aldis, *List*, 1852, *A Survey ... of Naphtali*, etc., pt. i. 1668; pt. ii. 1669; cf. Stewart's answer *Jus Populi*, etc., 1669; Wodrow, ii. 225; iii. 229 note; iv. 444.

[2] *Reg. Sec. Conc., Acta*, 36, 20th February 1668.

[3] 12th March: *Laing MSS.*, iv. Div. i. 137.

[4] Dodds, *Fifty Years*, 192, citing Letter in State Pap. Office.

[5] *Reg. Sec. Conc., Acta*, 62.

of the Bed-chamber to the pestilential Tolbooth, fining him in £200 sterling, and banishing him from Scotland.[1] That reckless hackster took to arms abroad, and met a soldier's death at the siege of Graves.[2]

Failure of Moray's policy.

With these bandits degraded and dismissed, and the Dalyell party temporarily checked, the executive made efforts, in the Spring of 1668, to stop conventicling, and to induce subscription of the bond of peace. The exiles in Holland wrote reviling the 'black bond' and recommending rejection of it. Some weak-kneed insurgents, such as Robert Cannon, younger of Mardrogat, in Galloway, who afterwards turned informer, gave in, but many preferred banishment to Virginia to defection. A warrant was issued in May to seize eighty notorious refusers of the Indemnity, among whom were some who evaded capture and afterwards became martyrs.[3] Conventicling spread even in Edinburgh, and the clergy were more despised than ever.[4] Local garrisons were established, and slave-ships transported irreconcilables to Virginia and Tangier, all with no perceptible effect.

Michael Bruce.

One of those sentenced to sail for Tangier was Michael Bruce, from Killinchy in Ireland, a great-grandson of the famous Robert, deposed for nonconformity, and seized while conventicling in Airth, not without a bloody bout in which soldiers and he were wounded. Bruce founded his defence on the authority of Scripture. They sent him to a higher authority meantime—the King, who, being influenced by courtiers, asked that Bruce should be sent to London, whence he transferred him to his work in Ireland. At the Revolution, Bruce was settled in Anwoth.[5]

Hog of Kiltearn.

Among the oppressed at this time was Thomas Hog of Kiltearn, who, taken from tolbooth to tolbooth, buffeted between the Bass and the Castle Rock, and by the Council designated 'a noted keeper of conventicles,' appears to have borne the malignity of Sharp in an especial degree. In a singular way Sharp acknowledged the invincible old Protester's talents and influence by advising the Council to immure him in a cell worse than that which had ruined his health; while he

---

[1] 10th April: *Laud. Pap.*, ii. 25, 26, 62, 83, 100, 116; *Just. Rec.*, i, 52; cf. Index.

[2] For Mr. Andrew Lang's futile attempt to turn Turner into a saint, see his paper, 'A Christian under the Covenant,' in *Blackwood's Magazine*, clxxiv., July 1903.

[3] Wodrow, ii. 108, 109 note.

[4] Tweeddale to Lauderdale: *Laud. Pap.*, ii. 113.

[5] Row, *Blair*, 520, 521.

asserted, 'that the prisoner did, and was in a capacity to do, more hurt to their interests, sitting in his elbow chair, than twenty others could do by travelling from this land to the other ... and ... if there were any place in the prison worse than another, he should be put there.'[1] To this 'closest prison' Hog was remanded, and there, to his own amazement, recovered health, for which he ironically blessed 'good Doctor' Sharp!

---

[1] *Memoirs of Mrs. William Veitch, Mr. Thomas Hog of Kiltearn*, etc., 104 (Edin., 1846).

Headstone of four Martyrs in the
churchyard, Hamilton

Graves of Pentland Martyrs in St. Michael's
Churchyard, Dumfries

Original Monument erected to the Martyrs in
Greyfriars Churchyard, Edinburgh

Martyrs' Monument in the
churchyard, Cupar (Fife)

The Grassmarket, Edinburgh

THE GRASSMARKET, EDINBURGH, AND MONUMENTS OF THE MARTYRS

CHAPTER TWENTY-FOUR

THE SCHEMES OF ANGELIC LEIGHTON AND IRON-HANDED LAUDERDALE

W HERE was the angelic Leighton all this time when the vice-gerent of Christ acted Nero, when ministers of justice crushed guilty and innocent indifferently, when feminine virtue was not safe from unbridled cavaliers, and clergy were not fit company for squeamish Turner?[1] What Robert Baillie said of Leighton in 1658 was true of him to the end: 'Mr. Lichtoun does not [nought] to count of, but looks about him in his chamber.'[2] The Episcopal ministers of 1666 reckoned this their golden age, and hailed the cavaliers as a divine legion of protectors. 'By the banks of Allan Water' Leighton dwelt apart, wishing the churchyard would open for him a door to heaven. He moped over his own sins and the lack of virtue in others. The Register of his Synod[3] proves that he strove to elevate the clergy of his 'precincts,' to inculcate domestic purity, and to promote religion of a public and liturgical kind especially; but there came not from him a Christian's proper reply to *Naphtali*, in protests against the brutalities of his peers and his coadjutors in Parliament and Council, nor even in any appeals for misguided fanatics and inhumanly treated innocents.[4] His was the conciliatory spirit of a disembodied soul, and the chilling

Robert Leighton visionary.

---

[1] Burnet, i. 379, 426.

[2] *Letters*, iii. 365.

[3] Wilson, *Register of Synod of Dunblane*, q.v.

[4] E.g. Agnes Anderson and ___ Hadden, starving prisoners, untried, even unaccused, petition for liberty, and are given to first skipper going to Barbadoes or Virginia: *Reg. Sec. Conc.*, *Acta*, 667, ult. February 1667.

purity of a corpse. Gilbert Burnet records that he had to be prevailed upon to go to court to expose the violence of the executive in planting religion which he said he did not approve of.[1] Yet he was one of the eleven Scots bishops who met on 16th September and subscribed a subservient letter to Lauderdale, signifying their concurrence in the new policy for remedying the evils in the Church.[2] Moray, the intriguer, and the diamond seal of Charles, also exalted Leighton into the peaceful heaven of resurrected Sharp. All were crying peace, save Archbishop Burnet and the swordsmen.

Leighton, however, was not so much a genuine champion of toleration as a juggler with concessions tending to uniformity, who maintained chimerical views, especially regarding the unimportance of distinctive Church principles.

The 'Accom-modation.'

Leighton, in a millennial vision, conceived a policy which was designated 'The Accommodation.' It proposed that the bishop, or 'constant moderator,' should preside in church courts, but have no negative vote; a dissentient presbyter on joining a 'precinct' (his name for a presbytery, or meeting of clergy under a bishop) might acknowledge the bishop under protest; a candidate for ordination might accept the bishop as the chairman of the presbyters; bishops were to submit themselves to the Synod for censure or approval every third year.[3] Of alternative schemes of conciliation—Kincardine's, imposing by law mutual terms of concession; and Tweeddale's, allowing field-preachers to minister in selected parishes—Leighton favoured the former. Conventicling was not in harmony with his veiled projects. The author of *Naphtali* had good foundation for his bitter accusation: 'Mr. Lighton, prelat of Dumblan, under a Jesuitical-like visard of pretended holiness, humility, and crucifixion to the world, hath studied to seem to creep upon the ground, but always up the hill ... and ... none of them all hath with a

Leighton's betrayal of The Cause.'

Kiss so betrayed the Cause, and smiten Religion under the fifth rib, and been such an offence to the godly.'[4] Leighton was no more clever than other schemers who had tried to busk the presbyter so as to hide the horns of Antichrist. It proved the shrewdness of the Covenanters that

---

[1] Burnet, i. 382.
[2] *Laud. Pap.*, ii. 59.
[3] Burnet, i. 497; Butler, *Life of Leighton*, 403, 422.
[4] *Naphtali*, 301.

they were able to detect what Burnet, Leighton's confidant, divulged regarding these concessions: 'He [Leighton] thought it would be easy afterwards to recover what seemed necessary to be yielded at present.'[1]

The strain of the times was too much for the ill-nourished mind of James Mitchell, 'a stickit minister,' then in his prime. A poor student from the Lothians, he graduated at Edinburgh; and doubtless the spare diet of a private tutor and chaplain made him a 'lean, hollow-cheeked man of a truculent countenance.'[2] Robert Blair, minister of Edinburgh, confidently recommended this 'honest young man,' in 1661, as fit to be a teacher or precentor.[3] He subscribed both Covenants when demanded by Principal Leighton, but, unlike the Principal, kept them. Enemies accused him of dealings with the bestial wizard, Weir. With Alexander Henderson he held that the bishops were the makers of the nation's woes. Believing Sharp to be the instigator of all the sufferings of the time, he imagined he had a call to remove him.[4] He joined the insurgents, and was sent to Edinburgh to interview Stirling, the author of *Naphtali*, and Fergusson of Caitloch. Thereafter he skulked about, under the name of James Small, armed with two loaded Scots pistols.[5] Sharp's mansion was on the High Street of Edinburgh, between the Netherbow and Blackfriars Wynd. On Saturday afternoon, 11th July, Mitchell, lurking on the north side of the High Street, saw Sharp, followed by Honyman, Bishop of Orkney, entering the Primate's coach. Mitchell fired through the window, but, being 'ane ill gunner,' missed Sharp, and shattered Honyman's wrist resting on the door of the carriage. Clearing a way with the second pistol, Mitchell dived down the Wynd, up Cowgate, into Fergusson's house in Stevenlaw's Close,[6] where he removed his disguise before descending to the street to join in the hue and cry, from which he sought retirement, it is said, in the very Tolbooth. The cry 'A man killed,' was soon hushed by the report, ''Twas only a bishop.' Mitchell was not suspected, and escaped. Sharp, however, got a glimpse of that mummified face beneath the odd periwig, which haunted him

James Mitchell— 'stickit minister.'

Mitchell shoots at Sharp, 11th July 1668.

---

[1] *Hist.*, i. 499.
[2] *Ravillac Redivivus*, 11.
[3] *Wodrow MSS.*, xxix. 4to, 94.
[4] *Laing MSS.*, Papers left by Mitchell, 269.
[5] *Laud. Pap.*, ii. 116.
[6] Others said Lord Oxenford's garden in Cowgate.

for years, till he identified it again at Robert Douglas's funeral and had Mitchell apprehended.[1]

Sharp was scared out of his wits. In a letter, dated 23rd July, he makes wild statements about a 'hellish design for murdering the King about that tyme,' and a combination of Pentland rebels and city conventiclers for rescuing the assassin; whereas Mitchell at his trial declared that no one was privy to his design.[2] These whinings were flouted in official circles. Gilbert Burnet politely visited Sharp to offer his congratulations. The Primate, assuming a pious visage, exclaimed: 'My times are wholly in Thy hand, O thou God of my life.' Burnet adds the cutting comment: 'This was the single expression savouring of piety that ever fell from him in all the conversation that passed between him and me.'[3]

As was to be expected, the authorities could not allow the outrage to go unavenged. All probable sympathisers with the criminal were haled in for examination; flying squadrons searched the wild west for phantom rebels; and former victims of the High Commission were more harshly treated. For giving unsatisfactory answers regarding her knowledge of certain suspects, Anna Kerr, relict of James Duncan, a minister, kept in prison with her two children for months, and sentenced to the plantations, was only saved from torture by Rothes saying that 'it was not proper for gentlewomen to wear boots.' Margaret Dury, relict of James Kello, a city merchant in Edinburgh, who gave Welsh an asylum, was sentenced to banishment, as well as to pay a fine of 5000 merks, and was kept in prison for months.[4] Many churches were vacant. Disorder had to be cured, for Lauderdale had sworn—

'I'll conform the Church and every man,
By placing calves at Bethell and at Dan.'[5]

The King invited Sharp to London, to win over that pliable courtier to the policy of toleration; and Sharp returned to Scotland in November, openly to promote what Burnet and he privately detested.[6] His vexed

---

[1] *Laud. Pap.*, ii. 109; *Hist. Notices*, 90; *Add. MSS.*, 23245, fol. 14, 15; Row, *Blair*, 518 Scott, *Fasti*, i. 348, gives February 1674 as date of Douglas's death.

[2] *Laing MSS.*, Papers left by Mitchell; *Just. Rec.*, ii. 307.

[3] *Hist.*, i. 502.

[4] Wodrow, ii. 118; *Laud. Pap.*, ii. 116-30, July 1668.

[5] 'The New Policie': *Laing MSS.*, 89, fol. 142.

[6] Burnet, *Hist.*, i. 502; *Laud MSS.*, 23130, fol. 42; 23131, fol. 26.

soul found vent in diatribes against the disaffected, especially those he styled 'she-zealots 'and 'Satanesses.'

At this juncture there came into prominence a brilliant young man, Gilbert Burnet, minister of Salton, a social pusher, able to worm out the confidences of public men, who considered himself as important a factor in the Church as Turner imagined himself to be the Bayard of the Army.[1]

Burnet, having picked the brains of Leighton, Sharp, George Hutcheson, the Hamiltons, and the leading Whigs, wrote to Tweeddale recommending the settlement of moderate Presbyterians in the vacant charges. Thereupon Tweeddale prevailed on some conciliatory ministers—Robert Douglas, Stirling, and others—to write to him in a similar strain. The communications were passed on to the King, who dispatched through Tweeddale an order to the Privy Council (7th June) authorising a conditional Indulgence.[2] The Indulgence provided for parish ministers resuming duty in their charges when vacant, in other parishes when presented to them by patrons, in consideration of being orderly, receiving collation, attending ecclesiastical courts, and receiving full emoluments; refusers of collation were allowed the use of manses and glebes; all were to attend the Presbyterian courts, and to restrict their services to their own parishes. Other orderly outed ministers were to be paid four hundred merks annually out of vacant parishes. Conventicles were to be suppressed.[3] This establishment of modified Presbyterianism was the public rebuke of prelatic incompetence, and Sharp was warned that, if the clergy and Church were not reformed, the King would turn disciplinarian himself.[4] When Sharp refused to recognise the reponing of an indulged minister, Tweeddale reminded him that censures were no longer canonical, but were now Parliamentary.[5]

Of the forty-three ministers reinstated in parish pulpits—a few being those from which they were ejected by the Council during 1669-70—some were conspicuous pastors, such as Robert Douglas, Edinburgh, indulged in Pencaitland; George Hutcheson, the well-known

Margin notes: Advent of Gilbert Burnet. — A conditional Indulgence, 1669. — Indulged clergy.

[1] Clarke and Foxcroft, *A Life of Bishop Burnet* (Cambridge, 1907), *q.v.*
[2] Burnet, *Hist.*, i. 496, 507; Wodrow, ii. 130, 131; Row, *Blair*, 524, 525.
[3] Brown, *History of the Indulgence*: in *Faithful Witness Bearing*, 135.
[4] *Laud. Pap.*, ii. 196.
[5] *Ibid.*, ii. 199.

commentator, Tolbooth, Edinburgh, sent to Irvine; William Vilant, Ferry-Port-on-Craig, transferred to Cambusnethan.[1]

On 3rd August, when twelve of these indulged preachers—'The Twelve Apostles of the Council,' or 'Council Curates,' as they were nicknamed—compeared before the Council to get their licences, 'it was a piece of pageantry to see them make their leg in receiving it.'[2] Hutcheson, in name of the brethren, thanked the King and Council; and, after asserting that the preacher's warrant came from Christ, said they would submit themselves to lawful authority in its exercise, and prayed for a blessing on the King, who had shown 'singular moder-

Opposition of irreconcilables. ation.' The irreconcilables, at home and abroad, vilified the Indulgence as a bare-faced Erastian breach of the Covenant, and adjured the people in red-hot language not to hear the intruded hirelings, and disguised prelatists, or any without 'a cleanly call.' The field-preachers, in apocalyptic ecstasy, summoned the conventiclers as 'angels of Michael' to a pitched battle with the Dragon, till Christ on His white horse should conquer the land.[3] While the Crown was thus endeavouring to mollify the people by unlocking the prison doors for those long-incarcerated knights, Cunningham, Mure, Maxwell, Stuart, and Chiesley, only a few parishioners, or, more probably, independent burglars, in some places were still molesting the curates and getting heavy fines imposed on the parishes. The cases of Balmaclellan and Urr only implicate six men in women's clothes.[4]

A new western Remonstrance. While to the Presbyterian the Indulgence was a licence to preach a Gospel without a Testimony to the times, to the Prelatist it was an illegal imposition nullifying the statutes establishing Episcopacy. Sharp, with the aid of Rothes, got behind the provisions of the Indulgence by keeping the indulged out of his diocese. Burnet took the bolder step of associating with his clergy in framing a Remonstrance, passed at the Synod, held in Glasgow in October, resenting this invasion

---

[1] He wrote a review of Brown's *History of the Indulgence*, and became Principal of the New College, St. Andrews. *A Review and Examination*, etc., 1681. Brown's *History … and Vindication* gives names of indulged—'By a Presbyterian. Printed in the year MDLXXVIII.' The preface is by MacWard.

[2] Kincardine to Lauderdale, 3rd August 1669: *Laud. Pap.*, ii. 192.

[3] Wodrow, ii. 154 note.

[4] *Ibid.*, ii. 145, 146. Row, minister of Bal, was again molested in Stoneykirk. He became a Papist: *ibid.*, 232. The Whigs knew their pastors.

of their rights, and blaming councillors for winking at dissent, and doing nothing to foster uniformity.[1] The Remonstrance was framed by Arthur Rose, afterwards Bishop of Argyle, Archbishop of Glasgow, and Archbishop of St. Andrews.[2] A smuggled copy reached Lauderdale. He detected treason. Soon the appellants were cited to the Council, the Synod books examined, the Remonstrance suppressed, and Burnet informed of his confinement in Glasgow during the approaching sitting of Parliament.[3] When Charles saw the document he exclaimed: 'This damned paper shewes Bishops and Episcopall people are as bad in this chapter as the most arrant Presbyterian or Remonstrator.'[4]

Lauderdale had the iron hand that was needed. As Commissioner to Parliament, indicted for 19th October 1669, after a royal progress, he arrived at Holyrood. He was no longer the noble Maitland of the Golden Age of Presbytery. If Mackenzie and others are credible authorities, Lauderdale was now a gross, loose, unbearable dictator, who bullied Parliament-men, terrorised Episcopal admirers, and disgusted Presbyterians by his 'bawdy discourses and passionate oaths.'[5] Lord Ailesbury's sketch of him depicts a grotesque, vulgar, fawning worldling.[6] *Character of Lauderdale.*

Lauderdale in his greed secured for himself seven salaries, gifts, imposts, minerals, shipwrecks, gold in Jamaica, and other grants; in his ambition he aimed at being great in the councils of England, by his becoming master of Scotland and indispensable to the King. Lauderdale informed Charles that the Estates began business 'after prayers by the Bishop of Dunblane [Leighton] for I would not have the Presbiterian trick of bringing in ministers to tell God Almighty news from the debates.' The first important bill passed was the Supremacy Act.[7] Its significance is indicated by its terms: 'His Maiestie and his successours may settle, enact, and emit such constitutions, acts, and orders, concerning all ecclesiastical meetings and maters to be proposed and determined therein.' Never had a Pope such power. *The new Royal Pope.*

---

[1] *Laud. Pap.*, II. xvi. 137; App. lxiv-lxvii.
[2] Burnet, i. 510. Ross was ejected in 1688.
[3] Mackenzie, *Memoirs*, 157, 158.
[4] Moray to Lauderdale, 6th October 1669: *Laud. Pap.*, ii. 139, 166.
[5] *Memoirs*, 182.
[6] *Memoirs*, i. 14, 18 (Roxburgh Club, 1890).
[7] 16th November, Act 2: *Act. Parl. Scot.*, ii. 554.

THE COVENANTERS

The Covenanters said the Act placed Charles as a Pope on Christ's throne.[1] It was suspected that Lauderdale, having an inkling of the royal leanings to popery, made a change in the national faith easier. The aristocracy hailed the Act as a relief from prelatic arrogance. Upon the introduction of the Supremacy Act Sharp in private reviled it, as savouring of the method of King Henry VIII., and tried to blunt its sting by adding the words 'as settled by law,' in reference to the Church; but when the debate came on he made his customary somersault and rated Bishop Rose for distrusting his Majesty.[2] A militia bill was also passed. Lauderdale then informed the King that he was sovereign of the Church, with twenty thousand armed men at his back, a power he had

Deposition of Archbishop Alexander Burnet.

not in England.[3] The King's gracious reply contained a command to Lauderdale to cause the hierarchy to depose remonstrating Burnet, 'as unfit to govern that sea [*sic*] any longer.'[4] Truly it was a *sea* of troubles in which Archbishop Alexander Burnet foundered. Lauderdale gave the bishops a dinner, and introduced the instruction as its *pièce de résistance.* Sharp was intractable, till his host silenced the primate by asserting that ministerial office was 'not *jure divino,*[5] but depended solely on the supreme Magistrate.'[6] Kneeling before this Grand Vizier, Burnet heard his doom: 'It's the King's will and pleasure that ye be no more Archbishop of Glasgow.' The unfrocked bureaucrat complaisantly departed to express his grief, that he 'hath not been so acceptable as I could have wished.'[7]

Bishop Leighton.

Leighton, with the tongue of an archangel, preached on pure religion, and, with the wisdom of the serpent, refrained from uttering a manly protest against the incubus crushing religion and its devotees.[8] Certainly 'one whose soul was like a star and dwelt apart' could scarcely feel the crushing deadweight. During the same Parliament many landlords obtained liberty to establish fairs—a simple method of exacting toll; and Lieutenant-General Drummond was ratified in a

---

[1] Burnet, i. 513.

[2] Mackenzie, *Memoirs*, 159; *Laud. Pap.*, ii. 151: Lauderdale to Moray, 2nd November.

[3] *Laud. Pap.*, ii. 163.

[4] *Ibid.*, ii. 166.

[5] [Latin: by divine law.]

[6] *Laud. Pap.*, ii. 171.

[7] *Ibid.*, ii. 17.

[8] Butler, *Leighton*, 420, 421.

grant of the lands of Inchaffray Abbey for proving himself 'the terror of his Majesty's enemies.'[1] The dethronement of Sharp was daily expected, and Leighton was marked out to succeed Burnet. Leighton pleaded excuses—disease, weariness, schism, the 'little or no good' bishops had done.[2] But the head of Leighton's church sent for him to be 'resurrected' and sent back to try and mollify the westland Whigs. King and courtier discussed the Accommodation which was satisfactory to Charles. Leighton was appointed Archbishop of Glasgow in April 1670, but did not resign Dunblane till after October 1672, thus administering the affairs of both sees, with a nominal salary for Glasgow which allowed the Crown to peculate the teinds. With the view of conciliating the opponents of Episcopacy, Leighton in the autumn selected six ministers to perambulate the west and recommend the Accommodation. These were Gilbert Burnet, James Nairn, minister at Holyrood, a fine preacher, Laurence Charteris, Yester, a refined scholar, afterwards Professor of Divinity in Edinburgh, James Aird, minister at Torryburn, nicknamed 'Bishop Leighton's ape,' Patrick Cooke, minister at Prestonpans, and Walter Paterson, minister at Bolton. In their debates nothing surprised them so much as the aptitude of the peasantry in meeting their arguments with quotations from Scripture.[3] The field-preachers followed them and nullified the work of 'Leighton's Evangelists.' The Bishop's six evangelists.

Parliament again met on 22nd July, and relentless Lauderdale reappeared as Commissioner. Sharp, Leighton, and other four bishops attended.[4] A new Act applicable to certain untried prisoners who would not divulge information was required, and was the second passed. It authorised fining and sending to prison or to banishment refusers to depone, and associates with suspects or rebels. It was a bad beginning for Leighton, who had not yet lifted his visor.[5] The Parliament of July 1670.

In furtherance of the desire of Charles for concord, Lauderdale summoned to Holyrood on 9th August six ministers, supposed to favour modified Episcopacy, to meet and confer with Sharp, Leighton, Rothes, Holyrood conference.

[1] *Act. Parl. Scot.*, vii. 618.
[2] *Laud. Pap.*, ii. 180.
[3] Burnet, i. 524; Row, *Blair*, 468.
[4] *Act. Parl. Scot.*, viii. 3.
[5] *Ibid.*, 7; *Laud. Pap.*, ii. 188.

Tweeddale, and Kincardine. The Whigs went into the conference with halters round their necks. Sharp kept away. Leighton waxed eloquent over soul-ruining schism and the need of compromise. Hutcheson, for his party (Wedderburn, Ramsay, Baird, Gemmel, Burnet, and himself), warily asked for the proposals in writing and leisure to consider them, the discussion of them being illegal as yet.[1] Parliament sat on making most obnoxious statutes, which Leighton, who kept away, afterwards stigmatised as inhuman. The fourth statute, 'Act against invading of ministers,' sent offenders to the gallows and indemnified apprehenders who slew resisting culprits.[2] The fifth statute was the notorious 'Act against Conventicles.' It imposed fine, imprisonment, or banishment on unlicensed preachers who prayed outside their own families; fine or imprisonment *sine die*[3] upon hearers of unlicensed preachers; fine upon master or mistress in whose house a conventicle was held, and, if held in a burgh, fine upon the magistrates. Unlicensed ministers or field-preachers, convening the lieges for religious services in conventicles (or houses which could not contain the worshippers assembled), were liable to death and confiscation.[4] Seizers of the field-preachers were to receive five hundred merks, and be indemnified should they slay their prey in the capture. Lauderdale boastfully wrote to Moray that Parliament had passed a 'Clanking Act' against conventicles, which had roused the Puritanic spirit of bold Cassillis, who alone voted 'no,' 'according to the laudable custom of his fathers.'[5] The more politic King was displeased with the brutal legislation, and told Moray: 'Bloody laws did no good: he would never have passed it had he known beforehand.'[6] The 'Act against disorderly baptisms' reached with heavy fines those who employed unlicensed preachers.[7] The eighth statute, 'Act against separation and withdrawing from the publict meetings for Divyne Worship,' was artfully drawn only to apply to 'all his good subjects of the Reformed Religion'—Papists were left out—and every

Margin note: Act against Conventicles.

Margin note: New 'Clanking Acts' in 1670.

[1] Burnet, i. 520; Wodrow, ii. 178.
[2] *Act. Parl. Scot.*, viii. 8.
[3] [Latin: indefinitely.]
[4] *Act. Parl. Scot.*, viii. 9: 13th August 1670.
[5] *Laud. Pap.*, ii. 200.
[6] Burnet, i. 523.
[7] *Act. Parl. Scot.*, viii. 10, Act 6.

absentee from church for three Sabbaths, without a good reason, was to be fined. Magistrates were given the fines of those under the rank of heritor; heritors who did not attend church and refused to sign the bond repudiating armed risings were to have their estates forfeited to the Crown.[1]

The 'moderate' Whig ministers often met to discuss the proposal of Lauderdale, which amounted to this—Can Presbyterians, allowed to have private opinions regarding Church government, meet in Church courts, presided over by a king-appointed bishop, deprived of his veto, and to whom no canonical oath of obedience has been taken? The answer was 'no.' Recent legislation had nothing to do with this determination.[2] It is clear that such an amalgamation was not in harmony with the genius of Presbytery, which opposed any moderatorship implying permanent ascendency of a pastor over his brethren. Tweeddale, anxious for a *modus vivendi*, went to the west to consult the indulged and to try and arrive at some 'regulation of episcopacy to a primitive model and the allowance of presbytery'; but he had to confess failure to Lauderdale, since 'some of that gang will not subscrive to the Lord's Prayer if asked'; and the diocese of Glasgow was ruined by scandalous curates and cruel soldiery.[3] The Moderates accused Leighton of playing fast and loose with them in secret communications which leaked out, and which the bishop explained away.[4] Leighton met in conference with twenty-six Presbyterian ministers in Paisley on 14th December 1670, of whom some were unfavourable to the Indulgence. The politic prelate began by asking, 'Who shall begin our conference with prayer?' 'Who should pray here but the minister of Paisley?' replied Ramsay, the indulged pastor, noted for his sweet temper.[5] Leighton pleaded for peace—of course, peace *plus* his Episcopacy, patronage, *et cetera*—'pleaded for it in a high and positive strain,' wrote Burnet, who was present. The customary wrangle over scriptural bishops and

Attempts at compromise.

Conference at Paisley, 14th December 1670.

[1] *Act. Parl. Scot.*, viii. 11.

[2] Wodrow, ii. 178, 179.

[3] Tweeddale to Lauderdale, 27th September 1670: *Laud. Pap.*, ii. 205, 207. The volume of Tweeddale-Lauderdale correspondence, which was exhibited in the Glasgow Exhibition 1888, was not available for consultation.

[4] Wodrow, ii. 179.

[5] *Analecta*, iii. 66.

presbyters ensued. Jamison, a learned pastor and Protester, pulverised EPISKOPOS, and drove Leighton into a corner, out of which Professor Burnet boasted he retrieved his ordinary. The battery of words was too much for the recluse, Leighton. His nose bled. He ran out, wringing his hands and crying, 'I see there will be no accommodation.'[1] The meeting dissolved without arriving at a compromise.

Leighton's Accommodation discarded. At a subsequent meeting held at Kilmarnock the indulged framed a reply to the Government. They came to Holyrood on 12th January and met Rothes, Hamilton, Tweeddale, Leighton, and other councillors, who again offered the 'Treaty of Accommodation' to the deputation. Hutcheson, for his party, laconically replied: 'We are not free in conscience to close with the propositions made by the Bishop of Dunblane as satisfactory.'[2] They declined to give their reasons. In their perilous circumstances they acted wisely. MacWard, however, recorded the reasons to this effect, that the bishop of the compromise suppressed the presbyter and ruling elder, and submitted to the wrongous supremacy of the civil ruler.[3] Theirs was the constitutional standpoint established since Melville's day. Sharp was jubilant over the disaster which followed Leighton's impracticable concessions to 'beasts,' whom he considered unappeasable until they got the mastery.[4] He also blamed Leighton for ruining the Church.[5] Leighton thus found himself in a most uncomfortable predicament, railed on by Sharp and his 'high' party as a traitor to Episcopacy, and banned by the Covenanters as a masked emissary of Rome.

Development of convent-icling. Out of common prayer-meetings at Corsock, Caitloch, and other asylums of homeless ministers, conventicles had developed into potent factors in the national life, which the Government, on reckoning with, found were neither to be ignored nor suppressed. Offences at common law had become so multiplied that any drunken trooper or officious informer was at liberty to apprehend any person on chance of discovering a rebel. Only a people debased by slavery could submit

[1] Wodrow, ii. 180; *Laud. Pap.*, iii. App. 233, 234: Law to Lady Cardross, 28th December 1670.

[2] Butler, *Leighton*, 444 *et seq.*

[3] *Case of the Accommodation*, etc., 12, 14, 19 (edit. 1671).

[4] Sharp to Lauderdale, 2nd February 1671: *Laud. Pap.*, ii. 213.

[5] Burnet, i. 606.

to such oppression without revolting. The Hillmen hit the happy medium of maintaining the conviction, expressed by Blackadder, 'that both ministers and people who used such meetings were peaceable, not set on revenge, but only endeavouring to keep up the free preaching of the Gospel in purity and power, in as harmless and inoffensive a way as possible.'[1] The persecuted looked upon a conventicle much as the Israelites viewed the Tabernacle and Ark in the wilderness, as the Presence of God. After the publication of the policy of reconciliation, conventicles became more frequent, of greater dimensions, and more influential, because the gentry also ventured to countenance them. In May 1668, Michael Bruce held a conventicle at Anstruther, under the very nose of Sharp, who demanded a commission to examine this 'gangrene' of implacable persons, as he styled their 'mad conventicling humour.' He now prophesied that 'their confident pranks will have some strange eruption.' John Blackadder left graphic accounts of his wanderings, conventicles, communions, baptisms in the west and around Fife, which, for their exquisite literary grace and style, are still well worth perusing.[2] He said, 'People seemed to smell him out in spite of his caution.' In Dundonald Wood the rapturous multitudes sat on trees, which broke with their weight. At Hill of Beath, on 18th June 1670, he was guarded by Barscob and a troop of Galloway men. A militia officer disturbed the peaceful meeting. Instantly Barscob and a comrade presented pistols. Blackadder, fearing bloodshed, stopped the service, rushed into the fray, exclaiming: 'I charge and obtest you not to meddle with him or do him any hurt … we came here to offer violence to no man, but to preach the gospel of peace.'[3] The officer was let go. Yet one of the results of such gatherings was the 'clanking Act against conventicles.' Some of the Hill of Beath conventiclers were seized, tried, and sentenced to the plantations of Virginia.[4] Illicit meetings were so popular that the authorities tried to nullify their influence by putting in force every repressive statute; and some zealots, in retaliation, exhibited their irritation by committing outrages in manses. Burnet's account of these enormities is exaggerated, as is proved by the records of the

Blackadder's reminiscences of conventicling.

[1] Wodrow, ii. 157 note.
[2] *Memoirs, passim.*
[3] *Ibid.*, 146, 147.
[4] Row, *Blair*, 536, 537.

Justiciary Court.[1] What Burnet refers to is the execution of four men—Smith, Robertson, Montgomerie, and Armour—who were tried for rebellion at Pentland, robbing the manses at Auchinleck, Cambuslang, and Closeburn, and wounding with sword and pistol Ramsay, minister of Auchinleck, whom they made swear never to preach there again. Mr. Andrew Lang thinks that this violence is ignored by Covenanting writers; but neither of these historians mentions that the Lord Commissioners of Justiciary forbade the filling of prisons with suspects, whom no one appeared to charge, and who were left in the jails to starve.

Conventiclers free from crime. The records prove that Covenanting districts were characteristically free from penal offences. Innocent persons, some untried, lay in the oubliettes, till they died; others long after the orders of liberation had been issued, but kept back by those interested.[2]

The trial of Lovell of Cunnoquhie, which was departed from, is worthy of note in its relation to Sharp's murder.[3]

An Episcopal kidnapper, 13th June 1672. In the Records there is no other case like that of Archibald Beith, Episcopal incumbent in Kilbride, Arran, and his servant, who on trial were condemned to the gallows for wiling with refreshments unwary travellers, and murdering them for their merchandise.[4]

Gilbert Burnet's ingenious project. The studied good behaviour of the nonconformists drove Lauderdale into 'the most frantic fits of rage possible,' and he declared to Gilbert Burnet his wish that they should openly rebel, so that he might have the chance to import Irish Papists to cut their throats.[5] Burnet devised, and induced Lauderdale to put into practice, a most ingenious plan for extinguishing the combustion, on the principle that fire confined in a chimney is less dangerous than flame spread about. Laodicean

---

[1] Burnet, in the Preface to the *Vindication*, makes the most of these cases in charging the Presbyterians with cruel molestation of the conforming clergy, but the indictment of the Lord Advocate puts a different face on the crimes, by designating the accused as common robbers living since Pentland 'in a constant habit of oppression and robbing of his Majesties good subjects, and particularly the ministers of the Gospell': *Just. Rec.*, ii. 114. Such felons could not be genuine Covenanters, any more than they could be pious Episcopalians: Burnet, *Vindication*, Pref. xix., 148, 149, 153, 154.

[2] Burnet, i. 604; Lang, *Hist.*, iii. 324; *Just. Rec.*, ii. 30, 31, 113, 115; Wodrow, ii. 187.

[3] Cf. *postea*, 245; *Just. Rec.*, ii. 58, 63.

[4] *Ibid.*, ii. 85-98, 113, 125, 127.

[5] *Hist.*, i. 605.

Lauderdale in his fury preferred the cut-throat method; in his cooler mood of diplomacy he tested Burnet's scheme, which provided for cantoning vagabond preachers in couples in selected parishes, wherein full ministerial power was given to them. This would confine the conflagration, he reckoned. Accordingly, the Council, on 3rd September, appointed one hundred and twenty ministers to charges in various disaffected parts: thirteen to parishes round Glasgow, thirty-two round Irvine, seventeen round Ayr, eight round Kirkcudbright, fourteen round Hamilton, twelve round Lanark, four round Linlithgow, six in the Lothians, ten in Argyleshire, and four were recommended to patrons.[1] This Second Indulgence provided that the indulged minister should get one-half of the stipend, and his colleague the other half; that pastoral duty should be confined to parishioners; that there should be simultaneous communion in each diocese; that preaching should be in churches only; that indulged ministers should not leave their parishes without a licence from the bishop; that dues be paid to, and discipline be taken up by, Presbyteries as before. Ministers outed since 1661 were ordered to attend the parish churches and be certified by magistrates, while disorderly preachers were to be reported on and apprehended. The vagabond ministry, with 'Holy Fairs,' private preaching, and conventicling, was declared criminal. The position of a Presbyterian was not to be envied: he was liable to be thrown into prison and kept there an indefinite time, charged with any offence by any person, who might depart from the accusation; fined or banished for not attending church, for sheltering or speaking to any rebel, for refusing to give satisfactory information regarding suspects, for listening to field-preachers, for being one of five strangers at a prayer-meeting, for whispering against or criticising the Government, for refusing to take the oath of loyalty, for refusing to own Episcopacy, for crossing the parish boundary to hear the neighbouring incumbent. Preacher and layman alike were liable to death for convening or praying at any outdoor meeting, such as a funeral gathering, unless they had licences.

The Second Indulgence, September 1672.

Charles, now practically thralled to Popery, and desirous to be freed from Parliamentary trammels, by encouraging courtiers who favoured toleration, became bold enough to publish a Declaration of Indulgence

The English Indulgence, 1672.

[1] *Hist. of Indulgence,* 179-81; Wodrow, ii. 203-10.

to all English nonconformists, 15th March 1672. Using his power to give relief when none is available under the law, he suspended all penal laws referring to matters of religion and gave freedom to all sects. Very few knew that the King was a Papist. More discreditable was his selling of his friendship and alliance to Louis XIV. of France.[1]

For helping the King in his autocratic designs Lauderdale was rewarded with a dukedom, garter, place in the Council of England, perpetual presidency of the Scots Council, and other lucrative privileges. He gratified another ambition by wedding Elizabeth, Countess of Dysart, daughter of the treacherous William Murray, the beautiful, brilliant widow of Sir Lionel Tollemache of Helmingham. This Delilah owned to having had some influence with Cromwell, and was not credited with many virtues. Fascinating, extravagant, rapacious, sticking at nothing to gain her ends, this 'Queen of Love' trafficked in government patronage; and, in promoting her parasites to places of power wherein they could fleece the unfortunate and pay toll to her, she created ruptures between her husband and his old friends.[2]

Lauderdale's 'Queen of Love.'

Early in summer, 1672, Lauderdale and the Duchess came to Edinburgh and made a great display. When the third session of Parliament assembled on 12th June, she had the audacity to order chairs for herself and her vice-regal court to be placed in the legislative chamber.[3]

Parliament in June 1672.

In view of the English Indulgence, Lauderdale expected the Scots Presbyterians to fawn at his feet, but found that they despised and avoided him. Consequently repressive legislation was renewed. The first statute ordained that all militia officers should be Episcopalians who had taken the oath of allegiance.[4] An 'Act against unlawful ordinations' made ordination by outed ministers punishable by confiscation and banishment, and declared marriages by them to be illegal and clandestine. This made the children of nonconformists illegitimate.[5] Act 22 imposed fines on those whose infants were not baptized within thirty days by accredited clergy; Act 23 ordained the keeping of Restoration

---

[1] Forneron, *Court of Charles II.*, 1-43.
[2] Burnet, i. 437.
[3] Mackenzie, *Memoirs*, 219.
[4] *Act. Parl. Scot.*, viii. 58.
[5] 24th July, Act 20, *ibid.*, 71.

Day with festivity, bells, and bonfires, and a thanksgiving sermon in every parish church.[1] The day after the promulgation of the Second Indulgence, 4th September, Parliament passed Act 41 'against keepers of conventicles and withdrawers from publict worship,' for other three years; amending the former Act, so that only four strangers might attend family worship, and that no outed minister could pray except in a house beyond the parish to which his licence referred.[2] Parliament rose on 11th September. It is evident that the legislators passed these Acts as precautionary measures, in the hope that the generous Indulgence might have a soothing influence through time.

Leighton did not return to Parliamentary life in order to mitigate the rigours invented by his friends, preferring to counsel peace where and while the sword of Damocles hung over the heads of doomed dissenters. His Christianity was not heroic. Had the first Christians evidenced no higher faith, the Gospel would never have crossed the Vale of Hinnom. In his diocesan work in the west he found, he said, the people so intractable that they 'would not receive angels if they committ ye horrid crime of going to presbyteries and synods.'[3] He continued throwing oil on the troubled waters until he was able to report that, through his complacency, 'the west sea is at present pretty calm.' He considered the Second Indulgence a forlorn hope, and recorded his belief that the Church would never recover from 'the fatal Act of Glasgow, laying so great a tract waste to make it quiet, and then stocking again that desert we had made with a great many howles and satyres.'[4] True, the moderate Presbyterians had got their Indulgence out of a mailed fist. Those ministers convened in Edinburgh to consider the Indulgence, 24th September, were afraid to express their views, and parted after concurring that the proposal was not universally acceptable. A concordat could not be framed to include a 'salvo' sufficient to prevent concurrence with magisterial encroachment. Six ministers who accepted office under the Second Indulgence, while resisting the right of King and magistrate to interfere in ecclesiastical affairs, were summoned to the Council. The Covenanters were again

Estimate of Leighton.

---

[1] *Act. Parl. Scot.*, viii. 72, 73.

[2] *Ibid.*, 89.

[3] Leighton to Lauderdale, 1st December 1671: *Laud. Pap.*, ii. 217.

[4] *Hamilton MSS.*, *Hist. MSS. Com. Rep.*, xi., App. vi. 149.

divided into two contending parties, the more dissatisfied opponents being incited by their exiled brethren to pass through the country abusing the Indulgence.[1]

Lauderdale ordered the laws to be put into execution.[2] Eleven landlords in Renfrewshire were fined in £368,031, 13s. 4d. Scots.[3] The outed clergy living in the Capital were ordered into the country; and the indulged who had not entered into their cantonments were cited for their contumacy and ordered to take up their parochial duties before 1st June. The indulged who ignored the Restoration Service were summoned for disloyalty, and nineteen were mulcted of half their stipends. For refusing to take ministerial instructions from the Government, Blair of Galston was thrown into jail, where he contracted a fatal malady.[4] Other refractory ministers were denounced and proclaimed for apprehension. King Charles, still pursuing his policy of toleration, on 31st May, wrote enjoining the Council not to press refusers of the Indulgence who would promise to select a vacant pulpit or to live orderly. At the same time he menaced the untractable, and, in order to stimulate the executive, he required them to commission a court, consisting of Hamilton, Linlithgow, Dumfries, Dundonald, and the Lord President, to quell the 'incorrigible rogues' in Glasgow diocese.[5]

The morose Leighton had to confess to Lauderdale that his undertaking had not succeeded, and that the bishops were a failure: 'for us of this order in this kingdom, I believe 'twere little damage either to Church or State, possibly some advantage to both, if we should all retire.'[6] Concluding that the national troubles were a '*querelle d'Alman,* or a drunken scuffle in the dark,' the invertebrate pacificator confessed he longed for this 'crazy turf of earth that I carry, which makes it an uneasy burden to mee,' to 'shortly drop into the common heap.'[7] Nevertheless he continued to approve of 'curbing that froward party' and did not object to 'those coercions and civill restraints ... found needfull

[1] *Hamilton MSS., Hist. MSS. Com. Rep.*, xi., App. vi. 142.
[2] Lauderdale to Rothes, 21st November 1672, *Hist. MSS.*, XI. vi. 143.
[3] Wodrow, ii. 227.
[4] *Ibid.*, ii. 217.
[5] *Hist. MSS. Com. Rep.*, XI. vi. 144.
[6] *Laud. Pap.*, ii. 238.
[7] *Ibid.*, iii. 75, 76.

to be renewed upon them.'[1] A popular clerical demand for a National Synod, which Leighton recommended to Lauderdale on the ground that it gave parties a freedom of discussion, and that the genius of the Church voiced itself in such conventions, was opposed by Lauderdale, whose recollections of the clerical petitions of 1638, as he said, made him fear evil, as a burned child dreads the fire.[2] At length, sick of the unhappy struggle, Leighton resigned office, retired in December 1674, and settled in Sussex. In the dark days that followed the murder of Sharp, and the rout at Drumclog, the King wrote inviting Leighton to return to Scotland to assist in restoring concord; but the development of events created a new situation in which the proposal came to nought. When on a visit to London, Leighton died in the Bell Inn, Warwick Lane, on 25th June 1684, aged seventy-four years. He was laid beside his brother, Sir Elisha, in the chancel of Horsted Keynes Church.[3] Resignation of Leighton, 1674.

With the light now fully thrown upon the bloody arena of which Leighton was a spiritual overseer, it is not surprising to find that the efforts of Leighton for conciliation, and his policy of comprehension, were distasteful to honest, godly men, who rightly protested against a legal Church having Charles for its Head, and believed that the Accommodation was only a sop thrown to Cerberus.[4]

With all Leighton's fame for piety and anxiety for concord among contentious preachers and distracted citizens, he was in reality a more inflexible Prelatist than any other of the bishops, who, however, were less nervous in occupying their perilous position. As overtly as he pleaded that the spirit of the Gospel only was necessary for salvation— the form of religion being quite indifferent—he as covertly worked for the enforcement of the letter of the inquisitorial law against which any revulsion of his was indefinite and ineffective. His saintliness was timorous and self-protective, not the complement of a soul, manly, magnanimous, and heroic. Leighton an inflexible Prelatist.

The rottenness in high places referred to by Moray[5] grew to such a pitch that universal corruption burst out. In their private letters the Rottenness in high places.

---

[1] 16th June 1674: *Laud. Pap.*, iii. 50.

[2] *Ibid.*, iii. 54.

[3] Burnet, ii. 63, 427, 428; Butler, *Leighton*, 506, 511.

[4] Cf. Burnet, i. 496-536, chap. xiii.

[5] He died in July 1673.

aristocrats undermined and betrayed each other like vulgar knaves. An Anglo-Scottish intrigue to humiliate Lauderdale had its inception, according to Lauderdale, in the ingenious brain of Gilbert Burnet, who incited Hamilton to disaffection. Lauderdale blamed Hamilton for defection, and the latter accused the former of malice. Hamilton had asked and expected much and got little. He opposed Lauderdale's scheme of Union, and had been badly treated by Hatton, so that he was ripe for a rupture. So were others. The secular affairs of the day make a sordid story.[1] The Lauderdale connection battened on ill-gotten gains, Hatton even sweating the coinage.[2]

Parliament met on 12th November 1673 to receive the King's demand for the suppression of 'insolent field-conventicles.'[3] The Hamilton party—Rothes, Tweeddale, Queensberry, Morton, Roxburgh, Drummond, Dumfries—met on the 11th, and arranged that it should be moved that the King's letter be not answered until they had discussed the national grievances.[4] This unexpected assault only temporarily disconcerted Lauderdale, who outmanoeuvred his opponents by introducing three bills discharging the unpopular import duties on salt, brandy, and tobacco. He wisely burked a proposal to introduce a liturgy. The King informed the opposition that they did him no good service who tried to unseat his faithful Commissioner. A similar attack upon him in the English Commons in January also failed.[5] Lauderdale knew how to humour his master, and thus wrote to him: 'I am your secretarie for Scotland, and by that place obliged to atend you, bot I lye at your feet, do with me what ye please.'[6] Hamilton and Tweeddale laid the public grievances before the King, and were 'dismissed with fair words.' Lauderdale was practically sole ruler in Scotland. He had Sharp so well in hand that he could afford to display his own satanic brilliancy in a profane expression of patronage: 'My Lord, sit down

Attacks on Lauderdale frustrated.

[1] *An Accompt of Scotland's Grievances, By Reason of the Duke of Lauderdales Ministrie* (1672), p. 29.

[2] Burnet, ii. 24; Lauderdale got in donations £26,900 stg.; Hatton, £15,300, and £2500 out of the Mint yearly; Atholl got £1500 of fines, and £1400 yearly: *An Accompt*, 29.

[3] *Act. Parl. Scot.*, viii. 208.

[4] Mackenzie, *Memoirs*, 256; Burnet, ii. 38.

[5] *Laud. Pap.*, iii. 21.

[6] 1st February 1674: *ibid.*, 26.

here at my right hand untill I make all your enemies your footstool.'[1] Those special spiritual favours which Mackenzie credits the Duchess of Lauderdale with promising to Welsh and other wandering preachers had practical illustration in an 'Act of Grace,' pardoning past offences of conventiclers, which Lauderdale in the King's name proclaimed, in March 1674, before proceeding south to Court.[2] It created fresh hopes, multiplied field-preachers, and made the multitudinous conventicles more influential, the gentry now countenancing them close to the Primate's palace.[3] Naturally Sharp was furious at the turn things were taking. Compensation was at hand, where he least expected it.

On Saturday, 7th February 1674, James Mitchell was apprehended by Sir William Sharp and two servants of the Primate, and lodged in the Tolbooth of Edinburgh. Unsuspected, he and his wife kept a little shop in the Capital for the sale of brandy and tobacco. Sharp himself in passing noted the interested gaze of Mitchell at his door, and caused his apprehension. He had also been discovered at the funeral of Robert Douglas.[4] He disclaimed identity with the assassin. He was instantly brought before the Commissioner and the Privy Council, and a committee, consisting of Rothes, Hatton, and Primrose, was appointed to examine him. Sharp sent Nicoll Sommervell, brother-in-law of Mitchell, to visit the prisoner and assure him of a pardon on his confessing his crime.[5] Mitchell was willing if he got an assurance in the King's name. Primrose said, 'It would be a strange force of eloquence to persuade a man to confess and be hanged.' Lauderdale authorised the committee to give this assurance. Rothes took him apart and conveyed the promise. Thereupon Mitchell upon his knees confessed his attempt upon the Primate, he and his examiners thereafter signing the written confession. Mitchell's papers, Hatton's letters to Kincardine, and the Minutes of the Privy Council bear this out, to this effect: 'He did then confesse vpon his knees he was the person, vpon assurance given him by one of the Committy, as to his lyfe, who had warrand from the

Apprehension of James Mitchell, February 1674.

Mitchell's confession and imprisonment.

---

[1] *An Accompt*, 38.
[2] Mackenzie, *Memoirs*, 273; Kirkton, 342.
[3] Blackadder, *Memoirs*, 164.
[4] Burnet, ii. 136; *Hist. Not.*, 90.
[5] Burnet, ii. 136; Wodrow, ii. 471.

Lord Commissioner and Councill to give the same.'[1] Two days later he adhered to his confession before the Privy Council, the members of this court condemning him to lose his right hand and to be forfeited; and for this doom passing him on to the Justiciary Court for indictment and sentence. On 2nd March, he appeared in the dock. As one of the judges, who hated Sharp, passed by the prisoner to the bench, he said, 'Confess nothing, unless you are sure of your limbs as well as of your life.'[2] Naturally Mitchell resiled from his confession, and brought about a deadlock in the court, which was adjourned, first till 9th March, then till 25th March, when the Lord Advocate deserted the charge.[3] Mitchell was committed to the Tolbooth, no doubt owing this respite to the fact that the King's abhorrence of bloodshed made the Council pause, before imprisoning him on the Bass, as they intended to do. The new state prison on the Bass Rock, a solitary islet in the Firth of Forth, was a recent acquisition of the Crown from a minion of Lauderdale, who advised its purchase at a great price, and then had himself appointed as its salaried captain.[4] It was the most vile and unwholesome of prisons.

Prison on the Bass Rock.

Every effort was made, but in vain, to suppress the conventicles and to apprehend the fugitive preachers. Militiamen and informers scoured the country in search of Welsh, Semple, Cargill, Blackadder, Veitch, Peden, Hog, Fraser, and others, £400 sterling being offered for the first two, and 1000 merks for each of the others alive or dead. Persecution made the field-missions prosper the more. Hosts of eight or ten thousand persons assembled to hear Welsh, Blackadder, and Welwood, when they perambulated Fifeshire. The parish churches were empty, Rothes and his household being the only worshippers in Leslie church one Sabbath. This happy interlude, which lasted for about a quarter of a year, was called 'The Blynk,' i.e. a glimpse of sunshine amid stormy showers and darkness.[5] Brushes with the military became more frequent, and in some cases prisoners were taken and blood was shed.

'The Blynk,' 1674.

[1] *Reg. Sec. Conc.*, *Acta*, 1673-8, p. 55, 12th February 1674; pp. 63, 64, 12th March 1674; Papers left by J. M., *Laing MSS.*, *Farrago*, 269; Wodrow, ii. 248; *Just. Rec.*, ii. 337.

[2] Burnet, ii. 137. For indictment and trial, cf. *Just. Rec.*, ii. 255-62; App., 307-39.

[3] *Just. Rec.*, ii. 268; *The Scots Worthies* (Carslaw's edition), 382-97.

[4] *Accompt of Scotland's Grievances*, 38; M'Crie, *The Bass Rock*, 17; Blackadder, *Memoirs*, 267.

[5] Blackadder, *Memoirs*, 155-69; Wodrow, ii. 234.

During these skirmishes the much excited worshippers imagined they saw supernatural beings protecting them from the harmless shots of the soldiery. The garrison of Mid-Calder surprised a conventicle conducted by Riddell, shot Davie, a heritor, and carried away some prisoners and their clothes, Bibles, and belongings.[1]

Robert Gillespie, an irregular preacher 'at the horn,' was taken after a conventicle at Falkland, and on 2nd April sent by the Privy Council to the Bass to be immured.[2] Gillespie was soon followed by the hitherto elusive Peden, whom Major Cockburn captured at Knockdow, Ballantrae, the house of Hugh Ferguson, and whom the Council, on 26th June, sentenced to the Bass, where Peden was kept for four years. Ferguson was fined 1000 marks for resetting Peden, and the captors were handsomely rewarded.[3]

[margin: Capture of Peden.]

On 16th June the Privy Council issued an Act for apprehending rebels, especially Welsh, Semple, and Arnot, and offering as a substantial reward to informers the fines exigible from conventiclers seized.[4] Two days later a proclamation made heritors liable for their tenantry, masters for their servants, and magistrates for burgesses, and offered the escheats to heritors and liferenters.[5] These orders accorded with instructions sent from the King, explaining, 'It is not for their opinions, but their traitorous practices, that we intend to punish them.'[6] This idea of Lauderdale Mackenzie afterwards repeated in his *Vindication* of the Government.

On 4th June 1674, the narrow Parliament Close was the scene of a remarkable incident which terrified Sharp into imagining that Jenny Geddes and her brigade of stool-throwers had seen a resurrection. Fifteen women, mostly in widows' weeds, blocked the entry to the Council-chamber, ready to thrust into each councillor's hand a petition lamenting their spiritual starvation and supplicating that liberty be granted to faithful ministers to provide the citizens with

[margin: The widows' petition.]

---

[1] Blackadder (*Memoirs*, 158) calls him John. A gravestone in Bathgate churchyard records: 'Here lies the Body of James Davie, who was shot at Blackdub, April 1673, by Heron,' etc.: *Martyr Graves of Scotland*, 237.

[2] Wodrow, ii. 223.

[3] Walker, *Peden* in *Six Saints*, i. 49; ii. 130; Wodrow, ii. 224, 356; M'Crie, *Bass*, 31-3.

[4] Wodrow, ii. 237 note.

[5] *Ibid.*, 235 note.

[6] *Ibid.*, 239 note.

a pure Gospel after the Presbyterian form. Rothes gallantly received the petition of Widow Livingstone with raised hat and insinuating speeches. The furtive Sharp, fearing a thrust under the fifth rib, hurried past amid a fusillade of vituperations, such as 'Judas,' 'traitor,' glad that only the gentle hand of a widow detained him while she prophetically exclaimed, 'that neck must pay for it ere all was done.' The Council decreed that the paper was seditious and that the tumult was a plot. The petitioners were summoned; a few were thrown into prison, and three—Mrs. Elizabeth Rutherford, Wariston's daughter Margaret, and Lady Mersington—were banished out of Edinburgh,[1] chiefly for refusing to implicate others. Absentees were denounced.

In March 1669, the city of Edinburgh was fined £50 for a conventicle held in Widow Paton's house; on 24th June 1674, the city had to pay £100 for a conventicle held in April or May by Weir and Johnston in the Magdalene Chapel. Some of the attenders at this conventicle were still in prison awaiting trial. Similarly the city of Glasgow was fined £100 for recent conventicles. On 25th June, the Council examined a batch of Fife lairds for hearing and harbouring Welsh and other preachers. They were mulcted in 20,000 merks, being sent back to jail till their fines were paid.[2] No favour was shown to any one. Linlithgow politely informed Atholl that Atholl's own steward had been fined 2000 merks for sheltering Veitch.[3] A long list of persons escheated to Sir William Sharp, cash-keeper to the King, shows how widespread nonconformity was in July 1674 in Fifeshire.[4] It includes fifty laymen, two ladies, and forty-two ministers, including Hog, Welwood, Kirkton, and Cargill. Some appear to be identical with the Magus Moor conspirators. Escheats were often sold by public auction. By an Act of 16th July witnesses were forced to give evidence on oath regarding conventiclers, or stand confessed themselves. That there might be no escape, a royal commission was granted to three influential courts, mostly composed of nobles, in three districts, for the purpose of exterminating conventicles.[5]

Fines, escheats, fugitations.

---

[1] Mackenzie, *Memoirs*, 273; Kirkton, 344; Wodrow, ii. 246, 268.
[2] Wodrow, ii. 238.
[3] *Hist. MSS. Com. Rep.*, viii. 32.
[4] *Wodrow MSS.*, lx.
[5] Wodrow, ii. 245.

As proving how weak was the policy of repression among good and thoughtful men, the case of Thomas Forrester, Episcopal minister at Alva, is prominent. After a minute study of the *Apologetical Narration* by Brown and similar works upon the question, Forrester felt himself constrained to inform his co-presbyters in Stirling that he was prepared to prove that the 'prelatic frame of government' was both unlawful and unscriptural. The brethren never asked his proofs. He left their meetings to associate with the persecuted. He was apprehended and imprisoned in Edinburgh in the spring of 1674, but took advantage of the indemnity in March to obtain freedom. On 29th April the diocesan Synod of Dunkeld deposed him.[1] He became a field-preacher, latterly an able polemic and defender of Presbytery, and, after the Revolution, was appointed Principal of St. Mary's, at St. Andrews, and Professor of Divinity.[2]

At this juncture the nonconformists were anxiously devising means whereby a succession of sound ministers might be maintained and united under Presbyterial rule. Regulations were suggested for licensing the wandering students who accompanied the outlawed preachers, for giving calls, for establishing Church courts, and for asking the protection of the Crown for loyal Presbyterians.[3] Large numbers of the outed ministers met in Edinburgh in June, and after drawing up a series of overtures, adjourned till October. These overtures were sent down to Presbyteries or 'societies' for discussion and approval, and the substance of them and of the facts relative to the Church was included in an address to the Government. The overtures were generally approved of.[4] The righteous desired ministers and meeting-houses; their rulers gave them General George Munro, the militia, and thirteen garrisons!

Not all the clergy of the Established Church had lost their interest in self-government, and many of them desired a national Synod wherein they might publicly appear as operative members of a Church with a constitution, and having some say in the administration of its own

[1] Wodrow, ii. 258.
[2] Forrester wrote *Rectius Instruendum* in 1681, published 1684; *The Hierarchical Bishop's Claim*, etc., 1699, a reply to Scott, Munro, and Honyman; *Review and Consideration*, reply to Sage, 1706.
[3] Wodrow, ii. 272.
[4] Row, *Blair*, 542; Wodrow, ii. 274.

distinctive affairs. This was considered the more necessary that the Established Church now had no authorised Standards, apart from the Presbyterian Standards. Some leading laymen also thought a Synod desirable. The movement took shape in May 1674. Sir William Sharp, at the instance of Atholl, Argyll, Murray, and Linlithgow, on 7th May, wrote to Lauderdale upon the subject,[1] who in turn informed Leighton that he could not concur in the proposal, since he could 'expect no manner of good' from a Synod. Some bishops were as friendly to the proposal as the Primate was inimical to it. Notably James Ramsay, Leighton's successor in Dunblane, the same enthusiast who bonfired the Covenant at Linlithgow, and rescued Hamilton while gallantly he fought for the King at Rullion Green, voiced the opinions of his diocese. Laurie, 'the nest egg,' now Bishop of Brechin, also favoured the proposal.[2] Four incumbents in the diocese of Edinburgh—Turner, Cant, Robertson, and Hamilton—tried to induce Young, the Bishop of Edinburgh, who was supposed to be sympathetic, to persuade the Primate to convene a Synod.[3] Sharp was incensed at the idea. He frantically wrote to the English Primate declaring 'the Gospel is at stake ... there is a fire set to our own bed-straw by sons of our own bowels, who viper-like seek to eat that which produced them. ... Cant, a presbyter, has shaken off all fear of God ... calling me a great grievance to the church ...' and unless Canterbury would come to his help he would suffer shipwreck and the Church be wounded.[4] Sharp entreated Sheldon to influence the King against the proposal. Meantime, in St. Andrews on 8th July, he called a meeting of the bishops of his province with some presbyters to discuss and practically to shelve the subject. Bishop Ramsay made an honest stand and gave reasons for the need of reform in the Church. Sharp rebuked Ramsay, who left the meeting. As soon, therefore, as opportunity offered, Sharp hurried up to London and stayed nine months croaking over incipient revolution. The peacemakers fell on trouble. Insubordination was insufferable to the bureaucratic Lauderdale, who got a royal mandate for the removal of the petitioning ministers from their charges, and for the transference of Ramsay, within fourteen days,

---

[1] *Laud. Pap.*, iii. 42, 54.
[2] Wodrow, ii. 300.
[3] *Laud. Pap.*, iii. 46.
[4] Wodrow, ii. 301; *Laing MSS.*, 81, 82.

to the See of the Isles, beyond the reach of 'meddling with affairs relative to the church.'[1] The warrior bishop, who denied all factious intentions, and admitted his desire for the authorisation of regulative formularies, was not to be suppressed. He carried his case to court. He wrote fierce letters to Sharp, accused him of tyranny, threatened him with the revelation of 'foul things,' and refused to attend meetings where there was no right of free speech.[2] After a conflict for more than a year Ramsay found himself outwitted by astuter diplomatists, and was compelled to submit obsequiously to the Primate after an inquiry in a court of bishops presided over by the Archbishop of Glasgow, and humbly to throw himself 'at his sacred Majesty's feet.'[3]

Sharp and Lauderdale suppress Bishop Ramsay.

The national Synod was not convened. With the retiral of Archbishop Leighton and the reinstallation of Alexander Burnet, 29th September 1674, the exterminators of the Covenanters had their hands strengthened, and the policy of 'blood and iron' was prosecuted with greater vigour than ever.

A rigorous winter followed by a blasting summer, 'making the heavens brass and the earth iron,' although it 'broke the staff of their bread,' was to the Covenanters a light affliction compared with the cruel humiliation imposed upon them by an order of the Privy Council, that all the lieges should assemble in the parish churches on a fixed Fast Day to confess sin, repent, and thereby avert the wrath of God.[4]

The indulged clergy were worst off, because some of them had got no stipends for years, and this hardship was a good reason for their ignoring their instructions and ministering beyond their licensed districts, in order to regain some popularity, and with it, bread. The Government at once prosecuted these breakers of the licence.[5] The fever of conventicling nowhere abated, although informers and troopers with dogs ranged everywhere in search of the elusive preachers in the

The policy of iron and blood.

---

[1] 16th July 1674: Wodrow, ii. 304.

[2] *Wodrow MSS.*, xxxii. 129.

[3] Turner, Cant, and Robertson also submitted: Wodrow, ii. 315, 342; Kirkton, 348; *Laud. Pap.*, iii. 64; Grub, *Hist.*, iii. 250-2; Law, *Memoirs*, 70, 71, 84. Ramsay was recalled, 27th April 1675, was translated to Ross in 1684, and died in Edinburgh on 22nd October 1696. Cant was afterwards appointed Principal of Edinburgh College.

[4] Wodrow, ii. 280 note: 15th July 1675.

[5] *Ibid.*, 296.

Lothians, Fife, and the south, and heavy fines were imposed on towns where illegal preachings took place.[1] A party of guardsmen with their hounds by night surprised the house of Cardross. They were disguised as civilians. They were in search of John King, chaplain there, Robert Langlands, tutor, and any incriminating papers. Sir Mungo Murray was the hero of this illegal and brutal burglary, in which they inhumanly treated the delicate Lady Cardross, as well as broke up lockfast places, and carried off King. The peasantry rose and rescued him. Rightly, Cardross petitioned the Council for redress, only to find himself in August charged with being associated with criminal rescuers of an irregular preacher; his wife, too, was accused of harbouring a rebel conventicler. The Council ordered Cardross to prison in the Castle of Edinburgh during the King's pleasure, and fined him in £1112, 10s. sterling. They also turned his house into a garrison. Not till February 1677 was he released, then to be charged afresh for his having two children baptized by unlicensed ministers, for which he was fined in one-half of his valued rent.[2]

Prosecution of Erskine of Cardross.

News of the rescue was sent to London, whence a letter came in June demanding an inquiry into the continued disorders. As a result of this the Council passed an Act, 13th July, establishing thirteen garrisons in the counties of Perth, Linlithgow, Kinross, Lanark, Selkirk, Roxburgh, Stirling, Renfrew, Ayr, Dumfries, and empowering the district commissioners of excise to quarter and victual the troops.[3] This novel exaction was resisted by some landlords in Berwickshire. Sir Patrick Hume of Polwarth boldly refused payment and lodged a bill of suspension against the decreet, which brought the whole subject before the Council. They gave Polwarth 'Jeddart justice,' imprisoning him till the King's pleasure was declared. In October, the King replied approving of this treatment of Polwarth as 'a factious person,' declaring him incapable of all public trust, and ordering him to a cell in Stirling Castle.[4] In his trials Polwarth was supported and encouraged to be firm by the Earl of Home, Lord Cardross, and the Duke of Hamilton, the latter promising

Jeddart justice' on the Borders.

---

[1] At a fight at Bathgate fifteen prisoners were taken—13th March 1675: *Laud. Pap.*, iii. 77.

[2] Wodrow, ii. 288-93, 357, 358.

[3] *Ibid.*, ii. 282.

[4] *Ibid.*, 294; Row, *Blair*, 562, 565.

him help.[1] The baffled Council devised a new method of striking at those who refused to compear in court, or to observe the terms of the Indulgence. This method was promulgated in the scandalous 'Letters of Intercommuning,' 6th August 1675.[2] This proclamation discharged the lieges from resetting, supplying with meat, drink, shelter, or intelligence, from intercommuning with certain rebels then 'at the horn' and therein designated, under pain of being prosecuted as 'art and part with them.' Twenty-one ministers were named, among the number being Cargill, Welsh, Semple, Arnot, Hog, M'Gilligen, Fraser of Brea, King, and seventy-three men and women, many of them heritors, ladies of title, and dames of influence. On 3rd August 1676, this black list was augmented by the names of Kirkton, Welwood, Donaldson, and other famous field-preachers. Thus the doom of traitors was applicable to the friends or suspected friends of the outlaws.

'Letters of Intercommuning,' 6th August 1675.

During the perpetration of the severities in Fifeshire, four outlaws distinguished themselves, and were largely instrumental in bringing about that state of affairs which ultimately ended in the triumph of Covenanting principles. These were Donald Cargill, Richard Cameron, John Balfour of Kinloch, and David Hackston of Rathillet. Cargill had, since October 1662, been the outed minister of the Barony, Glasgow, where he had served seven years. He was the son of Laurence Cargill, notary, and laird of a small estate in Rattray, and of his wife Marjorie Blair. He matriculated in St. Salvator's College in 1645, and was licensed by the Presbytery of St. Andrews on 13th April 1653.[3] At the height of this conventicling period he was in his prime, and well able to attempt the memorable long 'Cargill loup' over the fearful chasm in the Keith, when he was chased from the Haerchen Hill. A sad, silent, prayerful prophet was Cargill, mourning a dead wife, lamenting the destruction of the Church, and uttering malisons thus: 'Wo, wo, wo to him [the King], his name shall stink while the world stands for treachery, tyranny, and leachery ... if these men die the ordinary death of men, then God never sent me, nor spoke by me.'[4]

Outlaws in Fife: Donald Cargill.

[1] *Marchmont Papers*; *Hist. MSS. Com. Rep.*, xiv. App. iii. 112, 113.

[2] Aldis, *List*, 2058, 2077; Wodrow, ii. 286 note.

[3] Patrick Walker, *Some Remarkable Passages in the Life and Death of ... Cargill*, 1732; *Six Saints*, ii. 1-62, 119-222; *Biog. Presby.*, ii. 1-54 (Edin., 1837).

[4] *Six Saints*, ii. 8, 10.

Richard
Cameron.

Among the names of conventiclers in 1675 appear those of 'Allan Cameron, merchant in Faulkland, Margaret Paterson, his spouse, Mr. Richard Cameron, his son, Michael Cameron, indweller there.'[1] Richard Cameron was born in Falkland, matriculated in St. Andrews in March 1662, and took the degree of M.A. on 22nd July 1665. Thereafter he became schoolmaster and precentor in Falkland.[2] Cameron came under the influence of the stirring outlawed preacher, John Welwood, whom we find in 1675 writing to Richard: 'You have the honour to be persecuted for righteousness: have a care, be not lifted up, for there may be several tryals before your hand.'[3] Welwood also wrote from Dundee: 'My desire is that the Lord may help you to be holy and harmless in a crooked generation.' He accompanied Welsh in his wanderings, and won the esteem of that good man for his piety and gifts. When the itinerant Presbytery met at Henry Hall's house, Haughhead, Teviotdale, Welsh, Semple, and other ministers licensed Cameron, knowing that he was an enemy of the Indulgence. They sent him on a mission to the unregenerate in Annandale, and on his appearing timid, Welsh encouraged him with the moving benediction, 'Go your way, Ritchie; set the fire of hell to their tail.'[4] This the clerical Samson effectively did. That imported flame, stirring the inflammable Celtic disposition of Cameron, made him an uncompromising antagonist of the Government and of their lukewarm allies—the indulged. After joining Welwood and Kid in their perilous and discouraging campaign against the favourers of compromise with the regnant party in State and Church, Cameron deemed it expedient to seek a refuge on the Continent, whither Welwood sent him a letter, on 26th January 1677, grudging him his 'stay where no religion is.'[5]

John Balfour
—'Burly' of
Kinloch.

Among the auditors of the field-preachers in Fife, in the summer of 1672, was 'John Balfour, portioner in Kinloch,'[6] in the parish of

[1] *Wodrow MSS.*, xxxiii. 142.

[2] Patrick Walker, Life, in *Biog. Presb.*, i. 191-319; *Six Saints*, i. 218-365; ii. 155-98; Downie, *The Early Home of Richard Cameron*, 1-38; Herkless, *Richard Cameron* (Famous Scots Series, *passim*).

[3] Edin., 13th Dec. 1675: *Laing MSS.*, 359, fol. 4.

[4] *Six Saints*, i. 219.

[5] *Laing MSS.*, 359, fol. 33.

[6] John Balfour of Kinloch, son of John Balfour and Grizzel Hay, daughter of Hay of Paris, Perthshire, born *c.* 1640; served heir to his grandfather Robert, 26th

Collessie. He was a squat, squint-eyed, fierce-looking man, and was known as 'Burly.' With the strain of the wild unreliable Balfour of Burleigh blood in him, it was not singular that he should disobey the order of the court to compear and answer for conventicling, for which contempt of court he was under warrant for apprehension. In all likelihood he is the same criminal mentioned in a list of escheats granted to Sir William Sharp, and also in the 'Letters of Intercommuning.'[1] Balfour's brother-in-law, David Halkerstoun, or Hackston, proprietor of Rathillet, in Kilmany parish, succeeded his father in 1670.[2] He was esteemed a gallant country gentleman, at first of the prelatic party, and having employment of some kind from Rothes. A sordid transaction on the part of Archbishop Sharp resulted in his being brought into active alliance with the conventiclers. It is a story of agrarian outrage. The estate of Cunnoquhie in Monimail, a gift of James III. to the church of St. Andrews, was held by a family of Lovells, the last of whom, William, became bankrupt, and in resisting a distraint in 1671 killed the sheriff-officer, for which he was summoned to the Justiciary Court.[3] On the restoration of the hierarchy, Sharp became superior of Cunnoquhie, and, on Lovell's failure to pay the feu-duties, resumed possession of the fief, to the detriment of the heirs and creditors.[4] Hackston appears to have had two interests in the estate, being a creditor, and also acting as collector of the Episcopal rents for his friend, Sharp. For a bond of £1000 Scots, Sharp sold his interest to Hackston. Sharp was notorious for avariciousness. Hackston failed to implement his bargain, or to give satisfactory count and reckoning, with the result that Sharp threw him into jail, where he lay for months. On his release Hackston swore, 'God damn him if ever he went to church so long as there was a bishop in Scotland.'[5] The popularity of the Primate was not increased by the fact that his brother, as cash-keeper to the King, intromitted with the fines, and by the suspicion that Rothes and the Archbishop worked to

David Hackston of Rathillet.

February 1663; married Barbara Hackston, sister of Hackston of Rathillet. His confiscated property went to Lord Lindores: *Scot. Mag.*, i. 130 (September 1817).

[1] *Wodrow MSS.*, lx.; Wodrow, ii. 287, 288 note.
[2] Miller, *Fife*, ii. 318.
[3] *Just. Rec.*, ii. 58, 60, 63; *Book of Adjournal*, 17th July 1671.
[4] *Act. Parl. Scot.*, v. 449.
[5] *A True Relation*, etc., *Anal. Scot.*, ii. 388.

each other's hands.[1] The King blamed the authorities for winking at conventicles in order to get fines, and said to Monmouth that if Rothes and the other nobles had done their duty there would have been no conventicles in Fife.[2]

Brutal

The unsuccessful attempt of James Mitchell, in December 1675, to break the Tolbooth, gave the Privy Council an opportunity to examine that undischarged prisoner. The new charge was that he was in the rebellion of 1666; and his alleged confession to that effect before the Council, now produced to the Lords of Justiciary, he renounced. To elicit the facts, the Council authorised a joint bench of judges and nobles to torture him. In the vaulted chamber beneath the House of Parliament, where Linlithgow presided on the night of the 18th January, the inquiry began. The accused justly pleaded that he had stood his trial. Linlithgow set aside the plea, asserting that he was only asked to own a former confession. The first diet ended with the threat of 'a sharper thing.' At the second diet, 22nd, the ugly boots and wedges lay on the table, and Linlithgow said to the prisoner, 'I will see if that will make you do it.' Mitchell, who knew the law, argued that a confession extorted by torture could not be used against him or others. The judges hesitated and adjourned. At a third diet, 24th, the court met in the inner Parliament House, in full state. The executioner and his instruments were there. Mitchell was obdurate. The executioner tied him to a chair, and asked the judges which leg they selected for the boots. 'Either,' was the reply. Mitchell boldly exclaimed, 'Take the best of the two, for I freely bestow it in the cause.' He dropped the right leg into the frame. As the torture proceeded, Lord Advocate Nisbet and he debated on the question of magisterial function and power. The grand test of morale began as the wedges were slowly driven down, thirty queries being ejected amid the blows, followed by the rasping question of the judicial tongue, 'Any more to say?' As often repeated was the resolute reply, 'No more, my Lords.' At the ninth stroke, nature failed. 'Alas, my Lord, he is gone,' cried the executioner. The torturers vanished. As soon as Mitchell recovered from the swoon he was carried back to prison—his smashed limb being unable to support him. It was said that the torture

Brutal torture of James Mitchell, January 1675.

---

[1] MacWard Papers, *Wodrow MSS.*, lx, (Iac. 5. i. 10), 88.
[2] *Laud. Pap.*, 23242, fol. i.

would have been renewed had not Sharp received a warning that he would get a shot from a steadier hand. The injured man was kept in the Tolbooth till January 1677, when he was transported to the Bass with the devout Fraser of Brea. In direst misery he lay there another year, till Sharp discovered another prosecutor from whose clutches he could not escape. Peden might rove over his rocky Patmos, Fraser might pluck the cherries in its garden, but broken Mitchell might only hear in darkness the scream of the sea-gulls and the distant psalm of praise.[1] With this form of entertainment the governors of Scotland began the year 1676. Before they saw the end of it they had made many a home desolate and many a heart sad. The Government were not dealing with a few ignorant fanatical peasants, being forced to acknowledge that 'Schollars, merchants, and tradesmen are the chief persons who are ordinarily poisoned with factions and Schismatick principles.'[2]

Mitchell confined on the Bass.

The Council, attributing the decay of religion to absenteeism from church, sounded another blast on their horn, on 1st March 1676, in a 'Proclamation against Conventicles.'[3] It ordered the prosecution of Papists and other schismatics, the seizure of 'all such preachers as with their families do not attend public worship,' the fining of all magistrates and heritors for conventicles held on their property, with power to recover the fines from the culprits, the licensing of teachers and chaplains, the arrangement of rewards for informers, and the imposing of fines on remiss magistrates. A census was ordered of all who had taken the oaths of allegiance and supremacy; and special courts were commissioned to see the laws executed in every shire.[4] The inquisition began with the summoning of heritors and ministers in the west to confess their recent dealings with the intercommuned. The ministers not compearing were outlawed. Some gentlemen, refusing to declare on oath, were held as confessed, and sent to prison for months till their friends paid their fines. With such phenomenal activity of the law-officers, military, and spies, the outlaws and conventiclers practised wariness. Their gatherings were held in remotest places, and the sacraments were even dispensed by night. Welsh was untiring, even

A Fresh Inquisition, 1st March 1676.

[1] Wodrow, ii. 455-7; Law, *Memoirs*, 85; Fraser, *Mem.* in *Select Biog.*, ii. 344.
[2] 'Lauderdale's plan against Schism': *Wodrow MSS.*, xliii. (Rob. iii. 3. 16), 15.
[3] Aldis, *List*, 2081; Wodrow, ii. 318 note.
[4] Wodrow, ii. 320, 323.

preaching in the middle of the frozen Tweed, that 'two nations might dispute his crime.'[1] His friends paid dearly for their attachment to him—Durham of Largo being mulcted in £1200 Scots for resetting him, and 2500 merks for attending his preaching twice. Veitch held a conventicle of four thousand persons on the Blue Cairn on Lauderdale's land in defiance of him on 26th April 1676. In the wild uplands on the Borders, Welsh, Arnot, Semple, and Scott found a temporary asylum until the long arm of the law reached them. Others crossed to Ireland.

Convention of the outed clergy, May 1676.

On 20th May, some expelled clergy, fifty or sixty in number stealthily assembled in Edinburgh to discuss the situation. Alexander Forrester, minister of St. Mungo, was clerk of the meeting, which assumed the function of a Commission of the Church, and sat about a week transacting business competent to a Church court, regarding preachers, correspondence with the disunited portions of the Church, and the proposals of the Government. Forrester and his minutes fell into the hands of the authorities,[2] when Forrester was apprehended for the second time, after he had served a term of imprisonment in St. Andrews and on the Bass Rock. Among the preachers at this time summoned by the Council for intrusion was Hugh Campbell in Muirkirk, whom we shall afterwards find trying to overcome the scruples of John Brown of Priesthill.[3]

James Kirkton trepanned.

James Kirkton, formerly minister at Mertoun, and now at the horn for refusing to be indulged minister at Carstairs and for conventicling at Cramond, had a singular experience in June 1676 which he records in his *History*.[4] At noon, on the streets of Edinburgh, he was politely accosted by a gentleman and inveigled into a house, to find that he was trepanned into a dungeon by the notorious Captain Carstairs. Kirkton's friends, having traced him, arrived at the nick of time, when Carstairs, who had just drawn his pistol, found himself in grips and grounded by the more athletic outlaw. Kirkton's brother-in-law, Robert Baillie of Jerviswood, and others separated the combatants. Carstairs rushed to Hatton to complain of this rescue of a fanatic preacher, and to inflame the Council. Sharp demanded vengeance, lest punishers of disorder should be discouraged. The rescuers were apprehended. At their

[1] Kirkton, 372.
[2] Wodrow, ii. 355.
[3] *Ibid.*, ii. 323.
[4] *Hist.*, 367.

trial a warrant, fabricated after the fracas, purporting to be Carstairs' order for the seizure of Kirkton, was produced. That settled the case. For deforcing an officer of the Crown Baillie was fined £500 sterling and sentenced to lie in prison till he paid it; while his two comrades were also heavily fined and sent to prison. For four months Baillie lay in the cells in Edinburgh and Stirling Castles before he was released. Carstairs was encouraged in his villainy by receiving 3000 merks out of Baillie's fine.[1] Baillie was more than ever a marked man, being considered a bird out of a bad nest—a descendant of Knox and the son-in-law of Wariston. Kirkton was specially marked for punishment, his name heading the list of fifteen intercommuned ministers proclaimed on 3rd August 1676.

To render the punitive work of the Government more effective a royal commission, dated 20th July, was received instituting a 'Committee of Public Affairs,' consisting of the two archbishops, Argyll, Mar, Murray, Linlithgow, Seaforth, Kinghorn, Dundonald, Elphinstone, Lord Privy Seal, President, Treasurer-Depute, Advocate, Justice-Clerk, Lord Collington, or any three of them; Sharp to be vice-chairman, with plenary powers, 'to do all things necessary to his Majesty's service.'[2] It was another 'Star Chamber' instituted to engineer the persecution. *The Scots Star Chamber.*

The biographer of the Lord Advocates had justification for asserting: 'On taking office [in 1677] Mackenzie found the jails full of wretches whom Nisbet had left in chains, because he had neither been bribed to prosecute them nor bribed to release them.'[3] Prisoners, for whom no victuals were provided, lay long untried, often forgotten. This is proved by the petition of seven untried conventiclers who had lain in Stirling Tolbooth for fifteen months and now sought liberation, being, they confessed, 'poor old decrepit bodies … poor creatures with wives and families. We have been many times at the point of starving, and had long ere now died for want, if we had not been supplied by the charity of other people.' The Council disponed them to Captain Maitland for serfdom or military service in France, and they were smuggled away at midnight in fetters and guarded by soldiery,[4] one being discharged because he appeared to be dying. *Forgotten victims.*

---

[1] Wodrow, ii. 328; Kirkton, 370; Burnet, *Hist.*, ii. 114.

[2] Wodrow, ii. 324.

[3] Omond, *The Lord Advocates*, i. 213.

[4] Wodrow, ii. 342.

In the early winter of 1676, many clergy and laity, including ladies, were prosecuted, denounced, fined, or sent to prison till they found cautioners for their fines, among the number being Widow Guthrie, relict of the minister of Tarbolton, and Bessie Muir, relict of Alexander Dunlop of Paisley, mother of Principal Dunlop.[1]

Ker of Kersland. A fellow-prisoner in Stirling with Baillie in August 1676 was Robert Ker of Kersland, Dalry, who had been in various jails since 1670. After Rullion Green he escaped to Utrecht, whence he returned in the end of 1669 to see his estate enjoyed by General Drummond, and to fall into the hands of the Government through the treachery of Cannon of Mardrogat, the informer. The sufferings of his family were also grievous. In 1677 his punishment was relaxed and liberty allowed to him. He was once more taken and thrown into Glasgow Tolbooth, from which he was rescued by the people, when a great fire broke out in Glasgow. After consoling himself with the society and sermons of the hill-preachers till August 1678, he saw the prudence of withdrawing to Utrecht, where he died in 1680.[2]

Donaldson of Dalgetty. Very merciless was the action of the authorities in the case of Donaldson, the model minister of Dalgety, at this time resident in Inverkeithing. For daring to have a service in his own house for his family and friends, Donaldson, an old man, was carried from his bed to Linlithgow prison and immured there for a year without being prosecuted.[3]

Exiles in Holland. Not satisfied with harassing his subjects at home, the King molested them abroad, first sending a communication, and then Sir William Temple, to the Court of Holland to demand the expulsion of the Scots exiles, Colonel Wallace, and the ministers, MacWard and Brown. This the States declined to do, and at the same time testified that the three Scots had been good and faithful citizens, who had proved their 'zeal and affection for the advancement of the truth.'[4]

Assaults on parish ministers. With all these hardships and sufferings on the part of a large section of the people, one is surprised to find so few records of reprisals or revenge taken upon the persons or property of those blamable for the

[1] Wodrow, ii. 335.

[2] Ibid., ii. 330, 331, 361; M'Crie, *Veitch*, 423.

[3] Wodrow, ii. 343.

[4] M'Crie, *Veitch*, 367; Wodrow, ii. 344.

almost universal coercion and its baleful results. Henry Knox, Episcopal incumbent in Dunscore, complained that on the 28th December six or seven persons did burglariously invade his manse and, after maltreating him and his wife, stole his furniture. Somewhat similar assaults took place at Gargunnock and Abbotsrule, but no particular sect of the dissenters is specified as the burglars, who, after all, may have been the too common dissenters from the principles of honesty. The ministers got compensation. The heritors were summoned to the Council and ordered to assess themselves in 5000 and 6000 merks respectively for the ministers of Dunscore and Gargunnock.[1]

The reader would be surfeited by a hundredth part of the record of the activities of the servants of the Crown in carrying out Lauderdale's policy for stamping out disregard for the law by exhausting the resources of suspects, who at this time were reckoned to be seventeen thousand in number.[2]

Early in the year 1677, a convention of Presbyterian ministers of different parties met in Edinburgh to discuss the situation and to consider terms of union of indulged and non-indulged, so that peace might prevail among the nonconformists. Blackadder proposed fasting and humiliation for the sin of Erastianism as the first step, a suggestion disagreeable to a section that would have deposed Welwood, Cameron, and a third preacher, probably Kid, for their extreme views on separation from the indulged. Welwood and Cameron declined the jurisdiction of this irregular assembly at the time. One result of the conference was the expression of a general feeling that indulged and non-indulged should work harmoniously together, preaching where occasion offered, and that ministers should not be ordained to congregations which were not in a position to give a call and make proper provision for their pastors. The fugitive missioners were thus discounted.[3] Differences had separated parties too far to allow a millennial concord to be struck at a single conference.

Assembly of Presbyterian parties, 1677.

At the end of January another famous field-preacher was in the toils. This outlaw, James Fraser, son of Sir James Fraser of Brea, of noble extraction, born in 1639, was attracted to the side of the persecuted

James Fraser of Brea.

[1] Wodrow, ii. 341.
[2] Dodds, *Fifty Years*, 209.
[3] *Six Saints*, i. 208; Wodrow, ii. 346.

after his conversion, and considered it his duty to take licence from the nonconformists in 1670. In his *Memoirs*, one of the most extraordinary products of this age, he narrates how, after he married a pious widow, who died in 1676, the Bishop of Moray persecuted him out of pique. He took to field-preaching, and, ignoring citations, was denounced and intercommuned. Through the treachery of a maidservant he was apprehended in the house of a relative in Edinburgh during family worship, on Sabbath night, 28th January. Next day Sharp and Hatton, in Council, tried to trap him into admissions punishable by death. He was wary. They sentenced him to the Bass, where he arrived, along with James Mitchell, on 1st February.[1] His experiences as recorded afford a very painful picture of prison life on the Bass—petty tyrannies, bad food and worse water, oatmeal mixed with foul water or melted snow and dry fish, vindictive usage, gifts stolen, warders blaspheming in order to irritate, debauching the female servants and blaming the pious prisoners, and other horrors.[2] During his stay here for two years and

Fraser's opinions.

a half Fraser found leisure to study and write a *Treatise on Justifying Faith*, which maintained novel and uncommon views on the subject. These becoming known to his friends gave rise to much dissatisfaction and disputation long before the work was published. Fraser's absurd conclusion was that Christ had died for all—for the elect that they might obtain superlative blessedness, and also for the reprobate that they might justly receive a more awful judgment. The resuscitation of Fraser's opinions by some ministers in the Cameronian and Antiburgher denominations in the eighteenth century gave rise to angry debates and resulted in the deposition of one disciple. Fraser was liberated in August 1679 on a bond, but his troubles were not over.[3]

Prisoners on the Bass.

Confined in the rock-prison at the same time as Peden and Fraser were James Drummond, chaplain to the Marchioness of Argyll, Patrick Anderson, minister of Walston, Hog, minister of Kiltearn, John M'Gilligen, minister of Fodderty, Robert Traill, minister at Cranbrook, John Law, minister of Campsie, John Macaulay, Robert Ross, and William Bell, three preachers, and George Scot from Scotstarvet, at

[1] Fraser, *Memoirs: Select Biog.*, ii. 81-370.
[2] *Ibid.*, ii. 344.
[3] Hutchison, *The Reformed Presbyterian Church in Scotland*, (Edin., 1893).

first as stiff a lay Covenanter as any, but latterly the recalcitrant receiver of a shipload of banished fellow-conventiclers.[1]

Blackadder and Welsh, accompanied by their bodyguard, marched about on their rousing mission. The former left a graphic description of an immense conventicle at Eckford in Teviotdale, where Welsh, Riddell, Dickson, Rae, and he officiated.[2] It is a pity to mutilate the exquisite story by an epitomised paraphrase. A multitude from all quarters swarmed on to a mead through which the Whitadder flows. On preparation day, Saturday, tokens were given to intending commun- icants. On Sabbath morn three tables, covered with linen cloths, bore the Communion cups and elements. A bright sun glorified a cloudless blue sky. The slopes around were clustered with over three thousand believers waiting their turn to partake of the holy food. Though the God of Jacob was still their refuge, these hunted Christians had a fence of steel in the hands of horsemen round the feast, sentinels on the hilltops, and mounted scouts patrolling the vicinity. They expected the rash young Earl of Home and the Berwick militia to keep Home's threat to ride in and 'make their horses drink the communion wine and trample the sacred elements under foot.' Aristocratic elders served the tables. Dickson's theme was 'The Lord will provide.' 'Neither shall the Covenant of My peace be removed,' was Blackadder's consoling subject next day.[3] In such inspiring circumstances the rapturous host saw Heaven's King reflected in the beauty of holiness upon them, and as each night they retired to their various resting-places guarded by armed men, they experienced a sense of Divine Power 'encamping round about them.' Their earthly ruler was forgotten. In the middle of June Captain Buchan captured eighteen persons holding a conventicle at Culross with a faith which disdained precautions.[4] For releasing the prisoners the too lenient magistrates of Culross got into trouble.

Lauderdale, having complained to the King of the number and insolence of the conventicles, received the King's authority for seizing

A sacramental conventicle.

---

[1] In transporting them to the plantations, Scot and his wife perished at sea: cf. M'Crie, *The Bass Rock*, 169.

[2] Blackadder, *Mem.*, 183-9; Blackadder wore a Highland plaid to conceal his identity.

[3] Genesis xxii. 14; Isaiah liv. 10.

[4] Wodrow, ii. 363.

the principal ministers and laymen, and bringing them to condign punishment. If he had not local forces to effect this, he was to temporise until succour should come from Ireland.[1] One of these conventicles was held in the parish of Girvan under the presidency of Welsh and other four preachers on 21st October. There seven thousand persons assembled and two thousand took the communion, after having engaged to abjure the orthodox clergy and to 'pursue the ends of the Solemn League and Covenant.' The Government spy also reported to Lauderdale that Welsh not only preached rank treason, but presided over a Presbytery that made cautious preparations for a rising and a rabbling of the clergy.[2] In order to quell this incipient rebellion Lauderdale made arrangements in December with Viscount Granard to hold himself in readiness to transport horse, foot, and artillery into Galloway on demand. Instructions for hunting down Scottish nonconformists led to the apprehension of William Douglas, a preacher.[3] Douglas was betrayed in Belfast by Roderick Mansell, a Government spy: and of both these worthies Lord Granard wrote: 'Douglas is a mountebank and almost as great a knave as his prompter Mansel, who has treated me with so many and so great aspersions that I must fly to your Grace's justice for reparation.'[4]

Welsh and others held a great conventicle at Maybole, which had a more practical consequence. According to a Government report 'a great many swords were sold' at the autumn fair in Maybole, because it was determined that the people should rise if they were further provoked.[5] From a spy, the Government had information of a similar character, which Lauderdale judiciously forwarded to Hamilton, who was suspected of complicity with the rebels. The information bore that the hillmen, in October 1676, had signed a paper asserting it to be lawful and agreeable to the subscribers to take up arms—their likeliest leader being Hamilton; and that early in 1677 arms had been imported from Holland and concealed, for which subscriptions in London had been

Conventicle at Girvan.

Conventicle at Maybole.

[1] Coventry to Lauderdale, 19th November 1677: *Ormonde MSS.*, iv. 62.
[2] *Ibid.*, iv. 69.
[3] *Ibid.*, iv. 75, 88.
[4] *Ibid.*, iv. 94.
[5] *Rec. Off., State Papers* (Charles II.), 397, 398: 5th November 1677.

raised.[1] Hamilton was an opportunist and not strictly veracious; and in these uncertain days it is not surprising to find the Crown relieving him of his commission in the militia. A deeper estrangement from Lauderdale was the result.

Long before Cameron's day 'some hotheads were for taking the sword and redeeming of themselves from the hands of oppressors,' but these spirited Scots appear to have been kept in check by the calmer counsels of men of the type of Fraser, who considered retaliation unwarrantable.[2]

Lauderdale again visited Scotland in the summer of 1677. His intriguing wife had one daughter marrying Lorne and another ready to be 'a forced cast upon Atholl.' The great man's influence was soon felt. That the malcontents might be thrown off their guard a third Indulgence was mooted.[3] A hard case was that of Sir Alexander Bruce of Broomhall, a conformist, too considerate to his tenantry, who in July was fined in £100 for the conventicling of his tenantry, whom he had not bound over.[4]

Lauderdale in Scotland, 1677.

On 2nd August the Council published the proclamation of 8th June 1674 in more stringent terms, demanding a bond from both proprietors and tenants subscribed by the former.[5] The heritors of Ayr, met in conference, Loudoun presiding, resolved to inform the Council that the demand was impracticable, and that leniency was the only cure of the disorders. The heritors of Hamilton took a similar stand. Hamilton himself informed Queensberry that the Act was 'hardly practicable.'[6] In August about forty ministers, indulged and non-indulged, were summoned for breach of the regulations and Acts, but only one is recorded to have compeared and defended himself. He acknowledged attending a conventicle in his own parish in order to challenge its legality. The plea was successful and the suspect was dismissed.[7]

Heritors oppose the policy of the Crown.

In October the Council ordered the release of eight prisoners, including Peden, Hog, M'Gilligen, Ker of Kersland, and Fraser of Brea,

---

[1] Perth to Hamilton: *Hist. MSS. Com. Rep.*, xi. App. vi. 156.
[2] *Select Biog.*, ii. 325, 326.
[3] *Hist. MSS. Com. Rep.*, xv. viii. 224, 226.
[4] Fountainhall, *Hist. Not.*, i. 168; Wodrow, ii. 360.
[5] Wodrow, ii. 364.
[6] *Hist. MSS. Com. Rep.*, xv. viii. 222; Wodrow, ii. 368.
[7] Wodrow, ii. 348.

on certain conditions—Peden being ordered into exile. There were relays of prisoners to take their places in the noisome vaults.[1] Sir John Nisbet was forced to resign the office of Lord Advocate, and George Mackenzie, on 23rd August 1677, got his place[2]—

Sir George
Mackenzie of
Rosehaugh.

> 'By merit raised to that bad eminence.'

A recent writer has well classed him with sanguinary Jeffreys and 'Weir of Hermiston' as one of 'The Terrors of the Law.'[3] Mackenzie had distinguished himself as a fearless pleader, even daring to oppose Lauderdale, who afterwards showed a preference for Mackenzie for reasons of state more probably than of love. A fiery temper, a bold, biting tongue, absolutist views, and expressed loyalty qualified this young advocate for the post of adviser and draughtsman of laws for the party of extermination. He began by emptying the crowded jails of those either too poor or too conscientious to bribe his predecessor. His method was not always just or merciful. Two men, who had been confined for six years untried, he brought to the gallows on the most nebulous evidence.[4] He promptly earned his nickname—'The Bluidy Mackenzie.'

Affair at
Kinloch.

Early in October, an affair occurred whose importance was not underestimated by those seeking fresh incitements to suppress the nonconformists. The outlawed John Balfour of Kinloch stole home to meet his friend and neighbour, Alexander Hamilton of Kinkel, Robert Hamilton, son of Sir Thomas Hamilton of Preston, and other conventiclers. Captain Carstairs and a dozen troopers rode up to capture the meeting. A boisterous Irish soldier, called Garret, took a trial shot, to which the defenders replied by a volley which brought down Garret and put his comrades to flight.[5] The episode was exaggerated to the injury of those molested. As a corrective to these rumours, Hamilton informed Queensberry that 'there was only thrie soldiers that were beaten and disarmed.'[6] Carstairs had a similar experience of deforcement in April 1678, when invading a minister's house in Kintore. For this scuffle the

---

[1] Wodrow, ii. 356, 361.
[2] Omond, *Lord Advocates*, ii. 200-34; *Hist. Not.*, i. 174.
[3] Francis Watt, *The Terrors of the Law*, 1902.
[4] Omond, 213; *Hist. Not.*, i. 180.
[5] Wodrow, ii. 371.
[6] *Hist. MSS. Com. Rep.*, xv. viii. 225.

two Flemings of Balbuthy, elder and younger, were tried and acquitted.[1] These attacks irritated an already nervous and retaliatory peasantry, and at the same time created periodic hysteria in official circles. In October there was an alarm in Edinburgh over the news invented by the Earl of Nithsdale and coloured by the bishops, that the westland Whigs, armed to the teeth, and equipped with Irish horses, were on the eve of rising. Dundonald informed Lauderdale that the manse of Torbolton had been forced and the minister threatened with death if he preached again.[2] The Council instructed Glencairn, Dundonald, and Ross to convene the gentlemen of Ayr and Renfrew, to take order for the extinction of factious courses in 'the great seminaries of rebellion' in these counties. The gentlemen met in Irvine on 2nd November, and came to three resolutions: that it was not within the compass of their power to suppress conventicles: that toleration of Presbytery alone would restore peace: that the toleration must be similar to that granted to England and Ireland.[3] The three conveners mutilated the manly resolutions, and compressed them into a phrase: 'It was not in their power to quiet the disorders.' Lord Advocate Mackenzie made a worse paraphrase: 'That the peace could not be secured without abrogating Episcopacy'; and this he supplemented by an even worse corollary: 'The King and Council considered this as a sacrificing the Laws to the Humours and Fashions of private men ... and therefore the Highlanders were sent in to secure the Peace.'[4] Lauderdale informed the King that the Highland chieftains were ready to march with their redshanks to nip the rebellion in the bud, and he asked for instructions.[5]

The King replied, 11th December, placing Scotland under martial law, and, for the protection of the Crown and of the Established Church, authorising a muster of English troops on the Borders as well as on the northern shores of Ireland, a gathering of the Highlanders at Stirling, the embodiment of the militia, the disarmament of the disaffected, and other military steps. The instructions issued by the Council simply condensed the old repressive statutes and handed over army,

Hysteria in official circles, in 1677.

Scotland under martial law in 1677.

---

[1] *Reg. Sec. Conc. Dec.*, 4th April 1678, 43.

[2] *Laud. Pap.*, iii. 88, 24th October 1677.

[3] Wodrow, ii. 375.

[4] *Vindication*, 12.

[5] Mackenzie, *Memoirs*, 329.

magistrates, and subjects to the mercy of a Committee, consisting of Atholl, Mar, Glencairn, Murray, Linlithgow, Perth, Wigtown, Strathmore, Airlie, Caithness, and Ross, with full powers, any five to be a quorum, who were ordered to meet in Glasgow on 26th January. The day after Christmas, the 'Commission for raising the Highlanders' was signed.'[1] Hamilton expressed the view then held that this was a royal charter for the plantation of the Lowlands by Gaels.[2] It was nothing short of a licence to freebooters to devour at pleasure and be indemnified if blood were spilt, and of a charge to bankrupts in uniform to conduct an unholy crusade. Worse still, the right reverend fathers in God—the bishops—met and formulated ten suggestions for the suppression of conventicles, which, for drastic rigour, better became a cave of bandits than a conclave of religious men, the cruelest suggestion being, that the forces should 'move slowly.'[3]

Muster of 'The Highland Host,' 1678.

The fiery cross soon sped among the loyal clans. The Lowlands were the Eldorado of the Gaels. They termed the Whigs 'Figs,' probably also recalling the sweetest fruit they knew of—an article of commerce then heavily taxed.[4] Joy prevailed in all quarters favourable to Prelacy; but while visions of wealth glorified the castles and shielings of the north, a horror of the naked barbarians struck the southern Whigs and people generally. The isolated clergy complained that the upper classes were migrating to the Capital. A ravenous joy possessed the associates of Lauderdale, expectant of forfeitures, 'so that on Valentine's Day, instead of drawing mistresses, they drew estates.'[5] Queensberry informed Hamilton that 'the offishers off the whoill [militia regiment of Dumfries] ar the scum of the countray and all beggars save 2 or 3, and most overjoyt att the honourabell imployment.'[6] The sordid vision came to Captain John Graham of Claverhouse and Claypots,

Return of Claverhouse, 1678.

in Holland, and he, having resigned his commission in the Dutch army in December 1677, also hastened home, hoping to cover Claverhouse with glory and to fill Claypots with Whig gold. Sir Walter

[1] *Wodrow MSS.* (Advocates' Library), xcix.; Wodrow, ii. 376, 377, 379, 387.
[2] *Hist. MSS. Com. Rep.*, xv. viii. 230.
[3] *Laud. Pap.*, iii. 95.
[4] M'Crie, *Veitch*, 519.
[5] Burnet, ii. 146.
[6] *Hist. MSS. Com. Rep.*, xi. vi. 161.

Scott probably had good reasons for making Edith Bellenden say of Claverhouse, '"Root-and-branch work" is the mildest of his expressions. The unhappy Primate was his intimate friend and early patron.'[1] More patriotic, or at least more sympathetic, citizens were deserting the woeful country. Lauderdale promptly counteracted the threatened exodus to London of nobles and persons of property, who thus hoped to enlighten the King and his advisers regarding the true state of affairs. On 3rd January, Lauderdale, President of the Council, published a proclamation prohibiting all men between sixteen and sixty years of age leaving the kingdom without a licence, on pain of treason.[2] To test the loyalty of Hamilton, orders were sent to the gentlemen of Lanarkshire to muster when required by the Committee.[3] After Rothes got the heritors of Fife to sign the bond obliging all the inhabitants to keep the peace, Lauderdale returned the instrument along with the draft of a more stringent Bond binding them to refrain from intercourse with the nonconformists, and to apprehend them.[4] The Ayrshire heritors sent a deputation to the Privy Council to assure them of the quietness of the shire, the absence of conventicles in those parishes provided with indulged ministers, their own personal loyalty, and the impropriety of unloosing 'so inhumane and barbarous a crew' of spoilers upon the land.[5] Implacable Lauderdale refused to see the deputation. With Shylock he might say, 'I would have my bond.' The influence of Hamilton, Blantyre, and Carmichael was felt in Lanarkshire, where of the 2900 heritors and feuars all, save nineteen, refused to take the bond until they were coerced by the militia. Queensberry informed Hamilton that it was otherwise in Dumfriesshire, where all, 'save some few pitifull persons inconsiderable both as to parts and interests,' had signed. Although Queensberry had not yet subscribed, he had ordered the imprisonment and removal of his offending tenantry, of whom he wrote, 'Its remarkable most off thes ar Annandale people and knou no moir off religion or civell deportment than bruts.'[6] When Lauderdale

Protests of loyal heritors against 'The Black Bond.'

---

[1] *Old Mortality*, chap. x.
[2] *Reg. Sec. Conc., Acta*, 554.
[3] Wodrow, ii. 381.
[4] *Ibid.*, ii. 382.
[5] *Ibid.*, ii. 388.
[6] *Hist. MSS. Com. Rep.*, xi. vi. 159; xv. viii. 233; Wodrow, ii. 397.

learned how 'the gentlemen looked on and would no nothing' to make
the latest legislation effective, according to Burnet, 'this put Duke
Lauderdale in such a frenzy, that at Council table he made bare his arm
above his elbow, and swore by Jehovah he would make them all enter
those bonds.'[1]

These submissions grudgingly given were merely nominal, and
expressive of the universal horror at the thought of a descent of 'the
Irishes.' In May, Queensberry reported that hill-sermons were never so
numerous, at which 'they thunder anathemas against the blak-bonders
(as they call us), and ane maid his repentence publicly Sunday last for
tacking 't, befoir Mr. Welsh wood chrissen his child.'[2] To the consistent
Covenanter *The Black Bond* was an instrument of Satan, proving the
infidelity of the subscriber to God and Christ.[3]

The Highland Host mustered at Stirling on 24th January 1678.
Increased by regulars and militia, and equipped with artillery, shackles,
and instruments of torture, this force representative of heathenism
and religion, eight thousand strong, marched to Glasgow and Ayr in
search of the imaginary foe. Ploughmen in the furrows saw the legalised
marauders and the exterminating Commission pass by. The ingenious
Mackenzie was left behind to fabricate novel legislative measures
couched in damnatory language; and truly

> 'That crooked Vulcan will the bellows blow
> Till he'll set all on fire.'

Employers were now discharged from receiving servants or tenants who
had not taken the bond; and to secure the public peace the strange
device of 'law-burrows,' or caution given that nothing wrong would
be done, was resorted to. Mackenzie, in vindicating the Government,
declared this to be the ordinary surety whereby 'any private man may
force another by the law to secure him against all Prejudices from his
Men, Tenents, and Servants, and others of his Command, Out-hounding
and Ratihabition.'[4] Those who refused the Black Bond were required to

---

[1] *Hist.* ii. 145.
[2] *Hist. MSS. Com. Rep.*, XI. vi. 162.
[3] For 'Black Bond and Highland Host,' cf. *Wodrow MSS.*, xxxvi. (Rob. iii. 3. 11. 17).
[4] *Vindication*, 12.

give pledges that they and all their dependents would keep the ecclesiastical laws on pain of two years' valued rent.[1] To these unprecedented demands many great land-lords and influential citizens—Cassillis, Loudoun, Crawford, Balmerino, Melville, Newark, Callendar, Kilsyth, Roxburgh, Cochrane, Cathcart, Bargany, Cessnock, Kilbirnie, Montgomery, and others—refused to yield, and were denounced as traitors. Nothing was left to chance. It was the priestly function of the armed Commission to pursue every living soul into a state of revulsion from nonconformity. The claymore would produce uniformity.

The Gaels swept over south-west Scotland like a flood, and bore away whatever they fancied. Every church was converted into an armoury for discarded weapons, and the graveyard into a pound for commandeered horses; every cupboard was often searched and every sheaf devoured.[2] Strange to relate, the Whigs grew facile as the Israelites in Egypt. Goads of no kind—torture by hustling, blows, robbery, arson, match—availed to change their humour and resolution to give no ground for justifying the brutal policy of Lauderdale. The unhindered caterans had no inducement to soil their blades by cutting throats. There is no authentic record of atrocities committed, apart from the inevitable inconveniences of an enemy's visit. Alexander Wedderburn, minister of Kilmarnock, was badly injured by a blow from a Highlandman's musket. The author of *A Hind Let Loose* says that it would require several large volumes to record their barbarities; but in his later *Short Memorial*, the charge is minimised by the omission of the statement, 'by the sword of these Burrios,' when he repeats this record: 'Many houses were then left desolate in a winter flight, many lost their cattel and horses, and some in seeking to recover them lost their lives, by the sword of these Burrios.'[3] Wodrow published a statement of the losses incurred in Ayrshire, as prepared by the heritors for transmission to the King, and these amounted to nearly £138,000 Scots. He also reckoned that £200,000 Scots might represent the losses in Ayrshire; and from this fact one can imagine what the total 'sufferings' in the disaffected area must have been. At the end of February, the Council

[1] Proclamations, 11th Feb. and 14th Feb.: Aldis, *List*, 2113; Wodrow, ii. 396, 400.

[2] *Atholl MSS., Hist. MSS. Com. Rep.*, XII. viii. 35; *Wodrow MSS.*, xcix. 28.

[3] *Hind*, 190, 191; *Memorial*, 12; *A True Narrative … 1678: Published by Authority*; Aldis, *List*, 2143; Wodrow, ii. 442 note.

THE COVENANTERS

saw the necessity for recalling this punitive expedition, and the Gaels
returned loaded with loot, while Airlie and Strathmore were credited
with securing bags of money.[1]

King Charles
approves of
the expedi-
tion.

The King in a letter of 26th March indicated approval of all this
savagery.[2] The bold Cassillis first complained to the Duke of Monmouth,
hoping through that channel to reach the royal ear before he personally
came to Court. In March, Cassillis, Hamilton, Roxburgh, Haddington,
Atholl, Perth, some other nobles, and 'fifty gentlemen of quality,'
including Sir John Cochrane and Lieutenant-General Drummond,
went up to London to complain of the miseries of Scotland. Charles
would at first neither receive the petitions nor the petitioners. He sent
for representatives of the Council. Lauderdale dispatched Murray,
Collington, and Mackenzie to counter-act his accusers. Mackenzie was
no match for his brilliant rival, Lockhart. The King gave the petitioners
audience, and demanded their indictment in writing. They were not
to be caught in such a snare, and refused. Their stand augured ill for
Lauderdale. But that able tactician by a simple method outwitted his
antagonists. He persuaded the King to convene the Scots Estates on
26th June, while these members were from home, and then cozened
the others who were left, who outnumbered the Hamilton party, as five
to one.

Meeting of
Parliament,
June 1678.

The King's letter to the Estates praised Lauderdale for his fidelity.
The Parliament voted supply of £800,000 Scots, for the maintenance
of authority and an army—the cess to be payable in five years. When
Parliament, in replying to the King's letter, declared that Lauderdale's
'managment of affairs in this convention hath justifyed your Maiesties
choice of him,' that astute diplomatist had completely outwitted the
Whigs. They had to face a new peril on their return, for Lauderdale had
the satisfaction of issuing a royal warrant in May for the prosecution of
murmurers against persons in authority.[3]

Sharp had waited long enough for Mitchell's blood. He induced
Lauderdale to bring the prisoner from the Bass and send him to
the gallows.[4] The Council, 6th December, instructed Sir George

[1] Kirkton, 391.
[2] Wodrow, ii. 432.
[3] Burnet, ii. 147, 149; Wodrow, ii. 449, 453, 454, 490; Kirkton, 393; *Act. Parl. Scot.*,
viii. 213-30; *Hist. MSS. Com. Rep.*, XIII. ii. 49; xv. viii. 235, 236.
[4] Burnet, ii. 138.

Mackenzie, Mitchell's former counsel, to prosecute him afresh. The accused petitioned for counsel. The advocates, remembering Mackenzie's dictum at Argyll's trial, that the defence of a traitor was treason, refused to plead until they were licensed. John Ellis and Lockhart undertook the defence. Sir Archibald Primrose of Carrington, deprived of the post of Lord Register, now Justice General, with five judges, occupied the bench. Primrose narrated to Burnet what transpired. The trial began on 7th January with the indictment charging Mitchell with feloniously attempting to injure, demember, and murder an officer of the Crown, a bishop, and a subject—offences punishable with death; and further with associating with traitors.[1] To be even with intriguing enemies, who had arranged to perjure themselves at the trial Primrose, with 'a most exquisite malice,' sent to the counsel for the defender a copy of the pardon minuted in the Council Record. Mitchell refused the libel, and renounced his extorted confession. Lockhart forcibly pleaded that an extra-judicial confession was inadmissible as evidence. A long debate took place over the relevancy of the libel. The bench held that the Lord Advocate had proved the presumption that Mitchell had attempted assassination, and that his confession was judicial, and could not be retracted. The case was sent to a jury. The box contained selected soldiers and Anti-Covenanters.[2] Evidence was led. The confession, signed by Mitchell, Rothes, Primrose, Nisbet, and Hatton, was produced. It was pleaded that it was extorted on promise of life. According to Mackenzie's own work on the criminal law, 'a confession extorted by torture is in no law sufficient.'[3] Mackenzie, too, had seen the torture and compulsion. Notwithstanding, Rothes, Hatton, Lauderdale, Sharp, one after another, swore that they neither gave nor heard of 'any assurance to the pannell for his life, and that the pannell never sought any such assurance.' Rothes went further and deponed, 'any expressions in any paper which may seem to infer anything to the contrary, … it hath been insert upon some mistake.'[4] This was severe on the last discarded Lord Advocate and the Clerk of Court.

Trial of James Mitchell, 7th January 1678.

Defences of Mitchell.

[1] Wodrow, ii. 459 note; Burnet, ii. 140-3; *Hist. Not.*, i. 182-6; Mackenzie, *Memoirs*, 327-9; M'Crie, *Bass*, 71; Cobbett, *State Trials*, vi. 1207-62, 1270; Kirkton, 383; *Just. Rec.*, ii. App. 307.

[2] *Hist. Not.*, i. 186.

[3] *Laws and Customs*, 257.

[4] Wodrow, ii. 469.

Lockhart now showed his hand. He produced an authentic copy of the minute and demanded the production of the original. Not to be worsted, Mackenzie retorted that the record was closed; that he was not bound to produce evidence for his opponents; that the Lords of Council had sworn that no assurance was given; and that none can grant remissions except the King. Lockhart, however, was permitted to read the document, in which these words appeared: 'having retired a part with one of the s[ai]d Committy [*i.e.* Rothes] He [Mitchell] did then confesse vpon his knees he was the person, vpon assurance given him by one of the Committy, as to his lyfe, who had warrand from the Lord Commissioner and Councill to give the same.'[1] Nicoll Sommervell, brother-in-law of Mitchell, offered to depone in court that Sharp promised to get Mitchell spared if Sommervell went and persuaded him to confess. Sharp denied this, and 'called it a villanous lie.'[2] Lauderdale rose in court and menacingly demanded if the object

Perjury of Privy Councillors.

of the defence was to make the councillors out to be perjurers.[3] The judges, cowed, ruled that the defence was too late in asking diligence, and that the alleged assurance was nugatory owing to the depositions of the councillors. The court adjourned for the night. The minutes were inspected and found as Lockhart alleged. But unable to withdraw their perjury, they tried to explain the minute as a promise of intercession. On 10th January, the jury returned a verdict finding Mitchell guilty as libelled, that he had made a confession, but that there was no proof of any exculpation.[4] He was condemned to be hanged on Friday, 18th January, in the Grassmarket, and his goods and gear to be escheat.

Dilemma of Lauderdale.

Lauderdale now found himself in a quandary, caused by the fact that the Earl of Kincardine had in his possession letters from Hatton, written at the time the confession and promise were made, bearing out the contention of Lockhart: all of which Lauderdale knew full well and of which he had been reminded. Consequently, when a petition was sent to the Council in favour of the doomed man, Lauderdale favoured it. But Sharp, not to be cheated of his quarry, said that such a pardon

[1] *Reg. Sec. Conc., Acta*, June 1673-August 1678; 12th March 1674, pp. 63, 64.
[2] Wodrow, ii. 471.
[3] *Ibid.*, iii. 162.
[4] *Just. Rec.*, ii. 339.

would be a further invitation to assassination. Ready with an impious jest, the unfeeling Lauderdale retorted, 'Let Mitchell glorify God in the Grassmarket.'[1] The lack of truthfulness, honour, and trustworthiness in these high officers of state is almost incredible. Primrose also gloated over the fact that in this trial his enemies consigned the 'damnation of their souls in his hands.' Sharp had already been exposed. Hatton, afterwards impeached for his false testimony by William Noble, member for Dumbartonshire, was humiliated, and fined.[2] In his own writings Mackenzie left proofs of his unscrupulous and untruthful nature, as when he recorded that 'the Registers of Council were produced, but not the least mark of a promise was made to appear by either.'[3] In his *Memoirs* he also avers that 'Sir George Lockhart refused to speak for Mitchell, being unwilling to offend Lauderdale.'[4] With similar incorrectness he records that 'very famous witnesses ... deposed that Mitchell was upon a new plot to kill the same Archbishop'; and that he died 'glorying in his crimes and recommending to others *the sweetness of such assassinations.*'[5]

Mitchell spent his last days writing his Testimony, and, on the morning of the day on which he was executed, he wrote a letter in which he testified: 'I wish heartily that this my poor life may put an end to the persecution of the true members of Christ in this kingdom ... by the perfidious prelates.'[6] Through a crowd of sympathising women Mitchell was taken to the gibbet. A rescue was expected, and Major Johnson kept close to the prisoner to stab him if the attempt was made. He met his fate bravely, and was thrown over the ladder amid the rolling of drums. His unmutilated body was removed under a velvet pall to the Magdalen Chapel.[7] 'Thus they hunted this poor man to death,' wrote the diarist Fountainhall, 'a prey not worthy of so much pains, trouble, and obloquie as they incurred by it.'[8] The country was

Execution of Mitchell, 18th January 1678.

---

[1] Burnet, ii. 141.
[2] Cobbett, *State Trials*, vi. 1262-70; *Scot. Hist. Misc.*, 244.
[3] *Vindication*, 19.
[4] *Memoirs*, 328.
[5] *Vindication*, 19.
[6] Wodrow, ii. 473; *Laing MSS.*, 269; *ibid.*, 89, fol. 99; *Hist. MSS. Com. Rep.*, XIII. ii. 46.
[7] Hickes, *Ravillac Redivivus*, 53.
[8] *Hist. Not.*, i, 185.

roused and incensed by the sensational news of the trial and martyrdom of Mitchell and of the perjury of the 'famous witnesses,' and many scribes were busy penning and circulating poems, pasquils, satires, and papers bringing contempt upon the corrupt Government, and giving dark warnings to Sharp.[1] Denunciation of the murderers of Mitchell was made an article in the unwritten creed of the fugitive hillmen. The accusation of murder was hissed into the ears of the dying Primate on Magus Moor.

Punishment of the Whigs.

The Privy Council never rested from their infamous work. The noisome jails were emptied to be filled again with prisoners, including children, caught at the ever-increasing conventicles, and left in the cells without being charged till health gave way. Alexander Ross came to Edinburgh on tutorial business, and was clapt into prison with- out a reason for four months.[2] James Webster, afterwards minister in Edinburgh, for holding a private prayer meeting in Dundee, was kept praying in jail there for eighteen months, in spite of the indemnity applicable in his case.[3] George Hume of Kimmerghame and his wife, Lady Ayton, were imprisoned for three months in the Castle of Edinburgh for being married by an unauthorised minister.[4] James Lawson, a boy conventicler of fourteen years of age, was liberated; Alexander Anderson, aged sixteen, was banished. These were not uncommon cases.[5] Ex-Provost Sir James Stewart, old and infirm, was also released.

Transportation of prisoners.

Consignments of men, women, and boys were kept waiting their turn to be shipped off to the East Indies to be sold as slaves.[6] Peden was one of sixty-nine prisoners marched down to Leith harbour into the '*St. Michael* of Scarborough,' Captain Edward Johnston, all consigned to Ralph Williamson in London for transportation. The prescient Peden declared there was never a ship built that would take him to Virginia. At Gravesend, Williamson did not appear, and the skipper of the convict ship, expecting a gang of rogues, refused to take the holy men

---

[1] *Laing MSS.*, Mitchell's Ghost: *Manes Mitcheliani*, etc., Nos. 148, 149, 150, 151, 152.

[2] Wodrow, ii. 475.

[3] *Ibid.*, ii. 484.

[4] *Ibid.*, ii. 480.

[5] *Reg. Sec. Conc.*, *Dec.*, 178, 2nd January 1679; Wodrow, ii. 484.

[6] *Hist. Not.*, i. 204.

off Johnston's hands. The latter released them, and gaily they tramped away to Scotland.[1]

A conventicle on the hills of Whitekirk on 5th May was attacked by Ensign Maitland and some soldiers from the Bass, who were repelled, leaving one of their number, John Hogg, dead. Of some men afterwards apprehended, James Learmont, a chapman, and William Temple were tried and condemned, the former to be hanged on the 27th September in the Grassmarket and the latter to be transported.[2] Mackenzie, with his usual inaccuracy, calls the man executed 'George,' whereas George was acquitted. Learmont's defence was that he was unarmed and innocent— a plea which the Crown met with the charge of accession to murder. This incident gave Mackenzie ground for the following statement in his *Vindication*: 'As to the sending away People to the Plantations, it is answered that none were sent away, but such as were taken at Bothwell Bridge or in Argyle's Rebellion.'[3] The Council, on 16th January 1679, informed Lauderdale that several were shipped to the plantations.[4]

Scuffle at Whitekirk.

Among notable conventicles held in 1678 those conducted by Welsh and Blackadder at Meiklewood and Skeoch Hill were remarkable for numbers and for fervour. Blackadder describes the march of fully armed and mounted gentlemen from Lanarkshire down Enterkin Pass into Nithsdale and on to the Vale of Cairn or Cluden in Irongray, near Dumfries. Fourteen thousand persons assembled and remained for three days, the Communion Season, as it was called. The services were held and the Sacraments dispensed in the lone, bracken-clad amphitheatre of Skeoch Hill, where on a slope a mass of rough stones, still visible, formed a Communion-table and pulpit, and four rows of stones afforded seats for the communicants. While Blackadder, Welsh, Arnot, and Dickson in turn lectured, preached, and dispensed the Bread of Life, alert sentinels were posted on every coign of vantage to guard against surprise; and Earlston at the head of the Galloway Horse stood ready for every emergency. The timid garrisons from afar spied the convention, which was too strong to be disturbed.[5] In September

Blackadder's conventicle in Irongray parish.

---

[1] *Reg. Sec. Conc., Dec.*, 172, 12th December 1678; *Six Saints*, 52, 53.

[2] Wodrow, ii. 477-9; *Add. MSS.*, 23251, fol. 96.

[3] Mackenzie, *Vindication*, 11, 20.

[4] Wodrow, iii. 24.

[5] Letter, 23rd August 1678: *State Papers* (Charles II.), 396; Blackadder, *Memoirs*, 197-203.

Colonel Strother requested Lauderdale to send troops to the Borders to suppress Welsh's party of horse, which had lately shot his cousin Marly, and Carr of Cherrytrees.[1] So far north as Forgandenny, Stewart of Ballechin and some Highland soldiers scattered a conventicle and shot Andrew Brodie, wright, near Culteuchar Hill in October.[2]

Lauderdale was the fountainhead of power, and, as Dr. Matthew M'Kail at the time graphically wrote: 'In judgment a dog cannot move his tongue against him ... he values the Episcopal Clergy as little as the Presbyterians when it comes in competition with the King's supremacy.' In consequence of this, self-defence became an article of an outlaw's faith, and M'Kail reported, 'There is many a man in Galloway, if he hath but two cows, he will sell one cow for a pair of pistols.'[3] The saints had greater need of them than ever. In a letter from Edinburgh it is stated: 'There is invented (as is alleged) by the famous bishop of Galloway [Paterson] a certain screw to couple their thumbs together by pairs to disable them from defensive or offensive war.'[4] Worse still, on 23rd September, a captain's commission for a troop of horse was given to John Graham of Claverhouse, and soon the relentless harriers of the Whigs would be in the southern fields.[5]

Invention of thumb-screws.

At this crisis eight bishops met, not for prayer, but to commission the Primate, Sharp, to visit Lauderdale and concert still sterner measures for annihilating the Covenanters.[6]

[1] 15th September: *Add. MSS.*, 23251, fol. 99.
[2] *Martyr Graves of Scotland*, 215.
[3] *State Papers* (Charles ii.), 396.
[4] M'Kail to Adams, 16th November 1678: *State Papers* (Charles ii.), 408.
[5] Terry, *John Graham*, 38.
[6] 23rd November 1678, Letter of Sharp to Lauderdale: *Laing MSS.*, 784.

JOHN BALFOUR OF KINLOCH—'BURLY'

EFFIGY OF ARCHBISHOP SHARP IN THE PARISH CHURCH OF
ST. ANDREWS

CHAPTER TWENTY-FIVE

THE EXIT OF SHARP

S COTLAND had reached the nadir of degradation when Scotland's curse in 1679. Lauderdale occupied the vice-regal chair, when Sharp controlled the well-springs of religion, when Paterson, the inventor of the double thumbscrews, was advanced to the Privy Council and to the see of Edinburgh, when mendacious Mackenzie pleaded in the name of justice, when heartless Claverhouse rode out to guard the angel of peace in 1679. While King Charles, with an incredible dissimulation, himself a secret Papist, sanctioned the persecution of his co-religionists, even permitting death to overtake a sayer of mass, and allowed the people to be disturbed over popish plots and the dissolution of the Cavalier Parliament, the best Scottish minds were occupied with thoughts of salvation.[1] 'There are more converts than ever,' wrote Blackadder to exiled MacWard. Armies of believers met all winter. If there were more crowns there were more crosses. The Council proclaimed the Papists and Quakers, but refrained from prosecuting them.

The case of William Veitch indicates how differently Presbyterian The harrying of William Veitch. dissenters were harried.[2] Veitch, an unattached probationer, joined the insurgents in 1666, and being dispatched on business, just missed the fight but got into the rout after Rullion Green. After marvellous escapes he reached England, with other fugitives, and lurked all winter in Newcastle under the name of William Johnston. His wife followed. He farmed and taught, to maintain a home, ultimately settling at

---

[1] Hallam, ii. 443.
[2] *The Scots Worthies* (Carslaw's edition) 607-22.

Stanton near Morpeth. He was discovered and sent to Edinburgh, where he appeared before Sharp and the Committee of Council on 22nd February 1679.[1] His farm was displenished and thrown into lea, to obtain support for his wife and six children, till his fate was sealed. The old sentence of death and forfeiture stood against him. The Council examined him. 'Have you taken the Covenant?' asked Paterson, now Bishop of Edinburgh. The prisoner replied: 'All that see me at this honourable board may easily perceive that I was not capable to take the Covenant, when you and the other ministers of Scotland tendered it.' This telling retort sent the court into laughter. They ordered him to the Bass till the King considered his case. In March a reply came that Veitch was to be tried, or, in other words, to be hanged. To take his neck out of the halter great influence was brought to bear on Lauderdale and others. Gilbert Elliot of Craigend, the prisoner's agent, was sent up to London to prosecute the petition, and he was able to make political capital out of the case, with the result that Veitch, after various sordid intrigues and mean subterfuges, was liberated.[2] Long afterwards when Elliot, then Lord Minto, visited Dumfries, where Veitch was minister after the Revolution, Minto facetiously remarked to Veitch: 'Ah, Willie, Willie, had it no' been for me, the pyets had been pyking your pate on the Netherbow Port.' The equally humorous minister retorted: 'Ah, Gibbie, Gibbie, had it no' been for me, ye would ha'e been yet writting papers for a plack the page.'[3]

Stripping
conventiclers. The legal procedure for detecting a Whig or Cameronian had been brought to such a pitch of perfection that a suspicious sneeze, a diffident reply, or a misunderstood reference was enough to imperil a person's liberty. Another kind of evidence was pitched upon. Worshippers returning from conventicles were to be stripped as far as decency permitted and the clothing retained as evidence. Boys entering college or beginning trades were to produce certificates of church attendance.[4] It is too ludicrous to picture 'Bonnie Dundee' and his slashing dragoons returning from a Sunday raid with their saddles hung with the coats and breeches of men and the petticoats and shawls of women, and with

---

[1] M'Crie, *Veitch*, 94.
[2] *Reg. Sec. Conc., Dec.*, 275, 31st July 1679.
[3] *Memoirs*, 99 note.
[4] Wodrow, iii. 13, 14, 33.

nosebags full of Bibles and other oddments of the chase. Such was the work of heroes then! The Council blamed the three preachers, Welsh, Semple, and Arnot, for being the chief promoters of disorder, and offered 9000 merks (£500) for Welsh, and 2000 merks each for Semple and Arnot, as well as 900 merks for any vagrant preacher.[1] No bribe was sufficient to tempt the persecuted to betray their homeless pastors.

That the laws might not remain inoperative, the Council, on 27th February, added many names to the Commission of the Peace in all counties between the Grampians and the Cheviots, and also appointed active deputes to the sheriffs and bailies of regality. Several of these officials had already graduated in wickedness, and were yet to blossom red in the 'crimson iniquity of the time.' Claverhouse and Captain Andrew Bruce of Earlshall were commissioned deputes for Dumfries, Annandale, Wigtown, and Kirkcudbright. Robert Grierson of Lag, a youth of twenty-two, was associated with them in Wigtown, and Captain John Paterson in Kirkcudbright.[2] The depute for Fife and Kinross, with various regalities, was the notorious William Carmichael of Easter Thurston. Their courts were to meet weekly. Their duty was to extinguish dissent and dissenters. They were to be paid by results. Their instructions placed every one in their power. Fines exacted from those not heritors were to go to these depute-sheriffs, and fines taken from the landed proprietors were to fall to the Crown and to the commissioners in equal parts.[3] If the harriers were thus tempted to plunder, the sufferers were sorely tempted to resist and retaliate.

New Commissioners of the Peace.

Blackadder, an invalid hiding in a seventh-story garret in Edinburgh, records a scuffle which brought more tribulation to the persecuted. One night in March, some gentlemen met in the house of Mrs. Crawford in a quiet close in Edinburgh in order to transact commercial business. A mischievous boy informed Major Johnston of the City Guard, in order to see the sport of that zealous breaker-up of conventicles dispersing an orderly gathering. The gentlemen resented the Major's rude intrusion, and drawing weapons, gave him so sound a drubbing that he yelled, 'For

Drabbing of Major Johnston.

---

[1] Proclamation, 6th February; Aldis, *List*, 2158; Wodrow, iii. 15.

[2] William Douglas of Morton was afterwards associated with Claverhouse in Dumfries and Annandale. Lag Castle, Dunscore, stands eight miles north-west of Dumfries.

[3] Wodrow, iii. 17-23; 'Carmichael's Warrant': *Wodrow MSS.*, xliii. 26.

Christ's sake, send me not to hell,' and promised that he would never disturb a meeting again. One of his soldiers was mortally wounded by a pistol-shot. Richard Cameron's brother, Michael, blamed for having laid the trap for Johnston, was one of the flagellators, for whose capture the Council offered 1000 merks reward. The affront was further avenged by ordering all ministers and their families to leave the city, and the magistrates of Edinburgh and Glasgow were commanded to make a nightly census and to remove all visitors beyond their bounds.[1]

Fight at Lesmahagow, 30th March 1679.
A conventicle held at Cummerhead, Lesmahagow, on Sabbath 30th March, ended in a gallant affair. Lieutenant Dalziel and a party of soldiers, afraid to attack the main body, hovered at a distance and seized stragglers, stripping some women and detaining some men. The Whigs, marshalling the men of Strathaven and Douglasdale, boldly demanded the release of the prisoners, and in the fray Dalziel and seven of his men were captured. But for the interposition of William Cassils, a Douglas man, Dalziel, who was wounded, would have been put to death, and for this generous act Cassils got a royal pardon.[2] Before a commission got time to investigate this affair, and examine eleven prisoners lying in Lanark jail; another outrage took place near Loudoun Hill. Early on Sabbath morning, 20th April, two infantry soldiers, quartered upon a farmer who had not paid his cess, were roused from sleep. One of them on going to the door was saluted by an invitation, quite unlike a Covenanter's: 'Come out, you damned rogues.' A shot laid him low. A second shot and an assault also mortally wounded his comrade, who was able to identify John Scarlet as his assailant. Wodrow's picture of this villain is not inviting.[3] This Scarlet was well qualified to paint the country red. He was a tinker, confessedly illiterate, a soldier dismissed from the service, an unabashed polygamist who wandered about the country with his harem betimes, and then broke into piety, probably in the garb of a Whig, all the time he was a Government 'fly' or informer, ready to swear that he had been one of Welsh's bodyguard, and said

Murder at Loudoun Hill.

---

[1] Wodrow, iii. 31-3; Blackadder, *Memoirs*, 208.

[2] *Laud. Pap.* iii. 162; Wodrow, iii. 33-6.

[3] Wodrow, iii. 36, 37. John Scarlet, described as of 'Kirkness, Portmoak, tinker,' appeared before the Lords of Justiciary on 12th May 1679, and again on 31st January 1681, when he was sent down to Cunningham for punishment for his crimes: *Book of Adjournal.*

to have joined the bodyguard of Richard Cameron. The odium of the murder was cast upon the Cameronian party.

The landowners of Ayrshire met and resolved to send Lords Loudoun and Cochrane and Sir John Cochrane as a deputation to the Council to express detestation of these armed conventicles and outrages, which they attributed to the influence of 'a few unsound, turbulent and hot-headed preachers, most part whereof were never ministers of the Church of Scotland,' whom they also accused of fostering schism, separation, and rebellion.[1] This severe criticism, from a quarter where sympathy for the hunted was expected, could not fail to encourage the Council to proceed with their authorisation to the whole army to capture or kill Welsh, Cameron, Kid, Douglas, and other leaders of armed field-worshippers.[2] The breach between the moderate and the extreme sections of the Cameronians, as the disaffected generally for some time had been called, was being made wider every time the various leaders met to discuss the situation. There was a lack of unanimity and cohesion among these parties.[3]

Action of heritors in Ayr.

The atrocious procedure and vile acts of Carmichael, depute to the Sheriff-principal of Fife, the Earl of Rothes, were no longer endurable by the wanderers in Fife, whose feelings were outraged by the tales of robberies, rapes, adulteries, and other sins of the flesh, as well as of torture by match and maltreating of women and children, indulged in by the agents of the Crown.[4] During the month of April 1679, about twenty men, including David Hackston of Rathillet, met in Gilston, Leslie, and other places to pray and to consider probable action. The hapless Sharp was now devoted for sacrifice, at least by the determination of some of these outlaws.[5]

Enormities of Sheriff-depute Carmichael.

---

[1] Wodrow, iii. 38.

[2] *Ibid.*, iii. 39.

[3] The term 'Cameronian' as applied to the parties 'agin the Government' appears to have been in use before this time, probably in 1677. Cf. *Six Saints*, i. 241; ii. 167, note 9.

[4] Wodrow, iii. 42.

[5] The authorities for the following facts are *inter alia*: *Add. MSS.* (Brit. Mus.), 28747, fol. 23: Rothes to Lauderdale, 4th May 1679; *Cal. State Pap.* (Charles II.), 79, fol. 412; *A True Relation ...* (Lond., 1679); *Anal. Scot.*, ii. 389; *A True Account ...* (Lond., 1679) (by Mackenzie?); Hickes, *The Spirit of Popery ...* (Lond., 1680); Russell's 'Account' in Kirkton, 403-82; Guillan's 'Account,' *Wodrow MSS.* xliv.;

Since January, before the execution of Mitchell, 'several godly men' had been dogging the Primate between St. Andrews and Edinburgh; twice he narrowly escaped their sinister intentions; and 'other worthy Christians had used means to get him upon the road before.' The zealots at several meetings discussed the subject of the removal of Sharp and Carmichael, and concluded it to be their duty to hang both of them 'over the port,' much as Cardinal Beaton had been treated. Russell and other conspirators, feeling impulses to do something, consulted the oracle in the Scriptures and confessed having got encouragement therein for their homicidal mania. John Balfour of Kinloch, *alias* 'Captain Burleigh,' declared he was prevented fleeing to the Highlands, and, on asking God's mind, was turned back with these words, 'Go, and prosper.' Then he got this divine commission from Scripture, 'Go, have not I sent thee?' and he dared no longer question.[1] Smith, a godly weaver in Strutherdyke, prayed, then oracularly observed, that if God wished it He would place the persecutors in the avengers' way.

The result of these deliberations was the desire for an assize on horseback with Hackston at their head, if he would take command. It was also agreed to invite two stalwart fighters for the cause, then absent, John Balfour and John Henderson. On Friday, 2nd May, the thirteen conspirators met on the moor near Gilston, and, after discharging a weak associate, the lucky number proceeded to Baldinny to spend the night.[2] Robert Black's wife there was a veritable Judith encouraging the desperadoes, one of whom gave her a holy kiss at parting, when she

---

M'Crie, Veitch, 103; Blackadder, *Memoirs*, 210, 211; Burnet, ii. 236; Wodrow, iii. 40-52; *Mackinlay MS.*, *A coppie of the maner of the death*, etc.; Wodrow, iii. 49 note; 'Account … from two persons present,' Kirkton, 419 note; Stephen, *Life*, 578-619; Defoe, 248; Fountainhall, *Decisions*, i. 47, 62; *Hist. Not.*, i. 225; Aldis, *List*, 2160, 2170; Law, *Memoirs*, 147; Mackenzie, *Vindication*, 20; *Criminal Letters, Wodrow MSS.*, xxxiii. 48; *Book of Adjournal*, 1683; *Dict. Nat. Biog.*, art. 'Sharp'; *Reg. Sec. Conc.*, Dec., 1679; Pat. Walker (ed. Fleming), *Six Saints*, i. 214; ii. 160; 'Account of Balfour of Burley' in *Scots Mag.*, i. 130, September 1817; Scott, *Old Mortality*, chaps. iv., v., and notes. Cf. *postea*, pp. 277, 278.

[1] Russell's 'Account' in Kirkton, 408, 412.

[2] They were David Hackston of Rathillet, John Balfour of Kinloch, James Russell in Kettle, George Fleman or Fleming in Balbuthy, junior, Alexander and Andrew, sons of John Henderson in Kilbrachmont, James, Alexander, and George Balfour in Gilston, William Danziel in Caddam (Robert Dingwall in 'Hue and Cry'), Thomas Ness in P—, and Andrew Guillan, weaver in Balmerino.

replied: 'If long Leslie [minister at Ceres] be with him [Sharp], lay him on the green also.' 'There is the hand that shall do it,' was the response of the gallant.[1]

Early in the morning a scout was dispatched, and returned to report that Sheriff Carmichael, who loved to hunt a hare as well as to run a Whig to earth, was already riding with his dogs to Tarvit Hill. A party mounted and rode to the hill to find that Carmichael, warned by a shepherd, had gone back to Cupar. He had realised his peril. A night or two before, Hackston had fixed on the door of Cupar school a discharge to all parties buying Carmichael's poinded goods, thereby putting the people in reverence of Whig reprisals.

Escape of Carmichael.

When the scattered conspirators met again to consider the next move, a boy appeared with a message from Mrs. Black to the effect that the coach of the Archbishop was passing between Ceres and Blebohole. They saw it and exclaimed: 'Truly, this is of God; it seemeth that God hath delivered him into our hands.' All except Hackston avowed a clear call to kill, or, in their fatalistic terminology, 'to execute the justice of God' on the 'murtherer of His saints.' Hackston had scruples. There was 'a known prejudice betwixt the bishop and him,' so that his intervention now 'would mar the glory of the action.' When he refused to lead the band of nine in the chase Balfour cried, 'Gentlemen, follow me.' This bold avenger was described at Hackston's trial as 'a laigh, broad man, round, ruddy faced, dark brown hair, and had ane brown horse, armed with hulster pistols and a shable [sword].'[2] Hackston followed his brother-in-law on a white horse.

Discovery of the Primate.

We turn to the intended victim. He had done his worst for the Covenant he had sworn, his utmost against the faithful maintainers of it. His untiring assiduity in wiping out what he called the 'gangrene' of dissent had its most striking illustration on Thursday, the 1st of May, when he attended the Privy Council for the last time. He was one of twenty-six legislators who sat that day revising and authorising sanguinary measures. One of these was a proclamation 'Against being in arms at field conventicles,' afterwards published on 13th May.[3] This order virtually empowered any officer of the Crown—the meanest

The final labours of Sharp.

---

[1] 'Deposition' in Kirkton, 418 note.
[2] M'Crie, *Misc. Writ.*, 327 note. He was a burly man, known as 'Burly,' or 'Burley.'
[3] Wodrow, iii. 58 note; *Reg. Sec. Conc.*, Dec. 245; Aldis, *List*, 2161, 2162, 2163.

justice of the peace or youngest subaltern—to seize, try for treason, and execute on the spot any suspected conventicler carrying any 'weapon invasive.' The Primate, it was said, contemplated going to London to have the latest repressive legislation sanctioned, and this may have been one of the 'papers of moment' found when his coach was ransacked. It was an iniquitous Act quite to be expected at the end of a reptilious career, and a suitable accompaniment for the French pistols, which this high-priest carried along with his pictorial Bible.

Sharp on the road to St. Andrews.

On the 2nd May, the Primate, his daughter Isabella, and five servants, with the state-coach drawn by six horses, reached the village of Kennoway, where Captain Seatoun entertained them for the night. On Saturday forenoon the equipage halted at the manse of Ceres, where the social prelate had a comforting pipe with 'long Leslie.' As they proceeded homeward Sharp grew nervous as he approached Millar's farm at Magus, or Magask, and said to his daughter: 'There lives an ill-natured man, God preserve us, my child.'[1] It was a timeous presentiment.

The chase.

At noon, as the coach rumbled up to the ridge where Magus Moor slopes down into green Strathkinness, in sight of the cathedral towers of St. Andrews, three miles and a half away, the band of nine 'execrable fanatical assassinates,' as the Hue and Cry described them, were seen galloping, pistols in hand, and naked shables gleaming in the sun looped to their right wrists. The other three, James and Alexander Balfour in Gilston and Thomas Ness, did not join the assassins.[2] Suspecting their evil design, the prelate frantically urged coachman and postillion to 'drive, drive, drive.' Balfour, Russell, Henderson, and others fired at the fleeing coach, then threw their pistols and cloaks on the ground. Slashing the faces of horses and postillions, ham-stringing the leaders, and cutting the traces, they soon held up the coach. With execrations, 'dog,' 'villain,' 'apostate,' 'murderer of Mitchell, Guthrie, and Learmont,' they ordered him to 'come forth, Judas.' He descended yet unwounded.[3] More probably Balfour's last shot into the standing coach gave him the only gun-shot wound he got.[4]

---

[1] Wodrow, *Narrative*, iii. 46 note.
[2] Kirkton, 413.
[3] His son's Letter, Kirkton, 483.
[4] 'Russell's 'Account' in Kirkton, 417. Veitch mentions Burly's 'brazen blunderbus': *Memoirs*, 104.

The premeditated informal assize proceeded on the moorland, and the fierce accusers, hurling impeachments and taunts at the defenceless prisoner, in imitation of the Council's method, were prosecutor, jury, judge, and executioners in turn. Asseverating that 'he never wronged man,' he piteously begged his life. They told him to repent and prepare for death, judgment, and eternity, and bade him pray. He would not pray, or, in the circumstances, could not. Assuming a judicial air Balfour said that no spleen moved them; Sharp, murderer, betrayer, and enemy of Christ, must die. On his knees he looked up into the squinting eyes of little Balfour, fiercer looking with his ten weeks' beard, and probably recognising that beggared heritor, said: 'You are a gentleman ... have pity upon my poor child here and spare her life, and for this, sir, give me your hand.' Balfour's reply was a slash on his upturned face before he rode him down. Another account makes Sharp crawl to the feet of Hackston, who answered his entreaty, 'Sir, I shall never lay a hand on you.' At the sight of the cold steel the Archbishop shrieked. His daughter rushed between the avenging blades and her father, and was wounded too. With fiendish delight Russell recorded the brutalities—usually attributed to Balfour—which he himself perpetrated.[1] Guillan, who held the horses, implored the slayers to spare the old man's life, and was threatened by Balfour. He appealed to Hackston, who, mounted on horseback, 'his cloak about his mouth,' stood by looking on at the tragedy. But 'that once pious godly youth' refused to interfere. At length William Dingwall gave the victim the final thrust, and Russell exultingly exclaimed: 'Take up your priest now.' Wallace, one of the attendants, made a gallant defence before he was cut down.

The dead man's pockets were rifled. The coach and baggage were next ransacked. They found State papers, a Bible, a talisman, a tobacco-box, out of which flew a humming-bee (supposed to be his 'familiar'), some

---

[1] A post-mortem examination showed that the Primate had got a sword-cut over the left eye; many cuts on the back of the head with loss of brains; one shot-wound below the right clavicle; one dagger wound near the kidneys; three wounds on the left hand and one on the right-hand: *The Spirit of Popery*, 58. This was practically one wound for every outlaw present. Russell's boastful, self-glorifying, brutal narrative must be taken with a discount. For Guillan's fate, cf. *postea*. William Dingwall fell at Drumclog. Cf. *postea*, pp. 295.

nail parings—probably used for scaring witches—a case of pistols, and a few trifles belonging to his daughter.[1]

A monument marks the scene of the tragedy. In an adjoining field another marks the grave of five men put to death there to appease the *manes* of Archbishop Sharp: while in a clump of trees close by, still another stone indicates the spot where Guillan, after being hung in chains, was buried.[2] With almost regal pomp the body of the Primate was conveyed to St. Andrews, and, on the 17th May, buried in the parish church there. As was meet, Bishop Paterson, the inventor of the thumbscrews, preached the funeral sermon. A handsome monument representing the Archbishop in the attitude of prayer, and also portraying the slaughter, was erected to his memory, and (at least once repaired) still remains a striking memorial of the breadth of Presbyterian toleration.

The dispatch of Sharp was preconcerted.

That the dispatch of Sharp was premeditated seems certain, and, as the outlaws blasphemously expressed their determination, the accomplishment of it was left to the direction of God. John Welwood, when dying, is credited with saying in April to a hapless youth, then intercommuned—Andrew Ayton of Inchdarnie: 'You'll shortly be quit of him, and he'll get a sudden and sharp off-going, and ye will be the first that will take the good news of his death to heaven.'[3] The prophecy was fulfilled. In searching on the night of the murder for the perpetrators of the deed, a party of soldiers under the Justice-General and the laird of Lundy met, shot, and mortally wounded this 'comely sweet youth,' Ayton, riding peacefully down to Cupar to hear a preacher there, and they also took Hendry Shaw.[4]

Thus disappeared the much misguided champion of unpopular prelacy—hero and saint he was not—whose prowess was exhibited in the persistent audacity with which he, devoid of intellectual and moral strength, at the bidding of superiors in rank and authority, slavishly devoted himself to foisting, by ignoble means, on his country and Church, a system of government as unconstitutional as it was detestable

---

[1] Kirkton, 421; Wodrow, iii. 45.

[2] Cf. *postea*, p. 394 note 3.

[3] *Six Saints*, i. 214.

[4] *Ibid.*, 215; Wodrow, iii. 56; Rothes to Lauderdale, 4th May 1679: *Add. MSS.*, 28547, fol. 23. Letters found about Ayton's person and in Russell's house indicated preconcerted measures against Sharp: Kirkton, 424 note.

to honourable freemen. A competent and unprejudiced authority, Mr. Osmond Airy, has well declared what the knowing Covenanters always said, and died for saying: 'In the most comprehensive sense of the term, Sharp was a knave *pur sang*,[1] and one who, to retain the price of his knavery, either submitted to be cajoled, threatened, bullied, or ignored, by bolder men as served their turn.'[2] What more needs to be said? The most exalted Christian in Scotland—*absit omen*[3]—was a knave *pur sang*! Little wonder that that clearest-headed and largest-hearted of Scotsmen, who so long with dignity lived in the same sacred precincts, could write: 'But his [Sharp's] public career after the Restoration is without redeeming points; and even as one stands by his bloody grave, where I have stood more than once with the wisest and gentlest of modern Anglican teachers, it is hardly possible to start a tear of sympathy over his awful fate.'[4] After all, there may have been many who thought, what Judge Brodie wrote in his Diary: 'I heard that the Bishop of St. Androes was kild. It grewd my soul to hear that ane professing reall grace should fall in such an act. I abhor it perfectlie.'[5] As was to be expected, the Covenanters were divided into two parties when considering the justifiableness of the execution of Sharp by self-constituted judges—the extremists, such as the author of *A Hind Let Loose*, defending, and other sufferers reprobating it. Wodrow mentions the fact that the Scots congregation in Rotterdam would not allow the outlawed Balfour to have fellowship with them in the Communion on account of his indefensible life and character.[6]

The baneful influence of Sharp, so far from dying with him, found expression in the redoubled rigour with which his bereft associates persisted in executing old and new persecuting enactments.[7] The high-priest's mantle fell on the King's advocate—Mackenzie. On the

Estimate of Archbishop Sharp.

---

[1] [French: without doubt.]

[2] *Laud. Pap.*, i., Pref. x.

[3] [Latin: may it not happen!]

[4] Principal Tulloch, *Scottish Divines*, 138 (Edin., 1883).

[5] 5th May 1679: *Diary*, 412.

[6] Wodrow, iii. 47.

[7] Sir Walter Scott probably had a foundation for the vow which he makes Claverhouse take, never to excuse any from 'the ample and bitter penalty of the law, until I shall have taken as many lives in vengeance of this atrocious murder, as the old man had grey hairs upon his venerable head': *Old Mortality*, x.

4th May the Council issued a Hue and Cry, with the names of the assassins printed red, probably in blood, offering 10,000 merks for their apprehension, plainly attributing the murder to the conventiclers, and ordering heritors and masters in Fife to gather all the inhabitants at four centres for examination, the absentees to be reckoned assenters to the murder.[1] Another proclamation made heritors and masters responsible for the offences of suspects not apprehended or evicted from their lands or service.[2] Another forbade any one carrying arms without a licence.[3]

Vengeance of the Government.

The killing of a Crown dignitary afforded a pretext for further spoliation. There was little need for fresh incitements. On that very May day Lord Ross had to throw eight soldiers into irons for committing a wanton burglary and arson.[4] Innocents apprehended lay in prison long, untried, forgotten.[5] For holding private worship in a relative's house after canonical hours, William Hamilton, a preacher, was thrown into the cells, where dysentery cut him off before he could be tried, no engagement for his compearance being acceptable to the Council.[6] The jailors and Claverhouse were busy. The westlandmen burned with rage.

Flight of the assassins.

From Magus Moor the bloodstained gang, after gathering up their cloaks and pistols, rode away to hold a prayer-meeting for several hours, at which they praised themselves, gloried in their deed, and lauded God, 'seeing He had been pleased to honour them to act for Him and to execute His justice upon that wretch.' The disordered Dingwall avowed that he heard the Lord saying to him, 'Well done, good and faithful servants.' Thereafter they rode away, some to home, others into hiding. The Balfours, Hackston, and Russell rode together, deviously, and, after various adventures, came to Dunblane, where they had a stiff refreshment of brandy before proceeding to Kippen. There a preacher joined them, and while, on 18th May, they were preparing for a conventicle in Fintry Craigs, a party of horse from Stirling attacked and dispersed them, not until some of the soldiers were wounded, and

---

[1] Wodrow, iii. 52 note.

[2] *Ibid.*, 56, 57, 58 and notes; Aldis, *List*, 2160, 2170.

[3] Aldis, *List*, 2162.

[4] Napier, *Memorials*, ii. 203.

[5] *E.g.* the cases of James Stirk, Thomas Ness, William Falconer (bedfast): *Reg. Sec. Conc.*, *Dec.* 330, 425.

[6] Wodrow, iii. 54.

one of the Whigs, called Robert Rainie, received a spent shot, Burly only evading capture by flight over a bog. Often suspected, and even recognised, although never betrayed, they skulked and moved towards the safer west, where Richard Cameron's following were defying the Government.[1]

Richard Cameron, since obtaining licence in the spring of 1678, had developed into a fervid evangelical preacher and an implacable enemy to Erastianism, even in its compromise between the outed and the indulged ministry, which was favoured by Welsh, Blackadder, and other moderately inclined nonconformists. The latter, lamenting further divisions, worked for reunion and peace. The Cameronian or Cargill party with Douglas and others, encouraged by the trenchant advices and pamphlets of the exiles, Brown, MacWard, and others, deemed it their duty to hold denunciatory services in the parishes allotted to the indulged. Cameron would not brook any restraint or even counsel on these points, and continued banning the Indulgence and the State for interfering with the Church. The more prudent nonconforming ministers, who had licensed Cameron, cited him to compear at Sundaywell on 14th November 1678, and at Dindeuch in Galloway on 26th December 1678, to submit to presbyterial discipline and instruction.[2] Cameron, supported by Henry Hall of Haughhead, Robert Hamilton, Robert Gray, John Fowler, Michael Cameron, his brother, and others, attended at Sundaywell. Taking exception to the procedure, Cameron haughtily left the convention, unconcerned about the proposal to take away his licence.[3] Robert Hamilton objected to these unconstitutional meetings altogether.

Robert Hamilton was the younger son of Sir Thomas Hamilton of Preston and Fingalton (who signed the Covenant in 1638) and was born in 1650.[4] He was educated in the house of Professor Gilbert Burnet,

Richard Cameron and the irreconcilables.

Sir Robert Hamilton, 1650-1701.

[1] For the shelter which Hackston got from Allan of Elsrickle near Biggar, he presented his host with his ring, and remarked, 'I am uncolys [exceedingly] obleeged to you.' The ring is in the possession of Mrs. Pearson, Crofthead, Muirkirk, whose family preserve this anecdote.

[2] Sundaywell or Sundewal, a fine old house, Kirko's home, with the inscription 'J. K. S. W., 1651,' still stands on the road between Dunscore and Craigenputtock.

[3] Herkless, *Cameron*, 68-78; Howie, *The Scots Worthies* (Carslaw's edition), 423.

[4] J. B. Dalzell, *The Covenanters*, 8 (Hamilton, 1888). Janet Hamilton, his sister, married Alexander Gordon of Earlston. M'Millanites, according to Patrick Walker,

brother-in-law to his father.[1] According to Burnet, Robert was 'then a lively, hopeful, young man,' whom the company of dissenters turned into 'a crackbrained enthusiast.'[2] Blackadder describes him as the young incompetent convener of meddlers and sticklers, who held frequent deliberative meetings in 1678, before the times were ripe, to consider the propriety of rising in arms, and thereby did no good to the cause by making the people restless and the executive more rigorous.[3] Officers in the country warned the Government to expect a rising. Claverhouse, one of whose predatory soldiers had lately mortally stabbed the Provost of Stranraer, informed Linlithgow, the Commander-in-chief, that the peasantry possessed the arms of the militia, and that 'Mr. Welsh is accustoming both ends of the country to face the King's forces, and certainly intends to break out in an open rebellion.'[4]

Manifesto by the extremists.

Hackston and his associates came into touch with Hamilton, Douglas the preacher, and their party, who held a conventicle in Avondale on the 25th May. Now determined to make a public testimony, a deputation of these extremists—Hamilton, Hackston, Burly—went to Glasgow to meet Donald Cargill and John Spreul, for the purpose of settling the terms of a manifesto, first to be approved, as it was, at a meeting at Strathaven, before being formally published at Rutherglen.

Testimony at Rutherglen, 20th May 1679.

For this act they selected the 29th May, the unpopular statutory holiday in honour of the King's birth and restoration. To Rutherglen they rode, sixty or eighty in number, put out the bonfires on the streets, and compelled the magistrates to accompany them to the Market Cross. After Douglas prayed and addressed the crowd, the sympathisers sang a psalm. Hamilton then read out the manifesto in its seven sections, whereby they, 'as true members of the Church of Scotland,' added their testimony to that of the martyrs against all the statutes for overturning the work of Reformation, establishing Episcopacy, renouncing the

---

'should be called Hamiltonians, after Robert Hamilton, who was the only man … that led them in these untroden, dangerous paths of positive disowning of the State, and separation from the Church, and [from] all others that dare not nor will not go their lengths in principles and practices': *Six Saints*, i. 138, 139; Howie, *The Scots Worthies*, 597-607.

[1] Burnet's sister was the second wife of Sir Thomas Hamilton, and step-mother of Robert.

[2] *Hist.*, ii. 238.

[3] *Memoirs*, 214.

[4] Napier, *Memorials*, ii. 202; 21st April 1679.

Covenants, outing the ministry, imposing Restoration Day, setting up
the royal supremacy, authorising the Indulgence, and against the illegal
acts of the Privy Council.[1]

Hamilton affixed the Testimony to the Cross and threw the
obnoxious statutes into a fire. The zealots would have invaded Glasgow
had it not been strongly held by Lord Rose. Instead, they retired to
the wilds of Lanark and Ayr, to brood and pray over the wrongs which
goaded them into becoming revolutionaries.[2] There were many secret
sympathisers with their cause who had not the courage to oppose the
'Sons of Belial,' and who consoled themselves, meantime, with the
prayer of 'Burley's Litany'—

> 'From the Archbishop's Hector, ready att a call,
> From the Carrabine charged with a double ball,
> From John Whyt, the hangman, who is last of all.
>   Libera nos Domine.'

[1] Kirkton, 439; Wodrow, iii. 66.

[2] The *Register of the Privy Council*, vol. v., contains the *Acta, Decreta*, etc., from
4th July 1676 to 27th April 1678. Volume vi is in the press (1912), and will soon be
issued. It contains the minutes of the Council, etc., between 11th September 1678
and 23rd December 1680. The manuscript volume was transferred from the British
Museum to the Register House. I have been privileged to see the volume in print,
and to extract the following interesting item relative to Archbishop Sharp, p. 179;
'Edin., 1st May 1679, *Sederunt*, Chancellor, St. Andrews … Linlithgow … Dalyell
… The Lords warrant the Earle of Linlithgow with horse and foot to prosecute
and follow that party into whatsoever place Welsch, Cameron, Kid, or Douglas
keep their field conventicles, or any uthers whom that standing party follows, with
power to seize and apprehend, and in case of resistance to pursue them to the
death.' Very interesting short biographies of the leading Covenanters are found in
The Scots Worthies, by John Howie of Lochgoin. The excellent revised edition by
the Rev. W. H. Carslaw, M.A. (Edin., 1870), was consulted for this work. The Rev.
John H. Thomson's edition (Edin., 1871) of *A Cloud of Witnesses* (1714) presents the
'Last Speeches and Testimonies' of the sufferers. The complement of both is the
Rev. J. H. Thomson's *The Martyr Graves of Scotland*, edited by the Rev. Matthew
Hutchison, and containing a masterly introduction by Dr. D. Hay Fleming, entitled
'The Story of the Scottish Covenants in Outline' (1903). Exquisite characterisations
are presented by the Rev. Alexander Smellie, M.A., in his *Men of the Covenant*
(Lond., 1903). Mrs. Hugh Pryce has written a popular *Life of the Great Marquis of
Montrose* (Lond., 1912). Mr. Michael Barrington has retold the story of *Graham of
Claverhouse, Viscount Dundee* (Lond., 1911). The Marchioness of Tullibardine has
given a spirited account of the Battle of Killiecrankie and the death of Dundee in *A
Military History of Perthshire*, 1660-1902 (Perth, 1908).

John Graham of Claverhouse in 1681

Alexander Leslie,
first Earl of Leven

The Market Cross of Edinburgh

John Balfour
of Kinloch—'Burly'

Holyrood House

Monument to 'Old Mortality,'
The Holm, Balmaclellan

PORTRAITS OF CLAVERHOUSE, LEVEN, AND BALFOUR, ETC.

CHAPTER TWENTY-SIX

THE RISE OF CLAVERHOUSE

TO the chase after these defiant Whigs:

'There, worthy of his masters, came
The Despot's Champion, bloody Graham,
To stain for aye a warrior's sword,
And lead a fierce, though fawning horde,—
The human bloodhounds of the earth,
To hunt the peasant from the hearth.'

At this time Claverhouse had the repute of being a terror in the south, at the mention of whose name intending conventiclers disappeared. This John Graham, eldest son of Sir William, laird of Claverhouse and Claypots, near Dundee, and of Lady Magdalene Carnegie, fifth daughter of John, Earl of Ethie, afterwards first Earl of Northesk, was of aristocratic lineage. Born probably in 1648, he was left fatherless when five years of age.[1] The latter circumstance contributed to the comparative affluence of Claverhouse at his majority. Like Turner, Bruce of Earlshall, Lag, and other harriers of the Covenanters, he had a university education. No one could conjecture this from his compositions, wherein he expressed his thoughts in a rude, vulgar, and curiously spelled dialect, not employed by other students in St. Andrews. With six hundred pounds annually from his property, he had no need, like Turner, to become a mercenary, fighting for daily bread.

Lineage of Graham of Claverhouse.

[1] Terry, *New Scots Peerage*, iii. 325, says 'probably in July 1648'; Morris, *Claverhouse*, chap. i; Napier, *Memorials*, i, 178; *The Despot's Champion*, chap. i. I have searched twenty-five likely parish registers for the record of his birth, but in vain as yet.

Yet he had gone to, and returned from, France and Holland with the reputation of being a dashing officer, whose white plume had marked the track of his gallantry at Seneffe. At the instance of the King and his brother, Claverhouse was gazetted captain of a new troop of horse on 23rd September 1678. His duty in patrolling troublous Dumfriesshire that winter animated him with zeal and delight. He had peculiar, if not unique, views of soldiering at home, considering himself to be an armed high-priest, commissioned to sacrifice the enemies of the Crown as much for their own sake as for that of his employer; an Episcopal crusader inspired to do battle with dissent and cleanse away the gangrene likely to infect and destroy divine Episcopacy. Thus he confessed to Queensberry: 'For my owen pairt I look on myself as a cleanger. I may cur people guilty of that plaigue of presbitry be conversing with them, but can not be infected.'[1] He was the natural successor to Turner, who acted on the principle, 'that so as we serve our master honnestlie it is no matter what we serve,' since Claverhouse declared: 'In any service I have been in, I never enquired farther in the laws, than the orders of my superior officers.'[2] Even jovial Turner did not go so far as a hireling, who, given a warrant, would shoot incontinently, and sheathe his sword anywhere. With such a despicable want of principle, it is not surprising to find this fanatic, Graham, when revelling in his exterminating work, complimenting the Earl of Menteith on a similar assiduity: 'I rejoice to hear you have now taken my trade in hand, that you are become the terror of the godly.'[3] Although Sir Ewen Cameron asserted that Claverhouse died a 'good Christian,' there is no record of any pious thoughts or humane deeds in connection with his career, apart from the fact that he drove other sinners into church to inspect them, had family prayers, and attended the baptism of the son of the parson of Dundee.[4] Probably for the same undiscoverable reasons that Mr. Andrew Lang averred that Turner 'was infinitely more of a Christian than the saints of the Covenant,' Claverhouse has a title to be considered the Episcopal saint and martyr, which Sharp failed to be.[5] No unprejudiced historian

Views of Claverhouse.

[1] *Hist. MSS. Com. Rep.*, xv. viii. 287.
[2] Napier, *Memorials*, ii. 189.
[3] *Red Book of Menteith*, ii. 200.
[4] Terry, 218 note; Cameron, *Memoirs*, 278, 279.
[5] *Blackwood's Magazine*, clxxiv. 41, July 1903.

could place an aureole round the head of Claverhouse. Even Sir Walter Scott, when writing to Southey vilifying the Covenanters—at least the Poundtexts, Kettledrummles, Mucklewraths, and other oddities of his imagination—actually confessed of his hero: 'I admit he was *tant soit peu*[1] savage, but he was a noble savage; and the beastly Covenanters, against whom he acted, hardly had any claim to be called men, unless what was founded on their walking upon their hind feet.'[2]

Sir Walter Scott's opinion of Claverhouse.

None of the biographies of 'The Despot's Champion' gives a description of the personal appearance of John Graham, leaving readers to form their own opinions from the prepossessing portraits which enhance these works. The reason of this is, that writers on the subject believed that there was no delineation extant other than the prejudiced reference of John Dick, the student-martyr of 5th March 1684, who, in his Testimony, sneers at 'the pitiful thing,' escaping from Drumclog on account of the fleetness of his horse, where 'there fell prettier men on either side than himself.'[3] Obviously this was a gibe at the diminutive and plain person of the runaway from Drumclog. That Dundee was a very small man, not more than five feet six inches in height, with narrow sloping shoulders, is proved from his breastplate, preserved in Blair Castle, and whose genuineness has never been doubted. It measures but fifteen inches and a half in length from gorge to skirt, and only eighteen inches and a quarter across its broadest part.[4] The fine portrait of this 'bonny fighter' when young, preserved in Melville House (Leven portrait), and the other in Glamis Castle, attributed to Sir Peter Lely, are presentations of a Minerva rather than a Mars—of a soldier with a girl's face and a tiger's heart. They do not depict a Privy Councillor who could attend sanguinary cases, incite and pass bloodthirsty measures for shooting and maiming, drowning and abusing pious men and women. It is to be remembered, however, that in the bloated epoch of the Stuarts the geese were all swans to Lely and Kneller. Even M'Cries' description of Claverhouse as a 'handsome bloodhound' is but partly in harmony with the persistent tradition of the districts harassed by him that he

Personal appearance of Claverhouse.

Breastplate of Claverhouse.

---

[1] [French: ever so little.]

[2] *Life of Scott*, ii. 134.

[3] Terry, *John Graham*, 86 note; Dick, *The Testimony to the Doctrine*, etc. (1684), n.d.

[4] Lord Tullibardine kindly sent these measurements to the author, 19th February 1907.

was an ugly man. Moray's statement to the King in 1685 that 'he knew Clauerous to be of a hye, proud, and peremptor humour,' does not necessarily disagree with the opinion formed after viewing the good-looking soldier in the Melville and Glamis portraits. The miniature formerly in Hamilton Palace, now in possession of the Earl of Moray, portrays a sharp, clever man, with very round forehead, blue eyes, thin *retroussé* nose, firm mouth, open nostrils, and brown hair. He is wearing armour. We possess three accounts of Dundee, which corroborate the tradition of the southern Whigs that he was 'a small and fearsome man,' who rode 'Satan,' his black charger, along the face of the precipitous Stey Gail, down Enterkin Pass. John Morrison, a Terregles man, repeated to Sir Walter Scott, as they examined a portrait of Dundee, the following account of the exploits of Dundee in Dumfries seen by Joseph Robson: 'He [Claverhouse] attending the murder of two martyrs on the sands of Dumfries, rode his horse along the coping of a parapet wall built to guard off the waters of the Nith in time of floods, and when the horse had arrived at one end, he wheeled round on one of his hind legs as on a pivot, repeating the same manoeuvre. His arms were long, and reached to his knees, his hair red or frizzly, and his look altogether diabolical. Such would never be the face that painters love to limn and ladies to look on,' added Morrison.[1] This delineation partly harmonises with a portrait, recently sold in London, which represents a middle-aged man of sinister, vulgar lineaments, with red curly hair or wig, clad in armour, and wearing a cravat.[2]

Morrison's description.

A somewhat similar account is found in the curious, unreliable Memoirs of Thomas Brownlee, laird of Torfoot, which first appeared in the *National Gazette* in America. The laird asserted: 'I distinctly saw the features and shape of this far-famed man. He was small of stature and not well formed: his arms were long in proportion to his legs. He had a complexion unusually dark ... his cheeks were lank and deeply furrowed ... his irregular and large teeth were presented through a smile

Torfoot's delineation.

[1] Tait's *Edinburgh Magazine*, x. 628; 'Stey Gail' or 'Gyle,' Scots for steep gable.

[2] This oval miniature, measuring 3 by 2⅓ inches, was sold at Puttick and Simpson's sale, 29th May 1907 (item 71), to Colonel Horace Walpole, Heckfield Place, Winchfield, Hants. The inscription on the back of the silver frame runs: 'John Graham of Claverhouse, Viscount of Dundee. Given by himself to David Bethune of Balfour in 1681.'

which was very unnatural on his set of features. His mouth seemed to be unusually large. ... In short his upper teeth projected over his under lips, and on the whole presented to my view the mouth on the image of the Emperor Julian the Apostate.'[1]

These extraordinary delineations are partially corroborated by an old serving-woman, who served Claverhouse with wine in old Duffus Castle in 1689. She survived till 1760, and described him as 'a swarthy little man, with keen lively eyes, and black hair tinged with grey, which he wore in locks which covered each ear and were rolled upon slips of lead, twisted together at the end.'[2] If Torfoot was right in declaring that Claverhouse bore 'the strong expression given by our painters to those on the face of Judas Iscariot,' it is not to be wondered at that the Covenanters saw Apollyon himself in this Apollo Belvedere of the Royalists. There is disillusionment in these revelations. Hitherto Scottish heroes have been portrayed in the handsome mould and mien of Agamemnon; but to conjure up a 'pitiful thing,' diminutive, choleric, impertinently irrepressible, with too long arms, jumping up in Council to 'box in the ear' Sir John Dalrymple, creates a shock. Still greater is the shock on imagining this Carolan dandy with his curls in leads; yet after all it might have been expected of so close an imitator of the cavalier Montrose, who ascended the scaffold in all the bravery of a Covent Garden coxcomb.

Little wonder that such a horrid leader, followed by a troop of dare-devil riders, making over hill and dale, as the crow flies, forty or more miles, by day or night, could boastingly report to Linlithgow: 'No body lays in ther bed, that knowes themselfs any ways guilty, within fourty milles of us.'[3] Three days afterwards Claverhouse was appointed a Sheriff-depute of Dumfriesshire, Stewartry of Kirkcudbright and Wigtownshire, the most disaffected area in the country.[4] This untiring soldier was so punctiliously careful, that nothing would induce him to act contrary to the minutest terms of his commission. Scott, in a note to *Old Mortality*, describes him as 'the unscrupulous agent of the Scottish

[margin note] A serving-maid's reminiscences.

[margin note] Claverhouse appointed Sherriff, 27th February 1679.

---

[1] Brownlee, *A Narrative ... of Drumclog*, etc. (1823).

[2] Shaw, *History of the Province of Moray*, ii. 84; *Scott. Rev.*, July 1884, iv. 116. Scott in *Old Mortality* describes him as 'rather low of stature.'

[3] 24th February 1679: Smythe, *Letters of John Graham* (Bann. Club, 1826), 13.

[4] *Ibid.*, 16-18.

Privy Council in executing the merciless severities of the government in Scotland.' Self-interest was his constant monitor.[1] Turner's example, his reward too, stared him in the face. As soon as the proclamation of 13th May empowered all officers to proceed against traitors, Claverhouse got the unlimited licence which satisfied and gratified him.

Yet at the very time he was vigorously hunting down conventiclers, smashing up meeting-houses, and carrying off to jail 'old and infirm men with gravel,' he stole leisure to think of love.[2] Claverhouse was one of the rare solvent officers who then could afford the luxury. He began a correspondence with the childless, bankrupt, adulterous Earl of Menteith, whom he styled 'the last of so noble a race.'[3] With an assurance quite unsurpassed, Claverhouse offered himself for the purpose of perpetuating the manly stock of Graham by marrying the

Claverhouse's sordid love proposal.

heiress of Menteith, Helen Graham, the Earl's cousin; and in consideration of the Earl giving him patronage and help to secure the maid, whom probably he never saw, and also selecting him as heir to the falling title, the ambitious, speculating wooer agreed to settle a pension on the broken peer. Like other dragoons he swore he would take her in her 'smoak.' The needy noble saw business in the proposal which the fair Helen rejected. There was another Graham in the competition— Montrose—who complicated matters in this sordid affair. In Helen's praise, be it said, she chose her own match in Captain Rawdon, and kept her honour.[4] Claverhouse, in leading a clean life, was unlike his profligate contemporaries. With the exception of the hint of guilty familiarity with Lord Advocate Mackenzie's wife, in a scurrilous pasquil entitled *Mitchell's Ghost*, ascribed to Sir James Turner, there is no impeachment of his moral character.[5]

Capture of the conventiclers, May 1679.

Claverhouse was soon in pursuit of Hamilton and the Rutherglen Protestors. He had been recalled on some military duty, and on his route dispersed a conventicle near Galashiels, making some notable seizures of ladies, and Thomas Wilkie, a minister.[6] Close on Hamilton's

[1] Napier, *Memorials*, ii, 189.
[2] Letters, 18.
[3] *Red Book*, ii. 170.
[4] Terry, 84-101.
[5] Kirkton, 389 note.
[6] Wodrow, iii. 61.

party, he surprised and captured in or near the town of Hamilton the already famous John King and fourteen suspected conventiclers, whom he dragged along with him 'bound as beasts.'[1] He reached Strathaven on Sabbath the 1st of June, about six o'clock in the morning. Claverhouse got notice of a great conventicle mustering that day on Glaister Law or Hairlawhill, some eight miles away and two miles from Darvel. Blustering and boasting he rode to the fray. He declared that his men were eager to fight the rogues, and, in order to arouse this courage, he threatened to court-martial them if they quailed in the conflict.[2] No quarter was to be given.

The conventiclers, duly warned of his approach, appointed Hamilton, apparently the only man of standing among them, to be their commander. He had no military qualifications save that of stern resolve to fight, seeking no favour and giving none, in terms of this order: 'I, being called to command that day as head, gave out word that no quarters should be given.'[3] The preacher, Thomas Douglas, finally addressed the gathering and said: 'You have got the theory, now for the practice.' The Covenanters were marshalled and marched away singing psalms to meet the soldiery on a suitable arena at Drumclog, where the unarmed worshippers—men, women, and children—were massed above the combatants.

The scene of the encounter at High Drumclog, in Lanarkshire, was green slope of a ridge stretching between two tracts of moorland overlooked, at a distance of two miles, by the verdant dun of Loudoun Hill, which also gave its name to the fight.[4] Both forces chose firm ground. Alton writes: 'The ground on the north side of the bog where the Covenanters made their stand was rather steeper than that occupied by the military, but was also fair lying arable land ... the marshy ground between these arable fields was only a few yards broad.'[5]

Drumclog and Loudoun Hill.

[1] *Short Memorial*, 13; Wodrow, iii. 94 note.

[2] *Letters*, 25 (Bann. Club)

[3] Fleming, *Six Saints*, ii. 215; *Faithful Contendings*, 201.

[4] Professor Lodge in *The Political History of England* (Lond., 1910), viii. 202, writes: 'On the following Sunday, June 1, a large conventicle was held on (*sic*) Loudoun Hill, when it was interrupted by the news that James (*sic*) Graham of Claverhouse was approaching with a body of troopers.'

[5] The authorities consulted for this sketch are: Claverhouse, *Letter to Linlithgow*, 1st June 1679: Napier, *Memorials*, ii. 220-3; also in *Laud Pap.*, iii. 164; Russell's

The command of Claverhouse consisted of not more than one hundred and fifty mounted men. The armed force under Hamilton probably numbered fifty men on horse and two hundred infantry, some of whom carried swords and firearms, the rest being armed with homemade pikes, cleeks (halberds), pitchforks, or other rustic weapons. The officers acting under Hamilton were Hackston, John Balfour ('Burly'), Henry Hall of Haughhead, Robert Fleming, John Loudoun, John Brown of Priestshiel, and William Cleland. Cleland, then a poetic, brilliant, belligerent student of St. Salvator's College, St. Andrews, some eighteen years old, was a leader of the foot, and that day showed the prowess which distinguished him in the command of the Cameronian regiment which held Dunkeld in 1689.[1]

Claverhouse, leaving King and other prisoners under a small guard at North-Drumclog farm, reconnoitred the position of his foe before sending out a flag of truce. His demands were spurned. When the Covenanters reached their defensive position the whole host prayed and raised a cry to heaven in the words of Asaph to the melody of 'Martyrs'—the 76th Psalm: 'In Judah's land God is well known,' with its menacing finish—'By Him the sp'rits shall be cut off.'[2] That they stood under 'The Bluidy Banner,' a flag inscribed with vindictive threats, is a modern fiction already disposed of.[3] According to Russell 'a great gutter like a stank, being no way to get about it,' separated the combatants. Skirmishing parties answered each other's fusils and pistols across the gutter, without either force making much impression on his well-posted antagonist. At length, the fearless Covenanters, roused to a pitch of heroism, determined to cross the 'stank' and meet the military

---

'Account' in Kirkton, 442; Aiton, *Hist.*, 53; Wodrow, iii. 69, 94 note; Terry, *John Graham*, 52; Morris, *Claverhouse*, 65; Barbé, *Viscount Dundee*, 48; *The Despot's Champion*, 43; Burton, *Hist.*, vii. 224; Nisbet, *Diary*; M'Crie, *Veitch*, 455-61, 519; Thomson, *Martyr Graves*, 31; *Ayrshire Ballads*, 51; Nimmo, *Narrative*, 12; Dodds, *Fifty Years*, 239; Defoe, pt. iii. 238; Paget, *Paradoxes*, 121; Fleming, *Six Saints*, i. 86, 125, 241, 298; ii. 144, 148, 215, 216, 224; Scott, *Old Mortality*, notes; *Add. MSS.* (Brit. Mus.), 23244; *Faithful Contendings*, 201; Blacader MS. (Advocates' Lib.); J. B. Dalzell, *The Scots Army* (*Review*), Hamilton, 1909.

[1] Cleland entered college 2nd March 1677; Wilson, *A True ... Relation*, etc., 8 (1797).

[2] Brownlee (Torfoot), *Narrative*, 6.

[3] Dr. Hay Fleming's *Six Saints*, ii. 216.

in hand-to-hand conflict. Their advantage in having knowledge of the tracks through the marsh was counterbalanced by the odds of charging disciplined soldiers in their panoply of war. Yet there was no hesitation. Cleland, Nisbet, Dingwall, Weir, and others, some on horse, others on foot, made a dash through the harmless smoke upon the royal troops, whose firing was largely ineffective. This fierce onset of horse, men, and some gallant Amazons, with sword and pistol, with pike and pitchfork at the push, was too much for the dragoons, who fled helter-skelter, leaving thirty of their comrades dead upon the field. Graham's white plume at Seneffe was the white feather at Drumclog. 'His fine horse,' as Veitch called it, saved the runaway's life.[1] Claverhouse's exculpatory account must be taken with reserve. The farmers, some of whom came long distances 'to hear the sermon,' pursued him so long as their jaded horses could carry them. Not till Claverhouse reached Capernaum, a mile from High Drumclog, was his charger stabbed by the pike of Thomas Finlay, farmer, Southfield. The maddened, 'sorre horse' still galloped on one mile and three-quarters to Hillhead, and here, near the Trumpeter's Well, Claverhouse mounted the horse of his trumpeter, who was killed there. Cowardice in him and his men is proved by the smallness of the number of the peasantry who fell—one slain and five mortally wounded. Had Claverhouse been a hero-cavalier he would have turned and faced his pursuers. John Nisbet of Hardhill, on the other hand, was reputed to have slain seven troopers that day. Thomas Weir of North Cumberhead captured a royal standard which was afterwards retaken, and, though mortally wounded, continued pursuing. Cleland actually seized the bridle of Claverhouse's horse, and would have taken him had he been supported.[2] William Dingwall was mortally wounded, his horse having fallen as he gallantly supported Cleland's victorious foot. Dingwall on dying was so ravished with joy in his assurance of glory in Heaven, that his Testimony often constrained sympathisers to visit his grave in Strathaven, where they sat and wept.[3] The Covenanters killed were buried in local churchyards.[4] Early in the fight the bold

(margin note: Defeat and flight of Claverhouse.)

[1] Some have mistaken Claverhouse's 'sorre' (wretched from its wounds) charger for a sorrel: Scott called it a 'rone'; Veitch, *Memoirs*, 108, 'his fine horse.'

[2] *Memoirs*, 240.

[3] Kirkton, 446.

[4] Cf. Thomson, *Martyr Graves*, var. loc.

Nisbet had rescued the prisoners, and as Claverhouse galloped for life King facetiously hollaed to him to stay for the afternoon sermon.

The victors captured and gave quarter to some prisoners. Hamilton would have put them all to the sword had his associates not prevented him. One they did not save from their leader. Afterwards accused of his cruelty 'for killing of that poor man (as they called him) at Drumclog,' Hamilton vindicated himself in a letter, wherein he acknowledges his 'no quarters' order, and declares 'that there was 5 more that without knowledge gote quarters, quhom notwithstanding I desired might have been sent the same way that their neighbours were, and its not being doon I reckoned ever amongst our first stepping aside.'[1] Extremists of this type, like Walter Smith, maintained that the refusal to shed the blood of God's enemies was the cause of the curse resting on the unhappy Church.[2] The tale of the mutilation of Cornet Robert Graham's body, mistaken for that of Claverhouse, and the reports of the indignities shown to the fallen before the barricades in Glasgow, and practised by the Whigs on bodies in Glasgow Cathedral, may all be dismissed as fabrications.[3]

Hamilton and the 'No Quarter' order.

The beaten persecutor brought the news to Glasgow that night, and sat down 'so wearied and so sleepy,' to write the dispatch notifying, 'very confusedly,' his defeat to the Commander-in-Chief.[4]

The march of the insurgents.

With the arch-enemy of their cause buried and the most terrible of their oppressors humiliated, the credulous insurgents vainly imagined themselves to be compelling a blessing from a pleased God, and deemed it their duty to follow up their advantage. After a halt at Strathaven and a sleep in Hamilton they marched to Glasgow. Lord Ross had barricaded the central district of the city, and with the garrison stood to arms. The insurgents appeared on Monday, 2nd June, before noon.[5] Without artillery Hamilton found it impossible to force Ross's defences; and the gallant attacks by Balfour, Hackston, and other bold fighters, met

---

[1] *Six Saints*, ii. 215, 216 note.

[2] *Ibid.*, 77.

[3] Kirkton, 442; Terry, 57 note; Wodrow, iii. 71; Napier, *Memorials*, iii. 229 note; Creichton, *Memoirs*.

[4] It has been reprinted often, e.g. Napier, *Memorials*, ii. 220; *Martyr Graves*, 34; Scott, *Old Mortality*, notes. Cf. *Stowe MSS.*, 142; *Brit. Mus. Cat.*, 101, No. 61.

[5] Ross to Linlithgow, 2nd June 1679; *Laud. Pap.*, iii. 166; *Add. MSS.*, 23244.

by the sure fusillade of the soldiery, ended in the discomfiture of the assailants and the loss of lives. They were obliged to retreat to their camp at Bothwell Bridge and wait for reinforcements, munitions of war, and the help of God.

Claverhouse concluded his dispatch in these terms: 'The contry was floking to them from all hands: this may be counted the begining of the rebellion, in my opinion.' The Council thought similarly, proclaimed the victors of Drumclog traitors, ordered Linlithgow and the regulars to march west, and mustered the King's host, including the 'Highland Amorites' of Argyle. English reinforcements were promised. Ross left Glasgow and met Linlithgow at Kilsyth on 5th June. Hearing of the strength of his opponents, Linlithgow deemed it prudent to withdraw his force of 1800 men to Stirling, whence, on an order from the Council, they came to Edinburgh.[1] As soon as news of the rising reached London, the Duke of Monmouth, the King's illegitimate son, received a commission to quell the rising with the aid of English soldiers and guns.

Claverhouse's dispatch.

The insurgents, on the retiral of Ross, entered Glasgow and burned the mansions of the prelates and Lauderdale.[2] The Covenanters, in passing to their rendezvous, had by the way bloody scuffles with the garrisons and militia. The men of Ayrshire on the march removed the heads of those who suffered for the rising of '66 from the Tolbooth spikes in Ayr, Irvine, Kilmarnock, and Glasgow. The rebellious host fluctuated between five and eight thousand men. It was composed of four distinct classes, each a menace to the other. The victors under Hamilton, with the ministers, Cargill, Douglas, King (?), were the uncompromising opponents of the existing politico-ecclesiastical system, and avowing the tenets of Richard Cameron, were ready to adventure on action damaging to Malignant and Indulged alike.[3] The moderate Presbyterians, King and others, soon to be largely reinforced by Welsh and the men of Carrick, Gordon, and the Galloway outlaws, Ure of Shargarton and the Stirlingshire stalwarts, and others, came into camp willing to assist in restoring freedom, spiritual and civil;

Victors in Glasgow.

Four parties in camp.

[1] Wodrow, iii. 72-4 notes, 84 note; *Laud. Pap.*, iii. 168, 169.

[2] *State Papers* (Charles II.), 412, 268; Dr. James Colville, 'Claverhouse in Glasgow,' in the *Glasgow Herald*, 3rd and 10th February 1906.

[3] M'Crie, *Ure's Narr.*, 470.

and, while antagonistic to the indulgence, tolerated all the Indulged who safeguarded Presbyterial principles. There was a more peaceable section still, little represented however, who held with Blackadder and Fraser of Brea that 'the Lord called for a testimony by suffering rather than outward deliverance.'[1] There was a fourth, the worst class, the indifferent and ungodly associates, who joined expecting loot and a chance to fight where there was no danger. Of this order was Alexander Mackinnan, pipemaker in Glasgow, who fought at Bothwell, robbed ministers, and being brought to justice, got his ears nailed to a post and himself banished in 1680.[2] In order to maintain discipline the officers of the Covenanting host found it necessary to shoot a Glasgow butcher, named Watson, who drove a pitchfork through a godly brother, and they also nailed a thief by the ear to the local gallows.[3]

Hamilton was not the man of Napoleonic genius qualified to manage this incongruous, incoherent mob. His active policy of purgation might have turned out well had Cromwell been there to drill the holy remnant into irresistible Ironsides. There was no chance of a miracle. There was not a leader of any calibre to marshal that immense conventicle of wrangling theologians, unless we except the dauntless veteran of the Civil Wars and of Rullion Green—Captain John Paton of Meadowhead, who, with the men of Fenwick, Newmilns, and Galston, joined Hamilton after the affair at the barricades. Instead of entrenching a leaguer, gathering munitions, appointing officers, the leaders turned the camp into a general assembly of the hottest heads. Like stump orators the perfervid demagogues carried their pulpits with them. One little brass gun filched from Douglas Castle, with a few charges, was all their artillery. Both zealots and moderates desired to promulgate a new declaration similar, and supplementary, to that of Rutherglen, but as the age of building platforms suitable for differing sections had not emerged, and every would-be leader there had a stand of his own, the fabrication of a manifesto was so difficult that over it arose angry shoutings, rude jostling, forcible evictions from the pulpits,[4]

Hamilton a 'feckless' general.

---

[1] Blackadder's son. Dr. William, was at Bothwell Bridge: Blackadder, *Memoirs*, 220; *Select Biog.*, ii. 336.
[2] *Reg. Sec. Conc.*, *Dec.*, 379, 4th June 1680.
[3] M'Crie, *Ure's Narr.*, 460; Kirkton, 457.
[4] These portable pulpits were called 'tents.'

and threats of cold steel. The councils of war afforded the splitters Divided councils. of hairs the opportunity of producing internecine dissensions. The Rutherglen paper was unknown to many newcomers, and, on account of its extreme attitude to the Indulgence, required modification to suit the views of Welsh, David Hume of Coldingham, William Fergusson of Caitloch, and others, whose aim was to unite parties on the broad basis of Presbyterianism. At a meeting held at Glasgow in June the Hamilton-Cargill party mustered so strongly that the Welshites only succeeded in getting the terms of the Rutherglen protest against the Indulgence modified into the phrase 'declaring against popery, prelacy, erastianism, and all things depending therupon.'[1] Enough for all save splitters of hairs, harmonising with the stereotyped principles of Knox and Melville, almost like ecclesiastical papers of our day for delightful vagueness, this equivocal compromise would not do for the Welshites.

The Hamiltonians, in the spirit of Guthrie, wished a day of mourning The Hamiltonians or extremists. to avert the Divine wrath. Their opponents opposed the formation of a schedule in which their sins and defections were sure to be entered along with Restoration rejoicings, cess, supremacy, indulgence, and the compromises made by the Moderates for peace's sake. The list staggered Welsh, who, as a constitutionalist, protested that the enumeration of ecclesiastical offences was the function of the General Assembly only. Sin was sin whatever the Church might say, was the answer of Hamilton and Cargill, who held that if there was to be co-operation, the ministry led by Welsh should denounce the sin in the Indulgence. Hamilton, for the council of his party, went so far as to send a peremptory order to the Moderate preachers to preach against the Indulgence. The latter thought this interference an intolerable illustration of Erastianism as sinful as the acts of their common foe. Parties would not mourn together.[2]

The Moderates proposed a civil declaration to the effect that their The Moderates. insurrection against the Government was not a proof of disloyalty. They were monarchists. The Hamiltonians could neither reconcile this with their own declaration nor with their repugnance to a King who had broken the Covenant and other vows, ruined and disestablished the

---

[1] Wodrow, iii. 91.
[2] *Ibid.*, iii. 91, 92.

Church, slaughtered the godly, and waged war on his people. They would abide by that declaration which left the question of allegiance open. Theirs was the manly maintenance of a sacred contract against which the arguments of expediency could not prevail.

The Hamilton Cross Declaration, 13th June 1679.

During these wranglings some sympathisers with the insurgents, apprehensive of Hamilton's incapacity, deemed it advisable to frame a tentative declaration, which, through the agency of Robert Wylie, minister of Hamilton, then a prisoner in Edinburgh, and William Dunlop, afterwards principal of the University of Glasgow, was conveyed to the Moderates. Its strong terminology pleased Welsh; for lack of a definition of specific evils it was abjured by Hamilton. Welsh utilised the document in framing the new Hamilton declaration, which a majority passed before it was affixed to the Cross in Hamilton. The minority—Hamilton-Cargillites—intended amending it by adding references to the public defections, and they were disappointed, if not outwitted, on the appearance of the declaration in print in Glasgow on 13th June.[1]

Import of the manifesto.

The declaration narrates the woeful state of the land and Church through the brutal execution of the laws, and the refusal of redress from the magistrates, so that a defensive rising was necessary: the aim of the insurgents was (1) the preservation of the Church, Protestant, Presbyterian, Covenanted, with its legal standards; (2) the maintenance and defence of the King; (3) the obtaining of a free Parliament and a free Assembly. This manifesto did not heal the divisions. Hamilton declared that association with favourers of the Indulgence would bring the malison of God, who had signally owned the Precisians at Drumclog. Another week's wrangling and rioting demoralised the undisciplined crowd. Many sympathisers with the Covenanters' cause went home disaffected.

Arrival of Monmouth and an army.

Meantime the timid Government took heart and equipped the army. Monmouth arrived in Edinburgh on the 18th June, next day joined the army at Blackburn, and on Saturday evening, 21st, lay with ten thousand men before Bothwell Bridge.[2] Linlithgow commanded

---

[1] *State Papers*, 412; *Wodrow MSS.*, xxxiii. 7; Wodrow, iii. 96; *Laing MSS.*, 89, 102—'*The Declaration of the Presbyterians now in Armes in the West*'; *The Scots Worthies*, 598.

[2] *Add. MSS.*, 23244, No. 12, Privy Council to Lauderdale, 10th June, gives 10,000 men at Shotts; Blackadder, 224, gives 15,000 men.

the infantry division. Dalyell was overlooked, and left at Binns to comb his monumental beard till, too late for the battle, he got his commission. The extremists following Hamilton had already secured the appointment of officers—Balfour, Hackston, Paton, Henderson, Hall, Carmichael, Cleland, Fowler, and Major Learmonth—with Cargill, Douglas, King (?), and others as armed chaplains. The arrival on the 20th of a Galloway contingent of Welshites one thousand strong led to a discussion as to the advisability of selecting other officers. Quarrelling resulted. The newcomers were willing to abide by the Hamilton declaration and to refer differences to a new Parliament and Assembly: the Hamiltonians desired dissociation from Indulgers. Thus the quarrel stood as the advance-guard of the Royalists, on the 21st, had an outpost affair at a ford east of Hamilton and mortally shot James Cleland.[1] That day a great council of war was held, and the Hamilton party left the meeting in a body.[2] The Covenanters had become *distrait*, and, by their preoccupying infatuation, were blinded to the fact that their opponents were at hand.

The appointment of Monmouth, a Protestant, instructed to act with toleration, gave a new complexion to the crisis. English sympathisers with the persecuted forwarded communications advising the insurgents to negotiate with Monmouth, 'who would take it kindly.'[3] Monmouth himself, through Melville, made known his own kindly intentions and desire of peace, and promised good terms.[4] His power was unlimited, and he had authority to pardon all except the forfeited and the slayers of Sharp. Ultimately the contending parties agreed to forward a bare representation of the facts of the case to the Duke, and Cargill was one of a committee appointed to revise the draft. The document is a cultured address to the 'potent prince,' whose presence was declared to be 'a most favourable providence,' containing a simple request for liberty to send a deputation to give a true account of their deplorable sufferings. It is signed, 'R. Hamiltoune in name of the Covenanted Army now in armes.'[5] An angel might honestly have subscribed it.

The Duke of Monmouth, 1649-1685.

---

[1] Kirkton, 463.
[2] *Ure's Narr.*, 473.
[3] *Wodrow MSS.*, xxxiii. 8; Wodrow, iii. 101.
[4] *Ure's Narr.*, 474 note; M'Crie, *Veitch*, 110; *Act. Parl. Scot.*, viii. App. 57.
[5] 'Original document,' *Add. MSS.*, 23251, fol. 22; 23244, fol. 14; Laud. Pap., iii.

Bothwell Bridge.

As Sabbath morning, the 22nd June, broke, Hamilton's pickets saw the Royalist musketeers across the Clyde blowing their matches and ready for the advance to the bridge at Bothwell. The Covenanters, through their wranglings reduced in number to four thousand badly armed men, were drawn up in two bodies, the smaller battalion near the bridge, and the main body on high ground near the Little Park, Hamilton.[1] The fine old narrow with its guard-house and toll-bar, when barricaded with stones, and adjacent dwelling-houses, were an ideal strength for the brave defenders, none braver than Hackston, Hall, Turnbull of the horse, and Fowler and Ross of the foot. The little brass piece defended the approach. The men of Stirling, Clydesdale, and Galloway, the latter brave with banners and terrible with pikes and halberds, stood on the south side of the bridge, Hackston being in command on the left side, near the houses at Bridgend.

Skirmishes and truces.

By seven o'clock Monmouth's force was marshalled along the north side of the Clyde, before the bridge, and some skirmishing took place. During the preliminary confusion consequent on this advance William Blackadder, bearing the address to Monmouth, accosted Hamilton and got him to sign what he said he had not read, but took on trust as the work of Cargill.[2] Two envoys with a drummer, the former said to be David Hume, minister, and William Fergusson of Caitloch—other authorities mention Welsh, Captain M'Culloch, Murdoch—crossed the bridge carrying the address.[3] The drum of truce returned to Hamilton, who, learning that Monmouth would only treat with the Whigs if they first laid down their arms, cynically replied, 'and hang next.'[4] In turn Monmouth asked for Hamilton's ultimatum, which was 'no surrender.'

The fight at Bothwell Bridge, Sabbath, 22nd June 1679.

The English park of artillery was trained on the bridge and the foe, and when the gunners fired, the musketeers and the brass piece replied with such effect that the timid Royalists abandoned the guns. Incredible to tell, there was no brave Dingwall ready to leap the barricade and

---

260; Wodrow, iii. 105; Kirkton, 465; Wilson, *A True and Impartial Relation*, etc., 39 (Glas., 1797).

[1] Burnet, *Hist.*, ii. 240.

[2] *Faithful Contendings*, 195.

[3] Blackadder, 225; Wodrow, iii. 106; *Ure's Narr.*, 466; Terry, *John Graham*, 74 note (citing Smith, *Account*, 119).

[4] *Ure's Narr.*, 477.

spike the guns. They were manned again, and soon made a way for the pioneers. Hackston, Ure of Shargarton, and the men of Kippen and Galloway clung to their posts for two hours or more, calling out for supports and ammunition, and being supplied with raisins, till they were forced to retire, with 'sore hearts,' fighting as they retreated. Hamilton practically forbade a rally. Had he not been both incompetent and in the sulks, he would have reinforced the heroes, who, with a keg of powder, might have blown the bridge into the river. On a rising ground on the edge of the moorland, where the great public gibbet of the Nether Ward of Lanark stood, was posted the sullen horde of conventiclers, without a leader, helpless as a drove of sheep, while the army of Monmouth, headed by himself, marched across the bridge in unbroken order. Linlithgow was colonel of the foot-guards; Montrose was colonel of the horse-guards. On the first discharge of the cannon, the horses on both wings of the insurgents' main body grew restive and stampeded, and before ten men were killed in the action the foot was disordered as well.[1]

It was now ten o'clock. Monmouth loosed the cavalry under Oglethorpe, Maine, and Claverhouse, and their thirsty swords completed the *débâcle*. Hamilton was the first to flee; Claverhouse was among the last to quit the scene of slaughter, where 'and his troop, mad for blood, did the most cruel execution.'[2] 'When we fled there was not ten men killed of us all,' Ure recorded.[3] Some fugitives who sought safety in the parish church of Hamilton were butchered in the sacred edifice.[4] Before the dragoons could be got to desist from slaying, some 'were knocked down by gentlemen of the life-guard.'[5] From Hackston's account of the fight we learn that after he and the other defenders of the bridge had been compelled to fall back upon the main body of Covenanters, and, as the Royalist troops filed across the bridge, there was a movement of the Covenanters, which was checked by the cry that their officers had deserted them. This was followed by a stampede

Stampede of Covenanters.

---

[1] *Ure's Narr.*, 483.
[2] Blackadder, *Memoirs*, 227.
[3] M'Crie, *Veitch*, 483.
[4] Dr. John Wilson, *Dunning, its Parochial History*, 26 (citing *Secession Magazine*).
[5] Blackadder, *Memoirs*, 228. Major Rollo captured a flag now preserved in Duncrub House.

of two troops of horse under Thomas Weir of Greenrig, formerly a trooper under Dalyell at Pentland, apparently done wilfully to disorder the ranks of the infantry, as well in the main body as in the reserve, on the left wing.[1]

Credit was given to Peden, far away on the Borders, for seeing a vision which made him refuse to preach, and constrained him to send the people to pray, as he saw the soldiers 'hagging and hashing them down and their blood is running like water.'[2] It is not to the credit of the hair-splitting heroes that all escaped with sound skins, excepting Balfour, who was shot in the thigh, and Cargill, who was left for dead on the field and miraculously escaped death. Hamilton and his craven staff slept in Loudoun Castle that night. Kid was caught in the first bog. Many of the fugitives found refuge in the woods round Hamilton. Some innocent persons were killed in the chase.[3] Monmouth personally did not follow far, and mercifully restrained the pursuers. On riding to Crookedstone, near West Quarter, the dragoons met and slew William Gordon of Earlston, a notorious old conventicler, returned exile, and outlaw, on his way to join his son, Alexander, who married Janet, only sister of Robert Hamilton.[4] Alexander fled into a house in Hamilton, and disguising himself as a woman rocking a cradle, escaped the searchers.[5] Hundreds were slain in town and field.[6] Few Royalists fell.

Surrender of a craven mob. A large body of the Covenanters, seemingly converted to a policy of non-resistance, gave up their arms without striking a blow. According to

---

[1] Hackston to MacWard, *Faithful Contendings*, 199, 200 note.
[2] *Six Saints*, i. 53.
[3] Wodrow, iii. 108, 109.
[4] His tombstone in Glassford churchyard bears that he was sixty-five years of age: *Martyr Graves*, 253.
[5] Crookshanks, *Hist.*, ii. 15.
[6] The numbers of slain and prisoners are variously stated: Wodrow gives 800 killed and 1100 taken; Creichton, 700 or 800, and 1500; Burnet between 200 and 300, and 1200; Blackadder, 400 and 1200; Law, 800 and 300. The figment found in Creichton's *Memoirs* (p. 34), that the Whigs had the gibbet and a cart-load of ropes ready to hang the Royalists wholesale, is a piece of Swift's delightful sarcasm. Yet the 'carts' disturbed the sober judgment of Hill Burton (*Hist.*, vii. 232), and the 'new ropes' similarly affected Mr. Andrew Lang (*Hist.*, iii. 353). The head of the moor, at the junction of Muir Street with Bothwell Road and Almada Street, is still known as 'Gallowhill 'and 'Gallowsknowe,' and as the locality where the Nether Ward gibbet always stood.

Blackadder, 'after the retreat was sounded they fell on taking prisoners, which were above twelve hundred on the place, who were all gathered together about a gallows that stood there, and kept in that place all night (and made to lye flat on their faces on the ground) with a strong guard.'[1] He also mentions the barbarities with which they were treated. They were stripped. The wounded were prevented getting water, until some humane officers interfered. Monmouth with the feelings of a true cavalier spurned the counsel, attributed to Claverhouse and Major White, that all the prisoners should be put to death; and this humanity was afterwards animadverted upon both in Scotland and at Court.[2] The Duke of York thought what the King afterwards said, 'that if he had been there they should not have had the trouble of prisoners.' To this Monmouth made a true soldier's reply: 'He could not kill men in cold blood; that was only for butchers.'[3]

Sharp was fully avenged; the 'Blynk' was over. The tide of battle was turned before ten; at noon the Council in Edinburgh were discussing the news of victory, brought by a galloper, Lundin, thirty-five miles as the crow flies.[4] A courier left immediately for London, but found himself outstripped by a flying packet of Robert Mein, postmaster, whom the Council soon cited for his impertinence.[5] While Monmouth remained in Clydesdale a few days establishing the peace, and Claverhouse and other captains of horse rode through Ayrshire avenging Drumclog, the prisoners, a sorry gang roped in pairs, stripped in terms of the Act, some wearing 'mutches,' were on their way to Edinburgh, which they reached on Tuesday. Outside the city they were met by a jeering rabble, who insultingly inquired, 'Where's your God? Where's your God?' Their sufferings were intense. Any expression of sympathy rendered a friend liable to similar treatment under many statutes. All were martyrs of the Blackadder type, and by compulsion now, and Blackadder advised them to remain staunch in their bonds. Monmouth humanely mitigated their lot. For want of room in the common prisons

Twelve hundred prisoners enter Edinburgh.

[1] Blackadder, *Memoirs*, 228-9.
[2] Wodrow, iii. 112.
[3] Burnet, ii. 240.
[4] Council's Letter to Lauderdale, 22nd June: *Add. MSS.*, 23244, fol. 16; Wodrow, iii. 113 note.
[5] *Reg. Sec. Conc., Dec.*, 260, 11th July 1679.

the majority were penned in a vacant walled-in part of what is now Greyfriars' Churchyard—the 'inner' or 'new yard.' The wounded were confined in 'Heriot's Wark.' Fresh captures increased their number to fifteen hundred.[1] The enclosure, open to the elements, was shelterless till in winter some sheds were erected. Few of the prisoners were suitably clothed. Their ale was watered, their coarse bread stinted, and drinking-water ill supplied. They were robbed of their goods, and defrauded of the charities friends brought to them. They stood by day, and lay on the earth at night in inclement seasons. The militia sentinels were hostile, being made responsible for the captives; and, on an escape, they had 'to cast dice and answer body for body for the fugitive.' Some escaped. Surgeons were employed to succour and keep alive the wounded, because the Council had resolved to send the most influential rebels to the gallows and other four hundred to the plantations.

The fate of the fighters who escaped from the battle was nearly as unbearable. John Stevenson of Cumreggan, Girvan, author of *A Rare Soul-Strengthening and Comforting Cordial*, joyfully recorded how he lay for four months in winter in a haystack: 'One night when lying in the fields I was all covered with snow in the morning. Many nights have I lain with pleasure in the Churchyard of Old Dailly, and made a grave my pillow.'[2]

The Scots Privy Council did not delay issuing a 'Proclamation against rebels, 26th June 1679,' declaring sixty-five of the leading insurgents to be traitors, making it a crime to reset or have the slightest dealings with them, and ordering the pursuit and apprehension of them, persons failing in their duty being held to be accessory to treason. Some on this list were dead, others were abroad, and the rest were the rebel officers, small landholders, the slayers of Sharp, and thirteen ministers.[3] A very bad case of oppression at this time was that of John Hamilton, Lord Bargany, suspected of Covenanting, seditious leanings, study of denounced treatises, friendship with Welsh, expressing joy at the Primate's death, and other offences. Never brought to trial, he was thrown into Blackness Castle prison, a victim of the perjury

---

[1] Wodrow, iii. 124, 125; *Six Saints*, ii. 131; *Passages in the Lives of Helen Alexander*, etc., 4.

[2] *Select Biog.*, ii. 471.

[3] Wodrow, iii. 114 note.

and subornation of enemies who hankered after his estate. Bargany demanded a public examination, but was frustrated by the Duke of York. The little satisfaction which he had on his release on bail in June 1680 was increased at the Revolution, when he raised a regiment for the public service and King William.[1]

The King thanked the Council for their loyal communication, and while approving of their proposal to transport three or four hundred prisoners, authorised the use of torture to elicit the causes of the rising, and ordered the release of such as would bind themselves never to revolt again.[2] The clemency shown by Monmouth was to be more strikingly illustrated by a proclamation of 'His Majesties gracious pardon and indemnity,' which was to be interpreted with 'all possible latitude and favour.'[3] This document, bearing the stamp of the genius of Mackenzie and the callousness of Lauderdale, was a trap to cause the unwary to make new admissions. It concluded by giving increased powers to 'all *our other judicatures* to pursue and punish with all the severity that law can allow,' threateners of clergy, murmurers against courts and Crown officials, and disseminators of criticisms. The sting in the word *murmur* stabbed the nation to its heart. Every trooper's blade was now whetted, and every militia-man's fusil was charged anew.

The King's gratitude.

Monmouth, after having been fêted in Edinburgh, left Scotland on 6th July, the very day Claverhouse rode in Galloway close on the track of Balfour and a small party of his Fife comrades, who, after secreting their wounded leader in a den at Waterhead, escaped into Douglasdale.[4] Welsh and Balfour were in a tight corner, the more that the friendly lairds of Carrick warned Welsh of keeping company any longer with the notorious 'Burgle.' After many a chase and hairbreadth escape in the shires of Stirling, Perth, and Fife, the men of Magus Moor separated, and Balfour escaped to Holland in October. Claverhouse's westland route was marked by evidences of rapine, torture, and shedding of blood. He was in his element, for the sacrificial track of blood was now sanctified by law.[5] The soldiery may not have been

Chase of the men of Magus Moor.

[1] Wodrow, iii. 235, 236 note.
[2] *Ibid.*, iii. 116 note.
[3] Aldis, *List*, 2168; Wodrow, iii. 118 note; *State Papers*, 412, fol. 265.
[4] *State Papers*, 412, fol. 259; Kirkton, 473.
[5] Wodrow, iii. 120-2; Kirkton, 475; *Martyr Graves*, 124. In Galston Churchyard is

The Act of
Indemnity.

so inhuman as the persecuted made them out to be, but every fresh
instruction was an incitement to ferocity. The operation of the Act of
Indemnity was immediate. Many prisoners took the oath to rise no
more in arms—an acknowledgment of rebellion—and were released.
Unfortunately they received no written discharge, and at home found
themselves to be suspects still chargeable under other statutes. Visitors
were permitted to enter the prison and try conciliation. Four ministers,
Kennedy, Creighton, Jamison, and Johnston, tried to induce them to
take what the irreconcilables called 'The Black Bond.'[1] Blackadder wrote
dissuading them from being ensnared.[2] The slowness of the Council in
bringing the ringleaders to doom was displeasing both to the King and
to Lauderdale; and a process was ordered without delay. To mark the
royal detestation of the Archbishop's murder, the King commanded
that nine prisoners—one for every assassin—should be convicted, and
hanged in chains on Magus Moor, for owning the slayers.[3] This order
led to the examination of the prisoners with these questions: 'Was the
late rising rebellion? Was the death of the Archbishop murder?' The
result was the furnishing of a list of the most obstinate or conscientious opponents of the Government. The growing horrors of prison
broke down the fidelity of some who sought liberty on the Crown's
terms. This created a disruption, when a coterie of Adullamites, under
Robert Garnock, a fiery blacksmith from Stirling, refused longer to
worship with the supplicants, on the ground that their petition was
a defection acknowledging the rising to be sinful. To quell war in the
jail the Council gave the brawny leader of the disruption an oratory to
himself in the Iron House, and made secret arrangements for deporting
petitioners and disruptionists without distinction.[4]

Two clerical
victims—Kid
and King.

The Council had two notable field-preachers ready for the altar—
John Kid, captured in a bog a few miles from Bothwell Bridge, with a
sword in his belt, and chaplain John King, seized on his way to Arran
by Captain Creichton. This herald of peace had two pistols in his belt.

---

a memorial of 'Andrew Richmond ... killed by Bloody Graham of Claverhouse,
June 1679.'

[1] *Wodrow MSS.*, xxxvi. 17.
[2] *Six Saints*, i. 53, 54.
[3] Letter, 26th July: Wodrow, iii. 127.
[4] Wodrow, iii. 130; *The Scots Worthies*, 466.

The tale-weaving Swift makes Creichton at Bothwell Bridge spy this 'braw muckle kerl with a white hat on him and a great bob of ribbons on the cock o't,' a phenomenal dress for a Puritan, who swore he left the field before the battle began![1] The Council expected important revelations from the two, and put Kid in the horrid boots to assist his memory. They had no plot to reveal. At their trial, on 28th July, their story, told in evidence and petition, was that they were conventicle preachers, but so far from being disloyal rebels, they advised the armed brethren to return 'to loyalty and Christianitie.' Kid further pleaded that Monmouth had given him quarter, and that he carried a short sword merely to disguise himself from being known as a preacher. King went further, and protested that he did not know that the Balfour party were the assassins, was actually a prisoner of the insurgents, had deserted at Bothwell Bridge, and rested on the Proclamation. Their confession of being at conventicles and carrying arms was damnatory enough. Their request to lead proof was ignored. The altar was ready, and the judges were in a hurry. The assize sent them to the gibbet at the Cross and their heads and right hands to the Netherbow Port to preach there with Guthrie's.[2]

That day—14th August—on which Kid and King were executed was a gala day in Edinburgh. With every pomp, roaring guns, ringing bells, and other rejoicings at the Cross, the authorities in the morning proclaimed the Royal Indemnity, 'commanding all our judges to interpret this our remission and indemnity with all latitude and favour.' In the afternoon the interpretation took the form of the two preachers dangling with all possible longitude at the same gay Cross. Their testimonies are the delightful expressions of valiant manliness, Christian faith, and Covenanting honour.[3] Both victims repudiated the charge of disloyalty. King specially adjured the bystanders to pray for their persecutors and to obey the civil authorities 'in the Lord.' That sense of humour so seldom associated with men libelled as sour fanatics did not forsake the fearless pair as they walked hand in hand to the gallows.

Joy at their execution, 14th August 1679.

---

[1] *Memoirs*, 36; Wodrow, iii. 133; *The Scots Worthies*, 409-11.

[2] Wodrow, iii. 132-6; Petitions of Kid and King: *Add. MSS.*, 23244, fol. 45; *ibid.*, 47; *Laud. Pap.*, iii. 176, 177*b*; *Hist. Not.*, i. 228, 229; *Book of Adjournal*, 16th-28th July 1679.

[3] Cf. later editions of *Naphtali* for these.

Kid smilingly remarking to the 'braw muckle kerl' at his side: 'I have often heard and read of a *kid* sacrifice.' Each left a wife and one child to mourn his loss.

The smell of blood must have lingered long in the nostrils of the four judges who wrote assuring King Charles that the execution of Mitchell was a duty, and 'we are conscious of our own innocencie.'[1] Six bishops, also enthroned beside the bloody altar, wrote to Lauderdale, whom they styled 'the general patron of the Church under God and our Royal Magistie,' praying him to continue his care of the afflicted Church. So the political policy of rope and axe was the prelatic one as well.[2]

Trial of refusers of the bond.

On the 12th November, the trial of thirty-three prisoners in Greyfriars, who refused to take the bond, began. The judges treated them with a show of lenity, taking each one aside to persuade him to take the bond never to rise in arms.[3] Five or six held out. 'The justices by their sentence ordained the five to be hanged up in chains in Magus Moor [on the 18th November] to expiate and appease the Archbishop's ghost who was there murdered, for tho' they were none of the immediate actors of it, yet they were accessory for they would not call it murder.'[4] Their testimonies, recorded in *Naphtali*, afford indications of having been amended by some pious notary who frequented jails. The sufferers express themselves more naturally when 'settled upon the ladder.'

Thomas Brown.

Thomas Brown, an Edinburgh shoemaker, said it was his first and last visit to Fife; that he rose in defence of the Gospel, and 'if this day every hair of his head were a man, and every drop of his blood were a life, he would cordially and heartily lay them down for Christ and this cause for which he is now sentenced.'

Andrew Sword.

Andrew Sword, a weaver from Borgue, sweetly sang, 'O taste and see that God is good. ... None perish that Him trust' (Psalm xxxiv.). He had never seen a bishop in his life, and would not, he said, 'exchange my lot for a thousand worlds.'

[1] 17th July: *Add. MSS.*, 23244, fol. 33.
[2] *Ibid.*, fol. 41.
[3] Fountainhall, *Decisions*, i. 62.
[3] *Ibid.*, i. 63. A warrant, dated 26th July 1679, to hang the slayers of Sharp in chains on Magus Moor was sent down to Scotland: another, dated 15th August, ordered the execution of obstinate rebels: *Warrant Book*, 195, 241-2.

James Wood, from Newmilns, had never seen a bishop, and confessed James Wood.
that his infirm arm and halberd had been at Bothwell, and that it was
his desire to the Lord 'that He would let me die a martyr.'

John Waddell, from New Monkland, was a staunch Covenanter, John Waddell.
willing to become 'a hinging witness' against the evils of the day, and
'not a whit discouraged to see my three brethren hinging before mine
eyes.'

The most touching scene of all was when John Clide, 'a poor John Clide executed, 18th November 1679.
ploughman lad,' as he styled himself, left his weeping mother and
her family at the gallows-foot, in order to 'welcome Lord Jesus'—the
lad being certain that his dutiful execution of Watson, the butcher in
Glasgow, was no barrier to his sanctification and his elevation to angel-
hood. Men of that courageous and also devout type were a force in the
land not to be despised and not to be readily exterminated. On the 18th
November they were hanged, first on a great gibbet on Magus Moor,
then wrapped in chains, and left to rot there. A stone marks the place
of their execution.[1]

On the black morning of the 15th November, two hundred and fifty- Shipwreck of transported insurgents.
seven prisoners, in a gang, were hurried from Greyfriars down to the
Pier of Leith for transportation to a ship lying in the roads, chartered
by William Paterson, merchant in the city, to take them to the plantations.[2] For twelve days more the ship rocked at her anchor, with her
suffocating hold stowed full of the unfortunates: through other twelve
days of tempest she plunged seeking the Pentland Firth, with the
unsanitary horrors experienced in Greyfriars multiplying all the time.
On 10th December she tried an anchorage off Deerness. At night the
popish captain battened down the hatches, as the rising storm drove the
vessel ashore to be broken in halves; the captain and crew scrambled
ashore and barbarously battered those prisoners who had cut their way
out, back over the rocks into the raging sea, so that probably not more
than fifty were dashed to land alive. On bleak Scarvating the drowned
were buried.[3]

The Privy Council had its hands full of lists of processes against overt Legal processes and oppressions.
rebels and absentees from the musters, who were punishable by death;

[1] *Martyr Graves*, 182, 187, 193; Fleming, *Handbook of St. Andrews* (1902), 119-21.
[2] *Hist. Not.*, i. 246.
[3] Wodrow, iii. 131; *Hind Let Loose*, 193; Shields, *Hist. of Scot. Presby.*, 33.

but their extra labours were compensated for by the hope of forfeitures. The Council was instructed to announce the establishment of circuit courts at seven centres in the troubled districts, to have Porteous (portable) Rolls of rebels prepared, and to hang up in every county in Scotland lifelike effigies of the Magus Moor assassins, so that they might be recognised, 10,000 merks and an indemnity being offered for Balfour and Hackston.[1]

The clerks of court, with the aid of local informers, sheriffs, justices, incumbents, proceeded to make up the Porteous Roll of all rebels and to take an inventory of their goods. Innocent persons were often registered and falsely sworn against, a regular trade of bribing and perjury being initiated before the suspects were summoned to court to exculpate themselves. The result of this was that Court favourites and loyal gentry were enriched with the heritable property, and the officers and soldiery carried off the movables of the downtrodden Presbyterians, many of whom lay immured in jails for long periods. A striking instance is that of Alexander Hamilton of Kinkell, who having broken with Episcopacy, found himself outlawed, intercommuned, his house turned into a garrison and displenished, his family thrown out, his money filtered away, and himself cast into prison twice.[2] This was the kind of 'oppressions which make wise men mad,' as the grievances were described in the Supplication to Monmouth in 1679. The favoured of the Crown who received the forfeitures were designated 'donators,' and on their instructions the insolent soldiery became shameless spoliators where they pleased. Even the Duke of Hamilton had to complain of the violence of the agents of the Earl of Glencairn, who was donator of the movables in the parish of East Monkland, and he got the military recalled.[3]

Favourites enriched with forfeitures.

Monmouth's efforts for clemency.

The country groaned under these exactions, despite the kindly efforts of the Duke of Buccleuch and Monmouth to obtain a recall of obnoxious legislation. He succeeded in securing 'A Proclamation suspending laws against Conventicles, June 29, 1679,' which authorised the remission of fines and other disabilities to the confessedly peaceable, and the licensed enrolment of loyal field-preachers, one for each parish,

---

[1] Proclamation, 14th August 1679; Wodrow, iii. 140 note.
[2] Wodrow, iii. 145.
[3] *Ibid.*, iii. 146.

with authority to dispense the Sacraments, provided they were not in the last rebellion and gave a bond for good behaviour. The Act applied to the Lowlands south of Tay, and excepted the environs of Edinburgh, St. Andrews, Glasgow, and Stirling. The cautionary bond of six thousand merks, according to Brown, was a new form of disestablishment.[1]

This third Indulgence was of short duration. Early in July, the prison doors were opened for ministers and conventiclers willing to accept the terms of the Indulgence. Some refused, but were liberated on finding caution to appear when called upon. The emancipated ministry met in August and tried to rehabilitate their decadent system of Presbytery, and soon fifteen quasi-parish ministers took up their new role of Crown licensees in various districts.

The third Indulgence.

Monmouth returned to Court to report what he had spoken, that 'a gallanter gentry and more loving people I never saw.' After the return of the Duke of York from Holland the influence of Monmouth soon waned, and he was ostracised to Flanders on 24th September. Lieutenant-General Thomas Dalyell now commanded the forces in Scotland, and was accountable to the King alone. His commission is dated 1st November 1679. His men began the chase of the Balfour gang and all refusers of the bond. Sequestrators were appointed to manage the properties seized, and the country swarmed with these vampires.

Two other proclamations were published on 13th November—the first prohibiting parishioners who had not taken the bond going to hear the licensed preachers, and the second giving the peasantry who had not taken the bond still another chance to do so.[2]

The quarrel between some Scots nobles of the Moderate party and Lauderdale was still proceeding, and came to a height when, on the King's birthday 1679, the English House of Commons presented an address to the King, accusing Lauderdale of giving dangerous counsels, and demanding his removal from office. The grievances of the Scots politicians were expressed in a memorandum entitled 'Some particulars of fact relating to the administration of affairs in Scotland under the Duke of Lauderdale,' etc. It was a serious indictment of the executive, and an epitome of the iniquities of the period. In its printed form it

Indictment of Lauderdale and his policy.

[1] *Banders Disbanded*, 50; Wodrow, iii. 149, note, 152.
[2] Wodrow, iii. 157 note.

created a sensation. The Council defended itself. The King himself called the case, the complainants having advocates to explain it. Sir George Mackenzie answered for the Crown. The King, 13th July, decided that the faithful Lauderdale was 'most unjustly used,' that the judicatories were calumniated by libellers, who were henceforth to be silenced as poisoners of the people, and that the Council merited his thanks for hanging 'Mitchell, that enemy of society.'[1] Hamilton and the Moderate party, who had complained of Lauderdale's 'excessive greatness,' were outgeneralled again. The pronouncement boded ill for Presbyterians generally. It boded worse when the Duke of Albany and York crossed the Borders, and on 4th December, by the King's command, took his seat in the Privy Council in Edinburgh without taking the oath. This was an intolerable exercise of supremacy in view of the existing crisis in England over the exclusion of James from the throne, the debates on which he was glad to escape from. Rothes, Argyll, Moray, Hatton, and Mackenzie had the manliness to protest against York's intrusion.[2] Tweeddale imagined that York would checkmate Lauderdale in the north; and York, to serve his own purposes, pleaded for toleration.

Forfeiture of heritors in the south-west.

The Lord Advocate now made a dead set against the disaffected lairds in Dumfries and Galloway, and early in July had thirty-five of them forfeited and dispossessed. Among these were Patrick M'Dowall of Freuch, whose estate went to Claverhouse; John Bell of Whiteside, afterwards shot by Lag; John Gibson of Auchenchain; John Gibson, younger of Ingliston, afterwards shot by the dragoons of Douglas and Livingston, his property going to Douglas of Stenhouse; William Fergusson of Caitloch; Alexander Gordon of Earlston; James Gordon of Craichlaw—the lands of the last three were given to Colonel Edmond Maine, Major Theophilus Ogilthorpe, and Captain Henry Cornwall; and Robert MacLellan of Barmagechan, afterwards banished to New Jersey.[3] The absentees from the muster of the militia included many Covenanters who had not appeared in the rising. Lauderdale found the machinery of the Justiciary Court too slow to undertake the

[1] Wodrow, iii. 158-71.

[2] Letter, 6th November 1679: *Add. MSS.*, 23245, fol. 21; Letter that York was not to take oath, 30th November 1679: *Warrant Book*, 328.

[3] *Act. Parl. Scot.*, viii. 315, 323; *Martyr Graves*, 411, 444, 225-7; *Warrant Book*, 464, 21st April 1680, for Freuch.

multitudinous business of prosecuting these men, and he transferred its functions to the Privy Council, whose procedure was simplicity itself,—namely, summons of accused, his non-compearance, forfeiture, appearance of a donator or sequestrator on the land, and finally the disappearance of the victim. The year closed with the signing of a warrant that certain persons should be 'gratified with shares of the forfeitures,' and among the number was Claverhouse.[1]

[1] 27 December 1679: *Warrant Book*, 393.

BATTLE OF BOTHWELL BRIDGE

CHAPTER TWENTY-SEVEN

THE REMNANT

MORE than is warranted by evidence, writers prejudiced against the Covenanters have laid too much stress upon the alleged retaliatory actions and methods of parties of men who are supposed to have been illustrators of the Covenanting spirit. Harassed though the Lowland Covenanters were, their faith in most cases transmuted their sufferings into an ineffable delight and glory for Jesus' sake, rather than into yearnings for revenge. That ecstasy incited them to wish, pray for, and expect misery and martyrdom in Christ's interest, and the just judgment of God on evil-doers. Patient suffering, rather than wrestling, was the cult of all save the extremest hillmen, of the type of James Skene, who declared it to be his duty to kill soldiers, 'when they perse- cuted God's people.'[1] On the other hand, the gallant Hackston confessed 'we were forced to fight' at Ayrsmoss.[2] 'Rebellion to kings is unbeseeming Christ's ministers,' wrote Rutherford to Lady Kenmure.[3] The outlawed MacWard, in his *Poor Man's Cup of Cold Water*, counselled the persecuted, as 'Jewells surrounded by the cutting irons' ... to 'seal from your own experience the sweetness of suffering for Christ,' since 'there is an inherent glory in suffering for Christ.' His friend, John Brown, discussed this subject in ten chapters in his work entitled *Banders Disbanded*, and while stating

Suffering, the cult of the persecuted.

---

[1] *Cloud* (Thomson edit.), 83.

[2] *Ibid.*, 50.

[3] Letter, 4.

that there was 'a proper season of suffering,' declared that it required a divine revelation to tell when a tyrant was discharged.[1]

King, in his dying testimony, asserted: 'I have been loyal, and do recommend it to all to be obedient to higher powers in the Lord.'[2] Retaliation was no duty, according to Fraser of Brea, who declared: 'We are to be submissive to the commands of superiors, not to imitate their practice.'[3] Nisbet of Hardhill confessed: 'I have longed these sixteen years to seal the precious cause and interest of precious Christ with my blood.'[4] This was not the malignant spirit of a bigoted slayer of his fellows who held different views. Something more than irrational obstinacy, something nobler than frantic superstition, underlay the life and morale of martyrs who kissed the rope that hanged them. 'If we had a hundred lives, we would willingly quit them all for the truth of Christ,' was the gallant farewell of the Enterkin Pass rescuers when upon the scaffold.

Duke of York in Holyrood, 1680. While Holyrood House rang with the revelry of the Court of the Duke and Duchess of York, as it had never done since the lute of Rizzio roused the galliards of Queen Mary, the Lowland moors resounded with the plaintive psalms of the Remnant, who prayed and fasted on account of their latest misfortune, in the arrival of the popish heir to the Crown.[5] Claverhouse accompanied the Duke from England, and had the Prince's ear. Long after the slave-ship had recrossed the seas bringing him back from the plantations, John Mathieson of Closeburn wrote: 'None knows the marrow and sweetness that is to be had in suffering and contending for Christ, but them that has felt.'[6] In the same strain wrote John Wilson: 'The pleasantest time that ever I had was when I was joined with that suffering remnant, while hunted as partridges upon the mountains in following the persecuted gospel.'[7] These threnodies formed a marked contrast to the jubilations of the hierarchy and the 'orthodox clergy.'

---

[1] Brown, *Banders Disbanded*, 92, 93.

[2] *Naphtali*, 364.

[3] *Select Biog.*, ii. 368.

[4] *Ibid.*, 408.

[5] *Domestic Ann.*, ii. 403-5; *Arch. Scot.*, i. 499; Burnet, ii. 248, 254; *Six Saints*, i. 226; Terry, *John Graham*, 89.

[6] *Coll. of Dying Testimonies*, 187.

[7] *Ibid.*, 167.

Richard Cameron returned from exile in October 1679. In Holland he was preceded by the ill-natured gossip that he was a mere babbler against the Indulgence; but his intercourse with the ministers there proved that he was 'a man of a savory gospel spirit,' and, as MacWard announced, fit to 'go home and lift the fallen standard,' all alone, too, if the home ministry would not help him. Before leaving Holland, Cameron was ordained by Brown, MacWard, Hog, and Koelman, in the Scots Church, Rotterdam.[1] Before lifting his hand off Cameron's head, MacWard, as if reading off a mental vision, pathetically exclaimed: 'Here is the head of a faithful minister and servant of Jesus Christ, who shall lose the same for his Master's interest, and shall be set up in the publick view of the world before sun and moon.'[2]

Return of Richard Cameron, October 1679.

On his return, Cameron found the whole country seething with repressed discontent, met countless persons to whom Bothwell was a bitter memory, and discovered only a remnant who preferred suffering, to compliance with a hated rule, and death, to encouragement of those evils certain to follow the advent of a popish prince. Cameron, in the romantic enthusiasm of his youth, was mentally pledged to an idealised conception of Protestantism, shorn of every defection and innovation—Indulgence, Cess, Black Bond—a pietistic system demanding all for Christ. In this respect he was like Zinzendorf, but without his extravagances and fanatical errors, and like him, too, was almost apotheosised by his ardent followers. He acted as a spell on the wanderers as he vowed he would rather die than 'outlive the glory of God departing entirely from these lands.' A chivalrous nature, a reliant faith, a patriotic fervour, a seer-like instinct, a tender sympathy for the persecuted, a loyalty to righteousness, combined in him to rouse a crusading rather than an apostolic spirit, which, increasing his earnestness to recklessness, prejudiced the judgment of Cameron, so that he could only view the peace-loving and submissive tacticians of the 'Poundtext,' or Moderate, ministry as nullifidians. His pietistic ecstasy prevented him comprehending how conscientious men could accept instalments of liberty and political doles as the foretaste of heavenly treasures. Young and inexperienced, he expected victories won

The spirit of Cameron.

---

[1] *Six Saints*, ii. 163, note 18; Steven, *Scot. Church in Rotterdam*, 73 note.

[2] *Six Saints*, 225, 235-6.

by dash, and never contemplated triumphs to be won by waiting and diplomacy. Men, like Cameron, Cargill, Renwick, Peden, and their lay bodyguard—*milites Christi*[1]—never rose above the Petrine expectation of divine thunderclaps, irresistible legions, lethal swords of the Spirit, and visible judgments following upon their determinations, when they imagined that they were thinking and acting for Christ. This extreme and indefensible view clearly arose out of their belief in their personal union with Christ, with whom each had made an individual covenant. It resulted unfortunately in their proneness to bring the retributive sword to the ears of the servants of the high-priest before the gentle voice of persuasion had accomplished its diviner mission, as inculcated in the discipline of the Church.

Cargill, Douglas, and other field-preachers.

Cargill and Douglas associated themselves with Cameron. He spent some time explaining his views of the crisis, and was discouraged when ministers such as Hog, Dickson, and Welsh, and others too timid to climb his heights, did not enter the inflammatory council of the Cameronian field-preachers.[2] A constitutional party also thought that a preacher ordained abroad to a vagabond ministry was not upholding the law and practice of the church of Melville. Amid these disquietudes the homeless leader sought comfort in obedience to the primal law by entering into wedlock. Cameron soon obtained a staunch coadjutor in the fighting Borderer, Hall of Haughhead, who, after his escape from Bothwell Bridge to Holland, found the society of the dogmatical hair-splitters there too quiet for his active spirit, and returned home.

Movements of the extremists.

In April 1680, Cameron and Cargill convened a 'fellowship meeting of the Lord's people' at Darmead, Cambusnethan, where in fasting and humiliation they mourned over the sin of the land which had joyfully received York, 'a sworn vassal of Antichrist.' In May, on the Moor of Auchingilloch, Lesmahagow, they kept another fast-day for the purpose of stirring up the faithful to prayer and lamentation.[3] There was contagiousness in the spirit of Cameron throwing out its fiery floods of indignation along with the perfervid stream of evangelical truth which he could appositely pour from his eloquent tongue, to the refreshment and joy of his hearers. His style was simple and emphatic. His influence

[1] [Latin: soldiers of Christ.]
[2] *Six Saints*, i. 333, 334; ii. 225; 163 note 18.
[3] *Ibid.*, i. 225; ii. 163.

was indelible. James Robertson, who suffered in the Grassmarket in December 1682, testified to the rousing power of his preaching.[1] John Brown of Priesthill quoted Cameron as if he was the infallible mouthpiece of God.[2]

Henry Hall arrived in West Queensferry, where his friend Cargill was lurking. As they strolled between Bo'ness and Queensferry, James Hamilton, minister of Bo'ness, and John Park, minister of Carriden, a worthless creature, afterwards deposed for immorality, recognised Cargill, and made haste to inform Middleton, captain of Blackness Castle, who, with his men, was soon on the track of the outlaws. Middleton introduced himself in a friendly way to the travellers in a hostelry in Queensferry on 3rd June 1680. He even pledged a glass of wine to his guests before he announced that they were prisoners in the King's name. Hall instantly drew steel, and in grips worsted Middleton. Cargill, wounded, escaped on Middleton's horse. Had not George the waiter interfered and felled Hall with a carbine, he too would have escaped. At the gate he fell into the hands of some friendly women, who carried him off insensible to hide him. General Dalyell at Binns, near by, heard of the scuffle, and soon ferreted out the dying Covenanter. Next day he was dead before the escort with him arrived at Canongate Tolbooth. In Hall's pocket, or in Cargill's valise, a prolix paper was found, which on examination turned out to be an elaborate new Covenant in eight sections, entitled *The Queensferry Paper*.[3] The draft was understood to be 'drawn by Mr. Donald Cargill.'[4] It was also called 'The Fanatics' New Covenant,' 'The Camerons' Covenant.'[5] It was still without signatures. It was intended to bind acceptors—

Capture and death of Henry Hall, 3rd June 1680.

(1) To covenant with and swear acknowledgment of the Trinity and to own the Old and New Testaments to be the rule of faith.

The Queensferry Paper, June 1680.

(2) To advance God's kingdom, free the Church from Prelacy and Erastianism, and remove those who had forfeited authority.

---

[1] *A Cloud of Witnesses*, 252 (Thomson's edit.).
[2] *Muirkirk Sess. Rec.*, i. 67.
[3] *Laing MSS.*, 639, No. 20; Wodrow, iii. 206, 207 note; *Six Saints*, ii. 13, 206, 225; *Hind Let Loose*, 133-6; Mackenzie, *Vindication*, 41. Park afterwards applied for protection and was recommended for a reward: *Reg. Sec. Conc., Dec.*, 8th June 1680.
[4] *A Joint Testimony*, 1684; *Six Saints*, ii. 225.
[5] Row, *Blair*, 568.

(3) To uphold the Presbyterian Church of Scotland, with her standards, polity, and worship, as an independent government.

(4) To overthrow the kingdom of darkness, i.e. Popery, Prelacy, Erastianism.

(5) To discard the royal family and set up a new republic.

(6) To decline hearing the indulged clergy.

(7) To refuse the ministerial function unless duly called and ordained.

(8) To defend their worship and liberties, to view assailants as declarers of war, to destroy those assaulting, and not to injure any 'but those that have injured us.'

This was simply a patriotic effort, natural enough in the circumstances; yet it is impossible to harmonise the old Scottish principle *Nemo me impune lacessit*[1] with the teaching of the Redeemer. It was a bold revolutionary call to the people to overthrow the King, Government, and their Malignant supporters, and to afford posterity 'a debate they may begin where we may end.' This manifesto, according to others, was intended for transmission by Hall to Holland, to form a basis of discussion for the exiles in setting up a new Presbyterian platform in Scotland.

The Sanquhar Declaration, 22 June 1680. The principles polemically stated in the *Queensferry Paper* were, in less than three weeks afterwards, embodied in practical form in the Sanquhar Declaration. It is not improbable that the tenets of the protocol were known to the framers of the Declaration, even although Cargill, with his uncured wounds, lurking in the wilds of the Lammermuirs, had not yet seen Cameron's following, nor narrated how he escaped. The war Cargill waited to discuss, impulsive Cameron declared. As the insults of the Royalists were offered to their opponents on Restoration Day, so the Cameronians chose the anniversary of Bothwell Bridge to publish their Declaration of Independence. Claverhouse was in London on an amorous errand, and the sheriff, Queensberry, was absent from Crichton Peel that fateful day, when Cameron, at the head of twenty horsemen, rode down the crooked High Street of Sanquhar—two rows of mean thatched houses—'with drawn swords and pistols in their hands, and after a solemn procession through the town, did draw up at

[1] [Latin: no one attacks me and gets away with it.]

the Cross and published and affixed upon the Cross and other public places thereof a most treasonable and unparalleled paper disowning us to be King.' So ran the Royal Proclamation.[1] It recognised the religious significance of this 'solemn procession,' as if it had been the elevation of the Host in some awe-inspiring cathedral.[2]

On that day, turning down to a long winter of sorrow, one can imagine the Israelitish paean, 'Now Israel may say,' favoured of John Durie and other iron-shod veterans, rising to the green ring of Nithsdale hills. Here in the glittering-eyed preacher—Cameron—was the Judaic Samson in the cornfields of the Philistines loosing the 'fire of hell'; by his side his brother Michael ready to read what 'one Campbell' was ready to fix on the Cross; also Thomas Douglas, the conventicler, with brand in hand ready to bless where his namesakes had often cursed; Daniel MacMichael with his long ribbed claymore, of no use when they shot him fever-stricken at Dalveen; John Vallance, who that day fell in blood with the Camerons at Ayrsmoss and died in the Tolbooth of Edinburgh, and others. The declaration of war was short and soon read. 'The Declaration and Testimony of the True Presbyterian, Anti-Prelatick, and Anti-Erastian, Persecuted-Party in Scotland' announced that they, as representing a loyal, Protestant, Presbyterian, Covenanted nation, 'disown Charles Stuart, who hath been reigning, or rather (we may say) tyrannising on the Throne of Scotland ...; under the Standard of Christ, Captain of Salvation, we declare War against such a Tyrant and Usurper, and all the men of his practices, as enemies to our Lord Jesus Christ, His Cause and Covenants ... and against all such as ... have acknowledged him. ...'

Scene at Sanquhar Cross.

By the Declaration they homologated the Rutherglen Testimony and repudiated that of Hamilton, disowned the Duke of York, 'a profest Papist, repugnant to our Principles and Vows ...' and 'protest against his succeeding to the Crown.' The concluding paragraph concentrated its virulence—'rewarding those that are against us as they have done to us.' On this war to the knife a blessing was asked. Another psalm of triumph sought the skies, and thereafter the grim-looking zealots

Tenor of Declaration at Sanquhar.

---

[1] *Wodrow MSS.*, xliii. (Rob., iii. 3. 16.), 128, 129. King ordered 'Cargill's New Covenant' to be printed.

[2] Aldis, *List*, 2214; *Reg. Sec. Conc.*, Declaring Cameron and others traitors, 30th June; Wodrow, iii. 212 note, 214, 215 note; Mackenzie, *Vindication*, 54; *Hist. Not.*, i. 274.

rode off to the wastes round Little Cairntable. With no little prescience Cameron asserted that theirs was 'a standard that shall overthrow the throne of Britain.' If there was no justification for this unprecedented act of a wandering preacher and a band of insignificant guerillas, there was none eight years afterwards, when, using the identical arguments of the Cameronians, the Lords Spiritual and Temporal and the Commons of England, with the Estates of Scotland, ousted King James, and established William and Mary on the British throne.[1] Not a revolution, but a 'return to ancient principles' was aimed at.[2] They had but one King now. Consequently the sequel to the Declaration was a mutual bond of Covenant signed on the borders of Galloway, binding its subscribers to adhere to one another, to acknowledge the Rutherglen Testimony, to disclaim the Hamilton Declaration, and to disown the King, York, and other magistrates.[3]

On 30th June, a proclamation was issued offering 5000 merks for Cameron, dead or alive, 3000 for Cargill, Douglas, and Michael Cameron, 1000 for their comrades dead or alive; and ordering the citation of the parishioners of sixteen parishes round Sanquhar for the discovery of the traitors and their friends.

An important trial was begun on 15th July which ended in condemning to the gallows the captain of the ship *Fortune of London*, John Niving, who in his cups had spoken of York as a Papist and a plotter against the life of King Charles, who, after all, on the intervention of the politic prince reprieved the garrulous sailor.[4] The news of the Sanquhar declaration of war, of Cameron's fiery sermons lamenting the national sins and sorrows, and predicting the fall of the Stuarts, with other growing libels, reached the ears of the indulged ministers of Mauchline and Ochiltree, Veitch and Millar, and terrified them. Millar, on learning of the location of the Cameron party, informed Sir John Cochrane of Ochiltree, who showed zeal in suppressing them, and got Dalyell to send a strong force under Captain Bruce of Earlshall in search of the rebels.[5]

Doom of Captain Niving.

[1] *A Collection of Papers relating to the Convention*, 1689.
[2] Acton, *Lectures on Modern History*, 231.
[3] Wodrow, iii. 218, 228; *Cloud*, 500.
[4] *Decisions*, i. 108; *Hist. Not.*, i. 268.
[5] *Six Saints*, i. 228; Row, *Blair*, 569; *Aberdeen Letters*, 127.

On Wednesday night, 21st July, Cameron with his following of forty foot and twenty horse rested on a moor near Meadowhead in Sorn parish, and next day marched up the River Ayr, making for the safer wilds round Muirkirk.[1] They had reached Ayrsmoss, a bleak, undulating stretch of moorland, lying in the three parishes of Muirkirk, Sorn, and Auchinleck, when they descried the military. Hackston selected a stand where he posted the men—

'By the black and sweltering swamp,
A small green mound uplifts its brow,
'Twas their altar, 'twas their battle-ground,
'Tis their martyr-spot and death-bed now.'[2]

Cameron asked if all were willing to fight. All responded 'Ay'—John Gemmill with emphasis. Cameron prayed, three times exclaiming, 'Lord, spare the green and take the ripe.' The holy *crabhadh* (*pietas*, religious zeal) of the Celt, the untamable spirit of his race, moved him to vow like bold Gilnockie—

'It will never be said we were hanged like dogs,
We will fight it out most manfully.'

'Michael, come let us fight it out to the last,' he cheerily said, 'for this is the day I have longed for, and the death I have prayed for, to die fighting against our Lord's avowed enemies; and this is the day we will get the crown.' His comrades he thus inspired: 'All of you that shall fall this day, I see Heaven's gates cast wide open to receive them.'[3] Bruce had a mixed command of sabres and carbines—Airlie's troop and a troop of Strachan's dragoons—not in full muster.[4] The opposing commanders must have known each other, county gentlemen and magistrates, in the courts at Cupar.[5]

Hackston posted eight horse on the right wing under Robert Dick, and fifteen on the left, probably under Fowler. Bruce advanced a party

[1] At Meadowhead, the stone trough wherein Cameron performed his ablutions that morning is reverently preserved.
[2] Dodds, *The Battle of Airsmoss*.
[3] *Six Saints*, i. 232; *Cloud*, 46.
[4] Hackston reckoned them to be 112 well armed; Creichton minimised them to 30 horse and 50 dragoons, and boasted *magna pars fui:* [I play the major role].
[5] Minutes of local Courts of Justice.

of twenty horse to try the mettle of his undisciplined opponents, who foiled the movement by a destructive fusillade, emptying some saddles. The firing, however, threw the countrymen's timid horse into confusion. Hackston gallantly carved a way through the enemy till his horse stuck in the bog. While opposed on foot, in single combat, to an old acquaintance, David Ramsay, servant to Major Ramsay, three troopers from behind meanly cut him down, so that he was forced to take quarter. James Gray, younger of Chryston, fought gallantly before he was laid low. The Cameronians were defeated. The fighters on foot easily escaped over the swamp. The two Camerons and other seven of their comrades lay dead on the moor. Four prisoners were taken. The loss to the Royalists was trivial, according to Creichton, who took the credit of the victory. But Patrick Walker records that soldiers after the fight acknowledged the loss of twenty-eight men, and this is borne out by the testimony of Hackston: 'The field was theirs, but they paid for it; we compelled them to give us this testimony that we were resolute and brave.'[1]

The heads and hands of Richard Cameron and Captain John were lopped off and borne away in a sack as evidence for procuring the reward which Bruce and Ramsay applied for.[2] The slain were buried where they fell, and a stone with an inscription, tampered with re-cutting, marks the spot.[3] Hackston, with head slashed and gory, and four other prisoners, John Pollok, William Manuel, John Malcolm, and Archibald Alison, stripped, barefoot, bleeding, tied on barebacked horses, were taken the first night to Douglas Tolbooth, now the Sun Inn. Next day they reached Lanark, where General Dalyell and Lord Ross examined them. Hackston records that Dalyell 'did threaten to roast me,' for his unsatisfactory answers. After this, with his wounds merely stanched, not dressed, this 'bonny fighter' was again bound like a beast and cast into the Tolbooth for the night.[4] The escort with the sack entered the house of John Arcle in Lanark and asked his wife if she would buy

---

[1] *Six Saints*, i. 236.

[2] *Reg. Sec. Conc., Dec.*, 1680, pp. 418, 419; *Six Saints*, ii. 115. In the petition Bruce referred to 'the heavens having blessed them with success.' Bruce got £500 stg.; Cochrane, 10,000 merks.

[3] *Martyr Graves*, 154.

[4] Hackston's 'Account' in *Cloud*, 47; Wodrow, iii. 219 note.

calves' heads. They rolled out the martyrs' heads and played football with them. The sight of the bloody heads made her faint, when they exclaimed: 'Take up the old, damn'd Whig-bitch.'[1]

On 24th July, the Privy Council met and arranged a dramatic entry of the felons into the Capital on Sabbath afternoon. The magistrates were commanded to meet them at the Watergate, to have Hackston mounted on a white barebacked horse, his face to its tail, his feet roped beneath its belly, his hands tied behind his back; to make the disguised executioner drive his halberd into the mouth of Richard Cameron, and to elevate it with Cameron's hands and bear these bloody objects standard-wise before Hackston, while the executioner proclaimed: 'There's the heads and hands of traitors, rebels'; to tie to the white horse's tail the three prisoners bound to a bar of iron, and to march the wretches up Canongate and High Street to the Tolbooth. The strain was too much for Manuel, who died of his wounds as he entered the prison. One of the first visitors to Hackston was his old friend and employer, Rothes, who acted most inhumanly, stormed, called the prisoner a liar, twitted him with his former graceless life, and threatened him with boots and torture before his dispatch, even before his wounds were dressed by a surgeon.[2] The next act of brutality was the conveyance of the head and hands of Cameron into the cell where his old father still lay for unrepented conventicling. The devout Covenanter tenderly lifted them and said: 'I know them, I know them; they are my son's, my dear son's: it is the Lord, good is the will of the Lord, who cannot wrong me nor mine, but has made goodness and mercy to follow us all our days.' The hangman thereafter fixed them on the Netherbow Port, where many might see them and say with Robert Murray: 'There's the head and hands that lived praying and preaching, and died praying and fighting.' While these incidents were occurring in Edinburgh, Cargill in Shotts was preaching from the text, 'Know ye not that there is a prince and a great man fallen this day in Israel.'[3]

On 29th July, the Privy Council arranged the minutest details of Hackston's doom and dispatch. Next day they gave him public trial for Bothwell Bridge, Queensferry Paper, Sanquhar Declaration,

Entry of Hackston into Edinburgh.

---

[1] *Six Saints*, ii. 114.
[2] *Six Saints*, i. 231-4; ii. 114, 115, 221.
[3] *Six Saints*, i. 234.

Ayrsmoss, murder of Sharp, and the usual items of indictments since 1679. Bruce and three other witnesses were heard. Hackston declined the authority of the Court and laid his blood on their heads. The pre-arranged verdict was carried out that afternoon, 30th July, to the letter of the judicial menu for barbarous tastes: drawn on a hurdle to a high scaffold between St. Giles and the Cross; right hand severed; interval; left hand cut off; body drawn up by a pulley to top of gallows, dropped alive; heart cut out, thrown down, spitted and apostrophised—'Here is the heart of a traitor'; body disembowelled; entrails thrown into a fire on the scaffold; decapitation; quartering; filling and addressing the sacks which conveyed the gory relics to St. Andrews, Cupar, Glasgow, Leith, and Burntisland. Gilbert Burnet, who had his account from eye-witnesses, states that the victim, although dying of his wounds, 'suffered with a constancy that amazed all people.' He seemed all the while as if he were in a lofty rapturous trance, and insensible of what was done to him. 'When his hands were cut off he asked like one unconcerned, if his feet were to be cut off likewise.' He had liberty to pray on the scaffold, but was prevented speaking to the people. He had, however, utilised his time in prison writing a personal confession, and an account of Ayrsmoss, which are worthy of the hero who was among the last to leave the Bridge at Bothwell. These extant communications of a Christian gentleman who had found grace, and was able to say: 'I doubt not but God will save a Remnant. … If the free grace of God be glorified in me, ought not all to praise Him?'[1] exhibit the finest charac-teristics of the Covenanters, who believed in the ultimate triumph of their cause.

On the 13th August two of Hackston's associates, Archibald Alison from Evandale and John Malcolm from Dalry, in Galloway, were sent to the Grassmarket gibbet, and both left gallant testimonies, preserved in *A Cloud of Witnesses*. Malcolm was one of the few banished prisoners dashed ashore from the slaveship on bleak Scarvating.[2] Pollok endured the boots unflinchingly, and was sentenced to banishment.[3] The fallen

---

[1] Wodrow, iii. 222, 223; *Decisions*, i. 112; *Hist. Not.*, i. 270; Original Verdict and Warrant in Nat. Mus. of Antiq., Edin., OA. 26; *Cloud.*, 58, 68; *Laing MSS.*, Div. ii. 27; Burnet, ii. 306; *Martyr Graves*, 178.

[2] Alison's sword is preserved in Crofthead, Muirkirk.

[3] *Six Saints*, i. 233.

at Ayrsmoss and by these executions were the first aftermath of Bothwell Bridge fight. Papers said to have been of an incriminating character, and proving Dutch influences, were found upon Cameron's body, and were made use of in judicial examinations afterwards.[1] Probably the bond of mutual defence already referred to may have given rise to this statement.[2] After Ayrsmoss, troopers, informers, cess-collectors, excisemen, donators, and sequestrators roved about incessantly making life in the Lowlands unendurable. The recoil fell on the Government, which turned upon its own rapacious and brutal minions, several of whom were whipped, fined, and imprisoned for misdemeanours too gross to be palliated by such an executive.[3] The worthless character of the spies—'flies' they were called—may be gathered from Creichton's description of James Gibb, a praying Irishman, whom he employed to betray the conventiclers: 'If I had raked hell I could not find his match in mimicking the Covenanters.'[4]

The Sanquhar Declaration was virtually the pronouncement of a political party convinced of the righteousness of the new policy they intended to carry out, and which they notified to all concerned. The remnant, speaking from their own attenuated standpoint, might also call themselves the Church speaking in this crisis. Cargill was the surviving representative of the ministry uncontaminated by defections, the last veteran able to bear aloft the banner of the Covenanted Church. He considered his solitariness no barrier to him in exercising his spiritual functions as the *ultimus judex*[5] in the land, willing to act constitutionally in excommunicating the enemies of Christ's Church. Consequently, in September, the sad, silent, isolated old field-preacher convened a great conventicle in the Torwood, Stirlingshire, as if it were a General Assembly or Folk-mote.[6] He preached from the text (Ezekiel xxi. 25): 'And thou, profane wicked Prince of Israel, whose day is come'; also from 1 Cor. v. 13, Lam. iii. 32. Investing himself with the office of

---

[1] *Laud. Pap.*, iii, 202.

[2] *Cloud*, 500.

[3] Wodrow, iii. 249.

[4] *Memoirs*, 92.

[5] [Latin: final judge.]

[6] The spot was marked by a thorn-tree at the foot of the Old Toll Brae near the Glen.

a prophet and the dignity of a herald of the divine judgments, Cargill assured his hearers that he knew the mind of God, and had a clear call for doing on earth what was approved in heaven; and to show the seal upon his commission, he declared that those he excommunicated would live to confess in terror the truth of his malison, and would die no ordinary deaths.[1] After explaining the nature of and necessity for excommunication, Cargill solemnly said: 'I being a minister of Jesus Christ, and having authority and power from Him, do, in His name and by His spirit, cast out of the true Church and deliver up to Satan Charles Second, King,' etc., for reasons which were tabulated under seven heads—mocking God in 1650, perjury in renouncing the Covenants, disestablishment of Covenanted Protestantism, destroying the Lord's people, promoting Popery, pardoning murderers; 'lastly, to pass by all other things, his great and dreadful uncleanness of adultery and incest, his drunkenness, his dissembling with God and man, and performing his promises when his engagements were sinful,' etc. He proceeded to excommunicate the Duke of York, Monmouth, Rothes, Lauderdale, 'Bloody Mackenzie,' and General Dalyell—the last for 'his lewd and impious life, led in adultery and uncleanness from his youth with a contempt of marriage which is the ordinance of God.' Cargill's justification for this bold and extraordinary act was the demand of reason, which concluded that to appoint flagitious magistrates was 'to make a wolf the keeper of the flock.'[2] After cursing these authorities, Cargill went elsewhere to bless.

The Government, roused by the Torwood Excommunication, in vain searched for Cargill; but neither the torture of prisoners nor the offer of a reward of five thousand merks induced the faithful to betray the hiding-place of the fugitive.[3] The Council considered themselves more fortunate in securing the persons of James Skene, Archibald Stewart, and John Potter, ardent Cameronians and subscribers of Cameron's bond, whom they sent up to the Lords for dispatch to the gallows on

At Torwood Cargill excommunicates the King and his advisers, September 1680.

Execution of Skene, Stewart, and Porter, 1680.

---

[1] The miserable deaths of the six excommunicated are matters of history: *Six Saints*, ii. 8, 9, 10, 204, 205.

[2] *Hind Let Loose*, 138, 139, 140; *Cloud*, App.; *Laud. Pap.*, iii. 209.

[3] Proclamation, 22nd November; Wodrow, iii. 231: 3000 merks were offered for Douglas.

1st December.[1] These victims were cross-questioned before York and the Council, and made a clean breast of their extreme principles. Skene, brother of the laird of Skene, was an acolyte from the north who had been carried away by the spell of Cargill's oratory, and boldly avowed the duty of killing Sharp, the rightness of shooting poisoned ball certain to kill, and other extravagances. While Skene lay in prison Cargill wrote to him an inspiring farewell, concluding with the fine Tennysonian conception and prayer, that God might send him a full gale to carry him 'sweetly and swiftly over the bar.'[2] His two fellow-sufferers, Archibald Stewart, a Bo'ness man, who had fought at Ayrsmoss, and Potter, a farmer from Uphall and a servant of Lord Cardross, were less extreme in their views.[3] All three left their curses upon the Crown officials, and also upon 'this bloody Popish Duke [York], who must be welcomed with a draught of our blood now.' York was in the habit of attending the meetings of Council, and viewing the tortures as 'some curious experiment,' thus originating the idea that he was 'a man that had no bowels nor humanity in him.'[4]

Utilising the confessions of these three sufferers, the Government announced the existence of a hellish plot of persons encouraged by treasonable pamphlets—*Naphtali, Jus Populi, The Apologetical Narration*, and others—to destroy the King and his subordinates, the Protestant Church and its ministry, and to inaugurate a new regime. The proclamation (22nd November 1680) plausibly explained the necessity for using severity to suppress those disorders, which the leading councillors blamed each other for causing.[5] To extirpate what the authorities designated 'atheistical giddiness' another proclamation was published in spring (8th April), demanding that heritors should provide magistrates with a list of their tenantry attending conventicles; and, what was more unlooked for, a fast-day was appointed for averting famine and God's wrath for sin, and for praying for a blessing upon the Parliament about to assemble. Processes of forfeiture went on inces-

Proclamation of 'atheistical giddiness.'

---

[1] *Book of Adjournal*, 29th November 1680; *Decisions*, i. 117.

[2] *Cloud*, 13 (Thomson's edit.); *Six Saints*, ii. 16, 181, 206, 211, 213; Wodrow, iii. 228, 230.

[3] *Six Saints*, i. 232, 316, 325; ii. 16, 165, 181, 206; *Cloud*, 100, 107, 348.

[4] Burnet, ii. 420.

[5] Wodrow, iii. 229; *Hist. MSS. Com. Rep.*, XI. vi. 164.

santly, many westland homes being ruined and heritable estates given over to 'donators.' Wodrow gives instances of these oppressions. On 8th October 1681, a decreet was published empowering the sheriffs to eject from their lands, and, if resisted, to pursue to the death as traitors, forty-five rebels in Lanarkshire, ten in Ayrshire, four in Dumfriesshire, and twenty-eight in Galloway—some already dead, others to become famous as sufferers—with the proviso, that the pursuers would never be questioned.

Torture of John Spreul.

The Council considered it a fortunate circumstance to have in custody John Spreul, apothecary, Glasgow, related to nonconformists, a friend of Welsh and Arnot, an associate of the exiles in Holland and of the insurgents at home, and supposed to be in their secrets. A double hammering in the boots brought out no revelation beyond an intense loathing of Jesuitical practices, which, being expressed in York's hearing, made the inquisitors more pitiless. The brilliant advocate Lockhart obtained for Spreul, brought to trial on 10th June, a verdict of 'not proven.' Notwithstanding this acquittal, Spreul was detained by the Council, fined £500, and sent to the Bass, where he was immured nearly six years.[1]

The Gibbites or Sweet Singers.

Of all the fantastic dissenters who ever troubled the land, none could compare for mad extravagances with the Gibbites, or 'Sweet Singers of Borrowstounness,' who appeared at this time.[2] These mad-caps proved by their curious religious practices and tenets how dire are the results of living in an age where everything tends to exasperate human nature and to unsettle tender nerves and weak intellects. Inexplicable comets and portents filled the northern sky; Cargill's curses were reiterated everywhere; the appropriate psalm of the dying martyr from Bo'ness, Archibald Stewart, and his malisons also, rang in excitable ears: 'Why rage the heathen?' 'O Lord, what wilt thou do with this generation?' 'Meikle John Gibb,' a sailor, and 'a great professor,' was moved. A recent historian would feign canonise him as 'another Saint of the Covenant.'[3] He neglects to mention, however, that Gibb, in his manifesto, specially

---

[1] Wodrow, iii. 252-62; *Reg. Sec. Conc.*, Dec., 663, 14th July 1681; 12th May 1687.

[2] Gibb's Paper in Mackenzie, *Vindication*, 57; Wodrow, iii. 350-3 note; Pat. Walker, Cargill (*Biog. Presby.*, ii. 15-23); *Six Saints*, cf. Index; *Hind Let Loose*, 140; *Hist. Not.*, i. 300; *Dom. Ann. Scot.*, ii. 414.

[3] Lang, *Hist. Scot.*, iii. 359.

renounced 'all the Covenants' as well as the Covenanters' declarations.[1] Some individuals wiser than the Gibbites now believed that the little that remained right was growing bad, and that God's wrath was imminent. Certain Psalms—74th, 79th, 80th, 83rd, 137th—so exactly described the lamentable state of affairs, that bands of Sweet Singers began to sing them plaintively through the streets. Grief was assuaged by cursings; joy was intensified by prayer; fasting increased both faith and sorrow. The blood of Stewart and Potter, flaunted on a handkerchief, was a sight which added to excitement an element of ferocity. Gigantic Gibb came on the scene, declaring that he and the Holy Ghost would right the wrong by the destruction of all human inventions. The deluded ones hailed this deliverer, or king, as 'King Solomon.' Three men— Walter Ker, David Jamison, and John Young—joined Gibb's council; and twenty-six hysterical women, some carrying sucklings—among others, Elspeth Granger, Margaret and Ann Stewart—fell at Gibb's feet. Their idea was to leave the haunts of wickedness and to retire to the wastes, in order to become perfect by casting off every characteristic of unredeemed human nature. The unsaved world ate, drank, enjoyed comforts, used human contrivances for making themselves comfortable. These reformers, pretending to be guided by the Spirit, renounced everything save life itself—that life sustained, too, on bread and water—and the pure text of the Bible. Consequently they became teetotallers, haters of tobacco, ascetics, despisers of home comforts, destroyers of Bibles having human addenda,—such as metrical psalms, chapters, verses, pictures, prefaces, printers' marks—burners of the Covenants and relative documents, repudiators of the King and his officials, of educated clergy, of the calendar and its terminology, and of every imaginable thing, even to the fashions contrived by men. Gibb would refashion humanity into a temple perfect and worthy of himself—the Second Solomon. As a century later 'Divine White' and 'Moon-clothed Mother Buchan' led their vagabond flock into the wilds of Galloway in search of a Mount of Ascension, so Solomon the Sailor steered his following in their regenerative development through some of the wettest 'flow mosses.' On the Pentland Hills they sat and, like sirens, sang over Edinburgh, expecting to see the 'haar' enveloping

Tenets of the Gibbites.

---

[1] *Vindication*, 59, 61.

that frigid scene of martyrdoms turned into a conflagration like to that
which destroyed Sodom. Cargill, eager to guide and redeem his old
acquaintances, invited them to emerge from a morass, called the 'Deer-
slunk' (slough), so as to hear his interpretation of the will of the Holy
Spirit and his rendering of the 37th Psalm—'For evildoers fret thou
not Thyself unquietly.' Gibb disdained compliance with an imperfect,
conventicling apostate. Not to be baffled, Cargill went and interviewed
this herald of holiness and his associate, David Jamie, who was 'a stickit
minister.'[1] He found them armed like buccaneers, and, with all the
fidelity of Moslem eunuchs, guarding their holy zenana at Darngavel
from the irate husbands and friends of the votaries. Gibb was hospitable. The two spiritual warriors arrived at an understanding. A Sweet
Singer made one bed for the pietists. In the night watches Cargill,
however, had a vision of a cut throat, and rising, slipped away from the
slumbering buccaneer into the muggy slunk in order to pray. By break
of day Cargill had concluded, 'This man, John Gib, is an incarnate

devil.'[2] A troop of dragoons seized the sect at the Woolhill Craigs and
brought them into the Canongate Tolbooth.[3] Cargill wrote to them
there, warning them 'that the devil was sowing tares among your thin
wheat.' So it turned out. Their place of confinement was small, and men
and women were herded in one apartment. Gibb was subject to diabo-
lepsy. According to the superstitious views of the time his paroxysms
of madness were referable to the visible visits of the black dog, Satan,
who made Gibb roar and blaspheme while his fellow-prisoners prayed.
In May 1681, five Cargillite women threw offensive articles upon the
carriage of the Duke of York as he passed by their prison, and had
rigorous treatment meted out to them. But this episode did not prevent
him taking an interest in these mad folk, whose liberation he arranged
for in August 1681, on condition that they renounced disloyal principles
and gave bail.[4] Returning to their extravagant practices, Bible-burning
among the rest, Gibb, Jamie, and two women had to be immured a
second time. Again the roaring and 'gollering' (shouting) began. The
huge diabolist, however, had his match in a lithe young Christian lad

---

[1] 'A good scholar lost and a minister spilt': *Six Saints*, ii. 22.
[2] Cargill's Letter: Wodrow, iii. 353 note.
[3] 21st February 1681: *Dom. Ann.*, ii. 414.
[4] *Reg. Sec. Conc., Dec.*, 617, 674, 5th May 1681, 2nd August 1681.

of eighteen, George Jackson, who was there qualifying for an early martyrdom. He sat on Gibb, thrust a napkin in his mouth, battered his head into a dead silence, not even a growl. So unendurable was the vulgarity, profanity, and beastliness of this antinomian crowd that Helen Alexander, a pious Covenanter in the same cell, declared that she preferred the gibbet to another Sabbath in their vile company.[1] Yet Mr. Andrew Lang has the assurance to assert, 'On the whole, Gibb only went a little further than the other saints.'[2] The Council ultimately sent Gibb, Jamie, and two women to America, where Gibb's exhibitions of diablery brought him fame among the Red Indians. Jamie became a respectable clerk in New York, and associated himself with some sect which built a church there. Renwick was falsely blamed for Gibbism. The Societies, at Cainitable in October 1686, denounced the sect. No other heed was paid to these silly obscurantists.

On 5th April 1681, Major Johnston seized in Edinburgh the long-concealed field-preacher, Blackadder, 'commonly called Guess-again.' Johnston brought him to General Dalyell, whom the prisoner asked leave to address. The grim general rudely replied: 'You, sir, have spoken too much; I would hang you with my own hands over that out-shot.'[3] Next day Rothes, Bishop Paterson, Dalyell, and Mackenzie interrogated him. To the bishop he made no response; to the others he disclaimed sedition and king-killing principles. His conventicling could not be denied. Without further process he was sent off to the Bass, on 7th April. In his cage there, bad air, foul water, and want of exercise induced dysentery and rheumatism, which completed the wreck of the once powerful frame of the stalwart Covenanter, now an old man of seventy, whose petition for release was only answered on 3rd December 1685. It was too late. About that time the prisoner had, as his son Robert so consolingly wrote to his mother, 'breathed up his soul as in a fiery chariot, in the flames of that holy zeal, wherewith he burned for the honour and house of his God … a glorious and triumphant martyr for the name of Jesus.'[4]

Blackadder seized and sent to the Bass, 1681.

---

[1] *Six Saints*, ii. 207; Alexander, *Passages*, 8.

[2] *Hist.*, iii. 360.

[3] *Memoirs*, 248.

[4] *Ibid.*, 279; this letter is a beautiful composition, free from every trace of recrimination. He lies buried in North Berwick churchyard: *Martyr Graves*, 491.

Gabriel
Semple cap-
tured.

Blackadder's friend, Gabriel Semple of Kirkpatrick-Durham, who had long escaped the clutches of the persecutors, was apprehended in July 1681, and cruelly taken from Oldhamstocks to Canongate Tolbooth. He was suffering from ague. The attempt to make this old veteran of Rullion Green incriminate himself failed, and he took advantage of his release on account of sickness to seek a home in England, where he had long quietly ministered since his eviction, and where he continued residing until Charles II. died.[1]

Fraser of Brea again experienced trouble and a second term of imprisonment for preaching while out of the Bass on parole. He was falsely accused of conventicling, so that a large fine might be exigible. Argyll's escape from prison two days before Fraser's compearance made the Council bitter. Fraser, so far from being an extremist, so explained his position, and actually 'prayed the Lord to bless his Majesty with all his blessings, both spiritual and temporal,' that all but the bishops in the Council wished to exonerate him. Although suffering from a severe

Fraser in
Blackness
Castle.

attack of ague, Fraser was sent to Blackness Castle till he paid a fine of five thousand merks. From that melancholy promontory, with its dark, damp, filthy cell, filled with smoke for seven wintry weeks, he was glad to escape and go into exile in England, as arranged, unknown to him, by his brother-in-law. There his preaching and his principles soon brought him into Newgate Jail for other six months, and his persecution did not cease till the Revolution.[2]

Examination
of Isobel
Alison and
Marion
Harvey.

Cargillism was still the bane of the Government. The restless tongues of women reiterated the Torwood excommunications. Isobel Alison, a young unmarried woman in Perth, and Marion Harvey, from Bo'ness, a servant-maid twenty years of age, were readers of the Bible, staunch Presbyterians, disciples of Cargill and Cameron, and ready to utter and defend their principles. They were apprehended and taken to Edinburgh. They underwent a lengthy examination by the Privy Council, eager to have the unwary prisoners trapped into admissions before being sent to trial. Dalyell threatened Marion with the boots. They acknowledged sufficient to put the halters round their necks. Isobel knew Hackston, and 'never saw ought in him but a godly pious youth.' They owned

[1] Wodrow, iii. 268; he died in August 1706: Scott, *Fasti*, ii. 481, 590.
[2] *Mem. Select Biog.*, ii. 350-63.

following the great conventiclers and maintaining the Sanquhar and Queensferry Declarations. Neither would express commiseration for the fate of perjured Sharp. The inquisitors asked Isobel if she were mad; and they sent a surgeon to let her blood if he thought it necessary. They received the usual indictment—conventicling, harbouring the Magus Moor assassins, rebellion at Bothwell Bridge, declining the King's authority, treason, etc. Lord Advocate Mackenzie's wrangle in open court with these 'poor lasses' was a most miserable exhibition, and displayed the depth of degradation to which an educated Stoic can sink when he barters his conscience and honour for patronage, position, and pelf.[1] The doom—to be hanged—was a foregone conclusion. 'They say I would murder,' exclaimed Marion. 'I could never take the life of a chicken, but my heart shrinked.' Marion was bold and loquacious, and did not hesitate to call the prosecutors liars and the jurymen 'bloody butchers.' Both during the trial and long afterwards Mackenzie asserted, that it was not for religion but for treason that these women were tried. And the kind of treason he magnified into 'most heinous crimes which no sex should defend.' Marion as stoutly denied this to Mackenzie's face.[2] Archibald Riddell, the indulged minister of Kippen, was sent to their cell to persuade them to renounce their convictions, and for his pains he had their special dying testimony left against him. Bishop Paterson, with a malevolence quite in keeping with his unprincipled character, taunted Marion that, as she had previously refused the ministration of the curates, 'now you will be forced to hear one.' When the curate began to pray, Marion asked Isobel to join with her in singing the 23rd Psalm so that they might drown his voice. The date of their execution was the 26th January. On the scaffold Isobel sang the 84th Psalm and read the sixteenth chapter of St. Mark; Marion chose the 74th Psalm and the third chapter of Malachi for her devotions. Both of them in laying aside the sacred Word exclaimed: 'Farewell, sweet Bible. … Farewell, sweet Scriptures.' Thus, with the serenity of angels, these 'two honest, worthy lasses,' as Peden called them, exchanged the cross for the crown.[3] The execution, in April 1681, of a young woman who

(margin note) Lord Advocate Mackenzie's wrangle.

(margin note) Execution of Alison and Harvey, 26th January 1681.

---

[1] For Interrogations, Testimonies, etc., cf. *Cloud*, 116-46.

[2] *Vindication*, 20.

[3] Wodrow, iii. 275-7; *Cloud*, 116-46; *Six Saints*, i. 56, 338; ii. 132 note; Fountainhall, *Observes*, 26, 27; *Book of Adjournal*, 21st January 1681.

had murdered her child to escape the discipline of the Church had aroused the displeasure and sympathy of the Duke of York, and it was currently reported that at this period these and other victims of the law were offered their liberty by him if they would even say as much as 'God save the King.' This statement Patrick Walker, on the authority of witnesses, flatly denied.[1]

Borrowstounness, or Bo'ness, a seaport town on the Forth, into which trading-vessels from Holland brought these offensive publications denounced by the Government, was the centre of a disaffected district where Cargill long lurked, and his definite principles, with their corrupt offshoot in Gibbism, were upheld.[2] Early in March, the judges had at the bar representatives of revolt from the troubled area—John Murray and William Gougar, or Gogar, from Bo'ness, and Robert Sangster and Christopher Millar from Stirlingshire.[3] They got the usual indictment; and the distorted confessions dragged out of them having been used to incriminate them, they were condemned to the gallows, where three of them suffered on 11th March. Fountainhall records that the Earl of Roscommon was sent to offer them pardon if they would say 'God save the King.' Murray escaped by owning the supremacy of the King in civil affairs. Two of the heads were placed on the West Port, to take the places of those of Stewart and Potter, which had been stolen.[4] All three before dying repudiated the slander of being classed with killers of their enemies, and declared they only took up arms in defence of the Gospel and of themselves.[5]

The Justiciary Court, on 11th July, tried three Cargillite visionaries, simple peasants in Fife—Adam Philip, Laurence Hay, weaver, and Andrew Pitilloh, labourer, Largo. They were wont to secretly meet for prayer and denunciation of the defections of the age, and, having subscribed a bond entitled 'A Testimony against the Evils of the Times,' also framed a manifesto called 'The Sixth Month,' which fell into the

Execution of Gougar, Millar, Sangster, 11th March 1681.

---

[1] *Six Saints*, i. 293; Fountainhall, *Decisions*, i. 137.

[2] The fine old houses still preserved in South Queensferry, the house where Cargill was almost seized, and others in 'The Covenanters' Close,' indicate the importance of this town.

[3] *Book of Adjournal*, 8th March.

[4] *Observes*, 30.

[5] Wodrow, iii. 277; Testimonies in *Cloud*, 146-59. In the *Observes*, 30, the date is given thus, 'ii Martii 1681,' *i.e.* second.

hands of the authorities. It abjured the King and all the clergy save Cargill. All of them were condemned to die in the Grassmarket on 13th July.[1] The heads of Hay and Pitilloh were dispatched to Cupar for exhibition with a hand of Hackston on the Tolbooth there.[2] The testimonies these men left exhibit an invulnerable faith in the Bible and its doctrines, as well as an incredible personal heroism. To them death was sweeter than life. On the scaffold Pitilloh exclaimed: 'O sweet indictment! O sweet sentence for my lovely Lord! O sweet scaffold for contending for the Cause, Covenant, and work of Reformation!' When virtuous ecstasies of this kind possessed the cottars and weavers of Scotland, it was impossible for a loose Government to influence them in any way.

Hay and Pitilloh, martyrs from Fife

Rulers and ruled were living on different planes of thought and action. While these invincible disciples of Cargill were on their blissful of way to death, that hapless preacher was on the road by Lanark and Glasgow to Edinburgh securely roped on a barebacked horse. When sleeping in Covington Mill during the night of the 12th July, Cargill and two companions, Walter Smith, a preacher, and James Boig, a student of theology, were apprehended by a party of Stuart's dragoons led by James Irving of Bonshaw.[3] When that blustering Borderer and smuggler of horses discovered his luck he exclaimed: 'O blessed Bonshaw! and blessed day that ever he was born, that has found such a prize this morning!' Brought before the Privy Council on the 15th and 19th July, Cargill gave few satisfactory replies to the interrogations put to him regarding his connection with Magus Moor, Ayrsmoss, Bothwell Bridge, and the 'Cargill Covenant,' yet quite enough to prove, what he afterwards gladly testified, 'not acknowledging the present authority, as it is established in the Supremacy and Declaratory Act.'[4]

Capture of Cargill by Bonshaw.

At this time the Lord Chancellor, Rothes, was in the article of death, hastened by those 'great liberties in all sorts of pleasure and debaucherie' which he took. He must have risen from his bed, jaundiced, swollen, moribund, to meet his old excommunicating enemy in the Council

Moribund Rothes confronts Cargill.

[1] Lauder in *Decisions*, i. 147, gives 14th; *Book of Adjournal* and *Hist. Not.*, 302, the 13th.

[2] Cf. tombstone in Cupar churchyard; *Martyr Graves*, 178.

[3] *Hist. MSS. Com. Rep.*, xv. viii. 240.

[4] Wodrow, iii. 279; *Hind*, 141; *Cloud*, 1-26; 26-34; 35, 36; 172-8; 179-90.

Chamber. Cargill had given Rothes over to the devil, and assuredly he had gone. What a great gulf yawned between them since that happy time when together they signed the still extant Solemn League and Covenant in St. Andrews! According to Patrick Walker, Rothes now threatened Cargill with torture and a violent death. The prisoner was ready with a malison: 'My Lord, forbear to threaten me,' he said, 'for die what death I will, your eyes will not see it.'[1] The trial came off on the 26th July. Cargill, Smith, Boig, William Thomson, a serving-man in Fife, and William Cuthill, a seaman from Bo'ness, were arraigned together.[2] A fanfare of trumpets gave distinction to the indictment and made Cargill declare, 'The sound of the last trumpet will be a joyful sound to me.' Thomson had been at Bothwell; Cuthill went about fully armed. The confession of all five, that they only declined the royal authority when it was exercised unconstitutionally was sufficient in itself to justify judges and jury, demanding implicit obedience, in recording a verdict of guilty. The brutal doom for traitors was theirs—to be hanged and hashed at the Market Cross next day, and three heads impaled on the Netherbow, with two on the West Bow. When the clerk, in reading the sentence, came to the stereotyped phrase,[3] 'having cast off the fear of God,' this falsehood was too much for Cargill, who cried out 'Halt!' Then pointing to Lord Advocate Mackenzie, he defiantly said: 'The man that has caused that paper to be drawn in that form, hath done it contrary to the light of his own conscience; for he knows that I have been a fearer of God from my infancy; but, I say, the man that took the Holy Bible in his hand and said, "That it would never be well with the land until that book was destroyed," ... is the man that has cast off all fear of God.' This was a thunderbolt which the legal Stoic little expected.

On the very night of the trial Rothes was in the throes of death and seeking comfort in the prayers of Presbyterian ministers, notably 'old Mr. John Carstairs,' who 'dealt very faithfully and freely' with the dying sinner. The bystanders were moved. The Duke of Hamilton observed:

Trial of Cargill and others, 26th July.

Death of Rothes.

---

[1] Walker, 'Cargill,' in *Six Saints*, ii. 53. For Cargill's curses on Irving and Nisbet, cf. *Six Saints*, ii. 51, 52; Crookshanks, *Hist.*, ii. 108. Fountainhall thought Cargill was 'shifty.'

[2] *Book of Adjournal; Decisions*, i. 148; *Hist. Not.*, i. 305.

[3] *Six Saints*, ii. 55.

'We banish these men from us, and yet when dying we call for them; this is melancholy work.'[1] York, when informed of the scene, said: 'That all Scotland were either Presbyterian through their life or at their death, profess what they would.'[2] Such a sentiment, so true to fact, ought to have given pause to James himself.

The condemned had used their leisure in preparing their elaborate testimonies.[3] They appeared on the scaffold at the Cross serene and elated. 'This [27th July] is the most joyful day that ever I saw in my pilgrimage on earth; my joy is now begun,' exclaimed Cargill. He sang part of the 118th Psalm:

> 'I shall not die, but live, and shall
> The works of God discover.'

While he spoke the drums rolled. As he mounted the ladder he said: 'The Lord knows I go up this ladder with less fear and perturbation of mind than ever I entered the pulpit to preach.' In the act of praying he was turned over.[4] The other four as bravely met their fate; the student Boig, in his last letter to his brother, thus apostrophising: 'Welcome cross; welcome gallows; welcome Christ.' Smith, born in St. Ninians parish in 1655, was an erudite and brilliant student of Utrecht, perambulated the country with Cargill preaching, and left behind him two papers entitled 'Twenty-two Steps of Defection,' and 'Rules and Directions anent private Christian Meetings for Prayer and Conference,' etc. These compositions afford proof of the literary tastes and theological attainments of this gifted minister. As he hung on the gibbet his head reclined on the dead breast of Cargill.[5]

Probably Walker's story that Cargill would have escaped the extreme penalty but for an ill-timed interjection from Argyll, should be taken with reserve. He records that the collapse and fearful exit of Rothes, together with Cargill's curses, so terrified the Council that one-half of them were willing to commute Cargill's penalty into perpetual

[margin note:] Cargill, Smith, Boig, Thomson, and Cuthill on the scaffold, 27th July 1681.

[margin note:] Argyll's ill-timed interjection.

---

[1] *Six Saints*, ii. 54, 210.

[2] Wodrow, iii. 356.

[3] *Cloud*, 1-38.

[4] *Hist. Not.*, i. 305. The Bible which he handed down from the scaffold is still preserved.

[5] Walker, 'Account of … Smith,' in *Six Saints*, ii. 56, 63-104.

banishment in the Bass, had not Argyll given the casting vote and said: 'Let him go to the gallows, and die like a traitor.'[1] This was certainly in keeping with Argyll's earlier acquiescence in the policy of torture and cut throats. Soon his own neck was in peril.

Estimate of Cargill's life and work.

Sir Robert Hamilton of Preston left an estimate of Cargill which may be accepted as the current contemporary appreciation of him by his fellow Covenanters. It makes him out to have been a pious, warm-hearted, charitable, and devoted pastor, whose word could be trusted, and whose influence was as much the result of a life of honour as of his fervent oratory, which he punctuated with sighs and deep groans.[2] What influence Cargill personally had in guiding the political destinies of the nation into the channel where the angry torrent of popular passions swept the Stuarts and Prelacy out is less easily appraised. It may be said, however, that Cargill willingly died in

'Freedom's battle once begun,
Bequeathed by bleeding sire to son;'

and so long as he lived he was unwearied in declaring those religious and political principles which ultimately triumphed. The harsher corollaries from his teaching were the accidents of a troubled and cruel time which the Covenanters neither originated nor desired to see continue.[3]

The Parliament of 1681.

The day after Cargill's execution, 28th July, the Scots Parliament rode with all the Honours, and James, Duke of Albany and York, presented his commission as the representative of his brother. The convention sat till 17th September and passed 193 Acts, mostly ratifications of property and warrants.[4] Ironically enough, the first statute passed on 13th August, secured the Protestant religion and renewed the ban against Popery.[5] The second Act, passed the same day, asserted the right of succession to the Crown, declaring that the kings of Scotland derive their power from God alone, and succeed each other lineally, so that 'no difference in religion, nor no law, nor act Parliament made, or to be made, can alter or divert the right of succession and lineal descent of the Crown

[1] *Six Saints*, ii. 58.
[2] *A Relation, Cloud* (Thomson's edit.), 501.
[3] For Cargill's lectures and sermons, cf. Howie, *Collection of*, etc. (Glasgow, 1779).
[4] *Act. Parl. Scot.*, viii. 231-447.
[5] *Ibid.*, 239.

to the nearest and lawful heirs.' It specified as treason any endeavour by word or act to dispute or alter these facts.[1] This was a new blossom on the tree planted by King James. The time-honoured political dogmas of the Knox-Buchanan school on which the Covenants rested were taboo—were treason. To further ensure peace, an Act was passed (4) making heritors liable for the fines of the conventiclers, which were doubled, and empowering them to evict dissenters.[2]

On 31st August, the sixth Act, entitled 'Act anent Religion and the Test,' was passed.[3] This statute embodied the royal resolve to extinguish every vestige of dissent from legalised Protestantism—Papists, Separatists, and resetters of the intercommuned. Each parish minister was ordered to forward a signed list of withdrawers from public worship to his bishop, who, in turn, was to sign it and dispatch it to a magistrate (with a duplicate to be sent to the Council), the magistrates having orders to prosecute the suspects. The statute also ordered all individuals in places of office or trust, the King's lawful brothers and sons only excepted, to subscribe an oath before 1st January 1682, or be attainted. A subsequent Act (91) enlarged the scope of this Act, and brought in persons holding heritable offices of the King. Heritors were admitted, and Hamilton was among those who, holding no office, did not take the Test.[4] The tenor of the Test follows:—

The Act on the Test.

'I ... swear I ... sincerely profess the true Protestant Religion contained in the Confession of Faith recorded in the first Parliament of King James the Sixth [1567] ... shall adhere thereto ... educate my children therein ... never consent to any change thereto; renounce all such principles inconsistent with the said ... Religion and Confession ...; affirm ... the King's Majesty is the only supream Governour ... in all causes ecclesiastical as weill as civil ...; renounce ... all foreign jurisdictions ...; judge it unlawful ... to enter into covenants ... or to ... assemble ... in assemblies ... to treat ... in any matter of State ... without his Majestie's special command ... or to take up arms against the King ...; that there lyes no obligation on me from the National Covenant or the

The Test.

---

[1] *Act. Parl. Scot.*, viii., 239.
[2] 29th August: *ibid.*, 242.
[3] *Ibid.*, 242-4.
[4] *Hist. MSS. Coin. Rep.*; *Drumlanrig MSS.*, ii. 178.

Solemn League and Covenant or any other … to endeavour any change or alteration in the Government either in Church or State …; shall mantein … and … never decline his Majestie's Power and Jurisdiction …; swear that this is my oath … without any equivocation, mental reservation or any manner of evasion whatsoever.'[1]

When the bill was under discussion Lord President Dalrymple was credited with the intention of wrecking the measure by proposing the insertion of the clause explanatory of 'Protestant Religion,' namely, 'contained in the Confession,' etc (ratified by Parliament in 1567), because that standard embodied ultra-Presbyterian principles as to the Headship of the Church, and other points quite inconsistent with subsequent clauses in the Test. The bishops had never read the document.[2] Argyll argued that the exception in the Act should be confined to York himself. York rose and protested.[3] This roused Argyll, who, according to Bishop Paterson, 'had fired the kiln,' and he retorted: 'An exception would do more harm to Protestantism than many Acts would do good.' A majority passed the statute, the lairds of Saltoun and Grant entering their dissent. Of the Council, Argyll, Dalrymple, and Lord Clerk-Register Murray refused to take the Test. Dalrymple in vain sought an interview with the King to explain his position, and finally deemed it expedient to retire to Rotterdam, where he joined James Stewart and other exiled Presbyterians.[4] He would not resign his office, and was deposed, Gordon being made President in his stead.[5] York and the Council insisted on Argyll and Monmouth complying. Monmouth held that the Test was only binding in Scotland. Hamilton, Huntly, Hope of Hopetoun, Scougal of Aberdeen, Professor Charteris, and persons of lesser note, ignored the Test.[6]

Bishop Paterson, to allay the doubts of the clergy, prepared an explication of the Test which, when read aloud, became so wearisome to the Council that York remarked: 'The first chapter of John with a stone will

Discussions of the Test.

Paterson's explication of the Test.

---

[1] *Act. Parl. Scot.*, viii. 244; Wodrow, iii. 295 note.
[2] Burnet, ii. 314.
[3] He said, 'Stair had ruined all honest men by bringing in the Confession of Faith.'
[4] *Hist. MSS. Com. Rep..*, xv. viii. 175.
[5] Graham, *Annals … of Viscount … Stair*, i. 64 (Edin., 1875).
[6] *Observes*, 89: Charteris deprived.

chase away a dog.' It was approved.[1] The substance of the paper was that (1) the Test only bound subscribers to the Protestantism embodied in the Confession; (2) it authorised no encroachment on the Church's spiritual power; (3) it did not prejudice Episcopacy as then established.

On 6th September, Parliament ratified the royal charter disponing of the Barony of Freuch in Wigtownshire (formerly possessed by Patrick M'Dougall, a rebel, forfeited in February 1680), to Claverhouse, 'in consideration of the good and faithful services and sufferings of John Graham of Claverhouse and his predecessors for his Majestie.'[2]

The ministers of Aberdeen, in a paper under seven heads, stated their objections to the Test when examined in relation to the Confession. Bishop Scougal and the Synod drew up a careful explication of the Test as binding them to the uniform doctrine of the Reformed Churches; allowing the literal trimming of the Confession; reserving intrinsic spiritual power; permitting meetings for church discipline and for the conservation of Protestantism; and sanctioning alteration of government when not accomplished by arms or by sedition.[3] The Bishop of Dunkeld and his clergy also framed another pointless explanation. These ecclesiastical travails constrained the Council to issue an Act on 3rd November, drawn by Bishop Paterson, explaining the Test as simply acknowledging Protestantism free of Popery and fanaticism, spiritual independence of the Church, and Episcopacy. Many honest orthodox clergy thought this to be mere juggling with great principles, and preferred deprivation to compliance.[4] *The clergy and the Test.*

The re-allocation of heritable jurisdictions and appointments to places of trust were a fresh bait to the needy jobbers about Court. About this time a discreditable intrigue began for the crippling of Argyll in his already attenuated finances. He determined to refer his case to the King. York demanded and coerced Argyll into giving his subscription of the Test before the legal time had expired. Argyll obstinately held his ground, and before signing made this explanation: 'I take it as far as it is consistent with itself or with the Protestant Religion.' This *Argyll's caveat.*

---

[1] Wodrow, iii. 303; Burnet, ii. 317.

[2] Act 56, viii. 315.

[3] Wodrow, iii. 304, 308 note.

[4] Burnet (ii. 318, 319), says 80; Bishop Paterson acknowledged 30; Letters to Sancroft, 54.

caveat excited suspicion. York was playing fast and loose with Argyll. His advisers suggested treason. Mackenzie was sure of its existence. Accordingly next day, 4th November, York and the Council demanded a subscription without any reservation, and also with the reservation, both of which Argyll declined to give. Thereupon he was deprived of his seat in Council and of his Commissionership of the Treasury. A few days later, this harsh procedure was followed by an order for Argyll to enter the Castle of Edinburgh, by a warrant to Mackenzie to prosecute him for treason, and by a letter to the King explaining their diligent rascality.[1]

Trial of Argyll, 12th December 1681.

Argyll duly received his indictment and summons to a trial to be held on 12th December. The leading advocates at the bar gave an opinion that Argyll's act did not imply treason, leasing making, depraving the laws, or perjury. The trial proceeded before Queensberry and four judges. Argyll made a manly speech asserting his loyalty. His counsel, Lockhart and Dalrymple, alternately had interesting forensic duels with Mackenzie regarding the relevancy of the libel, and there being a division of opinion on the bench about it, Queensberry slyly sent out for Lord Nairn, then an invalid, to support the view for relevancy. The case was sent to proof. A jury of fifteen was sworn. Among the number were hereditary enemies of the Campbells—Montrose, Airlie, Claverhouse—and political opponents of the Argylls. Further defence was futile. They refused to plead. Montrose brought in the verdict of guilty of the crimes libelled except perjury.[2] Such mean injustice made the Earl of Halifax pertinently remark to the King: 'By the law of England that Explanation could not hang his dog.'[3] The King confirmed the judgment. Learning this, Argyll,

Escape of Argyll.

on the night of the 20th December, took advantage of the visit of his stepdaughter, Lady Sophia Lindsay, to escape from the Castle disguised as her page; quite an easy exploit for 'that little lord,' as York styled him. Argyll, after finding shelter with William Veitch in Northumberland, and a refuge in London not unknown to the King, passed over to Holland. The doom of traitors was publicly proclaimed, and the House of Argyll was for the second time in one reign reduced to a nullity.[4]

[1] Mackenzie, *Vindication*, 21; Fountainhall, *Decisions*, i. Wodrow, iii. 317 note, gives explanation in full.

[2] Wodrow, iii. 319-39; *Hist. Not.*, i. 341-4; Burnet, ii. 320-3; *Observes*, 53.

[3] *Observes*, 55.

[4] Willcock, *A Scots Earl in Covenanting Times*, 268-87.

This travesty of justice gave amusement to the children of Heriot's Hospital in Edinburgh, who tried, condemned, and hanged the watchdog, because when offered the Test it refused to take it, and because when the Test was smeared with butter (which they designated the Explication) the dog licked off the butter and spat out the Test.[1] The students of Edinburgh University had a procession on Christmas night, in which they bore an effigy of the Pope in canonical vestments and adorned with his regalia. In the High Street, at the head of Blackfriars' Wynd, they halted and burned the effigy. The apprehension of George Ridpath and other students infuriated the youths, who entered into a combination and threatened to burn the provost's mansion at Priestfield. It was burned on 11th January. The Privy Council dissolved the college classes, and passed an Act (1st February) requiring from every student money security for peaceable behaviour, the oath of allegiance, and an engagement to attend church, all at the sight of the professorial staff.[2]

(margin note: Pranks of students in Edinburgh.)

One praiseworthy purpose to which the fines were devoted was the employment of John Adair, mathematician, to correct Blaeu's maps and prepare a complete atlas of Scotland.[3]

One of the incidents of the Parliament was the impeachment, by William Noble of Kipperminshoch, commissioner from Dumbarton, of Maitland of Hatton for perjury in the Mitchell case, of which he had the undoubted proofs. York had the case stifled by referring it direct to the King.[4] But Hatton had the worse charges of peculation and tampering with the coinage to meet, he being deputy treasurer; and, by his insolent behaviour, having alienated powerful friends, he soon found himself a disgraced and discarded servant trying to scrape together a fine of £20,000—a composition for his villainy—which was bestowed on two creatures of the heir-apparent, Aberdeen and Claverhouse, whom Burnet not unfitly designated 'two raw oppressors.'[5]

(margin note: Impeachment of Hatton.)

In October 1681, the Privy Council sent to the judges for trial six prisoners—namely, Robert Garnock, smith in Stirling; Patrick Forman

(margin note: Six fresh victims.)

[1] *Observes*, 55, 303.
[2] Wodrow, iii. 347 note.
[3] *Ibid.*, iii. 56.
[4] Cobbett, *State Trials*, vi. 1262-70; *Hist. Not.*, i. 309; Burnet, ii. 311.
[5] Burnet, *Hist.*, ii. 325 and note *a*; *Observes*, 73, 78: Terry, *John Graham*, 132.

from Alloa; David Farrie; James Stuart; George Lapsley, miller in Linlithgow; and Alexander Russell. Garnock was a notable prisoner—a man of destiny. A harmless bullet whistled through his hair when the dragoons chased Cargill and his following from Loudoun Hill. Since May 1679 he lay in jail, having been removed from the Greyfriars' Yard, where he had displayed considerable animus against any of his fellow-prisoners who were willing to conciliate the Council by taking the bond.[1] This hammerman of thew and nerve was a typical extremist, a Cargillite, bold of tongue, heedless of fate, hostile to Popery and Prelacy, furious at the 'hell-hatched acts' of the Government encouraging these, thinking it 'a sweet lot' to give up as many lives as he had hairs on his head, to get 'a gibbet and bloody winding sheet' for 'Christ's cause,' and ever ravished with visions of Paradise. Dalyell was right in saying, from the Episcopal standpoint, that nothing short of extinguishing such men would cure their malady. When Garnock was brought before the Committee of Council for examination, Dalyell and he fell foul of each other, and he called the General 'a Muscovia beast who used to roast men.' The anvil responded to the hammer, and 'the general in a passion struck him with the pommel of his shable till the blood sprang.'[2] The youth, Stuart, testified that on his refusing to answer questions in the presence of York and Paterson, on 1st October, Mackenzie threatened to tear out his tongue with a pair of pincers.[3] The answers given, and the refusals to reply, were fabricated to get proofs of the charge made at their trial on 7th October, that all were guilty of treason in disowning lawful authority. All were condemned to die on 10th October, and to have their heads and Forman's right hand exhibited on the Pleasaunce Port. Nothing could save the head and hand of Forman, in whose possession was found a knife with an inscription, 'For cutting tyrants' throats,' which he would not further explain as referring to the King. He twitted the judges by saying it would form a suitable posy for the sword of justice. Before leaving the bar the prisoners proffered a protestation declaring that they only abjured unlawful authority, and accusing their rulers of 'destroying the laws of God, murdering his people against and without law.'[4]

[1] Cf. *antea*, 308.
[2] *Hist. Not.*, i. 332.
[3] *Cloud*, 221.
[4] Wodrow, iii. 285-7; *Observes*, 44.

Lapsley was reprieved; the other five suffered heroically at the Gallowlee in Leith Walk.[1] They emitted long testimonies, some of them 'leaving their blood' on York, and all expressing delight in their martyrdom.[2] James Renwick, student, saw them hanged and hashed. Patrick Walker, in his *Vindication of Cameron*, recounted with evident zest the story told him by 'the never-to-be-forgotten Mr. James Renwick,' that his 'first public action' was the convening of his adventurous friends in order to lift the bodies from the foot of the gibbet and transport them to the West Churchyard, and to remove the heads and hand from the spikes on the Pleasaunce Port and bury them in Lauriston Yards.[3]

Renwick's bold exploit.

The bloody dispatch of the Cargillites and the recent legislation had two marked results—they made York practically master of Scotland; they convinced the ardent Covenanters that in their increased peril their only safety lay in banding themselves in a Union or General Correspondence of the various Societies in existence, in order to protest against the tyranny and defections of the times.

Proposed union of Covenanted Societies, 1681.

The first convention met at the Logan House, Lesmahagow, on 15th December 1681, and resolved to have a Declaration published at Lanark, on 12th January 1682, in the presence of adherents attending in arms on horse and foot. Arrangements also were made for the transmission of a circular letter every fortnight, and for a quarterly meeting, the first to be held at Priesthill on 15th March 1682.[4] James Renwick was one of forty horsemen and twenty men on foot who gathered round the Cross of Lanark, which they defaced with forehammers, where they burned the obnoxious statutes and decrees, and affixed the Declaration at

Lanark Declaration, 12th January 1682.

---

[1] Lapsley was before the judges on 4th May 1683.

[2] *Cloud.*, 190-224.

[3] On 7th October 1726 the latter remains were discovered and with honour removed to the Martyrs' Tomb in Greyfriars: *Biog. Presby.*, i. 283-9; *Six Saints*, i. 323-33; ii. 185. Walker, in contrasting these fearless heroes of Gallowlee and Grassmarket with the weaklings rabbled in 1688, wrote: 'How would they tremble and sweat, if they were in the Grassmarket, and other such places, going up the ladder with the rope before them, and the lad with the Pyoted coat at their tail. But they were speechless objects of pity': *Biog. Presby.*, i. 281.

[4] *Resolutions of the True Presbyterians*, Laing MSS., *Farrago*, No. 234; Michael Shields, *Faithful Contendings Displayed*, 9 (Howie's edit., 1780).

noon.[1] This manifesto entitled 'The Act and apologetic Declaration of the true Presbyterians of the Church of Scotland,' afterwards incorporated in 'An Informatory Vindication,' homologated the Declarations of Rutherglen and Sanquhar, and repudiated all the unconstitutional acts of the King, and also the statutes of the Parliament presided over by York—'professedly Popish.'[2]

The Privy Council fined the magistrates of Lanark in 6000 merks for their slackness in not dispersing these 'desperate villains,' but this exaction was a mere tithe of the £25,443 which the town had paid in connection with the Covenant, not to mention personal sufferings, strippings, and rapine.[3] The Council also ordained the complete Town Council of Edinburgh to go to the Cross on market-day, 18th January, and see the common hangman burn the Covenants and all these recent Declarations; and this they did.[4]

Unpopularity of the Test.

The unpopularity of the Test among the aristocracy was soon proved by the long list of hereditary jurisdictions and offices which reverted to the Crown on account of the refusal of their holders to take the new oath; among them being Buccleuch (Monmouth), Hamilton, Haddington, Nithsdale, Galloway, Cassillis, Rothes (Countess), Sutherland, Kenmure.[5] Some of these dissentients formed a syndicate for which they asked a royal charter for the planting of a colony in Carolina, where they hoped to see the angel of peace hovering over the unmolested homes of devout Covenanters. Among the subscribers were Callander, Cardross, Haddington, Yester, Polwarth, Sir John Cochrane, Sir George Campbell, and others.[6] But even this innocent proposal brought suspicion on its promoters. Needy nobles and gentry were gaping for every possible vacancy. It was not so easy to fill the empty pulpits. In the diocese of Edinburgh twenty-one ministers preferred ejection to subscription. In other dioceses subscription was delayed long after the appointed time, and these waverers were compelled to petition to be reponed.

[1] *Extracts from Burgh Records*, 208.
[2] *Inform. Vindic.* 250.
[3] *Burgh Records*, 229-30.
[4] Wodrow, iii. 362-3; *Hist. Not.*, i. 346.
[5] List in Wodrow, iii. 359.
[6] *Ibid.*, 368-9.

In 1682, Sir George Gordon, afterwards first Earl of Aberdeen, became Chancellor; Queensberry was Treasurer, and Perth, a Papist, became Justice-General. Finally, in May, York returned to England after giving the Council the sinister advice to suppress the Whigs, and to foster the orthodox clergy. The Council in turn gave York a good character for 'kindness, justice, and moderation,' which was an echo of a fulsome encomium forwarded in March by the prelates to the Primate of England, in which they traced the improvement in their Church and order to his princely care, and the tranquillity of the kingdom to his zeal and prudence.[7]

Of more importance in the spiritual life of the country was the new *duodecimo* from Anderson's press, entitled *The Pilgrim's Progress*, by John Bunyan, fifth edition.[8] Thus so early as 1681 there must have been a demand for the greatest prose classic of the seventeenth century, as there had been for Bunyan's other works some years previously.

Influence of the Duke of York.

---

[7] Wodrow, iii. 365 note. Paterson writing to Sancroft, 7th March 1683, acknowledged that York's presence in Scotland kept the fanatics 'under the greatest terror': W. N. Clarke, *A Collection of Letters ... to Sancroft*, 58-62. The minutes of the Privy Council indicate the almost uninterrupted regularity of the Duke of York and Albany in attending their meetings during 1681, and on till 13th May 1682; and this assiduity was an unmistakable proof of the Prince's assent to the policy which the Government was pursuing.

[8] Aldis, *List*, 2253.

Battlefield of Drumclog

Old Blair Church; burial place of Dundee

The Magdalen Chapel; and
Martyrs' Monument in Greyfriars
Churchyard, Edinburgh

Memorial spot on Magus Moor
where Archbishop Sharp fell

Monuments of Alexander Hende
and Principal Carstares in Greyfr
Churchyard, Edinburgh

Dalgarno Churchyard, with graves of the
Harknesses—the Enterkin rescuers

Kirko's Monument in St. Michael's
Churchyard, Dumfries

MEMORABLE SCENES AND PLACES OF BURIAL

CHAPTER TWENTY-EIGHT

THE POLICY OF ROPE AND GUN

THE heir-apparent returned to Court, assured that his succession to the throne would never be disputed in the northern kingdom, where he had left the Test as a touchstone to prove the loyalty of the Scots. His suave manners and conciliatory policy confirmed many aristocratic and disreputable friendships, which, meantime, he did not forget—soldiers being recommended for 'any little forfitur or fine,' and reverend spies for 'some little thing.'[1] In Chancellor Gordon, son of that Sir John Gordon of Haddo who, on being executed for Royalism, left his six children to the care of the King, he had an influential supporter in Parliament, council, and judicature, active and willing to champion the unpopular cause of York.[2] Gordon was accomplished. In his youth he acted as professor in Aberdeen University. He studied law abroad. He succeeded to his elder brother in the baronetcy, passed the Scottish bar in 1668, sat in Parliament in 1669, supported the Lauderdalian policy, and qualified for the Presidency, from which the Test drove Sir James Dalrymple. He was in his forty-fifth year when he was promoted to the Chancellorship, an honour which was followed in November by his elevation to the peerage as Earl of Aberdeen.[3] Unfortunately this 'glied carl,' as John Dick, the martyr, called Aberdeen, was noted for his crooked person and vulgar manners, which, his opponents said, prevented him adorning his exalted position. York trusted him.

Chancellor Gordon, a rising Royalist.

[1] *Hist. MSS. Com. Rep.*, xv. viii. 182, 189.
[2] Spalding, ii. 390.
[3] *Letters*, Preface, i-i (Spalding Club).

The Marquis of Queensberry.

A coadjutor was William Douglas, third Earl of Queensberry, Lord Justice-General, Treasurer, created Marquis on 11th May 1682, and Duke on 3rd February 1684. The magnificent pile of Drumlanrig, at this time being built on the site of the House of the Hassock, in Mid-Nithsdale, fitly immortalises the ambition of this thrifty Treasurer, who, notwithstanding that he flourished while other aristocrats were in penury, bitterly wrote on his accounts, 'Deil pike oot the een o' him wha looks herein.' All the peculating officers of the Crown might have docketed their papers in the same terms. The Earl of Melfort was bold enough to tell the King in 1685 that 'Duke Queensberry was an atheist in religion, a villain in friendship, a knave in business, and a traitor in his carriage to him [James].'[1] Yet this intriguer, according to Perth, posed as an angel of light.[2] The Earl of Moray was appointed Secretary of State in room of Lauderdale, who realised his increasing decrepitude.

Secretary Moray.

Exit of Lauderdale, 24th August 1682.

Middleton was his deputy. Lauderdale, discredited at Court, worn by his excesses and cares, became apoplectic, and merely existed in his overgrown body, as impotent as before he was all-powerful, and died at Tunbridge Wells on 24th August 1682. York, when communicating news of his demise to Queensberry, one of the courtiers waiting for the dead man's shoes, made no comment, further than that he had recommended Hamilton for the coveted Garter, and Queensberry for the captaincy of the Castle of Edinburgh.[3] Thus the great politician, who for years had moulded the regal and prelatic policy and hammered his native land, was never missed by the princes he served, because they had younger and more active agents to carry on their nefarious undertakings. The country did not mourn for what the Court did not miss. Lauderdale's body was laid in Inveresk Church in October 1682 and buried in Haddington in the following April. Bishop Paterson preached a funeral sermon from the text, 'O death, where is thy sting; O grave, where is thy victory?' The solemnities were rendered more memorable rurally by the fact that a drunk beggar, quarrelling over the alms, stabbed another in the churchyard and was hanged next day over the town bridge.[4] Thus passed Lauderdale, ignominiously too, like all the other

[1] *Hist. MSS. Com. Rep.*, XI. vi. 171.
[2] *Ibid.*, XI. vi. 171.
[3] *Ibid.*, XV. viii. 173.
[4] *Observes*, 76, 93.

Grand Viziers of the Stuart despots—Hamilton, Traquair, Middleton, Rothes—unblessed by his master and cursed by his countrymen. He lived to belie the promises of an honourable youth, when Presbyterian patriots belauded him high, also the assurances of a manhood which made Mackenzie, in dedicating to him a work on the criminal law, designate him 'The greatest statesman in Europe, who is a scholar; and the greatest scholar, who is a statesman ... who spends one-half the day in studying what is just, and the other half in practising what is so.'

According to a reliable authority, Mr. Osmund Airy, Lauderdale's *Estimate of Lauderdale.* career up to the Restoration had been 'a carefully arranged hypocrisy' of a cunning fellow, 'a bold and unabashed liar,' who lived to exemplify the French proverb 'Jeune hermite, vieux diable.'[1] Lauderdale's misgovernment of Scotland gave rise to the rebellion in the West and to countless woes consequent upon it, but when honester politicians endeavoured to bring Lauderdale to his knees for his maladministration, all the satisfaction that these patriots got from the King for their anxiety was the unanswerable retort of the despot that the 'many damned things' urged against his political paramour proved nothing hurtful to the interests of the King. Like master, like slave—Self was the God of them both. Another worshipper at the same shrine was ready to take up the uncompleted task of the dead viceroy.

That obliteration of dissent desired by Lauderdale, which grim *Agents for obliterating dissent.* Dalyell could not effect by means of torture, hair-shirts, sleepless dissent, tormentors, and other brutalities, was to be assured by the new protégé of York—Claverhouse—with his eager dragoons, relentless bailiffs and beagles, and his own pistols. As a spiritual power, and an effective administrator of ecclesiastical affairs, the hierarchy had become a nullity in the land. The bishops were mere automata. Equally happy in the torture-chamber and on the primatial seat, Archbishop Alexander Burnet, the 'Long Face' of earlier politicians, feline in his opposition of Whiggery and self-tormented by a horror of imaginary plots, found solace in promoting severer punishments for the extermination of nonconformists. The Test, which was the aversion of Bishop Scougal, was the exact measure of the toleration of Burnet.[2] In January

[1] Airy, *Charles II.*, 264-9. [French: 'The young hermit, the old devil.']
[2] Scougal died on 16th February 1682, aged seventy-five.

The Reformed Bishop.

1680, Burnet presided in a Synod which deposed James Gordon, Episcopal minister of Banchory-Devenick, who, in an anonymous work, published abroad, entitled *The Reformed Bishop*, advocated the establishment of a moderate Episcopacy, as favoured by King Charles I. Gordon also animadverted on the innovations of Puritanism, pointed out the weakness of the existing Episcopacy, denounced corruption, lashed, without naming, black sheep in high places in the Church, and reprobated conversion by inquisitorial methods.[1] Gordon submitted, and, after an interval, was restored to his charge. A contemporary epigram hit off the episode thus:—

'If your book had never been seen
You had been Bishop of Aberdeen;
If you had been Bishop of Aberdeen,
Your book had never been seen.'

Authorisation of Liturgy.

On 12th February 1680, the Privy Council authorised the use of the Liturgy in family worship, which resulted in the sale of many copies of the Prayer Book.[2] Nevertheless, Presbyterian rites and customs died hard. In October 1683, the Synod of Edinburgh ordained ministers to stand throughout divine service; to pray for archbishops and bishops; to pray for the King as the Head of the Church in all causes; and ordered the people to sing the doxology and to stand at prayers.[3]

The refusal of the Test by the ministers of Lothian was to Archbishop Burnet 'the mystery of Iniquity.' As if the ghost of Sharp was re-incarnated in him, he informed Sancroft: 'If an Indulgence be allowed to any person upon any consideration whatsoever, our labour will be lost, and this poor Church utterly undone.'[4]

Archbishop Ross.

Burnet's hands were strengthened by his colleague in Glasgow, Arthur Ross, of the House of Kilravock, who, according to Burnet the historian, was 'always a proud, ill-natured, and ignorant man, covetous and violent out of measure.' In another passage Burnet declared that in him 'obedience and fury were so eminent, that these supplied all

[1] Grub, iii. 272.
[2] Wodrow, iii. 232; *Letters to Sancroft*, 29.
[3] *Hist. Not.*, i. 456.
[5] *Letters*, 35, 36.

other defects.'[1] It was while he was parson at Glasgow he drafted the acrimonious Address of the Synod of Glasgow against the Indulgence.

All the time Paterson was Bishop of Edinburgh he never mitigated his hatred of the Covenanters, and rendered himself such a nuisance to the advisers of the Crown that Drummond, afterwards Earl of Melfort, wrote to Queensberry that Secretary Middleton and he were planning Paterson's relegation to the Orkneys, because 'he is the most impudent of mankinde, for he attests me as a wittness of his litle medling.'[2] Paterson wanted a house in Edinburgh to be built out of Moodie's Mortification, left for building a church in Edinburgh, then lying in the Treasury. This meant raising the Deil of Drumlanrig.[3] Before Paterson ceased to trouble he had his cruel thumbscrews to perfect and introduce, pensions to secure by fraud, and stipends, from parishes purposely kept vacant, to hold up for his own self-aggrandisement. Thereafter the King and the Privy Council removed him from their choice society.[4] These were the damning facts which 'opened the Whigs' mouths,' as the English prelates then observed. In the correspondence of the diplomatists Paterson figures as 'Mr. Pious' and 'Pope Pious'; but to the Covenanters this unblushing votary of Venus was nicknamed 'Bishop Bandstrings,' in allusion to the gossip that Paterson when preaching sometimes made use of his bands to convey amatory signals to neurotic women in the audience.[5] The other bishops, Atkins in Galloway, Falconer in Brechin, afterwards in Moray, Maclean in Argyle, Bruce in Dunkeld, Wood in Caithness, and Archibald Graham, minister of Rothesay and Bishop of the Isles, were not very prominent men of affairs.

One of the most distinguished ornaments of the Church, who preferred eviction to taking the Test was Laurence Charteris, Professor of Divinity in the University of Edinburgh, and formerly one of Leighton's perambulating evangelists. A dissenter against unconstitutional prelatic jurisdiction, and heaving definite views regarding the worthlessness of 'large Confessions of Faith … imposed in the lumps as tests,' Charteris was, as Burnet described him, one of the sanest, most

Bishop Paterson.

Professor Laurence Charteris.

---

[1] *Hist.*, i. 510; ii. 430.
[2] *Hist. MSS. Com. Rep.*, (*Drumlanrig MSS.*), ii. 124, 125.
[3] *Ibid.*, i. 119, 121, 123, 170; ii. 82, 83.
[4] *Observes*, 133.
[5] *Packet of Pestilent Pasquils*, 10; Ridpath, *An Answer*, 87; Row, *Blair*, 542.

learned, and deeply spiritual ministers of his age.[1] In 1692 he sought and got admission into the Presbyterian Church. A manuscript containing some of his sermons is preserved in the Laing Collection, Edinburgh University. These discourses are chaste and readable compositions of an evangelical character.

Twenty of the Scots clergy, expelled for the Test, sought refuge in England, and through the influence and patronage of Gilbert Burnet, found comfortable settlements in the Church of England.

The public records indicate that during the year 1682 many rural ministers were molested in their manses, and, of course, the Covenanters were blamed. But in view of the light in the same records upon the doings of Government servants, it would be rash, if not unjust, to attribute any of the outrages even to the extremest section of the Cameronians. Writing in his *Observes* at this very time Fountainhall states: 'Let soldiers commit as great malversations and oppressions as they please, right is not to be got against them. Witnesse John Cheisly of Dalrye's usage with Daver [Davis] and Clerk in the King's troop; and Sir John Dalrymple's with Claverhouse.'[2] The attempt to discredit Wodrow's extensive record of the horrors of this epoch, many of them vouched for in writing by the sufferers or onlookers themselves, entirely fails on the production now of the evidence of the public registers and of private diaries brought to light since Wodrow's day. Wodrow prided himself in his aim of being accurate, and more often minimises than magnifies the brutal stories he had to disclose. Many striking instances of persecution are omitted by him. For instance, Wodrow omits the villainous case of Rollo *versus* Craigie, recorded in the *Decreta* of the Privy Council on 21st June 1681, from which it appears that Lord Rollo brought up the oppression of John Craigie of Dunbarnie, who, for ten years, was guilty of coercing women, seizing goods, citing suspects and releasing them for fines, imprisoning and binding Andrew Weightfoot, and other crimes. The result of this interposition was that Craigie was mulcted in 5000 merks, and thrown into the Tolbooth of Edinburgh. The case referred to by Fountainhall shows that Cheisley accused a party of the Life Guards of invading his house, wounding and beating

Wodrow's stories of brutality now corroborated.

Invasion of Chiesley's house by soldiers, 1682.

---

[1] *Hist.*, i. 385; ii. 318.

[2] *Observes.* 87; *Hist. Not.*, i. 353, 363; *Just. Rec.* 12th July 1682.

him and his servants, turning out his horses, and other criminal acts committed in April 1682. The Lords of Justiciary tried the culprits on 6th July, sentenced Davis to banishment, degraded Clerk, another guardsman, making him find caution.[1] On 6th March 1684, the case of Captain Kilpatrick,[2] 'one of the Dutch officers at Thornhill,' is brought before the Council by two petitioners, David Ralston and Robert Young, merchants, who accused him of stealing their packs and money, binding them, and dispatching them to prison in Edinburgh. A process was ordered. Another case of the same kind in Stirling is recorded. Various petitions prove that many men, women, mothers with babes, and youths lay for long periods without being charged, some dying of neglect and others from the foulness of the dungeons. Fountainhall mentions that Marion Purdy died of cold and poverty at Christmas, because the Lord Advocate had no time to indict her for witchcraft.[3] A strange sidelight is thrown upon the honour of the prisoners who bribed the jailer to let them out at night and returned unobserved to the foul dens in the morning; one prisoner being caught in the act.[4]

Horrors of this epoch.

The unspeakable brutality perpetrated by dragoons on the two Nisbet boys, one aged ten, the other fourteen, is detailed in the Diary of Sergeant James Nisbet, the elder of the two. They were the children of John, the fighter at Drumclog, and afterwards a martyr. The soldiers came to Hardhill and seized the younger boy. To try to discover from him the refuges of the hunted, they terrified him with drawn swords, and fired pistols, blindfolded him, set him up to be shot, beat him with swords, fists, and feet, 'kicked him several times to the ground,' called the speechless child 'a vile, ugly, dumb devil,' beat him down and left him in his blood.[5] Wodrow records two similar atrocities perpetrated on boys; that of a boy, in his fifteenth year, resident at West Arnbuckles, in New Monkland, examined by Archibald Inglis, an officer, whose men beat the boy till he bled, and dragged him by the hair to a fire, where they held him till his eyes were like to jump out of their sockets, wrung

Enormities practised on children.

---

[1] *Hist. Not*, i. 353, 363; *Reg. Sec. Conc., Dec.*, 632.
[2] *Book of Adjournal*, 12th July 1682.
[3] *Decisions*, i. 304: 1st October 1684.
[4] *Reg. Sec. Conc., Dec.*, May 1682, p. 618.
[5] M'Crie, *Veitch*, 521.

his nose till it bled, beat him amid curses into insensibility.[1] He gives a parallel instance from Dumfriesshire, when William Hannah, not sixteen, ague-struck, was taken, trailed along by soldiery, threatened with execution, sent to Edinburgh, thumb-screwed there, robbed, and sold into Barbadoes, whence he returned to become minister in Scarborough.[2] These were not singular incidents. Patrick Walker, to whom we are indebted for many strange reminiscences of an evil time, took pride in narrating the share he had, as a youth of sixteen, in the dispatch, by a pocket pistol, of a lecherous ruffian of Meldrum and Airlie's command, named Francis Gordon. On the morning of the 2nd March this debauchee, unable to sleep, ran amok with drawn sword, threatening to send to Hell three fugitives whom he started at Mossplat, near Lanark. In the fray, Gordon fell dead with a shot in the head. In his pocket Patrick found a list of suspects which he tore in pieces, and some popish books and money which he replaced. In the exuberant zeal of his youth, and with the pride of a Masai warrior drawing his first blood, Patrick wished that all the blood of the Lord's enemies had so 'gone out with a gush.'[3] That the soldiers were far from tender with orderly and innocent persons is substantiated by a complaint sent by the Duke of Hamilton to Meldrum of Urquhart, declaring that the soldiery took away the peasantry's butter and cheese, 'kills their sheep and hens, takes them from their own harvest, and forces them to shear other cornes and gives them no allowance or satisfaction therefor.'[4] Nevertheless, retaliation from the side of the Covenanters was casual and generally unpremeditated. On 15th May 1682, William Kegue was tried for complicity in Gordon's murder, and executed in December.[5]

Claverhouse, distinctly the man of the hour, recommended for the perilous office of subjugator of the westlands, with the title of 'Scherif of Galoua,' was soon to be in the saddle speeding to 'Drumbfrich in Galaua,' as he proudly wrote in a *billet doux*.[6]

Patrick Walker's youthful exploit.

The subjugating of the westlands.

---

[1] Wodrow, iii. 389.

[2] Wodrow, iv. 176.

[3] *Six Saints*, i. 354; Scott in *The Heart of Midlothian*, vol. ii. note ii, refers to this Gordon, Gardin, Gairden, or Gairn, as he is variously named.

[4] Hamilton to Urquhart, 4th October 1683: *Hist. MSS. Com. Rep.*, xi. vi. 167.

[5] *Book of Adjournal*, 15th May 1682; Wodrow, iv. 177.

[6] [French: love letter.]

His heart was in his work. His commission to be Sheriff of Wigtown, and Sheriff-Depute of the Stewartries of Kirkcudbright and Annandale, and county of Dumfries, was signed on 31st January 1682, and was tenable during the King's pleasure.[7] A subsequent order associating him with Dalyell in the pacification of the shires of Ayr and Lanark, virtually made Claverhouse a military dictator from the Mull of Galloway to the Pentland Hills.[8] His commission was unique not only in giving him shrieval power in two other counties, 'when he is first attacker,' but in instituting him as a justice to administrate the laws in assize to all persons, not being heritors, who were in the late rebellion and were not indemnified. He inaugurated a new system of victualling the forces, which simply robbed the peasantry.[9] Soldiers were to pay for supplies: refusers of their demands were to be fined and imprisoned: soldiers seizing without payment were to be sued at common law. The result may be guessed—the troops were three months in arrears of pay. The inquisitor held every one in the hollow of his mailed fist. No Mephistopheles could have worked out his scheme with greater cunning or deliberation. He divulged it to Queensberry.[10] He found the district wasted, cereals eaten up, kine too worthless to kill or too lean to drive to mart, and the inhabitants in 'great dreed.' He made rapid marches through peaceful vales, sent flying squadrons hither and thither, made conciliatory visits to friends, displayed the velvet glove to ladies while he was spying out the strongholds of their male relatives, for whom he had decreed decimation piecemeal—rebels first, and, in their order, resetters, conventiclers, fanatics generally. He confidentially informed Queensberry, 'for what remains of the lawes against the fanatiks, I will threaten much, but forbear sever excicution for a whyll, for fear people shall grou desperat and increase too much the number of our enimys.'[11] This was the policy of a butcher, not of a soldier. His greedy eye spied some movables left, and he asked Queensberry's leave to take them to pay outlays, if 'I can find probation against' their owners. Three weeks' experience made the rebels elusive, their wives

Method of Claverhouse.

7 Wodrow, iii. 370 note; Terry, *John Graham*, 104.
8 Wodrow, iii. 373.
9 Letters to Aberdeen, 107.
10 Cf. Letter 37 in *Drumlanrig MSS., Hist. MSS. Com. Rep.*, xv. viii. 264-94.
11 Cf. Letter 37 in *Drumlanrig MSS., Hist. MSS. Com. Rep.* 265.

intractable, and Claverhouse bound to confess, 'I can catch nobody, they are all so alarumed.'[1] He hit on three cures—first, to enlist one hundred roughriders mounted on horses taken from 'suffering sinners here,' and paid sixpence a day; secondly, to seize the lairds who blamed their wives for encouraging the unlicensed preachers (Stair was hinted at)—thus befooling the Government; thirdly, to order the heritors to convene the inhabitants of several parishes into one church, where, after explaining the royal clemency, he might give them a final chance of submission. He was convinced, 'it will be mor of consequence to punish on[e] considerable laird then a hondred little bodys,' who 'only sin by the exemple of those.' He would stop the jest of nonconformity in the pulpit.

Capture of
rebels.

The success of his night-riders in capturing Maclellan of Barscob, M'Kie of Drumbuy, 'the great villain MkClorg, the smith at Minnigaff, that made all the clikys, and after whom the forces has trotted so often,' cowed the Whigs. Claverhouse's report to Queensberry on 1st April, that 'this contry nou is in parfait peace,' was more of a boast than a fact.[2] He continued: 'All this is don without having received a farthing mony … or impresoned any body'... all by 'attacking first.' 'Barscob is very penitent' and willing to turn informer and save his neck. In the

Claverhouse's
opinion of
the situation.

next report, 17th April, he wrote: 'We ar nou com to read lists evry Sonday after sermon of men and weomen, and we fynd feu absent. … I have examined every man in the shyr, and almost all the Steuartry of Galouy, and fixt such a guilt upon them, that they ar absolutly in the King's reverence. … Did the King and the Deuk knou what those rebellious villans, which they call minesters, put in the heads of the people, they would think it necessary to keep them out. The poor people about Menegaff confess upon oath that they wer made reneu the Covenant, and believe the King was a Papist, and that he desseined to force it on them.'[3] In these circumstances of millennial transformation Claverhouse judged a new indulgence hinted at to be madness. Had the soldier really counteracted the influence of the ministerial 'villans'? Or was he in the conspiracy to burke authentic news from Scotland, lest York should be dispatched north again, which deceit Perth insisted

[1] *Hist. MSS. Com. Rep.*, 267.
[2] *Ibid.*, 271.
[3] *Drumlanrig MSS.*, *Hist. MSS. Com. Rep.*, 272, 273.

362

on when writing Aberdeen thus: 'For God's sake, let all be keept in as quiet a condition as may be; and give timous accounts of all things of that nature [rebellion]'?[1] The Gallovidian jest of nonconformity would soon have sad reiteration, soon a joyful echo. For the Whigs were well informed.

In the last week of March, Claverhouse led Barscob, Neilson, and other malcontents in a string of Galloway prisoners into Edinburgh. To his superiors he then, and later, explained his tactics, and, on the 15th May, he was awarded a special vote of thanks by the Privy Council for his assiduity.[2] His own written Report, explaining his method of reducing Galloway 'without blood ... without severity or extortion,' does not harmonise with his letter to Queensberry, of date 1st April, nor with Wodrow's information. In the letter he stated he had received no money nor imprisoned anybody: in the Report he owned to having 'rifled so their houses, ruined their goods ... that their wyfes and schildring were broght to starving ... feu heritors being fyned, and that but gently.'[3]

[margin note] Gallovidian malcontents marched into Edinburgh.

Till Wodrow's day there still lived a remembrancer of Claverhouse's gentle tact. This Thomas Greg, merchant in Carrick, more than once informed Wodrow that while he was travelling with his pack he was seized on the public road by Claverhouse, robbed of his goods and money, brought through New Galloway to Dumfries on a barebacked horse, kept without food or drink, and in a famishing condition thrown into Dumfries jail along with other prisoners captured at this time, and kept there eleven days. The food brought to them by sympathisers was dashed out of their hands and tramped on by the soldiers. Without trial, Greg was removed to Leith, put on a ship going to Holland, being given away as a recruit. Greg returned to recite this tale of brutality, and fixed the date, 4th April 1682.[4]

[margin note] Robbery by Claverhouse.

The rank and file were often more considerate than their commanders, whose conduct they resented, as is shown by the case of a prisoner who was rescued from Colonel Douglas by the soldiers of Captain Cairns's company, in April 1682, Douglas being badly handled.[5]

---

[1] *Letters*, ii.: 23rd March 1682.
[2] Wodrow, iii. 371.
[3] Cf. Report in *Letters to Aberdeen*, 107-11; Napier, ii. 276.
[4] Wodrow, iii. 402.
[5] Moray to Council: *Mar MSS.*, 211.

For about a month Claverhouse helped Dalyell to pacify the shires of Ayr and Lanark, which could be no easy task, if Secretary Drummond was right in designating the inhabitants 'a sort of mungrell currs, half heritor, half common and whole brute.'[1] On his return to his own shrieval duties in the middle of June, Claverhouse was nearly entrapped by a commando of hill-men at The Bille, probably The Crook Inn, on the road to Moffat.[2] His party just missed these Society-men as they dispersed from their quarterly convention held at Talla Linn in Tweedsmuir, on 15th June, at which they ratified a resolution to send Earlston to Holland, disclaimed any connection with the extreme views of James Russell who advocated the non-payment of customs at toll-bars and ports, and discussed the reliability of Peden.[3]

Convention of the Societies, June 1682.

During autumn Claverhouse scoured the country executing a new Council order, of date 9th September, instructing him to cure absenteeism from church, and to establish Lord Livingston in the properties of forfeited Stewartry men.[4] He had craved more stringent orders and got them.[5] Wodrow records an epoch-making incident in the seizure by Claverhouse of several non-churchgoing parishioners in New Glenluce in August. They were kept twelve weeks in the Castle of Stranraer before Claverhouse sent them tied in pairs on barebacked horses to Edinburgh for trial.[6] On the way the prisoners were constrained to sign a bond finding caution for 1000 merks, and were released. Meantime soldiers rioted in their homes. This studied despotism brought its contriver into conflict with Sir John Dalrymple, afterwards first Earl of Stair, hereditary Bailie of the Regality of Glenluce, the same magistrate whom Claverhouse had referred to as 'fooling the Government.' The House of Stair openly favoured the Whig cause. When Claverhouse, as 'the first attacker,' seized these conventiclers, Sir John and his father protested against the sheriff overriding his authority, and, in presenting a bill of suspension to the Council, Sir John pled that he

Claverhouse opposes the Dalrymples.

---

[1] *Drumlanrig MSS.*, ii. 187.

[2] *Hist. MSS. Com. Rep.*, xv. viii. 273; Aberdeen, *Letters*, 23.

[3] *Faithful Contendings*, 21. Claverhouse put their number down at 120; the proclamation ordering their seizure fixed their number at 80.

[4] *Reg. Sec. Conc., Dec.*, 9th September 1682.

[5] *Letters to Aberdeen*, 77.

[6] Wodrow says four (iii. 385); Dalrymple said six or seven; Napier, *Dundee*, ii. 288.

had already dealt judicially with the culprits. The reply of Claverhouse was one calculated to move his self-aggrandising superiors, namely, that the complainant was acting in collusion with the criminals and fined conventiclers too little. The case was taken to avizandum. Claverhouse having soon learned that he had the sympathy of the Government, formally accused Dalrymple of obstructing him in his duty, and of actually bribing him to condone the irregularities of his Whig mother, sisters, and others. The bill of complaint in the form of criminal letters was read to the Privy Council on 14th December 1682.[1]

Dalrymple, himself an advocate, employed the two eminent counsel, Lauder and Lockhart. Mackenzie acted for Claverhouse. In the discussion arising out of the complaint regarding the irregularities of Claverhouse, when Sir John Lauder asserted that the Gallovidians 'were turned orderly and regular,' Claverhouse retorted, 'There were as many elephants and crocodiles in Galloway as loyal or regular persons.'[2] An attempt was made to induce Dalrymple to substantiate his charges by producing witnesses, but the complainant was too wary to bring the sufferers into greater peril. The Court dismissed Dalrymple's complaint, and found 'that the said John Graham has done his duty ... and acted ... faithfully and diligently,' and gave him 'thanks for his good service, and praise for outwitting a sharp Whig lawyer.' On the other hand, Dalrymple was found guilty of employing disorderly persons, imposing sham fines, slandering Claverhouse and interfering with his courts; was deprived of his bailiary, and sent to the castle till he paid a fine of £500 sterling with expenses.[3] After paying the fine the worsted litigant made for safety in Holland, and joined his father and other noble exiles there. It boded ill for friendless Cameronians, who could not flee, when thus a little spitfire of a dragoon, who actually threatened to box Dalrymple's ears in court, had influence enough to cause the expatriation of a powerful family whose movements abroad were chronicled by the Duke of York himself.[4] The effect was instantaneous. Other officers and justices were now eager to win their spurs

Triumph of Claverhouse.

[1] Fountainhall, *Decisions*, i. 201; *Hist. Not.*, 373, 391, 416, 420; Napier, *Dundee*, ii. 285-309; J. G. Graham, *Annals and Correspondence of ... Stair*, i. 352, App.
[2] *Decisions*, i. 191.
[3] Napier, ii. 304.
[4] *Hist. MSS. Com. Rep.*, xv, viii. 175.

and spoil; and a uniform experience was recorded in the disaffected areas—domiciliary visits, drives to churches, fugitations, evictions, eating up, legalised rapine, and worse offences by men capable of doing such merciless acts.

Trials of Patrick Vernor.

Wodrow gives details of the apprehension in February 1682 of a very interesting minister, Patrick Vernor or Warner, who, after serving as a missionary on the Coromandel Coast, returned to Scotland in 1667, and thereafter wandered about assisting John Welsh.[1] After the defeat at Bothwell Bridge he fled to Holland, where he spent his savings in printing David Calderwood's *History*, twenty copies of which he brought home in 1681 to sell along with hundreds of copies of the *Second Book of Discipline*. He was resident in Edinburgh in the house of the widow of William Guthrie of Fenwick, his mother-in-law, when he was seized and had all his goods, along with a trunk full of Guthrie's manuscripts, impounded. Claverhouse was glad to hear of his capture, and volunteered to Queensberry information, supplied by some mendacious 'fly,' that he was a dangerous man, and that 'from such men flous all our evills.'[2] His examination by the Council produced nothing incriminating. After incarceration for three months and a half in the Tolbooth he was liberated. He crossed the borders and got into jail again. He eventually reached Rotterdam, whence he returned at the Revolution to settle as minister of Irvine, dying Father of the Church in the first quarter of the eighteenth century.

Henry Erskine.

One of the most notable sufferers in this period was Henry Erskine, outed minister of Cornhill near Berwick, father of the still more famous preachers, Ebenezer and Ralph Erskine. Erskine's ministrations, appreciated in the district round Dryburgh where he settled, were unmolested until Urquhart and his men seized him in April 1682 and carried him before the Council. When Lord Advocate Mackenzie pressed him for a bond to desist from preaching in the fields, Erskine replied: 'My Lord, I have my commission from Christ, and though I were within an hour of my death I durst not lay it down at any mortal man's feet.'[3] He was sentenced to pay 5000 merks or go to the Bass. To him, afflicted with ague and colic, imprisonment meant death. His friends got his sentence

[1] *Hist.*, iii. 393-401.
[2] *Hist. MSS. Com. Rep.*, xv. viii. 270.
[3] Wodrow, iii. 403.

mitigated on condition that he left Scotland. Soon he was thrown into an English jail. The touching story of his playing his guitar in the night-time, in order to soothe his children who could not sleep for hunger, is recorded by William Veitch in his *Memoirs*.[1] Erskine returned, and after the Revolution Settlement became minister of Chirnside, where he died in 1696.

A cold-blooded murder is laid to the charge of Claverhouse at this time. It is first recorded in 1690 in *A Short Memorial of the Sufferings and Grievances, past and present, of the Presbyterians in Scotland, Particularly of those of them called by Nickname Cameronians.* This interesting treasury of Covenanting facts and hagiology was written by the Reverend Alexander Shields, the friend and biographer of Renwick, and a man whose other statements show that he was exceptionally well informed.[2] He is definite in associating the incident with the year 1682. He avers: 'John Graham of Claverhouse, Viscount of Dundee, in the year 1682, with a party of his Troup, pursued William Graham in the parish of [blank] in Galloway, making his escape from his Mother's house, and overtaking him, instantly shot him dead.'[3] Defoe, who declares that he 'talked with many sober and judicious persons who lived in that part of the country at the time and were eye-witnesses to much of it,' is specific in numbering Graham among those whom Claverhouse 'barbarously murdered … with his own hands.' He designates him 'one of his own name, viz. Graham of Galloway,' evidently trusting to the *Memorial*, but adding these details: 'Claverhouse rode after him and overtook him; and although the young man offered to surrender, and begged him to save his life, he shot him dead with his pistol.'[4] The epitaph on the little gravestone in Crossmichael churchyard, which is copied into *A Cloud of Witnesses*, repeats Shields's narrative, and gives his name as William, and his fate—'shot dead by a party of Claverhouse's troup for his adherence to Scotland's Reformation, Covenants, National and

[margin note:] Claverhouse shoots William Graham 1682(?)

[1] Veitch, *Memoirs*, 204.

[2] Alexander Shields, 1660-1700: M.A., Edinburgh, 1675; Bass, 1686; Renwickite; submitted to General Assembly, 1690; chaplain to Cameronian Regiment. 1691; minister of second charge of St. Andrews, 1697; went to Darien; died in Jamaica, 1700.

[3] *Memorial*, 34.

[4] *Memoirs*, 238, 289.

Solemn League, 1682.'[1] Wodrow omits this incident entirely from his published *History*. Therein he gives a detailed narrative of the seizure of James Graham when coming home from his work to his mother's house,' when 'he was overtaken in the highway by Claverhouse and a party of soldiers.' He was sent to Edinburgh, and after trial was hanged there on 9th December 1684. As regards date and the trial, at least, Wodrow is accurate, as falls hereafter to be shown.[2] Professor Terry, in his *Life of John Graham*, reduces the story of William's death to a legend, and the rural epitaph—'Here lyes William Graham'—to a sepulchral lie. He confidently asserts that 'there is no room to doubt his [James's] identity with the William Graham whose grave is in Cross-michael churchyard. … The most probable date for William Graham's arrest is about 17th or 18th December 1684. Claverhouse was then in the neighbourhead. …' He also ventures to give the motive for the arrest.[3] But this academic method of disposing of an ugly charge is not satisfactory, and by such an unscientific device the three John Brouns from Muirkirk, who occupy martyr-graves, may be slumped into one buried far from Priesthill, and the body of any martyr may be spirited away altogether. The author of *The Despot's Champion* tries to whittle away the accusation by the averment that the fact was never alluded to by Sir John Dalrymple when accusing Claverhouse, and that 'the inference is necessarily' that William's death, 'if not due to unmis-takable accident, was accounted for either by his active resistance, or in some other way which prevented any accusation from being at the time founded upon it.'[4] Certainly not—'necessarily'! Imaginative histo-rians are by no means safe guides; and a simple reference to authorities produces a convincing explanation. Dalrymple's complaint was that Claverhouse 'meddled within his regality'; and when he attempted to lead irrelevant evidence, he, according to Fountainhall, was checked by the Chancellor and confined to instances of acts done to himself and his tenantry, 'without he had a commission from the rest of the shire.'[5]

Professor Terry's assertion.

The Despot's Champion.

---

[1] *Martyr Graves*, 365.
[2] Wodrow, iv. 166, 167; *Book of Adjournal*, 8th and 9th December 1684: cf. *postea*, pp. 433, 434.
[3] *John Graham*, 172, 173 note, 176, note 3.
[4] *The Despot's Champion*, 207.
[5] Napier, ii. 289, 302; Fountainhall, *Decisions*, i. 191, 201, 217.

Crossmichael was far outwith the regality, and is in the neighbouring shire of Kirkcudbright.

A reference to the *Wodrow Manuscripts* clears up the matter. The basis of Wodrow's narrative is a circumstantially detailed account of the sufferings in Crossmichael parish in a well-written letter, to all appearances by a ministerial hand. It records that John Maxwell of Miltoun caused soldiers to visit Graham's mother's house in search of suspects lurking there, and that the youth William tried to escape, staff in hand only, but was taken, and, without being allowed to speak, was shot before his mother's eyes.[1] Wodrow, in two places in his manuscript, *Scotia Sub Cruce*, under date 1684, mentions the two Grahams.[2] In the former case, while referring to the executions on 9th December 1684, Wodrow writes: 'The same day James Graham, taylour in the parish of Crossmichael in Galloway, suffered. This good man was Brother to William Graham who was so barbarously cut of by the souldiers ye 15 of March this year [*i.e.* 1684]. When coming home from his work to his mother's house, He [*i.e.* James] was overtaken by Claverhouse and a party upon the High road. They had nothing to lay to his charge but His having a Bible upon him.' Wodrow next details his removal to Kirkcudbright, Wigtown, and Edinburgh.[3] The letter did not specify the military commander of William's slayers on the 15th March. Claverhouse, however, was not in attendance on the Privy Council between the 13th and 20th March.[4] If Wodrow's informant is to be credited, the date 1682 in the *Memorial* and on the tombstone should read 1684. That Wodrow is not to be disbelieved, the authentic facts connected with James Graham's arrest and trial, to be afterwards[5] detailed, abundantly show.

The case of James Gray of Chryston, father of the youth who fell so gallantly fighting at Ayrsmoss, illustrates the persistency with which the persecutors harassed any heritor with means, on account of his religious opinions. Long before the crisis in 1679, Gray's Presbyterianism was definite, making him a marked man; and, on his refusal to sign

The Graham tragedies in the *Wodrow MSS.*

James Gray's case.

---

[3] *Wodrow MSS.*, xxxvii. No. i, p. 11, No. 65.
[2] *Ibid.*, xli. (4to, Rob. iii. 14) 214; xlviii. (Rob. iii. 4. 2) 910.
[3] *Ibid.*, xli. 214.
[4] *Reg. Sec. Conc., Acta*, 275, 284; *Reg. Sec. Conc., Dec.*, 661, 666.
[5] Cf. *postea* p. 437.

the Highland Bond, the dragoons rode in, turned out his household, and made his homestead a desolation. For a time he was a fugitive at the horn, until after a trial he got relaxation from this hardship, but no relief from persecution. His place was again devastated, his family dispersed, and his wife left in 1681 to subsist on the milk of one cow. In January 1682, Gray stole home, was spied, taken, and sent into Glasgow and Edinburgh. The Council made nothing of him. Untried, he was left languishing in prison for three years and a half, till, in August 1685, he was included in a batch of prisoners dispatched to the slave-marts of Jamaica. There the old man was unsaleable, because he was squint-eyed, infirm, done. Only the menace of death and the offer of fifteen pounds induced his owner to free him from custody. He long survived the Revolution.[1] There were worse cases of oppression than eviction of lairds and families, such as of Fergusson of Finnart, for nonconformity.

Robert Nairn, Bonhill.

The chronicle of the sufferings of Robert Nairn is reverently treasured by his representatives to this day, and corroborates Wodrow's tale of woe. Robert Nairn, a thriving shoemaker in Napierston, Bonhill, on the lands of John MacAlister, did not relish Episcopal services, absented himself from church, and was hunted about in 1682. His wife, with a babe at her breast, also fled, leaving a maid to care for their other three children. The officers of the Crown arrested the Whig's effects. Mother and maid were caught and clapped in ward, till caution was forthcoming. Outdoor severities were too hard upon a domestic tradesman, and he contracted a mortal malady. He crept into a neighbour's barn to die. Before the bailiffs arrived to hale him to prison, Nairn's spirit had fled. The parish incumbent, William M'Kechnie, Master of Arts, refused the use of the mortcloth, and locked the churchyard gate in the face of the burial party. Even these churlish acts were outdone by the sheriff-officer, who arrived, before the bakemeats were eaten, to summon widow and heir for the crime of removing the dead body of a rebellious dissenter.[2]

---

[1] Wodrow, iii. 129, 220, 263, 264, 391, 393.
[2] *Ibid.*, iii. 405. A modern gravestone in Bonhill churchyard gives the date of Nairn's death, 15th April 1682. M'Kechnie was rabbled at the Revolution. In the *Wodrow MSS.*, xxvii. 143, the account of Nairn is signed 'James Baines,' the parish minister of Bonhill (1675-1755). Nairn's residence may have been at Auchincarroch.

Nonconformity was not confined to the peasantry and humbler classes of the community. Many dames of quality—in those days designated 'Ladies'—Douglas, Longformacus, Moriston, Gordon—figure in the records as patronesses and followers of the preachers, as Cargill, Arnot, Semple, Douglas, Renwick, and others. A notable sufferer was the widowed Lady of Cavers, Catherine Rig, Lady Douglas, who rather than satisfy the Council, 16th November 1682, by paying a fine of £500 and giving a bond abjuring conventicling, preferred two years' incarceration in the castles of Edinburgh and Stirling. Her son, Sir William, on his return from abroad, in 1684, petitioned the Council to liberate his mother on condition that she lived regularly or expatriated herself. She accepted the latter punishment.[1]

The 'Lady' of Cavers.

Wodrow gives an epitome of a credible account of the hardships endured by James Ure of Shargarton, in the parish of Kippen, in Stirlingshire, a centre of nonconforming disaffection.[2] From 1670 Ure was leading the disorderly life of a dissenter, having his children baptized by outed ministers, now skulking in the Wood of Balwhan, anon in Ireland, and again an intermittent visitor at home. He was foremost among the braves who held the Bridge of Bothwell. When the trial of the fugitive came off on 9th January 1682, all the political crimes of the day, as well as 'throwing off the fear of God,' were charged against him, and the traitor's doom and forfeiture were accorded him. The soldiery exhausted his estate. This severity merely confirmed the faith of his family. His septuagenarian mother was captured at a conventicle at the Gribloch and was one of a crowd marched down to Glasgow Tolbooth, which was overcrowded. Her petition to be allowed out on bond, 'at least to win to the prison doors for air'—those able to jostle took their turn at the chinks—was refused, so that the pestilential ward killed the old lady. Among the prisoners was Margaret Macklum, wife of Arthur Dougall, miller at New Miln, Kippen, a non-churchgoer, who was apprehended in April 1681 and liberated on a bond.[3] Some of these

Use of Shargarton.

Prisoners in Glasgow Tolbooth.

---

[1] Wodrow, iii. 406; iv. 55, 56.

[2] The original MS. by Ure is preserved in the Advocates' Library: *Wodrow MSS.*, xxxvii. Rob. 3. 12. Art. 147; cf. M'Crie, *Veitch*, 435-54, 455-83: *Notices of, and Narrative by Ure*; Wodrow, iv. 408, 409.

[3] Wodrow, iii. 194, 196; M'Crie, *Notices of Ure*, 446, 447. Dougall's Toor is a rock in the glen of Balwhan, where Dougall, according to the tradition among his descendants, was shot.

prisoners were sent to Dunnottar and others were banished. The offer of £100 reward for information regarding the hiding-places of Ure did not tempt those in the secret. For intercommuning with her husband, Ure's wife, with a baby at her breast, was carried off first to Stirling, then to the Canongate Tolbooth, to be examined by the Council. After four weeks' detention she was released and returned to her devastated home, in which her husband spent only three nights during nine years of wandering. The gallant laird, however, survived to become a potent factor at the Revolution, to get a commission in Argyll's regiment, to have his forfeiture rescinded by Parliament, and to see the extinction of the Jacobite Rising.[1] Ure's neighbour, John Flockhart in the Hole of Kippen, another conventicler, who was married by a nonconformist, was punished by the quartering of seventy troopers, under Bruce of Clackmannan, and by condemnation to prison for several months.[2]

The Bloody Vintage, 1682. The Lords of Justiciary, assisted by Lord Advocate Mackenzie, who entered with the keenest zest into his incriminating function and work, pressed a bloody vintage in 1682.[3] Prisoners were first examined by a Committee of the Council, and their answers, or refusal to answer, gave the prosecutor material to form a statement, or so-called confession, usually framed to incriminate the prisoner. The interrogations generally were the following: Can you read the Bible? Were you present at Drumclog, Bothwell Bridge, Ayrsmoss, or other skirmish? Do you own the Declarations made at Rutherglen, Sanquhar, Lanark, etc.? Do you know, have you heard, had you ordinances from Cargill, Cameron, or other field-preachers named? Have you intercommuned with the outlaw, whose name was mentioned? Do you own the King's authority? Will you say 'God save the King'? Will you pray for the King? Do you adhere to the Acts of Parliament? Have you taken, or will you take, the Oath of Abjuration, the Test, etc.? Is rising in arms rebellion? Will you give a bond not to rise in arms? And so forth. Refusal to reply was considered an acknowledgment of the crime referred to.

A gravestone in Lanark churchyard attests that 'William Hervi sufered at the Cros of Lanerk the 2 of March 1682, for his adhering to

---

[1] *Act. Parl. Scot.*, lx. 165 note.
[2] Wodrow, iii. 406.
[3] *MS. Book of Adjournal.*

the Word of God,' etc.[1] Harvey was a weaver indicted for participation in the rebellion and in the publication of the Lanark Declaration in 1679, and for these offences he was sent back to Lanark to make a personal testimony on the gibbet. He was of the Moderate party, and on the scaffold declared his belief in 'kingly Government according to God's Word,' and that the 'people should obey the King in his lawful authority … so far as the Word alloweth'; and actually said 'God save the King.' The Government considered his dispatch to be necessary as their reply to the burning of the Test at Lanark on 12th January by the Cameronians.[2]

Of quite a different type was Christian Fyfe, a Fifeshire woman, actuated by a spirit similar to that of Jenny Geddes. This 'bangster Amazon,' full of visions of Sharp, who she thought had been righteously finished, and of Cargill, whom she mourned as foully murdered; and impelled by the delusion that Ramsay, preacher in the Old Kirk of St. Giles, was 'a Judas and a devil,' one Sabbath fell on belabouring that unfortunate counterfeit of a true preacher; and, according to Christian, 'there was not an honest minister left in Scotland.' For this sacrilege, confessed to the Privy Council, and for vilifying the King, dishonouring the judges, and approving of the slaughter of bishops, the Lords of Justiciary condemned her to be hanged in the Grassmarket on 7th April.[3] But afterwards, concluding that her fanaticism was a proof of madness, the Council reprieved this woman.[4]

On 7th April, four notable prisoners stood at the bar—Major Joseph Learmont, the 'bonny fighter' at Pentland and Bothwell Bridge, now almost an octogenarian, Robert Maclellan of Barscob, whose Covenanting zeal was soon blighted, Robert Fleming of Auchinfin, and Hugh Macklewraith of Auchinflower. For years these fugitives had lain under the doom of traitors, till now, after identification, that doom with all its horrible details was pronounced in their presence.

[1] Wodrow and Fountainhall give 3rd March: Wodrow, iii. 409; *Hist. Not.*, i. 348; *Decisions*, i. 176; *Book of Adjournal*, 24th January, ordered execution on 3rd March.

[2] Wodrow, iii. 409; *Martyr Graves*, 265, 266. It was pleaded that he had been compelled by *vi majore* [superior force] to proclaim the Declaration at Hamilton; and his case was considered hard, since he had also cried out 'God save the King.'

[3] *Book of Adjournal*, 27th March 1682: *Reg. Sec. Conc.*, 21st March.

[4] *Hist. Not.*, i. 350.

On their petition, clemency prevailed and they escaped the brutal tragedy: Barscob going free to make himself useful and to meet a bitter fate; Learmont remaining steadfast and for punishment relegated to the Bass, whence he issued in five years to look forward to the happy Revolution, which he saw; and the other two prisoners, probably after taking the Test, being dismissed.[1]

This judicial procedure of raking out old sentences was an easy method of expediting the public business and of bringing in money.

Gray, an English sufferer in May.

On 15th May, Robert Gray, a Northumbrian, confined in Canongate Tolbooth for ten months, after emitting an incriminating confession before the Committee of Council, was passed on to the Lords for trial, for disowning the royal authority and repudiating the 'black test.'[2] A letter written by him to a prisoner in Dumfries, in which he gave reasons why King Charles, as a tyrant and patron of murderers and other criminals, should not be owned in Church or State by Christian men—afforded damnatory evidence. He boldly confessed that he was justified in writing thus to a perfect stranger. The Lords deemed it imperative to quench zeal of this undesirable character by the rope in the Grassmarket four days later—19th May. Gray was not a whit daunted, and in his written testimony, as well as in that spoken with the halter round his neck, proved himself to be a fearless upholder of the Covenants, which he upbraided the Scots for breaking. He had been a disciple of Cargill and Cameron in Northumberland and gloried in their uncompromising principles for which he died. Before ascending the ladder he sang the 84th Psalm, and read the fifteenth chapter of St. John's Gospel.[3]

Another tassel.

On the 16th August the gallows at the Market Cross of Edinburgh had another tassel in Thomas Lauchlan, whom the Justiciary Lords sent there, having revived a former sentence of death and forfeiture recorded against him in 1681 for complicity in the rebellion of 1679.[4] The Justice-General, Perth, and his colleagues on the bench did not incline to pity. In the middle of December, they held an assize upon fifteen

---

[1] Wodrow, iii. 410; *Wodrow MSS.*, xxx. 60; xxxvii. 82, 83; *Book of Adjournal*, 7th April 1682.

[2] *Book of Adjournal*, 15th May 1682.

[3] Wodrow, iii. 411; *Hist. Not.*, i. 358; *Cloud*, 225-37; *Decisions*, i. 185.

[4] Wodrow, iii. 412.

gentlemen of Dumfries and Galloway, and two ministers—Arnot, late of Tongland, and Warner, late of Balmaclellan—of whom only two, Alexander M'Kie of Drumbuy and Anthony M'Kie of Glencard, were at the bar. All were formally sentenced to be executed and demeaned as traitors on the first Wednesday of July; Grierson of Dalgonar (being deceased) was excepted. His kinsman, William of Lochurr, made more famous by the Enterkin rescue, was among the number.[1] The M'Kies were reprieved.

Not so favoured were James Robertson, from Stonehouse, Lanarkshire; William Cochran, from Carnduff, Evandale; and John Finlay, Muirside, Kilmarnock, who after trial were dispatched, amid ruffling drums, in the Grassmarket, on the 15th December.[2] All three were staunch Cargillite-Cameronians; and, while refusing to say 'God save the King,' thereby meant to indicate that they did not approve of the policy of that Government of which he was the consenting head. Their guarded answers to the Committee were construed into the evidence that brought them to the gallows. Their striking testimonies supported the case of the authorities against them. Robertson, a pious packman, garrulous and vituperate, was a complacent perfectionist, who boasted: 'I am a true Christian, truly anti-Popish, anti-Prelatic, anti-Sectarian, anti-Schismatic, anti-Erastian, a true Presbyterian, owning the true Protestant religion, now owned and professed by the poor, wrestling, and suffering remnant in Scotland.' The hardened town-major, Johnston, gave him a sound drubbing with his cane and stopped his flood of oratory at the ladder foot. Finlay, who had been at Bothwell Bridge without arms, left his blood on his enemies. Cochran evinced the more refined spirit of a young martyr. All three ended valiantly.[3]

Three Cargillites hanged, 15th December 1682.

The case of Alexander Home, portioner in Humetoun, appears incriminating enough in the charge-sheet. Patrick Hume in vain defended him. It was averred that he had fought at Bewly Bridge, besieged Hawick Tower, and roamed about the Borders armed, in search of more arms in Mackerston House and elsewhere. He confessed attendance at two conventicles, and that on his way home he and his servant had made a harmless commercial visit to Mackerston to buy a

Intrepidity of Alexander Home, martyr.

[1] Wodrow, iii. 413; *Book of Adjournal*, 18th December 1682.
[2] *Cloud*, 240, 260, 269.
[3] Wodrow, iii. 415.

bay horse. The assize was on 21st December; eight days afterwards he swung at the Market Cross of Edinburgh, to the last maintaining his innocency and loyal patriotism, and declaring the discrepancy between the evidence and the verdict. The 'Last Words' of this composed and brave sufferer are singularly chaste, free from those ill-advised tirades found in many testimonies, and indeed redolent of a gracious spirit. His loyalty he expressed thus: 'I am loyal, and did ever judge obedience unto lawful authority, my duty, and the duty of all Christians.' His love he left thus: 'Farewell, my dear wife and [five] children, dear indeed to me, though not so dear as Christ, for whom I now willingly suffer the loss of all things, and yet am no loser. I leave them on the tender mercies of Christ.' With the rope round his neck he sang—

> 'But as for me, I thine own face
> In righteousness will see;
> And with thy likeness when I wake
> I satisfyed shall be.'

It was reported that his friends obtained a remission, which Perth held up till he was executed.[1]

Reward of Claverhouse.

On Christmas Day 1682, Claverhouse was rewarded for his strenuous services by a commission 'to be colonell of his Majesty's new formed regiment of Horse in Scotland,' as 'also captain of a troop therein.'[2] The regiment was embodied in four troops, of sixty men each and their officers, and was captained by Claverhouse, Adam Urquhart of Meldrum, William, Lord Ross, and the Earl of Balcarres. Claverhouse's lieutenant was the unsavoury Andrew Bruce of Earlshall. Three years later King James honoured it with the title of 'His Majesty's Own Regiment.' The colonel soon set about equipping them in their red tunics, and stone-grey cloaks to render them invisible in the rocky Rhynns.[3] Four months later, May 1683, Claverhouse was further honoured by promotion to a seat in the Privy Council.[4]

[1] His forfeited estate went to Sir John Gordon, advocate. After the Revolution the forfeiture was rescinded. George Dickson, the servant, became an outlaw: *Book of Adjournal*, 21st December 1682; Wodrow, iii. 416-20; iv. 27 note; Gunn, *Early Hist. of Stitchell*, 62; *Act. Parl. Scot.*, viii. 637; ix. 166.

[2] Terry, 119; App. i.

[3] 31st May, *Reg. Sec. Conc., Dec.*, 515; *Reg. Sec. Conc., Acta*, 101.

[4] Terry, 132.

Now there was no rest for the various officials of the Crown. During 1683 a persistent effort was made to sweep into Edinburgh the remnant of the rebels who hitherto had not been registered on the Porteous or fugitive rolls, and finally to register all persons guilty of intercommuning, as well as witnesses able to prove this misdemeanour. Complications arose regarding the fines exigible from dissenting wives, widows, and children, so that the Committee of Council had to draw up fresh instructions (11th January) exonerating husbands who produced their rebellious wives, and parents who sent children over seven years old to church.[1] The Council concluded that many rural justices ignored the law, and winked at religious offences—a theme Claverhouse harped on. In a note of instructions (1st March) to Claverhouse, Meldrum, and White, the Council ordered these officers to call for the records of rural magisterial courts, and examine them for proofs of collusion or illegal mitigation of fines, to report cases of offenders, to exact the appointed fines, and to give suspects two months to come in under a passport.[2] Sir John Harper of Cambusnethan, Sheriff-Depute of Lanark, was thrown into prison for suspected collusion.[3] Unfortunate cautioners were also asked to produce their fugitive friends or lose their bail. Never were known such acts of legalised rapine. The Council did not always right the wrongs, when appeals to their dread tribunal were taken even by influential men like Hamilton.[4]

New repressive rules and regulations, 1683.

To prevent the aristocracy harbouring disguised Presbyterian preachers, all tutors and teachers were again required to take the Test and get a bishop's licence. The mills of justice ground exceeding small. An unpopular or suspected parishioner had a miserable fate. There was the incumbent, usually called 'the curate,' to satisfy, then the blackmailing informer to pay off, Major White or some such to provide with forage and pay, the justice of the peace to meet with a fine for some neglect of the innumerable laws, and, when all these were sent away happy, there was the sheriff, or his depute, to encourage with some forfeit to justify his loyalty. The pinching laws were not made to be fruitless of those pitiable illustrations whereof Wodrow faithfully

Variety of oppressors and oppressions.

[1] Wodrow, iii. 422.
[2] *Ibid.*, 424.
[3] *Ibid.*, 434.
[4] Hamilton *v.* Meldrum, *Hamilton MSS.*, XI. vi. 167; Wodrow, iii. 442.

recorded only a moiety. With a Claverhouse or a Lag in the pulpit, a red-coated clerk in the 'latron,' the mean curate with his Porteous roll at the communion-table, and the sheep pent in the fold, a clever creature he would be who escaped the fleecing.

Dr Jasper Touch.

Jasper Touch, surgeon in Kilmarnock, wrote for Wodrow a memorial of his exasperating persecution at this time. This young leech, with an apprentice, opened a modest drug-store in Kilmarnock. George Pollok, the incumbent there, failed to attract him often enough to church, and White's booted elders were sent to lay him in the Tolbooth, where he began to pay fines, fees to jailers, and charges for bonds of caution to enable him to get out free. Pollok was less attractive than ever, and the doctor found himself in prison again, then out of it heavily bonded. He absconded, leaving his apprentice dispensing. He ventured back, and was in town in April 1685, when the rebels came in from the rescue at Newmilns with wounds and bruises needing his Samaritan touch. For this illegal act of charity he went to prison again, and was not released until he had paid the fullest scot to Colonel Buchan.[1]

Muir of Glanderston.

William Muir of Glanderston, afterwards of Caldwell, also informed Wodrow of his peculiar case. While sympathetic with the nonconforming party, Muir had lived regular and orderly, keeping out of the clutches of the despots. Unhappily he took fever. His household sent for a respectable apothecary in Paisley, of the unfavoured name of James Sprewl, to bleed him in his unconsciousness. That was enough. Sprewl was a registered suspect, and the Council would bleed more if need be. Muir was sent to prison and to the bar of the Justiciary Court on 8th August, from which he was discharged, the indictment being departed from.[2]

Michael Potter sent to the Bass.

The calendar of offences for 1683 was a heavy one. The Council began the year, 4th January, by sending Michael Potter, a field-preacher, to the Bass for two years. A year bygone, Potter, having returned from Holland, was caught in ill-favoured Bo'ness.[3] A week later they remitted to the King the case of Andrew Herron of Kerrochtree, against whom the extreme penalty was passed for his intercommuning with his own second son, Patrick, in the way of cattle-dealing, both, however, being

[1] Wodrow iii. 425.
[2] *Ibid.*, 468, 469.
[3] *Ibid.*, 433.

accused of Bothwell Bridge. A payment of 5000 merks satisfied the authorities.[1] On 15th January the justiciary lords pronounced the doom of traitors upon Thomas Cunningham of Mountgreenan in Ayrshire, who had already been apprehended for a share in the rebellion, released, charged anew, and now condemned.[2]

John M'Gilligen, formerly minister at Fodderty, had in many prisons tasted that sweetness which martyrs find there, and was now out of the Bass on parole upon the bond of Sir Hugh Campbell of Calder. His loyalty was as pronounced as his Presbyterianism. In order to get the security, the Council summoned M'Gilligen on the old charge of irregular ministry. M'Gilligen, expected to flee, actually compeared. By refusing to answer the libel, except in his own way, he was held as confessed, fined 5000 merks, and sent to the Tolbooth and Bass till it was paid. Worse still, the few bolls of victual from his land in Ross, which hitherto saved his wife and eight children from starvation, were seized by the authorities. The prisoner's health gave way, and on his petition he was liberated, after July 1686, on finding bail.[3]

M'Gilligen again sent to the Bass.

William Laurie, tutor of Blackwood,[4] who had constituted himself an intermediary between the Rullion Green reformers and Dalyell, now found himself accused of participation in the rising, inasmuch as he permitted the rebels to carry off the two guns from Douglas Castle to Bothwell Bridge, employed the disloyal, and restored rebel tenantry to their farms on the Douglas estate. Laurie's defences were strong—the rebels were not convicted nor banned, he was not a heritor of their lands, his intercommuning was a public affair. The lords repelled all defences. On 7th February, the assize returned a verdict of guilty, and the ignominious doom of traitors was passed on Laurie. The King was pleased with this brutal diligence, and sent the Council thanks. A reprieve was obtained for Laurie, who was kept in prison under sentence of death during the rest of the year, and was ultimately pardoned on the petition of his master, Douglas, to whom he was indispensable, and with whom he had not settled his estate affairs.[5] The Council had a precedent

Laurie of Blackwood.

---

[1] Wodrow, iii. 422, 439, *Privy Counc. Rec.*

[2] *Ibid.*, 433, 449.

[3] *Ibid.,* iii. 435; M'Crie, *Bass*, 248. He died minister of Inverness in 1689.

[4] He married the widow of the proprietor of Blackwood, Lanarkshire.

[5] *Book of Adjournal*, 8, 31st January, 7th February 1683; Wodrow, iii. 449-552; *Reg.*

for this remission in the case of Robert Hyman, a bailie too useful for the Duke of Buccleuch to be sent to the Grassmarket or cane-brakes.[1] Many of the sentences passed, especially by the Privy Council, were more severe on account of the impolitic obstinacy with which the accused replied to or contemned their interrogators. John Archer, brother of Thomas, the associate of Argyll, a nonconforming candlemaker in Strathmiglo, was a fugitive, by turns in and out of prison, untried for complicity in Sharp's murder, of which he was innocent. He, his wife, and five delicate children were seized and carried off to jail in Kirkcaldy. He was dispatched to Edinburgh. In the course of an examination by the committee of Council he was not deferential enough in giving the Right Reverend Father in God, Archbishop Burnet, his titles, and his punishment was to lie in irons. He was liberated without further trial.[2]

Among minor cases which terminated in discharges on contracting to lead orderly lives, were John Hamilton of Gilkerscleuch, fined 2000 merks for his wife's conventicling; John Gibson of Auchenchain, Glencairn; Robert Fergusson, Letterpin; William M'Culloch in Cleuchred, registered rebels; John Menzies of Dalquharn, sentenced to death for boasting: when drunk of getting a letter from Burly, and for intercommuning; and James Laurie, writer in Lanark. The latter was an outlaw, and thinking to get an easy discharge compeared, was tried on 4th April and sentenced to the gallows, from which he barely escaped in answer to his petition.[3]

The disgrace of Sir John Dalrymple was the main topic of the day. The most immediate result of this victory for militarism was the public acknowledgment of Claverhouse to be a power at Court as well as in the field. Consequently, the great officers of the Crown were as eager to utilise their henchman for their own base purposes as he was to profit by their recommendations. All were playing for great stakes—Aberdeen for a share of Lauderdale's ill-gotten spoil, Queensberry for the dead duke's title and blue ribbon, Claverhouse for Dudhope Castle and the Constabulary of Dundee, and York for Claverhouse and his ready

Sec. Conc., *Dec.*, 24th May, 510, petition; Burnet, ii. 331, 332; *Hist. Not.*, i. 380, 409-13.

[1] *Reg. Sec. Conc.*, *Dec.*, 1st May 1679. Paterson, Hamilton's factor, was in Hamilton jail in May; *ibid.*, 501.

[2] Wodrow, iii. 55, 389, 439.

[3] *Ibid.*, 438, 452.

carbines. Jobber in all these causes, Claverhouse crossed the Borders on the 1st or 2nd of March, and began the sordid intrigues intermittent between the King's cock-fighting, coursing, and other less worthy royal pastimes.[1] The Council were in terror of this fiery agent. He kept his eye on the main chance. With studied abbreviation of the truth, in writing to Queensberry asking his patronage regarding his own tidbit, Dudhope, a fair expectation in return for the pretty things he was saying in London, Claverhouse stated, 'I have no house, and it lays within half a myl of my land.'[2] The deal ended in Hamilton getting the garter, Aberdeen and Claverhouse obtaining £20,000 out of the modified fine of Hatton, now Duke of Lauderdale; or alternatively, Hatton's Dundee estate was to go to Aberdeen, from whom Claverhouse might purchase Dudhope and the Constabulary. Queensberry received gracious messages. In May, Claverhouse was invited to Windsor, where his honours were augmented by a commission as a Scots Privy Councillor, and a warrant to his brother, David, to be Conjunct-Sheriff of Wigtown.[3]

Queensberry henceforth had a suspicion that his agent had diverted his influence to the side of his rival, Aberdeen, and took an umbrage at Claverhouse. York, who considered the army his tool, had a trusty ally in Claverhouse. York took credit for his protégé's success in Galloway, and not only approved of the soldier's method of subjugation but recommended it, so that 'the King is very resolved it shall be followed.'[4]

While Claverhouse was in London influencing the heir-apparent, the King authorised the Privy Council to issue a proclamation, 13th April 1683, promulgating the conclusion that the plea of the Covenanters—'difference of religion and tenderness of conscience'— was a mere pretext to cloak their disloyalty and disaffection, in order that they might disturb the peace; ordering the laws to be put into execution, especially against those having dealings of any kind with rebels, even converse with relatives; establishing circuit courts of justiciary at six convenient centres, namely Stirling, Glasgow, Ayr, Dumfries, Jedburgh, and Edinburgh, and appointing other justices for

[1] *Aberdeen Letters*, 101; Claverhouse to Queensberry, 9th March 1683-3rd May: *Drumlanrig MSS.*, *Hist. MSS. Com. Rep.*, xv. viii. 275-81.
[2] Claverhouse to Queensberry, 9th March 1683-3rd May: *Drumlanrig MSS.*, *Hist. MSS. Com. Rep.*, xv. viii. 276.
[3] Terry, 132, 133.
[4] Claverhouse to Queensberry, 13th March: *Hist. MSS. Com. Rep.*, xv. viiii. 276.

THE COVENANTERS

the purpose of punishing recusants; but announcing, in order to show the royal clemency, a complete indemnity to any person taking the Test on his knees before the 1st of August 1683, and also promising that no more processes, except for new offences, would be undertaken during the years 1684-7.[1] 'This was perhaps such a proclamation as the world had not seen since the days of the Duke of Alva,' was the pertinent comment of Burnet the historian on the document.[2] Thus Claverhouse began to meddle with the national policy at its fountainhead, and the sequel will show to what purpose this fell executioner of ruthless decrees, which he helped to shape and heartily carried out, stiffened other less unfeeling councillors.

At a meeting of Council on 21st August, at which Claverhouse was present, the Council agreed to ask the King to extend the truce and time to take the Test till 1st March.[3] This request was granted. On 29th September, the Council, Claverhouse being among the number, issued a proclamation ordaining all officers of justice 'to punish with all rigour that our law will allow all such as will refuse this our last offer of mercy.' But this last offer of mercy was not applicable to persons apprehended before they applied for remission, nor yet to persons guilty of crimes other than resetting and intercommuning.

The last offer of mercy, 1683.

Largess of this kind was a royal invitation to come through the rows of carbines, to try the halter on, and discover how pleasant it was to escape through it by the skin of one's teeth, or confidingly to enter the oubliettes and the slave-ships for peace's sake. In further pursuance of these exterminating Acts, the Council, Claverhouse being of the number present, on 29th November 1683, gave justiciary powers of 'pit and gallows' to certain Border sheriffs, sheriff-deputes, stewards, and officers, including Captain John Dalyell and Lag, any two to form the bench. This was a commission to Claverhouse himself, then a depute-sheriff in Dumfries, Annandale, and Kirkcudbright.[4]

When Claverhouse took his seat in the Council on 22nd May he had definite views on religion and politics.[5] He was a thorough Jacobite,

Claverhouse a military high-priest.

[1] Aldis, *List*, 2409; Wodrow, iii. 475 note.
[2] *Hist.*, ii. 333.
[3] *Reg. Sec. Conc., Dec.*, 546, 547; *Reg. Sec. Conc., Acta*, 145; Wodrow, iii. 429, 430.
[4] *Decreta*, 584; *Acta*, 166; Wodrow, 333, 432, 370 note.
[5] *Decreta*, 501; *Acta*, 100; *Hist. Not.*, i. 441.

believing that Presbyterianism ill agreed with monarchy, that Episcopacy was the best antidote to dissent, and that he had an irresistible call to become the official cleanser of the infectious plague of Presbytery—a high priest of the vindictive order of Caiaphas. York promptly recognised the genius he was in search of under the iron skull and jack of Graham, and gave him the altar where he might use his sacrificial and redemptive blade. The newcomer was a potent acquisition to the board whereat sat Aberdeen, Queensberry, Perth, Linlithgow, Balcarres, Glencairn, Kintore, Livingstone, Archbishop Burnet, Bishop Paterson, Mackenzie, Castlehill, Dalyell, Drummond, and others.

It has been repeated *ad nauseam*, even by well-informed writers, that Claverhouse was merely the executive hand of the Lord Advocate, 'The Bluidy Mackenzie,' himself the official executant of laws presumably righteous and defensible. Claverhouse was now a legislator, and an assiduous attender of the meetings of the Council—his name appearing on the sederunts thirty-three times in 1683 from 22nd May, fifty-nine in 1684, and thirty-eight in 1685—'the killing times.' He was present when the worst forms of legislation were devised, and assisted in preparing them; looked on while torture proceeded; visited the prisons to select those fit for transportation; and sanctioned the use of the stigma and the cropping of ears of prisoners.[1]

Claverhouse now a Privy Councillor, 1683.

During Claverhouse's absence his comrades in arms were untiring in their hunt, terrorising the people and scooping in fines. The brutalities of Irving of Bonshaw and his drunken dragoons at Coltness were reported to the Government and amends were made. 'This Mr. Irvine, some months after in a drucken quarell at Lanrick, was stabbed to death on a dunghill by one of his own gange; a proper exit for such a bloodhound.'[2] Three prisoners of Meldrum accused him to the Council of improperly exacting fines, and on proof led, got their freedom, but Meldrum was not cashiered.[3]

Barbarities of Bonshaw and other officers.

One of the hardest cases was that of Dame Barbara Cunningham, or Lady Caldwell, relict of William Mure of Caldwell. Her nephew, Sir William Cunningham of Cunningham, chronicled her experiences.[4]

Sufferings of the Caldwell family.

[1] *Reg. Sec. Conc.*, *passim*; *Decreta*, 547; *Acta*, 484.
[2] Coltness *Collections*, 76: 10th April 1683.
[3] Wodrow, iii. 442: 18th April.
[4] *Wodrow MSS.*, xxxiii. 57.

Since her return in 1670 from Rotterdam, where she nursed her dying husband, outlawed since Pentland, she and her three daughters supported themselves in Glasgow by the work of their hands. When Dalyell got her husband's estate he also seized her marriage jointure, threw her out of Caldwell, and actually retained her private furniture.[1] The suspicion raised by an informer that a conventicle had been held in her home led to her apprehension, and her incarceration in Blackness Castle, along with her daughter Jean, in the month of May. In six months, Jean, a maid of twenty, was broken in health and was released. The mother, however, was kept a close prisoner—the cell is a miserable fog-swept hole—till her liberation in June 1686, being even refused the gratification of visiting her second daughter, Anne, who died in Linlithgow, but four miles distant. Lady Caldwell survived till the Revolution. The name of Caldwell is the first mentioned in the special Act of Parliament, rescinding the forfeitures of Caldwell, Kersland, and Veitch.[2]

John Nisbet hanged, 4th April 1683.

Major White, by his justiciary power, brought to the gallows in Kilmarnock, on 4th April, John Nisbet, younger of Glen in the parish of Loudoun, charged with the 1679 rebellion, disowning the curates, maintaining the Cameronian cult, and refusing to pray for the King. He joyfully acknowledged the truth of the indictment, and like a gallant soldier went to the scaffold to pray, to sing the latter half of the 16th Psalm, and to read the eighth chapter of Romans, before rejoicing that he was one of God's elect children, and sealing his testimony with his blood.[3] That same day James Lowrie, writer, Lanark, condemned on 21st March by the Justices, would have suffered in Edinburgh, had he not obtained a reprieve.[4]

John Wilson's dying testimony, May 1683.

One of the most interesting and instructive testimonies left by any of the later Covenanters, is that of John Wilson, preserved in *A Cloud of Witnesses*, and also recorded by Wodrow in the more reliable form given to him by the sons of the sufferer. It is the genuine revelation of the mind of an astute man. Wilson was one of seven prisoners brought

---

[1] Morrison, *Dict. Decisions*, 4685-9.
[2] *Act. Parl. Scot.*, ix. 164, 199; Anderson, *Ladies of Covenant*, 262-90. Jean married Col. John Erskine of Carnock.
[3] Wodrow, iii. 452; *Cloud*, 288, gives 14th for date; *Martyr Graves*, 131, 292.
[4] *Book of Adjournal*, 27th March 1683.

to the Justiciary bar on 4th May. He was a lawyer, son of the town clerk in Lanark, and in his own modest reckoning, a 'most timorous man.' Yet he had been a captain at Bothwell, and got his deserts by being condemned in absence on 1st March 1681. He had the characteristics of his professional tribe. His friend, Peden, very clever in eluding martyrdom, hit him hard when he declared that the martyrs, 'going off the stage in full sails ... if you saw them ... would fley [terrify] you out of your wits.' Laying his hand on the shoulder of the timorous scribe, Peden thus emboldened him: 'Encourage yourself in the Lord, and follow fast, John, for you'll win up yonder shortly, and get on all your bras [fine garments].'[1] Less than a year afterwards, 16th May, Wilson was in the Grassmarket halter, 'winning' up: the others took the Test and 'won' down. Probably on the principle that 'hawks never pyke out hawks' een,' Mackenzie and Sir William Paterson, when examining Wilson, took great pains to convince this backslider from their elastic order that he was a sinner against his wife and family, and a martyr by mistake. Wilson, whose acute replies embarrassed his interrogators, confessed that religion sharpened the mind, directed the affections, and rewarded the soul. They even forced a fellow-prisoner, M'Gilligen, into his cell; but that feeling preacher would not intrude into Wilson's soul. What is very noteworthy in his testimony is his appeal to the truth of the cause for which he suffered, and which, he contended, was publicly proved by the martyrdoms. 'I have read of some single ones dying for opinion (not truth), yet could I never read of a track of men such as has been in Scotland these twenty-two years, laying down their lives for naked opinion, so calmly, so stolidly and composedly, with so much peace and serenity.'[2]

On the scaffold with Wilson was David MacMillan, of whom very little is known, except that he must have been living an orderly life after he fled from Bothwell, since he was captured by Claverhouse in church, 'when retired to it for reading the scriptures.' MacMillan was one of seven prisoners tried on 4th May. His replies to the Council were of the usual indefinite, equivocating character, and implicated him as a sympathiser with the rebellion, Sharp's death, and refusal of the Test.[3]

David MacMillan.

[1] *Six Saints*, i. 57.
[2] *Cloud*, 301-19; Wodrow, iii. 457-62; *Book of Adjournal*, 4th May 1683.
[3] Wodrow, iii. 456; *Book of Adjournal*, 4th May 1683.

There was no surcease of the high ardour which demanded such Governmental treatment. Children caught the ecstasy and confirmed themselves in their faith by subscribing holy leagues, of which one signed by some maidens in the Pentland district is still to be read with interest.[1]

'A Covenant Transaction with the Lord, by a society of Young Children, who met together in a meeting in Pentland Town, in the time of Persecution, when there was no faithful minister in Scotland, anno 1683, ere that great burning and shining light, Mr. James Renwick, came an ordained minister from Holland.

'This is a covenant made between the Lord and us, with our whole hearts, and to give up ourselves freely to him, without reserve, body and soul, to be his children, and him to be our God and Father; if it please the holy Lord to send the Gospel to the land again. That we stand to this covenant which we have written between the Lord and us, as we shall answer at the great day, that we shall never break this covenant, which we have made between the Lord and us. That we shall stand to this covenant which we have made; and if not, it shall be a witness against us in the great day, when we shall stand between the Lord and his holy angels. O Lord give us real grace in our hearts to mind Zion's breaches, that is in such a low case this day; and make us to mourn with her; for thou hast said, "them that mourn with her in the time of her trouble, shall rejoice when she rejoiceth; when the Lord will come and bring back the captivity of Zion." When He shall deliver her out of her enemies' hands. When her King shall come and raise her from the dust, in spite of all her enemies that will oppose her, either devils or men. That thus they have banished her king Christ out of the land, yet He will arise and avenge his children's blood, at her enemies' hands, which cruel murderers have shed.'

Upon the back of this covenant was written as follows:—

'Them that will not stand to every article of this covenant, which we have made betwixt the Lord and us, that they shall not

---

[1] *A Collection of the Dying Testimonies*, etc., 188 (Kilmarnock, 1806).

go to the kirk to hear any of these soul-murdering curates, we will neither speak nor converse with them. Any that breaks this covenant they shall never come into our society. We shall declare before the Lord, that we have bound ourselves in covenant, to be covenanted to him all the days of our life, to be his children and Him our covenanted Father.

We subscribe with our hands these presents.

Beterick Uumperston,	Agnes Aitkin,
Janet Brown,	Margaret Galloway,
Helen Moutray,	Helen Straiton,
Marion Swan,	Helen Clark,
Janet Swan,	Margaret Brown,
Isobel Craig,	Janet Brown,
Martha Logan,	Marion M'Moren,

Christian Laurie.

Psal. viii. 2.— 'Out of the mouths of babes and sucklings hast thou ordained wisdom.'

This remarkable document is in all likelihood a youthful expression of devotion of a spontaneous character, certainly to be expected when those harrowing incidents, which have been recorded, were occupying the minds of men and women not yet brutalised and bereft of reason and sympathy.[1]

With Scotland no longer the peaceful home of contented citizens, and, after the prolonged and still imminent tract of persecution, become 'as insecure to them as a den of robbers'—so Hume described the situation—some leading Presbyterians revived a project for establishing a colony in Carolina in 1682. This escape from tyranny was suggested by the brilliant advocate, Lockhart, ten years before. Thirty-six noblemen and gentlemen—among others Callander, Haddington, Melville, Cardross, Yester, the two Cochranes of Ochiltree, the two Campbells of Cessnock, Crawford of Crawfordland, Stewart of Coltness, Baillie of

The projected Carolina colony, 1682.

---

[1] Beatrice Umpherston was probably a daughter of Charles, tenant in Pentland, then dead, whose widow married James Currie, and who personally suffered in prison for the Covenant. Beatrice, according to Dr. Hay Fleming, married Rev. John M'Neil and died in her ninetieth year: *Martyr Graves*, Pref. xxxv.; *Passages in Lives of Helen Alexander*, etc., 68, 69.

Jerviswood, Patrick Hume, Lockhart, and Gilmour—began negotiations with the patentees of the colony for the purchase of a settlement wherein they might live in the undisturbed enjoyment of political and religious liberty. This business brought them into contact with that party of discontented English Whigs, who were maturing a plot for the exclusion of the Papist James from the succession, and for the restoration of constitutional government. Communications also passed between them and Argyll and other exiled Covenanters in Holland. While negotiations were proceeding, the Rye House Plotters in England were discovered, Lord William Russell and Algernon Sydney sent to the scaffold, and other associates driven into exile. Baillie and the Campbells were apprehended in London and sent down to Scotland to be tried for complicity in this treasonable conspiracy.[1]

The Rye House Plot, 1683.

In Scotland extreme views had hitherto run in religious channels; in England it was otherwise. Formed in political grooves, they resulted in 1683 in the Rye House Plot, to seize the King and York on their return from Newmarket, and in a combination of Parliamentary Whigs for the purpose of coercing the King into summoning another Parliament. As a precaution, the dragoons of Claverhouse and other troops were sent to patrol the Borders. A greater trust was placed in the soldier: Claverhouse was one of a committee of three appointed to deal with the crisis and to frame a proclamation, issued on 4th July, offering a large reward for the capture of the Duke of Monmouth, Lord Gray, Sir Thomas Armstrong, Robert Fergusson—a preacher, Rumbold, and other conspirators.[2]

The Courts on circuit.

The circuit Court began its work at Stirling on 5th June 1683. The judges were Perth, Justice-General, Maitland, Justice-Clerk, and Lords Foulis, Forret, Lockhart, and Balfour, the Sheriffs also sitting with them. Mackenzie prosecuted. By command, Claverhouse and other selected officials, with their clerks, charge-sheets, Porteous rolls, and ledgers, ready to prove many a shameful charge against the innocent, were in attendance. In flocked the inhabitants of the shires of Stirling, Clackmannan, Kinross, Fife, and Perth. The procedure was of the simplest.

[1] Bishop G. Burnet was in touch with the plotters at this time, and recorded their movements: *Hist.* (Airy), ii. 333, 355, 361-3, 368, 397; Foxcroft, *Suppl.*, 108-31, 158; Wodrow, iii. 368, 369: *Fergusson the Plotter*, chap. x. 190-212.
[2] Wodrow, iii. 499 note; Terry, 141; *State Pap. Dom.* (Charles II.), 426.

All were judicially called to make public confession, and to take the Test. Refusal meant apprehension followed by demand for caution for compearance in Edinburgh when cited. Absentees, one hundred and eighty in number, were denounced and registered on the huge Fugitive Roll of 1683-4.[1]

The long arm of the law had at last reached the recesses of the disaffected country, so that, with the judges unanimous and Mackenzie 'doing wonders,' according to Claverhouse, the masses were cowed into compliance and few left to flee.[2] The pitiful case of William Bogue, or Boick, tenant of Auchinreoch, evidences the irreconcilable spirit which really actuated Claverhouse and Mackenzie in dealing with a culprit, whose very vacillation showed he was not worthy of the martyrdom the court conferred upon him.[3] Bogue was on the Porteous roll and came in and answered to his name. He produced a certificate signed by the clerk of Council, Paterson, but it omitted his Christian name. The judges suspected him of forgery and cross-questioned him as to signing the bond and other matters. With excessive caution, amounting to stupid obstinacy, he at first refused to depone, to declare the rebellion wrong, to acknowledge the death of Sharp to be murder, and to take the Test. Bench and bar were incensed and had him tried and found guilty of high treason. Then he softened, and developed Lauderdale's facility to take a cartload of oaths, an unexpected acquiescence which upset the calculations of the judges temporarily. The question arose whether article two of their instructions, authorising the desertion of a charge against a person willing to take the Test, was applicable in Bogue's case. Mackenzie advised negatively, holding that Bogue's chance was past. Bogue went so far as confess the justice of the sentence. The Lords, not unwilling to save Bogue, referred the matter to Chancellor Aberdeen and stayed the execution meantime.

At this stage Claverhouse, acting under the instigation of Mackenzie, at least with his connivance, meanly interposed to tighten the halter on the simpleton's neck. He wrote a long letter to Aberdeen, practically demanding the execution of the sentence on Bogue, who, he declared, 'would doe anything to saive his lyf: but nothing to be reconciled to

Bogue, an unworthy martyr.

Claverhouse demands Bogue's death.

---

[1] Cf. roll, Wodrow, iii. 13 note; Erskine, *Journal*, 2.
[2] *Hist. MSS. Com. Rep.*, xv. viii. 282.
[3] *Decisions*, i. 235: *Hist. Not.*, i. 443.

the goverment.' He argued that 'the King's Indemnity should not be forced on villains. All I can hear of inconvenience is, that it may terify those in his circumstances to come in. ... Above twenty have taken the Test since he was condemned. ... If this man should not be hanged, they would take advantage ... that we durst not venter on this.' Then with a bathos, quite in keeping with his heartless nature, he concludes his special pleading thus: 'I am as sorry to see a man day [die], even a whigue, as any of themselfs; but when one days justly for his owen faults, and may sawe a hondred to fall in the lyk, I have no scrupull.'[1] The Chancellor approved of the sentence and of the reasons for it furnished by the military high priest. The Lords carried Bogue with them to Glasgow to emphasise his vicarious sacrifice there, since 'it was thought the execution would be more terrible at Glasgow then heir, and he will succeid to him who wes so villainously resscewed.'

Before the court rose, news came that a prisoner had been rescued from a military escort of whom some had fallen in the fray. This did not give the judges pause. On the contrary it fired Claverhouse to write: 'This murder they have comitted gives us all neu vigeur.' Indeed justiciary work was exhilarating to him, and he confessed to Aberdeen: 'I am impatient to be at Glascou, when we will have neu mater.'[2] Not so Mackenzie, whose miserly soul could express itself thus: 'I shall not see on[e] doller in all this circuit.'[3]

Five guardsmen were escorting a prisoner, Alexander Smith, a Cambusnethan Covenanter who had fought at Bothwell, been captured and had escaped from jail in women's clothes, a feat he afterwards repeated at Dunnottar, when the cavalcade fell into an ambuscade. A cottage near 'a strait pass on the highway' at Inchbelly Bridge, near Kilsyth, afforded a sconce for seven bold men on foot, on 8th June. Shots were fired; David Murray, guardsman, fell dead beside a wounded comrade, and in the confusion agile Smith, covered by his armed rescuers, escaped over the moss. The Sheriff, the Duke of Hamilton, showed unusual alertness in dispatching search-parties. Next day two Lesmahagow men, John Wharry or MacQuarrie and James

Rescue at Inchbelly Bridge, 8th June 1683.

---

[1] Claverhouse to Aberdeen, Stirling, 9th June 1683: *Aberdeen Letters*, 121; *ibid.*, 115-23; Terry, 138, 139; *Hist. Not.*, i. 443; *Hist. MSS. Com. Rep.*, xv. viii. 281.

[2] *Aberdeen Letters*, 123.

[3] *Ibid.*, 120.

Smith, lurking unarmed in Stevinson Wood, were seized by Hamilton's retainers and brought before him. Tolerant though Hamilton was, he thought them uncivil and taciturn: 'the insolentest rogues ever I spoke to.'[1] He marched them off to their fate in Glasgow.

The Lords made an almost royal progress into Glasgow on the 12th June, welcomed by a huge concourse of apparently loyal gentry and citizens, many of whom convoyed them from the boundaries of Stirling. Next day, Bogue paid his penalty in the market-place.[2] The satisfied judges further informed the Chancellor: 'We have ordered the gallowes to stand, for the better instruction of the great numbers of rebells who are cited to appeir.'[3] The gallows, more than the wondrous eloquence of Mackenzie, was the most effective agent of conversion; and of the commons the court could write, 'All took the Test most cheirfully.' On the 13th June, the Advocate 'gave ane indytment to tuo ruffians,' so the judges designate Wharry and Smith, and before these men were tried they inform the Chancellor, 'and they are to dye to morrowe [14th].'[4] This was Jeddart justice with a vengeance! Wodrow had the testimony of persons present at their trial to the effect that no witnesses were produced against them.[5] The judges owned that they believed the men had fought at Bothwell, burned the Test at Lanark, and called the King a tyrant. It was enough to have been found near Inchbelly. They were sentenced to have their right hands cut off, to be hanged till dead, and their bodies to be hung in chains at Inchbelly Bridge. On the scaffold, on the 14th June, these young men displayed a marvellous courage, serenity, and ecstasy of soul. When Wharry was ordered to place his hand on the block, he laid down his head boldly. Major Balfour angrily told him that it was his hand that was demanded. Wharry cheerfully replied that he was willing to lay down hand, neck, all the members of his body for Christ's cause. When his hand fell, he lifted up the bleeding stump and called it 'the blood of the Covenants,' or, as Wodrow tells the story, 'this and other blood now shed will yet raise the burned Covenants.'[6]

Margin notes: Bogue hanged in Glasgow, 13th June. | The gallows an instrument of conversion. | Gallant deaths of Wharry and Smith.

[1] *Hist. MSS. Com. Rep.*, xv. viii. 282; *Observes*, 96.

[2] Erskine, *Journal*, 5.

[3] Bogue was buried in Campsie churchyard, where a tombstone records his fate, on June xiv: *Martyr Graves.*, 244.

[4] *Aberdeen Letters.*, 126. The letter is dated 13th June.

[5] Wodrow, iii. 484.

[6] Erskine, *Journal*, 5; Wodrow, iii. 485; *Cloud*, 281-7; *Observes*, 97. Wodrow gives

The last letters from these sufferers to their relatives are very touching and chaste expressions of pious men, who found themselves rooted and grounded in the faith. There is no mention of their trial, no recriminations, no malisons on King and judges, nothing but rhapsodies praising their Redeemer; both of them glorifying Christ, 'that ever He honoured the like of me with cords on my arms and stocks on my legs.' Said Wharry to his mother, 'O bless Him, for dealing so with me.'[1]

Claverhouse, an informer.

The court assiduously exhausted the large Porteous rolls, and the Justice-Clerk and Claverhouse showed such zeal and despotic assumption, that Hamilton confessed to Queensberry his grave alarm, not only at the trend of affairs, but at the fact that Claverhouse had become a mean informer against his class.[2] Sentences of forfeiture, demeaning, and death were recorded against many of the accused, whose indictments for participation in the rebellion were easily proved relevant by such witnesses as swore before such judges.[3]

The justices in Ayr.

The judges had no sanguinary cases at Ayr. Colonel John Burns, two preachers, and eight other typical rebels were summoned, and of these only two had the temerity to appear; and after all of them were sentenced to the degradation and death of traitors, the two prisoners, Robert Lockhart of Bankhead, and Andrew Brown of Duncanyeamer, were put into the custody of Claverhouse for safe delivery on Lammas Day.[4]

Renunciation of property.

Sir John Cochrane of Ochiltree and his son, John of Waterside, were classed among the rebels on the Porteous roll. The father repudiated the suspicion and wrote the Chancellor boasting of his activity against the Cameronians; the son sought safety on the Continent. Those persons who compeared to take the Test had first to renounce all they possessed in favour of the King before they were allowed to subscribe it. One of these was William Torbran, formerly Provost of Stranraer, who just escaped the halter by his timeous confession of being guilty of 'having been att a councill, wherein it was resolved the whole toune should

---

date of execution, 13th; *Cloud*, 11th; tombstone near Inchbelly Bridge, 13th: *Martyr Graves*, 239. The *Cloud* says they were carted away half dead.

[1] Wharry's Bible was in the Dick Museum, Kilmarnock.
[2] *Hist. MSS. Com. Rep.*, xv. viii. 253.
[3] Wodrow gives instances pitiable enough, iii. 485-9.
[4] Wodrow, iii. 490.

goe out to the rebellion.' He renounced his estate, and on his knees craved the royal pardon. He was given a safe-conduct home under Claverhouse, of whose tender mercies in past years he had no pleasant recollections. He also found it necessary, a ruined man, to seek a refuge abroad.[1] These renunciations, nominally enriching the Crown, actually aggrandised the officials, from the highest functionary to the lowest mercenary, who came in for some picking in the business of devolution. The Lords of Justiciary gave much credit to the eloquent Lord Advocate for the undoubted success of their new netting policy, but Bogue's high gibbet in the market-place of Glasgow was the most potent preacher of conversion in the west.

While the itinerant court had no sanguinary cases at Dumfries and Roxburgh, where they next sat, they returned to Edinburgh for their final labours, followed by several companies of Border lairds and other heritors, some prisoners, others summoned, whose cases were for reset and converse with rebels—in many instances mere inadvertencies—to be taken up in the Capital.[2] Scores of these influential gentlemen were detained ten days in the pestilential prisons until their bail-bonds were adjusted, and many were immured for long periods, as for example that much-mulcted laird, Sir William Scott of Harden. *Justices in Dumfries and Roxburgh.*

Several serious cases demanded the attention of the Justiciary Court when it resumed its sitting in Edinburgh on the 12th July. Claverhouse was still in attendance, and sat that day in the Privy Council.[3] Since June, the authorities had in custody Andrew Guillan, an alleged murderer of Sharp, Alexander Gordon of Earlston, a plotter, and his associate, Edward Livingston or Atkin, a preaching drover. Guillan was a weaver in Balmerino. Since the day he ruefully witnessed the tragedy on Magus Moor, he had been a fugitive in Angus and Lothian, and a Society-man acquainted with devotees like Helen Alexander. While resident in Cockpen he did not attend Wood's Sabbath ministrations, and was suspect and recalcitrant. He was uncommunicative, refused to drink the King's health, and was obstinate to the curate, who had him haled off to Dalkeith and Edinburgh prisons. Before the Council he appeared to be an obtuse, 'silly fellou,' and confessed being *The Justiciary Court in Edinburgh, 12th July 1683.*

---

[1] *Ibid.* 491: *Aberdeen Letters*, 129.

[2] Wodrow, iii. 491, 492.

[3] *Book of Adjournal*; *Reg. Sec. Conc.*, Dec., 516.

present with 'eight mor' at the assassination. Mackenzie wormed out this damning fact by cunningly expatiating on the horror of killing a suppliant at prayer, an assertion which made the veracious simpleton exclaim, 'O dreadful! he would not pray one word for all that could be said to him.'[1]

Trial and doom of Andrew Guillan.

At the trial his alleged confession, a fabricated document declaring he could not write—Wodrow asserts he could write—was presented to the court. The jury had no alternative to a verdict of guilty. Guillan was sentenced to die next day (13th), to have both hands lopped off, then to be hanged, to have his head cut off, and, with one hand, to be publicly set up on the Netherbow, the other hand set up on Cupar Tolbooth, and to have his body carried to Magus Moor and there hung in chains on a high pole.[2] In his dying testimony, to be found in *A Cloud of Witnesses*, Guillan takes up the same position as Claverhouse, who considered himself a cleanser, and therefore a justifiable manslayer, 'bound, I say, to meet him [Sharp] by the way.' He maintained that it was only 'justice that was executed on that Judas that sold the Kirk of Scotland ... and no other having appeared for God at that day but those who took away his life; therefore I was bound to join with them in defending the true religion.'[3] In the brutal finish on 13th July,

Heroic exit of Guillan.

Guillan made the exit of a heroic martyr. After the bungling hangman had hashed off his hand, the sufferer held up the oft-chopped stump and unconcernedly exclaimed: 'My blessed Lord sealed my salvation with His blood, and I am honoured this day to seal His truth with my blood.' This kind of demise was what Fountainhall designated dying 'hardened and insensible of any guilt.'[4]

The judges on the 12th July also sentenced to the gallows on the 20th Edward Atkin, 'a ranke Cameronian,' guilty of intercommuning with

---

[1] *Drumlanrig MSS.*, ii. 118; Wodrow, iii. 463.

[2] *Book of Adjournal*, 12th July 1683.

[3] *Cloud*, 276; Hay Fleming, *Guide to St. Andrews*, 121. Friends who removed the body and buried it in the wood at Claremont Farm were sentenced to banishment in May 1684: *Martyr Graves*, 194, 195, citing *Privy Counc. Reg.*, 27th May 1684; *Reg. Sec. Conc.*, *Acta*, 357 (*Decreta*, 742), Claverhouse present.

[4] Lauder in *Observes*, 96, and *Hist. Not.*, i. 447, dates death on 13th July; Erskine's *Journal* also gives 13th; 20th, given as a correction in the last edition of *A Cloud*, etc., is incorrect.

the habit and repute rebel, Gordon of Earlston.[1] The Council reprieved Atkin till the 3rd of August.[2]

Since February 1680, Alexander Gordon of Earlston, alias Pringill, had been at the horn, a demeaned traitor. He threw in his lot with the United Societies of the True Presbyterian Church of Scotland, and at a convention held at Priesthill, on 15th March 1682, he and John Nisbet were commissioned to go to foreign nations in order to 'represent their low case to the reformed churches there.'[3] He had gone, returned, and was on his way back with further dispatches, when he and his body-servant, Atkin, an alleged preacher, were apprehended at Newcastle, on 9th June, on the eve of his ship sailing for Holland. The 'papers of consequence,' which Earlston dropped into the sea, were fished out and confirmed the suspicions of the mayor regarding the suspects. Their tenor could not be misinterpreted—'After they have dispatched the Old Cotin Stufe, they uil then think of what new commodetys will be best.' Old Cotton Stuff—C. S.—was a designation of the King, as appropriate as it was comical. Here was inkling of a plot. The prisoners were hurried off to London. The King ordered their examination in Scotland.[4] For the first time the Government seemed to realise that the Cameronians held 'meitings who keep life in their shizme.' In Edinburgh nothing was disclosed by the examination of Earlston, who asserted that his papers were harmless church and business documents.[5] The Council distrusted the apparent ingenuousness of Earlston, and resolved on having him tortured, which was an illegal act in the case of a man already condemned. Authority from the King was craved, and as the Lord Advocate, Mackenzie, was at Court, and, on being consulted, was of opinion that torture to expiscate new matter was legal, the necessary order was sent to the examiners. To influence and make Earlston a little more communicative his execution was announced for the 28th September. Several reprieves were granted to him. On

Gordon of Earlston apprehended.

Examination of Earlston.

---

[1] Erskine, *Journal*, 9; *Book of Adjournal*, 12th July; *Decisions*, i. 236; Wodrow, iii. 463; *Hist. Not.*, i. 447, 454.

[2] 19th July; *Reg. Sec. Conc., Dec.*, 519, Claverhouse present. Aitken, or Atkin, was with Dick among the happy number who in September broke prison and escaped the gallows.

[3] *Faithful Contendings*, 18.

[4] *Aberdeen Letters*, 134, 135; *Drumlanrig MSS.*, ii. 113, 117.

[5] Wodrow, iii. 470-2.

the 25th September the inquisitors sat, and into their presence were brought Earlston, the hangman, and the boots, with the desired result that the accused promised to give the fullest assistance in interpreting his papers. He had previously accused General Dalyell, Drummond, and others, not without being suspected of having been suborned by intriguers at home; and when his examination produced no startling revelations the councillors were not satisfied. Fresh instructions arrived ordering torture. News of this intention unnerved Earlston.

Earlston in the boots, 23rd November 1683.

On the 23rd November the Council met—Claverhouse among the number—to put Earlston in the boots. With difficulty brought to the torture-chamber, Earlston, on being ordered to the boots, rose in fury, 'roared out like a bull,' and, being in his prime, like a shaggy Galloway, tossed macers and soldiers about the chamber to the dismay of his tormentors. The councillors imagined that he was shamming, but four physicians certified that the trouble of the distracted Covenanter was *alienatio mentis, furore latente laborans.*[1] They recommended for him the fresh air of the Castle Rock, and there he was sent and kept till April, when he was brought down to the foul Tolbooth again. He petitioned for the benefit of 'the air of the rock.' The Council gratified him with a fortnight's stay on the Bass Rock in August.[2] On his return to the

Earlston in several prisons.

Tolbooth he made a futile attempt to escape, for which he was loaded with irons. In these he was transmitted to the Castle of Blackness in September, where again he petitioned for air and to be relieved of his irons. In that damp fortress he lay till January 1689, when he was liberated before Donald Ker of Kersland, the leader of a rabbling party, could demand his release from a not inconsiderate governor.[3] Earlston

---

[1] [Latin: out of his mind, beset with latent madness.] *Reg. Sec. Conc., Acta,* 164; Erskine, *Journal,* 23; *Hist. Not.,* ii. 463, 465, 555; *Decisions,* i. 238, 240, 300, etc.; Wodrow, iii. 472; *Drumlanrig MSS.,* ii. 136; *State Papers* (Charles ii.), 1683, No. 427. Earlston was seventy-four years old in 1725 (?): P. Walker's *Peden, Biog. Presby.,* i. 117.

[2] *Book of Adjournal,* 21st August.

[3] *Six Saints,* ii. 146, 229; *Reg. Sec. Conc., Acta,* 486, 644. The Gordon estates of Earlston and Kenmure, forfeited to the Crown and disponed to Maine, Ogilthorpe, and others, were ultimately restored to the laird when the attainder was rescinded in 1690: *Act. Parl. Scot.,* viii. 823, 491, 586; ix. 165, 28, supp. 53. Gordon became the commander of the Kirkcudbright militia, commissioner of supply, and lived till after 1726.

always asseverated his loyalty to the Crown, and even prayed for his Majesty's health; but no excuses or defences availed with the suspicious authorities.

The case of Robert Hamilton, proprietor of Monkland, exhibits the persecuting spirit which completely possessed the despots on the Council. Hamilton was brought to the bar on the 24th and 27th July 1683, to answer to the charges of 'keeping a council of war,' of converse with the homicides of Magus Moor, and of encouragement of other rebels, was found guilty, condemned to death, and thereafter reprieved.[1]

Robert Hamilton condemned.

Crowds of suspects came into court to answer to their names on the Porteous rolls and to take the Test. Of these thirty-six gentlemen were sent to prison on the 24th, fifty-four on the 25th, twenty-two on the 30th July, while twenty-one who made no compearance were put to the horn and forfeited on the 25th July.[2] Indulged ministers were also summoned; and while some fled, others were fined or imprisoned, and many were never tried at all. So numerous were the cases that new commissions were granted to military and magistracy to force all to take the Test. Apprehensions were often cruelly effected.[3] The conforming clergy alone were pleased with the state of affairs. The prelates blessed the King and ordered the clergy to pray for him as head of the Church in all causes and to sing the doxology.[4] Papists were very little disturbed, Quakers were kept under surveillance, and inquiry made as to the proprietors of the sites of their meeting-houses.[5]

Effects of repressive measures.

One of the hardest cases at this epoch was that of Sir William Scott of Harden, who in 1662 was fined £18,000.[6] This knight refused to take the Test so long that he was thrown into prison in Edinburgh, charged along with Lady Scott with recusancy, absence from church, conventicling, and hearing in Harden a minister not licensed to preach in the parish. The public prosecutor himself, Mackenzie, was expecting and got the monster fine £46,000 Scots, modified to £1500 sterling, a job

Hard case of Scott of Harden.

---

[1] *Book of Adjournal*, 24, 27th July 1683; Wodrow, iii. 464, 465; his forfeiture approved by Parliament in 1685: *Act. Parl. Scot.*, viii. 472; restored in 1690: *Act. Parl. Scot.*, ix. 166, 228.

[2] Wodrow, iii. 465-8, gives names.

[3] *Ibid.*, iii. 428, 447.

[4] *Hist. Not.*, i. 456.

[5] *Privy Counc. Rec.*, 1st February.

[6] *Act. Parl. Scot.*, vii. 422.

which the Duke of York concurred in on the principle, 'ue most make the best of him ... for he is a good tool if rightly used at any time'; and, he being 'bred at Duke Lauderdale's scool,' sold his conscience dearly.[1] The septuagenarian laird lay long in prison, and got out on giving a bond, which was forfeited when later, on being summoned, he failed to compear—an offence which made him liable to another exorbitant fine.[2] The gallant sufferer had the satisfaction of living long after the Revolution Settlement, and of obtaining from Parliament a decree restoring the fine exacted on account of his wife's religious irregularities. His son William, the younger, answered to his citation in 1685, and was one of a party indicted for high treason.[3]

An almost incredible statement of Wodrow substantiated.

The prisons were filled to overflowing by sufferers, gentle and simple without distinction, to whom the prospect of transportation was the only relief which came to mitigate the brutality of their treatment. The most extraordinary and almost incredible statement of Wodrow, that the authorities deliberately deserted 'a great many processes for sodomy, adultery, murder, theft,' etc., to permit the Council and Lords of Justiciary to take up the more remunerative cases of gentlemen and heritors, for whom there was no accommodation in the prisons, is true.[4] A reference to the *Book of Adjournal* shows that, on 12th November 1683, twenty-one such criminal charges were departed from. The godly were stuffed into noisome cells; the vilest felons were emancipated in order to lurk around like ghouls and commit those crimes for which there was no cause traceable by the law officials, at least, beyond the Covenant.[5]

Blockhouses for Claverhouse.

There was a sullen show of peace. Claverhouse knew it was counterfeit, and proved it to Generalissimo Dalyell, before insisting, 12th September, that watch-towers should be established at Dumfries, Caitloch in Glencairn, Locherben, near Queensberry—the moorland home of the Harknesses who ambuscaded in Enterkin—Earlston in Glenkens, Machrimore in Minnigaff, and Ballagan Tower. It mattered

---

[1] Drummond to Queensberry, 20th October 1683: *Drumlanrig MSS.*, ii. 156; Wodrow, iii. 447; *Hist. Not.*, ii. 462.

[2] Wodrow, ii. 41, 137, 147.

[3] *Act. Parl. Scot.*, viii. 32*a*; ix. 357.

[4] Wodrow, iii. 473; *Book of Adjournal*.

[5] Claverhouse was present in Privy Council on the 3rd, 5th, 9th, and 14th November 1683, supporting this iniquitous procedure: *Reg. Sec. Conc., Acta*, 155, 157, 159; *Decreta*, 568.

not to Claverhouse, who saw the wife of Fergusson of Caitloch, with her children, wandering off to seek a home in Holland and to die there: it was his business as cleanser to purify the stream of Scots life at its well-eyes. He kept an eye upon Ballagan, a peel two miles from Queensberry's growing towers of Drumlanrig, where dissent had defiant devotees and willing martyrs.[1] Chased from their homes, many refusers of the royal clemency perished in the wilds, it being a long winter of frost and snow.[2] The objection of Chancellor Aberdeen to the punishing of the heads of families for the delinquencies of their dependants—a hardship less grievous than the taking children as hostages for their parents, as approved of by the King—led to his being suspected of weakness in his fealty and to his ultimate displacement. Public life was rotten to the core, and every man's hand was turned against his neighbour.

On 8th November, the Duke of Hamilton was prosecuted for not dispersing a field conventicle at Shotts in his jurisdiction, which, according to his statement, he did not hear of till fourteen days after the meeting. He was assoilzied. *Prosecution of Hamilton.*

The escape, on 16th September, of twenty-five prisoners, two of them being Covenanters under sentence of death, created a commotion in Edinburgh. They sawed through the iron bars of the Canongate Tolbooth. The convicts were John Dick, a graduate, a student of theology, son of David Dick, an Edinburgh solicitor; and George Lapsley, miller in Linlithgow. They were staunch followers of Welsh, in politics Monarchists, and in practice positive opponents of Episcopacy and Erastianism. They had fought at Bothwell Bridge, where Lapsley was wounded. Lapsley had lain in prison since 1681, when he just escaped the gallows.[3] *Escape of prisoners.*

Dick's plain dealing with the authorities, who examined him previous to his trial on 4th September, so incriminated him that sentence of death was the complement of his admissions.[4] He designated the executions of the Covenanters 'murders.' Next spring, Dick was recaptured

[1] The site of this home of a family called Hunter—a green moot-hill—is still visible.

[2] Chambers, *Annals*, ii. 454.

[3] Cf. *antea* pp. 348-9; *Cloud*, 398-400; Wodrow, iii. 445; iv. 58-61.

[4] *Book of Adjournal*, 4th September 1683; *ibid*.. Trial and doom, 4th March 1684.

The valiant
ending of
John Dick,
5th March
1684.

and brought to the scaffold on 5th March 1684; Lapsley escaped to London. Dick's composure at execution was phenomenal. To him it was simply going home with joy. Young Erskine of Carnock accompanied him from prison to the Grassmarket. There he was ecstatic, waiting for the potsherd to break and let his soul rise into glory. He sang the 2nd Psalm, and read the ninth chapter of Ezekiel. He looked down, and Erskine recorded, 'I got a smile from him.' Referring to the sacrifice of Isaac, and '"Now," said he, pointing to the gallows, "here is the altar," and to the tow, "here is the fire, and I give myself a willing and a cheerful sacrifice."' His body was first borne to the Magdalen Chapel.[1] He left for publication *A Testimony to the Doctrine, Worship, etc., of the Church of Scotland*, etc., in which he refers to 'that bloodthirsty wretch, Claverhouse,' of whose future on the day of judgment he inquires: 'Is it possible the pitiful thing can think to secure himself by the fleetness of his horse?'—the loss of which he lamented more than his fallen men at Drumclog.

The advent
of James
Renwick in
September
1683.

If the breaking of the Tolbooth was the cause of a great sensation, a greater was the advent in September of James Renwick, who had returned from his studies abroad to lift the banner of the Covenant which fell in blood at Ayrsmoss. The times were exciting. The Rye House plotters were now occupying the attention of the Privy Council, who appointed a small committee, Claverhouse being one, to ferret out the conspiracy, in which Sir John Cochrane was suspected to be implicated. Claverhouse was invalided in October, but he attended eleven meetings of the Council in November, and four in December, thus safeguarding the interests of his patron York.[2] The King expressed his sense of thankfulness for the assiduity of the Scots councillors by appointing in December seven great officers of state—Aberdeen, Queensberry, Perth, Atholl, Lundin, Tarbat, Mackenzie (Advocate), and the Secretary when in Scotland—with full power to manage the national affairs.[3]

Close of the
blood-stained
year 1683.

The Privy Council brought the bloodstained year to a fitting close by remitting to the judges for dismissal to the hangman three unfortunates: John Whitelaw in Stand, New Monkland, Arthur Bruce in

---

[1] Erskine, *Journal*, 44; *Six Saints*, 334; ii. 188; *Hist. Not.*, ii. 505.
[2] *Reg. Sec. Conc., Acta*, 155-64; *Decreta*, 568-84.
[3] Napier, ii. 381 note.

Dalserf, and John Cochran, shoemaker in Lesmahagow. Unsatisfactory were their answers to the stereotyped charge—having arms at Drumclog and Bothwell, approving of the Primate's death, refusing to say 'God save the King,' without reservations. There was unanimity in their aversion to Episcopacy, Popery, the Test, and in their cheerful justification of the unregretted rising. Cochran, leaving behind him a wife and six children, could say of his prison and his irons: 'That was no discouragement to me; for when the storm blew hardest, the smiles of my Lord were at the sweetest. It is a matter of rejoicing unto me, to think how my Lord hath passed by many a tall cedar, and hath laid His love upon a poor bramble-bush, the like of me.' All died in peace—the only peace in troubled Scotland![1]

---

[1] 30th November 1683; *Hist. Not.*, i. 406; Wodrow, iii. 474; *Cloud*, 279.

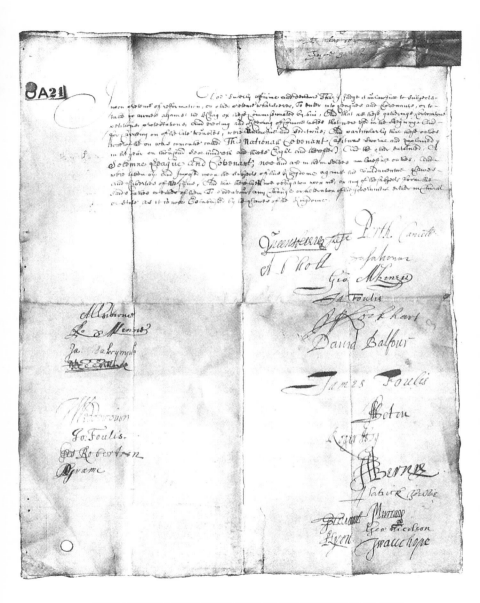

DECLARATION IN 1685 THAT THE COVENANTS WERE ILLEGAL

CHAPTER TWENTY-NINE

THE ADVENT OF RENWICK: CLAVERHOUSE AND THE KILLING TIMES

D URING these dismal days ubiquitous Peden, mysterious as 'Prester John,' fleeting as a phantom, lurked betimes in Ireland, stirring up the faithful fugitives there. Prospect-glass in hand, the seer was wont to stand on the shore longingly scanning the coastline of 'the bloody land,' as he designated Scotland. Ill at ease and wishful to return, he sometimes prayed, anon confessed, 'The devil and I puddles and rides time about upon [each] Other.' In one of his raptures he exclaimed: 'What comes of the poor, young, kindly, honest lad, Renwick (that shames us all, staying and holding up his fainting mother's [the Church] head, now when of all the children she has brought forth, there's none will avowedly take her by the hand), and the poor, cold, hungry lads upon the hills?'[1] Thus was it easy for this wary and self-conscious preacher, wandering about in a mask, to lament and criticise the cowardice of his fellows less proficient in the art of concealment. Peden here referred to a youth long known to the Societies, of which he was the pride and hope, whose repute for boldness was enhanced by his recent advent as the successor to Cameron in raising the banner of the Covenant again. In the beginning of September 1683, Renwick arrived in Scotland from Holland, where he had completed his theological studies.

James Renwick, Rannie, or Rennie, was born to Andrew Renwick, a humble weaver, and Elizabeth Corson, his wife, who resided at Knees

Ubiquitous Peden, 1626-1686.

James Renwick, 1662-1688.

[1] *Six Saints,* i. 69.

Cottage, Moniaive, in the parish of Glencairn, Dumfriesshire.[1] His birth, on 15th February 1662, was the long-expected answer to prayer made by a mother inconsolable for the loss of all her children. Consequently he was dedicated to the service of God. His precocity early exhibited itself and made the mother glad when she saw her babe of two years 'aiming at prayer, even in the cradle and about it,' and reading the Bible when only six years of age.[2]

Glencairn in 1662.

It was fitting that the Vale of Cairn, doorway to wild Galloway, home of sufferers, arena of martyrdoms, whose every hearth has its story of persecution, should give birth to one who, as much as any other, embodied the genius of the Covenant. The site of his birth had been forfeited for the cause of the Covenant by William Fergusson of Craigdarroch and Caitloch. Across the glen he could see Barndennoch, where outed Blackadder and his lively family found temporary shelter; at the village school he might play with the Blackadder boys. He was old enough to remember Barscob, Corsock, and other heroes of Rullion Green, escorting Turner out of Glencairn Kirk and past his father's door, then returning beaten to skulk in the glens. Probably he accompanied his parents when they attended the services of vagrant Semple. He lost the guidance of his pious father in 1676. In his student days he must have known intimately the braves from Glencairn who fought at Bothwell Bridge. He was nurtured in scenes fitted to inspire any youth with pious and patriotic sentiments.

Renwick at first loyal.

Friends assisted him to pursue his studies in the College of Edinburgh; and he was one of twenty-six students who, in the summer of 1681, publicly took their degrees. Contrary to what his biographer, Shields, states, Renwick subscribed the oath 'in the purity and truth of the gospel, in loyalty and obedience to his royal Majesty (in the Lord).'[3] Immediately afterwards we find him an 'indweller in Lanark,' who accepted the royal indemnity and took the bond, 'being desyrouse to be admitted burges of the said burgh.'[4] Soon he manifested his preference for, and sympathy with, the persecuted nonconformists. Seven weeks

---

[1] An old 'gean' tree marks the site of the cottage.

[2] *Biog. Presby.*, ii.; Shields, *Life of Renwick*, 7, 8.

[3] *Record of the Laureations from 1589 till 1809.* He appears to have written 'Renwick' over 'Rennie' or 'Rannie,' a name he was well known by.

[4] *Extracts from Lanark Records*, 9th June 1681, p. 205.

afterwards, the sight of dying Cargill 'so commoved' Renwick that his last doubt disappeared, and his revulsion against the horrid despotism cruelly exhibited that day was followed by the stern resolve of the patriot to fight and die for liberty. The hashing of the five men at the Gallowlee in October, and his brave exploit in removing their remains, stiffened his resolution.[1] He and other devotees met in secret Societies in order to counsel and comfort each other. There he used to refresh them with the testimonies of sufferers which he collected and recorded. The desire of these pious Societies to correspond with each other, and to be amalgamated in a General Meeting, or Correspondence, led to a convention of these scattered witnesses to defections, hillmen, wanderers, remnant, Society-people at the Logan House, Lesmahagow, on 15th December 1681.[2] Approving of the Lanark Declaration, except some of its ill-advised phraseology, Renwick accompanied the insurgents who published that paper, and with forehammers broke up the Cross of Lanark on 12th January 1682. On 19th May 1682, as he stood watching the execution of Robert Gray for calling the King a tyrant, he had a premonition of his own execution.[3]

The Societies of nonconformists.

Up till 12th October 1682, he attended all the meetings of the Societies and proved to be 'so soon [sound] in both the matter and the manner' of their proceedings, that he was accredited to the exiles in Holland as a student of parts, and a worthy candidate for the pastoral office. After a few months' study, along with other young men sent out by the Societies, at the University of Groningen, Renwick, after a prolonged examination in Latin, Greek, Hebrew, and Theology, obtained ordination from the 'classis' of Groningen, after the Presbyterian form, on 10th May 1683 (O.S.). He grew impatient to be back, to testify, and die for Christ. As 'James Bruce' he appeared in Dublin on 24th August 1683, and soon thereafter he was in Edinburgh.[4]

Renwick studies in Holland, 1682-1683.

On 3rd October, the General Meeting was held at Darmead, Lanarkshire, and at it Renwick compeared, handed in his Presbyterial certificates and testimony or confession of his principles and opinions on the controversies of the time, after which he received a call to be minister

Renwick's call.

---

[1] Cf. *antea* pp. 349.
[2] *Faithful Contendings*, 9; cf. Appendix iii.
[3] Wodrow, iii. 452.
[4] Carslaw, *Life and Letters of Renwick*, 33-65.

to the Remnant. A great multitude assembled at the same place on 23rd November, to hear his first public lecture and sermon in the fields, when he discoursed on Cargill's last theme—'Comfort ye, comfort ye, my people,' and on Isaiah xxvi. 20. Thus began his vagabond ministry, in which one of his most important coadjutors was a fleet fresh horse standing bridled at his hand. All the righteous did not rally to his flag. The superfine splitters of hairs, who paid customs at boats and bridges but refused to pay them at ports and markets, did not own him. Other Puritans withdrew on the ground that he was ordained by 'those who had the organs,' an evident slander. Still others distrusted him, attributing his hairbreadth escapes to his being a spy and a Jesuit priest.[1]

Results of Renwick's fugitive ministry. Nevertheless, after the return of Renwick, there was a recrudescence of disaffection and of conventicles. Hundreds of admirers brought their children to him for baptism. News of his activity reached London and induced York to compliment Queensberry thus: 'If every body would bestur themselvs and be as diligent as you, it would not be so easi for them to meett.'[2] This was a palpable hit at Hamilton, within whose jurisdiction the conventicles were held. Need we wonder that this fearless and cultured evangelical preacher at once became a favourite spiritual guide to the wandering ers of Knoxian Presbytery? He was endowed with a rapturous poetic spirit, like Rutherford's, which a refined pure mind and clear judgment so restrained that he was never led into excess of zeal either in writing or in action. The letters of this simple peasant, for grace, elegance of diction and delicacy of feeling, are comparable with the best productions of his age, and afford a striking contrast to the miserable, vulgar, ill-spelled compositions of the fashionable hacksters who hunted the rebels to death. His hereditary *Renwick's fearlessness.* instincts of piety and morality became his native source of strength when he found and acknowledged Christ for himself, and, standing on the Rock of Salvation, exclaimed: 'Let us be lions in God's cause and lambs in our own!' He fully realised the responsibility of his office and the end of his mission: 'O to be framed for the work of the day! … If I give the ark a wrong touch, it will be through blindness, not through biassedness.' The shadow of his cross preceded him in all his

---

[1] *Faithful Contendings,* 114; *Passages in Lives of Helen Alexander,* etc., 11; *A Vindication of the Presbyterians in Scotland,* 17.

[2] *Hist. MSS. Com. Rep.,* xv. viii. 198; XI. vi. 166.

weary pilgrimage, forcing him to say: 'I am daily looking out either to be presently killed ... or else dragged into a prison or scaffold.' He had no fear. His testimony to the Reformed Church and Faith, he vowed, he would seal with his blood. Renwick had not that 'body of the flesh' whose possession Captain Paton lamented, being but a fragile, bodiless soul, more a phantom than a suffering man carried about by others. It was natural to him thus to express his yearnings, 'Death to me is as a bed to the weary,' and to offer himself a reconciling sacrifice: 'If my blood were a means to procure that end I would willingly offer it.' Influenced by these principles and aspirations, this pure herald of the Cross, and champion of the Presbyterian Church of Scotland, could not countenance the workers of iniquity, regal, lay, or ministerial.[1]

The new Scots Cabinet took York's rebuke to heart and soon incited loyalists and rebels alike. Their drag-net searched every pool. Even indulged ministers who had exceeded the terms of their licence were proceeded against,—Campbell in Sorn, Veitch in Mauchline, and Shaw in Newmilns losing their licences. They got the option of exile or finding caution. Others were sent to jail. To extinguish any trace of clemency, magistrates and heritors were again commanded to give in a list of their decreets with count and reckoning of the fines paid or unpaid.[2] To reach the peasantry, tradesfolk, and others under the standing of heritors—the class from which the Cameronians were largely recruited—another plan was devised. On 3rd January 1684, a commission giving full justiciary power was granted, and to continue till recalled, to the Provost of Glasgow, Bailie of Regality, Sheriff-Depute of Lanark, Sir James Turner, and Lieutenant-Colonel Winram, for the shires of Lanark and Dumbarton, and to James Alexander, James Johnston of Westerhall, Thomas Lidderdale of Isle, David Graham, brother to Claverhouse, Andrew Bruce of Abbotshall, Captain Strachan, and Cornet William Graham, for Dumfriesshire, Kirkcudbrightshire, and Wigtownshire—three to form a bench of judges.[3] Theirs

A new drag-net for Covenanters.

Military judges and their penalties.

---

[1] Carslaw, *Life and Letters of Renwick*, passim.

[2] Wodrow, iv. 2, 37, 38.

[3] Claverhouse attended twelve meetings of Privy Council in January 1684, being present on 2nd and 3rd January. In Dalgarno churchyard, two miles from Thornhill, are the gravestones of Harkness, Hoatsons, and other families implicated in the rescue: cf. Appendix.

it was to 'pass sentence, and see justice done accordingly, conform to law.'[1] In February a similar commission was granted for the shires of Ayr and Renfrew, Lord Ross being associated with Turner, Winram, and others, of whom five were a quorum. Meldrum got a special commission for Lanarkshire. This was bringing justice by court-martial to men's doors. The in-calling of the fines led to unexpected results, on the one hand, by giving Queensberry an opportunity of pulling up Claverhouse, who had never explained his intromissions with the fines, and, on the other, by constraining Aberdeen to express views of clemency in regard to husbands fined for intractable wives. The cases of Harden and of others were referred to the King, who indicated his willingness to remit the fines of loyal husbands willing to deliver up to justice their obstinate spouses.[2]

Another trio hanged, 22nd February 1684.

On 11th February, the Lords of Justiciary tried for treason and condemned three men, namely, George Martin, a notary, formerly the teacher and reader in Dailly, John Kerr, wright in Hounam, and James Muir, in Cessford-boat. Martin had lain prisoner for over four years. Their examination afforded the Crown sufficient evidence to warrant a conviction, inasmuch as all three refused to say 'God save the King,' in the prelatic sense of acknowledging the absolute authority of the King in all causes. The trio suffered on the 22nd February.[3]

Trial of slayers of Barscob, March 1684.

In March the important trial of the slayers of Robert Maclellan of Barscob, Balmaclellan, took place in Edinburgh. In reference to this Mr. W. L. Mathieson makes the following most extraordinary and unwarrantable statement: 'The Cameronians, however, were unable to clothe the hideousness of this doctrine in the technicality of legal forms (*i.e.* executing murderous enemies of Covenanters); and they had done enough to make it impossible that their threat of cutting off all who attacked them, directly or indirectly, should be regarded as no more than a threat. The outcome of their tenets, and of the merciless persecution to which they were exposed, had lately been illustrated by several murderous assaults, the worst of which had occurred in the previous year, when Maclellan of Barscob, one of the Bothwell heritors, had

---

[1] Wodrow, iv. 6.

[2] *Ibid.*, 5.

[3] *Ibid.*, 57; Erskine, *Journal*, 36; *Cloud* (319-26) calls Kerr 'Gilry'; *Book of Adjournal*, 11th February.

been strangled in his own house, because he had procured his liberation by signing the bond of peace.'[1] So long as groundless accusations of this kind are made by a judicious writer, always unimpassioned and generally well informed, it will be impossible for trustful readers of history to arrive at accurate conclusions regarding the Covenanters. The story unfolded in the Justiciary Record is to this effect: Maclellan, Robert Grierson of Milnemarke and William, his brother, all Glenkens men, after attending the funeral of William Edgar's child, retired to Barbara Gordon's tavern to drink, then adjourned to that of William M'Ervail in the Clachan of Dalry to continue the entertainment. Barbara, who was then *enceinte*, wroth and disappointed, arrived and volleyed out most indecent language, especially against the wife of William Grierson. He retaliated with a blow which the delicate woman could ill stand, and gallant Barscob resented, the latter in turn striking Grierson. Grierson seized the laird by the hair. Noses bled. In the brawl Barscob fell in the fire and sustained fatal injuries. The prosecution was at the instance of Elizabeth Logan, widow of Barscob, and her brother-in-law, James Maclellan of Sundaywell, against the two Griersons and John Henrysone. The jury acquitted the prisoners, and found that Barscob was subject to epileptical fits, and had beaten the accused. Not one of the parties was on the Porteous roll, otherwise a different ending might have ensued.[2]

The homicide of Barscob, an affair of tavern brawlers, not of Covenanters.

Of the many atrocities perpetrated at this time no one can equal for cold-blooded infamy the attempt made to ruin and hang Sir Hugh Campbell, laird of Cessnock. This estimable baronet was of Lollard stock and his ancestors were friends of Alesius and other Reformers. His sympathies were with the Presbyterians. After Rullion Green he was sent to prison lest he might become involved in the rising; and thereafter, although he avoided all complicity with the disaffected, he was a suspect to the Crown officials. His mansion, Galston Tower, dominated the region where the stiffest Covenanters lurked, notwithstanding the fact that he chased them out of his barony and showed a good example by

The infamous Cessnock case.

---

[1] *Politics and Religion*, ii. 311. Professor H. M. B. Reid recounts a similar erroneous version in Maxwell's *Guide to the Stewartry of Kirkcudbright* (1902), Introd. 8.

[2] *Book of Adjournal*, 13th March 1684; *Hist. Not.*, ii. 508; cf. Widow Maclellan's Petition to Privy Council, 21st February 1684: *Reg. Sec. Conc., Dec.*, 637; *Acta*, 255; *Decisions*, i. 280.

attending Galston Church. On the strength of the boast of Lord Advo-cate Mackenzie to the King and the Duchess of Portsmouth that he could bring the guilt of treason home to Cessnock, his estate was promised to an illegitimate son of the King before the suspect was tried. A trial was arranged and began on 24th March. Mackenzie prosecuted. In order to prejudice the prisoner Sir George Lockhart was commanded to assist the prosecutor. Cessnock retained nine counsel, including Sir Patrick Hume and Sir John Lauder of Fountainhall. Perth was Justice-General. After prolonged debates on the relevancy of the indictment Mackenzie nar-rowed the charge to one particular, namely, that the accused had been guilty of inciting rebellion, inasmuch as he had spoken to fugitives from Bothwell Bridge and chid them for cowardice. The Crown relied on two suborned witnesses—Ingram and Crawfurd. When Ingram was put in the stand Cessnock adjured him: 'Take heed now what you are about to do, and damn not your own soul; for as I shall answer to God, I never saw you nor spoke to you before.' This appeal staggered Ingram, who resiled from his perjured recognition. The pressure of the court failed to induce the witness to remember anything. This unexpected *dénouement* made sympathisers with Cessnock clap their hands. Judges and prosecu-tor were furious and came into conflict with the jury, who refused to be browbeaten. The second perjurer also withdrew his incriminating tale.

Another scene ensued. The jury acquitted Cessnock, whose liberation was refused by the authorities until they received the King's orders. The witnesses were also sent to prison.[1]

On being liberated Sir Hugh and his son Sir George associated them-selves with other malcontents in London, which led to their apprehen-sion and to their being indicted by Parliament for accession to the con-spiracy against the King. They were offered an assurance of their lives on condition that they confessed their crimes and permitted forfeiture to pass. To the chagrin of the King's advisers the Cessnocks confessed. Parliament passed sentence of forfeiture on 13th June 1685. This Act was soon followed by the royal order for incarceration in the Bass. Sir Hugh did not long survive this nefarious treatment, and regained freedom to die in Edinburgh in September 1686.[2]

[1] Omond, i. 221; *Hist. Not.*, ii. 510-21; *Reg. Sec. Conc., Acta*, 367; Burnet, ii. 416; Wodrow, iv., *passim*; Fountainhall, *Decisions*, i. 286-92; *State Trials*, x. 919-88.
[2] *Drumlanrig MSS.*, i. (*Hist. MSS. Com. Rep.*, xv. viii.) 98, 127; ii. 84, 99; *Act. Parl.*

The Justiciary Commissioners in Glasgow—Winram, Fleming, Turner, Buchan, and Stirling—gave the usual indictment for treason to five men—John Richmond, younger of Knowe, Galston; James Winning, tailor, Glasgow; Archibald Stewart, a peasant lad from Lesmahagow; James Johnston, Cadder; and John Main, Old Monkland. The stereotyped charge of rebellion, converse with rebels, and reset brought out the unsatisfactory answers desiderated regarding Ayrsmoss, Bothwell Bridge, the royal supremacy, and the slaying of Sharp, so that only a verdict of death was possible. Two days afterwards (19th March) all five were hanged at Glasgow Cross and their bodies buried in the Cathedral Churchyard.[1] The scaffold made these sufferers rapturous. 'Welcome, gallows, for the interest of my sweet Lord,' cried Main; 'O if ye knew what I have met with since I came to prison … what matchless love for my sweet and lovely Lord, ye would long to be with Him and would count it nought to go through a sea of blood for Him,' said Richmond; Stewart testified: 'My soul blesseth the Lord that ever He made choice of me to suffer for His noble cause and interest. I am going to reap the fruit of my wounds in fetters, irons, and imprisonment for my lovely Lord.' These victims were clearly assured that it was not for selfish whims and political nostrums they were dying, but as witnesses for a persecuted Christ. Renwick, in one of his letters, proved that the result of these executions was the reverse of what the rulers expected, and that the fearless joy of these victims thrilled the people with a fresh enthusiasm which the exterminators dreaded. That fervour, he declared, reached the home of Winram himself and ravished his dying children, who implored their merciless father to quit his evil career in 'shedding the blood of the saints,' for which 'the Lord's hand was stretched forth against them.'[2]

James Nisbet came from Highside Farm, Darvel, to attend the funeral of his kinsman, John Richmond, and, being recognised by his own cousin, Lieutenant Nisbet, was apprehended. To a man who was already on the register of denounced rebels and fugitives, and was

Marginal notes:
Five men hanged in Glasgow.

Joy of victims on the scaffold.

Nisbet executed for sympathizing with Cameronianism

Scot., viii., App. 57, 69. The forfeiture was rescinded on 22nd July 1690: *ibid.*, lx. 207.

[1] Wodrow, iv. 62, 63; *Martyr Graves*, 124, 138, 139; *Cloud*, 326-57. The original tombstone stands in the chapter-house.

[2] Carslaw, *Letters of Renwick*, 99.

willing 'to set to my seal to the faithfulness of these two men's doctrines' (Cargill and Cameron), there was no chance of escape. He also disowned the authority of his judges. His explosive testimony wherein he abjures 'that monstrous beast,' the King, indicates that Nisbet was an invincible Cameronian whose supreme felicity was to write: 'Now I am brought hither this day, to lay down my life for the testimony of Jesus Christ, and for asserting Him to be Head and King in His own House … indeed I do it willingly, and not by constraint.' He was hanged at the Howgate Head, Glasgow, on 5th June 1684.[1]

Early in April the Lords of Justiciary considered the indictments of over sixty landed gentlemen, businessmen and tradesmen, including Sir John Pollok of Nether Pollok, Sir John Riddell of that Ilk, Sir William Scott of Harden, some of whom were in custody, and as they were prepared to 'thole an assize' the charge was deserted in the meantime.[2] More important processes were pending, criminal letters having been issued against the Earl of Loudoun, George, Lord Melville, Sir John Cochrane of Ochiltree, and his son John of Waterside, all of whom were charged, in their absence, with being concerned in the rebellion of 1679. The Parliament in 1685 dealt fully with them and others.[3]

At this time a notable rebel and gallant veteran of the Covenant, Captain John Paton of Meadowhead, lay waiting the judicial ending of a long warfare. His native Fenwick was too quiet for this lusty, passionate ploughboy, who was to qualify for the honours of Rullion Green and Bothwell Bridge on the bloody fields of the Continent, and at home on Marston Moor, Kilsyth, Mauchline, Leith, Dunbar, and Worcester. For a time he sheathed his thirsty, well-notched blade, and took up the eldership with William Guthrie, till his blood grew hot again and forced him into the ranks at Rullion Green, after which he was a fugitive. Cornet Lewis Lauder easily captured Paton in the house of Robert Howie in Floack, in Mearns, where the septuagenarian warrior was resting without even the defence of his sword. On his way to Edinburgh he met his old comrade of the Continental wars, General Dalyell, who, to his credit, exclaimed: 'John, I am both glad and sorry

---

[1] *Cloud* 364-73; *Martyr Graves*, 133, 141.

[2] *Book of Adjournal*, 1st, 2nd, 8th, 12th, and (John Paton) 16th April 1684; Wodrow, iv. 64.

[3] Wodrow, iv. 93, 94; *Act. Parl. Scot.*, viii. App. 32, etc.

to see you. If I had met you in the way before you came hither I should
have set you at liberty, but now it is too late. But be not afraid, I will
write to his Majesty for your life.' Dalyell kept his promise, and Bishop
Paterson was blamed for holding up the pardon till after Paton was
executed. The trial was held on 16th April. He was 'not clear to deny
Pentland or Bothwell,' he wrote. He would acknowledge what authority
was according to the Word of God. He was first sentenced to die in the
Grassmarket on 23rd April, but the Council had him reprieved till the
30th, and then till 9th May, when he suffered, leaving a wife and six
little children.

His recorded testimony reveals the fearless heart and the pious soul
of a Christian warrior and Reformer, willing to die as a protest 'against
the horrid usurpation of our Lord's prerogative and crown-right,' and
with an instinctive hatred of blood-shedding, in keeping with his statement on being examined, that he never heard the killing of officials
discussed.[1]

The prisons were now so crammed that the Council petitioned
the King and got consent to transport the less obnoxious prisoners,
styled 'penitents,' to the American plantations. Batches of the hapless
Covenanters were disponed to Walter and James Gibson, who sailed
the *Carolina Merchant* from Greenock in midsummer. They also took
passengers under false pretences, and even went the length of kidnap-
ping an innocent woman, who came to bid farewell to her kinsfolk.[2]
Both this woman, Elizabeth Linning, and John Mathieson of Rosehill,
Closeburn, survived to tell the sad tale of the brutal usage the convicts
received on their nineteen-weeks' voyage to Carolina.[3]

Claverhouse never rested until, in April, he had equipped and vict-
ualled the ring of blockhouses from Lesmahagow and Crawford-Muir
to Minnigaff and Kenmure, and he returned to Edinburgh to make

Marginal notes:
Chivalry of General Dalyell.

Paton's testimony.

Prisons crammed; emptied into the plantations.

---

[1] Wodrow, iv. 65; *Cloud*, 359; *Scots Worthies*, 479; *Martyr Graves*, 84, 114-21; Erskine,
Journal, 55, 60. Paton's sword and Bible are preserved in Lochgoin.

[2] *Acta*, 12th April; Wodrow, iv. 8, 9, 10, 11; Erskine, *Journal*, 5th July 1684.

[3] Mathieson was before the Council on 19th June 1684. He returned to his native
parish in time to hear Renwick, and died in 1709. Cf. 'Nathaniel; or the Dying
Testimony of John Mathieson,' etc., in *A Collection of the Dying Testimonies*, etc.
(Kilmarnock, 1806); tombstone in Closeburn; *Martyr Graves*, 433. At this crisis
there were so many prisoners in the Tolbooth of Dumfries that some were transferred to the castle vaults there.

THE COVENANTERS

the vain boast: 'Nou that the troups ar so posted I shall answer for the peace and good order of all these contreys, which in a maner is all the fanatick pairt of the Kingdom.'[1] The Government further provided the troops, the justices and ministers, with the most powerful engine of destruction they had yet received, namely a 'Proclamation, with a List of Fugitives, May 5, 1684,' giving authority to 'all officers and ministers of our law' to apprehend no fewer than 1956 denounced fugitive persons, whose names were included in a printed Porteous roll accompanying the Proclamation, unless they had taken the Bond or Test before 1st August. Sixteen of the number were preachers and twelve were women.[2]

Two letters which Claverhouse addressed to Queensberry from Edinburgh, on 19th May, contained an explanation of a step which he was about to take, and which might raise the suspicion that the Persecutor, as he was now designated, was himself tainted with the Whig disaffection.[3] Claverhouse, now commander of the forces in Ayr, had won the heart of the Honourable Jean Cochrane, grand-daughter of the Earl of Dundonald, and niece of the notorious rebel Sir John Cochrane. Her father was dead; her mother was a daughter of Covenanting Cassillis. Her cousin was Lord Ross, comrade-in-arms of her lover. These letters prove that Claverhouse could wield a pen as incisive as his sword, and present to us several sharply defined portraits of persons he is referring to: Dalyell 'in a terrible huff'; Dundonald scorning to take Claverhouse's mean advice and profit by his son's escheat and his grandchild's forfeiture; Sir John Cochrane, 'a mad man and lait him perish. They deserve to be damned would owen him'; the distressed mother unable to prevent her daughter's declension from 'right principles'; and the inimitable delineations of the little Draco himself, confessing how he had 'raire cases prepared, if it be the King's interest the rigeur of the lawe be used against all.' With no lack of self-assurance, he tries to add another cubit to his moral stature when looking down to survey the religious life at his feet, and cynically to mock it thus: 'For my owen pairt I look on myself as a cleanger. I may cur people guilty of that plaigue of presbytry be conversing with them, but can not be infected, and I see very little of that amongst those persons but may be

The great Porteous roll of 1684.

Claverhouse woos Jean Cochrane.

The *billets-doux* of Claverhouse.

A cleanser, persecutor, Churchman.

[1] Claverhouse to Queensberry, 19th May: *Hist. MSS. Com. Rep.*, xv. viii. 287.
[2] Wodrow, iv. 12 note; Aldis, *List*, 2477.
[3] *Hist. MSS. Com. Rep.*, xv. viii. 287, 288, Nos. 221 and 222.

414

easily rubed of. And for the young ladie herself, I shall answer for her. Had she been right principled she would never in dispyt of her mother and relations made choyse of a persicutor, as they call me. So who ever thinks to misrepresent me on that head will fynd them selfs mistaken; for both in the King and Churches interest, dryve as fast as they think fit, they will never see me behynd.'[1] Nor was this an empty boast. On his marriage day he proved that 'it is not in the pouer of love, nor any other folly, to alter my loyalty.'[2]

The wedding took place in Paisley on Tuesday, 10th June. One nuptial joy was vouchsafed to Claverhouse that day, in the recorded certainty that a marriage dowry of forty thousand merks Scots had been secured to his bride before he up-saddled for the moors. For Claverhouse never rose above considerations of pelf, however urgent was his business. A few days before this, he wrote to Queensberry—and Claverhouse was by no means shy in promoting his own worldly interests—'I hop when your great concerns are over, you will mind your friends.'[3] At sermon on Sabbath, 8th June, Dalyell was startled to hear that an armed conventicle of some eighty men and twenty women were worshipping that day at the Blackloch, under the spiritual leadership of Renwick.[4] Lieut.-Colonel Winram, sent to disperse them, just missed them as they disappeared through the mosses westward towards the Clyde and into the military district of Claverhouse. He reported to Dalyell, who sent the news by Ross to Claverhouse on his marriage morn. A soldier of the suspicious nature of Claverhouse was not to know that this call to duty was not a trap. As such he took it, vowing what three days later he wrote: 'I shall be revenged some time or other of this unseasonable trouble these dogs give me. They might have let Tuesday pass.'[5] As soon as the ceremony was over, Claverhouse and all his command of horse and foot were on the move for several days, marching and counter-marching through the valleys of Clyde, Douglas, Ayr, and Nith, as he reported to the Archbishop—'through all the moors, mosses, hills, glens, woods; and spread in small parties, and ranged as if we had been at hunting … but

Marriage of Claverhouse, 10th June 1684.

The disappointed bridegroom in the saddle.

[1] *Hist. MSS. Com. Rep.*, xv. viii. 287.
[2] *Ibid.*, 289.
[3] *Ibid.*, 289.
[4] Erskine, *Journal*, 65; Napier, ii. 395.
[5] Napier, ii. 398.

could learn nothing of those rogues.'[1] After this unsuccessful raid the persecutor's honeymoon began, and he was absent from Privy Council meetings from 29th May till 1st July.[2]

Punishment of suspected heritors.

The heritors in the district where the Blackloch was situated—Shotts, Cambusnethan, and Monkland—together with William Violant, indulged minister at Cambusnethan, were summoned to the Council for remissness of duty in not raising the hue and cry and tracking down the rebels. The Stuarts of Allanton and Hartwood were heavily fined, and Violant was imprisoned and banished.[3]

Shooting of Shillilau, July 1684.

Wodrow had authority for assigning to July 1684 the date of the killing at Woodhead, Tarbolton, of a ploughboy named William Shiringlaw, or Shillilau, aged eighteen years, employed on the neighbouring farm of Stairhead. The youth was seized by Lieutenant Lauder and a party from Sorn garrison, and being found to be an absentee from church reported by the curate, and making unsatisfactory replies to the usual interrogations, he was shot on the spot. His employers were also threatened with instant execution.[4]

The Privy Council turned its attention to the unravelling of the connection between the English Rye House conspirators, the English Whigs, and the Scottish malcontents, notably some influential prisoners who had lain all winter in the Tolbooth, being the alleged allies of Argyll, the Cochranes, and other fugitives from justice, as well as friends of Shaftesbury, Russell, and Sidney. Of these suspects the two Campbells of Cessnock, Fairly of Bruntsfield, Crawfurd of Crawfurdland, and the Reverend William Carstares, who, under the name of Swan, was apprehended at Tenterden in Kent, had the rigour of their imprisonment for a time mitigated, and the two Mures of Rowallan were liberated on bail.[5]

---

[1] Napier, ii. 403.

[2] Viscountess Dundee in her widowhood married Viscount Kilsyth, and, with her babe, was killed in Utrecht on 16th October 1695. Her embalmed body lay long exposed to view in a mausoleum in Kilsyth churchyard. She had lovely yellow hair. For account of her death cf. *Hist. MSS. Com. Rep.*, XII. viii. 49; Napier, *Memorials*, iii. 678.

[3] Wodrow, iv. 28, 46, 47.

[4] *Ibid.*, 172. Shillilau's gravestone in Tarbolton churchyard gives the date 1685: *Martyr Graves*, 315.

[5] Wodrow, iv. 94 *et seq.* William Carstares (1649-1715), nicknamed 'The Cardinal'

The spirit moving the governors of Scotland at this juncture may be understood from the tenor of the letter which the Council, Claverhouse among the number, sent to the King on 15th July, which asserts 'that there is no securitie in complying with turbulent and disaffected people ... it being truely much easier, nobler, and safer to disable your enemies than to flatter them.'[1]

Government's investigation into the national discontent.

The judicial inquiry began by putting in the boots, on 26th July, William Spence, M.A., who had acted as secretary to the late Earl of Argyll, and was supposed to be the depositary of the secrets of the Whig party. He had been minister of Glendevon till his recusancy led to his suspension, imprisonment, deposition, and excommunication by the Bishop and Synod of Dunblane in 1679-80.[2] The torture in the boots failed to break down Spence's resolution to reveal nothing of incriminating import, and the Council instructed General Dalyell to send soldiers in relays to his cell with orders 'not to suffer him to sleep by night or by day,' so that exhaustion would compel him to confess and to decipher the letters of Argyll. On 23rd July, the Council authorised the 'use of a new inventione and ingyne called the thumbikins which will be very effectual,' their minute declares, for expiscating facts.[3] The thumbikins were first tried upon Spence on 7th August, and he, realising the futility of resistance, agreed to decipher the correspondence. The Council assured him of his life. The information extracted resulted in an order to put Carstares in irons that night. His turn came next on 5th September. Dalyell, Drumlanrig, and Claverhouse were among the twenty-seven interested spectators who heard the Chancellor question the obstinate prisoner in vain before he ordered in the executioner and thumbscrews. The clerk of court appears to have delighted in detailing in his minute how they 'put him in the torture by applying the thumbscrew to him, which being accordingly done and his having for

Torture of William Spence.

The Thumbikins introduced, 23rd July 1684.

Claverhouse, Dalyell, and others interested in the torture of William Carstares.

---

on account of his influence with William of Orange; became Principal of Edinburgh University, 1703, and minister of Greyfriars, Edinburgh; Willcock, *A Scots Earl* (Argyll), 308 *et seq.*

[1] *Reg. Sec. Conc., Acta*, 401.

[2] Wilson, *Register of Synod*, 144, 146, 152, 159, 250; *Acta*, 427.

[3] Claverhouse was present in Council on 1, 2, 15, 17, 23, 24, 25, 26, 29, 31 July; 1, 12 August; 4, 5, 6, 16, 30 September, when the brutal procedure was conceived, ordered, and executed: *Reg. Sec. Conc., Acta*, anno 1684, 382-517; *Reg. Sec. Conc., Dec.*, 749-819.

near the space of ane hour continued in the agonie of torture, the screw being by space and space streatched and forced untill he appeared near to faint.'[1] The torturers, not able to break him down, tried the boots, but as the executioner was not expert in making them effective, the torture was deferred for the night. Bruised, he was sent to the Castle with a surgeon to cure his wounds, and an emissary to persuade him to depone respecting the Monmouth conspiracy. He was promised the fullest pardon for his depositions, which he understood were not to be used against any one, as he was never to be called as a witness. At length Carstares deponed. The authorities at once meanly printed his statements, and used them as an adminicle of evidence at Jerviswood's trial, now in course of preparation. Carstares and Spence were incarcerated in Dumbarton Castle, from which Carstares was removed to Stirling Castle and Spence to the Bass.[2]

Taiket, a tailor, tortured and hanged. On the 22nd July, the Council examined two prisoners, a young man, Arthur Taiket, tailor and heritor in Hamilton, and Patrick Walker, aged eighteen, son of Patrick in Cleuch. Since 1681 the former was a traitor demeaned for Bothwell Bridge, and lately had been conventicling at Blackloch with the Remnant when caught. Walker was wanted for the murder of Francis Gordon of Meldrum's troop in March, as before narrated.[3] The boots, now the medium of disclosures, were ordered for them. The prison surgeon said that the boots would break the spindle-shanks of the tailor, and the thumbikins were tried instead. Malloch, the slave-master, in a petition said that it was a pity to maim the boy, and he craved him for a slave. Patrick thus escaped torture. Taiket had nothing material to divulge beyond confessing to have fought at Bothwell 'merely in self-defence,' and to have followed the conventicling Renwick. That was enough for the judges on 24th July, who sent him to the Grassmarket gallows six days later. Believing that he had a 'tryst' with God, 'upon the sweet Cross of Christ' he could thus testify: 'If every hair of my head and every drop of my blood were a life, I would willingly lay them down for my lovely Lord and Master, Jesus Christ.'[4]

Walker was kept in prison fourteen months, was examined eighteen

---

[1] *Reg. Sec. Conc., Acta*, 484.
[2] *Ibid.*, 487, 492, 500.
[3] Cf. *antea* p. 360.
[4] *Book of Adjournal*, 24th July 1684; Wodrow, iv. 66; *Cloud*, 376.

times, had his first sentence of banishment to the plantations pro- Patrick Walker's experiences.
nounced by Archbishop Burnet himself, not long before his death, was
liberated on bail, brought back and dispatched to Dunnottar in May
1685, sent down to Leith Tolbooth on 18th August, whence he escaped
to become the ardent disciple of Renwick. He survived till March 1745,
and became the quaint biographer of Peden, Cargill, Cameron, and
other heroes of the Covenant.[1]

On 2nd July, General Dalyell was ordered to bring to Edinburgh The Dumfries prisoners.
from 'The Stone Jug' and the vaults of Dumfries Castle the condemned
of the Justiciary Court there. Some were men of good social standing—Alexander Gordon of Kinstuir, William Grierson of Lochurr,
near Craigenputtoch,[2] John M'Kechny (or Macchesny in Hole?), James
Welsh of Little Clouden, and others. Their fate was settled. They were
to join Malloch's gang of vagabonds and prostitutes netted in the purlieus of the Capital, and to sail for the canebrakes.[3] In Carolina, Malloch would get ten pounds for each of them.[4] Luckily for Claverhouse
he did not lead his troop escorting the prisoners. Their route was by
Thornhill, Carron Water, Drumcruil, and romantic Enterkin, on Tuesday, 29th July.

The upper pass of Enterkin is a grand, deep, green defile, sloping The Pass of Enterkin.
from the Lowther Hills down to the River Nith, seven miles due north
of Thornhill and six east of Sanquhar, in Dumfriesshire.[5] A noisy-
mountain streamlet tumbles down the cleft between the hills. Parallel
with the stream, on the northern hill-faces winds a narrow pathway,
part of the old drove-road from Galloway, Moniaive, through Nithsdale, on to Edinburgh. This was the 'Via Dolorosa' of Nithsdale up
which fearful men dragged rural suicides on sledges to their burial on
'No Man's Land,' on the Lowthers.

---

[1] No student of the Covenant can now dispense with Dr. David Hay Fleming's
edition of the *Biographia Presbyteriana*, entitled *Six Saints of the Covenant*, 1901; cf.
ibid., Introd. xxiii; i. 349-52; ii. 191-5; Wodrow, iv. 47.

[2] William Grierson, a Pentland rebel, was liberated from Edinburgh Tolbooth:
Reg. Sec. Conc., Acta, 11th February 1669.

[3] *Acta*, 387; *Decreta*, 750.

[4] Lauder notes in the *Decisions*, i. 299 (5th August 1684): 'Fifteen prisoners, for
being in Bothwell Bridge rebellion, are delivered to Robert Malloch, to be transported in his ship to Carolina, where he will get £10 sterling for them.'

[5] Mr. Andrew Lang places it in Moffatdale; the embouchure is in Nithsdale.

ENTERKIN PASS

MONUMENT OF STEWART AND GRIERSON IN THE CHURCHYARD OF ST. JOHN'S DALRY

Here and there on the route the bridle-path hangs perilously over the treeless gorge, and the slip of a foot or a hoof would mean sudden destruction.

Ambuscade and rescue of prisoners in Enterkin, 29th July 1684.

Lieutenant Patrick Muligan, in command of half a troop of Claverhouse's horse, escorting the party of prisoners tied in couples to horses led by 'pedees,' had safely reached the upper part of the defile at its most dangerous point, when he found himself menaced by armed men. On either side there was a party: looking backward he saw in Glen Valentine a third command barring his retreat. The ambuscade was perfect. There was a demand for the prisoners, a refusal, a dragoon's oath, a volley, the unerring shot of Black MacMichael—the fowler of Maxwelton—and the tumbling dead of Sergeant Kelt into the linn which tradition has named after him. The horses bolted, and in the confusion some prisoners escaped. One assailant or prisoner, Robert Smith, was killed; Grierson was left for dead among the brackens of the Dry Cleuch, into which he was trailed, and from which he was conveyed to the shieling at Thirstown, where nursing restored to him his strength, except his eyesight shot away; M'Kechny in a rally was recaptured and taken to Edinburgh, where he died of his gangrened wounds.[1] The story which soon reached Edinburgh was to the effect that some of the prisoners 'were slain in the conflict; two of them broke their necks over the precipices, and other two were brought forward to Edinburgh, and one or two of the King's forces were killed.' The Council ordered a judicial inquiry and Depute-Sheriff James Alexander of Knockhill, all the lairds of Mid-Nithsdale, the garrisons, and all the parishioners of the vale, were ordained to assemble at the romantic Church of Dalgarno to give evidence, on 4th August.

The heroes of the ambuscade.

It was then proved that the rescue was a well-planned affair. James Harkness of Locherben, 'Long Gun,' a youth of twenty-three, James MacMichael from the Clachan of Dalry, and John Grier, chapman from Glencairn, were the prime movers in the matter. Their associates were Thomas Harkness, junior, of Locherben—'White Hose,' Adam Harkness of Mitchellslacks, James Corsane, Jedburgh in Glencairn, James

[1] J. K. Hewison, *Scotsman*, 1st April 1901—'Fresh Light on Enterkin'; Defoe (who personally visited the spot), 237; Wodrow, iv. 173, did not know about Smith (Smith may not have been a Covenanter); *Hist. Not.*, ii. 546, 547, 552; *Observes*, 136; *Decisions*, i. 299.

Tod, William Herries from Kirkcudbright, Gilbert Watson, a spy, and others to the number of forty. On 28th July, sixteen of them met by night in the house of Rolland Thomson in Auchengeith to lay their plans and try their pistols. Most of the rescuers were on the fugitive roll.[1] One witness deponed that he heard that the wife of John Hoatson of Nether Dalveen gave winding-sheets to 'the killed prisoners'; another saw the people take away the 'corpse of Thomas Smith.'[2]

Margaret Frissell Harkness in Mitchellslacks, who swore an alibi for her sons William and Thomas, and her grandson, Thomas, was retained in custody for harbouring and resetting her own fugitive children.

Claverhouse was soon in the saddle for the southern hunt. In August, he appeared only twice at Council. His usual luck attended him. On 9th August, he stumbled upon six men sleeping in the open in the parish of Closeburn, Dumfriesshire, who defended themselves, three being wounded, and all taken prisoners. They were James Harkness, Thomas Harkness, junior; Andrew Clark, a smith, a youth of nineteen from Leadhills; Samuel M'Ewen, an orphan lad of seventeen from Glencairn; Thomas Wood from Kirkmichael, and another. James Harkness escaped, probably out of the prison in Dumfries.[3] Claverhouse escorted them through Annandale to Edinburgh, and secured them in the Canongate Tolbooth. There Patrick Walker saw them.[4] On 15th August, they were tried before Lord Linlithgow for 'being in arms, and that one of them presented a gun to the King's forces, that they had ball upon them, that they had conversed with rebels, denied authority, and fled from his Majesty's forces.'[5] They declared themselves innocent of Enterkin: three soldiers deponed otherwise. The defence of one was

(margin: Claverhouse captures six of the rescuers.)

(margin: Trial and execution of the Enterkin rescuers, 15th August 1684.)

---

[1] Wodrow, iv. 23; Hoatson's evidence in *Minute Book of Commissioners*.

[2] *Privy Council Papers*, 1684, Supp. 2; *Minute Book of Commissioners*, etc., Report by Queensberry, Drumlanrig, and Claverhouse. MacMichael and John Grier were afterwards shot at Auchencloy: *Martyr Graves*, 380-2, 405; Robert Grierson was shot at Ingliston, Glencairn, in 1685: *ibid.*, 387, 444. In Dalgarno churchyard, two miles from Thornhill, are the gravestones of Harknesses, Hoatsons, and other families implicated in the rescue: cf. Appendix, and photograph in this volume.

[3] The tombstone of James Harkness in Dalgarno churchyard is sacredly preserved. Beside is that of Thomas, posthumous son of Thomas Harkness, who was executed. Cf. Appendix II.

[4] *Six Saints*, ii. 97, 217.

[5] *Book of Adjournal*, 15th August 1684.

that he was fowler to Queensberry and had a licence for arms. Tried at noon, found guilty, and condemned to die between two and five o'clock, the victims had little time to compose their testimonies before they were dangling in the Grassmarket amid rolling drums, one of them being tumbled over the ladder, while in the act of prayer, to save time. In their joint testimony these valiant countrymen declared: 'If we had a hundred lives, we would willingly quit all for the truth of Christ.'[1]

Two zealots die for their faith, Nicol and Young. Two sympathisers stood sadly watching the execution—John Erskine, who quietly expressed his thoughts in his *Journal*, and James Nicol, merchant burgess in Peebles, too incensed to keep quiet, and muttering too loudly: 'A cow of Bashan has pushed these three men to death at one push, contrary to their own laws, in a most inhuman manner.' He was instantly seized. He was on the proclaimed list of vagabonds. His examination elicited the facts that he had been at Bothwell Bridge, justified the death of Sharp, called Hackston's execution murder, and was so uncompromising a recusant that he told the Council: 'For your Prelates' kirks, and Baal's priests, I never heard any of them, nor ever intend to do, if I were to live an hundred years.' Nicol was the most typical zealot possible. On 27th August, Nicol, and William Young, a lunatic, quiet anon dangerous, an Evandale tailor, were tried and condemned to die. That afternoon another 'push' made two more victims of tyranny. William Young was one of the prisoners who escaped from Canongate Tolbooth, and could not conceal that fact; nor his intense hatred of his dis-covenanted King.[2]

Patrick Walker dated 'The Killing Times' from 15th August 1684—the date of the execution of the Enterkin rescuers; Shields dated them from the death of Charles II. in February 1685.[3]

The Campbells of Over-Wellwood. During the hunt for fugitives in Ayrshire in August, Lord Ross's troopers captured two youths, John and William, sons of William Campbell of Over-Wellwood. Their name was of evil omen; two Bibles found in their pockets on Wellwood Hill were damning accusers. They were savagely maltreated before they reached the iron house in the Canongate Tolbooth. The Council could not break down their loyalty to Covenanting principles, in spite of cruel threats. With the help of

[1] Wodrow, iv. 67; *Cloud*, 404; *Hist. Not.*, ii. 551; Erskine, *Journal*, 76, 77.
[2] Wodrow, iv. 69; *Book of Adjournal*; *Cloud*, 388; *Observes*, 136; Defoe, 296.
[3] *Six Saints*, ii. 97; *Hind Let Loose*, 200, § iv.

two gimlets, a chisel, and a piece of iron they were able to cut their way out of prison on 21st August, eleven prisoners following them. Of these, Young was recaptured, as well as one injured in the descent.[1]

Some very important Acts were passed by the Privy Council, in the summer of 1684. The 'Act anent the Committee for public affairs, July 15,' empowered certain of their number, including the two archbishops and Claverhouse, three being a quorum, to call magistrates to account for their dealings with fanatics, and to imprison or dismiss all prisoners.[2] On 22nd July, a proclamation was issued which was virtually a Hue and Cry against the followers of Cameron and Renwick and calling on all to seize them.[3] On 1st August, an army order was passed for the redistribution of the troops, and giving new powers to Claverhouse and Buchan for the discovery of desperate rebels.[4] On the same day the Council ordered reports on the prisoners in custody, 'that it may be recommended to the justices to proceed and pronounce sentence of death against them immediately, which sentence they are to cause execute within six hours after pronouncing it (within three hours in Glasgow and Dumfries.)' This method of emptying the jails was quite in keeping with the cleansing spirit of the Rhadamanthus of the Committee—Claverhouse. It is one of the most inhuman decrees on the Scottish Record. It amply avenged Enterkin.

Fresh legislation in 1685.

Claverhouse was present on 6th September, that red-letter day in the calendar, when the Council, acting on the royal command to extinguish disaffection, granted a commission to certain of their number, including Hamilton, Mar, Livingstone, Queensberry, Drumlanrig, Balcarres, Claverhouse, or any two of them, to hold four circuit justiciary courts.[5] They received twenty-eight definite instructions as to disarming and fining non-jurors, licensing horses, sending in unlicensed preachers, punishing conventiclers—and for women their husbands—enrolling fugitives, examining indulged ministers, ferreting out inciters to rebellion, apprehending pedlars without passes, searching letter-carriers,

A red-letter day, 6th September 1684.

---

[1] Wodrow, 50, 51. John survived and became a captain of horse under King William. William died in 1686 of decline caused by his privations.

[2] Wodrow, iv. 31.

[3] *Ibid.*, note.

[4] *Ibid.*, 33; *Decreta*, 775; *Acta*, 432—Claverhouse present in Council.

[5] *Acta*, 490; Wodrow, iv. 113.

interviewing penitent rebels, ordering military, evicting the wives and families of forfeited and fugitive who do not clear themselves by oath that they have not conversed with their relatives, rendering account of quartering and fining, hunting down fugitives, suffering only loyal gentlemen to bear arms and no yeoman to travel three miles without a pass, offering the oath of allegiance, and banishing men and women refusing to take it, examining any one regarding his loyalty, and: 'You shall put in execution the power of justiciary to be granted unto you by our Privy Council, with all rigour, by using fire and sword, as is usual in such cases; and we do empower our Privy Council to insert an indemnity to you, or any employed by you, for what shall be done in the execution thereof.' This commission was to endure till the 1st December, 'unless we think fit to prorogate the same.' As if the mesh in the judicial net were not small enough, ship-captains were ordered to proffer the oath to all passengers, and no traveller was permitted to leave one jurisdiction for another without a magisterial permit.[1]

Use of fire and sword.

How were the elusive Renwick, Peden, and other preachers to break through this cordon of bayonets, detectives, and traitors? Frequently summoned by the Council, Renwick was tried in absence by the Lords of Justiciary on 16th September, and adjudged and proclaimed a traitor, rebel, and outlaw.[2] While the defenders of a religion pure and undefiled were thus in cruellest of straits, their opponents, the Prelatists, were not without their own troubles and heartburnings from the same source of tyranny.

Renwick outlawed.

In vain did the Scots hierarchy endeavour to obtain some say in the promotions within their own order, whose members were intruded like soldiery, moved obliquely like their namesakes on a chess-board, or peremptorily removed by royal fiat. On the 10th August, Archbishop Burnet was present in St. Andrews, 'near the ancient church of St. Rule,' at the consecration of Cairncross, parson of Dumfries, a protégé of Queensberry, and at the installation of the Bishops of Ross and Dunblane. Twelve days afterwards the Archbishop was dead, and soon thereafter was laid in St. Salvator's Church.[3] In the movement of the pieces, Rose, of Glasgow became Primate; Cairncross came to Glasgow,

Changes in the hierarchy, and death of Burnet.

[1] Wodrow, iv. 116 note, 117 note.
[2] 20th September 1684; Aldis, *List*, 2484; *Book of Adjournal*.
[3] Fountainhall, *Decisions*, i. 300; *Hist. Not.*, ii. 549; Grub, iii. 278; *Letters to Sancroft*, 65.

till, in 1687, he was turned out to make room for the discredited Bishop Paterson of Edinburgh; Dr. Drummond of Muthil got Brechin, when Douglas went to Dunblane; Bruce in Dunkeld, who was removed by order of King James, was succeeded by John Hamilton of Edinburgh. Truly the officials of the State-bureau of religion walked in slippery places. It required the courage of Andrew Cant, by heredity a defiant Protester, to declare that the clergy only elected Rose of Murray to the vacant throne of Paterson of Edinburgh on the King's order. The new Primate, with the blood of the Kilravock family in him, added no fresh lustre to the archiepiscopal see, and infused no happier spirit into the administration.

As if his thoughts turned to loving-kindness, when he reflected on Dudhope and his lonely young bride looking out on the local gallows, Claverhouse, on 10th September, petitioned the Privy Council for liberty for him, Constable of Dundee, to relax the death penalty on some petty stealers and pickers then lying in the local tolbooth.[1]

This unique instance of pity, by admirers of Claverhouse attributed to a humanitarian spirit, can be explained on utilitarian grounds. All judges already had, by long usage, a discretionary power as to the penalty for theft.[2] No military martinet, realising the hazards of the day, would venture to use a prerogative if his action was reviewable by his opponents. His letter to Queensberry shows how nervous Claverhouse was about the consequences of that legislation which he approved of, when its curse came home to roost: 'For I declair I think it a thing not to be desyred, that I should be forfaited and hanged, if my tenents wife, tuenty mille from me, in the midest of hilles and woods give mate or shelter a fugitive.'[3] Hangings were expensive, and not so profitable as the disponing of criminals to be home slaves, there being still a white slave mart in Scotland.[4]

The judges on circuit began their work religiously.[5] Dr. Ross, Professor of Divinity in Glasgow, must have been either a cynic or a grim humourist when he took for his text in Glasgow court—'Almost

Claverhouse credited with pity.

The circuit judges at work again, autumn 1684.

---

[1] Napier, ii. 410; *Privy Counc. Rec.*, 10th September.
[2] Hume, *Commentary*, i. 85 (edit. 1819).
[3] 30th October: *Hist. MSS. Com. Rep.*, xv. viii. 291.
[4] Hume, *Commentary*, ii, 528. Inscribed slave-collars were still in use in Scotland.
[5] Wodrow, iv. 113-36.

thou persuadest me to be a Christian.' The loyal heritors compeared, many with their tongue in their cheek, to bless 'the best of princes ... next to the Providence of God,' to ban the conventiclers, and to offer to pay cess. Twelve hundred recusants and indulged still preferred prison to feigning allegiance.[1] Consequently the sight was common of gangs of miserable bedraggled prisoners, heritors, ministers, men, women, and even children, without distinction, being driven like bestial by pitiless soldiery through wintry tempests to the State prisons, and to far Dunnottar, whence some, overdriven, did not return. Wodrow devotes a chapter to details of this subject.[2] Glasgow prison was so overcrowded for twenty days, that prisoners had to take turn about in lying down.[3] Justice had passed into insanity when Nithsdale women were tried for succouring a woman at the birth of a child of an Enterkin rescuer—in all likelihood the executed Thomas Harkness.

Wodrow, in giving an account of these hardships, had to depend on 'written accounts,' he wrote, 'there being no register of these itinerant Courts that I can meet with.' In vindication of Wodrow's narrative, there is a supreme satisfaction in now referring the student to the minute-books of those Justiciary Commissioners, which are preserved in the Register House. The subsidiary documents and lists of persons 'phanatically inclined,' prepared by the parish ministers, are most interesting; (that of Morton, signed by Greenshields, contains 260 names of persons living under the shadow of Drumlanrig). The minutes of courts held at Glasgow, 2nd-25th October; Ayr, 3rd October; Tynron, 19th September; Dumfries, 2nd October; Kirkcudbright, 7th-13th October; Wigtown, 14th October; Berwick, Roxburgh, Peebles, September-October 1684, are now accessible.[4]

Queensberry, Drumlanrig, and Claverhouse, opened the court at Dumfries on 2nd October 1684, and had a long list of suspects to try for reset of rebels and other treasonable acts, with the result that thirty men and four women (the latter from the Drumlanrig estate) were sentenced to the plantations. The justices proceeded to Kirkcudbright, and at a court held on Monday, 13th October (fol. 76), they had a band

---

[1] *Drumlanrig MSS.*, ii. 180.
[2] Wodrow, iv. 113-36.
[3] *Ibid.*, 136.
[4] *Ibid.*, 113. The Minute Books and Depositions are in the Register House.

of fifteen prisoners, men and women, including the well-known Mr. William MacMillan of Caldow, Balmaclellan; John Grier (the Enterkin rescuer?), and 'James Graham in Crofts of Corsmichaell,' said to have been brought in by a party of the King's forces.[1] Twelve of the men and women were sentenced to the plantations, but Graham and MacMillan were remitted to the Justiciary Lords in Edinburgh.[2]

The justices next proceeded to Wigtown, and held a court on the 14th October, at which the 'good wife of Arioland' and others compeared, and were sentenced to banishment. The three judges returned to Dumfries, preceded by a gang of convicts, who, to the number of eighty men, women, and children, were lodged in Dumfries Castle, whence they were marched out to Moffat on the 22nd November, and on to Edinburgh, which they reached two days afterwards. There, many of them lay in the Tolbooths of the city until they were dispatched to Dunnottar in May 1685, their names appearing in the report on the prisoners at that time.[3]

Such harrowing scenes could not fail to fire the Border blood, and to engender in the Remnant a defensive and retaliatory spirit, as they would have roused any citizens still endowed with a trace of self-respect and manliness. The nefarious system under which they groaned had created a class of oppressors worse even than the mercenary officers of justice, namely the 'flies,' delators or informers who ran from conventicle to barracks, so that the safety of any recusant outside the wildest uplands was impossible. 'There comes the devil's rattle-bag,' said farseeing Peden, when he noticed a noisy fanatic, named David Manson, afterwards a spy, crushing through a crowd of conventiclers for a good stance. Fountainhall records that: 'At Privy Counsell one Mr. William Houston is brought up by the soldiers as a Feild-preacher, with Rainy [Renwick]; but, it is said, he discovered himself to the Chancelor to be a Benedictine monk, and shewed his commission; so he was passed over in silence.'[4]

The 'flies' or informers.

---

[1] Wodrow gives a detailed account of MacMillan's sufferings: iv. 122-4, 216, 222, 322, 325.

[2] I have not traced Graham to a meeting with the Privy Council: he next appears before the Lords of Justiciary in December. Cf. *postea*, pp. 436, 437

[3] The report is printed in *Martyr Graves*, 497-507.

[4] *Decisions* (3rd March 1687), i. 451; *Hist. Not.*, ii. 788.

A cordon of
bayonets.

The Remnant saw the cordon drawing closer. Their prospects were terrible—the Grassmarket gibbet or the canebrakes with a free conscience: a perjured oath with an unpopular King, a hated Church, and a detested heir-apparent! The felon's burial-pit in Greyfriars Churchyard was the only refuge for honest men. Peden prophesied, 'The day is coming in these lands that a bloody scaffold shall be thought a good shelter.' Renwick as truly said, 'Death to me is as a bed to the weary.' 'Flimsy sophistries,' comfortably replies Mr. Andrew Lang.[1]

The wander-
ers at bay
issue a
manifesto.

At bay the wanderers were forced into self-defence. The Convention of Societies determined on a Declaratory Vindication, which Renwick, averse from it at first, was coaxed into preparing and publishing. Wodrow prints it from Renwick's copy, which is dated 28th October, and ordained to be affixed on market crosses and church doors on 8th

Society
People's Dec-
laration, 8th
November
1684.

November 1684.[2] It is there entitled 'Society People's Declaration, especially against Informers and Intelligencers, November 8, 1684.' It is a short manifesto of the religious and political principles of the Renwickian Remnant, announcing a declaration of war conditionally, inaugurating a supreme Court of Justice under the auspices of the Remnant of the Faithful. It begins with a reference to the present persecution by apostates, and re-states former resolutions to maintain the Covenants and other engagements in faith, 'wherein we have disowned the authority of Charles Stewart (not authority of God's institution, either among Christians or heathens) and all authority depending from him'; 'jointly and unanimously … we utterly detest and abhor that hellish principle of killing all who differ in judgment or persuasion from us, it having no bottom upon the word of God, or right reason'; 'to pursue the ends of our Covenants … we … declare … that whosoever stretch forth their hands against us (justiciary, military, assenting gentlemen, "viperous and malicious" clergy, intelligencers, delators, raisers of hue and cry), all and every one of such shall be reputed by us enemies to God and the Covenanted Work of Reformation, and punished as such, according to our power and the degree of their offence.' In order to emphasise

---

[1] *Hist.*, iii. 384.

[2] Wodrow, iv. 148 note; *Biog. Presby.* (*Life of Renwick*), ii. 67; *Faithful Contendings*, 150; *Testimony Bearing Exemplified*, 255: 'The apologetical declaration, and admonitory vindication of the true Presbyterians of the Church of Scotland: especially anent intelligencers and informers.'

the fact that their intention was to establish a righteous judicatory for punishing illegal shedders of innocent blood—they maintaining that lawful magistracy had expired—one paragraph states: 'Finally, we do declare, that we abhor, condemn, and discharge any personal attempts, upon any pretext whatsomever, without previous deliberation, common or competent consent, without certain probation ... confession ... or the notoriousness of the deeds'; and inhibiting private judgments. The persecuted therein avowed themselves 'a people by holy covenants dedicated unto the Lord ... for defending and promoting this glorious work of Reformation.' Theirs was a re-announcement of the opinions of Knox and his successors a century bygone; and the tone of the manifesto is less virulent than was to be expected from firebrands whom the Lord Advocate styled devils and wildcats.[1]

The Declaration drove many informers and unpopular curates to flight, and alarmed the officers of State. Their only remedy was heating the furnace of affliction seven times hotter. The Government resolved to convert the offensive document into a touchstone for dissenters. The Law Lords were asked by the Council whether or not the refusal to answer on oath the question of the lawfulness of killing the King's officers implied treason. They reported 'Yes.' The Council met on 22nd November and unanimously (Claverhouse among the rest) resolved: 'It being put to the vote in Councell whether or not any persone who ounes or does not disoune the late traitorous declaratione upon oath, whether they have arms or not, should be immediately killed before two witnesses: and the persone or persones who are to have instructions from the Councell to that effect: caryed in the affirmative.'[2] Thus Claverhouse voted for the cruel decree, which afterwards nerved his hand to pistol John Brown of Priesthill, and signed the Instructions relative to it.

Next day the Council, apprised of the murder of two soldiers, issued stringent instructions to Lord Livingstone and other justices, which Claverhouse signed, authorising the convocation of all persons over fourteen years of age in the Mid-Calder district, the instant military execution of approvers of the Declaration, and of the assassination of the soldiers, the trial, before a jury of fifteen, of refusers to disown, or

---

[1] Mackenzie to Queensberry, 20th November: Napier, ii. 424.
[2] *Acta*, 559.

to answer questions, who also were to suffer summary execution, the examination of all persons in reference to all matters of nonconforming, with powers to burn houses, seize goods, and carry off for the plantations all unsatisfactory individuals over twelve years of age—the Nimmos being specially wanted.[1] To make the terrible engine of extirpation complete, all that was needed was the Abjuration Oath, which the Council approved of, on 25th November, in the following terms:—

'I ... do hereby abhor, renounce, and disown, in the presence of the Almighty God, the pretended declaration of war lately affixed at several parish churches, in so far as it declares a war against his sacred Majesty, and asserts that it is lawful to kill such as serve his Majesty in church, state, army, or country, or such as act against the authors of the pretended declaration ... I ... disown the villanous authors thereof,' etc. This oath made its swearer own the Church to be a department of State.[2]

It must have been an extraordinary event in Christian Scotland to see that assembly of old, young, halt, decrepit, some tied to horseback to prevent them falling, others—fierce stalwarts—bending to the yoke, as they entered into that ring of glittering sabres on the fields of Livingston. The administration imagined that all this retributive severity was imperative, the more so after the receipt of a report that two

soldiers of the Life-Guards, Thomas Kennoway and Duncan Stewart, had met a foul death in Carmichael's hostelry at Swyne Abbey, in the shire of West Lothian, on the night of the 19th-20th November.[3] Kennoway, a native of Calder, his hands filled with loot and stained with blood, had been a terror to the Whigs for eighteen years. His portrait, preserved by Wodrow, is not attractive: 'He was notourly wicked and profane, a known adulterer, and a fearful drinker, and blasphemous curser and swearer.' He was depute to Captain Adam Urquhart of Meldrum, the legal inquisitor in Haddington, Selkirk, Berwick, and Peebles, and Sheriff-Depute of East Lothian. Urquhart died in a chair shortly after leaving a tavern ten days before his depute's exit.[4]

---

[1] *Acta*, 561-3: 23rd November—'J. Grahame' signs; Wodrow, iv. 154-6.

[2] *Acta*, 565.

[3] Wodrow, iv. 152, 156; Erskine, 94; *Narr. of Nimmo*, 69, 70; *Hist. Not.*, ii. 579; *Observes.*, 141; Terry, 174.

[4] Napier, ii. 424.

Kennoway arrived with his Porteous roll and his legal nets for catching criminals and fines, and with hopes thereafter of being rich and great. He and Stewart sat down to mingle the dreams of Alnascar in the steaming fumes of Carmichael's bowl; but when they emerged into the night some assassins made them pay in blood for many an old lawing, and then fled. Three years before, the authorities announced that Kennoway was doomed to removal by the Whigs. Now Whig blood alone could expiate the deed. The godly naturally were blamed, as if ruffians of the type of Kennoway injured none but the saints; and the blame of King and Council fell on gentle Renwick and his declaratory party. Livingstone and an influential commission were appointed to sift the matter. The slain men were dragged on sledges into Linlithgow for the ordeal of blood to be tried on Covenanters.

Some victims were ready tied to the horns of the altar. John Semple, from Craigthorn, Glassford, was the son of a Covenanter who fell at Rullion Green, and his mother and sister were inmates of Dunnottar.[1] John Watt came from Kilbride. Of Gabriel Thomson, a lad of eighteen years, nothing is known. Torture by the thumbscrews to discover their connection with the Declaration, on 13th November, threw them into a speechless swoon, and resulted in eliciting nothing incriminating. Semple owned the proclamation; the other two refused to disown it. They were sent to the Justiciary Court on the 24th November, and were sentenced to die that afternoon at the Gallowlee.[2] They died as boldly as they endured the thumbscrews—singing praise. The crowd afforded Captain Peter Graham an opportunity for testing the loyalty of the onlookers. Those who refused to acknowledge the justice of the doom were marched off to jail in Haddock's Hole. Night had fallen. Hangmen and guard were about to strip and bury the dead, when some students broke in and dispersed them. A band of women hurried the bodies into coffins and made for Greyfriars. At the very gate they were intercepted. They dropped the corpses, which lay on the streets all night, and next day were dragged back to the place of burial at the gallows'-foot. Before the day was done, the Council ordered the prosecution of the maker and painter of the three coffins.[3] For receiving

Victims at the altar.

A weird incident.

---

[1] Wodrow, iv. 152; *Six Saints*, ii. 98; *Cloud*, 415; *Martyr Graves*, 505.

[2] Wodrow and *Cloud* give 14th; *Book of Adjournal*, 24th; *Acta*, 24th.

[3] *Acta*, 564; *Hist. Not.*, ii. 574; *Six Saints*, ii. 96, 98, 101, 217, 220.

the Bible which Watt threw down from the gallows, Janet Fimerton, a godly old maid, resident in Edinburgh, was seized that night. Her mission was to attend executions and chest the sainted dead. She was relegated to Dunnottar, brought back, sentenced to banishment for disowning King James, sailed in Pitlochy's slave-ship, and found a watery grave.

Porterfield adjudged a traitor.

John Porterfield, the old laird of Duchal, a suspect and sufferer of long standing, lay in prison awaiting his doom. He was accused of conversing with and resetting his brother Alexander, a fighter at Rullion Green, and George Holms, a fighter at Bothwell, as well as of concealing the fact that Sir John Cochrane had asked and been refused the loan of fifty pounds for assistance to the Earl of Argyll. On 28th November, the day before Porterfield appeared at the Justiciary bar, the Council, anticipating the verdict, recommended the judges to leave the place and date of his execution to the King. The doom of traitors was duly passed.[1] Undismayed, Porterfield retained the dignity of a gentleman and simply replied: 'My Lords, I have little to say; I pray the Lord may save the King, whatever come of me.' The Parliament of 1685 approved of this harsh procedure and annexed the barony of Duchal to the Crown. In 1686, the King granted the personal and heritable estate of the prisoner to the Earl of Melfort. Porterfield and his son were long incarcerated, but ultimately were liberated, the old laird to hail the Revolution and get back his estate, to which in time was added the property of John Maxwell of Overmains, his overreaching betrayer.

Indulged ministers to be 'outed,' 27th November 1684.

Claverhouse kept the Council lively with his ill-temper; the Covenanters restless through his projects. In 1682 he wrote: 'Did the King and the Deuk knou what those rebellious villans, which they call minesters, put in the heads of the people, they would think it necessary to keep them out.' He was present in Council on 27th November 1684 when his advice prevailed, and they ordered 'all the indulged ministers to be "outed," because they kept not their instructions, and some of them did not keep the thanksgiving in September last year.'[2] The evicted had to find caution that they would not exercise their ministry. Soon the rural oracles were dumb and the Tolbooths had a superfluity of non-juring

---

[1] Wodrow, iv. 138-41, 212, 272; *Book of Adjournal*, 29th November 1684; *Drumlanrig MSS.*, ii. *passim*.

[2] *Hist. MSS. Com. Rep.*, xv. viii. 272; *Acta*, 565; Wodrow, iv. 40, 41.

chaplains for fellow-prisoners. Military counsels were in the ascendant. Claverhouse was present on 4th December when Lieutenant-General Drummond was commissioned to march a thousand foot and horse, including four troops of Claverhouse's cavalry, into the western and southern shires, quartering where he chose, and taking, trying, and killing rebels and their abettors. This commission continued till New Year's Day. A similar commission was given to William Hamilton of Orbiston to raise two hundred Highlandmen, and to range over Dumbarton and Renfrew, apprehending suspects, of whom 'outed' ministers were to be dispatched to Edinburgh Tolbooth. He was to be indemnified for the slaughter of any persons resisting.[1]

All these rigorous measures seemed to have no effect in restraining the more unmanageable opponents of the Government. About the middle of November a miserable assassination took place in Carsphairn Manse, Kirkcudbrightshire, when Peter Peirson, the incumbent there, was sent to his account by a fell shot of Black MacMichael.[2] Peirson was a middle-aged bachelor and a recluse. Formerly minister of Carmichael, he succeeded to the pulpit of three true-blue Covenanters—Semple, Erskine, and Gilchrist—and probably to little else of goodwill in the wilds of Carsphairn. A braggart, he boasted of his broadsword and blunderbuss, declaring 'he feared none of the Whigs, nor anything else, but rats and mice'—the latter, probably, his only company. He was bold in the pulpit, flagellating the Whigs. When Lag rode up to Garryhorn to hold his courts, Peirson took a seat at his side. He was therefore blamed for informing, suspected of Popery, and accused of immorality.[3]

The assassination of Peter Pierson, November 1684.

Night had fallen when MacMichael, Robert Mitchell, from Cumnock, a nephew of James Mitchell (Sharp's assailant), William Herron from Glencairn, Robert Pedzen from Sanquhar or Glencairn, probably an instigating 'fly,' afterwards a dragoon, and also, according to others, Andrew Watson, another 'fly,' visited the manse. Their business can only be conjectured. What seems to be a reasonable account of the incident

The assassins.

---

[1] Wodrow, iv. 158, 159; *Hist. MSS. Com. Rep.*, xv. viii. 212.

[2] Fountainhall (*Hist. Not.*, ii. 581) gives 11th December; the informant of Wodrow (Napier, i. 89) dates as above.

[3] Wodrow, iv. 197: 'Account of the Curate of C. by John Mathewson, Glencairn'; *Wodrow MSS.* (Edin.), xxxiii. 103; xxxvii. 5, 200 (Catal. 60); *Immoralities of Peirson*, xl. 934, 969; xxxvii. (Rob. iii. 3. 12), Nos. 44, 60, 61.

is, that Mitchell and Herron were a deputation to the curate to exact a timeous promise that he would cease troubling the wanderers. The fowler and trooper held back waiting results. From Renwick and Shields we learn that Peirson was 'a man of death, both by the law of God and man'—whatever that may mean.[1] Born in a contiguous parish, Renwick was likely to know something of Peirson.[2] The 'man of death' took an impolitic step, which the unerring fowler misunderstood and stopped with a fatal shot. One account makes the minister hold up the deputation, who cried for help; another, that he but peered through the partly opened door in response to a knock. Whatever happened, Renwick and the Societies expelled the perpetrators from their communion, and in *The Protestation* condemned the 'fact not materially murder,' as gone about 'contrary to our Declaration, without Deliberation, common or competent consent (the conclusion and deed being known only to three or four persons) in a rash, and not in a Christian manner.'[3] In this way Renwick and the Society-men disapproved of the excesses of those irreconcilable fugitives supposed to be of their following.

Black MacMichael's fatal shot.

The Renwickian Declaration was duly affixed on market-crosses and parish-church doors on 8th November, and apprehensions of those refusing to disown it began. Wodrow states that on 9th November ten men were seized, who ultimately were charged before the Justiciary Court on 8th December for owning, or not disowning, this 'most barbarous and hellish proclamation.' Their names were Thomas Wood (Enterkin rescuer?), Alexander Heriot, George Jackson, Thomas Robertson, James Graham, Patrick Cunningham, John Watt, James Kirkwood, Alexander Vallange, and James Glover. Wood, Jackson, Robertson, and Graham resolutely adhered to their principles, and were sentenced to die at the Gallowlee on the afternoon of the day of their adjourned trial—9th December. The other six recanted.[4]

Four assenters to the Declaration hanged.

Jackson, a tenant of Nether Pollok, left a record of his harsh examination by Lord Advocate Mackenzie, wherein he states that he had lain

Jackson's testimony.

---

[1] *The Protestation*, 267.

[2] The Renwick family were in the habit of attending John Semple's ministrations in Carsphairn: *Six Saints*, i. 196.

[3] *The Protestation … Sanquhar*, 267; *Biog. Presby.* (*Life of Renwick*), ii. 76.

[4] *Book of Adjournal*, 8th and 9th December; Wodrow, iv. 166, 167.

in prison since May.[1] Thus Wodrow has fallen into some confusion as to the dates of seizure, but is right as to the date of trial.

Wodrow's account of James Graham is that he was a tailor in Cross- James
Graham's
case. michael, Kirkcudbrightshire, and that when returning to his mother's house carrying his Bible and his tools, he was seized by Claverhouse, taken to Wigtown, Dumfries, and on to Edinburgh—acts which took time. But Professor Terry insists on naming him William—the name of Claverhouse's victim in 1682, whom he identifies with the later criminal, James—in face of the *Book of Adjournal* and the *Cloud*, which designate him correctly—the Professor not referring to these authorities. To suit this theory Professor Terry writes: 'The most probable date for William Graham's arrest is about 17th or 18th December 1684. Claverhouse was then in the neighbourhood.[2] At this date, James Graham was eight days under the Gallowlee, happy in his fate, which he preferred, as he declared: 'For it is all too little I can do for Him [*i.e.* Christ].'[3]

---

[1] *Cloud*, 411.

[2] Terry, *John Graham*, 172, 173 note, 176 note. It is fortunate that the Minute-books of the Commission of Justiciary are preserved in the Register House and are now available for reference. Accompanying them are bundles of depositions of suspects and witnesses. Cf. *Depositions, Sentences, etc. … at Ayr, Dumfries, etc.* Fol., 94 pp.

Minutes of Court of Justiciary held at Kirkcudbright on Friday, 17th October. Present—Queensberry, Drumlanrig, and Claverhouse (p. 76):—

> 'Fryday the saids Lords having caused call before them Marie Macleer or Marley, … Lady Gordon of Holm, Isobel Gordon, Lady Craig, … Mr. William M'Millan, and James Graham in Crofts of Corsmichaells—prisoners apprehended and brought in by a partie of the forces, have remitted and hereby remitt the said Master William Macmillan and James Graham to be tryed before the Justice-General and remanent lords of justiciarie att Edinburgh, and to continue prisoners in the meantime till they be conveyed thither.'

'KIRKCUDBRIGHT, 13 *Oct.* 1684.

> 'The Lords Commissioners ordains the persons above written (Mr. William M'Millan to be transported to Edinburgh; James Graham in Croftis of Crosmichell to be caryed to Edinr. to be tryed by the Justrs.) to be carried prisoners to Edinr., that they may be tryed there by the Justiciars.

'(Signed) QUEENSBERRY, I.P.D.'

Privy Council Papers, 1684. *Supplementary Papers.*

[3] Cf. his detailed testimony, *Cloud*, 423. Cf. William's case, *antea* pp. 367-9.

Reprisals by the malcontents.

Reprisals were not uncommon. Armed bands grew bold in the south-west and broke into Isle Tower, on Nithside, the residence of the Depute-Sheriff of Kirkcudbright; and, on 16th November, a band of over a hundred persons broke open and emptied the prison in Kirkcudbright, after killing the sentry at the Tolbooth.[1]

If any member of the administration had reason to be enraged, it was Claverhouse, who had boasted of a pacified Stewartry. He and his hacksters were soon in the saddle searching the fastnesses above Black

A deadly scuffle at Auchencloy, 18th December 1684.

Water of Dee. On 18th December, Claverhouse chased and overtook a party of eight fugitives, who made a last stand on Auchencloy Moor, near Loch Skerrow, in Girthon. Five were cut down and three were captured. Tradition tells that Claverhouse's steel bonnet saved him from Black MacMichael's sword. The slain were: James MacMichael, Robert Fergusson (Foremuligan?), Robert Stewart (Ardoch, Dalry), John Grier (Blackmark?), and, according to Defoe, Archibald Stewart. Robert Smith (Glencairn) and Robert Hunter (Tarbolton?) were captured and reserved for a Justiciary trial in Kirkcudbright, at which Claverhouse and his two coadjutors, Lieutenant-Colonel Douglas (*i.e.* James, Lord Drumlanrig), and Captain Andrew Bruce, presided. They were found guilty of treason, hanged, and beheaded.[2]

Claverhouse exhumes the fallen wanderers.

The other four were carried to ancestral graves in Dalry churchyard. Claverhouse, no doubt conversant with the law of *laesa majestas*,[3] as expounded by his friend Mackenzie in a recent book, and as soon as he learned the quality of the dead rebels—murderers of Peirson and victors at Enterkin—ordered their corpses to be exhumed and to suffer the degradation of traitors by being exposed on the local gibbet.[4]

Hardships of many landed gentlemen.

While scores of families were plunged into grief over these sanguinary cases, many landed gentlemen in the Lowlands experienced the direst straits from unceasing courses of fining. Some cases were appealed to

---

[1] Napier, ii. 428; *Memoirs of Dundee*, 11; Wodrow, iv. 177.

[2] *Wodrow MSS.*, xlviii. 934; xl.; *Hist.*, iv. 177; *Hist. Not.*, ii. 585, says five killed, three captured; *Chron. Notes*, 115. A table-stone covers the headless bodies in Kirkcudbright churchyard, and mentions 'Captans Douglas, Bruce, Grahame of Claverhous' as the judges: *Martyr Graves*, 402. Lord William Douglas was also a Captain under Claverhouse, Wodrow mentions six only.

[3] [Latin: treason.]

[4] *Martyr Graves*, 380; Mackenzie, *Laws and Customs of Scotland*, etc., 1679, p. 29; Defoe (p. 286) says four were betrayed praying in a house, taken out and shot without inquiry.

the merciless Council—such as that of Chalmers of Corsehill in Fife, a loyalist fined for his wife's abstention from church while she was nursing; M'Micking of Killantringan, Ayr, fined ten years' rent, modified to one, for hearing irregular preachers, he being old and unable to go to church eight miles; Ker of Chatto, fined £21,000 Scots for his wife's recusancy; twenty-six heritors of Roxburghshire were fined £274,737 Scots for non-churchgoing.[1]

On 2nd December the Privy Council fined, for a long course of disorderliness—hearing rebel preachers, intercommuning with proscribed persons, and other acts of treason: Sir John Maxwell of Pollok £8000 sterling, or £5000 if paid before 1st January; Alexander Cunningham, senior, of Craigends, £6000, or £4000; John Caldwell of that Ilk, £500 and imprisonment for life; Alexander Porterfield, £40,000 Scots, reduced one-half; Zacharias Maxwell of Blawarthill, 20,000 merks and imprisonment for life; James Pollock of Balgray, 15,000 merks, modified to £500. On a somewhat similar indictment the Council, on 4th September, fined Robert Baillie of Jerviswood £6000.[2]

Everything was now in train for raising on the common altar one of the most satisfying sacrifices ever immolated there—the moribund person of Robert Baillie of Jerviswood. To Royalist and Prelatist he was the embodiment of Scottish iniquity, being a descendant of Knox, a nephew as well as son-in-law of wicked Wariston, and a disorderly, anti-popish zealot already convicted. To Yorkist politicians he was the sole repository of the machinations of Argyllians and English Whigs. Secretary Melfort declared him to be 'the greatest villan of the pack, and desuerves the uorst.' Gilbert Burnet designated him 'a gentleman of great parts, but of much greater virtue.' Doctor Owen concurred. The world generally knew him to be a gentleman, scholar, and scientist. To the King and his brother Baillie was obnoxious. He had foiled James in the course of his examination.[3] *Baillie of Jerviswood.*

The irons, ordered by them, broke him down. In August he lay in Edinburgh Tolbooth at death's door. His sister-in-law, Helen Johnston, *Baillie in the Tolbooth.*

[1] *Reg. Sec. Conc., Acta, passim.*
[2] Wodrow, iv. 143; 105; *Reg. Sec. Conc., Acta*, 571, 580. Claverhouse attended Council on 4th September and 2nd December. For the distresses of the Nimmo family, cf. their *Narrative*, 55.
[3] Burnet, ii. 366.

Lady Graden, became a voluntary prisoner to nurse him. His invalid wife might see him in the presence of the prison doctor. These comforts were soon taken away. The chill of winter was killing him too soon, and the Council listened to Lady Graden's petition to be imprisoned with the sick man, and allowed her into the cell on condition that she would 'not go out of the room … without order from the council.' The Council soon saw that unless they hurried his trial, another and higher Tribunal would claim their victim. They examined him on 8th and 18th September, and on 22nd December. Mackenzie visited him in prison, pretended friendship, and wormed out facts, which he utilised with damnatory eloquence at the trial.

Trial of Baillie.

On 23rd December, Baillie, clad in a nightgown, was forced to totter on swollen legs to the Justiciary bar. Lady Graden revived him with stimulating cordials. To deprive the accused of the brilliant help of Lockhart and Lauder, these two advocates were ordered to assist Mackenzie. Patrick Hume, younger of Polwarth, lately liberated from prison, and four juniors undertook the defence.[1] The charge bore that the prisoner conspired to overturn the Government, debar York from the succession, and, under pretence of settling a colony in Carolina, to rebel, associating himself with Shaftesbury, Russell, and the English conspirators, with Argyll, Melville, Cochrane, Veitch, Fergusson, and the Scots plotters. The evidence of the Earl of Tarras and other witnesses indicated that Baillie, after the decision in the Blackwood case, went to London and discussed the peril in which Protestantism was placed by the passing of the Test Act. Carstares' extorted confession was introduced. Mackenzie taunted the prisoner with his relatives, and

Defence of Baillie.

demanded a capital sentence for the conspirator. With composure the dying man replied: 'I find I am intended for a public sacrifice in my life and estate, my doom being predetermined. I am only sorry … that my trial has given the Court so much trouble by staying here till past midnight.' Turning to the jury he assured them (Sheriff Graham of Wigtown was one of them) that he abhorred killing king or any man, was a monarchist, no conspirator, but a Protestant and humanitarian reformer. Then, like a lion at bay, he attacked the Advocate for charging with abominable crimes the man whom he assured of his belief that he

---

[1] *Reg. Sec. Conc.*, *Acta*, 615; on 4th December. Hume took Test and was discharged.

was innocent. In his fury Mackenzie proved himself to be more a caitiff, as he replied: 'I own what you say; my thoughts there were as a private man.' Then pointing to the clerk of court, he said, 'He knows my orders.' 'Well, my Lord,' retorted Baillie, 'if you keep one conscience for yourself and another for the Council, I pray God to forgive you. I do. I trouble your Lordships no further.' The jury returned a verdict of proven. The usual sentence followed: to be hanged, drawn, quartered— the parts fixed on the Netherbow and on the Tolbooths of Lanark, Ayr, and Glasgow—confiscated, demeaned, 'blood tainted,' that day. Like sanctimonious Jews, the inquisitors wished the awful deed over 'before the holy days of Yuile.' So wrote Lauder himself.

His final hours Baillie spent praying God to make him an 'acceptable sacrifice' and to 'put a merciful stop to the shedding of the blood of His people.' Too weak to walk, Baillie was carried to the city Cross to suffer. Lady Graden mounted the scaffold with him. When he began to address the bystanders thus, 'My faint zeal for the Protestant religion has brought me to this end,' the drums rolled, and the hangman turned him over. Lady Graden waited on and saw the hangman hash, oil, tar, and haul away to the Thieves' Hole the mortal fragments of her beloved relative. This was the hideous introduction to Christmas Eve—a holy season which ushered in no peace or goodwill to the Remnant.[1]

Baillie on the scaffold, 23rd December 1684.

Appropriately enough here might that heroine of the Covenant and friend of Jerviswood, Grizzel Hume, elder sister of young Patrick the advocate, have sung to a different strain her love-song, 'Were na my heart licht I wad dee.' But this brave maid of nineteen had yet to live for her ostracised father. Sir Patrick, in his perilous hiding, and for her lover, George, the son of the executed Baillie, whom she first met in a prison. Sir Patrick, once, and to be again, adjudged a traitor, with the hue and cry out for him as an associate of conspirators, found an unsuspected refuge in the family burial-vault in Polwarth churchyard, until

Grizzel Hume.

[1] *Book of Adjournal*, 23rd December; *State Trials*, x. 647-724; Fountainhall, *Decisions*, i. 324-7; *Hist. Not.*, ii. 587-95; Omond, i. 223; Erskine, *Journal*, 100; *Ladies of Covenant*, 383-5; Wodrow, iv. 104-12; *Analecta*, iii. 78-80. Parliament in 1685 approved of the forfeiture and granted Mellerstains to the Duke of Gordon; Parliament in 1690 rescinded the forfeiture: *Act. Parl. Scot.*, viii. 473, 594; ix. 158, 166a; App. 144a. He left a written speech: Wodrow, iv. 110. Lady Graden survived till 1707.

he escaped to the Continent. Into this weird and eerie charnel-house was faithful Grizzel wont to come at midnight hour, stumbling over graves as she went, fetching food, inspiring hope. Her mother was a Ker of Cavers. Only those of Border blood could do such romantically heroic deeds. It boded ill for the success of menacing Popery when such bravery characterised the Covenanting lads and lasses.[1]

The Council completed their business for the year by publishing a proclamation, 30th December, denouncing the Declaration and ordering its upholders to be 'executed to the death,' commanding all living south of Tay to assemble and take the oath renouncing the Declaration and its principles, so as to get a certificate or free pass, held indispensable for all travellers over sixteen years of age; forbidding keepers of inns and lodgings to shelter persons without certificates, and empowering them to examine holders of suspicious passes; and offering a reward of five hundred merks for the discovery leading to the conviction of a Society-man.[2]

Subsequently, on 9th January, burghal magistrates were ordered to exact the Abjuration Oath. Every parish was to be taken separately, and all the parishioners were to subscribe the Abjuration Oath 'on a large sheet of paper.' On the same date a commission, to endure till 1st March, was given to five or six influential nobles and landholders in the disaffected counties to punish the 'inhumane monsters' said to be 'debauched with schismatical and seditious principles,' and 'daily committing bloody and execrable murders,'—three to be a quorum, and nonconformists in the least jot or tittle to be their prey.[3] Eleven Lowland counties were embraced in this commission. Claverhouse was not nominated for this duty; his rival, Colonel James Douglas of the footguards, afterwards was. In Dumfriesshire the commissioners were the Earl of Annandale, Sir Robert Dalziel of Glenae, Sir James Johnston of Westerhall, Thomas Kirkpatrick of Closeburn, Sir Robert Grierson of Lag, and Robert Lawrie of Maxwelton. For the shires of Kirkcudbright and Wigtown John, Viscount Kenmure, Sir Robert Grierson of Lag, David Dunbar of Baldoon, Sir Godfrey M'Culloch of Mireton, and Sheriff-Depute David Graham were appointed. The justices in Ayr were

---

[1] Wodrow, iv. 505, 224-7; *Ladies of Covenant*, 546-87.

[2] Wodrow, iv. 160 note; *Acta*, 617-34.

[3] Wodrow, iv. 163-6.

Baron Hamilton of Bargany, Blair of Blair, Wallace of Craigie, Cathcart of Carlton, Provost Hunter of Ayr. It is noteworthy that Claverhouse was present in Council on 13th January 1685, and, with Perth, Queensberry, Douglas, Winton, Linlithgow, Southesk, Tweeddale, Balcarres, Yester, George Mackenzie, William Drummond, William Hay, and J. Wedderburne, prepared and signed the instructions given to the commissioners. The second instruction had painful results:—

'If any persone oune these principles [*i.e.* of the Cargill-Cameron-Renwick party], or doe not disoune them, they must be judged by at least three, and you must immediately give them a lybell and the names of the inqueist and witnesses, and they being found guilty are to be hanged immediately upon the place according to law. But at this time you are not to examine any women but such as hes been active in these courses in a signall manner, and these are to be drowned.'[1]

Instructions for 1685—warrant for drowning.

This was the warrant which empowered Sheriff Graham, Lag, and other commissioners to drown the Wigtown martyrs. In palliating the deeds of his hero. Professor Terry vauntingly writes: 'Of the refinement of cruelty which condemned the Wigtown martyrs to a lingering death there is in Claverhouse not a trace!'[2] That signature appended to the 'Instructiones'—'J. Grahame'—still exists to destroy this too charitable imagination, and for ever exhibits Claverhouse in his proper character.[3]

---

[1] 13th January 1685: *Reg. Sec. Conc., Acta*, 654-6; Wodrow, iv. 165.
[2] *John Graham*, 212.
[3] *Acta*, 654-6.

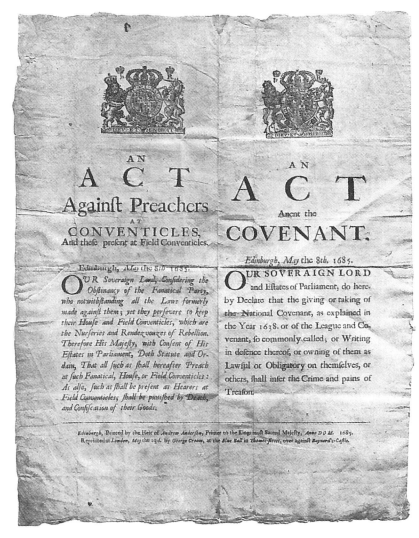

Edinburgh, Printed by the Heir of Andrew Anderson, Printer to the Kings most Sacred Majesty, Anno DOM. 1685.
Reprinted at London, May the 23d. by George Croom, at the Blue Ball in Thames-Street, over against Baynard's-Castle.

AN ACT AGAINST CONVENTICLE-PREACHERS.
AN ACT DECLARING SUBSCRIPTION OF THE COVENANT TO BE TREASON.

CHAPTER THIRTY

THE INLET OF POPERY

A T the end of the year 1684, Claverhouse was in disfavour at Court, as a result of the persistent efforts of Queensberry to undermine his recognised influence. From the time Queensberry concluded that Claverhouse preferred to promote at Court the interests of Aberdeen, he conceived an animosity which he expressed through the secretaries of State, thereby creating the impression that Claverhouse was fractious, impudent, fraudulent, avaricious, and overbearing to the great officers of the Crown. It was even hinted that his recent marriage into a Whig family made him no longer to be trusted with State secrets. The dislike was mutual. York took umbrage at Claverhouse, probably more out of policy than of pique. To the inconvenience of the soldier, who had paid his way out of the fines, and kept no accurate reckoning, Queensberry succeeded in getting an order calling up all the fines which Claverhouse had exacted, demand for payment of the forfeited estate of Freuch, granted under conditions to Claverhouse, the reprimand and removal of him for a time from the Privy Council,[1] and the promotion of other officers over his head.[2] The faithful slave of the Stuarts was cast down into the dust. With nothing left save his colonelcy, himself and his men at the call of less important officials, Claverhouse could only hope to retrieve his position by fidelity to his patron, soon to be king. It is in his role of sacrificer, with the

Claverhouse and Queensberry quarrel.

Claverhouse humiliated.

---

[1] 3rd March till 11th May.

[2] *Drumlanrig MSS., Hist. MSS. Com. Rep.*, xv. viii. *passim*; ii. *passim*; Terry, 181, 188-93; *Chron. Not.*, 128.

blood of John Brown upon his soul, that we next see Claverhouse approaching the proud Douglas as if to appease that god of his fortunes by an exhibition of his relentless hate of the antagonists of the King.

The year 1685 was notable for the activity of the various officials and forces of the Crown. To the military the south-west was an open execution ground. The well-authenticated instances of the enormities of the soldiery are too numerous for more than reference. Still many a Lowland family hands on from sire to son its own unrecorded story of suffering, and the public records are now substantiating narratives hitherto valued as mere tradition. Daniel Defoe fixes on the barbarities of this year to support his opinion that the Scottish persecution was worse than that of the Roman emperors and Popish inquisitors. Defoe investigated the subject when information was available, visited the blood-stained scenes, interviewed eye- and ear-witnesses and survivors, and, in the main, collected facts difficult to gainsay. Thus he records: 'The writer of this has heard the late Lieutenant-General Maitland express great abhorrence of the cruelties committed by Major Balfour, Captain Douglas, General Dalziel, and several others, who would take pains to search out such men as they thought did but shun to be seen, and with little or no examination, shoot them upon the spot, which he, being then under command, could no way prevent.'[1] Corroborating this statement is that of Wodrow, who, having learned from bystanders at the execution of the martyrs at Polmadie that Captain Maitland was heard protesting against it, sent his narrative to Maitland, who acknowledged its accuracy.[2] After all, Defoe may not be far from the mark when he reports that he heard that Claverhouse 'killed above a hundred men in this kind of cold-blooded cruelty.'[3] Wherever the history of Scotland is read, the names Dalyell, Graham, Grierson—a trinity of military persecutors—are associated with the contemporary undying epithet, 'bluidy.'[4]

Sir Robert Grierson, related to Queensberry by blood and marriage, son of William Grierson of Barquhar, born 1657, succeeded his cousin in the estate of Lag in Dunscore, Dumfriesshire. In his youth he was

Defoe's opinion on the persecution.

General Maitland's extraordinary testimony.

Grierson of Lag, 1657-1733.

---

[1] *Memoirs*, 281.
[2] Wodrow, iv. 251.
[3] *Memoirs*, 285.
[4] *Memorials*, 35, 38.

like Turner and Claverhouse, a university man, also an author. In his old age he was a smuggler, debtor, alleged debaser of the coin, a litigant put to the horn.[1] In the South he took a prominent part in all the political and military transactions between 1678 and 1688. He was in his twenty-second year when he was attached to Claverhouse's force at the demolition of the conventicle-house at the Brigend of Dumfries in 1679. This prototype of Sir Walter Scott's Sir Robert Redgauntlet was created baronet on 28th March 1685, and died in Dumfries in December 1733, having lived to see his son William go out in the '15 and be forfeited.[2] Patrick Walker, having published his animadversions upon Grierson six years before he died, must have had good authority for stating that Lag was 'a great persecutor, a great swearer, a great whorer, blasphemer, drunkard, liar and cheat, and yet out of hell.'[3]

For the student of the period, leaving out of account the military executions, it is impossible to conceive that the innumerable finings, driving to jail, burning of houses and implements, forcible quartering and victualling, encouraged a stainless soldiery. One would fain believe it untrue that the troops 'behaved themselves in so beastial a manner that no marriageable woman could with safety stay at home,' while the children could not be fed till 'the soldiers first lapped the broth.'[4]

Estimate of the common soldiery.

The soldiers were not always permitted to ride 'red-wat-shod' over the Galloway peasantry. In January, a fight took place in which Captain Urquhart and two soldiers were killed and Colonel Douglas just saved himself by pistolling his opponent.[5] Being hounded into church to take the Test and then to be told by Lag, 'Now you are a fold of clean beasts, ye may go home,' was not the worst occurrence. The records

---

[1] Grierson was tried for clipping and coining in Ruthwell old castle, The trial, begun on 3rd June 1696, was adjourned to 15th June. The charge was deserted by the Crown on 22nd June. Cf. *Book of Adjournal.*

[2] *Act. Parl. Scot.*, viii. 214; W. Dickie, 'The Griersons of Lag' in *Dumfries Standard*, cxviii. 1 and 2; Fergusson, *The Laird of Lag*, q.v.

[3] 'Vindication of Cameron,' *Six Saints*, i. 330. Lag's neglected grave, covered with rank weeds in a ruinous sepulchre in Dunscore old churchyard, was long an object of awe and contempt to visitors there. A monument now marks the burial-place.

[4] *A Brief and True Account of the Sufferings of Scotland*, 5 (Lond., 1690).

[5] *Reg. Sec. Conc., Acta*, 28th January 1685, p. 663; *Observes*, 146; Wodrow, iv. 198. Col. James Douglas of the foot was added to the Commission for Galloway on 28th January.

of the Privy Council remain to tell of the awful scenes in the judicial shambles—branding, bone-crushing, ear-lopping, starving to death, pestilence, and other horrors. A few instances, culled at random, may suffice.[1]

Marie Normand and baby to be liberated (*Acta*, 275). Patrick Maxwell, Dundee, aged eleven, gives bond (9th May, 85). John Fleming, 'ane old decrept paralike guttish creature,' detained till he take the oath. 'Patrick Jackson, a poor dyeing creature not able to stand, overgrown with scurvie' (21st May). Two women, soon to be mothers, went to Dunnottar to see their husbands, and were kept in the vaults by the governor (11th September, *Acta*, 157). Sick women dragged into prison leaving infants—Margaret Lithgow (2nd April 1685, *Acta*, 34). Dame Anna Scot, Lady Schelmerk, innocently distrained, proved guiltless, kept in ward while her children lay ill and dying, allowed out on caution (3rd June 1685, *Acta*, 77). Many such dames of quality were herded with other sufferers—Ladies Colville, Tealing, St. Ford, Hope, Abdean, Longformacus—and had to pay sweetly for freedom.[2]

The ordinary judges now had repose from sanguinary business, since the carnival of blood was managed by the soldiers in the country. Only

once in January, they sat to dispose of a capital case for the Covenant, namely that of Robert Pollock, shoemaker in East Kilbride, and of Robert Miller, mason in Rutherglen, who preferred death to the abjuration of Renwick's principles, and were accordingly dispatched at the Gallowlee on 23rd January 1685.[3] Several prisoners who were condemned to death by the Commission in Ayr had their sentences commuted to banishment. Quintin Dick was of the number.[4]

An early sacrifice to the Abjuration Oath was Andrew MacGill from Aryclyoch in Ballantrae, a registered fugitive, who was executed in Ayr in January.[5] On 23rd January, Colonel James Douglas, Lieutenant Livingstone, and Cornet Douglas surprised at prayer at Caldons, Minnigaff,

---

[1] When the *Acta* and *Decreta*—Minutes of the Privy Council meetings—are published, the eyes of Scotland will be opened and Wodrow will be vindicated. These manuscripts are preserved in the Register House, Edinburgh.

[2] Wodrow, iv. 213. Dames were by courtesy styled 'Ladies.'

[3] *Book of Adjournal*, 19th January; Wodrow, iv. 226; *Cloud*, 425-35.

[4] Wodrow, iv. 199.

[5] *Ibid.* 336.

six men. Their names were James Dun; Robert Dun (Bewhat, fugitive?); Robert Stevenson, Barbeath, Straiton; John Stevenson, Star, Straiton; Andrew M'Call (Alexander M'Aulay or M'Kale); James M'Clive (or John M'Lude, M'Leod, M'Clure, Maclave) from Straiton.

They were shot. One of the Duns escaped by plunging into Loch Trool and hiding there.[1] David Dun, farmer in Closs, Ochiltree, and Simon Paterson, returning from a conventicle held by Renwick at Dalmellington, were taken at Corsegellioch and shot by a party of Highlanders at Cumnock.[2] On 30th January, John Dalziel, son of Sir Robert of Glenae, and Lieutenant Straton or Strachan, surprised a party of Covenanters at Lurgfoot, a farm near Morton Castle, Dumfriesshire, and, after a skirmish on the moor, captured Daniel MacMichael, wounded and too sick to escape.[3] Daniel, a registered fugitive, brother of James, was lurking there fever-struck. The soldiers bore him to St. Cuthbert's Church, Durisdeer, for the night. Apparently they intended taking him to Edinburgh by snow-bound, revengeful Enterkin, where he had been a rescuer. The escort reached rebel Hoatson's farm at Nether Dalveen next day, when prudence and fear of an ambuscade made them halt. The sick man was interrogated and failed to satisfy the court-martial. Ordered to prepare for death on the hillside, Daniel read: 'A little while and ye shall not see me. … In the world ye shall have tribulation. I have overcome the world.' He fervently prayed. Then resounded in melody and words:

> 'O why art thou cast down, my soul,
> Why thus with grief opprest?'

That was enough. The sulphurous blast of four carbines made re-echoing discord through Dalveen Pass, and gave Amen to song and singer.[4]

Other victims of the law.

The heroic death of Daniel MacMichael, 31st January 1685.

---

[1] Wodrow, iv. 239, 240; *Memorial*, 35; *Martyr Graves*, 337, 357.

[2] 'Hanged,' writes Wodrow, iv. 252; *Martyr Graves*, 328, 336, 338, 357. Tradition says that Margaret Dun was also shot. David was on fugitive roll. *A Short Memorial*, 38, includes Joseph Wilson and other two unnamed, probably John Jameson and John Humphrey, who are buried on Corsegellioch: *Martyr Graves*, 339.

[3] Wodrow preserves (Advocates' Library MSS., xxxvii., 4to) an account of the brutal treatment of a woman thrown into the dungeon of Morton Castle for Covenanting.

[4] Wodrow, iv. 239; *Martyr Graves*, 459-62; *Memorial* (36) states Sir Robert D. MacMichael is buried in Durisdeer churchyard. Peden planted an ash-tree on his

Dispatch of
William
Adam.

An execution
at Paisley.

Conversion
through
terror.

The
Lochenkit
martyrs.

There is no more pathetic spot in Ayrshire than 'Wellwood's dark valley' where Dalziel and Strachan, in February or March, finding William Adam 'hiding himself in a bush, did stick him dead without ever speaking a word unto him.'[1]

Wodrow had the authority of Matthew Crawford, the historian, and parish minister of Eastwood, for his account of the vile treatment of John Park and James Algie, joint tenants of the small farm of Kennishead in Eastwood. They had ceased going to the church. The Commissioners tried them, and finding that these young men had doubts about taking the Test, although they were willing to take the Abjuration Oath, sent them to the gallows at Paisley Cross on 3rd February 1685.[2] Robert King, miller at Pollokshaws, also lived to inform Wodrow that, while these victims were still suspended before the Tolbooth, wherein the Commissioners were holding the court, he, apprehended for nonconformity that day, was brought in for examination. His answers were indefinite, equivocating, by their nature incriminating. He refused the Test. He was led to the window to view the dangling corpses of his neighbours and friends, and threatened with a like fate. He was sent to prison to wait three blasts of a trumpet, which were to sound in an hour. If he did not take the Test before the third blast he too was to swing. After the second call the terrified miller broke down, took the Test, escaped the halter, and to his dying day mourned his defection.[3]

On the uplands of Kirkpatrick-Durham, near lonely Lochenkit, Captain Bruce brought six or eight wanderers to a stand. Their names were William Herron, Glencairn; John Gordon (elder in Garryhorn?); William Stuart (Crofts, or Larg?); John Wallace (Rosehill?); Alexander M'Cubin (M'Robin, Marwhan, Glencairn?); Edward Gordon (Blacke?); Robert Grier; Lochenkit; and one named Edgar. The majority of them bore the names of registered fugitives. The four first-named were shot and buried on the moor. The four prisoners were marched down to

---

grave. It still lives. The late Mrs. Gracie, East Morton, gave the author Daniel's sword.

[1] Cochrane of Watersyde gave this account, which differs from Wodrow's; cf. *Wodrow MSS.*, xxxvii. 4to, with Wodrow, iv. 241; *U. F. Church Magazine*, July 1905; *Memorial*, 36; *Martyr Graves*, 150.

[2] Wodrow, iv. 189; *Martyr Graves*, 281.

[3] Wodrow, iv. 190-1.

Bridge of Urr where Lag, the Commissioner, was engaged proffering the Abjuration Oath. They refused to take it. Next day Lag took them as far as Irongray Church, where the invincible stalwarts of that parish had lately insulted the incumbent. He strung two of them—M'Cubin and Gordon—up to an oak-tree, as a warning to the tenant of Hallhill and other local dwellers at hand. Grier and Edgar, it is said, were banished to the West Indies, from which Grier returned home after the Revolution.[1] *A Short Memorial* records the shooting by Captain Douglas of a tailor named Mowat, taken between Fleet and Dee, simply 'because he had some pieces of lead belonging to his trade'—these being looked on as ammunition; also another case of shooting without trial—that of Edward M'Keen (M'Kean or Kyan) caught with 'a flint stone upon him.'[2] Wodrow gives details of the latter execution from an attested deposition, which shows that Kyan was a corn-dealer from Mennock Water, and had arrived at Dalwin in Barr on business. A party of soldiers under Cornet James Douglas surrounded the farm on the night of the 28th February. He tried to escape. The narrative states that Douglas himself first pistolled him after asking a few questions, and that the soldiers otherwise treated the inmates of Dalwin barbarously, even beating the women,[3] and taking away some suspected visitors. Well might those apprehensive of their country's fate ask: 'If they do these things in the green tree, what shall be done in the dry?'

On 6th February, King Charles II. breathed his last in somewhat dramatic circumstances. At the close of his mortal illness Archbishop Sancroft and Bishop Ken came to give ghostly counsel, to adjure the dying sinner to repent, and to offer him the Sacrament. The sweet voice of earnest Ken availed nothing, and the King politely declined the Sacrament, saying, 'It was time enough.' On their retiral York asked his brother if he preferred a priest, and he assented. Huddlestone, a Benedictine priest, was at hand, and was introduced by a private stair into the death-chamber. Charles received his old friend with joy, and exclaimed: 'You that saved my body is now come to save my soul'—a grateful reference to Huddlestone's services at Worcester. In the words of

Examples at Irongray.

Shooting men without trial.

Death of Charles II., 6th February 1685.

---

[1] Wodrow, iv. 240; *Martyr Graves*, 363, 481-3. *Memorial* (36), at p. 38 calls the two 'Alexander Mellubie and John Gordon.'

[2] *A Short Memorial*, 36.

[3] Wodrow, iv. 241.

York, Charles 'made his confession to him, was reconciled, receved the blessed Sacrament, had the Extreme Unction … and died unconcerned as became a good Christian.'[1] This acceptance of the viaticum was not the mere perfunctory, timid recognition of the Church of Rome by a dying man, for the act was in accord with the King's long-concealed opinion regarding Popery. His brother attested 'two papers written by the late King Charles II. of blessed memory,' which he vouched for as found in the King's 'strong box written in his own hand.' Therein Charles avowed his belief that there is 'one Church … that none can be that Church but that which is called the Romane Catholick Church.'[2]

The belief of Charles II.

Standpoint is everything. That day, Melfort wrote to Queensberry: 'He died as he lived, the admiration of all men for his piety, his contempt of the world, and his resolutions against death.'[3] This base trick of the moribund Monarch was a fitting termination to a long life of chicanery. His niggardly brother gave a suitable finish to a sordid career by the mean burial of Charles. The character and achievements of the dead Sovereign are too well known to require further comment.

The poet, Dryden, in a jejune ode, sang:

'Our Atlas fell indeed, but Hercules was near.'[4]

James VII. proclaimed King, on 10th February 1685.

On 10th February, an express messenger brought to the Scots Council the new King's letter announcing his accession, and also a copy of the Proclamation of the fact. Claverhouse was present and signed the Proclamation, which bore that James was 'righteous king and sovereign, over all persons, and in all causes, as holding his imperial crown from God alone.'[5] This assumption of authority was not according to the law of Scotland. It saved the King taking the coronation oath—an omission urged against James in 1689. It is also of importance to note that Claverhouse was also present in Council on the 12th February, when it was announced that King James 'by his royal proclamation, allowed all his judges and officers to act as formerly until they receive

---

[1] 'Account of the Death,' etc., in York's calligraphy: *Cal. Stuart Pap.*, i. 3-5; Airy, *Charles II.*, 411-4.
[2] *Brit. Mus. Add. MSS.*, 27402, fol. 153, 'Coppies of two papers.'
[3] *Drumlanrig MSS.*, ii. 212.
[4] *Threnodia Augustalis … 1685.*
[5] *Reg. Sec. Conc., Acta*, 1; Wodrow, iv. 201 note.

new Commissiones.' At the same sederunt certain commissions were referred to as continued.[1] The royal clemency was shown in a proclamation of indemnity, on the face of it merciful, but in reality harsh, since it was confined to persons under the rank of property holders, landward and burghal, and exempted vagrant preachers, persons under sentence of fining, and the murderers of Sharp, Peirson, Kennoway, and Stewart. Pardoned fugitives were to take the oath of allegiance or agree to leave the country.[2] But who all had paid fines? Who were the backbone of the country but the heritors and burgesses—still a prey for the Crown?

Although by subsequent orders the Council modified the terms of the undertaking of loyalty in order to bring in the lukewarm, there was no real intention of exhibiting genuine toleration. The boldness of gangs of rebels marching about Ayrshire in March was the reason advanced for granting a special justice's commission to Colonel Douglas of the Guards, to act in conjunction with the authorities then in office in all the southern and western shires, from 27th March till 20th April. A long list of magistrates and officers includes that of David Graham, styled Sheriff of Galloway, but not that of his brother, John. The latter was presently under reprimand. Still, Douglas's commission, given 'in pique to Claverhouse,' according to Lauder, did not supersede 'persons as were formerly commissionate.'[3] His orders were 'to extirpate these rebels.' Claverhouse was present in Council, and must have been galled to see this pleasant duty conferred on his rival.[4] The results of the expedition of Douglas were far from satisfactory.

Colonel Douglas's commission.

The King pressed the vintage of blood. His managers confessed, in the commission granted to Lieutenant-General Drummond on 21st April, and continuing till 1st June, that the disaffected in the Lowlands increased in number and insolence, so that the new justice needed extraordinary powers for 'utterly destroying all such fugitive rebels.'

Fresh vintage of blood.

[1] *Acta*, 2, 6, 7; Wodrow, iv. 204. Claverhouse attended Council seven times in January, twelve in February, eleven in March, two in April, and none thereafter till 16th July: *Proclamation for 'persons in office'*: Aldis, *List*, 2574, 2575. Thus Professor Terry is wrong in saying that Claverhouse's commission expired with the late King's death: *John Graham*, 190 and note 4.

[2] Wodrow, iv. 205 note; Aldis, *List*, 2578, 26th February.

[3] *Decisions*, i. 345.

[4] *Reg. Sec. Conc.*, *Acta*, 31; *Decreta*, 107; Wodrow, iv. 207 note.

Regulars, militia, and Highlanders were to accompany him. All persons found in arms were to be shot immediately. He was to inquire into any suspicious case and punish according to law. Meantime all other commissions for trying or punishing were withdrawn, and the military despot was given a free hand to secure peace.[1]

Man-hunting in 1685. The instructions given by Douglas and Drummond to their subalterns are not before us. Man-hunting was the order of the day. Meantime the Council busied itself with a scheme for emptying the overflowing jails. It was better to banish them to the cane-brakes than to let them die of cold and hunger, as the beggar witch, Marion Purdy, did. The Glasgow magistrates, 'pestered with many silly old women,' were ordered to whip, brand, and dismiss them.[2] Disloyal prisoners were to be liberated on a bond by a heritor, that they would be ready to go abroad in May. Those taking the Test and giving caution would be freed. Irreconcilables were to have their ears cut off, their cheeks stigmatised with letters, and be banished.[3]

March of prisoners to Dunnottar Castle. In May, it was reported that the Argyll expedition had sailed. Prisons would be needed. It was determined to transfer the most obstinate prisoners from Edinburgh to inhospitable Dunnottar Castle. A more miserable procession never walked out of or in to the Capital than this straggling band of above 134 men and 50 women—young, old, lame, sick, paralytic, dying—who were escorted by the foot-guards down to Leith, on 18th May. With other prisoners in Leith they numbered 224. In small boats they were ferried across to Burntisland. There they were examined by Gosford and Major John Wedderburne, and the oaths were pressed upon them. Wedderburne's notes are instructive: 'John Broun ane old decrept creature; Thomas Peticrew ... old age ... being paralitick; Nicolas M'Night a dyeing woman; Michael Smyth a lame and decryped man; John Wmson (Williamson?) mad and furious; Jean Stodhart, big of child and in hazard of dying if forced to travell.' Forty prisoners were sent back to Edinburgh, some having resiled from their principles and taken the oath. Roped like cattle, the miserables were marched northward, arriving at Dunnottar on Sabbath, 24th May.

[1] Wodrow, iv. 208, 209.
[2] *Acta*, 104, 4th July 1685.
[3] *Ibid.*, 107-35; Wodrow, iv. 198, 210, 216.

Seventeen escaped by the way.[1] Among the number immured were three preachers—John Fraser, minister of Alness, who left an account of his experiences, William MacMillan, and John Doning.

Sheriff-Depute George Keith of White-ridge received the crowd into his custody. Beneath the lordly chambers of the Earl Marischal remain intact two stone-vaulted stores, one above the other. Neither has a *garde-robe*.[2] The upper vault, probably a granary, with one small window looking on the German Ocean, and one bole, measures 54 feet 9 inches long by 15 feet 6 inches broad and 12 feet high. It communicates by a shoot with a small, wet, vaulted chamber beneath it, measuring 15 feet long, 8 broad, and 9 high, lighted and ventilated through the orifice of a small drain on the floor level, where the prisoners in turn lay down to suck in air.[3] These are called *The Whigs' Vaults*. The almost incredible barbarity with which the wretched Covenanters were treated does not rest merely on the local tradition that refractory inmates were lashed to hooks on the walls and burned with match, and otherwise tortured by the soldiers on guard. The petition of Grissell Cairnes and Alison Johnston, on behalf of their husbands and the other prisoners, is recorded in the minutes of the Privy Council.[4] They refer to their 'most lamentable condition,' and to 'one hundred and ten of them in one vault, where there is little or no daylight at all, and contrarie to all modestie men and women promiscuouslie together, and fourtie and two more in another roume in the same condition, and no person allowed to come near them with meat or drink, but such bread and drink as scarce any rationall creature can live upon, and yet at extra-ordinary rates, being twentie pennies each pynt of ale, which is not worth a plack the pint, and the pocke of dustie sandie meal is afforded to them at eighteen shilling per peck. And not so much as a drink of water allowed to be caryed to them, whereby they are not only in a starving condition but must inevitably incurr a plague or other fearful

'The Whigs' vaults.

Barbarity to prisoners.

---

[1] Wodrow, iv. 322-6; Gosford's report in *Reg. Sec. Conc.*, printed by Dr. D. Hay Fleming in *Martyr Graves*, App. 495-507.

[2] [French: a room in a medieval castle; originally a store-room for valuables, but by extension, a private room, a bed-chamber; also a privy. Its most common use now is as a term for a castle toilet.]

[3] Measured by author. Cf. Longmuir, *Dunnottar Castle*, 61, 62; *Martyr Graves*, 217; *Six Saints*, i. 352; ii. 99.

[4] *Reg. Sec. Conc.*, *Acta*, 86, 18th June; Wodrow, iv. 325.

diseases.' The Council ordered a mitigation of these severities, especially that the prisoners should be confined 'without throng.'[1]

Horrors well-nigh incredible.

The horrors did not cease here. At first sight one is inclined to disbelieve Wodrow's account of the brutality of the governor towards the wife of James Forsyth, were it not that an almost similar case was humanely treated by the Council in September, after the prisoners came back to Leith. James Forsyth in Carthat, Annandale, a registered fugitive, was caught, sent to Edinburgh, included in the batch removed to Dunnottar, and was visited by his wife, who, of course, was apprehended for converse and added to the tale of captives. She was *enceinte*. The governor refused to allow her to leave the crowded vault, where she had to be confined of her child and where she died of neglect.[2] No wonder the contemporary author of *A Hind Let Loose* asserted that 'the wildest and rudest of savages would have thought shame of' such barbarity.[3] Wodrow, however, gives the governor's wife the credit of prevailing upon her husband to mitigate the lot of the captives. Of twenty-five men who tried to escape, fifteen were caught and subjected to castigation and torture by match, as one of the sufferers, William Niven, informed Wodrow.[4] Alexander Dalgleish died from the torture, and others from harsh treatment.[5]

Stock of prisoners.

The Council again took stock of their prisoners, on 24th July, and found that of 283 persons, 177 were banished, 49 cut in the ear, 15

---

[1] Patrick Walker, one of the prisoners, asserted that 168 prisoners, some in irons, were driven into one vault: *Six Saints*, i. 316.

[2] Wodrow (iv. 332) does not give her maiden name. Forsyth's name is on Wedderburne's list, also Jean Stodhart, 'big of child.' Cf. *Reg. Sec. Conc.*, *Acta*, 157: the Council order Janet Bell (on Wedderburne's list) and Marion Wallace, apprehended going to Dunnottar to see their husbands, to be liberated, being *enceinte* (11th September 1685).

[3] *Hind*, 201.

[4] *Hist.*, iv. 324; Erskine, *Journal*, 154.

[5] Sir Walter Scott met 'Old Mortality' in Dunnottar parish churchyard, repairing a stone with the following inscription:—

'HERE LYES JOHN STOT, JAMES ATCHISON, JAMES RUSSELL, AND WILLIAM BROUN, AND ONE WHOSE NAME WEE HAVE NOT GOTTEN, AND TWO WOMEN WHOSE NAMES ALSO WEE KNOW NOT, AND TWO WHO PERISHED COMEING DOUNE THE ROCK, ONE WHOSE NAME WAS JAMES WATSON, THE OTHER NOT KNOWN, WHO ALL DIED PRISONERS IN DUNOTTAR CASTLE, ANNO 1685, FOR THEIR ADHERENCE TO THE WORD OF GOD AND SCOTLAND'S COVENANTED WORK OF REFORMATION. REV. XI. CH. 12 VERSE.'

detained, 2 remitted, and 4 dismissed. Before the slavers sailed, there were additional recruits at the muster. Other tragedies were being enacted in the sad south-west. John Bell, proprietor of Whiteside, David Halliday, Mayfield, Robert Lennox, Irlandton, Andrew MacRobert, and James Clement were surprised at prayer on Kirkconnel Moor, in Tongland parish, by Lag, accompanied by some of Claverhouse's horse and Strachan's dragoons, on 21st February. Bell was fugitive and forfeited since 6th July 1680, and was on 8th October 1681 proclaimed among other gentlemen in Galloway wanted by the authorities. His mother, Marion MacCulloch, daughter of Ardwell, took for her second husband Viscount Kenmure. Claverhouse's men rioted on Whiteside. Bell's fine monument in romantic Anwoth churchyard records that 'Douglas of Morton did him quarters give.' Notwithstanding, when the young man begged a respite for prayer, Lag retorted: 'What, Devil, have you been doing? Have you not prayed enough these many years in the hills?' They were shot instantly. Clement alone was buried where he fell. When Lag, Claverhouse, and Kenmure next met, Kenmure challenged Lag for his brutality, and on Lag retorting, 'Take him, if you will, and salt him in your beef barrel,' Kenmure drew his sword to run Lag through, when Claverhouse interposed.[1] *Shooting of Bell and others, February 1685.*

On the Racemuir, Moniaive, a rough slab marks the place where William Smith, a youth of nineteen, was shot. It is in view of the hill where his father and mother dwelt, also visible from Renwick's home. Cornet Baillie of the Caitloch garrison took Smith on the fields of Hill, in March. He refused to answer questions. The cornet handed him over to Robert Laurie, laird of Maxwelton, who, with Douglas of Stenhouse and Sir John Craik of Stewarton, examined the youth in Glencairn church. He was accused of converse with rebels and refused to disclose their hiding-place. Probably he was a Renwickite. Laurie, whose justiciary commission expired on 1st March, and who could hardly have got notice of a new one from Colonel Douglas, ordered Baillie, also a justice, to shoot him. Baillie, it was said, protested against the illegality of a sentence without reference to an assize presided over by three justices, but obeyed orders. It is more likely that the procedure *Shooting of William Smith, March 1685.*

---

[1] *Short Memorial*, 37; Wodrow, iii. 180, 249; iv. 242. For their graves see *Martyr Graves*, 369, 393, 395, 399, 411.

was according to the Privy Council's orders. Smith died like a hero. Local tradition maintains that Laurie ordered him to be buried under the doorstep of Hill. After the Revolution he was buried in Tynron churchyard, where an 'Old Mortality' stone records these strange features of the case.[1]

Captain Peter Inglis, of the dragoons stationed at Newmilns, had an unenviable notoriety for ferocity when harassing the Ayrshire Covenanters. At Greenock Mains, Muirkirk, lived an aged man, over seventy, Thomas Ritchart, whom the indulged minister of the parish. Hew Campbell, had induced to resume church-going, but whose heart was with the persecuted. His son James was on the fugitive roll. Early in April, Inglis, with a few of his men, disguised as Whigs, came to the hospitable farm and ingratiated themselves with the unsuspecting host, and trepanned him into making incriminating allusions in his prayers, and admissions in his talk. They conveyed him to Cumnock, where the Commissioner Douglas was holding a court. He was ordered to be shot at the gallows on the Barhill on 4th April 1685, for his proved confession of sheltering 'the honest party.'[2]

A somewhat kindlier fate awaited Allan Aitken, indweller in Cumnock, John Pearson, tailor there, and James Napier, mason in Ochiltree. Douglas sentenced them to die at Cumnock on 20th April. They petitioned the Council, took the Abjuration Oath, were reprieved, and liberated in July.[3]

Nemesis soon overtook Inglis. About this time (April) Inglis, 'By birth a Tyger rather than a Scot,' surprised a conventicle at Little

---

[1] *Short Memorial*, 37; *Martyr Graves*, 440. Wodrow (iv. 242) gives 3rd March, the tombstone 29th March, for date of execution. Douglas's joint commission with Laurie, Baillie (not Craik), is dated 27th March: cf. Wodrow, iv. 207 note; 164. Craik was 'convener' of Glencairn, holding a commission from Queensberry, Drumlanrig, and Claverhouse: cf. Papers in Register House, October-December 1684. Laurie, Douglas, and Craik held a court in Tynron kirk on 19th September 1684, and examined witnesses regarding James MacMichael and the Enterkin rescue: *ibid*. This proves that they had a commission.

[2] *Muirkirk Sess. Rec.*, 67; *Short Memorial*, 35; Wodrow, iv. 252; Cochrane of Waterside, Letter, 2nd October 1714: *Wodrow MSS.*, xxxvii. 104; 89; *Martyr Graves*, 336.

[3] *Reg. Sec. Conc.*, *Acta*, 42, 56, 78, 94: 9th, 30th April, 5th, 30th June; Wodrow, iv. 234.

Blackwood, and, according to the *Memorial*, 'killed one James White, struck off his head with an ax, and plaid at the football with it.' Some prisoners were lodged in Newmilns Tower. The peasantry were roused. Renwick and armed bands were conventicling at Loudoun Hill and Cairntable. Sixty men led by Browning, a blacksmith at Lanfine, and John Law, brother-in-law of Captain Nisbet, with sledge-hammers broke into the Tower and rescued the prisoners, Law being shot in the exploit by the meagre guard. The authorities degraded Inglis for his remissness. The soldiers had speedy revenge by shooting, at Croonan, , who gave the escaping rescuers some refreshment.[1]

Rescue of prisoners in Newmilns.

Before Douglas's commission expired he made a descent upon Nithsdale, accompanied by Lieutenant Livingstone and eighteen dragoons, and was guided by 'knavish [Andrew] Watson' to a 'hidie hole' on Ingilston farm, overlooking the Racemuir, Moniaive. A conventicle had just dispersed. In this asylum he found John Gibson, fugitive brother to the laird of Ingliston, James Bennoch, Glencairn, Robert Edgar, a Renwickite and non-juror from Balmaclellan, Robert Mitchell, Cumnock, and Robert Grierson from Galloway (Reglen?) A volley wounded the men in the cave. Douglas gave them short shrift. First John Gibson prayed, then sang the 17th Psalm ending:

The Ingliston tragedy, April 1685.

> 'And with Thy likeness when I wake
> I satisfied shall be.'

He read from the sixteenth chapter of St. John—'Yea, the time cometh, that whosoever killeth you will think that he doeth God service.' His mother and sister ran in before the muskets, only to be comforted with the confession, 'this was the joyfullest day ever he had in the world.' Douglas was inexorable. After Gibson fell, the others were shot. When weltering in his blood, before John Fergusson thrust him through, one of the victims (Gibson) exclaimed: 'Though every hair of my head were a man, I am willing to die all those deaths for Christ and His Cause.'[2]

---

[1] Norman Macleod in *New Stat. Acc.* (Loudoun), 838; *Observes*, 160; *Hist. MSS. Com. Rep.*, xv. viii. 292; *Martyr Graves*, 129, 110. White is buried in Fenwick; Law lies close to the Tower. Inglis had other slaughters to his account in his district. Cf. James Smith, and John Barrie, *Memorial*, 37: date 25th April (?).

[2] Cf. tombstones: one in Ingliston Garden, three in Glencairn, one in Balma-clellan: *Martyr Graves*, 443, 386; *Memorial* (35) says Watson was then—1689—in

Drummond's commission.

Douglas's commission expired on the 20th April; General Drummond's was signed next day. It was comprehensive—'to do everything'—shoot, hang, fine, fire, let loose the Highland horde—'for securing peace.'[1] Nothing made for peace. The impolitic treatment of the indulged ministers, some languishing in prison, others 'at the horn,' still others like David Simson of Killean (and Southend) in Kintyre, glad to escape from trouble by joining the slave-ships, was irritating those moderately inclined.[2] Armed conventiclers, societies, secret schools of rustic acolytes of Renwick, still increased in number and influence, and often held the field unmolested listening to Peden and Renwick, whom none betrayed. The only genii of bliss moving over the unhappy land were these two holy, homeless wanderers.

Claverhouse in the chase.

Great events were at the birth. Parliament was about to sit. Argyll was about to sail. Claverhouse, now dropped out of the Council, and with no seat but his hot saddle, was about to make welcome amends for his indiscretions. At the end of April, Claverhouse, leading one hundred horse and three hundred redshanks, searched the uplands of Lanarkshire, between Douglas and Newmilns, for those spectral preachers of the mist and the mountain, Peden and Renwick, and just missed the former and his company. Serjeant James Nisbet was there among the hunted, and left an account of the fearful chase lasting for days.[3] Peden escaped and found refuge in the wild waste of Priesthill at Over-Priestshiel, the home of his friend, John Brown, 'the Christian Carrier.' He stayed all night and wisely left at daybreak of what he called 'a fearful morning, a dark misty morning.' It was May Morn.[4]

Priestshiel or Priesthill.

Priestshiel was a little croft on the melancholy moorland between Muirkirk and Lesmahagow. There Brown lived with his two boys and Jonet Ritchart, his first wife, till she died, leaving him barely solvent with twenty sheep, one cow, a stirk, and 'ane old meir,' together with debts to pay—two years' rent to Loudoun, a loan to a relative, a debt

---

Dumfries prison; Defoe, 287; Wodrow, iv. 243, 244. Glencairn stones give date, 28th April, probably a mistake.

[1] Wodrow, iv. 209.

[2] *Ibid.*. 340.

[3] Nisbet, *Memoirs*, 103-5; M'Crie, *Veitch*, App. 522.

[4] Walker, *Peden, Six Saints*, i. 84; Wodrow (iv. 244) calls the house 'Priestfield.' It is locally pronounced 'Preshil.'

to the minister, one fee to a lass, and another to the herd laddie, John Brouning.[1] Peden married Brown to Marion (or Isabel) Weir, and of their two children one was yet unborn. Brown, abhorring the indulgence, cess, and Prelacy, had developed out of an absentee from church into a pronounced Cameronian. As a resetter of all such he was proclaimed.[2] A rarely gifted, pious intelligence—like that of William Burness—distinguished this peasant, who attracted to his home earnest youths, so that it became a rustic school of theology. In Peden's eyes, Brown was 'a clear, shining light, the greatest Christian that ever I conversed with.'[3] Of the many John Browns who professed the Covenant, three of that name in Muirkirk were martyrs in that epoch: this one was the least offending.

There are two main accounts of the tragedy which occurred after Peden left—that of Claverhouse including John Brouning's alleged information, and that founded upon Widow Brown's narrative and that of others likely to know. In the latter, Brouning's part was ignored, or unknown.[4] After family worship, Brown, spade in hand, left home, between five and six in the morning, for a peat-face to flay peats. Claverhouse was then being led by guides—without them that waste is still impenetrable on a misty day—towards the shieling. Whether these guides were the Brounings from the Plewlands, the goodman of which farm Claverhouse mentions as in his hands (along with John Brouning, said to be captured beside his uncle, John Brown), or John Hamilton of Meadow, who 'rode in the guard,' it is now impossible to say.[5] Brown was surrounded and escorted home for examination and for a domiciliary search. When offered the Abjuration Oath Brown refused

---

[1] Testament of Jonet Ritchart: *Glasgow Com. Rec.*, June 1678. (Copy lent by Mr. J. B. Dalzell.)

[2] Hewison, 'The Martyrdom of John Broun' in *The U.F. Church Magazine*, July 1906, for authorities, facsimile, and photographs.

[3] *Six Saints*, i. 87.

[4] Letter of Claverhouse to Queensberry, dated 3rd May 1685, in *Hist. MSS. Com. Rep.*, (*Drumlanrig MSS.*, vol. i.), xv. viii. 292; Walker's *Peden*, in *Six Saints*, i. 84, 85; Cochrane and Aird's accounts in *Wodrow MSS.*, .xxxvii. 89, 102, 104, 105; *Short Memorial*, 35; Terry, *John Graham*, 197-202; Napier, *Memorials*, i. 141; iii. 457.

[5] Thomas Brouning of Plewland died 1669: *Glasgow Com. Rec.* John, son to William Brounen in Evindaill, baptized 26th July 1668: *Muirkirk Sess. Rec.* This date is suitable for the informer's birth.

to take it, declaring 'he kneu no King.' The 'yong fellou and his nephew' would take it. The search revealed bullets, match, and treasonable papers, which were no unlikely possessions lying in a carrier's home. 'I caused shoot him dead, which he suffered very inconcernedly,' was Claverhouse's account of the incident.[1]

Widow Brown's account of the matter.

The widow had a more pathetic story to tell as she sat on her husband's gravestone, recounting how he was brought home, ordered to his prayers, interrupted in them by irascible Claverhouse, peremptorily commanded 'to take goodnight' of her and his—that father's farewell and blessing sealed with tender kisses of her soon again to be a mother, and of his two children, one in her arms, a boy at her side— how six carbines shot, and 'her eyes dazled.'[2] Worse followed when the hero-cavalier sneeringly inquired 'What thinkest thou of thy husband now, woman?' 'As much now as ever,' said she. The framer of the law for drowning of women then exclaimed: 'It were but justice to lay thee beside him.' The fearless widow said: 'If ye were permitted, I doubt not but your cruelty would go that length; but how will ye make answer for this morning's work?' He retorted: 'To man I can be answerable; and for God, I will take Him in my own hand.' He rode away. Alone in that dreary spot she gathered up the scattered brains of her husband, laid him out under his plaid, and weeping watched the dead till humanity arrived. John Brown was buried where he was shot, before his own door.[3]

Claverhouse's treatment of Brouning.

Seemingly proud of his work, Claverhouse further rehearses all he did to the boy Brouning. He ordered him to prayers preparatory to execution, presented carbines at his head, then offered him a respite, and promised to plead for him if he would reveal anything of importance. The boy had much to tell, wrote Claverhouse, of his uncle's career at Bothwell, his arsenal stocked with arms, which they discovered, the Newmilns rescue, and local covenanting. Brouning was passed on to Drummond at Mauchline, and whatever pleadings of his captor may

---

[1] Claverhouse reported: 'We perseued tuo fellous a great way through the mosses and in end seized them.' Were they not Peden and Nisbet? Walker records that the Highlanders 'apprehended one John Binning [*i.e.* Brouning] waiting upon cattle, without stocking or shoe': *Six Saints*, i. 297.

[2] *Ibid.*, 86.

[3] The tombstone there gives his age as fifty-eight: *Martyr Graves*, 144.

have gone with him, that judge hanged the barefooted boy. But is Claverhouse's story to be credited?

Wodrow emphasises two statements, which he accepted as sufficiently vouched for by his informants—John Cochrane of Waterside, grandson of the Earl of Dundonald, and James Aird, a dweller at Priestshiel—that Claverhouse, on the refusal of his men, 'in a fret, shot him with his own hand,' and that Brown's dying prayer could never be effaced from his executioner's memory.'[1] Might not Cochrane have been told this latter fact by his own cousin, Jean, Viscountess Dundee, the only person likely to know of this secret revulsion?

On 2nd May 1685, another red-letter day in the Martyrology of the Covenant, the Wigtown martyrs were drowned.[2]

On the 13th April 1685, the Justiciary Commission held a Court at Wigtown. Wodrow states that Grierson of Lag, Sheriff David Graham, Major Winram, Captain Strachan, and William Coltran of Drummoral, provost of the burgh, and member for the county, took part in the proceedings.[3] The *Short Memorial* mentions only Colonel Douglas, the Commissioner, Lag, and Winram.[4] A jury was sworn. At least four female prisoners were brought to the bar, namely, Margaret Lauchlison (or Lauchlan, or M'Lachlan, or M'Lauchlison), Margaret

The Wigtown martyrdom, 2nd May 1685.

Justiciary Court at Wigtown, 13th April 1685.

---

[1] Wodrow, iv. 244; *Wodrow MSS.*, xxxvii. 102.

[2] Wodrow's printed *History* gives 11th of May, the usually accepted date as found in the Penninghame Kirk Session Record. But the two manuscripts of Wodrow's *History*, entitled *Scotia Sub Cruce*, etc., in the Advocates' Library (vols. xli., xlvii., xlviii.), give '11. of May' and 'May 11,' which read along with another sentence, 'This ii of May hath been a black day,' creates doubt. In the manuscript Wodrow places the Wigtown tragedy immediately after Priestshiel (*Scotia*, bk. iii., 234, 235, 236*b*; in vol. xlviii., 1022, 1026, 1027). The 2nd May is the most suitable date in reference to the useless reprieve. For authorities cf. Hewison, 'The Romance of Wigtown Martyrdom,' *Glasgow Herald*, 16th November 1901; Dr. A. Stewart, *History Vindicated*, 1867; 2nd edition, 1869; Mark Napier, *The Case for the Crown*, 1863; *History Rescued*, 1870; *Short Memorial*, 35; Kirk Session Records of Kirkinner and Penninghame; P. Walker in *Vindication of Cameron, Six Saints*, i. 329; *Reg. Sec. Conc., Acta*, 56 (30th April 1685); Wodrow, iv. 246-9. Wodrow's informant was the Rev. Robert Rowan, Penninghame, who had his account vouched by witnesses. Walker's account was given to him by Margaret Maxwell, a prisoner along with the martyrs, and by other intimate friends: *Six Saints*, i. 330. Defoe (266) gives the story of witnesses.

[3] *Wodrow MSS.*, xlviii. 1025.

[4] *Short Memorial*, 35.

and Agnes Wilson, sisters, and Margaret Maxwell. Their offence was nonconformity. All four were registered on the Porteous rolls as 'disorderly,' or absentees from church. Margaret Lauchlison was an old woman, widow of John Milliken, wright in Drumjargan, Kirkinner parish, and of reputed piety. Margaret Wilson, a maid of eighteen, and her sister Agnes, aged thirteen, daughters of Gilbert Wilson, farmer of Glenvernock, Penninghame, had, with Thomas their brother, become vagrant conventiclers. Margaret Maxwell was a servant of the laird and lady of Barwhannie, who also were sufferers for the Covenant. Gilbert Wilson and his wife were regular hearers of the Episcopal parish minister.[1] The usual indictment was given—treason by rebellion at Bothwell and Ayrsmoss, conventicling; in fine, Renwickism. The widow and the Wilsons refused to take the Abjuration Oath, and were sentenced to be drowned. Maxwell was sentenced to be flogged through Wigtown streets, and to be put in the 'jougs' for three days. This was done by the hangman. Time was allowed for an appeal to the Privy Council. Gilbert Wilson gave a bond of one hundred pounds for the release of Agnes, who thus narrowly escaped her sister's fate, and hurried to Edinburgh to petition for Margaret. The widow did not or could not write, and friends prepared her petition confessing the justice of her sentence and containing the abjuration demanded.[2] The Council was pitiful, no military being present, when, on 30th April they discharged the 'Magistrates of Edinburgh' (*sic*) from executing the widow and Margaret Wilson, and recommended the Secretaries of State to interpose with the King for a remission.[3] That was as good as a pardon if the resolution was announced, which was by no means unlikely: as good as salvation, if a bold rider could post over a hundred miles in a day and night. It is to be presumed that, in face of such a decreet, the officers in Wigtown dared not have executed on the 11th May. If Gilbert were the horseman, he was too late on the 2nd May.

The indict-ment and verdict.

Appeals to the Privy Council.

---

[1] The *Short Memorial* makes Lauchlison 'upward of 60 years,' and Margaret 'about 20'; Kirkinner Session Minutes make Lauchlison 'aged about 80'; her own petition says seventy.

[2] The original petition lies in the Register House, Edinburgh—*Miscellaneous Papers*, 1685. The petition for the Wilsons has not been found.

[3] *Reg. Sec. Conc., Acta*, 55, 56. 'Edinburgh' in the minute was evidently a mistake for Wigtown.

In any case, before the pardon could be expedited the tragedy was accomplished.

The conception of the execution was as diabolical as the work of carrying it out. 'Redgauntlet' and Winram's blood-red ring of guardsmen marched to Solway shore. The two sacrifices were loosely tied to stakes driven in that sludgy bight, where the swelling tide of Solway slowly rolls over the fresh stream of Blednoch to lave the green bank below the old parish church of Wigtown and its holy acre where their bodies now rest.[1] The old woman was bound furthest out, to bob like a fisher's float on every advancing wave, in order to terrify the maid into timeous reasonableness. This aspect of the case struck a letter-writer who visited the spot so early as 1689—'the sea overflowed them, when the stroke of every wave coming on them was as so many repeated deaths.'[2] The menace availed not. The Record of Penninghame prettily tells how the maid full joyfully exclaimed: 'What do I see but Christ wrestling there? Think ye that we are sufferers? No, it is Christ in us.' Bible in hand, Margaret Wilson sang part of the 25th Psalm—

'My sins and faults of youth
do Thou, O Lord, forget:
After Thy mercy think on me,
and for Thy goodness great.'

She also read the eighth chapter of Romans with its gospel of hope. Before the cadences of the tide silenced the melody and prayers of the virgin martyr, the authorities in vain pressed upon her the Abjuration Oath, and a ghoul-like hangman was at command with his Galloway 'cleek' to lift up the drooping form or dash it back as she exclaimed: 'I am one of Christ's children, let me go.' Patrick Walker recounts what the Kirk Session Minutes could hardly record, statements by no means unworthy of the 'sons of Lucifer.' 'The old woman was first tied to the stake, enemies saying, "'Tis needless to speak to that old damn'd bitch, let her go to hell." But say they, "Margaret, ye are young; if ye'll pray for the King, we will give you your life." She said, "I'll pray for salvation for all the elect, but the damnation of none." They dashed her under the water, and pulled her up again. People looking on said, "O Margaret, will

Margin notes:
Two sacrifices at the stake.

Margaret Wilson's faith.

Margaret Lauchlison's testimony.

---

[1] A stake has been renewed to keep the spot in remembrance.
[2] *Hist. MSS. Com. Rep.*, XIV. iii. 171.

ye say it?" She said, "Lord, give him repentance, forgiveness, and salvation, if it be Thy holy will." Lagg cry'd, "Damn'd bitch, we do not want such prayers; tender the oaths to her." She said, "No, no sinful oaths for me." They said, "To hell with them, to hell with them, it is o'er good for them." Thus suffered they that extraordinary and unheard-of death.'[1]

The Mauchline tragedy, 6th May 1685.

The next tragedy was enacted at Mauchline on 6th May, when the commissioner, Drummond, after the customary formalities—a field assize, which Covenanters never acknowledged to be a legal trial—sent four men and a youth to the gallows. The first four were intimate friends of Patrick Walker, who left a credible account of their seizure by the Highlanders when marching down to reinforce Drummond in the south-west. Unfortunately he does not name their leader. Does not this suggest the exploits of that body of Highlanders under Claverhouse who chased Nisbet at the end of April 1685, as already narrated?[2] Defoe, indeed, places the whole responsibility for these executions upon Claverhouse.[3] Professor Terry challenges Defoe's story as 'not true' and essays to 'undermine the silly fable.'[4] From Muiravonside parish they carried away Peter Gillies, waulker there, a registered fugitive and married man, together with a customer who had come to transact business with him. This visitor, named John Bryce, was a weaver in West Calder. They got William Finneson of Fiddison and Thomas Young in Carluke; and coming further west they 'apprehended one John Binning waiting upon cattle, without stocking or shoe.'[5]

Shield's *Short Memorial* associates Claverhouse, the Earl of Dumbarton, and Colonel James Douglas in the deed.[6] In reference to the part taken by Lockhart's footmen in the apprehension of Thomas Young and Finneson, 'the Laird of Lee' is specified in the old epitaph on their monument —

---

[1] *Six Saints*, i. 329. Cf. also Fergusson, *Laird of Lag*, 70; Paget, 'Paradoxes and Puzzles' (*Blackwood Magazine* articles), 252-63; Maxwell, *Dumfries and Galloway*, 282; *Martyr Graves*, 420-31.

[2] Cf. *antea* p. 460.

[3] *Memoirs*, 285.

[4] *John Graham*, 205. In face of Walker's narrative, Professor Terry identifies Muiravonside, near Linlithgow, with Muirside, in Old Monkland! (*ibid.*, 204).

[5] *Six Saints*, i. 297.

[6] *Short Memorial*, 34.

'Bloody Dumbartoun, Douglas, and Dundee,
Mov'd by the Devil and the Laird of Lee,
Drag'd these five men to Death with gun and sword,
Not suffering them to Pray, nor Read God's Word.
Owning the Work of God was all their Crime.
The Eighty-five was ev'n a Killing Time.'

The connection with this case of the Earl of Dumbarton, lately commissioned to be commander-in-chief, and still in London, is not obvious. He left on 10th May and was expected in Edinburgh on the 13th May. The contemporary authorities did not specify the date of the execution, which Wodrow assigned to the 6th of May. Is this a mistake for the 16th?[1]

Another execution in which Claverhouse was a chief actor was that of Andrew Hislop, son of a widow who lived near Gillesby, in Hutton, Annandale. This kindly widow had sheltered a dying wanderer, and, assisted by her sons, buried him by night in the field adjoining her home. News of this reached Sir James Johnstone of Westerhall, the Steward-Depute, who caused the corpse to be exhumed for identification, and, as a punishment for reset, levelled the widow's cottage, turning her household into wanderers.[2] Claverhouse captured Andrew and brought him, probably on the 10th May, to Westerhall, then at Craighaugh, Eskdalemuir. What occurred thereafter is very indefinitely stated by Wodrow; and the reason why Johnstone judged the case is not stated. By the commission given to Drummond, on 21st April, all other commissions were rendered 'void and extinct,' and, unless Drummond renewed the commission granted to Johnstone concurrently with Douglas, which had expired, then Johnstone had no right to interfere. Where Claverhouse was a precisian, Johnstone was a practical sheriff with the fearless spirit of his tribe in him. Parliament had just set its seal upon the sanguinary policy of King and Council, and passed the Act of 8th May condemning preachers and hearers at conventicles to death and confiscation. Johnstone ordered the execution of Hislop on 11th May, and Claverhouse, now reduced to a mere executioner, was, despite

[margin note:] Westerhall and Claverhouse execute Hislop, 11th May.

---

[1] *Hist.*, iv. 246; *Martyr Graves*, 162; Todd, *Homes, Haunts*, etc., 70-83. *Wodrow MSS.* xxxvii., No. 102, refers to Mauchline cases.

[1] Act 1681, c. 4, *Act. Parl. Scot.*, viii. 242.

his protest, forced to obey. Wodrow declares that Claverhouse desired the commander of the Highland infantry to carry out the order, but that more righteous officer drew his men off and 'swore he would fight Claverhouse and his dragoons before he did it.' Protesting, 'The blood of this poor man be upon you, Westerhall, I am free of it,' Claverhouse ordered his troopers to shoot Hislop. The peasant lad, refusing to be blindfolded, stood, Bible in hand, facing his three executioners, whom he adjured that they would answer for their crime at the Great Day. After prayer and the singing of some verses of the 118th Psalm, another fearless believer won the martyr's crown.[1]

Wodrow does not include in his published work the case of Matthew M'Ilwraith, whose tombstone in Colmonell churchyard bears the inscription —

'I Matthew M'Ilwraith in this parish of Colmonell
By bloody Claverhouse I fell,
Who did command that I should die,' etc.

According to Defoe this innocent man ran across the street in sight of the troops under Claverhouse, who, imagining that the man was trying to escape, commanded him to be shot without inquiring into the case.[2]

The omission of these incidents is easily accounted for, Wodrow confessing that he had grown weary of enumerating the barbarities of Claverhouse and Drummond, for 'particulars would be endless.'[3] He left sufficient well-attested reports to substantiate the accusation that Claverhouse ranged around like an insatiable demon, and even outrivalled Turner in the odium attached by the peasantry to his Brigadier name. In May and June, Claverhouse, now advanced to be Brigadier, with Highlanders and horse, continued his sweeping

[1] Wodrow on the margin of his manuscript *Scotia Sub Cruce* wrote: 'Androu Heslop killed May ii,' *i.e.* second. Wodrow, iv. 249; *Memorial*, 37; Terry, *Graham*, 208; *Act. Parl. Scot.*, viii. 461; *Martyr Graves*, 453, epitaph; *Wodrow MSS.*, xli. 236; xlviii. 1027.

[2] Defoe, 286; *Memorial*, 35; *Martyr Graves*, 323. Wodrow also omits the cases of John Murchie and Daniel M'Ilwraith shot by Drummond near Cross Water of Duisk, Colmonell: *Memorial*, 36; *Martyr Graves*, 319.

[3] *Hist.*, iv. 255.

movements through the disaffected Borders, on the outlook for the rebels under Argyll, eager to catch the little 'White Devil,' as Renwick was called, and indulging his fierce fanatical hatred of Presbyterians in atrocious acts such as have been described. Soon Dumbarton with 6000 men followed in his tracks. Wodrow specifies the methods of these hero-cavaliers. With a cordon of troops the Brigadier rounded up all the inhabitants of selected districts into a common centre for examination as to their loyalty. Some were driven into a ring of soldiers, then blindfolded, terrified by the discharge of carbines, threatened with death if they did not comply, and, when found immovable, were dispatched to Edinburgh. Worse still; children under ten years of age were ordered to pray before being shot, were terrified by discharged carbines—Claverhouse himself indulging in this violence on one occasion—and forced to tell about their relatives.[1] To lend effect to his method the Brigadier dragged about with him little 'parcels' of captives roped together, whom he did not fail to taunt with their former nimbleness of foot in following field-preachers; and there were always in his train the more desirable *spolia opima*[2] of the ruthless chase. Blood marked his trail.

Brigadier Graham chases Renwick.

The subordinate officers followed the example of their superiors. Shooting without inquiry was not a unique incident. In Kirkmichael churchyard, Ayrshire, lies Gilbert MacAdam of Dalmellington, who was shot by Kennedy of Culzean and the laird of Ballochmyle, while he essayed to escape from a prayer-meeting in a house near Kirkmichael House.[3] Claverhouse was about to shoot James Brown in Coulter, for carrying a powder-horn, when the laird of Coulterallers prevailed on him to delay the execution and to send him to prison, whence he escaped.[4] Defoe records that Lieutenant-General Maitland informed him that some of his fellow-officers shot men after 'little or no examination,' and that he himself humanely warned suspects who escaped from their peril.[5] Defoe instances the execution of three weavers at Polmadie, near Glasgow, an account of which Wodrow was fortunate

Shooting without inquiry.

[1] Wodrow, iv. 255-6. This was quite in harmony with the King's latest advice that children should be kept as hostages for their rebel parents: *Drumlanrig MSS.*, ii. 66.

[2] [Latin: rich spoils.]

[3] *A Short Memorial*, 38; Wodrow, iv. 329; *Martyr Graves*, 494.

[4] Wodrow, iv. 329.

[5] *Memoirs*, 281.

enough to obtain, attested by eye-witnesses, and in a particular part by Maitland himself.[1]

On 11th May, Major John Balfour, Captain Maitland, and a mixed force surrounded the hamlet of Polmadie and captured Thomas Cook and John Urie at their looms in the mill there, Robert Thom, a labourer, and the other residents. Balfour examined the three, and their answers to his queries, especially as to the sense in which they would pray for the King, not being satisfactory to him, he swore, and ordered them to prepare for instant death. They were shot and stripped. But when the soldiers saw their dogs lapping the flowing blood they cast the clothes upon the fallen to hide their hideous work. Wodrow's informants heard Captain Maitland exclaiming, 'As the Lord liveth, I have no pleasure in the death of those men.' A quarter of a century afterwards, Maitland regretfully confessed to Wodrow that the narrative of the witnesses was fact. Of the other prisoners taken that day several men were dispatched to prison. Colonel James Douglas, on 10th May, captured Adam Macqwan or Macwhan, a registered fugitive, while lying sick of fever near New Galloway. Dissatisfied with his replies to the customary interrogations, Douglas caused him to be shot next day at Knockdavie, an eminence overlooking the Tolbooth there.[2]

Two days afterwards, 13th May, a very interesting Covenanter, James Kirko of Sundaywell, Dunscore, betrayed by James Wright in Holywood, where he lurked, was shot on the White Sands of Dumfries. His name is not on the fugitive roll.[3] Captain Andrew Bruce, who apprehended Kirko, offered him the Abjuration Oath, which he refused to take. He was told to prepare for death. He sang part of the 116th Psalm,—'Dear in God's sight is His saints' death'—then prayed, and read the Scriptures. He was offered pardon if he would betray other fugitives. This he disdained. He would not buy back his life at so dear a rate, he replied. He asked a respite for a day. 'No, no,' said the captain, 'no more time, the devil a peace you now get made up.' Kirko answered, 'Sir, you mistake it, you cannot mar my peace with God.'

[1] Attested Account in *Wodrow MSS.*, xxxiii. 106; Wodrow, iv. 251; Defoe, 282; *Memorial*, 37; *Martyr Graves*, 70.

[2] Wodrow calls him Andrew, iv. 251; *Memorial*, 35; monument in Kells, *Martyrs Graves*, 389.

[3] Sandywell, or Sundowall. Cf. p. 94 and note 1.

This retort enraged Bruce, who cried to his men, 'Dogs, make ready, for the devil a peace shall he get more.' Before he could pray again the muskets laid him low.[1]

Other commanders had their share in adding to the martyrology. The Earl of Annandale and his command captured two men, David Halliday in Glengap, and George Short. Short was on the fugitive roll, likewise William Halliday in Glengap. Annandale gave them quarter for the night. Lag arrived and found them roped like bestial. He ordered their death at once. They begged a night for preparation. He was implacable, and ordered them to be shot as they lay bound.[2]

Other instances of these summary executions are recorded in *A Short Memorial*, in Wodrow (book in chapter ix.), and in *The Martyr Graves of Scotland*.

A Scots Parliament, summoned by King James, as his letter asserted, to 'defend and protect your religion as established by law and your rights and properties, against fanatical contrivances, murderers, and assassins,' met in Edinburgh on 23rd April, and rose on 22nd August 1685. William, Duke of Queensberry, was Commissioner, and demanded in the King's name that Parliament should legislate to destroy 'that desperat phanaticall and irreclameable pairtie who have brought us to the brink of ruine and dissgrace ... enemies of mankind, wretches of such monstruous principles and practises that past ages never heard, nor those to come will hardly believe.' He accused the disaffected of being the executors of the 'most hellish and barbarous designs that were ever contrived.'[3] In a more vulgar tirade, the Chancellor, Perth, declared 'we have a new sect sprung up among us from the dunghill, the very dreggs of the people who kill by pretended inspiration ... whose idoll is that accursed paper the Covenant. ... These monsters bring a publick reproach upon the nation in the eyes of all our nighbours abroad ...

Other victims.

The rival Parliaments.

William, first Duke of Queensberry, 1637-1695.

---

[1] A cross on the causeway still marks the spot where he was shot. He is buried near to Robert Burns: *Martyr Graves*, 472; Wodrow, iv. 251; *Wodrow* MSS., xli. 237; *Memorial*, 36. A James Kirko was served heir to his father John in 1647. He was a friend of James Guthrie, and a fighter at Rullion Green: M'Crie, *Veitch*, 49 note; Wodrow, ii. 78.

[2] Wodrow, iv. 252, gives date 10th June; tombstone in Balmaghie gives 11th July: *Memorial*, 38; *Martyr Graves*, 369, 370.

[3] *Hist. MSS. Com. Rep.*, xv. viii. 146.

they bring reproach upon our religion, and are our great plague.'[1] What contrast this vituperation of Queensberry makes with the testimony of his daughter Anne, Lady Elcho, when dying: 'I die in the faith that the Presbyterian Church is the true Church of God, and they are the true servants of God who die in the faith of it.'[2] Parliament proved itself to be invertebrate, and wholly subservient to the Despot's will. Statutes, curt and severe, display the temper of the time. The first Act confirmed the Acts securing the Protestant Religion in the Episcopalian form.[3] The second Act gave the King an army of men between the ages of sixteen and sixty, as well as the excise. A subsequent Act gave him supply. The fifth Act declared it treason to take or own the Covenant of 1638 or 1643.[4] The sixth Act made husbands liable for the fines of non-churchgoing wives. The eighth Act ordained the death penalty and confiscation of goods for preachers and hearers at field conventicles.[5] Other statutes provided for the taking of the Test (13), empowering justices (16), obliging heritors to keep orderly tenants (34), apprehending rebels and resetters (30), and forfeiting rebels, Argyll, Baillie, Hamilton, and others, whose estates annexed to the Crown were parcelled out to Jacobites. An 'Act for the Clergy' made assault on the orthodox clergy punishable by death, and confirmed and re-established the hierarchy in its dignities, immunities, and possessions.[6]

For all this obsequiousness and assiduity, Queensberry was rewarded in a libel presented to the King by Melfort, accusing him of exceeding his instructions, which drew from the King a letter of approbation and exoneration.[7] The Acts of this Parliament were the decrees of King James.

Another Parliament of a different order sat down in discomfort on the Moss of Blackgannoch,[8] between Muirkirk and Sanquhar, on 28th May. It was the senate of Scotland's best sons. Narrow although their vision was, it, at least, included those important factors in the

Acts of Parliament, 1685.

The rival Parliament of Blackgannoch.

---

[1] *Hist. MSS. Com. Rep.*, xv. viii., 147-48; Wodrow, iv. 259-63 note.
[2] *Select Biog.*, ii. 516.
[3] *Act. Parl. Scot.*, viii. 459.
[4] *Ibid.*, 461.
[5] 8th May, Act 8: *Ibid*, 461.
[6] 13th June, Act 46: *Act. Parl. Scot.*, viii. 486.
[7] *Hist. MSS. Com. Rep.*, xv. viii. 135-51.
[8] Or Blagannoch.

national life which would have been obliterated altogether had not this convention of defiant men demanded their conservation; and, in so doing, they forestalled the more timid revolutionaries of 1688, who later recovered the ancient rights of the Fatherland. On this occasion James Renwick was the Commissioner of a King greater than James Stuart. His councillors were two hundred persecuted fugitives in arms. Their decrees were few and unambiguous—(1) 'not at all to join with Sectarians, Malignants, nor any other, their confederates'; (2) 'the said day the Protestation … against proclaiming James, Duke of York, King … was concluded and agreed upon and ordained to be published the same day at the Burgh of Sanghair.'[1]

As soon as this business was over, the Remnant marched to Sanquhar Market Cross. On arrival there, they sang a psalm, heard Renwick invoke the blessing of God, published their Protestation, and affixed a copy of it to the Cross, then retreated into the wilds whence they emerged. This manifesto is entitled: 'The Protestation and Apologetical Admonitory Declaration of the True Presbyterians of the Church of Scotland against the proclaiming James, Duke of York, King of Scotland, England, France, and Ireland, the lawfulness of the present pretended Parliament, and the apparent inlet of Popery,' etc.[2]

The Remnant's 'Protestation' at Sanquhar Cross, 28th May 1685.

The document began by homologating previous Declarations bearing upon the unconstitutional usage to which the Church had been subjected; and it proceeded to express the protest of the 'contending, suffering Remnant of the true Presbyterians,' against the proclamation of James as King, on the ground that he was a murderer, 'who hath shed the blood of the saints of God'—an idolater, a Papist, an enemy of religion, who was disqualified by statute and by the Covenant and practice of the Church. The Protestation further renounced as unlawful the Parliament in session, some of whose members were alleged to be 'convicted of avowed murder'; protested against all kinds of Popery; adjured the Churches of England and Ireland to rise and help their 'bleeding Remnant,' and called on other Protestant Churches to bestir themselves against infidelity and Popery. It condemned the slanderous misrepresentations against the cult of Renwick (probably hinting also

Tenor of the Protestation.

---

[1] *Laing MSS.*, 234; *Faithful Contendings*, 166; Shields, *Life of Renwick—Biog. Presby.*, ii. 84.

[2] It was published at Sanquhar, *Testimony Bearing Exemplified*, 260.

at the slanders against the extremists current in Holland); disclaimed all connection with unwarrantable acts, done 'not in a Christian manner'; and it concluded by avowing the intention of the Remnant to abide by a pure Covenanted Christianity.

It is evident that Renwick and his disciples were taking, in a literal sense, the last words of David, King of Israel: 'But the sons of Belial shall be all of them as thorns thrust away, because they cannot be taken with hands. But the man that shall touch them must be fenced with iron, and the staff of a spear; and they shall be utterly burnt with fire in the same place.'[1]

As soon as these hillmen retreated into their fastnesses Brigadier Graham was at their heels.[2] The efforts, originated in Holland, to induce the Renwick party to rise in arms along with the Argyll confederacy failed. The wanderers were incensed at the accusations urged against them abroad—that they were antinomian revolutionaries, bent on establishing some unscriptural proletarian form of autocracy and on cutting off dissentients, and that they were a corrupt body—no Church—with impure doctrine and corrupt students.[3] The Societies therefore resolved that they could not conscientiously join a mixed faction which included Malignants untrue to the Covenants, such as Sir John Cochrane, whom they reprobated as the betrayer and slayer of the faithful who fell with Cameron at Ayrsmoss, and Argyll himself, whom many blamed for sending Cargill to the scaffold.[4] According to the Blackgannoch protesters the declaration of Argyll was 'not concerted according to the ancient plea of the Scotch Covenanters.' They were willing, however, 'to do what lay in their power against the common enemy.' After the defeat of Argyll, two ministers, George Barclay and Robert Langlands, who accompanied the hapless Earl on his expedition, were conducted to conferences with the United Societies in order to discuss the differences between the Remnant at home and the purists abroad. But the dissentient spirit causing the cleavage could not be cast out even after days of prayer and fasting.[5]

The Renwickites refuse to join the Argyll insurgents.

[1] 2 Sam. xxiii. 6, 7.
[2] *Faithful Contendings*, 167.
[3] *Ibid.*, 171.
[4] *A Collection of Dying Testimonies*, 345; *Biog. Presby.*, ii. 85, 86.
[5] *Faithful Contendings*, 166, 167.

What may be called a third Parliament—a convention of exiled Scots politicians—met in Amsterdam on 17th April 1685 (O.S.).[1] The plotters present were the Earl of Argyll, his son Charles, Sir John Cochrane of Ochiltree, Sir Patrick Hume of Polwarth, George Pringle of Torwoodlee, William Denholm of Westshiels, George Hume of Bassindean, John Cochrane of Waterside, George Wisheart, William Cleland, James Stuart, advocate, Gilbert Elliot, and William Spence. Sir John Cochrane presided. It was unanimously resolved that these and other Scots gentlemen become 'a Council for the recovery of Religion against the Duke of Albany and York, and that Argyll to be Captain-General.'[2] Argyll now ventured to illustrate practically what he meant by refusing the Test.

On 2nd May, Argyll and his force of three hundred men sailed in three ships from Holland, and four days later reached Cairston Bay. The intention was that Argyll's command, reinforced by clansmen, Presbyterians, and patriots generally, would act in Scotland in conjunction with an armed expedition led by Monmouth into England a little later. In face of the military preparations ordered by Parliament, and in view of the popular distrust of the character and military skill of Argyll, the disaffected at home showed a saving prudence and did not move. On arriving in Kirkwall, Argyll sent ashore his secretary, Spence, and Dr. William Blackadder, to obtain intelligence. They were seized and hurried down to the Justiciary Court. Bishop Mackenzie soon informed the Privy Council of the descent of the rebels, and before Argyll could reach his own lands and summon his vassals, the country was in 'a posture of defence.' The Campbells dared not rise after the Government had made Atholl lieutenant of Argyleshire and put torch and rope into his free hand. When Argyll arrived at Campbeltown, on 20th May, he had printed from his portable printing-press 'The Declaration and Apology of the Protestant People ... for defence and relief of their Lives, Rights, and Liberties, and recovery and re-establishment of the true Protestant Religion, in behalf of themselves and all that shall join with and adhere to them.'[3] James Stewart, afterwards Lord Advocate, was the author of

---

[1] Fergusson, *Ferguson the Plotter,* chap. x. 190-212: cf. also 113.

[2] Original Minute signed John Cochrane in *Laing MSS.,* 639, No. 149.

[3] *Laing* MSS., fol. 3, 85; Wodrow, iv. 286 note; *Hist. MSS. Com. Rep.* (Athole), XII. App. viii, 12, etc.; M'Crie, *Veitch,* 311-23; *Observes.,* 164-77; Erskine, *Journal,* q.v.

this remarkable manifesto, which was intended to justify their rising against 'this hellish mystery of antichristian iniquity and arbitrary tyranny ... of James, Duke of York, a notorious apostate and bigot Papist,' etc.[1] A similar summons was sent to his vassals. A few obeyed on seeing the fiery cross. The force arrived at Glendaruel; and the islet in Loch Ridden, called Eileanghirig, where Duncan Campbell had a keep, was fortified and made into an arsenal. His council was divided as to the plan of campaign. He had English warships in his rear and a strong force of Lowlanders and Highlanders under Dumbarton and Douglas on the mainland. He abandoned the arsenal, which an English squadron soon took. Among the booty was Argyll's standard with the motto: 'For God and Religion, against Poperie, Tyrannie, Arbitrary Government, and Errestianisme.'[2] Cowardice overcame Argyll when he saw himself and his party of eight hundred men dwindling away on the road, and forced to march he knew not whither for safety. He had a presentiment that he would die at the Cross of Edinburgh in expiation of Cargill's death.[3]

They crossed the Clyde at Kilpatrick Ford. Argyll deemed it expedient to part company with Cochrane, Polwarth, Balfour of Burley, and other braves, who determined to cut their way through friendly districts into England. After a slight skirmish, in which the honours lay with the rebels, at Muirdyke, Lochwinnoch, Cochrane and the rest scattered and sought safety in night marches. Assuming the disguise of a peasant in a blue bonnet, Argyll tried alone to pass the lines near Paisley on the 18th June. Lord Cochrane's troop noticed a horseman alight to cross the Cart on foot, and a militiaman named Semple, a weaver, was sent to take him. Argyll's pistols missed. The weaver drew his rusty blade and gave his opponent 'a great skelp on the head,' who, as he fell stunned, exclaimed, 'Ah, unfortunate Argyll.'[4] The Privy Council made preparations for his reception into Edinburgh as a felon. An eye-witness describes the scene: 'We wer all wating to see Ar[gyll] cum in and go up the way, in great disgrac, which he was not much conserned in; yet, when the hangman tayd his hands about his

The fiery cross fails.

Capture of Argyll.

---

[1] Fergusson, *Ferguson the Plotter*, 203.
[2] *Chron. Notes*, 50.
[3] *Six Saints*, ii. 61.
[4] *Atholl MSS.*, 22; *Observes*, 181.

back, with ane tow tyd about his midell, and then to the hangman who went befor him, I confess it mad him chang colours.'[1]

As soon as the King heard of the capture of Argyll, he ordered his execution to take place within three days of receipt of his command. On 29th June, the Lords of Justiciary met, and, in terms of the former doom and sentence of forfeiture of 23rd December 1681, adjudged the traitor to be beheaded at the Market Cross next day and his head to be affixed aloft on the Tolbooth.[2] He met his death with that counterfeit of bravery with which a final reversion to the comforts of religion invested the lordly Campbells when they faced their doom. Following the example of Montrose, he composed his mind to frame a Testimony interlarded with texts punctiliously quoted, and to cast his assurances into poor rhyme: *The King orders Argyll to be executed.*

> 'Though my head fall, that is no tragic story,
> Since going hence I enter endless glory.'

He expressed some kindly thoughts for his family, whose misery he had effected, and for many clansmen whom he dragged into ruin. Up that High Street he had carried the crown before the Duke of York, who now sent him down that *Via Dolorosa* to claim a martyr's crown. Dean Annand and ex-Professor Charteris ministered to his timorous soul. The sight of The Maiden so unmanned him that he had to be blindfolded before he was led on to the scaffold. In the dark his equanimity returned, and he boldly declared: 'I die, not only a Protestant, but with a heart hatred of Popery, Prelacy, and all superstition whatever.' On kneeling and laying hold of The Maiden he also pleasantly exclaimed: 'It was the sweetest Maiden ever he kissed, it being a mean to finish his sin and misery, and his inlet to glory, for which he longed.'[3] Before the loaded blade fell, he prayed, 'Lord Jesus, receive me into Thy glory!' It was of the temperament of this sufferer to resign all to his Maker when there was no other alternative; and to the amazement of an acquaintance, he even slept the sleep of the just a short hour before his headless body 'started upright to his feet till it was held doune' in its fountain *Argyll beheaded, 30th June 1685.*

---

[1] *Atholl MSS.*, 23. Letter to the Marchioness of Atholl; *Reg. Sec. Conc.* 20th June; *Observes*, 185.

[2] *Book of Adjournal*, 29th June 1685.

[3] Wodrow, iv. 306.

of blood.[1] Fountainhall also properly recorded that 'tho Argile was very witty in knacks, yet it was observed, he has never been very solid sen his trepaning of his scull in 1653; he was so conceitty he had neir 20 severall pockets, some of them very secret, in his coat and breeches, and brought a printing press with him, and artificiall bullets and pistolls.'[2] These idiosyncrasies indicate the ill-balanced nature of this whimsical liberator, whose greatest distinction was that he died, as Wodrow phrased it, 'in the plerophory of the faith' of the Covenanters, which, however, did not include any benediction for the Papist on the throne.

Fate of Monmouth, 15th July 1685. Misfortune and disaster followed Monmouth, the champion of the extreme Protestants and dissenters in England, whose army of five thousand men was defeated at Sedgemoor on 6th July. Soon Monmouth was captured. No trial was needed. Already an attainted traitor, he was executed on the 15th July.[3] Judge Jeffreys, in the Bloody Assizes, completed the cleansing work in the south. Among the confederates of Argyll who fell into the hands of the Scots Government were Colonel Richard Rumbold (1622?-1685) and Thomas Archer. Mark Ker, bailie in Lesmahagow, afterwards paid with his life for apprehending Rumbold. Rumbold was an Englishman, a maltster, a Cromwellian veteran and fighter at Dunbar, owner of the Rye House, Hertfordshire, who had fled to Holland on being indicted for conspiracy. Thomas Archer, *alias* Urquhart, was a minister of the Gospel, a graduate, a licentiate set apart by the Scots ministers in Holland, and had a great reputation for linguistic and theological scholarship. Lest death should balk them of their prey, since both of the prisoners were sorely wounded, the Council, Ferocious finish of Rumbold. the archbishops present, arranged for their immediate dispatch. They met to ferociously conceive a fitting finish for the moribund Rumbold, and practically ordered the Lords of Justiciary to meet next day, 25th June, and to find the accused guilty. They specified in their minutes the exact details of the execution settled on—the magistrates to erect a high gibbet, have a fire prepared upon it, order the hangman to hoist the victim up by the neck, then let him drop half strangled, to cut out and spit his heart upon a bayonet, to perambulate the scaffold exclaiming, 'Here is the heart of a bloodie traitor and murderer,' to cast the heart

---

[1] *Observes*, 194.
[2] *Ibid.*, 195; *Hist. Not.*, ii. 653; *Decision*, i. 362, 366; Willcock, *A Scots Earl*, 395-421.
[3] *State Pap. Dom.* (James II.), 2 (June to July).

into the fire, and finally to dismember the body and see its parts distributed.[1] In excruciating torment the veteran tried, amid rolling drums, to ejaculate his malison on Popery and Prelacy, and his benediction on the Protestant cause, declaring that if every one of his grey hairs was a man he would willingly give them all up for the Lord's glory.

The fever-stricken condition of Archer for a time prevented his presentation for examination and trial. He showed great resoluteness in refusing to incriminate his associates. On 6th August the Lords sentenced him to die eight days afterwards in the Grassmarket, but he was reprieved until the 21st August.[2] He might have escaped from prison, but preferred to make a public testimony in 'the interests of Christ.' This erudite young man of thirty-two years went to his fate praying, singing, rejoicing. *(Fate of Thomas Archer.)*

Other sentences of death, followed by reprieves, were passed upon David, afterwards Sir David Stewart of Coltness, Spence, Blackadder, Charles and John Campbell, sons of Argyll, and Archibald, son of Lord Neil Campbell, the doom of forfeiture being allowed to remain on the Campbells.

Sir John Cochrane and his son William were also captured, the father being led ignominiously, bound and bareheaded, by the hangman into the Tolbooth of Edinburgh, on 3rd July. Only the influence of his father, Dundonald, and a well-placed bribe saved from the gallows this fickle rebel, already doomed and forfeited for his accession to the Rye House Plot—so the report ran. But more likely the pardon was occasioned by 'ane itching curiosity to hear his discoveries.'[3] These, however, were scarce, for neither political party trusted Sir John with important secrets. Other less influential followers of Argyll were ordained to be transported to Jamaica and New Jersey along with some Covenanters lying in Dunnottar and other prisons. At the same time, the Council ordered that those men who refused to take the Oath of Allegiance should have their left ears *(Pardon of the Cochranes.)* *(Ear-lopping.)*

[1] *Acta* 87: 20th June, 25th June, 4th August; *Book of Adjournal*, 25th June 1685; Wodrow, iv. 314; Fountainhall, *Decisions*, i. 365.
[2] *Hist. Not.*, ii. 659, dates execution on 14th; Wodrow, iv. 317, gives 21st; *Book of Adjournal*, 6th August, appoints 14th August.
[3] *Observes*, 240. *Book of Adjournal*, 16th July: Sir John, born 1636: Waterside, b. 1663.

lopped off, and the women should be stigmatised on the cheek or branded on the hand.[1]

Claverhouse again took his seat as a Privy Councillor on the 16th July, and, after being present in Council on the 20th, did not return till the 31st August, immediately before Dalyell's funeral.[2] That old field-marshal attended Council on 20th August, and was appointed on a committee to examine the prisoners going into banishment on Scot's ship. Three days afterwards the veteran died, seventy years old, wine-glass in hand, looking up to the glory of the celestial bodies painted on the ceiling of his mansion in Big Jack's Close, Edinburgh. His colleagues arranged a befitting military funeral and display of force.[3] Defoe's estimate of this soldier-politician is not exaggerated: 'A man as void of humanity as most that heaven ever permitted to live.'[4] Drummond got the vacant post.

Claverhouse's absence from Council may be accounted for by his attention to duties in the field. The proclamation of 24th June, against traitors and fugitives, gave Atholl in the West Highlands and Dumbarton, and Claverhouse in the Lowlands, that licence which these callous officers were not slow to utilise in crushing out any spark of freedom visible. 'The White Flag of the Devil,' as the Royalists dubbed the anti-Popish movement of Cameron, Renwick, and the Remnant, was always reappearing in the lone retreats of the hunted ministers— Peden, Renwick, Robert Langlands, George Guthrie, John Black, and Duncan Campbell.

Now that the Argyll and Monmouth expeditions had ended in a fiasco, the authorities gave attention to the burdensome prisoners, for whom convict-ships were being chartered to convey some to slavery in New Jersey and others into voluntary exile. Robert Barclay of Urie got a gang of twenty-three prisoners, including the notorious John

Death of General Dalyell, 23rd August 1685.

'The White Flag of the Devil.'

Miserable convicts.

---

[1] *Acta*, 24th July, 73 sentenced; 28th July, 14; 30th July, 53; 31st July, 24; 11th August, 14; 17th August, 51 men and 21 women; 9th December, 17. Among the 33 men whose left ears were cut off on 4th August was James Gavin. He returned to Douglas from the plantations, built a house, and carved his initials and a pair of scissors above the door. It is still extant: Wodrow, iv. 216-23.

[2] Hugh Mackay of Scourie, sent for out of Holland to assist in putting down Monmouth's rebellion, took his seat in the Council on 23rd July 1685: *Acta*, 107.

[3] *Acta*, 142, 145, 150; Wilson, *Memorials of Edinburgh*, 290; Hewison, 'The Muscovie Beast,' *Scotsman*, 26th November 1904; *Scot. Eleg. Verses*, 38 (Edin., 1842).

[4] *Memoirs*, 256.

Gibb, the Sweet Singer. George Scot of Pitlochie got another batch of nearly one hundred prisoners—sixty-seven men and twenty-six women—from whom some, who had, in the interval, taken the Oath of Allegiance, were withdrawn. In their place others were added. The foul vaults of Dunnottar were emptied of their sickly and emaciated crowd, who, with hands tied behind their backs, were marched, such as were able, back to Leith by way of Montrose, Arbroath, Dundee, Cupar, and Burntisland.[1] The Council inspected them at Leith on the 18th August.[2] Patrick Walker escaped from Leith Tolbooth that night.[3] Among those who sailed on 5th September were several dames of good family and several ministers—John Frazer, William Ged, William Aisdale, Archibald Riddell, minister of Kippen, long a prisoner in the Bass, and, after his return from banishment, minister in Wemyss, Kirkcaldy, and Edinburgh. On the voyage rotten provisions, malignant fever, and other troubles cut off seventy of the passengers, including Scot and his wife. Scot, however, made a disposition of the prisoners to his son-in-law, who was a hard task-master. Many died in bondage. Some returned to narrate their bitter experiences.[4]

Robert MacLellan, laird of Barmagechan in Galloway, fighter at Rullion Green and Bothwell Bridge, wanderer for years with three of his family, twice forfeited for his principles, had his sufferings in Dunnottar crowned by transportation in Scot's ship. Three children accompanied their father. He was manumitted, and purchased an estate at Woodbridge, New Jersey, of which district Archibald Riddell was invited to become the Presbyterian minister. There they remained till news of the Revolution came, when they set sail homewards, arriving off the English coast on 2nd August. Their ship was captured by a French man-of-war, and the prisoners were badly used and thrown into various prisons, MacLellan being cast into a hulk at Toulon, with his one eye dashed out by a warder's whip, while Riddell was thrown into the verminiferous vault of Dinan Castle. At length they were released on an exchange of prisoners. But MacLellan's sufferings were not over.

The MacLellans of Barmagechan.

[1] 30th July: *Acta*, 123, 140-2.
[2] Wodrow, iv. 221, 222; *Reformed Presbyterian Witness*, September 1901.
[3] *Six Saints*, i. 352; ii. 195.
[4] For an account of Riddell see M'Crie, *Mem. of Veitch*, 523; Appendix No. xiii.; Wodrow, iii. 191, 196, 197, 200, 202, 264; iv. 335.

He had to sail home by Cadiz. A storm forced his ship into Bantry Bay. The callous Irish stripped to nakedness the broken man, who, after a long illness, reached his home at Barmagechan on 31st October 1691.[1]

Trials in August 1685. In spite of all these terrors the justices had no lack of culprits to try for treason. Of twelve prisoners tried on 6th August for treason, rebellion, refusing to own the King's authority, Thomas Stodhart, Gavin Russell, and James Wilkieson, being intractable in not taking the Oath of Allegiance, were hanged in the Grassmarket on 12th August; Cunningham, Muirhead, and Jackson were banished; Alexander Shields, the preacher, took the oaths, was sent to the Bass, then brought to Edinburgh, whence he escaped in 1686; and four, Matthew Bryce, Archibald Campbell, Edward Stit, and David Low, said to have been executed, were sent back to prison.[2]

Captain John Nisbet hanged, 4th December 1685. Early in November, Lieutenant Nisbet and his men captured at Midland in Fenwick, after a tough fight, the redoubtable Captain John Nisbet of Hardhill. This handsome soldier, bred of Lollard stock, saw service in the Continental wars, and returned to fight and fall at Rullion Green, to rise again and do hero's work at Drumclog as well as at Bothwell Bridge. At Midland three other Society-men fell at his side—Peter Gemmel, George Woodburn, and John Ferguson, or Fergushill.[3] Nisbet confessed to the Council his valiance on the field, his irreconcilable enmity to the Popish regime, and his joy in the Cross for the sake of Christ and the Covenant. The Lords of Justiciary, on 30th November, tried him and sent him to the Grassmarket on the 4th December.[4] The court also passed a similar doom on Edward Marshall, farmer, Kaemuir, Muiravonside, a fighter at Bothwell, an invincible Cameronian, and on John Welsh of Cornley, Kirkcudbrightshire. Both were registered fugitives. Welsh, by a timely submission, slipped out of the noose, and returned to Irongray.[5] The other two made gallant

---

[1] Wodrow, iv. 334-6; *Wodrow MSS.*, xxxiii. 111, 117; xxxvii. 26; *Mem. of Veitch*, App. 523. For John Mathieson's sufferings in Carolina, cf. *A Collection of Dying Testimonies*. Mathieson returned to Closeburn and died in 1709.

[2] Wodrow iv. 234, 235; *Book of Adjournal*, 6th August 1685; *Cloud*, 443-6; *Hist. Not.*, ii. 658. The fate of the last four is difficult to trace.

[3] *Martyr Graves*, 109.

[4] *Book of Adjournal*, 29th, 30th November 1685; *Hist. Not.*, ii. 681; *Decisions*, i. 381.

[5] The gravestones of the family are close to the church door. *Book of Adjournal*, 4th December.

ending, welcoming death. Marshall, commending his wife and seven children to the Divine Father's care, said he died out of love to Christ. Nisbet, in his prolix testimony to his fidelity to Covenanting principles, as maintained by the extremists, manifested that assurance with which these 'Captains of the Lord's people,' of whom Nisbet considered himself one, longed to seal the cause with their blood.[1]

Before the year 1685 expired, the Privy Council felt the inlet of the power which was to disintegrate the administration. In a letter dated 7th November, Secretary Melfort conveyed an order of the King that the Duke of Gordon, the Earl of Seaforth, the Earl of Traquair, and other twenty-three Popish landlords should not be required to take the Test.[2] This decree was the logical outcome of the persecuting policy of the Killing Times, and the firstfruits of the victory over Argyll, Monmouth, and dissent generally. Another result was the displacement of Queensberry, who was inimical to the re-establishment of Popery. Perth and his brother, Melfort, both gone over to Rome, contrived to poison the King's mind that Queensberry was a vindictive, tyrannous traitor, unworthy of trust.[3] Perth wrote to a confidant: 'Duke Queensberry has impudence enugh to resist all the King can say, and make a jest of it over a bumper.'

Signs of the times.

The Royal Commissioner soon realised that he had lost his Sovereign's confidence, and he returned under a shade to Crichton Peel, Sanquhar. It was the reward he deserved from one he had untruthfully described in Parliament as 'the greatest and best of kings.' Fortune had veered to the side of Claverhouse. He too went to Court, and found that his royal master's displeasure was slight and easily exchanged for lasting favour. When Claverhouse returned to Edinburgh on Christmas Eve his baleful star was in the ascendant.

Queensberry under a shade.

Chancellor Perth, the guileless Nathaniel of Burnet, and devotee of Episcopal Protestantism, also returned from the royal presence an avowed Papist, who celebrated his perversion by rocking a child in a cradle on Christmas Day. He was enriched with £8000, which the King gave him to purchase the 'ornamenta' necessary for restoring the full Romish service in Holyrood Chapel. The effrontery of priests,

Perth, a well-paid pervert, 1648-1716.

[1] *Cloud*, 447, 449-72.
[2] Wodrow, iv. 347.
[3] *Hamilton MSS., Hist. MSS. Com. Rep.*, XI. vi. 169, 171.

become plentiful in the Capital, roused the perfervid spirits of many haters of Popery. The stories of the French refugees, exiled because of the Revocation of the Edict of Nantes, were sickening and unsettling. Alexander Ramsay, for declaring from his pulpit that there were 'fallen stars,' and that the pillars of Church and State were shaking, was silenced by the bishops. At the end of January the apprentices of Edinburgh, in a reforming mood to coerce priests, brought on a causeway brawl, which ended in fatal shots and in legal reprisals—a drummer shot and a fencing-master hanged.[1] The King instructed the authorities to examine and torture the brawlers in order to discover any possible connection with a plot.[2] Loyalists now were divided into 'King's men' and 'No Popery politicians.' Gordon, a Papist, displaced Queensberry as captain of Edinburgh Castle. His treasury was placed in the hands of a committee. The Duke of Hamilton, President Lockhart, and General Drummond were invited to London to be won from opposition.[3] The Primate (Rose) and the Bishop of Edinburgh (Paterson) went to Court in February, in order to signify their concurrence with the King's desire for the abolition of the penal laws against those of the King's religion, as Popery was now euphemistically designated; but others, who saw that the toleration ostensibly favoured the fanatics, and pointed this out, incurred the displeasure of those leaders possessed of the King's secret regarding the succeeding steps in his policy of rehabilitation.[4] The shrewd clergy in Aberdeen, in April, petitioned their ordinary to oppose the intended relaxation, and Melfort wrote demanding their punishment.[5]

In January and February, Fletcher of Saltoun, Dalrymple of Stair, the clan Campbell, and other fighters and Cameronian Protesters were prosecuted.[6] The only martyr who flowered the field this year was David Steel, tenant of Nether Skellyhill, near Lesmahagow, a friend of Renwick, who was betrayed, captured, and brought back to his home

Marginal notes:

Religious brawlers in the Capital, 1686.

Prosecution of Cameronians.

Shooting of Steel, 20th December 1686.

---

[1] *Book of Adjournal*, 22nd February 1686; *Observes*, 241-4; *Hist. Not.*, ii. 700; *Decisions*, i. 399, 407; Napier, iii. 467.

[2] Woodrow, iv. 397.

[3] *Hamilton MSS.*, 172.

[4] *Collection of Letters to Sancroft*, 96-8.

[5] Wodrow, iv. 358; *Hamilton MSS.*, 173.

[6] *Book of Adjournal*, 4th January; 5th, 21st February; Wodrow, iv. 354-6.

on the 20th December and there shot by Lieutenant Creichton, in the presence of his wife and child. According to local tradition, neighbours found the widow, Mary Weir, binding up the shattered head, while she apostrophised the slain thus: 'The archers have shot at thee, my husband, but they could not reach thy soul; it has escaped like a dove far away, and is at rest. Lord, give strength to Thy hand-maid that will prove she has waited for Thee, even in the strength of Thy judgments.' Dean Swift, in his *Memoirs of Creichton,* makes his hero discover Steel's retreat in a dream, and gives a dragoon's account of the episode, concluding with this burlesque on Steel's epitaph in Lesmahagow churchyard:—

> Here lies the body of Saint Steele,
> Murdered by Jolin Creichton that dee'l.[1]

King James artfully concealed his deep design to re-establish the ancient faith when he convened the Scots Parliament on 29th April, and appointed the Earl of Moray, a Papist, Commissioner.[2] The ostensible purpose was to recognise loyalists who had supported the Crown through the crisis. Quakers were liberated to prove the royal clemency.[3] The King's letter asked for toleration for Catholics who had hazarded life and fortune for his person and crown, and offered an indemnity to his opponents. The Commissioner enlarged upon the King's paternal solicitude for the welfare of all.[4] With native caution the Estates courteously replied that, in considering the claim for equal rights to Catholics, they would 'goe as great lengths therein as our conscience will allow, not doubting that your Majesty will be carefull to secure the Protestant Religion by Law.' The 'Conscience' of Perth, Queenberry, Grierson of Lag, Dalziel of Glenae, Provost Coltran of Wigtown, and other red-handed legislators, is certainly the last factor which the ecclesiastical historian would expect to find in such men and such a place. Archbishop Ross and Bishop Paterson declared for the toleration. When the proposed bill was debated in the Committee of Articles it was carried by a majority of four in a chamber of thirty-two. The Bishops of Glasgow, Galloway, Brechin, and Aberdeen were in the minority.[5]

The King's veiled projects.

---

[1] *Martyrs Graves,* 257.
[2] Alexander Stewart, fifth Earl of Morray; Justice-General, 1647; d. 1701.
[3] *Act. Parl. Scot.*, viii. 576-653.
[4] Speech, Aldis, *List,* 2646.
[5] Mar *MSS.*, 217, 219.

Royal
largesse.

The King began the game he was playing by throwing largess. Soon the first statute showed the way the wind was blowing, and greedy cavaliers—Melfort, Perth, Dumbarton, Gordon, Arran, Tarras, Drummond, Stewart of Bute—and other Jacobites were 'fleshed' with the lands of their neighbours. Parliament was by no means pliant, and the Bishops of Galloway, Ross, and Dunkeld were inimical to the toleration. Melfort warned the opposition of long memories for priests meddling in Kings' matters. The threat was made practical. Melfort in returning a draft Act to Hamilton significantly wrote: 'Any more jangleing will give him [the King] the pet past all our power to cure.'[1] Seeing that this Act giving the Papists liberty to worship in private was not to be passed pleasantly, the Chancellor had it withdrawn and Parliament dissolved. James now took the matter in his own hand.

James
becomes
lawgiver.

Fortified by the opinion of English judges that his *nobile officium* gave him power to repeal the penal laws, James revoked them. First he made a change in the personnel of the Scots Council, and wrote to that now loyal body, on 21st August, putting in force the 'Act anent the Penal Statutes, 1686.' It authorised the Catholic worship in private homes and in Holyrood, and assured the Papists of protection from assailants and critics.[2] The clergy were made to realise the import of Melfort's comment to Hamilton: 'Surely the devill never inspired a man with a more hellish divise to hinder the King's service, and it ought not to be tollerat in a clergyman of any kind.'[3] Bruce was removed from his see in Dunkeld, and his chapter was coerced into electing his successor. Dr. James Canaries, an apostate from Popery, in a sermon in St. Giles, animadverted on his former co-religionists.

Deposition
of Archbishop
Cairncross.

Perth and Claverhouse demanded his prosecution,[4] Cairncross, Bishop of Glasgow, winked at the affair, and let Canaries slip across the Border till the storm blew past. Notwithstanding the order of Council, 5th October 1685, forbidding unauthorised treatises, the sermon was printed— '*Rome's Additions to Christianity*, Edinburgh, 1686.'[5] Too late, Cairncross suspended Canaries. An inquisition resulted in Cairncross

[1] *Hamilton MSS.*, 173.
[2] Wodrow, iv. 389.
[3] *Hamilton MSS.*, 173.
[4] Fountainhall, *Decisions*, i. 404.
[5] Aldis, *List*, 2634.

being reported to the King, and removed from his archbishopric, to which Paterson was promoted. The thumbscrews amply enriched that inventor. The orthodox clergy meanly submitted to the discipline of their Erastian rulers.

A nobler spirit animated the Remnant. Renwick, in his mossy dens in the wild watershed of the Lowlands, and in North England, was composing his masterly letters in defence of his party, and in combating the false charge that he was creating 'a popular confusion,' and imposing unscriptural restrictions upon the ministry. He was also framing the famous *Vindication*, and writing inspiring letters to prisoners urging them not to be coerced into surrendering the citadel of the Covenanters' faith. A blessing followed his thrilling sermons at Sanquhar under the very shadow of Queensberry's towers.[1] Nevertheless dissension crept in among the various bands of wanderers, and much of their spiritual energy was lost in wrangles over points of difference. The legality of Renwick's ordination was one of these. Some maintained that Renwick was an intruded preacher, because his ordination had not been approved by a competent court of the Church of Scotland.[2] Even the shrewd but timid Peden was alienated from him, and bitterly vowed that he would make the young preacher's name 'stink above the ground.'[3] When Death, however, laid its clutch upon Peden in his earthen 'hidie-hole' at Ten Shilling Side in Auchinleck parish, on 28th January 1686, he sent for Renwick to examine him. The wearied youth soon proved to the spent prophet that no defections existed to justify the enmity of that dying witness to the Covenant. Peden penitently confessed his regrets that he had listened to slanders which quenched his love in bitterness. Drawing the innocent youth near to be embraced and kissed, the old minister said: 'Sir, I find you a faithful servant to your Master: go on in a single dependence upon the Lord, and ye will win honestly through and cleanly off the stage, when many others that hold their head high will fall and ly in the mire, and make foul hands and garments.' At the beginning of this extraordinary interview the sarcastic seer, after viewing the puny Protester, exclaimed: 'I think your legs too small, and your shoulders too narrow, to take on the whole

The influence of Renwick.

Renwick interviews Peden, 28th January 1686.

[1] Carslaw, *Life*, 137, 153-71, 180, 197.
[2] Shields, *Life of Renwick*, Biog. Presby., ii. 113-7; Wodrow, iv. 393-5.
[3] *Six Saints*, i. 106.

Church of Scotland upon your back.' When soul met soul, before they parted, Peden prayed and blessed the herald he had almost cursed.[1] At last, this benediction was a great victory for the party which styled Renwick 'the only minister in Scotland.'

Peden found his rest after a joyful confession that God 'had been both good and kind to poor old Sandy thorow a long tract of time.' He was buried in Auchinleck cemetery. He foretold the exhumation of his body. About forty days after his burial, Lieutenant Murray and a party of horse lifted his coffin and summoned his acquaintances to identify the decaying corpse. Satisfied it was a traitor's, they removed the body two miles to Cumnock, where they intended hanging it in chains on the gallows at the Barhill there. From this hideous act they were dissuaded by the Countess of Dumfries and Dame Boswell. He was buried at the gibbet-foot with Ritchart, Dun, and others. The once dishonoured spot became the parish graveyard.[2]

Peden was a subtle, shrewd, and prescient preacher whom the people credited with gifts of second-sight and prophecy, of which traditional illustrations were from his day indelibly fixed in rural memories, and averred to have been amply fulfilled. As a patriot and Churchman, Peden was lacking in that constructive faculty which distinguished so many of the great Presbyters, and gave them that force by which they made their mark in Scots history. The extraordinary elusiveness of the shaggy prophet, wearing the fabled coat of darkness,[3] betokened a spirit as cunning as it was determined, as uncompromising as it was caustic and bereft of that sweet grace distinctive of the bolder champions of the Covenant.

Renwick lived down the foul slanders attaching to his name. The over-righteous runaways from peril could in Holland defame him as 'a poor blown up illiterate person' who, with 'a hundred silly, poor, daft, bodies' went about the country robbing.[4] These slanders made

---

[1] *Six Saints*, i. 107, 108.

[2] John Cochrane's statement that Peden was buried in David Boswell's aisle in Auchinleck is not substantiated: *Wodrow MSS.*, xxxvii. 104; *U. F. Church Magazine*, July 1906; *Six Saints*, i. 97, 217; ii. 139, 140; *Memoirs of Nisbet*, 184, 185; Wodrow, iv. 396; *Martyr Graves*, 327; Todd, *The Homes*, etc., i, 52-70.

[3] His mask is still preserved.

[4] *Biog. Presby.*, ii. 129; *Six Saints*, 33, 142; *Faithful Contendings*, 242.

it imperative that the General Meeting held at Blackgannoch, on 7th April 1686, should authorise Renwick, Boyd, Hill, Wilson, and Michael Shields, brother of Alexander, to draft a Vindication of the Remnant.[1] At this meeting it was also resolved that members should come to conventions armed 'for their own and the brethren's defence.' The Vindication, after various references to the meetings, was finally prepared for the press by Renwick, and, at Friarminion, on 4th March 1687, authorised for publication in Holland at the price of 'eight pence per book and at seven pence unstitched.'[2] Alexander Shields superintended the printing.

Its title runs thus: *An Informatory Vindication of a Poor Wasted Misrepresented Remnant of the Suffering Anti-Popish Anti-Prelatic Anti-Erastian Anti-Sectarian True Presbyterian Church of Christ in Scotland united together in a General Correspondence. By Way of Reply to Various Accusations in Letters Informations and Conference given forth against them.* The Vindication is a very able defence of the principles of Renwick and the Remnant, and ascribes the reason for their existence to the habitual tyranny that forced men back on their native liberty. It challenged the allegation that the Remnant were revolutionaries setting up an unjustfiable regime of the Covenanted Reformation, and declared that they were neither Separatists nor a new Church, but only the unconquered Remnant of the historic Church of Scotland. To publish their shame for the defections of the Church, royal encroachments, and popular indifference, the Remnant held a Fast in April. The best account of the principles of the Societies, ministered to by 'Rabbi Renwick' and his elders, is found in Michael Shields' letter to 'Friends in Ireland.'[3] There we are informed of a fact not generally known, that these intractable hillmen were ready to 'embrace all ministers as are clothed with Christ's commission in an orderly way,' and only withdrew from usurpers of the prerogatives of Christ. They were in the apostolic succession of Knox and Melville. Before the end of the year the frail preacher, Renwick, got assistance from David Houston and Alexander Shields—the latter confessing shame at swearing allegiance and taking the Abjuration Oath.[4] On 9th December 1686, the Government issued

An Informatory Vindication.

Toleration of the hillmen.

---

[1] *Faithful Contendings*, 243.
[2] *Ibid.*, 287, 319.
[3] *Ibid.*, 287-307; 2nd March, 1687.
[4] Carslaw, 198.

a second proclamation against Renwick, and offered a reward for his apprehension. A third proclamation followed on 18th October.[1] Renwick held on his way, with joy declaring: 'There is now strange thirsting after my blood, but that moves me not.'

Daily the Catholic interests in Britain were growing stronger, and the King, imagining that his authority was now paramount, resolved to carry out his own desire for the enfranchisement of his co-religionists and their restoration to place and power, for which they were legally incapacitated. What Parliament failed to do, James accomplished by a letter addressed to the Scots Council, 12th February 1687, enclosing a proclamation announcing his moderation, care for tender consciences, regard for the conformists, and hatred of conventiclers. The proclamation bore that the King, realising that dissent was ruining the realm, by his supreme power created a *modus vivendi* by the dispensation of toleration—

(1) to moderate Presbyterians, who were to be allowed to worship in private houses and to hear indulged ministers;

(2) to Quakers, with licensed meeting-houses;

(3) to Roman Catholics, with liberty to worship in private houses and chapels, not in the fields or Protestant churches, that worship not to include public processions in the High Streets of Royal Burghs. The penal laws were abrogated and political equality was restored to the Catholics. The concessions were granted on condition that acceptors signed an oath acknowledging the absolute authority of the King, his heirs, and his successors.[2]

The proclamation disclaimed any intention on the part of the King to violate individual consciences, and promised to maintain the existing clergy and to advance public officials irrespective of religious beliefs.[3]

In this way constitutional government was abolished *per saltum*,[4] and a Popish King, in spite of the law, assumed an autocratic power whose plenitude was never acquired by any Pope. The Council obsequiously accepted the papal indulgence, and acknowledged the royal prerogative.

[1] Aldis, *List*, 2665, 2715.

[2] *Ibid.*, 2709: Granting toleration to all religions—First Indulgence.

[3] Wodrow, iv. 417 note.

[4] [Latin: by a leap, *i.e.* without going through the necessary legal proceedings.]

The *habituès*[1] of that sanguinary body signed the new bond of Slavery. For refusing to acquiesce, Hamilton, Panmure, and Dundonald fell under royal displeasure. Panmure and Dundonald were removed from the Council by royal fiat.[2]

It included a worse order—that Presbyterian preachers were not to be permitted to preach without a Council licence. This act of tyranny had to be modified, so that ministers who scrupled at the oath were allowed to preach if the Council judged them to be orderly.[3] The granting of liberty of conscience in England, 4th April, was followed by a Scots proclamation, 5th July, giving freedom of worship to all sects, if loyal, in buildings notified to, and approved by, local magistrates.[4]

All penal enactments against dissenters, conventiclers always excepted, were annulled. In this way the Romanists obtained power to erect places of worship, so long as they had them reported to the magistrates. In November, the 'ornamenta' for Holyrood arrived at Leith, in the royal yacht, and thereafter the chapel was re-consecrated for its ancient rites and for the use of the Knights of the Thistle.[5] In the precincts, schools and printing-presses were established by the priests.[6]

On the other hand, news of the King's *Irenicon* caused many exiled ministers to return home to become useful pastors again—among the number being 'that signalie holy man of God, Mr. Thomas Hoge [Kiltearn], who was a true father in our Israell,' Kirkton, the historian, Professor George Campbell, James Veitch, and Patrick Pitcairn. The country, except in Episcopal districts, rang with praises of the King for his charitable considerateness. Some Presbyterian ministers met in Edinburgh, and on 21st July framed an address to the King, in which they pawkily stated their gratitude, their adherence to the Confession of Faith, and their habit of praying for his 'divine illumination.'

The citizens of Edinburgh also blessed the King for 'this late refreshing and unexpected favour.'[7] The Episcopal party were highly

Return of exiles.

---

[1] [French: the frequenters, *i.e.* the members of the Council.]
[2] Wodrow, iv. 423 note.
[3] *Ibid.*, 424 note.
[4] *Ibid.*, 426 note; *List*, 2711, 2712; Third Indulgence, 2713.
[5] Fountainhall, *Decisions*, i. 430, 432.
[6] Aldis records Holyrood House publications.
[7] Woodrow, iv. 428 note.

incensed at the new policy, but dared scarcely express their hatred of the Indulgence, to which they traced the subsequent disestablishment of their Church.[1] That the disaffected and hypercritical might not imagine that they were overlooked and pardoned upon no show of repentance, the public prosecutor, Sir John Dalrymple, cited Dr. Gilbert Burnet, formerly Professor of Divinity in Glasgow, to the Justiciary Court to answer to a charge of treason.[2] Burnet was the most perfect specimen of a subtle intriguer the Crown could light on. In Scots parlance he was 'a pawky chiel.' From his earliest youth Burnet evinced an inquiring, if not a meddling, spirit, and pushed himself into an intimacy with aspiring leaders and patriots, more with a view to get information and appear influential than to act as a leader.[3] The Government, however, reckoned him to be a malicious plotter associated with the plots of Argyll, Stewart, and Fergusson the Plotter, and produced for testimony the Cochranes, Carstares, and others. Burnet declined to compear, alleging that he was a naturalised Dutch subject, also about to marry a Dutch wife. In place of himself he would send to his judges an explanation, in which he showed that he had slight acquaintance with the rebels, and that the charge was trumped up and provocative. After a second citation Burnet was put to the horn.[4] According to Fountainhall, the reason for the indictment was the discovery of a letter from Burnet, in which he stated that in Rome he had seen the original text of the League binding James and other Popish sovereigns to extirpate the Protestants.[5]

Renwick and his party consistently rejected the truce, and transmitted a Testimony against the Toleration to the meeting of ministers in January. The Societies appointed a Fast in January 1688, in order to pray for the success of their own mission, and that God 'would bring down the throne of iniquity, and give us godly and faithful magistrates.'[6]

[1] Balcarres, *An Account*, 8, 14; *An Account of the Present Persecution*, anno 1690, p. 10.

[2] *Book of Adjournal*, 21st February 1687; 29th August, Burnet at the horn. Sir John Dalrymple, first Earl of Stair (1648-1707), then Lord Advocate.

[3] For instances of Burnet's deftness in dealing with records of public affairs, cf. Foxcroft's *Supplement* with the published *History*; also *Scot. Hist. Rev.* iv. 16, 'Burnet on the Scottish Troubles.'

[4] Wodrow, iv. 408-11 note.

[5] *Hist. Not.* ii. 793.

[6] *Faithful Contendings*, 322; Johnston, *Treasury of Covenant*, 361.

The long-continued tragedy of a proud and pious people panting for freedom, while brutal betrayers of their own flesh and blood crushed down the meek and patient, and sent to bloody graves, or burning fields of slavery, the untameable, was about to reach the final act. The long tract of barbarity was to have its consummation on the scaffold in the offering of an almost spotless victim to the insatiable Moloch who sat on the throne under the delusion that he ruled the fate of the Covenanters. That oblation was James Renwick. Busy in all directions, preaching even so near the Capital as on the Braid Hills, comforting, writing, after many a race and chase, the bold youth ventured again into Edinburgh to stay in the Castlehill with John Luckup. Luckup's house was a rendezvous of wanderers and the store of uncustomed English goods. There lay safe the papers of Henry Hall's son, and of Alexander Shields. Luckup was a suspect. John Justice discovered Renwick and brought a party of 'tollers' or excisemen, ostensibly to examine Luckup's merchandise on 1st February, in reality to apprehend Renwick and get the reward. Pistol in hand, Renwick cleared a way for himself and friends through the ring of searchers and made down Castle Wynd for the Cowgatehead. In his flight he got a disabling blow from a staff, and, after several falls, his feeble frame was caught and held by a lusty pursuer. When the comely youth was brought into the presence of Patrick Graham, Captain of the Guard, he exclaimed: 'What, is this boy Mr. Renwick, that the nation hath been so much troubled with?'[1] To save himself from torture he explained the diary he carried; and even this seeming betrayal of his friends hurt his sensitive nature.[2] Otherwise he was ravished with joy at the thought of his martyrdom—what he called 'his marriage and coronation hour.' The Council examined him on 1st February, and found that he was an irreconcilable opponent of the King and his Government, although he disclaimed all 'antinomian and anti-magistratical principles.' On 8th February, Philip Standfield, a reviler of John Welsh, stood in the dock, and received sentence of death for parricide.[3]

The indictment was drawn by Sir John Dalrymple, although at the time Mackenzie (Rosehaugh) had superseded him in the office of

The grand oblation.

Capture of Renwick, 1st February 1688.

Indictment of Renwick.

[1] *Biog. Presby.*, ii. 146-50; *Six Saints*, ii. 232; *Decisions*, i. 495; *Hist. Not.*, ii. 850.
[2] *Laing MSS.*, *Farrago*, 223; Carslaw, 254.
[3] *Book of Adjournal*, 8th February 1668.

Lord Advocate. The large roster of jurymen was another test to catch sympathisers with the rebels. At length fifteen men were selected, and Ninian Bannatyne of Kames, elder in the parish church of Rothesay, was appointed their chancellor. Among the witnesses were Bishop Paterson, Claverhouse, and James Boyle, a prisoner. Boyle, a fighter at Bothwell, a conventicler and acquaintance of Renwick, was lying under sentence of death since 7th November.[1]

Trial of Renwick, 8th February. The trial took place on 8th February under Linlithgow, Justice-General.[2] Renwick, in challenging the jury, adjured any professed Protestant, Presbyterian, or Covenanter to sit on the assize to his own condemnation. He denied the terms of the indictment, that he had shaken off the fear of God, since the fear of offending God had brought him there. He justified his principles and confession that the King was no longer lawful Sovereign according to God's Word, the ancient laws of Scotland, and the Covenants; that it was unlawful to pay cess to suppress the Gospel; that it was lawful to use arms to resist unjust violence. For one holding such anti-Royalist views only one doom was possible. It was not necessary to call witnesses. He was condemned to be executed in the Grassmarket two days later, 10th February 1688. Linlithgow asked him if he wished a longer time for preparation. The fearless devotee replied: 'It was all one to him. If it were protracted it was welcome, if it were shortened it was welcome: his Master's time was the best.'

Renwick in prison. While Renwick lay in prison, an incessant assault was made by his prosecutors, and by the clergy, in order to break down his fidelity to Covenanting principles. A certain glamour rested on the hapless young preacher, and constrained even his enemies to wish a happier fate for him. The Chancellor declared that he had the courage of his opinions, convictions which other Presbyterians had not. Other observers rightly judged that he was of 'Old Knox's principles,' which only recent legislation had denounced as treason, so that he was a martyr for Presbyterianism.[3] Bishop Paterson, Dr. Munro, and other influential Episcopalians did

---

[1] *Book of Adjournal*, 7th November, 7th December 1687; *Biog. Presby.*, ii. 152-6; Wodrow, iv. 447.

[2] *Ibid.*, 8th February 1688.

[3] *Biog. Presby.*, ii. 177. Viscount Tarbat is credited with saying that if Renwick 'had lived in Knox's Days [he] would not have died, by any laws that were then': *ibid.*

what Leighton did not do to Guthrie— visited Renwick in prison; for Paterson thought him 'a pretty lad,' and would fain have had him reprieved.[1] The Lord Advocate, Dalrymple, apparently smitten by conscience, did not leave him to die without personally trying to save him by endeavouring to procure from him some acknowledgment of the King's authority. His biographer declares that a pardon 'was offered to him if he would but let a drop of ink fall upon a Bit of Paper; it should satisfy, but he would not.'[2] His cell was a scene of levèes. Priests, Prelatists, and indulged Presbyterians were allowed to try him as if he were a Jesuit, and to tempt him from the course that assured him of happiness.[3] His execution was delayed a week in order that the effect of the Royalists' blandishments upon the condemned might be seen. Renwick was steadfast and immovable.

His mother and sisters arrived to comfort him. They found him 'ravished with the joy of the Lord.' He soothed his mother's fears as to his comely head and hands, which he prophesied would never appear on the jail spikes. He owned a shrinking from torture, but a greater horror of defection, since he would 'rather choose to be cast in a caldron of burning oil, than to do anything that might wrong truth.'[4] He longed for 'the crown of martyrdom, an honour the angels are not capable of.' He believed himself to be an instrument in God's hand for the redemption of Scotland. 'I am persuaded,' said he to his mother, 'that my death will do more good than my life for many years has done.'[5] By such mothers and such sons has Scottish freedom been fostered and regained.

Renwick comforted by his mother.

The fatal day arrived—17th February. When the drums beat for the guard to take him to execution, he said to his mother: 'Yonder is the welcome warning to my marriage; the Bridegroom is coming. I am ready. I am ready.' In a transport of joy he walked to the scaffold. Amid the tattoo of drums he sang the 103rd Psalm, read the twentieth chapter of The Revelation, prayed, and addressed the audience till he was forced

Renwick on the scaffold, 17th February 1688.

---

[1] *Biog. Presby.*, ii. 163-5.

[2] *Ibid.*, 168.

[3] The respite was attributed to the report that he was a Jesuit: *A Vindication of the Presbyterians in Scotland* (Lond., 1692), 17.

[4] *Biog. Presby.*, ii. 158.

[5] *Ibid.*, 169.

up the ladder. 'Spectators,' said he, 'I am this Day to lay down my Life for these three Things:—

'(1) For disowning the Usurpation and Tyranny of *James Duke of York.*'

'(2) For preaching that it was unlawful to pay the Cess, expresly exacted for the bearing down of the Gospel.'

'(3) For teaching that it was lawful for People to carry Arms for defending themselves in their Meetings for the persecuted Gospel-Ordinances. I think, a Testimony for those is worth many Lives; and if I had Ten thousand I would think it little enough, to lay them all down for the same.'[1]

The drums never ceased until the struggles of one of the noblest martyrs for religion and Fatherland had ended. Another romantic incident occurred, when Helen Alexander of Pentlands, long time a prisoner for the same cause, rolled him in his winding-sheet, and, with his relatives and friends, had him laid in the same dust as other sufferers in Greyfriars' cemetery. Renwick was twenty-six years and three days old when he was hanged.

Appreciation of Renwick.

The verdict of Renwick's associates was that he was 'a ripe Christian.' That is the highest appreciation. A cultured mind, capable of a comprehensive grasp of revealed truth and of political principles, which expressed itself in gracious thrilling oratory, as well as in the chaste language of polemical manifestoes, distinguished Renwick. There is no trace of a plebeian spirit in the literary remains of this author. He had a kindly sympathy for his opponents—the Papists excluded. He told Patrick Walker, 'He never durst preach withdrawing from all the ministers of Scotland, for many might get good of them that did not know about them what he knew.'[2] His exalted aims were in keeping with his prescience, which found expression thus: 'There is a Storm coming, that shall try your Foundation. *Scotland* must be rid of *Scotland* before the Delivery come. ... I die in the faith that Thou wilt not leave Scotland, but that Thou wilt make the blood of Thy Witnesses the Seed of Thy Church, and return again, and be glorious in our Land.'[3]

[1] *Biog. Presby.*, ii. 174; Wodrow, iv. 454; *Cloud*, 472-91.
[2] *Six Saints*, i. 292.
[3] *Biog. Presby.*, ii. 175-6.

The spirits of the unconquered heroes of his Fatherland seem to have been reincarnated in this fascinating leader of the wanderers. A rare genius inspired him who could say that he died a witness for 'the incommunicable Prerogative of Jehovah.' That phrase illuminates the religious war in Scotland waged for one hundred and thirty years. The pioneers of Protestantism, evangelists after Wishart, reformers after Knox, polemics after Melville, protesters after Guthrie, plotters after Argyll, excommunicators after Cargill, fighters after Wallace and Cameron, and conventiclers before and after Renwick, all, in one form or other, contended and bled for the Crown Rights of our Redeemer in His own Church, and against the impious and insufferable usurpation by the Stuart kings of this 'incommunicable Prerogative of Jehovah.'

'The incommunicable Prerogative.'

How clearly did Carlyle see this root of the matter: 'Yes, Reader, here is the miracle. ... Since Protestantism went silent, no Luther's voice, no Zisca's drum any longer proclaimed that God's truth was not the Devil's lie; and the last of the Cameronians (Renwick was the name of him, honour to the name of the brave!) sank, shot,[1] on the Castle-hill of Edinburgh, there was no partial impulse of Faith among nations. Herein we say in that astounding faith of theirs lies the miracle. It is a Faith undoubtedly of the more prodigious sort even among faiths; and will embody itself in prodigies!'[2] True! The Covenanters declared they saw portents in the sky: we come to see the prodigies right soon.

Thomas Carlyle on Renwick.

The death of Renwick was duly reported at a meeting of the Societies at Blackgannoch, on 7th March, and appraised as a 'dash' to their enemies, and as another witness to the Covenants. Nowise daunted, the irreconcilables resolved to appoint another watchman in Mr. Thomas Lining, to be 'cleanly' ordained by the *Classis* in Embden. Renwick's colleague, David Houston, was apprehended in Ireland and sent back to Edinburgh. The Hillmen attacked the escort at Bello Path, or Crichton Path, three miles from Old Cumnock, and rescued Houston. In the fray, which took place about the 20th June, some soldiers were killed and some wounded; and one of the rescuers fell—John M'Gechan, Auchingibbert. Houston was badly wounded in the scuffle,

Effect of Renwick's death on his associates.

---

[1] Perhaps Carlyle here refers to some tradition that Renwick, in his flight, was wounded by a shot. Carlyle must have known well that Renwick was hanged, not shot, in the Grassmarket.

[2] *French Revolution*, iii. 102.

and incapacitated for the ministry.[1] The usual proclamation followed, and Claverhouse, Douglas, and the forces were soon rounding up into the burghs gentle and simple alike, with the indulged ministers, to determine 'the hounders-out of the said desperate rebels.'[2] King and Council meant what they enacted, that all worshippers should be licensed, and all conventiclers must die.

The last mar-tyr, George Wood, July (?) 1688. Probably in this last military drive the last martyr fell. In Sorn churchyard an old slab tells: 'Here lyes G[e]org[e] Wood who was shot at Tinkhorn by John Reid Trvper for his adherence to the Word of God and the Covenanted Work of Reformation, 1688.' Wood was a boy of sixteen, whom Reid shot without asking him a question, afterwards justifying his ruthless act by saying: 'He knew him to be one of the Whigs, and they ought to be shot wherever they were found.'[3]

According to the author of The Scots Worthies, and other author-ities, the number of sufferers for the Covenants, by imprisonment, banishment, and death, was 18,000—a computation which is probably too great. Of these 1700 were transported; 750 were banished to the North Isles; 2800 suffered imprisonment; 7000 went into exile; 680 were killed fighting; 498 were dispatched in the fields; 362 were judicially executed; and many others perished in their wanderings.[4]

[1] M'Gechan's monument at Stone Park bears date 28th July 1688: *Martyr Graves*, 341; *Faithful Contendings*, 336, 337, 338, 352, 359; Wodrow, iv. 442; *Proclamation*, 22nd June; Aldis, *List*, 2737. M'Gechan 'was a singularly pious man': Cochrane's Letter, *Wodrow MSS.*, xxxvii. 104.

[2] Aldis, *List*, 2737.

[3] Wodrow, iv. 457; *Martyr Graves*, 343. This incident took place shortly before 1st August 1688: Shields to Hamilton, *Faithful Contendings*, 355.

[4] *The Scots Worthies*, 626; M'Crie, *Sketches*, ii. 239; Defoe, 319; *A Short Memorial*, 33-8. The author of *Answer to the Scotch Presbyterian Eloquence* (pp. 40-1) declares that, of 1310 who suffered banishment and death, 700 were banished, 400 slain in skirmishes; 140 executed judicially; and 70 murdered in cold blood—in all 610. Of the 700 who were banished, 200 died abroad. Among the exiles who perished abroad was John Balfour of Kinloch, said to have been drowned on his return from Holland. But accounts differ as to the fate of this fugitive, and nothing certain is known of his last deeds and days.

Scene of the martyrdom at Wigtown

Graves of the Wigtown Martyrs

Ayrsmoss and Cameron's Monument

'Wellwood's dark valley'

William Adam's grave at Wellwood

Priesthill and John Brown's Monument

MONUMENTS OF THE MARTYRS

The Cross, Moniave

The Parish Church, St. Andrews

Monument to the Earl of Angus, Douglas

Dalgarno: tombstone showing dress of a
Covenanting preacher

Graves of Peden and of Martyrs in the
Cemetery, Cumnock

Martyrs' Monument, Irongray

PEDEN'S GRAVE AND OTHER HISTORIC SPOTS

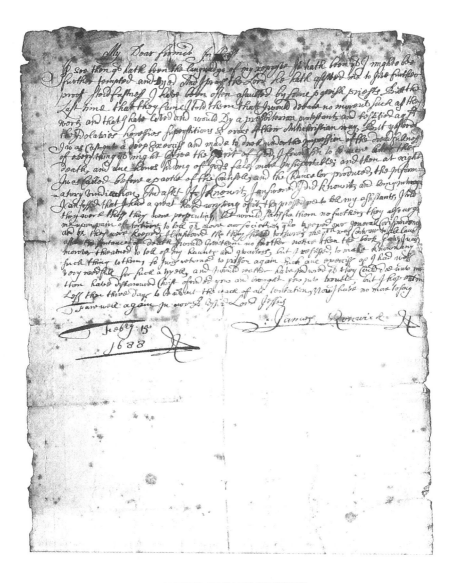

LETTER OF JAMES RENWICK

BATTLEFIELD OF KILLIECRANKIE

CHAPTER THIRTY-ONE

THE REVOLUTION

DELIVERANCE was at hand. The good sense of the nation re-asserted itself, and found expression in the joy of the people, who almost universally hailed with acclamation the overthrow of the unconstitutional dominion after a bloodless campaign. The identical arguments used by the Cameronians for justifying their renunciation of the Stuarts became the reasons offered to Europe for the righteousness of the invasion of Britain by a foreign liberator. The Society-men took credit to themselves for inaugurating that successful revolution for which they had long been reproached and persecuted.[1] Although the throne was trembling, the myopic Government pursued as hot a persecution as that proceeding before the Toleration was published. The whole *catena* of Covenanting literature was proclaimed as pernicious treason—such as *De Jure, Lex Rex, Jus Populi, Naphtali, The Cup of Cold Water, The Scots Mist, The Apologetical Relation, Mene Tekel, A Hind Let Loose,* and the various Declarations of the later Covenanters.[2] The soldiery was active.

A tottering throne.

For long, British Protestants at home and abroad had been looking to William Henry, third Prince of Orange, as the Joshua who would complete their flight from bondage and lead them into the Promised Land. This Protestant sovereign had strong claims on them. He was the son of one British princess, the husband of another—Mary, the heiress of the Crown, also a Protestant—and the nephew and son-in-law of

William, the Protestant Joshua.

---

[1] *Faithful Contendings*, 392.
[2] 15th August: Aldis, *List*, 2791; Wodrow, iv. 444 note.

Birth of
James
'the old
Pretender.'

the King. He had at his ear gossiping Gilbert Burnet. How far, if at all, the Prince of Orange encouraged the onfall on Britain of the unsuccessful invaders—Argyll and Monmouth—and intrigued with the exiled dissentients, has not been made clear. Two events changed the relationship of William to James, namely, revocation of the Edict of Nantes, and the birth of the 'hopeful prince,' James—'the Chevalier de St. George'—on 10th June 1688. The Council and Claverhouse hailed the birth as 'so extraordinary a mercy.' William saw in it the menace of a Popish dynasty. Whig and Tory perceived that and the peril of an alliance with belligerent Louis of France. The acts of James, in his autocratic madness, brought matters to a head. The Indulgence, the dissolution of Parliament, the prosecution of seven bishops accused of sedition, and other intolerable doings, incensed the people and incited the courage of seven influential patriots, who invited William to come and protect the liberties of Britain.

Declaration
by William
of Orange,
October
1688.

William promulgated a Declaration of the reasons inducing him to appear in arms in defence of Protestantism and of the liberty of Scotland.[1] These, in fine, were the new unconstitutional régime, the miseries of the downtrodden, the violation of anti-Popish statutes, the despotism of the governors, the illegal, brutal persecution, punishment, and slaughter of the lieges, the subversion of Protestantism, the spurious birth of Prince James, and William's interest in Mary's heritage. No mountain man—Cargill, Cameron, Renwick, or Patrick Walker— could have issued a more explicit proclamation of extreme Covenanting principles than was therein published by William of Orange. William and his fourteen thousand men—'Butterboxes,' the Jacobites called them—landed at Brixham, Torbay, on 5th November. In his *entourage* were Sir James Dalrymple, Carstares, and Burnet. On touching British soil they consecrated their mission by worship. On the 18th December, the Prince of Orange reached St. James's Palace; five days later the absconding monarch, James, left England for ever. The country was soon in a ferment of excitement.

James's futile
move.

So early as September, King James commissioned the Earl of Perth, who employed Sir Patrick Murray, to discover if the Presbyterian party generally, in consideration of the clemency he had displayed towards

---

[1] 10th October: Wodrow, iv. 470; Aldis, *List*, 2828.

them, would not out of gratitude adhere to his cause in this crisis. The leaders equivocated, and declared that they 'would meddle no more with him' or his officials, and would act as God inspired them.[1]

The Society-men, realising that they were escaping martyrdom by the skin of their teeth, resolutely testified against both Jacobites and Dutch, styling the latter 'a promiscuous conjunction of reformed Lutherans, Malignants, and Sectaries.' At a meeting held at Wanlockhead on 24th October, they resolved to put themselves in a 'posture of defence' when circumstances were favourable; to league themselves with unadulterated Covenanters only; to refuse amalgamation while operating with the Dutch and accepting their ammunition and drill-sergeants. At a subsequent convention they testified that the Prince of Orange's Declaration was 'too lame and defective,' having ignored 'the Covenanted Work of Reformation.'[2] They showed their practical sympathy with the invasion, by proceeding with phenomenal activity to purge the churches in south-west Scotland of their 'intruded hireling curates.'[3] *The Society-men testify against Jacobites and Dutch.*

On the 3rd of November, the Scots bishops, all but two, met in Edinburgh and subscribed a letter to the King, whom they styled 'the darling of Heaven,' so 'miraculously prospered with glory and victory.' They could not more fawningly—such a contrast to the conduct of the bishops in England at this crisis—have lauded the Archangel Michael than James, for whom they prayed God to give him victory with 'the hearts of your subjects and the necks of your enemies.'[4] They appointed a deputation of their number to go to London and watch over their interests. This mission of Bishop Rose accomplished nothing.[5] *The Scots bishops support James.*

The Scots Privy Council, seeing the tight corner they were driven into, resolved with the wisdom of the serpent to display the harmlessness of the dove, and discharged the punitive measures that were ordered after the rescue of David Houston; and, in order to evince a more marked show of magnanimity and tenderness of feeling towards Presbyterians, gave instructions that the heads of the martyrs were to be removed from the public gaze on the jail spikes. Shields naively remarks on this *The wily Scottish Council.*

[1] Balcarres, *An Account*, 24.
[2] *Faithful Contendings*, 365, 370, 371.
[3] *Ibid.*, 71.
[4] Wodrow, iv. 468.
[5] *Letters to Sancroft*, 89; Grub, iii. 295.

expedient act— 'for fear lest these monuments of their cruelty standing might occasion the question to be moved, By whom and for what were they set up.'[1] In December, the Council disarmed Papists and threw them on the protection of heritors, who were summoned to a muster 'for security of the Protestant Religion.'[2] The obedient soldiers, taking an example from their masters, drove their swords into their scabbards.

Representative conventions. Two important conventions met in January 1689—a meeting of Scots nobles and gentlemen summoned to St. James's by William, and a convocation of Presbyterian ministers frequently assembling in Edinburgh. Each of these representative gatherings framed an Address to that Prince, and concluded with definite requests regarding political and ecclesiastical freedom. The laymen asked for a free Parliament at which no oath was to be taken, at which 'no bishop or evil counsellor be called to sit to be our judges.' The ministers demanded the extrusion of Episcopacy, alleged to be 'contrary to the genius of the nation,' the restoration of Presbytery, and a 'quiet harbour' for 'this poor weather-beaten church.'[3] The Societies still held aloof from their Presbyterian brethren, till they owned their defections, only agreeing to attend meetings for the purpose of convincing of error, but not to amalgamate with the unreformed.[4] They also lent a willing hand in the newly begun rabbling.

Claverhouse on the march. Since the appearance of Claverhouse as a witness against Renwick, he had been busy with his new duties in the Provostship of Dundee and other civil business, which he performed with military exactitude. In September, the standing forces in Scotland, the chief garrisons excepted, received orders from Whitehall to march to Carlisle in view of the anticipated invasion. Lieutenant-General Douglas had three thousand men of all arms, including eight hundred and forty-one horse and dragoons under Major-General Graham. They continued their march till they reached London in the end of October.[5] They pushed on to join the royal army lying at Salisbury. Before James left London he

---

[1] *A Short Memorial*, 28.

[2] Wodrow, iv. 475; Aldis, *List*, 2742, 2743—14th and 24th December.

[3] Wodrow, iv. 477-82; lay desire for the expulsion of the bishops was due to their own indiscretions—Queensberry to Sancroft, 24th December 1688: *Letters*, 99.

[4] *Faithful Contendings*, 421.

[5] *Terry*, 236.

raised the loyal Claverhouse to the peerage with the titles of Viscount of Dundee and Lord Graham of Claverhouse, in recognition of that soldier's 'many good and eminent services,' and his 'constant loyalty and firm adherence (upon all occasions) to the true interests of the Crown.' James threw away any opportunity left to him at this crisis. Nothing could induce James to act boldly and give his daring generals a chance of victory. He skulked away, leaving his army to be disbanded. William failed to win Dundee and Balcarres over to his party—Dundee only promising that 'unless he were forced to it he would live quietly'; but William did not interfere with their return to Scotland, Dundee riding home at the head of his own troop, at the end of February.[1]

The advent of the Liberator gave the students an opportunity of burning an effigy of the Pope in Glasgow. On 10th December a rabble, some Cameronians among the rest, proceeded to Holyrood Abbey to purge that ancient fane of its monuments of idolatry, and were met by the deadly fire of Captain John Wallace and a guard, which killed twelve of the assailants and wounded thrice as many. The enraged townsmen, led by the provost and Captain Graham, formerly of the town-guard, surrounded the palace, put Wallace to flight, killed some of the guard, wrecked the chapel, looted the Jesuits' quarters and schools, drank dry the cellars of Chancellor Perth, and fired themselves into a fit condition for plundering every Papist's house they knew.[2]

Mêlée at Holyrood, 10th December 1688.

Perth thought it was time to seek safety with the King in France, but was captured near the Bass, brought back to Kirkcaldy jail, and sent to Stirling, where he lay for four years.[3] In many parishes mobs of angry men and women emptied the manses and showed violence to the inmates.

Capture of Chancellor Perth.

The Society-men considered this disorderly method of 'rabbling out' the ministry to be improper and wanting in ecclesiastical formality and dignity, and resolved to prepare a warrant of ejection to be politely forwarded to all obnoxious incumbents, inviting them to cease from official duty, and to deliver up the church keys and communion plate before the inevitable eviction took place.[4] Rabbling was brutal

The Society-men and rabbling.

[1] Balcarres, *An Account*, 58.
[2] *Ibid.*, 38-43.
[3] *Ibid.*, 47.
[4] *Faithful Contendings*, 375; *The Case of the present Afflicted Clergy* (Lond., 1690),

procedure. Christmastide was reckoned to be a seasonable time for commencing it. By day and by night bands of despoilers and immodest viragoes sallied forth to find the curates, and broke up doors of church and manse in their quest. They made free of meat and drink, turned the plenishing upside down or out into the open, and drove into the snow and frostbound fields women, children, and cattle. The incumbent, invested in his canonical robes, they bore to the market cross or into the churchyard. They cudgelled him on the route. They tore up his vestments into ribbons, and cast these with his hat into an improvised fire, before which the shivering wretch was made to beg his life, give up the keys, and swear that henceforth he would desist from his hateful office.

Barbaric rabblings.

Captain James Harkness, in all likelihood a hero of Enterkin, at the head of a band of Amazons, invaded the manse of Kirkpatrick-Juxta, in Annandale, and seized Archibald Fergusson, the minister. Each from her girdle drew an ugly knife, and began incontinently to undress the prostrate pastor. An eye-witness said that 'their modesty could not prevail against their zeal as to spare his shirt and drawers, but all were cut in pieces and sacrificed to a broken Covenant.'[1] Then the barbarians allowed the naked wretch with bruised bones to crawl back to his wife —she was *enceinte*—who was also maltreated in trying to protect her husband. Robert Bell, minister of Kilmarnock, left a graphic account of his forced compearance in a crowd of howling fanatics, who burned the Prayer-Book at the Cross of Kilmarnock, and cut off and burned his gown—'the garment of the Whore of Babylon,' as they designated his robe. Patrick Walker, who attended fifteen rabblings, narrates with what delight he essayed this public duty, especially of raiding Traquair House, whose 'Popish Wares' were carried to the Cross of Peebles and burnt. The curates were in terror of these cleansers. Patrick asked them: 'How would they tremble and sweat if they were in the Grassmarket and other places, going up the ladder, with the rope before them, and the lad with the pyoted coat at their tail?' Patrick also notes that his honest party of official rabblers are not to be identified with the loose ruffians who were then spoiling manses.

21-71. This pamphlet was answered by Gilbert Rule in *A Second Vindication*, 1691.
[1] G. M. in the *Case*, 61.

The Society-men took the precaution to publish a vindication at the Cross of Douglas, on 4th January 1689, clearing themselves of aspersions on that head, an occasion on which Shields addressed the meeting, which sang the significant psalm—the 76th—'In Judah's land God is well known.'[1] Yet at this time Scotland had little appearance of the Holy Land.

The iron gates of the wind-swept dungeons of Blackness Castle opened to permit Alexander Gordon of Earlston, after years of incarceration, to attend a meeting of the Societies in Sanquhar on 23rd January 1689, where he more than satisfied that inquisition that his past defections were pardonable; and that bold freeman in turn even went the length of animadverting upon the defection of the Remnant in associating with Malignant sympathisers with the Prince of Orange.[2] After all their bickerings they became unanimous in resolving to renew the Covenants, to prepare a list of defections, and to organise their supporters before the Estates met. Another great meeting of the Covenanters assembled in Lesmahagow Church, and marched up to Borland Hill, on Sabbath, 3rd March, when, after William Boyd and Thomas Lining preached, 'Mr. Lining read before the Congregation the Acknowledgment of Sins, and Engagement to Duties, and next the Covenants—National and Solemn League—which were fairly written at length, with some alterations which the circumstances of the times of necessity called for, such as when they mention the King, in place thereof is put the Civil Magistrate.' The people with uplifted hands swore the two Covenants. In the evening many subscribed them in Lesmahagow Church.[3]

Liberation of Alexander Gordon, 1650-1726.

Covenants subscribed at Lesmahagow, 3rd March 1689.

A wave of violence spread over the south-west counties of Scotland, as if the worst passions of a rude enslaved people had been unleashed, and got beyond control, the more they recollected the indignities and sufferings to which they had been for a generation subjected. The peasantry, as much as the zealots, rebels, and mountain men, had their own scores to settle with callous governors and pitiless sympathisers with the late misgovernment. All the sufferings were not for the Covenant's sake. There was many a roofless home, empty cupboard,

Explanation of the violence of the victors.

---

[1] *Six Saints,* i. 321; 183, 184.
[2] *Faithful Contendings,* 373.
[3] *Ibid.,* 381.

lonely green grave, many a footsore vagabond as well as unkempt saint, to testify to the truth that the authorities had not always been scrupulous in discriminating whose farms were fired, whose goods were spoiled, whose lives were gangrened out in dungeons, rotted on the moorland, wasted in the cane-brakes, ended by bullet, rope, or rising tide. William's Declaration mentioned these facts. No religion has ever yet subdued the Scottish spirit to a clemency willing to overlook and excuse the long course of barbarity which met a paltry retribution in the rabbling of about two hundred Episcopal pastors. It was in keeping with William's own tolerant spirit that one of his first proclamations was that of 6th February 1689—'For the Keeping of the Peace'—in which he adjures all lovers of concord to bear with one another, and not accentuate differences. Only the violent disregarded this order.[1]

An English convention, 1689.

William, well advised, summoned a convention of English legislators, which met on 22nd January 1689. First the Commons and afterwards the Lords resolved that James II., having violated the fundamental laws, and having withdrawn himself out of the kingdom, had abdicated the Government, and that the throne had thereby become vacant. Both Houses united in offering the Crown of England to William and Mary as joint Sovereigns. Sovereignty thus became the result of a Parliamentary vote, and the theory of divine right was exploded. Here again was light out of an old window by which the more prescient Covenanters had been guided through the valley of humiliation for half a century, and even longer; for by this resolution the political dogmas of Knox, Buchanan, and Melville, and the ecclesiastical doctrines of Henderson, Guthrie, Cargill, Cameron, and Renwick, received the national imprimatur. Soon the Protestant dissenters in England were satisfied by a Toleration Act, but the demand that all officials should take the oaths of supremacy and allegiance, resulted in the removal of Archbishop Sancroft, six bishops, and four hundred clergy, who refused to take the oaths. They too were tolerated as a new sect of Non-Jurors.[2]

Scots Convention of Estates, 14th March 1689.

The Scots Convention of Estates, summoned by a letter from William, duly met in Edinburgh on 14th March. Test and disability were ignored. The Anti-Jacobite party secured the chair for William,

[1] Aldis, *List*, 2931,
[2] Foxcroft's *Supplement* to Burnet, 315, 317, citing *Hist*., ii. 6, 12.

third Duke of Hamilton (1635-94).[1] The sederunt of one hundred and eighty-nine members was highly representative. Among others sat these blood-stained executioners of the expiring Government—Dundee, Sir John Dalrymple, Dalziel of Glenae, Johnstone of Westerhall, and Coltran of Wigtown. Nine bishops also sat for the last time. A debate arose as to which letter should be read first—that of the King or that of the invader. The latter was preferred.[2] Thereafter the legislators passed an Act declaring the Convention a free and lawful Parliament. 'Dundie' actually subscribed this Act.[3]

The Duke of Gordon, a Papist, still held the Castle of Edinburgh for King James. When Balcarres and Dundee returned from England, they lost no time in communicating with Gordon, and in inducing him to hold the arsenal for the King, as also to menace the Capital with its guns. How Dundee could harmonise this intrigue with his promise to live quietly, only he could explain. Afterwards he might justify it on the ground that the lives of 'Bluidy Mackenzie' and himself were reported to be in jeopardy from Whigs lurking in the purlieus of the city, and ready to defend the Anti-Jacobites and to dispatch the persecutors. Dundee's fellow-legislators flouted his demand that these conspirators should be arrested. Then he thought it was time to be gone. Mackenzie also found it wise to seek stimulus in the invigorating waters of Knaresborough.[4] The bold design to hold the Castle till the forces of James could muster and declare the Convention illegal fell through. Fearing to fall into a trap, Dundee made a final attempt to confirm the loyalty of Gordon. At the head of his troop, Dundee rode out of the city and round to the west front of the Castle. The smart cavalier mounted the steep rock to the postern-gate, and there interviewed Gordon. He descended and rode for safety into the Constabulary of Dudhope. Mar, the quasi-friend of James, did not open Stirling gates until Dundee crossed Stirling Bridge. The daring exploit of Dundee enraged Hamilton, who ordered the doors of Parliament to be locked, so that the caged opponents of the provisional Government were forced to submit to the inevitable.

Dundee's intrigues and exploits.

[1] *Mar MSS.*, 222; *Act. Parl. Scot.*, ix. 3.
[2] Letter, Aldis, *List.*, 2987.
[3] Cf. facsimile in *Act. Parl. Scot.*, ix. 9.
[4] *Leven and Melville Papers*, 32 (Bannatyne Club, 1843).

Gordon submitted; Dundee was denounced rebel; Papists were dismissed from place and privilege; Perth, Balcarres, and others, were soon in jail; the country was ordered to arms; Hugh Mackay, commander of the Scots Brigade, was appointed generalissimo. The very next day, Dundee was commissioned by James to muster 'the ancient cavalier party.' That party had reached its nadir.[1]

Action of Scots Estates. On 3rd April, a Committee appointed to frame the proposal to settle the Government, laid their report before the Convention, and next day the Estates, all but unanimously, passed the resolution that James had forfeited the throne.[2] When Sir Patrick Hume declared that York never had legal title to the crown, some auditors said: 'Ye will be as wild as ever Renwick was.' 'Wild!' exclaimed the Laird of Blair, 'we have been hanging and shooting honest men for wildness, and now we are all turned wild together.'[3] This Act afforded the opportunity for the secretary of the despised Societies to record in his 'Account of the year 1689': 'A few months ago, Prelacy was arrived at the greatest hight of arrogancy and pride. Behold it thrown down from the top of its grandeur! This is also remarkable that the Meeting of the Estates, having by an Act declared King James to have forfeited his right to the Crown, gave the same reasons for it, that the United Societies formerly had given, and for which they protested against his instalment. ...'[4] Verily time sees strange revenges. The same might be said of the Declaration of the Estates containing the Claim of Right and the offer of the crown to William and Mary—a document which Hume had a hand in Knox and the Covenanters justified. drafting—passed on the 11th April. No zealot in the moss-hags could have hurled a more bitter indictment at persecutors, no revolutionary could better have described Prelacy, as an 'unsupportable grievance' which was 'contrary to the inclinations of the generality of the people.' This last idea was a fresh bud on the old stock planted by Knox, watered by the tears of Melville, and nourished on the blood of the martyrs.[5] Hamilton went forthwith to the Cross of Edinburgh and proclaimed

---

[1] 29th March, *Drumlanrig MSS.*, II. i. 39: *Hamilton MSS.*, XI. vi. 175-8: *Act. Parl. Scot.* IX. 11-33. For siege of the Castle, cf. Terry, *Scot. Hist. Rev.*, ii. 6, 163.

[2] *Act. Parl. Scot.* ix. 33, 34.

[3] *Six Saints*, i. 254.

[4] *Faithful Contendings*, 392.

[5] *Leven and Melville Papers*, 47; *Act. Parl. Scot.*, ix. 37-40; Wodrow, iv. 482.

William and Mary as Sovereigns. When the proposed Coronation Oath was adjusted, it was found to make no mention of the Confession of Faith or the relative Acts of Parliament, and, while including the persecuting clause referring to heretics, only provided for the maintenance of the 'true religion ... now received and preached.'[1]

Meanwhile the Cameronian party was not idle. A committee of ten watched affairs in Edinburgh, and the influx of large numbers of the armed wanderers gave security to and influenced the opponents of Jacobitism. But they could not refrain from harking back upon the dangers of 'sinful association,' and upon the demand for Providence to protect the righteous minority. Adherence to this distinctive principle had practical illustration in the proposal of the Laird of Blackwood to the Estates to raise a regiment of westlandmen, true blue Covenanters, under Colonel James Douglas (Angus),[2] Lord Douglas, and Lieutenant-Colonel William Cleland, in order to support the new Sovereigns and the Protestant cause.

The General Meeting of the Societies was held in Douglas church, on 29th April, and before they separated, assenters and irreconcilables thrashed out in debate every detail of Malignancy, before an agreement, framed by Sir Patrick Hume, could be made, on 14th May. The enthusiasts lay in companies on the Holm of Douglas. Cleland had the terms of the engagement read to the recruits and explained by Shields, to the effect that they 'engage in this service of purpose to resist Popery and Prelacy, and arbitrary power; and to recover and establish the work of Reformation in Scotland, in opposition to Popery, Prelacy, and arbitrary power in all the branches and steps thereof, till the government in Church and State be brought to that lustre and integrity which it had in the best times.'[3] The distinctive feature of the regiment was that it was to be a separate peripatetic congregation of armed Presbyterian, Covenanting worshippers, led by regular officers, and, at the same time, in spiritual matters led and disciplined by one minister and twenty elders—one for each company—for the purpose of promoting piety, moral discipline, worship, and catechising, at times

[1] *Act. Parl. Scot.*, ix. 48, Act 46, 18th April; Oath, *ibid.*, App. 127.

[2] James Douglas (1646?-1700), grandson of William, first Marquis of Douglas; Earl of Angus, 1655.

[3] *Faithful Contendings*, 393-404.

compatible with military duties. Before the Convention of Estates adjourned, commissions were granted to Angus and Cleland for the embodiment of the Cameronian regiment of foot, and to Viscount Kenmure for his regiment.[1]

Argyll, Sir James Montgomery, and Sir John Dalrymple were the deputation sent to London to proffer the Coronation Oath to William and Mary. When William came to the persecuting clause—'We shall be careful to root out all heresies and enemies to the true worship of God, that shall be convicted of the true Kirk of God,' etc., William hesitated and said: 'I will not lay myself under any obligation to be a persecutor.' The deputies assured him that the formulate implied no such obligation. 'In that sense, then, I swear,' replied William, and the Revolution was consummated by their Majesties signing the oath.[2]

The Convention was adjourned till 5th June to permit it being raised to the dignity of a Parliament, at which the new Sovereignty was duly ratified.[3] The Duke of Hamilton was made Commissioner, Crawford elected President. The bishops stayed away. 'The bishops, I know not where they are,' Claverhouse facetiously wrote to Melfort, 'they are the Kirk Invisible.'[4] During this critical period King William had the able and shrewd advice of George, first Earl of Melville (1634?—1707), whose spirit of moderation and sympathy for the persecuted had brought on himself trouble, the doom of traitors, and exile. He well merited advancement to the office of Secretary of State. William trusted in him for the adjustment of the religious settlement, with due regard to the rights of minorities.[5]

Parliament was advised by the King to settle Church government according to their own 'desires and inclinations.' Consequently, on 22nd July, Parliament passed an 'Act (4) abolishing prelacie.'[6] 'Not a dog wagged his tongue against the Presbyterian establishment, not a

Marginal notes:
King William repudiates the persecuting clause.

A legal Scottish Parliament, 5th June 1689.

Settlement of the Church.

---

[1] *Act. Parl. Scot.*, ix. 55, 56.

[2] *Ibid.*, ix. 93.

[3] *Ibid.*, 99.

[4] Napier, *Memorial*, iii. 601.

[5] Cf. instructions 7th March 1689: *Leven and Melville Papers*, 2. Burnet considered Melville to be 'a weak, narrow-hearted, low-minded man,' Foxcroft, *Supplement*, 324.

[6] *Act. Parl. Scot.*, ix. 98, 104. Wodrow, iv. 484.

mouth gave a vote for Episcopacy,' wrote Defoe.[1] The form in which the national religion was to be established required the maturer consideration of another session of Parliament.

We turn to Viscount Dundee. The fiery cross had summoned some two thousand men to his standard—the lithe sons of many clans and septs loyal to Pope and King. General Mackay, followed by the Scots Brigade, Scots Greys, and Colchester's horse, chased him by many devious ways in the central Highlands,[2] without bringing him to a stand. Dundee wisely waited for promised Irish reinforcements and for the rousing of the clans. Colonel Cannon and the Irish force arrived in Mull on 12th July. Six days later, the Government offered 18,000 merks for Dundee dead or alive.[3] Dundee secured the Castle of Blair, the seat of Atholl, and placed in it a garrison under Stewart of Ballechin. He hoped to win over Atholl's son, Lord John Murray, with his clansmen, but these joined Mackay at Pitlochry on his northern march.[4] Mackay advanced by Perth and Pitlochry towards Blair.

The Pass of Killiecrankie only was between the Jacobites and their foes—a gorge sublime to the peaceful traveller, terrible and impassable to hostile invaders when defenders are at hand. Dundee chose to let Mackay pass through.

Mackay must have breathed freely when he saw that his rearguard had passed safely out of those jaws of death, and that his army was resting on the lovely Haugh of Urrard, girdled with the mountains in their variegated vesture, and watered by the Garry, just where it begins its angry descent into the romantic linns of Killiecrankie. Sunshine gilded the fields of ripening corn in a scene of apparent peace. No foe was visible. Blair Castle stood passively on guard miles away. Dundee had recently left it, and seemingly retreated up Glen Tilt. Nevertheless Mackay's comfort was short-lived. Dundee's movement was merely a feint—a masterly strategic movement by which his kilted force might march unseen behind the hills, Craig Caillaiche and Cnoc a Ghiuthais, and swing round into a strong position above the Haugh. In two divisions, approaching each other from opposite directions, they lined

---

[1] *Memoirs*, 327; *Leven and Melville Papers*, 145.
[2] Terry, 270, 291.
[3] Aldis, *List*, 2946.
[4] *Chronicles of Atholl*, 287-97.

up in clans and septs, on the hill face above the present House of Urrard, in a line from Tomgoulach nearly to Orchilmore. They were a horde of two thousand five hundred badly armed and indifferently fed braves. Dundee and a troop of miserable horse under Sir William Wallace of Craigie were posted in the centre below Lettoch.[1]

Opposing Dundee stood Mackay with about four thousand two hundred men. As soon as Mackay realised the menace in this disposition of the mobile command arrayed against him, he changed his front and marched his force across the meadow and up over the old river-bank to ground where a chain of fields afforded a suitable arena for the marshalling of his army between a stream, called Allt Chluain, on the left hand, and the roaring Girnaig Burn on the right. This battlefield is a little over a mile in length—1910 yards—and a quarter of a mile in breadth. With gentle ascent it stretched up to the stand of Dundee. On this cultivated ridge stood the House of Urrard, then also bearing the older name of Runraurie. It was to the right of Mackay's centre; and, with its houses, garden, and orchard a little behind the centre, formed another Hougomont. Mackay, fixing his centre at the old drove-road ascending to Lettoch, disposed of his five foot-regiments in ten half-battalions in a line three deep, between Low Mains and the Girnaig Burn. Three leathern guns and some petards were posted in the centre, and behind them stood one hundred horse ready to dash through the intervening spaces between the battalions.[2]

Mackay's position.

Waiting for the fray, 27th July 1689.

One hundred paces separated the combatants, who faced each other for hours like wild cats ready to spring. Dundee could not stir; he had but one charge for his few fusils, and the July sun glared in his eyes. Mackay was too experienced to charge up hill. To wile away the time Dundee rode in burnished armour from clan to clan adjuring all to fight for King, country, and religion, then doffed that panoply for a trooper's jerkin to prove the blood-thirst that was in him—his consuming desire

---

[1] Napier, *Memorial*, iii. 626-46, 724; Mackay, *Memoirs*, 41-60, 264; Terry, 319-45; Balcarres, *Account*, 103-8; Balhaldy, *Memoirs of Lochiel*, 256-9; Macpherson, *Original Papers*, i. 368-71; *Hist. MSS. Com. Rep.*, XII. vii. 252-5.

[2] Professor Terry (*John Graham*, 338-43) places the centre of the battle too near Allt Chluain, whereas it should be nearer Urrard House. His arena gives too little room for the line of Mackay to stand on. Thirteen hundred men, each having a stance of thirty inches, would extend nearly eleven hundred yards, or past Urrard a quarter of a mile.

to do his 'Shear-darg,' or harvest-day's work. Mackay, too, addressed his men in terms of his own 'Rules of War,' assuring them that a soldier's safety lay in his victorious fighting.[1]

The clansmen, stripped to their shirts—grey-headed Lochiel casting off his shoes—impatiently waited for the onslaught. The hours were monotonous, save for a few sniping shots and the bursting of Mackay's harmless leathern guns. Dundee's hour had come when the red rays of the sun, disappearing beyond Strath Garry into Benalder Forest, began to embarrass the army of Mackay. Shortly after seven at night he ordered the attack. The mountaineers answered with slogans, and the pipers with their pibrochs. Despite a galling fusillade they rushed upon the Lowlanders, reserving their own one volley, 'like one great clap of thunder,' threw the muskets away, and, wielding with terrible dexterity their great broadswords, mowed down their defenceless opponents before they could fix bayonets. Camerons, Macdonells, Clan Ronald, and Macleans rolled the Scots Brigade, part of Leven's regiment, and Mackay's regiment, down over the bank to the river 'in the twinkling of an eye'—so Mackay declared. Sir Alexander Maclean took the royal standard.[2]

Dundee's onslaught.

Having unleashed the mountaineers, Dundee soon followed with his horse to capture the guns, and put the troopers of Annandale and Belhaven to flight. Mackay himself tried in vain to rally his own men, and, accompanied by his servant, cut his way through the clansmen on to the stricken field, where he could see the debacle before him, except on the right wing which stood firm. This also Dundee perceived, and the reason—the Macdonalds had not advanced against the pikemen of Hastings on the extreme right. Riding back from the slope below the captured guns, athwart the field, to lead the Macdonalds on his left wing against Leven's Borderers and Hastings, Dundee fell mortally wounded by a shot. Local tradition, handed down in the House of Urrard, declares that the fatal shot came from that house as Dundee passed by, and that he was borne to a mound still pointed out in the garden. This is not improbable when it is conceded that Mackay's line extended beyond Urrard. Mackay's own regiment took the credit of

Mackay's bravery.

The fall of Dundee.

[1] Mackay, 52, 54; Macpherson, *Original Papers*, i. 371.

[2] Macpherson, *Original Papers*, i. 370.

shooting Dundee, the huge Haliburton of Pitcur, and Ramsay, at the first onset.[1]

It is now absolutely certain that 'my Lord Dundee was shot dead one the head of his horse,' and did not survive long enough to write the fabricated dispatch to the exiled King announcing his victory.[2] The story of Johnston, who said that he caught the General as he tumbled out of his saddle, need not be doubted. Lieutenant John Nisbet, prisoner in Blair, testified that a soldier named Johnston informed him that he had caught the General as he fell from his horse. Dundee inquired 'how the day went.' Johnston answered: 'The day went weel for the King [James], bot that he was sory for his Lord, and that the Viscount replied it wes the less mater for him seeing the day went weel for his master.'[3] His body was carried in two plaids to the hostelry of Blair, and, encased in his armour, was buried along with gallant Haliburton, in the parish church of Blair.[4]

How Dundee passed.

The clansmen instinctively turned to looting the baggage. Had Mackay and his staff, who made for the ford opposite West Balrobie, when by sunset they saw that the Highlanders had overrun the post which Lauder and his fusiliers held, boldly formed and led the gallant battalions which held the field against the demoralised plunderers, they might have turned a bitter defeat into an easy victory. The officers fled: the unbroken regiments marched down the pass in the darkness and escaped.[5]

Flight of Dundee.

Thus ended 'The Day of Rinrorie,' as the peasantry in Athole called the battle. A contemporary ballad well described the fate of Mackay, who thus

---

[1] Mackay, *Memoirs*, 265; *Hist. MSS. Com. Rep.*, XII. vii. 255. The distance from Aldclune to Urrard House is 2950 feet, to the mound, 3400 feet. According to Balhaldy (*Memoirs of Lochiel*, 270) Leven held Urrard. There is a Border tradition that Ringan Oliver of Smallcleuchfoot, Jedwater, slew Dundee.

[2] Newsletter, 10th August 1689, *Hist. MSS. Com. Rep.*, XII. vii. 255. 'It is certain that Lieutenant-Colonel Mackay is dead, he being the man that gave Dundee his passport to heaven or hell, and was afterwards himself shot': Macpherson, *Original Papers*, i. 372; Terry, App. iii.

[3] *Act. Parl. Scot.*, ix. App. 56, 57, 58.

[4] *Hist. MSS. Com. Rep.*, XII. vii. 254; viii. 5, 6, 41; *Chron. of Atholl*, 302, 304.

[5] Balcarres, *Account*, 106.

'Met the Deevil and Dundee
On the Braes of Killiecrankie, O.'

Of Mackay's army 1800 fell in the fray and 500 were taken prisoners. Of Dundee's force 600 are reckoned to have fallen. A few days after the defeat, Mackay accused his would-be allies—the Athole men—of slaying in the retreat three times more of his men than were slain in the battle. But for the greed of loot all might have been swept into the remorseless Garry.

It is difficult to fix in the Scottish Pantheon the place which should be assigned to the victor of Killiecrankie. History and romance have thrown a glamour around him which is calculated to lead the superficial student to the unwarrantable conclusion that Dundee was a great military genius. The heroics of the *Grameid* must be discounted. Balcarres best described the secret of Dundee's reputation—'Wherever your Majesty's Service, or Ambition prompted, he stuck at nothing.'[1] He left no proofs of the possession of the talents of a great soldier or a wise statesman. No feat of prowess is recorded to the credit of this untiring and merciless executer of the orders of his superiors, and of the cruel decrees he assisted in framing. No attractive ordinance displays the prudence and kindliness of a councillor who understood his fellow-citizens. On the contrary, there abide reminiscences of a martinet, a mercenary, a miserable clamourer for spoil, and a ruthless reveller in the blood of his countrymen. The gruesome libel that the Atholl Murrays raised the skull of Dundee and used it as a drinking-quaich is less likely to have been a taunt of the Jacobites in reference to the alleged double-dealing and irresolution of Atholl, than the suggestion of some sardonic Whig that at last a temporary use had been discovered for the cranium of a small Scot whom his unhappy Fatherland could well have spared.[2]

Estimate of Dundee.

The triumph of Dundee gave a great shock to the new Government for a short time, until authentic information of his death came to embolden the Protestant party to take fresh courage and end the campaign. James, in Dublin, informed Sir Donald Macdonald by

Alarm of the Government.

[1] *Account*, 107.

[2] *Chron. of Atholl*, 51, 52; *Account of Engagement*, in Nairn Papers: Macpherson, *Original Papers*, i. 368-71.

letter, that words could not express his grief for the loss of 'so brave a man,' whom he intended still further to honour.[1]

The command of the Jacobite troops devolved upon Colonel Cannon, who tried to extinguish the Cameronian regiment, which marched north too late to join Mackay against 'the grand enemy to the country.' As the Cameronians marched along they emitted declarations which at least enkindled in themselves a martial fire. Under Lieutenant-Colonel Cleland they reached Dunkeld, which they were commanded to hold as an important outpost.[2]

To have annihilated that sacred band, about 800 strong, would have been a sacrifice sufficient in Prelatic eyes to have satisfied the shade of the dead victor in Blair, and restored joy to the implacable haters of the Covenanted particularists. The latter, however, conceived the delusion that they had been sent into a trap there, and Cleland had to refute the slander by proving that he was there to die at their head. He intrenched without delay, 17th-18th August. Dunkeld, a primitive town girded by menacing hills, with its hoary Cathedral, laird's house, narrow streets, walled enclosures, was quite the place consecrated for the last stand in a great religious cause. Its very name implied the seat of a holy war. Into this basin, on 21st August, Cannon poured his elate clansmen and Irish, who drove the Lowlanders, contesting every yard, back to the Cathedral. The attackers took and occupied the houses round the church, and poured in a steady and galling fusilade upon the penned-in

Cameronians. Early in the action, Cleland and other officers fell to the deadly musketry, leaving the command to Captain Munro. Not to be annihilated, the Covenanters made a gallant sally and set fire to the houses, giving the musketeers ensconced therein to a horrible death. Other feats of valour proved to their assailants, who soon deemed it expedient to seek safety by a retreat to the hills, the invincibility of the Cameronians. The Highlanders would no longer follow their officers, and declared 'they could fight against men, but it was not fit to fight any more against devils.'[3]

[1] *Cal. State Pap.* (William), 338, 30th November 1689.
[2] *Faithful Contendings*, 413; *Life of Blackadder*, 88.
[3] *Life of Blackadder*, 98, 89-100; for 'Exact Narrative of the Conflict,' etc., also 102-5; Macpherson, *Original Papers*, i. 371. Young Cleland is buried within Dunkeld Cathedral, where his monument remains.

Through the terrible fray the defenders stimulated each other by outbursts of psalmody and displayed extraordinary bravery, fighting all day against odds—six to one. Of their number fifteen were slain; of the enemy three hundred fell. This fight practically ended the campaign. The final bout and rout took place in the Haughs of Cromdale on 1st May 1690, after which the Highland host, again mustered under General Buchan, dwindled away, and peace was gradually restored. To the Cameronian regiment thus belongs the prestige of consummating the rebellion with a victory for Protestantism, which could never have been achieved unless these 'bonny fighters' had been unified in an invincible legion by the spirit of the Covenant for which their leader, Cleland, lived, fought, and died. On the other hand, the hopes of James and his supporters 'were quickly dashed,' Balcarres wrote.[1]

The proclamation which the Convention enjoined all ministers to read on the 14th, 21st, and 28th April, discharging obedience to the deposed King, and ordering public prayers for the new Sovereigns, was not universally promulgated, so that a few delinquents were removed from office by the Convention and others by a Committee of Estates. Notwithstanding the royal order that unacceptable pastors were to be left unmolested, many rabblings occurred, with the result that another stringent order was promulgated on 6th August 1689.[2] It protected ejected ministers, provided for informing on disobedient clergy, and made rabbling, without legal process, a criminal offence. Nearly one-fifth part of the ministry found themselves homeless outcasts. By the first week of November, one hundred and eighty-two pulpits were empty,—some Presbyteries losing nearly all their members through deprivation—Cupar, all but one; St. Andrews, 17; Edinburgh, 13; Auchterarder, 12; Jedburgh, 11.[3] In some cases this drastic treatment is not to be wondered at, when, for example, we learn that Blair, minister of Scoonie, declared that the victory at Killiecrankie was 'the best news in the world'; and that, among other hilarious Jacobites, William Murray, minister of Crieff, on the Sabbath after the battle, significantly chose for singing the 118th Psalm —

Proclamations in 1689.

Evicted clergy.

---

[1] *An Account*, 114, 142— fight at Cromdale.
[2] Aldis, *List*, 2950; *The Case*, 84.
[3] Matheson, *Politics and Religion*, ii. 353, citing *The Scots Episcopal Innocence*, 1694.

THE COVENANTERS

'This is the day God made, in it
We'll joy triumphantly.'[1]

The surprising restraint of the Presbyterians.

In troublous times toleration and charitableness are not born in a day. How could the unconverted abettors of an unjustifiable persecution expect immediate forgiveness from men of the one ear, women with the branded cheek, soldiers whose tongues were bored with red-hot irons for 'blaspheming officers,'[2] the wizened survivors of malarial fever colonies, the sons of hunted heroes with twenty-eight notches on their consecrated blades, the many sufferers from Prelatic cruelty, who for years had lived on moors and sheltered in 'hidie-holes'?[3] It is surprising that so few wigs rolled on the green. With a commendable restraint the ascendant Presbyterians and the Covenanters generally were averse from vindicating their Gospel principles in the pains of others in the Grassmarket and at the Gallowlee. The deprivations were civil, not ecclesiastical acts, and Crawford, the President, justified them as such.[4]

The bishops, who, as a rule, lived out of their Cathedral cities, had to use their office with great circumspection, ordaining clergy, without maintaining diocesan rule. Archbishop Rose died in Edinburgh on the 13th June 1704; the notorious Paterson, Archbishop of Glasgow, died on the 9th of December 1708; the last of these titular bishops, Gordon of Galloway, joined the Church of Rome and died in 1726.[5] Cairncross, whom James deprived, had no scruples about the Oath of Allegiance, and, through the influence of Bishop Burnet, was appointed Bishop of Raphoe in 1693. He survived till 1701, and left money for help to the suffering clergy.

Fate of the hierarchy.

The Episcopalians in Scotland were divided into two parties—those that maintained their allegiance to James, and those who took the Oath of Allegiance to William and Mary. The incumbents, too, were split

Two Episcopal parties.

[1] Scott, *Fasti*, iv. 560, 755.

[2] *Mar MSS.*, 211.

[3] In Covenanting districts kindly people were wont to put out into the fields, especially in harvest-time, victuals for the 'fays,' 'little green men,' and other invisible genii, who, when thus kindly treated, were wont to help in securing and bringing the harvest by night. The 'queer folk' were sometimes the persecuted hillmen, who thus profited by the retention of a primitive superstition.

[4] *Act. Parl. Scot.*, ix. 111; *Leven and Melville Papers*, 376, 377.

[5] Keith, *Catalogue*, passim.

522

into two parties. Both alike were in unhappy circumstances, and many of them were in poverty. Some of the outed clergy, like Cairncross, took the oath and obtained appointments in England and Ireland. Among the laity generally, Presbyterianism, most prevalent in the counties south of the Forth, cannot be said to have been the overwhelming interest, since in northern counties Episcopacy was mostly in favour; in the midlands there was an almost equal distribution of Prelatists and Presbyterians; while in the Highland area the Romanists had a strong hold. The upper classes inclined to the old way. The Presbyterians had the influence in Parliament, and there expressed the will of the masses and middle classes with a zeal which was as potent as majorities usually are. What made Episcopacy more difficult to resuscitate was the fact, that, for twenty-eight years, the Episcopal ministers, without surplice or ceremonies, practically conducted the Presbyterian rites and used the discipline of the Presbyters, being under very little Episcopal jurisdiction.[1]

The Popish King was gone, the equally despised bishops were gone, and gone too was unanimity on any subject—civil or sacred. The seat of government was in a foreign land, for the Scots still reckoned England to be more than 'over the Borders.' At home contending political parties dug pitfalls for each other. It looked as if there was not a statesman capable of laying the foundation of the Revolution Settlement, among the would-be leaders—indifferent, elastic, moderate, extreme, as they variously were. *Conflict among political parties.*

The party shibboleths were Prelacy, Presbytery, Covenants. The malcontents might have added Place and Power. The Church, now rent by schisms, did not realise its inherently independent status and power, nor did it of itself rise into form and commanding station. A mere *corpus vile*,[2] it waited to be galvanised into life by the touch of the civil ruler. Long a bureau of State, ordered to pray and preach as required, it had no voice: its oracle was dumb. There was no Nehemiah on the walls, clarion and sword at hand; no Knox deputed by the brethren to trumpet danger and defiance; no strong patriot to summon the folk-mote and demand whether the people wished a Pope, Prelate, *The deadness of the Church,*

---

[1] Mackenzie, *Vindication*, 9.
[2] [Latin: cheap body.]

or Presbyter to lead them to heaven. There was a wild maelstrom of conflicting opinions out of which the strongest, steadiest current ran into the old Presbyterian channels. To return to the pre-Reformation allegory, the mariners—the country pastors—whichever way the wind blew, were content to remain in the ark, drifting, as far as they were concerned, into settled waters. The hands at the helm were laymen and Presbyterians—Melville, Crawford, and Dalrymple (Stair). By their adroitness they laid the weather-beaten Church on a safe Presbyterian basis, with the least ostensible indication of Erastian buttresses afforded by a willing civil magistrate. Behind these, at the King's right hand, was 'Cardinal' Carstares, wise, conciliatory, far-seeing. They had cunning factions to out-manoeuvre.

Episcopalian manoeuvres.

Strange influences and intrigues complicated the situation. Their story properly belongs to a narrative of civil transactions. The Episcopalians sowed dragons' teeth by republishing the extremest treatises of the Covenanters to prove to southern clergy the dangerous extravagances of Presbyterians. The Episcopal clergy of the Synod of Aberdeen, after conforming, craved Parliament to call a National Synod, doubtless with a view to resuscitating Prelacy. Invertebrates, like Atholl, 'on conscience,' declared for Episcopacy and sided with its opponents; vacillating Hamilton inclined to some mongrel form of Episcopacy, such as that which, since his day, other weak temporisers have conceived without having the power to materialise it. As an illustration of impudent hypocrisy, nothing equals the somersault made by Queensberry, who told the Parliament of 1685 that the Covenanted Presbyterians were the 'enemies of mankind,' and now (1689) stood 'not only for the King, but will concurr in Presbytry as now fitt for the King and nation.'[1]

'The Club.'

A group of malcontents, of various shades of opinion, who gave the new Government a great amount of trouble, was 'The Club.' This faction was composed of place-seekers, Malignants, visionaries, and was led by a rogue—Sir James Montgomery of Skelmorlie, the same emissary who rode with the Coronation Oath to William.[2] Associated with him, till they betrayed each other, were Annandale and Ross, and one of the coterie was Sir Patrick Hume, who, according to a contemporary,

---

[1] *Leven and Melville Papers*, 100.
[2] *Ibid.*, passim; *Fergusson the Plotter*, 270.

'rydes always the first horse.' Montgomery's plan was to form a coalition with the Jacobites and get hold of the reins of government. The astuter advisers of the Crown coaxed and bought up influential opponents, and when the staunch Presbyterians saw that they were being imposed on, they backed out of the association, which collapsed. The exiled King was in correspondence with the conspirators and promised them great honours. Out of them he actually nominated a provisional oligarchy, and Montgomery was subsidised from abroad. The bubble soon burst. Atholl, Queensberry, Balcarres, and others turned on Montgomery, and the triumvirate of scoundrels—Montgomery, Ross, and Annandale— made haste to confess their treachery in order to procure an escape from the doom they deserved. Unpardoned by the King, Montgomery disappeared into a miserable exile.

The second session of William and Mary's first Scots Parliament met in Edinburgh on 15th April. Melville, Secretary of State, now created Earl, was Commissioner. The Royal letter assured the Estates of their Sovereigns' affection and care 'in relation to the establishment of Church Government in that way which may be most conduceable to the glory of God and agreeable to the inclinations of the people.' This was the diplomatic stroke of a ruler whose circumstances made him a latitudinarian governing by majorities—an Episcopalian in England, a Presbyterian in Scotland.[1] Melville had already been instructed to adjust the religious settlement according to 'that interest is strongest,' and to allow no vindictive recriminations beyond forfeitures at the instance of Presbyterians.[2] Melville in his punctiliously guarded address pleaded for moderation.[3]

Second session of Parliament, 15th April 1690.

The first statute, passed on 25th April, rescinded the second Act of the Parliament of 1669—the Supremacy Act, making Charles II. supreme in all causes. That Act had been at the root of all the distempers and sufferings for twenty years.[4] On the same day, the Estates did an act of justice in passing the statute which restored to their charges the Presbyterian pastors evicted since January 1661, and ordered their Episcopalian

New statutes.

---

[1] *Act. Parl. Scot.,* ix. 109.
[2] Instructions, 7th March 1689: *Leven and Melville Papers,* 2.
[3] *Act. Parl. Scot.,* ix. App. 38.
[4] *Ibid.,* ix. III; viii. 554.

successors to quit the manses and glebes at Whitsunday.[1] This order was not implicitly obeyed, and some of the old incumbents continued in office.

On the 26th May, the Westminster Confession of Faith was produced, read, and considered word by word, 'and being voted and approven, was ordained to be recorded in the Bookes of Parliament.'[2]

Act ratifying Confession and settling of Presbyterian Church government.

Thereafter, on 7th June, was passed the new Charter of Presbyterianism in the seventh statute—'Act ratifying the Confession of Faith and setteiling Presbyterian Church Government.'[3] After citing the declaration of the Claim of Right that Prelacy is 'a great and insupportable grievance and trouble to this nation,' this most important Act first ratifies all previous Acts against Popery; ratifies and establishes the (Westminster) Confession of Faith, 'as the publick and avowed Confession of this Church containeing the summe and substance of the doctrine of the Reformed Churches'; establishes the Presbyterian Church government and discipline; annuls all Acts and orders contrary to or 'derogatory from the Protestant Religion and Presbyterian Government now established'; restores to office the ministers and elders ejected since 1st January 1661; appoints 'the first Meeting of the General Assembly of this Church as above established, to be at Edinburgh the third Thursday of October next to come in this instant year, 1690'; and authorises the Church to 'purge out all insufficient, negligent, scandalous, and erroneous ministers' from office and benefice. Thus Parliament settled and secured, as the Act declares, 'the true Protestant Religion according to the truth of God's Word, as it hath of a long tyme been professed within this land,' thereby indicating that the legislature authorised the upholding and retention of the Confession because it considered it to be true, and containing the doctrine long held by the people of Scotland. The other

Standards ignored.

standards—Catechisms and Directory—were ignored. A motion to ratify the Scottish edition of the Confession, with the clause relative to the Assembly's resolution in 1647, that the Church had the inherent right to call her own assemblies, was lost.[4]

[1] *Act. Parl. Scot.*, ix. 111, Act 2; Wodrow, iv. 485 note.
[2] *Ibid.*, ix. 117-31.
[3] *Ibid.*, 133; Wodrow, iv. 485.
[4] Peterkin, *Records of Kirk,* 475.

On 19th July, the Estates, by Act 53, abolished patronage in churches and transferred the right of presenting to heritors and elders in each parish, who were to nominate a minister to the congregation, who were given the right to appeal to the Presbytery if the appointment was not acceptable. Compensation to the amount of 300 merks, with the teinds not disponed, was awarded to the patrons.[1] The same day the Estates rescinded the laws demanding conformity and other statutes prejudicial to Presbyterianism.[2] Special Acts were also passed rescinding the forfeitures of notable Covenanters and sufferers, including Melville, James Guthrie, Patrick Hume, James Stewart, Gilbert Elliot, Cardross, Fletcher of Saltoun, Jerviswood, Cessnock, Wariston, Fergusson of Caitloch, and others.[3] The Covenants were not made the subjects of special legislation.

The Covenanters had won much they had contended and suffered for; the exponents of the Covenants among the Societies did not obtain all they had struggled for. On 8th April, at Leadhills, the Society-men met and subscribed 'The Humble Petition of the Persecuted People of the West and Southern Shires.' This embodied their faithful lamentations for manifold defections, a supplication for a Free Assembly, and a demand for the 'vindicating and approving these reproached Covenants.' It was intrusted to Sir John Munro of Foulis for presentation to Parliament, but to the embitterment of these consistent defenders of the faith, it was rejected by the Committee for Church affairs and never considered by Parliament. What more could these disappointed votaries do than personally testify to the land by the dissemination of two thousand printed copies of the Covenants, and sadly wait the opportunity for presenting their final and futile plaints to the first General Assembly? But that unsettled convention, while accepting the services of three licentiates of their number, Lining, Shields, and Boyd, imprudently turned a deaf ear to their call.[4] Thus the

[1] *Act. Parl. Scot.*, ix. 196.

[2] *Ibid.*, 198-202.

[3] *Ibid.*, passim.

[4] *Six Saints*, ii. 173; *Faithful Contendings*, 438, 447, 448, 459. Thomas Lining became minister of Lesmahagow, and died in October 1733. Alexander Shields, chaplain to the Cameronian regiment, became minister of the second charge in St. Andrews, went in 1700 to Darien, and died in Jamaica. William Boyd became minister of St. John's, Dalry, and died in 1741.

most faithful adherents of the Covenanted Church were turned away from the national Zion, veritable scapegoats consciously burdened with the sins of the people, and again driven into the wilderness. The Society-men were quite logical and accurate in their conclusion that the Covenanters had paid too dearly for all that their Protestant patrons and protectors were offering in return for their sacrifices. Conscience alone rewarded them. They still had the redress left to manly Christians—that of protesting, dissociating themselves from upholders of a tainted Church and State, and of purging their own remnant of all persons untrue to the Covenants. To them these bonds were indissoluble. In this action they were assisted by Sir Robert Hamilton and his 'Tinwald Paper.'[1]

The General Assembly again meets, 16th October 1690.

At length, on 16th October 1690, the General Assembly—*magni nominus umbra*[2]—met in the Capital. As was meet, Hugh Kennedie,[3] a surviving Protester, was called to the Moderator's chair. From the very nature of the circumstances in which it met, it was merely a regulative directorate. It did little more than appoint a Fast. Parliament had already settled the Confession of Faith, in an unacceptable English edition, and the form of Government, which were to obtain in the revived Church, without giving that institution even an opportunity of considering any possible amendments upon that Puritanic document. Before the Church met to contract with the State as to their relations, Parliament had judged the Confession to be the test for all the national teachers.[4] This disregard for the spiritual independence of the Church, and intrusion upon its special province, was one which both Knox and Andrew Melville would have resented. William soon made the leaders of the National Church feel the tightening of the bonds, when he indicated that the doors of the sanctuary should be wide enough to take in conforming Episcopalians as well as Presbyters.[5] This emphatic suggestion of toleration was so inconsistent with the legislature's stigma on Prelacy as 'an insupportable grievance,' that the ministers began

---

[1] Hutchison, *Ref. Presby. Church*, III; Carslaw, *Life of Renwick*, 178.

[2] [Latin: a shadow of a great name.]

[3] Hugh Kennedie, 'Father Kennedy,' 'Bitter Beard,' minister at Mid-Calder, deposed 1660.

[4] Act 25, 4th July, *Act. Parl. Scot.*, ix. 164.

[5] Innes, *Law of Creeds*, 77.

to stiffen themselves against further encroachments upon their jurisdiction, and ultimately triumphed over the King and his untimely
policy of Comprehension.

This work, by reference to the long series of documents issued by
the Protestant Presbyterian parties in Scotland, during one hundred
and thirty years, and also to the confessions of those witnesses who
justified their warfare and death on behalf of the Covenants, proves that
the genuine Covenanters, from first to last, never resiled from those
definite principles on which the Reformed Church in Scotland was
founded. These principles, in fine, were the absolute authority of the
Word of God over all men: the exclusive jurisdiction of the Church
in spiritual concerns: the exclusive power of the ruler in civil affairs
only, according to the Word, and in Scotland, according to its ancient
Constitution. It is now manifest beyond doubt, from the authoritative
documents issued by the Scottish Presbyterians, that the reason for their
persistent Covenanting was an inextinguishable dread of, and revulsion
from, Popery—the antithesis of their cherished principles. They also
feared that diocesan Episcopacy was Popery in disguise.

This fear of Popery was like an epidemic fever seizing hold of the
spirit of the Scots people, and making itself felt recurrently with the
intermittent revelations of the crooked negotiations which went on
between the successive Stuart sovereigns and the Popes, and regarding
which the sapient Protestant leaders obtained accurate information
from their well-informed foreign agents.[1]

The quarrel of genuine Covenanters, therefore, was with (1) despisers
of the Word, (2) troublers of the Church, (3) breakers of the Constitution. To them Prelacy (or superiority of certain clergy) was the 'insupportable grievance' created by men in the first category: the illegal acts of
the Stuart kings placed those rulers and their abettors among men of the
second and third categories. Consequently the various Covenants were
simply republications of the fundamental principles of the Reformers,
made suitable to the epochs that called them forth. They were, as they
were intended to be, plain standards to guide Christians, Churchmen,
and Constitutionalists. Through the malignant misunderstanding

[1] Gardiner, *Hist. of England*, i. 116, 221: *Add. MSS.*, 37021, fol. 25; *Eng. Hist. Rev.*,
xx. 127 (1905).

and resultant opposition of the ill-advised and worse-guided Stuart autocrats, the peaceful Covenants became Standards, in a different sense, in a Holy War, which ended in the dismissal of a family whose scions despised the Word, troubled the Church, and broke the Constitution. Robert Burns saw the true significance of these Covenants when he thus answered a critic, who judged them to be fanatical and ridiculous:—

> 'The Solemn League and Covenant
> Cost Scotland blood—cost Scotland tears:
> But it seal'd Freedom's sacred cause—
> If thou'rt a slave, indulge thy sneers.'

What the National Poet by a flash of genius thus so vividly portrayed, the English historian, Froude, after years of labour, spent among historical records and unassailable State documents, also discovered; so that he was constrained to acknowledge the place of the Covenanters among the benefactors of mankind, in these terms: 'The Covenanters fought the fight and won the victory; and then, and not till then, came the David Humes with their essays on miracles, and the Adam Smiths, with their political economies, and steam-engines, and railroads, and political institutions, and all the blessed or unblessed fruits of Liberty.'[1] Characteristically, too, Carlyle summed up the merits of fellow-countrymen, whom he regarded with reverence: 'Many men in the van do always, like Russian soldiers, march into the ditch of Schweidnitz, and fill it up with their dead bodies, that the rear may pass over them dry-shod, and gain the honour. How many earnest rugged Cromwells, Knoxes, poor Peasant Covenanters, wrestling, battling for very life, in rough miry places, have to struggle, and suffer, and fall, greatly censured, be-mired,—before a beautiful Revolution of Eighty-eight can step over them in official pumps and silk-stockings, with universal three-times-three!'[2]

---

[1] Froude, *The Influence of the Reformation on the Scottish Character—Short Studies*, i. 180. Cf. also Dr. James Begg, *The Covenanting Struggle: What was gained by it?* (Edin., n.d.).
[2] Carlyle, *Heroes*, Lect. iv.

LITERARY MEN AND THEIR WORKS
FROM 1625 TILL 1690

A seperate volume would be required to do justice to this subject. Only a small survey is attempted here.

As far as Scotland was concerned, there was a deficiency in literary productiveness during the reign of Charles I., and the works obtaining recognition and in demand were, as was to be expected from the temper of the time, disputative in character. While fewer than seven hundred items, including proclamations, college theses, and pamphlets, issued from northern presses, many important works were printed abroad and in London. Deficiency of literature.

Of poets, poetasters, and panegyric authors still a few poured out ephemeral verse—William Cargill, Alexander Forbes,—Fairley, Arthur Johnston, Drummond of Hawthornden, David Dickson, Sir Thomas Hope, Sir William Mure, and the well-known Zachary Boyd, minister of the Barony, Glasgow. Boyd's *Last Battell of the Souk in Death* (1629), *Balm of Gilead* (1629), *Garden of Zion* (1644), *Holy Songs* (1645), and other rhymed effusions, are more notable for quaintness and quantity than for inspiration. Dickson's *True Christian Love* (1634) is of the same character. Scots poets.

The hands of that day had nerves better fitted to grasp Ferrara blades than direct Boyd on his quills moved by the poetic spirit. This is what Zachary Boyd himself felt when thus wrote in his booklet—*The Sickman's Sore*: 'There was never an age more fertile in reproofs and reproches than this: we are come to the dregges of dayes, where it is Boyd on his age.

counted vertue to point out the imperfections of our brethren. Many are like the Flee that can not rest but upon a Scabbe.'[1]

Authors in Aberdeen. Raban's press in Aberdeen was busy with the theses and pamphlets of Scrogie, Sibbald, Strachan, and that indefatigable antagonist of Popery, Dr. William Guild. From 1608 till his death in 1657 Guild untiringly produced: *The New Sacrifice of Christian Incense, The Only Way to Salvation, Moses Unveiled, Harmony of all the Prophets, Purgatory, Papist's Glorying in Antiquity, Limbo's Battery*, and other works assaulting Popery. Guild's contemporary, Dr. John Forbes, Professor of Divinity and Church History in Aberdeen (1593-1648), was no less industrious with his *Irenicum amatoribus veritatis* (1629), *Gemitus Ecclesiae Scoticanae* (1630), *Theologiae Moralis* (1632), and *Instructiones ... de doctrina Christiana* (Amsterdam, 1645).

David Calderwood. David Calderwood, minister of Crailing, from the time he opposed the Perth Articles and flagellated the bishops, was too prominent to have his treatises published at home. His anonymous work, *The Pastor and the Prelate*, etc. (1628), was a bitter morsel to the prelates. Abroad, Calderwood elaborated his *Altar of Damascus* (1621) into *Altare Damascenum ceu politia ecclesiae Anglicanae obtrusa ecclesiae Scoticanae*, etc. (1623), and continued writing his indispensable *True History of the Church of Scotland*, published in 1678, after his death. The polyglot, Hume of Godscroft, published his *Origin and Descent of the Family of Douglas* in 1633, and in 1655 Sir Thomas Craig's *Jus Feudale* was published.

Archbishop Spottiswood. Calderwood's contemporary, Archbishop Spottiswood, who died in London in 1639, left a valuable MS., *The History of the Church of Scotland*, which was published in 1655. This, and a treatise in reply to Calderwood's *Regimine Ecclesiae Scoticanae*, represent the literary productiveness of this scholarly prelate. His son, Sir Robert, left a MS. of *Practicks of the Law of Scotland*, afterwards published by his grandson.

Bishop Maxwell. Bishop Maxwell, afterwards Bishop of Killala, was a vigorous polemic and wrote *The Epistle Congratulatorie of Lysimachus Nicanor*, etc. (1640); *Episcopacie not abjured* (1641); *Sancro-Sancta Regum Majestas* (1644), which called forth Rutherford's *Lex Rex*; and *The Burden of Issachar*, etc., which drew out Baillie's *Historical Vindication*.

---

[1] Preface (Glasgow, 1628).

A freer time had arrived when George Gillespie (1612-48), minister in Edinburgh, took up the burning questions of the day in *A Dispute against the English Popish Ceremonies*, etc. (1637), *Nihil Respondes* (1645), *Male Audis* (1646), *Aaron's Rod Blossoming* (1646), *A Treatise of Miscellany Questions* (1649), and in other trenchant treatises, of far-reaching influence. Every Scots brain was afire with these questions. George Gillespie.

Samuel Rutherford published, in London in 1642, his *A Peaceable and Temperate Plea for Paul's Presbytery in Scotland*, etc.; he gave his name on the title-page; but two years later, when he issued *Lex Rex—The Law and the Prince*—he suppressed the author's name. This unanswerable defence of the supremacy of the law, detested of royalists, had its highest encomium as an epoch-making work when it was destroyed by the common hangman in the interests of King Charles. The Professor's other works, *The Due Right of Presbyteries* (1644), *Divine Right of Church Government* (1646), *Survey of the Spiritual Antichrist* (1648), *Liberty of Conscience* (1649), *Arminianism* (1668), illustrate the learning and polemical vigour of a mind which was happier dealing with *The Covenant of Life opened*, etc. (1655), *The Trial and Triumph of Faith*, than even with his scholastic *Disputation on the Divine Providence* (1649); happier still penning those delightful letters, *Joshua Redivivus* (1664), of which Richard Baxter said: 'Hold off the Bible, such a book as Mr. Rutherford's *Letters*, the world never saw the like.' Professor Samuel Rutherford.

Robert Baillie's pen was never idle from the time he penned those letters descriptive of the Covenanting crisis, till his death in 1662. A large catalogue indicates his polemical industry: but now only his *Letters and Journals*, edited by David Laing, in 1841-2, are of abiding interest. Robert Baillie.

Few preachers, and these only the leaders—Henderson, Gillespie, Rutherford, Cant, etc., speaking in great crises—used the medium of the press for circulating sermons. But these incisive pamphleteers could write sermons as chaste as those given in English pulpits. Consequently, for opponents of the Covenanters to select the sermon preached in St. Giles by James Row, sometime minister in Strowan, as illustrative of the sermons in vogue in this age, is an indication of prejudice and ignorance. Row declared there was 'a Pockmanty, and what was in it, trow ye, but the Book of Cannons and of Common Prayer, and the 'The Pockmanty [portmanteau] Sermon.'

High Commission,' etc.[1] Eccentricity was not the characteristic of the preachers of the Covenant.

Alexander Henderson.

Although the sermons and pulpit addresses of Alexander Henderson have only appeared in the rustic dress given to them by some unknown reporter, and unrevised by Henderson, the able hand that penned *The Government and Order of the Church of Scotland* (1641), we can in them recognise the masterly spirit of a great preacher.[2]

William Narne.

Parish ministers, ponderous in learning, ready of pen, like Robert Baillie and others, were not illiterates exhibiting vulgarity in the exposition of sacred themes. The very title of the parson of Dysart's work, *The Pearle of Prayer most precious and powerful*, etc., shows the almost Judaic reverence with which the Scots ministers approached holy things.[3] The superfine merit of those spiritual works for which Archbishop Leighton has been superlatively lauded, and which were composed when he was yet a zealot for Presbytery and the Covenant, was not uncommon among his more rugged contemporaries.[4]

Archbishop Leighton.

For the leisure of the recluse, Leighton, there is no corresponding literary output. His excessive timidity prevented him publishing his works. As an author he would never have been heard of had not Principal James Fall, in 1692, printed his Sermons, and, in 1693, his professorial lectures and ethical meditations entitled *Praelectiones Theologicae*, etc. He also published *A Practical Commentary upon the First Epistle General of Peter*, and other critical works.

According to the Rev. Alexander Smellie, 'In Leighton's soul the master-power was the hunger of holiness.' This accounts for the products of his genius being somewhat deficient in virility. There is a hyperbolical generosity in an estimate by Professor Flint, who concludes, regarding Leighton's treatises: 'His works, owing to the marvellous fullness and perfection of the spiritual life which pervades them, are worth many times over all the writings of all his Scottish contemporaries.'[5]

David Dickson.

The expository works of David Dickson, Professor of Divinity in the University of Edinburgh (1583-1663), *Hebrews* (1637), *All the Epistles*

---

[1] Laing MSS (Edin.), No. 611, p. 4.
[2] *Sermons*, edit. R. T. Martin (Edin., 1867).
[3] By William Narne (Edin., 1630)
[4] *The Whole Works of Leighton*, ii-vi., edit. West (Lond., 1869-70).
[5] *Men of the Covenant*, 186; St Giles Lectures (1883), 204.

(1645), *The Psalms* (1653-5), *Therapeutica Sacra*, display an evangelical richness to be expected of that chaste singer of *True Christian Love*. Nor did his friend, the minister of Kilwinning, James Ferguson (1621-67), another Resolutioner, fall below the gracious standard of the Professor in his full expositions of the *Pauline Epistles—Philippians and Colossians* (1656), *Galatians and Ephesians* (1659), *Thessalonians* (1675). James Ferguson.

In James Durham, the popular preacher of Blackfriars, Glasgow, who died young (1622-58), the Church had an ornament whose captivating works, breathing his own gentle and peaceable spirit, remained in demand long after his demise. He had completed at his death his *Commentarie upon ... Revelation* (1658). Shrinking from the turmoils of the time, he busied himself writing acceptable works on *Christ Crucified* (1683), *The Law Unsealed* (1676), *Great Gain of Contenting Godliness* (1685), *The Unsearchable Riches of Christ* (1695), and other popular works published posthumously. James Durham

Another expositor was George Hutchison or Hutcheson (1615-74), minister of Tolbooth Church, Edinburgh, whose sermons were not printed till 1691. His expositions of *Job* (1669), *Twelve Small Prophets* (1657), *John* (1657), give evidence of scholarship and literary skill. George Hutcheson.

A book, which, on its publication in 1659, created no little sensation was *The Christian's Great Interest*, by William Guthrie, the genial and tender-hearted minister of Fenwick (1620-65). This book, which John Owen made his *Vade Mecum*, which charmed Dr. Thomas Chalmers, and which is referred to in the testimonies of Covenanters, is a faithful and chastely expressed offer of the Gospel riches to the sinner, and is a worthy specimen of the ideas and the works which influenced the persecuted Presbyterians who preferred ejection from home and charge to distasteful servitude in a corrupt Church. William Guthrie.

One remarkable result of the change of government and the re-introduction of the Episcopal regime was the sudden fall in the publication of books, at least in Scotland. The following table[1] will indicate the numbers of works issued from the Scottish press during the three decades preceding the Revolution:—

---

[1] Cf. Aldis, *A List of Books printed in Scotland* (Edin., 1904).

1661, 45	1669, 32	1677, 23	1684, 54
1662, 18	1670, 32	1678, 45	1685, 124
1663, 20	1671, 17	1679, 35	1686, 51
1664, 20	1672, 34	1680, 55	1687, 57
1665, 22	1673, 39	1681, 84	1688, 97
1666, 20	1674, 33	1682, 44	1689, 170
1667, 13	1675, 30	1683, 72	1690, 122
1668, 13	1676, 17		

When it is considered that these numbers include newspapers, statutes, proclamations, theses, pamphlets, etc., it is easily concluded how barren the native intellect was, or how effective was the ban upon free expression of opinion.

Treatises on vexed questions had to be printed abroad and smuggled into the country, or secretly printed with imperfect titles. Among these, and creating no small alarm on their appearance, were *An Apologeticall Relation of the Particular Sufferings of the Faithful Ministers, etc.*, from

Indictments of the Government.

1660, a trenchant indictment of the Government 'By a Well Wisher to the Good Old Cause, 1665'—John Brown of Wamphray; *Naphtali*, or *Wrestlings of the Church of Scotland*, etc., 1667, from the mordant pens of James Stewart, afterwards Lord Advocate, and James Stirling, minister at Paisley, the former writing the first part. Stewart is also credited with writing *An Account of Scotland's Grievances by Reason of the Duke of Lauderdale's Ministry*, etc., 1675.

Andrew Honyman.

Andrew Honyman, Bishop of Orkney, who had written *A Seasonable Case of Submission to the Church Government*, in 1662, replied to *Naphtali* in a *Survey* (two parts, 1668, 1669), and was answered by Stewart in *Jus Populi Vindicatum*, 1669, who vindicated the legality of defence by the people.

Alexander Shields.

A similar polemical work, *A Hind Let Loose*, etc., was issued in 1687 'By a Lover of True Liberty,' Alexander Shields, afterwards minister at St. Andrews.

John Brown.

In exile, John Brown, ejected from Wamphray (died 1679), published *An Apologeticall Relation of the particular sufferings, etc.* (1660), *Christ the Way* (1677), *The Banders Disbanded*, with preface by

MacWard, *The History of the Indulgence* (1678), *De Causa Dei contra Anti-Sabbatarios*, and other erudite works.

Another untiring polemic was Robert MacWard, minister at Rotterdam, who edited Rutherford's *Letters* in 1664, wrote the *Poor Man's Cup. of Cold Water* (1678), maintaining 'the inherent glory for suffering for Christ,' also *A Testimony against Paying of Cess*, etc., and *Epagounismoi; or Earnest Contendings for the Faith* (1723). In a *True Nonconformist* (1671) MacWard replied to Burnet's *Conference*, and drew out Burnet's *Vindication … of the Church and State in Scotland*, 1673. Robert MacWard.

Robert Fleming, ejected from Cambuslang in 1662, accepted a call to Rotterdam, whence he issued in 1669 his much-read work, *The Fulfilling of the Scriptures*, etc., and other religious treatises. Robert Fleming.

For ten years after the Restoration, no book on theology or morals of much importance issued from the press with the exception of the posthumous works of two very gifted evangelical preachers, who died young, Hugh Binning (1627–53), minister in Govan, and Andrew Gray (1634–56), of the Outer High Church, Glasgow.

Binning's early work, *The Common Principles of the Christian Religion*, passed through several editions. His rich evangelical sermons, afterwards published, compare easily with the writings of Leighton, and contain sublime ideas, couched in telling and chaste language, comparable with the best productions of modern preachers.[1] Hugh Binning.

Gray, with Binning and Leighton, had 'the new guise of preaching,' and made a profound impression on his time with his *Directions, etc., to Prayer, Great and Precious Promises, The Mystery of Faith opened up*, and *Spiritual Warfare*, all published posthumously between 1669 and 1693.[2] Andrew Gray.

From the Aberdeen press George Keith issued his *Help in Time of Need* (1665), *Immediate Revelation, Salutation of Dear and Tender Love*, and *The Way Cast-up* (1677); while John Menzies produced his *Papismus Lucifugus* (1668). Quakerism also occupied some writers in Aberdeen. Mackenzie (Sir George—'the Bluidy') 'At the Sign of the Sun,' Brown's press in Edinburgh, was issuing, 1663–9, *Religio Stoici, Moral Essay, Moral Paradox, Moral Gallantry*, as preliminaries to his more solid and Aberdeen press.
George Mackenzie.

---

[1] *The Works of Binning*, edit. Leishman.

[2] *Works of Gray*, edit. Weir (Paisley, 1762).

permanent works on law, heraldry, and history, 1681-4. The killing times demanded that facile hand to direct the hangman's lethal blade, and thereafter he wrote nothing of consequence.

English classics.

Few English classics were printed in Scotland. Shakespeare and the dramatists were taboo. Richard Baxter's *Full and Easy Satisfaction* appeared in 1674, and Bunyan's *Pilgrim's Progress*, printed in 1681, went into a second edition in 1684. No edition of any of Milton's works was published in Scotland in the eighteenth century. Nor is the political and literary influence of Cromwell's blind Foreign Secretary upon his Scottish contemporaries easily appraised, so few are the references to him. What effect Newton's new theories of Light had upon the dark places in the miserable land can easily be imagined.

Milton.

Gilbert Burnet.

Bishop Gilbert Burnet (1643-1715) encouraged the Scottish press. He became Robert Baillie's successor as a chronicler of trivial events. His untiring pen produced even more *Vindications* (1673), *Observations* (1673), *Reflections, Tracts, Discourses, Sermons*, as well as the invaluable *Memoires* of the Hamiltons (1677), the *History of the Reformation of the Church of England* (1679-81), and a *History of His Own Time* (1724-34). He also sent to press the MS. of the gifted Professor Henry Scougal's devotional treatise, *The Life of God in the Soul of Man*. As a general rule, the Episcopal clergy in Scotland were not inclined to authorship.

Demand for poetry.

No book by Knox, Melville, Henderson, Bruce, Calderwood, issued from the Scottish press in the Episcopal period. The books reprinted were the Bible, Psalm-book, and the poems of Blind Harry, Lindsay, and Montgomery, and some *Songs and Fancies*. Buchanan reappeared in print twice. His life in vulgar chap-books never died. No poet seemed to sing aloud unless we accept John Forbes in Aberdeen,[1] Samuel Colvill, and William Cleland, who rhymed and not too well.

Law Books.

From 1681 till 1685 there was a slight impulse given to the literary spirit, yet no great work appeared. Dalrymple (Stair) produced *The Institutions of the Law* in 1681. Sir George Mackenzie's *Institutions*, as well as his *Jus Regium*, appeared in 1684.

Forrester.

A telling volume dealing with 'the monstrous dragon of Erastian prelacy,' entitled *Rectius Instruendum*, etc., was published in 1684 by

---

[1] Forbes, *Cantus, Songs and Fancies*, 1682 ; Colvill, *Mock Poem or Whig's Supplication*, 1681 ; Cleland, *A Collection of Several Poems*, posth., 1697.

Thomas Forrester, a conventicler, who became Principal of St. Mary's College, St. Andrews.

One of the last defenders of 'the good old way' was Gilbert Rule, Rule. once a prisoner on the Bass, Principal of Glasgow College, who vigorously trounced Stillingfleet (1680), Sage (1696), Munro (1697), and wrote two *Vindications of the Church of Scotland* (1691).

Worthy of mention, on account of the author's connection with Hew M'Kail, are the works of the apothecary and physician, Matthew M'Kaile, M.D., who wrote: *Description of the mineral wells at Moffet ... oylywell at St. Catherine's Chapel.*, etc. (1664); *Noli me tangere: seu tractulus de cancri curatione* (1675); *Diversitie of Salts*, etc. (1683); and *Terrae prodromus theoricus* (1691). He was son of Hew Mackaile, minister of Trinity College Church, Edinburgh, whose brother Matthew, minister of Bothwell, was father of the martyr Hew. In 1657 Sharp employed Matthew on Church business in London.[1]

In that marvellous exhibition of prejudice, entitled 'An Examination Buckle. of the Scotch Intellect during the Seventeenth Century,' Buckle[2] tries to illustrate his untenable thesis—that the Scotch Kirk was a most detestable Tyranny—by selected excerpts from the books of a very few authors, some of whom, such as Halyburton and Boston, wrote in the eighteenth century, and others of no known influence, such as Abernethy, whose *Physicke for the Soul* has quite disappeared even from the large national libraries.

But no ideas, religious, moral, political, are reproduced from the productions of the leading intellects of that age to indicate the ideals set before the people by Henderson, Gillespie, Brown, MacWard, Wedderburn, King, Kid, Welwood, Welsh, Dickson, Semple, Cameron, Cargill, Blackadder, Trail, Forrester, Rule, and Renwick, and many others. It is not to be wondered at that Buckle could confess that reading the sermons of the Scots preachers was the 'most painful literary task I ever undertook,' when one realises that he read with one eye shut and the other obscured with prejudice.[3]

The theology of the Covenanters is simple and easily understood. It Theology is identical with the Reformed Theology in the main, being founded of the Covenanters.

[1] Scott, *Fasti, q.v.*
[2] *Hist. of Civil, in England*, iii. 191-280.
[3] *Ibid.*, 275.

upon the idea that God is revealed in man and more fully in His Holy Word given to man. God, Man, the Bible, were the Covenanter's certainties. To the Covenanter the consciousness of God was correlative with man's consciousness (by conscience) of responsibility to God. On this fundamental experience was based the contention that no third party has a warrant to stand between the Soul and God—the child and his Father. Consequently the Covenanter conceived God as his Father, Lover, Friend, grasping him by the hand. The acceptance of this deduction conditioned the thought and action of the Covenanter, and fully explains the reason why he persistently opposed the attempts of civil and spiritual overseers to deprive him of his right to approach the Father in the way the Spirit or the Word guided him. He considered his own Cause to be that of God. The struggle against regal, papal, and prelatic supremacy had thus first a theological, not a political basis.

This conception originated the custom of personally covenanting with God, as if the Most High was just at hand to declare His Will and conclude a compact with His son. Personal covenants, dedicating individuals to God, are still extant. Children, too, gave themselves up, by covenant, to God and Christ. The idea of a Christian political constitution rested on the same basis. There was a God of the nation as well as of the individual. So a National Covenant was also necessary. The idea of a God, creating, regnant, perfectly good, made the Covenanter, especially in troublous times, more to incline to bend reverently to the Sovereign will—predestinating will it seemed—than extravagantly to thrill with reciprocated affection for a loving Father. Yet men of the most diverse types, Knox and Rutherford, equally held Predestinarian (supra-lapsarian) views, the one exhibiting Divine Justice in frigid terminology, the other illustrating Divine Love with the florid ornaments of the Hedonists.

Predestinarians.

Theological determinations were more a result of temperament than of anything else.

Covenanters Calvinists.

The schools of Knox and Rutherford were not antagonistic. All were pure Covenanters, yet not fatalists, ever aiming at subjecting man's will to God's, as ever being the best. The Divine plan centred in the Atonement, which the Covenanters believed was meant for all, and must be preached to all. The Covenanters thus had the missionary spirit. Believing in the Unity of the Catholic Church, they stood for its government by such officers as are clearly referred to in Holy Writ— and none others affecting priestly 'empire.' Schism was unscriptural.

It was environment which made the Covenanters unflinchingly cling to the Presbyterian form of the Church and love its 'rigidness,' which was not without a high, indeed indispensable, function.

Between the Roman anvil and the hammer of the tyrannical Stuart monarchs the Covenanted Church of Scotland was beaten into that rigid shape which best resisted and ultimately shattered these alien crushing agencies.[1]

The Church of Scotland early recognised her great place in Chris- tendom, and rejected all doctrines which made the Father's Voice a mystery again, and which set up a distinctive class of preachers and teachers, who assumed a preternatural grace in unfolding that mystery. In fine, the aim of the Covenanting teacher was to impress men with the elementary idea of the Holy Word, and of the Reformers, that Justi- fication is by faith of the individual sinner.

Aim of the Covenanters.

[1] Alexander Henderson, *Sermons*, 279: 'The Kirk is a Studdy (anvil) which has worn many hammers, and broken many arms, with striking upon her, and yet she is to the fore.'

EPITAPHS ON THE MONUMENTS OF SOME OF THE MOST FAMOUS OF THE MARTYRS

T HE inscriptions upon the gravestones of many martyred Covenanters are entitled to respect as far as their credibility is concerned. So early as 1686, the Societies had under consideration a proposal for collecting and publishing the testimonies of the martyrs, and on 21st April 1697, a resolution to this effect was come to, 'that a true and exact account of the persecutors' be brought to the next General Meeting. In April 1699, it was enjoined that an Index of the Martyrs' Testimonies should be made. In October 1701, it was resolved that 'all the Correspondences provide and make stones as signs of honour to be set on the graves of our late Martyrs,' with their names furnished, 'in order for the epitaphs, and also an account of these Martyrs' carriage and behaviour in the time of their martyrdom.'

Thus about fifteen years after the time of the hottest persecution, steps were being taken to record the facts of the case, so long as eye and ear witnesses were alive. Some of the inscriptions written in metre, probably by one of the Secretaries to the Societies, Hugh Clarke, suggest the idea that they were to be sung, to such a melody as the Old 124th Psalm tune, when the wanderers met beside the dust of their departed friends.[1]

---

[1] Thomson, *A Cloud of Witnesses*, Introd. x.; Hutcheson, *The Reformed Presbyterian Church*, 132.

James Currie and others erected the monument to the Martyrs in Greyfriars' Churchyard, Edinburgh.[1]

'OLD MORTALITY'

Robert Paterson, stone-mason, the prototype of Sir Walter Scott's 'Old Mortality,' was the youngest son of Walter Paterson and Margaret Scott, and was born at Burnflatt or Haggiesha, a mile out of Hawick, on the 25th April 1716. He became lessee of Gatelawbridge Quarry, Morton, Dumfriesshire, about 1745. In his peregrinations through the south-west of Scotland erecting tombstones he also re-cut the inscriptions on the gravestones of the Covenanters. He died at Bankend, Caerlaverock, on the 14th February 1801. For an account of his work see a series of articles by the author in the *Dumfries Standard* in 1898-1900, entitled 'Chiselprints of Old Mortality.' His monument, executed by John Currie, Dumfries, is erected in the grounds of Dumfries Observatory. A replica, stands in the grounds of Holm, Balmaclellan.

[1] *Edin. Town Council Minutes.* 28th August 1706; *Passages in the Lives of Helen Alexander.*, etc., *q.v.* The original slab is preserved in Edinburgh Corporation Museum. A photograph of it appears in this volume, p. 214.

INSCRIPTION ON THE MONUMENT IN ST JOHN'S CHURCHYARD, DALRY, KIRKCUBBRIGHTSHIRE (See photograph p. 421)

HOUSE ANNO 1684 FOR THEIR ADHERENCE

MEMENTO MORI

ROBERT STEWART OF ARDOCH AND JOHN GRIERSON WHO WERE MURDERED BY GRAHAM OF CLAVER

TO SCOTLANDS REFORMATION AND COVENANTS NATIONAL AND SOLEMN LEAGUE

BEHOLD! BEHOLD! A STONE'S HERE FORCED TO CRY
COME SEE TWO MARTYRS UNDER ME THAT LY
AT WATER OF DEE WHO SLAIN WERE BY THE HAND
OF CRUEL CLAVERHOUSE AND'S BLOODIE BAND
NO S'OONER HAD HE DONE THIS HORRID THING
BUT'S FORCED TO CRY STEWART'S SOUL IN HEAVEN DOTH SING
YET STRANGE! HIS RAGE PURSUED EVEN SUCH WHEN DEAD
AND IN THE TOMBS OF THEIR ANCESTORS LAID
CAUSING THEIR CORPS BE RAIS'D OUT OF THE SAME
DISCHARGING IN CHURCHYARD TO BURY THEM
ALL THIS THEY DID 'CAUSE THEY WOULD NOT PERJURE
OUR COVENANTS AND REFORMATION PURE
BECAUSE LIKE FAITHFUL MARTYRS FOR TO DY
THEY RATHER CHUSE THAN TREACHEROUSLIE COMPLY
WITH CURSED PRELACIE THE NATIONS BANE
AND WITH INDULGENCIE OUR CHURCHES STAIN
PERJURED INTELLIGENCERS WERE SO RIFE
SHEWED THEIR CURSED LOYALTY TO TAKE THEIR LIFE

HERE LYETH ROBERT STEWART SON TO MAJOR

INSCRIPTION ON STONE AT CLAREMONT FARM
MAGUS MOOR, ST. ANDREWS

The Grave Ston of
Andreu Gullin who Suffred
At the Gallowlee of Edinburgh
July 1638 & Afterward was
hung upon a pol in Magus
Muir and lyeth hiar

A faithful martyr her doth ly
A witness against perjury
Who cruelly was put to death
To gratify proud prelates wrath
They cut his hands ere he was dead
To Magus Muir they did him bring
His body on a pole did hing
His blood under the altar cries
For vengeance on Christ's enemies

EPITAPH ON FLAT SLAB AT PRIESTSHIEL (PRIESTHILL), MUIRKIRK
(See photograph on p. 499)

HERE LYES THE BODY OF JOHN BROWN WHO WAS MURDERED IN THIS PLACE BY GRAHAM OF CLAVERHOUSE FOR HIS TESTIMONY TO COVENANTED WORK OF REFORMATION, BECAUSE

HE DURST NOT OWN
THE AUTHORITY OF THE THEN
TYRANT DESTROYING THE
SAME WHO DIED THE FIRST
DAY OF MAY A.D. 1685 AND
OF HIS AGE 58

IN DEATH'S COLD BED THE DUSTY PART LIES
OF ONE WHO DID THE EARTH AS DUST DESPISE
HERE IN THIS PLACE FROM EARTH HE TOOK DEPARTURE
NOW HE HAS GOT THE GARLAND OF THE MARTYR
BUTCHERED BY CLAVERS AND HIS BLOODY BAND
RAGING MOST RAVENOUSLY OVER ALL THE LAND
ONLY FOR OWNING CHRIST'S SUPREMACY
WICKEDLY WRONGED BY ENCROACHING TYRANNY
NOTHING HOW NEAR SOEVER HE TO GOOD
ESTEEMED, NOR DEAR FOR ANY TRUTH HIS BLOOD

INSCRIPTION ON SLAB AT MAUCHLINE

HERE LIES THE BODIES OF PETER
GILLIES, JOHN BRYCE, THOMAS YOUNG
WILLIAM FIDDISON, & JOHN BRUNING
WHO WERE APPREHENDED AND HANGED
WITHOUT A TRIAL AT MAUCHLINE ANNO
1685. ACCORDING TO THE THEN WICKED'S
LAWS FOR THEIR ADHERENCE TO THE
COVENANTED WORK OF
REFORMATION. REV. XII. 11

BLOODY DUMBARTON, DOUGLAS AND DUNDEE
MOVED BY THE DEVIL AND THE LAIRD OF LEE
DRAGGED THESE FIVE MEN TO DEATH WITH GUN AND SWORD
NOT SUFFERING THEM TO PRAY NOR READ GOD'S WORD
OWNING THE WORD OF GOD WAS ALL THEIR CRIME
THE EIGHTY FIVE WAS A SAIN KILLING TIME

Erected by subscription in 1850. The old decayed tombstone from which the above inscription is copied lies below.

INSCRIPTION ON MONUMENT AT CRAIGHAUGH, DUMFRIESSHIRE
ERECTED IN 1702, REPAIRED IN 1825

HERE LYES ANDREW HISLOP
MARTYR SHOT DEAD UPON
THIS PLACE BY SIR JAMES
JOHNSTON OF WESTERHALL
AND JOHN GRAHAM OF C
LAVERHOUSE FOR ADHERI-
NG TO THE WORD OF GOD
CHRIST'S KINGLY GOVERRN-
MENT IN HIS HOUSE AND
THE COVENANTED WORK OF
REFORMATION AGAINST TYRAN
NY PERJURY AND PRELACY
&C &C.

THE COVENANTERS

INSCRIPTION ON STONE IN CROSSMICHAEL CHURCHYARD KIRKCUBRIGHTSHIRE

HERE LYES
WILLIAM GRAHAM
WHO MAKEING HIS
ESCAPE FROM THE
MOTHER'S HOUSE
WAS PERSUED AND
TAKEN AND INSTANT
LY SHOT DEAD BY
A PARTY OF CLAVER
HOUSE'S TROOPS FOR

(*other side*)

MEMENTO MORI
HIS ADHERENCE
TO SCOTLAND'S
REFORMATION CO
VENANTS NATION
AL AND SOLEMN
LEAGUE 1682

INSCRIPTION ON STONE IN COLMONELL CHURCHYARD

I MATTHEW M'ILWRAITH IN THIS PARISH OF COLMONELL
BY BLOODY CLAVERHOUSE I FELL
WHO DID COMMAND THAT I SHOULD DIE
FOR OWNING COVENANTED PRESBYTERY
MY BLOOD, A WITNESS STILL DOTH STAND
'GAINST ALL DEFECTIONS IN THIS LAND

INSCRIPTION ON STONE IN SORN CHURCHYARD,
Commemorating the Last of the Martyrs

HERE LYES GEORG
WOOD WHO WAS SHOT
AT TINKHORNHILL BY BL
OODY JOHN REID TRVPER
FOR HIS ADHERENCE TO
THE WORD OF GOD AND
THE COVENANTED WORK
OF REFORMATION 1688

INSCRIPTION ON MONUMENT IN FENWICK CHURCHYARD

HERE LIES THE BODY
OF
JAMES WHITE
WHO WAS SHOT TO DEATH
AT LITTLE BLACKWOOD
BY PETER INGLES AND
HIS PARTY 1685

(*other side*)

THIS MARTYR WAS BY PETER
INGLES SHOT
BY BIRTH A TYGER RATHER
THAN A SCOT
WHO THAT HIS MONSTROUS
EXTRACT MIGHT BE SEEN
CUT OFF HIS HEAD & KICKT IT
OER THE GREEN
THUS WAS THAT HEAD WHICH
WAS TO WEAR A CROWN
A FOOTBALL MADE BY A PROFANE
DRAGOUN

THE COVENANTERS

INSCRIPTIONS ON MONUMENTS TO 'THE WIGTOWN MARTYRS' CHURCHYARD, WIGTOWN.

(See photograph on p. 499)

I

LET EARTH AND STONE STILL WITNES BEARE
HERE LYES A VIRGINE MARTYRE HERE
MURTHERED FOR OUNING CHRIST SUPREME
HEAD OF THE CHURCH AND NO MORE CRIME
BUT NOT ABJURING PRESBYTERY
AND HER NOT OUNING PRELACY
THEY HER CONDEMD BY UNJUST LAW
OF HEAVEN NOR HELL THEY STOOD NO AW
WITHIN THE SEA TY'D TO A STAKE
SHE SUFFERED FOR CHRIST JESUS SAKE
THE ACTORS OF THIS CRUEL CRIME
WAS LAGG STRACHAN WINRAM AND GRHAME
NEITHER YOUNG YEARERES NOR YET OLD AGE
COULD STOP THE FURY OF THERE RAGE

HERE LYES MARGARET WILSON DOUGHTER TO GILBERT WILSON IN GLENVERNOCH WHO WAS DOUNED ANNO 1685 AGED 18

II

MEMENTO MORI
HERE LYES
MARGRAT LACHLANE
WHO WAS BY UN
JUST LAW SENTENC
ED TO DIE BY LAGG
STARCHANE WIN#RAME AND GRHAME
AND TYED TO A
STAKE WITHIN THE
FLOOD FOR HER
ADHERENCE
TO SCOTLANDS RE
FORMATION COVE
NANTS NATIONAL
AND SOLEMN LEAGUE
AGED 63   1685

III

MEMNETO MORI

HERE LYSE WILLIAM JOHNSTO[n]

JOHN MILROY GEORGE WALKER

WHO WAS WITHOUT SENTE

NCE OF LAW HANGED BY MA

JOR JOR WINRAM FOR THEIR ADHER

ANCE TO SCROTLAND'S REFOR

MATION COVENANTS NATION

AL AND SOLEMN LEAGUE

1685

INSCRIPTIONS IN DALGARNO CHURCHYARD, DUMFRIESSHIRE,

COMMEMORATING AN ENTERKIN RESCUER

Here lies the body of James
Harkness in Locherben who
died 6th Dec. 1723 aged 72 years
Belo this stone this dust doth ly
Who indured 28 years
Persecution by tyranny
Did him pursue with eho and cry
Through many a lonesome place
At last by Clavers he was taen
Sentenced for to dy
But God who for his soul took care
Did him from prison bring
Because no other cause they had
But that he ould not give up
With Christ, his Glorious King,
And swear alligence to that beist
The duke of York I mean
In spite of all there hellish rage
A naturel death he died
In full assurance of his rest
With Christ eternaly

(Cf. photograph, p. 352)

Here lyeth the body of
Thomas Harkness who
Departed this life June 3th
1756 aged 71 who was
son to Thomas Harkness
who suffered myrter
dum in the time of the
leat Persecution for the
intrist of Jesus Christ

[This Harkness was the posthumous son of the martyr referred to on pages 422, 428 in this volume.]

THE UNITED SOCIETIES

A Copy of the Minute Books of the United Societies is in the possession of Mr. J. B. Dalzell, Larkhall, who, during the progress of this work, has given me much information; and to him I am indebted for this account of the aims and work of the Societies—

'The peculiar dangers to which the Covenanters were exposed from 1660 to the Revolution demanded the adoption of certain precautions, if they were to retain their lives and freedom. Accordingly it was agreed among themselves that no public action was to be taken by any individual independently of the general body, and it followed, as a natural consequence, that if a common understanding were to be maintained amongst them, a permanent union of some sort would require to be inaugurated.

'That union eventually took the shape of the UNITED SOCIETIES, and delegates from each district of societies met quarterly for consultation and united action.

'The various grades of organisation of the members of the United Societies were: General Meetings (held quarterly); Shire Meetings or Correspondences; Societies; and lastly, Fellowship Meetings.

'The results and productions of the General Meetings were: various declarations; the renewing of the Covenants; the printing of the *Cloud of Witnesses* and other volumes; the placing of memorial stones over the graves of the martyrs; the guarding of the Convention; the raising of the Cameronian Regiment in 1689 at Douglas; and many others that have exercised a more or less perceptible influence over the destinies of the country.

'Care was stringently exercised to prevent the entrance into membership of spies who might give information to the "curates" or to the military, and also of persons who might, by their unseemly carriage, bring discredit upon the others. Applicants for admission were bound to answer satisfactorily certain *queries*.

'Various sets of these queries were in use at one time or other. One set was composed by Mr. Hepburn, another by Mr. Walter Smith, whilst a third exists in the Hamilton of Calderhead MSS., though the use of that one is believed to have been confined to a sect somewhat limited in numbers, of much later origin, and holding very extreme views.

'The set most generally in use, however, was from the pen of the youthful martyr Renwick. Many references to the one composed by him are to be found in the minutes of the General Meetings both before and after the Revolution. The minute of the General Meeting— Cabinet meeting it might be called, so limited and exclusive it would be—held at Douglas Water on May 20, 1696, reads:

> "Concluded that every soceity provide and have for themselves ane correct copy of the paper called the artickles or methods to be used for Receiving members into the societie published by Mr. James Renwick in order to destinct understanding and putting them exactly in practice and execution according to the queiries of the Gen. meeting."

'Eventually the employment of these queries for admitting members would seem to have fallen into disuse, as the minute of the General Meeting held at Crawfordjohn on May 1, 1714, reads thus:

> "(3) That for the futter Intrants into Societies who are not under personall scandall or guilty of imoralities but only of the public Defection of Church & State be not required to give any other Obligation under their hand, save the consciencious superscription of the Covenants with the Acknouledgment of Sins and Engagments to Dutys."—(Extracted from copy of the "Minuts.")

'The late Rev. J. H. Thomson of Hightae had a copy of Renwick's set, but it was so faint that he had a difficulty in deciphering it. In November 1888 Mr. Thomas Binnie, 3 Park Gate, Glasgow, had then an imperfect copy.'

Mr, Dalzell's copy forms part of a thin duodecimo manuscript volume, covered quaintly with a portion of a 'barn wecht.' It is in the handwriting of several persons. It contains the—

> 1692 Declaration,
> The hitherto unpublished Tinwald Paper, which was the means of gathering together in 1691 what eventually was known as the Reformed Presbyterian Church,
> An abridgment of *Some Causes of the Lord's Contraversie*,
> The 1695 Protestation,
> Renwick's Letter and Queries,
> And a complete copy of *Some Causes of the Lord's Contraversie*, with curious marginal notes.

From the history of this copy it is probable that it was compiled for the use of a Society in or in the vicinity of Newmilns.

APPENDIX FOUR

THE CESS

THE Acts for taxation or 'Cess,' so much objected to by the Covenanters on the ground that the money assessed was unjustly applied to the suppression of the upholders of Presbyterianism and of the Covenant, were:—

1661, c. 128, *Act. Parl. Scot.*, vii. 88. Act raising £40,000 yearly for King's use.

1665, vii. 530-535. War tax—forty shillings annually for five years off each pound land, old extent.

1667, vii. 540*a*. £72,000 monthly for one year in shires and burghs.

1670, c. 3. viii. 8. £360,000 Scots for King.

1672, c. 4. viii. 62, £864,000 Scots for War against States General—out of *personal* as well as real property. *Ibid.*, 62*b*.

1678 (10th July), viii. 221-9. Supply for forces to suppress *field conventicles*, £1,800,000 Scots approved.

1681, c. 3, viii. 240. Supply continued for five years. *Ibid.*, 241*b*, heritors to be relieved by tenantry, retired gentlemen, tradesmen, cottars, and servants.

1685, c. 12, viii. 463. Act of supply offering James VII. £216,000 yearly, granted for life in 1681.

1685, c. 38 (June 4), viii. 483. Act for poll-money from parishioners to relieve heritors in paying supply.

THE WODROW MANUSCRIPTS

THE Wodrow MSS. form a large and valuable collection of papers recording facts in the history of Scotland, more especially in the period between 1560 and 1690, and embrace original documents, extracts from written and printed books and from minute-books of various Courts, copies of deeds, declarations, papers, covenants, original letters and copies of letters from leading politicians and pastors, biographies of leading Reformers and Covenanters, and thousands of communications from correspondents. This extraordinary treasury was made by the Rev. Robert Wodrow, parish minister of Eastwood, near Glasgow, who was born in the famous year 1679 and died in 1735. When the mass was complete in 1722 it consisted of 40 folios, 100 quartos, and 30 octavos; other volumes must have been added after that date. Of the volumes preserved there remain in the Advocates' Library, Edinburgh, 22 vols. 8vo; 73 vols. 4to; 50 vols. folio; *Letters*, 4 vols. 8vo; 22 vols. 4to (containing 3880 letters); *Analecta*, 6 vols: in the Library of Glasgow University 15 vols. 4to; 9 vols. folio: in the Library of the General Assembly of the Church of Scotland, 4 vols. folio (numbered 26, 28, 29, 31).

With the aid of these documents Wodrow composed his *History—Scotia Sub Cruce*, begun in 1714 and published in 1721-2. Cf. *supra*, p. 151. The press marks of this MS., *Scotia Sub Cruce*, in the Advocates' Library are vol. xli., Rob. iii. 3. 14; xlvii., Rob. iii. 4. 2; xlviii. Rob. iii. 4. 3. The most important of the manuscripts, as far as the Covenanting period is concerned, are those original letters and papers, descriptive of personal sufferings on the part of the writers or of the sufferings of their friends in time of the persecution. These are many in number.

ACTS OF PARLIAMENT
REPEALED IN 1906

BY the *Statute Law Revision (Scotland) Act*, 1906, 6 Edw. VII., ch. 38, the following Acts of Scots Parliament were repealed, but under the qualifications that 'the repeal of any words or expressions of enactment described in the said schedule shall not affect the binding force, operation, or construction of any statute, or of any part of a statute, whether as respects the past or the future ... nor shall this Act affect any principle or rule of law or equity ... revive or restore any jurisdiction, office ... or other matter or thing not now existing or in force.' The effect of the Act is to declare these Acts 'as spent,' and no longer available for practical purposes.

Year	Record Edition	12mo. Edition	Title of Enactment and Extent of Repeal
1560	Cap. 3		Anent the abolitioun of Idolatrie and of all Acts contrair to the confessioun of fayth publyst in this Parliment.
”	” 4		Anent the Abolition of the mess.
1567	” 2	Cap. 31	Act concerning the Religioun.
(Dec. 15)	” 3	” 2	Anent the abolissing of the Pope and his usurpit authoritie.

Year	Record Edition	12mo. Edition	Title of Enactment and Extent of Repeal
”	” 4	” 3	Anent the annulling of the actis of Parliament maid agannis Goddis word and mantenance of idolatrie in ony tymes by past. The Confessioun of the faith and doctrine belevit and professit be the Protestantis of the Realme of Scotland exhibitit to the estatis of the same in Parliament and by thair public votis authorisit as a doctrine groundit upon the infallibil word of God.
”	” 5	” 5	Anent the messe abolischit and punisching of all that heiris or sayis the samin.
”	” 6	” 6	Anent the trew and haly kirk and of thame that ar declarit not to be of the samin.
”	” 7	” 7	Anent the admissioun of thame that sal be presentit to benefices havand cure of ministerie.
”	” 10	” 10	Anent thriddis of benefices grantit in the moneth of December the yeir of God 1561 yeiris for sustening of the Ministeris and uther effairis of the Prince.
”	” 12		Anent the jurisdictioun of the kirk. In part, namely: From 'And forther' to the end.
”	” 31	” 24	Anent priviligeis grantit to kirkmen.
1571	” 2	” 35	Ratificatioun and approbatioun of the actis and statutis maid of befor anent the fredome and libertie of the trew kirk of God.

Year	Record Edition	12mo. Edition	Title of Enactment and Extent of Repeal
1572	" 2	" 45	Anent the trew and haly kirk.
"	" 3	" 46	That the adversareis of Christis evangell sall not injoy the patrimonie of the kirk.
1578	" 3	" 61	The ratificatioun of the libertie of the trew kirk of God and religioun.
"	" 19		Anent the policie of the kirk.
1579	" 7	" 69	Anent the jurisdictioun of the kirk. In part, namely: From 'And further our Soverane' to the end.
"	" 9	" 71	Anent the youth and utheris beyond sey suspectit to have declinit frome the trew religioun.
"	" 10	" 72	That househaldaris have bybillis and psalme buikis.
1581	" 1	" 99	The ratificatioun of the libertie of the trew kirk of god and religioun with confirmation of the lawis and actis maid to that effect of before.
1584	" 1		Anent the libertie of the preching of the trew word of God and administratioun of the Sacramentis.
1587	" 2	" 23	Ratificatioun of the libertie of the kirk of God.
1592	Cap. 8	Cap. 116	Act for abolisheing of the actis contrair the trew religioun. In part, namely: From 'and all and quhatsumever' to 'of the trew kirk,' from 'And becaus thair ar' to 'haldin of pashe and yule,' and from 'Item oure said soverane' to the end.

Year	Record Edition	12mo. Edition	Title of Enactment and Extent of Repeal
”	” 14	” 122	Againis Jesuites seminary preistis and thair resettaris.
”	” 18	” 125	Quha hes not gevin confessioun of thair faith sall not enjoy the benefite of pacificatioun.
1593	” 7	” 164	For puneisment of the contempnaris of the decreittis and judicatoriis of the kirk.
”	” 11	” 168	Aganis the sayaris of messe and ressattaris or interteneyaris of excommunicat papistes.
1594	” 4	” 197	Anent satisfactioun to the kirk be papistes.
1600	” 25	” 16	Ratificatioun of the actis maid of befoir in favouris of the kirk.
”	” 26	” 17	Act anent non communicantis.
”	” 27	” 18	Ratificatioun of the act anent Jesuittis preistis excommunicat and traffiquing papistis.
1604	” 2		Act in favouris of the kirk
1607	” 2	” 1	Act aganis the sayaris and wilfull heiraris of mess.
1609	” 7	” 5	Act aganis jesuitis seminarie priestes and resettaries of thame.
”	” 15	” 8	Act of the apparels of judges magistrattis and kirkmen.
1617	” 2	” 2	Anent the restitutioun of chapteris.
1633	” 4	” 4	Ratificatioun of the actes touching religione.
”	” 5	” 5	Ratificatioun of the act of counsall anent plantatione of Schooles.

Year	Record Edition	12mo. Edition	Title of Enactment and Extent of Repeal
1633	" 7	" 7	Act anent invading of ministers. In part, namely: The words 'Archbischops, bischops, and,' and from 'and becaus the malice' to the end.
"	" 9	" 9	The Kings generall revocatione.
1661	" 11		Act and Proclamation aginst the Remonstrators, and for order in the toun of Edinburgh.
"	" 12	" 4	Act anent his Majesties prerogative in making of Leagues and the Convention of the subjects. In part, viz.: From 'and declares that' to the end.
"	" 18	" 6	Act annuling the Convention of Estates 1643 and rescinding any acts ratifieing the same.
"	" 19		Act and Proclamation against the meitings of Anabaptists, Quakers, etc.
"	" 22	" 7	Act concerneing the League and Covenant and dischargeing the renewing thereof without his Majesties warrand and approbation.
"	" 37	" 8	Act against saying of Meese seminary and Messe Preists and trafficquing Papists.
1661	Cap. 46	Cap. 9	Act approving the Engadgment of 1648 and annulling the Parliament and Committees 1649.
"	" 126	" 15	Act rescinding and annulling the pretendit Parliaments in the yeers 1640, 1641, &c.

Year	Record Edition	12mo. Edition	Title of Enactment and Extent of Repeal
”	” 127	” 16	Act concerning Religion and Church Government.
1662	” 1		Act for calling in the Bishops to the Parliament.
”	” 8		Act for keiping the anniversary thanks-giveing for the Kings Majesties birth and restauration.
”	” 12	” 2	Act for preservation of his Majesties Person Authoritie and Government.
”	” 50	” 8	The Kings Majesties generall Revoca-tion with a Declaration thereanent.
1669	” 6	” 5	Act for the security of the persons of Ministers.
1670	” 4	” 4	Act against invading of Ministers.
1672	” 22	” 11	Act against such who do not Baptize their Children.
”	” 58	” 22	Act against Profaneness.
1681	” 80	” 14	Act restraining the exorbitant expence of Marriages, Baptisms and burials.
1685	” 1	” 1	Act for security of the Protestant Religion.
1689	” 1	” 2	Act declaring this to be a free and law-ful meeting of the Estates.
”	” 7	” 7	Proclamation against Papists.
”	” 4	” 3	Act abolishing Prelacie. In part, namely: From 'And hereby rescinds' to the end.
1690	” 2	” 2	Act restoreing the Presbyterian Min-isters who were thrust from their Churches since the 1st of January 1661.

Year	Record Edition	12mo. Edition	Title of Enactment and Extent of Repeal
"	" 7	" 5	Act ratifying the Confession of Faith and settling Presbyterian Church Government. In part, namely: From 'Lykeas, In pursuance' to 'take further course therewith.'
"	" 53	" 23	Act concerning Patronages In part, namely: From 'considering that' to 'continued in this Realme'; the word 'Therefore' next there-after occurring; from 'Dis-charge, cass annull' to 'with advyce and consent forsaid' where these words lastly occur; and the word 'said' twice occuring next thereafter.
"	" 57	" 27	Act Rescinding the laws for Conform-ity.
1693	" 38	" 22	Act for Settling the Quiet and Peace of the Church. In part, namely: From 'for the more effectuall Settleing' to 'said Office and lastly.'
"	" 39	" 23	Act Renewing the Commission for Plantation of Kirks and Valuation of Teinds. In part, namely: From 'and it being fitt and convenient' to the end.

ORDINATION IN THE CHURCH OF SCOTLAND

THERE are several instances in the Records of the Presbytery of Dumbarton of 'Expectants' or Probationers having been admitted to the ministry of parishes without any Act of Ordination 'by the laying on of the hands of the Presbytery.' Such admission was said to be 'conform to the Acts and Practise of this Kirk.' The Presbytery seems to have laid stress upon three things necessary to a competent ministry, viz. a proper appointment, examination in the several pieces of 'tryalls,' and a call or 'consent and content' of the elders, heritors, and parishioners; but nothing was said with respect to ordination. The Minutes bear that when the 'Edict' of admission was returned duly served from the pulpit of the vacant church, the Presbytery 'ordained,' *i.e.* instructed or appointed, two, three, or four ministers to go to the vacant church on the following Sunday 'to admit' the 'Expectant' to 'the functioun of the Ministrie at the said Kirk, where of Intimatioun was made to the sayd parochiners.' At the following meeting of the Presbytery it was reported that the 'admissioune' to the 'Ministrie' had been given 'by the brethren as was appointed, with common consent and content of all the elders and parochioners of the sayd Kirk, present for the tym in great numbers.' This seems to have been sufficient to constitute the new minister as a member of the Presbytery, for his name appears in the sederunt of the meeting. The next step taken is to 'ordain Institutioune to be given him by the moderator and brethren who war befoir appointed for his admissioune,' which was duly reported to the following meeting of the Presbytery.

Such was the procedure of the admission of John Stewart to the 'Ministrie at the Kirk of Bonnull [Bonhill], on Sunday the 29th December 1639,' and his institution at Bonhill on Monday the 3rd February 1640; and of the admission of James Wood to the 'Ministrie' at Kilpatrick, on Sunday the 24th May 1640, which was reported on the 2nd June, when the Presbytery 'ordains Institutioune to be given by Mr. Archibald Cameron and Mr. John Stirling,' two ministers, members of the Presbytery, who reported on the 16th June that they had done so.

I am indebted to the Rev. William Simpson, Bonhill, for the above extracts from the Minute Books of the Presbytery of Dumbarton.

Holyrood, 58; menace of Protestantism, 58; marries and flees with Bothwell, 62; writes to Elizabeth about marriage, 62; explains Bothwell marriage to Elizabeth, 62; taken captive to Edinburgh and Lochleven, abdication of, 63; Carberry, 63; Langside, 64; her demission ratified by Parliament, 71; subsidises Scots students, 92; execution of, 128
— accession of William, and, II.513
— Queen-Regent, I.15, 17, 20, 23, 28; dies, 31
Masson, Professor David, estimate of Covenanters, I.291-2
Mathieson, Mr. W. L., cited, I.431, 158, II.408
— John, of Closeburn, II.318
—— of Rosehill, banished, II.413 and note
Mauchline, skirmish at, I.434; tragedy at, II.466
Maxwell, imprisoned for saying Mass in Lincluden, I.135
— Bishop, his share in making Liturgy, I.217; his Prayer Book thrown into the sea, 272; advises Charles not to concede, 279; faults of, 297
— of Monreith, proscribed, II.196
— Sir John, of Pollock, II.448
— Margaret, II.464
Mein, John, ousted from Anwoth, II.172; letters to Williamson, 200;
—— merchant in Edinburgh, I.199, 228
— Robert, imprisoned, II.305
— Mrs. Cf. 'Jenny Geddes', I.199
Melfort, gone over to Rome, II.486
Melville, Andrew, advent of, I.81; sketch of his early life, 81-2; fame as a professor in Glasgow, 81-2; views on Church and State, 82; debates on Episcopacy, 83; threatened by Morton, 84; presides in Assembly of 1578, 84; his views of the jurisdiction

of ministers and magistrates, 90; at Dundee Assembly, 95; libels Montgomery, 107; at Perth, 110; attempt to silence, 118; summoned before Privy Council, 118; defence of, 118-19; flight to England, 120; incident with the Hebrew Bible, 119-20; answers Adamson, 126; his religious trek, 127; accuses the king of causing national misery in 1593, 135; interferes in Black's case, 137; at Cupar meeting, 139; fulminations of, 146; on *Basilikon Doron*, 148; at Montrose, 1600, 149; literary works, 165; protests at 'Red Parliament', 178; and other seven ministers invited to London, 178; at Hampton Court Conference, 1606, 179-80; his famous Latin epigram, 180-1; languishes in the Tower, 181; his death and character, 181-2
Melville, Lord, I.220
— George, first Earl, II.514, 525
— Professor James, preaches against Adamson, I.127, 132; at Cupar meeting, 1596, 140; on *Basilikon Doron*, 148; protests, 1602, 152; literary works, 157
rails, 178
Memorial, A Short, cited, II.261
Menteith, Earl and Countess, adulterers, II.114
Mersington, Lady, II.238
Michael, St., the, of Scarborough, II.266
Middleton, at Mauchline fight, I.434; humiliation of, 441; excommunicated, II.22; restored in Dundee church, 27; reward offered for, 48; flouts Sharp for his trickery, 70; Earl of, at Holyrood, 74-5; Commissioner to first Restoration Parliament, 66; conducts burial of Montrose, 75; expedites Argyll's execution, 83; coach stained with Guthrie's blood,